ABOVE THE BOTTOM LINE

An Introduction to Business Ethics
Second Edition

Robert C. Solomon

Quincy Lee Centennial Professor
of Business and Philosophy
University of Texas at Austin

Harcourt Brace College Publishers

Fort Worth Philadelphia San Diego New York Orlando Austin San Antonio
Toronto Montreal London Sydney Tokyo

Editor in Chief	Ted Buchholz
Acquisitions Editor	David Tatom
Developmental Editor	Mary K. Bridges
Project Editor	Sara Schroeder
Senior Production Manager	Tad Gaither
Art Director	Jim Dodson

Cover Image: © 1992 Ron Lowery/The Stock Market

Address for Editorial Correspondence:
Harcourt Brace College Publishers
301 Commerce Street, Suite 3700, Fort Worth, TX 76102.

Address for Orders:
Harcourt Brace, Publishers
6277 Sea Harbor Drive, Orlando, Florida 32887
1-800-782-4479, or 1-800-433-0001 (in Florida).

Printed in the United States of America

3 4 5 6 7 8 9 0 1   090   9 8 7 6 5 4 3 2 1

Library of Congress Catalog Card Number: 93–77629

ISBN: 0-15-501051-4

In memory of my father,
Charles M. Solomon
(1915 – 1986)

Contents

6. RATIONALITY, ENDS AND MEANS, COOPERATION AND COORDINATION   168

7. CONFLICTS OF INTEREST AND THE MEANING OF MORALITY   199

PREFACE

"The business of America is business," said more than one U.S. president. Business and the American way of life are inseparable, not only because the American business spirit is largely responsible for our unparalleled prosperity, but because business sets the values and provides the context for so much of American life. It molds our conceptions of work and success, our concern for selling our time and our talents, and our emphasis on "the things that money can buy."

Life was not always so bound up with business. Not so long ago, merchants, traders, and moneylenders were considered the lowest class of society, inferior even to peasants, who at least toiled the earth and produced food and materials. Aristotle made it quite clear that such people were considered "parasites" in ancient Greece: "Others exceed in taking anything and from any source, for example, those who ply sordid trades, pimps and such people, and those who lend small sums at high rates. . . .What is common to them is a sordid love of gain" (*Ethics,* iv. 1). Saint Thomas Aquinas insisted that society try to do without them, and even Martin Luther condemned business and "avarice" (what we call "the profit motive") as sin. Since Jesus chased the moneylenders out of the temple (John 2:13–16), businesspeople continued to be scorned and chased out of society until the eighteenth century.

In other words, for thousands of years, business existed at the fringes of society. Society thought little of people in business, and people in business expected little of society. Profit was their only reward because power, social status, and even social acceptability were closed to them. In this context, the idea that business and making a profit were activities quite apart from the rest of society and the idea that making a profit was the only goal of business might have made some sense. But business is no longer Babylon (Rev. 18:11–17) and the role of the businessperson is no longer that of the outsider. The values of the business world have come to determine the ethos of our entire society.

In the past ten years, it is as if the world of business has been through a great awakening. Across both oceans, the world has opened up to business. The collapse of socialism and so-called communism throughout eastern Europe and what used to be the Soviet Union has ended the Cold War and opened up markets in one of the most dramatic (and surprisingly bloodless) turnabouts of the twentieth century. China, though still nominally communist, is opening its doors, cautiously, to the old devil capitalism, and southern China is filled with factories and small, privately owned shops. Japan, of course, has beaten us in the car business and isn't doing badly with electronics, and Korea, Singapore, and Taiwan, along with other Asian nations, are making impressive moves into the international business world. At home, the excesses and scandals on and off Wall Street in the late eighties and the conviction and jailing of major business figures have started off the new decade with soul-searching. What are the rules of "good business"? Is a bigger corporation always better? What sort of constraints should there be on mergers and (hostile) acquisitions? What is the ultimate point of the practice of business — to make a buck for the stockholders or something more? To serve the public good, to create a satisfied consumer, to help produce a free and healthy society? What sort of example should we be in and for the world market? How should we think of ourselves as individuals in a business world?

This book is an attempt to understand the ethics of the current business world — "business ethics" — in this modern American environment. The starting point is the inseparability of business and society and the importance of seeing business in the larger context of the values of that society. In the second edition of *Above the Bottom Line,* I have tried to develop a textbook in business ethics that considers the nature and the values of American business life, emphasizing positive goals such as justice and social responsibility rather than crisis and failure. Given the assumption of the importance of the business enterprise in every facet of American life, understanding the ethics of business becomes essential for all of us.

I have not tried to develop any particular point of view, other than that just stated. While I have tried to give some attention to the peculiarly *moral* problems encountered in business, I have not tried to emphasize moral problems and principles at the expense of the more day-to-day ethical questions of value concerning work, competition, life in the corporation, the meaning of "management," and the nature of success. I have written this book for students who cannot be presumed to have extensive backgrounds in philosophy and who are primarily interested in the more practical concerns of ethics. At the same time, however, I have tried to provide an introduction to some of the more abstract philosophical concepts as well, but these are by no means my only concern.

In this second edition of *Above the Bottom Line* I have updated much of the material and added chapters and sections on regulation and taxation, the nature of the corporation, the managerial revolution, the ethical dimension of mergers and acquisitions, small businesses and the entrepreneur, individual responsibility and corporate responsibility, consumer responsibility, stockholder responsibility, loyalty, "stakeholders," corporations and the environment, distributive justice, the fairness of the free market, the problem of poverty, the underclass, affirmative action, "reverse discrimination," international business and cross-cultural ethical dilemmas, human rights and the multinational corporation, conflicts of rights, privacy, moral mazes, rights in the workplace, whistle-blowing, the nature and meaning of work, employee rights and duties, work satisfaction, work as creativity and expression, "alienated labor," the role of labor unions, workers and management, sexual harassment, women in business, working mothers (and fathers), family values, the nature of success, and new cases. The format of the book remains the same with study questions and informative boxes with key definitions, observations, quotations, short cases, and practical situations. Optional "Historical Interludes" at the end of each chapter cover the most important movements and authors in macroethics. Together they provide a brief history of attitudes toward business, its critics (Karl Marx), and its advocates (Adam Smith).

What is special about this book is that it approaches the questions of business ethics not only from an abstract theoretical and policy level but also from a person level—that is, from the perspective of the individual working in business at all levels of the organization or as an individual entrepreneur. In terms of contemporary ethical theory, the book places its primary emphasis on what is sometimes called "virtue ethics," the ethics of personal (and corporate) character. In more familiar terms, the emphasis is placed on what business life, business pressures and business decisions are like to live, to cope with, to make. The idea behind this book is that business is part of life, and the ethics of business has everything to do with becoming the sorts of people we want to be and living the kind of life we want — on serious reflection, to live.

How to Use This Book

The book is divided into 15 chapters, allowing a chapter a week for most standard one-semester courses. Each is concerned with a particular aspect of business life. These chapters are as self-contained as possible so that the student or instructor can use them in a variety of ways, omitting some or leaping ahead to others. I have included as much detail as possible, perhaps more than every student might want — for example, the extensive introduction to game theory in Chapter 5. I have also provided a range of study questions and cases for class discussion, as well as a large number of inserts for entertainment and further reflection. The book may be combined with detailed case studies for extended discussions or a short philosophical text providing more detailed analyses and arguments of such key ethical concepts as "responsibility," "morality," "justice," and "rights." I have not attempted to provide either detailed cases or such analyses and arguments here. Some instructors may prefer additional readings more critical of capitalism and the business world or more theoretical discussions of what I have called "macroethics" — the morality of the business world as such.

This book is designed to be used in a full-semester course. However, if it is to serve for less than the full term, I suggest the following selections: For a half semester use Chapters 1 – 4, 6, 7, 8 or 9, and 10. If the book is supplemented with one of the more traditional books that emphasize the problems of morality, justice, and rights, use Chapters 1 – 4, 5, 6 and a selection from 12, 13, and 14. For a class of a shorter term, use Chapters 1, 3, 7, 9, and 10 or 11; or if also supplemented with a traditional book, Chapters 1, 3, 4, 6, and 12 or 13 or 14. The chapters are also divided into clearly marked sections, and these can be selected and arranged independently.

ACKNOWLEDGMENTS

I am indebted to a number of friends and colleagues who encouraged this work and helped it along with their advice and criticism. In particular, I would like to thank Susan Zaleski for her painstaking work with the book at its various initial stages and David Zimmerman for his expert advice and criticism of some of the more technical parts of the book. I would like to thank Sylvia Stern, Phyllis Green, and Paul Nelson for their encouragement and suggestions for working out these ideas in a business context. Richard Rodewald and Karl Henion gave me advice and encouragement at the inception of the book. The entire philosophy department, together with the management school at the University of Auckland, gave a delightful forum for the initial writing. Eric Lander was an inspiration and a good friend at Harvard Business School, and Annette Weiner helped me immensely in putting the American business world in anthropological perspective. Thanks are also due to the reviewers: Patrice DiQuinzio, University of Scranton; Jack Williams, CPA, Tulsa Junior College; John T. Granrose, University of Georgia; W. Michael Hoffman, Director, Center for Business Ethics, Bentley College; Mark Pastin, Center for Private and Public Sector Ethics, Arizona State University; and Milton Snoeyenbos, Georgia State University. I also thank the University of Texas School of Business and the Harvard Business School, and Janet Byrnes, Melinda Phelps, and Sue Gath for helping with the index. Thanks to Winifred Conlon just in general.

For this second edition, I especially would like to thank Clancy Martin and David Sherman for their valuable advice and research assistance. Thanks again to Bill McLane of Harcourt Brace College Publishers for his foresight in encouraging the project when the field of business ethics was still in its infancy, and to David Tatom, Kristin Trompeter, Sara Schroeder, Tad Gaither, Jim Dodson, and Mary K. Bridges for their help with this second edition.

I owe a special and continuing debt of gratitude to Kristine Hanson, for her effort, research, and encouragement in preparing the first edition of *Above the Bottom Line*. Were it not for her interest and enthusiasm, this book — and several others in the field of business ethics — would never have been written.

Introduction: Business Ethics

T his is a textbook about business ethics. It is a new subject in the business and liberal arts curriculum, but a very old topic of discussion, both among businesspeople and everyone else. It revolves around the question, "What are the values of business life, and how do these values fit into the rest of life and society?" There is no simple answer to this question, but in general we can safely say that the values of business life and the values of the rest of life and society are rarely far apart; after all, people in business are people with private lives and a sense of community. The ethics of business life is just the ethics of people in business, and no different, basically, from ethics in general.

In response to public suspicion of business, "business ethics" has become a distinct subject and, often, a required course in the business curriculum. But, in a more positive light, it is a subject that is beneficial and essential to business, an intrinsic part of business life. In fact, *business ethics is just the broad understanding and appreciation of business life.* It is not just criticism of business practices and businesspeople. It is not a series of sermons on right and wrong, as if businesspeople were somehow particularly ignorant or neglectful of morals. It is not just abstract theory about the nature of business values. It is, ultimately, nothing more than careful and far-reaching thinking about a certain way of life in which money and profits play a prominent, but by no means exclusive, part. It is seeing the intimate interconnections between business activities and the rest of life, between business and society, between "free enterprise" and the values that such enterprise presupposes.

On the other hand, there is a simple quip, often presented as a joke among business students required to take a course in "business ethics," that "there isn't any ethics in business." For most students, this now tedious quip is nothing more than an innocent comment. But it signifies an attitude that, translated into the public domain, has had disastrous consequences for the public image of business in America and elsewhere. We can argue that the motivation behind offering "business ethics" courses has been the vague concerns of society and public offi-

---

The Image Problem ——

A recent Harris Poll shows that public confidence in the executives running major corporations has declined drastically from 55% ten years ago to 16% today. In one poll 87% of those interviewed agreed that too many businessmen are more interested in profits than in serving the public's needs. And 53% felt that many major companies should be dismantled.

Business and Society Review, #19

---

cials, that business has forgotten about the public interest and is concerned only with its own profits. This is, however, untrue of most people in business and of most businesses. But we should realize that what is said about business ethics these days is important and has enormous consequences. And realizing the ethics of business may well be the key to survival for American business today. The

---

Business ethics, in any civilization, is properly defined by moral and religious traditions, and it is a confession of moral bankruptcy to assert that what the law does not explicitly prohibit is therefore morally permissible. Yet curiously enough this is what businessmen often seem to be saying—therewith inevitably inviting government to expand its code of prohibitions. And the reason why this has happened is that businessmen have come to think that the conduct of business is a purely "economic" activity, to be judged only by economic criteria, and that moral and religious traditions exist in a world apart, to be visited on Sunday perhaps.

Irving Kristol, *The Wall Street Journal,* March 20, 1979

---

alternative is more public suspicion, more bad press, and, inevitably, more government regulation and consumer group antagonism.

Business education naturally focuses on concepts and concerns that are essential to business—the theories and techniques of finance, management, accounting, and marketing. Business ethics, on the other hand, focuses its attention on the purposes and roles of these techniques and on the activities they define. It concerns itself with such concepts as "the public interest," "social responsibility," "human rights," and "justice." However, even if these are not part of business as such, concepts and concerns are still essential to business life. Indeed, lack of attention to these broader concerns, writes "neoconservative" journalist Norman Podhoretz, has been extremely costly:

> While businessmen were minding their own business, intellectuals were busy developing a powerful case against capitalism. This cause went largely unanswered and eventually bore fruit in the form of regulatory and other government policies to which the business community was unhappily forced to pay attention.*

It is to provide business students with a sense of those arguments and concerns—and a broad sense of the significance of their own activities—that I have written this textbook. I have not tried to develop any new philosophical arguments but rather help business students master some of the oldest and most basic concepts of ethics, which are too conspicuously absent from the current vocabulary of business. My aim is to combat and correct the antagonism and suspicion that is popularly directed against business. *The appreciation of business is just as much a part of "business ethics" as its criticism.* Accordingly, I have tried to develop a textbook and a subject that emphasizes seeing business in a philosophical and social perspective, not without, however, some constructive criticism. The social success and importance of business is my starting point; and the ideas that define business life—not the failures and criticisms of business life—form my point of departure.

> Once again, modern business is paying the price for conceiving of itself as representing an abstract species of 'economic man,' rather than as men and women engaged in a fully human activity. It is this self-delusion that has helped so significantly to create the divorce between the business communities and academic-intellectual communities—a divorce that leaves the business community so defenseless when ideas (about morality or anything else) are used unscrupulously as weapons against it.
>
> Irving Kristol, *The Wall Street Journal,* March 20, 1979

One of the more pointless distractions and debates that interrupts the discussion of business ethics is the somewhat absurd question of whether one is "probusiness" or "antibusiness." Free market guru Milton Friedman, when he

---

The Harvard Business Review (March/April 1981).

once felt compelled to explain himself to some of his critics, insisted, "I am not pro-business. I am pro-free enterprise." Many of the books on business ethics have been admittedly antibusiness, indeed, arguing that business and justice, for example, were incompatible. In this book, I have tried throughout to be both fully sympathetic to the practical concerns of most managers and be critical where criticism is due. Capitalism and the free enterprise system have their vices as well as their many virtues, and it is no sign of support to praise only the virtues and leave the problems unspoken. Thus Irving Kristol called one of his books, following a title by E. M. Forster many years ago, *Two Cheers for Capitalism.* So, too, a qualified free enterprise system is taken as the starting point here. But it is important to remember that there is more than one kind of capitalism and it is not always obvious, given the world market today, that the American system remains unique or superior. Chauvinist cheerleading may be good for morale, but the

> With all the greed, hubris, and corruption now being showcased worldwide, perhaps it's heartening that a growing number of U.S. corporations are embracing in-house ethics programs. In fact, the Center for Business Ethics at Bentley College in Waltham, Mass., recently found that 45 percent of the 1,000 largest U.S. companies now have ethics programs or workshops, up from 35 percent five years ago. . . . Aside from the obvious public relations value in maintaining a commitment to ethics, companies have a wary eye on [tough] new U.S. sentencing guidelines that [took] effect November 1, 1991.
>
> —*Business Week*
> September 23, 1991

point is to create and maintain an economic system that prospers, and that we can be proud of.

Ethics, like economics, can be conveniently (but cautiously) divided into (1) the small, concrete questions about individual and personal transactions and (2) the larger questions about our society as a whole. We can call these *microethics* and *macroethics,* respectively. *Microethics* consists of our personal and professional concerns for living well and doing what is right. In business ethics, this includes the search for the good life, questions of morality, and the rewards and responsibilities of a business position. It also includes attitudes toward work and toward the people living and working around us and with us in society as a whole. *Macroethics* consists of larger and impersonal concerns, about the kind of society we live in and the kind of economic system that serves the society. It is a more global and theoretical analysis of the business world, like economics, but with an ethical and value-oriented, rather than explanatory, orientation. Every macroeconomic theory has its macroethical presumptions, about the source of value and who should get what, about the role of government and the social responsibilities of business, just as every microeconomic theory about individual transactions has its built-in views about fair exchange and the rights and responsibilities of everyone involved.

The "business" of business ethics is not to add another subject to the business curriculum but rather to help break down some of the artificial and unfortunate barriers between business and the business schools and the rest of humanity and "the humanities," as if business weren't also "human." But the few yards that separate the business school from the rest of the campus in most universities might as well be miles. At the University of Texas at Austin, for example, a mere thirty-five feet separates the "business-economics" building from the classics and philosophy departments, but they might as well be at opposite ends of the state for all that each knows about what is going on in the other. At Harvard, the split is a bit more graphic, with the "B-school" separated from the rest of the university by the Charles River, which not insignificantly resembles a great moat, protecting the "fast track" students on the Boston side of the river from the envy and disdain of the scholars on the Cambridge side. The sad truth seems to be—or at least, it seemed to be until very recently—that those students who choose one direction or the other are forever bound, by peer pressure and prejudice, to despise and avoid the other. But business also has its history and its culture, and it is an intrinsic part of American history and culture. It too has its philosophy, which only by mistake has been isolated from larger philosophical concerns and, through defensiveness, has come to dismiss philosophy and "ideology" altogether as impractical, foreign and unalterably unsympathetic to business.

■ SUMMARY OF GOALS

1. To clearly and distinctly define a subject matter deserving of the name "business ethics."

2. To present a fair and realistic portrait of the business world and business life and its values.

3. To present in a concrete and practical way some of the most important concepts and theories of ethics.

4. To present a variety of examples, cases, situations, and personalities that exemplify the options and circumstances of business life.

5. To present a perspective on the history of business and "free enterprise" in the context of history and modern American society.

Business, Ethics, and the Good Life

The good is that at which all things aim . . . and men are agreed, that this is called happiness.

—Aristotle

The life of the business world is a distinctive life, that is true. But life in the business world is also just a part of life, and the goals and rewards of business success are merely means to something more for each of us. This "something more" we call "the good life." It may include success and a modicum of wealth but this is surely not the whole of it.

Twenty-five hundred years ago, Aristotle described the good life in terms that are, despite some obvious cultural differences, still appealing and applicable to us today. He equated the good life with what the Greeks called *eudaimonia,* sometimes translated as "happiness," but what might better be understood simply as "living well." Aristotle insisted that having a healthy income and elevated status in society were both necessary for the good life, though life in business repulsed him and was actually considered to be incompatible with living well. He also stressed the essential importance of good health, living in a good city, being raised well, and having friends and a good family. He insisted that pleasure and enjoyment of life were essential too, though not, he argued, as goals in themselves. Also essential were having respect, being a good and patriotic citizen, and living a life steeped in culture and learning as well as filled with sports and pleasures. What we call "success" in our activities is just as important. Aristotle emphasized what he called *the virtues*—those special qualities that make a good person, but all of these had to fit together in what he called "a complete life."

The Good Things in Life ──

How important are these to you? Rate them on a scale of 1 to 10; 1 is lowest, 10 is highest.

_____ Wealth and financial success
_____ Love
_____ Being loved
_____ Having a good time
_____ Freedom to do what I want
_____ A happy family
_____ A sense of accomplishment
_____ Doing something meaningful
_____ Contributing to my community
_____ Helping others
_____ Social status
_____ Power over other people
_____ The respect of my friends
_____ The respect of strangers
_____ Inner peace
_____ Adventure and excitement
_____ Being comfortable
_____ Being challenged
_____ Religion, a sense of spirituality, salvation
_____ Wisdom

Fleeting enjoyment was never enough; temporary victories added up to nothing unless a person's whole life was lived well. And this included not only a full life in the sense of living a long time, but a full life in the sense of being filled with *all* of the above aspects of life. A life of extreme pleasure was not the good life, if it did not include success and community respect. A successful life was not the good life unless it included love and friendship, social participation and political responsibilities, and also pleasure and parties, and a fair amount of the carrying-on that we still sometimes refer to, with more vulgarity than Aristotle, as "the good life."

This conception of the good life as a complete life, in which wealth and success play an essential but only partial role, may sound obvious, and it would have sounded obvious to the students to whom Aristotle lectured so long ago. But people tend to forget in their everyday lives what they know quite well in their more philosophical moments. In business life, there is always the danger that has recently been named "workaholism"—excessive dedication to a job virtually to the exclusion of everything else. At the other extreme is the equally contempo-

Aristotle's Virtues ——

Courage—particularly courage in battle.

Temperance—which includes the enjoyment of pleasure as well as moderation; a man who abstained from sex, food, and drink would not be considered virtuous by the Greeks, as he might be by some people today.

Liberality—what we would call charity.

Magnificence—spending lavishly and doing great deeds.

Pride—appreciation of one's own worth (humility was a vice).

Good temper—but it is important to get angry when appropriate.

Friendliness—a very important virtue for the Greeks, not just a personal pleasure or necessity.

Truthfulness—honesty about oneself.

Wittiness—people who can't tell or take a joke aren't virtuous. Aristotle would not equate "seriousness" with being moral, as some people do.

Shame—being sensitive to one's honor and feeling appropriately bad when it is besmirched. "Feeling guilty," on the other hand, did not even seem to be worth talking about.

Justice—the sense of fair treatment of others.

From *Nicomachean Ethics*

The virtues, according to Aristotle, are those characteristics or features of "character" that make a man "good" and lead to "the good life" as well. Make your own list of virtues, and explain those that are different from Aristotle's. Which virtues do you insist upon in the people you work with? In your friends?

rary tendency to dismiss work altogether as a mere necessity, a way to "make a living," but nothing more. The fact is, however, that in our culture what we "do for a living" is also one of the major determinants of our personal self-identity, our sense of self-worth, our conception of who we are and how we fit into our society. Indeed, what we do also determines what we think about that society, who our friends are, and what sorts of activities we enjoy—or don't enjoy. Businesspeople naturally tend to see American society as a business society, and their conceptions of themselves mirror that image. To reject our work or career as a mere "necessity," therefore, may also carry with it the danger of rejecting ourselves and an entire society; but to take our work or career *too* seriously, on the other hand, is also to misunderstand our own life and the nature of society as well.

Ethics is, first of all, the quest for, and the understanding of, the good life, living well, a life worth living. It is largely a matter of *perspective:* putting every activity and goal in its place, knowing what is worth doing and what is not worth doing, knowing what is worth wanting and having and knowing what is not worth wanting and having. It is keeping in mind the place of a business career in our life as a whole, not allowing limited business successes or even business success in general to eclipse our awareness of the rest of life. It is also, within business itself, keeping in mind what is ultimately important and essential and what is not, what serves our overall career goals and what does not, what is part of business and what is forbidden to business, even when increased profit—the most obvious measure of business success—is at stake.

Business life has an unusual forthrightness about it—which is so often subjected to criticism by more "idealistic" people: The whole point of entering life in business is to lead the good life, to participate in the mainstream of American society. Business life provides and businesspeople enjoy the material goods that this society provides in such abundance, as well as a level of health and security that is unique in the world. However, it is a mistake to conclude that business is without its ideals, that life in business is solely directed at the fulfillment of individual desires and security, and that the business world is not aimed at the good of society in general rather than the well-being of its own members. Indeed, business ethics is essential as a reminder to people in business that they are, after all, in it for the good life. But the good life envisioned in business is itself often misunderstood and taken to be much more limited than it is.

In the sketch of the good life in the first few sentences of this chapter, the features listed pertained not to isolated individuals and their well-being but to people as members of society with family and friends, who have the need to be loved and respected. The good life requires personal health, security, and a certain amount of wealth and pleasure, but it also requires a healthy community in which to live, a kind of security that is not the need to hide behind locked doors all of the time, jealously guarding possessions. It requires friends and family—*other people*—to enjoy and share life's wealth and pleasures. Also, what is easiest for Americans to forget, it requires a culture and tradition and an established set of symbols and institutions within which our wealth is worth something, within which there are legitimate activities and possessions to enjoy, and within which our lives mean something. It means being able to see ourselves as something more than specks in eternity, whose pleasures and profits result in nothing, amount to nothing, and reduce to nothing more than the passing self-indulgence of creatures who might just as well have never existed.

The popular philosophy of "selfishness" and "pulling your own strings," however therapeutic for certain people at certain times, has always been false and dangerous. Our well-being as well as our brute survival depends on the mutual cooperation of friends and society. Success depends on other people who will recognize that success, and even wealth, depends in an obvious way on a stable society in which the value of a dollar—or of a coin, a lump of gold, even a loaf of bread—is established and more or less constant. Our sense of immortality, our fundamental desire to have our lives mean something after we die, can only be fulfilled by serving goals beyond ourselves, whether these be the well-being of our children, the good of our country or the company, "good works" or doing the will of God—goals that will outlast us and reflect back on our lives in a positive way. This too is an essential part of the good life. Living well is virtually never leaving well enough alone.

Life in business is possible, in an obvious way, only because other people are in it too, as bosses and as workers, as mentors and as competitors, and, needless to say, as customers. Without "the market"—which ultimately consists of individuals whose concerns and desires it is the business of business to fulfill—there would be no business. But in more subtle ways, life in business is possible only because of the approval of the society it is part of. Aristotle's society of ancient Greece considered business a disgraceful way to spend a life and regarded the good life as almost impossible for a person in business to achieve (this perspective lasted until, roughly, the fourteenth or fifteenth century). Today achieving the good life through business still depends on attitudes of society towards business, even if we tend to take the importance of business for granted in our society. But business is possible and the good life through business is available only insofar as society recognizes the place of business in the good life and in the good society in general. It is here that business ethics plays its most important role.

What are some of the main ingredients of the good life in America today? For each individual, of course, the proportion of these ingredients will vary considerably. Some people are more prone to seek pleasure and some prefer power; for others, respect, love, and friendship count for everything; and for still others, success and achievement are much more important. But the important function of ethics is to make us think about these various ingredients in our own lives, how much we value them, how much we *should* value them (if we are to live well, that is) and how we try to fit them together in a single harmonious life.

A. THE PURSUIT OF WEALTH

> As an end, the acquisition of wealth is ignoble in the extreme; I assume that you have saved and long for wealth only as a means of enabling you to do some good in your day and generation.
>
> —Andrew Carnegie

Whatever else it may include, being "in business" means intending to make money. Success in business is measured, whatever else it may involve, by profits, and personal success is measured, at least in part, by one's financial security and status. But for too many Americans, the quest for the good life and the pursuit of money have come to be taken to be virtually the same. Money means security, freedom, more goods, and "everything that money can buy." But even this description of the pursuit and aims of wealth shows us quite clearly that wealth is but a *means,* a means to do things and buy things, and not an *end* or goal in itself. This distinction between *means* and *ends* will be crucial to any discussion of ethics; indeed, we might well define the subject (as some authors have) by saying that ethics is the identification of the *ends* of our actions that make up the good life, distinguishing these from mere means as well as the false goals that sometimes lead us off the track. Wealth has been argued throughout history to be both merely a means and a false goal; in either case, it has virtually never been confused with the ends of the good life itself. Aristotle argued quite bluntly that

---

The Price of Wealth ──

You are offered a job that will make you fabulously wealthy, but the results of your success will be the death of hundreds if not thousands of innocent people and the destruction of whole communities. Indeed, the consequences of your actions will be so intolerable that you will be despised and abandoned by your friends and family. What you will have done, however, is legal, so no official sanctions can be raised against you, but your name will be known and loathed across the country (and in other parts of the world). You will, of course, not be lonely, for you will undoubtedly be appealing to hundreds of free-loaders and gold-diggers who will "admire" you for your money. And money, whatever else it might buy, will also purchase power, the ability to do pretty much what you want—so long as it doesn't involve being genuinely liked or admired by other people. Now, do you want the job?

---

wealth, though perhaps essential to the good life, could not possibly be the good life itself. What good is wealth, he asked, if we are not also healthy and respected by our peers, if we are miserable in our family life or unable to enjoy the things that money can buy? Christianity, throughout its existence (at least until very recently) has always argued that "mammon"—wealth—is a false god, that the "things" of life are worthless compared to the eternal value of the *spiritual* goals preached by religion and the salvation of one's immaterial *soul,* even to the point of insisting that "it is easier for a camel to pass through the eye of a needle than it is for a rich man to enter the Kingdom of Heaven" (Matt. 19:21).

Ends and Means ———

We have been using the terms "ends" and "means" throughout our discussion; they are crucial to any conception of ethics. An *end* is a goal; it is the *aim* of an activity. A *means* is a method of reaching that goal; it is the *instrument* or *strategy* of an activity. Sometimes, we talk of an "end in itself," in order to distinguish ends that are ultimate, the *final* goal of an activity, from ends that may in turn be means to another end. For example, taking an assignment to win a certain account for the company and winning that account would then be the end of certain activities (for which a number of meetings, phone calls, demonstrations, and letters probably would be the means.) But that end is itself a means to other ends for the company, a means to expand its activities and increase profits; and for the individual, it is a means to prove his ability and to receive more responsibilities and rewards. Working for the right ends by the best means is called *rationality*.

When we Americans tend to think of the good life, we quite naturally tend to think of the good *things* in life first—a magnificent house, rooms full of Victorian or Corbusier furniture, the best food and wine, a Rolls-Royce or a Jaguar. More modest generations might substitute a Volvo or a Toyota for the Jaguar, health food for the more traditional porterhouse steak, or a townhouse for the mansion, but our materialistic bias is undisputed. Even so, it is clear that such things are valuable not in themselves but largely as *symbols,* a special kind of means, to display and manifest our success in the world. A century ago, the American economist, Thorstein Veblen, called the more ostentatious displays of material success "conspicuous consumption." But conspicuous or not, the luxuries we consume nevertheless symbolize our success, if only to ourselves. But notice how far we have come from the ends of the good life: money is a means to buy things that are themselves symbols of something else—success. Is success, therefore, the key ingredient to the good life?

B. SUCCESS

> Success is counted sweetest,
> By those who ne'er succeeded.
>
> —Emily Dickinson

Success, unlike pleasure and more explicitly money, is a *social value;* it is defined within a particular society, depends upon standards set by a particular society, and involves comparisons with other people as well as "doing well" according to a person's own goals. (Money, ultimately, is also a social value, of course; it is worth only what an economy says it is worth.) It is impossible to imagine what it would mean for a person to be concerned with success but oblivious to any status in society with regard to other people and standards shared with other people.

In business, success is often taken to be a straightforward matter; one businessperson summarized this view by saying, "you can always just look in your wallet." There is a difference, however, between financial success and success as the mark of the good life. The business world as well as the worlds of art and scholarship are full of examples of success without commensurate financial reward. Of course, our American mythology is equally filled with examples (many of them real) of millionaires who by no means live the good life and in fact are downright miserable and who might well be said to be failures instead of successes, despite their financial gains. Howard Hughes, who was one of the wealthiest men in America when he died several years ago, was nevertheless a miserable recluse, without friends or pleasures. His wealth and financial success did not enable him to live well, and most Americans found him pathetic. In the nineteenth century, American social critic Henry Adams commented that America then "contained scores of men worth five millions and upwards, whose lives were no more worth living than those of their cooks" (no doubt being unfair to some of the cooks).

The word "success" sounds as if it represents a single goal; in fact it summarizes the whole of the good life. This is hidden by the fact that the same word is often used to apply to much more specific and particular goals. For example, if my goal for the afternoon is to clear all of the paperwork off my desk, I can be "successful" in that sense, without invoking any of the complexities I have hinted

Success

Robert Scheller was a graduate student, at the age of 26 a $10,000-a-year research fellow in biology at the California Institute of Technology. He is also a millionaire, holding 15,000 shares of Genentech stock, worth about "1.1 million at $71+ per share." Scheller worked for Genentech, trying to synthesize a hormone in the new bio-engineering revolution. He was paid in stock (half of which he returned when he left because of "too much pressure from the investors"). But the synthesis succeeded, and Mr. Scheller reaped the benefits. What is he doing now? He still works as a research fellow at Cal Tech. He still lives in the same small apartment, doesn't own a car and mainly wears T-shirts. "I'm interested in being a professor at a good university," he insists. "You can't buy that."

Reported in *The Wall Street Journal,* Oct. 15, 1980

at above. If a businessperson takes as a goal becoming vice-president of the company within ten years or making a million dollars in two years, it is easy to see what will count as being "successful." The problem becomes fully evident only when we start to ask what it is that makes for a successful *life,* not just the fulfillment of some specific goal. Wealth is surely not enough. Fulfilling the goals and realizing the dreams of a particular enterprise comes closer to the general idea of success; however, these may well vary among businesspeople. One wants power, another prestige; one wants to be feared, another wants the ear of presidents; one wants to build a building that would be the envy of the Babylonians, another wants to bring off a coup that would make Cornelius Vanderbilt sit up in his grave and take notice. Success, in other words, can take on many forms, depending on the context and the kinds of expectations of businesspeople in a particular sector of business society—for an investment banker, for a strategic planning consultant, for a middle-manager of a large corporation, for a professor in finance at a prestigious university, or for an advertising executive.

Success as the goal of the good life, however, is something more than these particular successes. It includes not only the achievement of this goal or that one, but people who think that they are successful just on such a limited basis have an extremely limited conception of success. Nevertheless, the emphasis on success in our society shifts our attention to two extremely important features of our conception of the good life—first of all, that it necessarily involves fulfilling certain *social* goals and expectations and earning the recognition of other people; second, that it is firmly based on the idea of *achievement.* The good life is one to be achieved by effort. One can be successful, however, and still not be happy. Indeed, it is possible to achieve one's goals, be a big success, or even help humanity but still be miserable. Many very successful people work obsessively, worry a good deal of the time, and rarely have the opportunity to enjoy the fruits of their success. Success is no guarantee of the good life. One must, it seems, also enjoy one's success and, just as important, enjoy the activities and efforts that are successful. But could this mean that it is the enjoyment as such that is really our goal, the main ingredient in the good life?

C. Enjoying Life—and the Life of Pleasure

> Pleasure is never permitted to interrupt business. . . . Even mealtime [for the American businessman] is not a period of relaxation . . . it is only a disagreeable interruption of business.
>
> —Michael Chevalier
> (a young French engineer touring America
> in the mid-nineteenth century)

On any list of possibilities or ingredients for the good life, one of the most prominent entries is usually pleasure, "enjoying oneself." Philosophers usually call life in search of pleasure *hedonism.* "Short-run hedonism" is the life of immediate gratification that many people in our society live through as teenagers. If they survive that, they probably discover "long-run hedonism," which involves the skill of "delayed gratification," working for distant rewards and stretching out pleasures so that they last, perhaps for a lifetime. Hedonism, in general, is both the satisfaction of desires and the stimulation of desires so that they can be satisfied. The second is just as important as the first. Our first desires in life are rather simple—thirst, hunger, the desire for warmth or sleep. Satisfying these is simple but hardly constitutes a "lifestyle" for most of us. Our satisfactions tend to be concerned more with achievements and social status than with the biological "basics" of life. These achievements tend to be long-term, even lifelong, aspirations rather than more or less immediate gratifications. Notably, success in business is a relatively long-term effort, even in those activities that in business are considered "short-term investments." Friendship and love are not momentary pleasures but long-term or lifelong developments that never need come to an end. Psychologists sometimes speak of this as "delayed gratification," but the truth is rather that these are pleasures—if we want to call them that—that are indefinitely protractible, in the continuous activity itself. There may be no point in a successful career in which success can be said to have been finally achieved.

A devoted hedonist might reply that such views are irrational and that denying pleasure for too long a time is like "hitting yourself with a hammer because it feels good when you stop." But pleasure alone may not be satisfying for very long. Pleasure too easily gained may be pleasure too easily taken for granted and forgotten. Desires too easily satisfied could be too small to satisfy us. We sometimes think of hedonism as simple and basic, requiring nothing but constant self-pampering. However, hedonism can also be an art, a set of skills with increasingly subtle pleasures as its reward.

There is a critical and essential difference between *satisfying a desire* and *satisfying ourselves;* we can satisfy a desire without feeling the least bit satisfied, for example, if the desire satisfied is "not what I really wanted." On the other hand, the most satisfying life often consists of desires perpetually unsatisfied or only partially unsatisfied. All ambitions worth the name are like this, for example. In the search for more lasting and satisfying pleasures, we learn to enjoy hobbies and sports, great works of art or books, the life of the intellect and great (not "pleasant") conversation—and, perhaps most importantly—work. In the business life, our division of life into "work and pleasure" guarantees disaster, because we use this distinction against ourselves by then thinking that what we do "for a living" is something *not* to be enjoyed; we design jobs for others with the preconceived idea that work is not to be challenging or enjoyable. Many words have been written in defense of interesting and enjoyable work—on the grounds that it is more "productive" or "boosts morale." But enjoyable work is its

Theories of Work: X, Y, and Z ——

The motivation of work and its relationship with other values and activities has always been central to management concerns. Indeed, management largely consists of motivating and coordinating other people's efforts, and so understanding *why* people work is essential to business success. If work is an end in itself, for example, something that people want to do whatever the rewards, the job of the manager would be quite easy—simply to coordinate the various workers' efforts. If, on the other hand, people work only because of its rewards—in other words, if work is only a means—then the job of management must be to offer them rewards sufficiently enticing to make people want to work. Theories of work, ultimately, are also theories of value.

In recent management theory, these various alternatives have been replaced by somewhat more subtle theories about why people work. The Puritans may have believed that work was an end in itself and good for its own sake; many people, thinking mainly of unpleasant and tedious jobs, thought that a sane person would work only for some external reward, such as a salary. But since World War II, theories of work have proliferated rapidly, and with Douglas McGregor's *The Human Side of Enterprise* management theorists have talked about two contrasting theories with the blandest of names, Theory X and Theory Y. Theory X assumes that people are basically lazy and dislike work, and so have to be both tempted by rewards and threatened by punishments. Work itself, in other words, is an undesirable means to the good life. Theory Y, by contrast, assumes that people want to work and want to assume responsibilities. It is, in effect, a psychological version of the puritan work ethic—that not only should people work, but by nature, they want to work.

These two somewhat simplified theories of human nature have been recently challenged by a third theory, appropriately called Theory Z. Theory Z has been proposed by William Ouchi, by way of his characterization of the successes of Japanese industry in the past few decades. Theory Z does not stress the individual self, and where Theories X and Y both stress the individual's isolated attitudes towards work, Theory Z points out the importance of membership in a supportive institution of which the worker feels an important part. A worker is not motivated just by external rewards, but neither should the work be taken to be valuable in itself. It is work as part of the group, part of the company, and ultimately, as part of the nation (accordingly dubbed "Japan, Inc."). It is a theory of *participation*

> rather than a pure psychological theory of motivation. And given its success in Japan, it is not surprisingly being tried out by a significant number of American companies too.

own defense, or rather, it needs no defense; enjoying one's work is one of those values that we consider an *end in itself*. It is an end and not necessarily a means to anything. Completing a job that has been enjoyable can satisfy our desire and satisfy ourselves as well.

Work and Reward ——

No one regards it as remarkable that the advertising man, tycoon, poet, or professor who suddenly finds his work unrewarding should seek the counsel of a psychiatrist. One insults the business executive or the scientist by suggesting that his principal motivation in life is the pay he receives. Pay is not unimportant. Among other things, it is a prime index of prestige. Prestige—the respect, regard and esteem of others—is in turn one of the more important sources of satisfaction associated with this kind of work. But, in general, those who do this kind of work expect to contribute their best regardless of compensation. They would be disturbed by any suggestion to the contrary.

John Kenneth Galbraith, *The Affluent Society*

There are only a few people who would completely reject the life of hedonism as "not for me." Many self-declared hedonists, however, turn out to praise the *idea* of the life of pleasure far more than they actually live it. It is not uncommon for someone to work very hard for success or money—claiming that she worked only to provide the means for a later, more enjoyable life—when that person's real goal was just the success or the money. A good test of this claim is to ask "why then am I not just enjoying the pleasures I have available to me now?" or "if I could get the leisure and pleasure without having to work so hard or be successful, would it still be as valuable to me?"

Pleasure is important to the good life; indeed, we would have great difficulty imagining what it would be to "live well" without it. But this is quite different from insisting that pleasure itself is our goal in the good life. At most, it is an ingredient. It appears on analysis to be more of an *accompaniment* to the good life rather than a component. Aristotle argued this with the hedonists of his own day, and his view seems just as justifiable today. We do not do what we do in order to get pleasure, but

rather we get pleasure from doing what we want to do. It is not pleasure that constitutes living well, but rather, living well that gives us pleasure. It goes without
saying that we enjoy the good life; what does not follow is that enjoyment itself is
what the good life is about.

The Happiness Box ——

Suppose you were offered a machine with cushions in it, not unlike a
casketlike container in which an astronaut may sleep on a long space
voyage. The box is equipped with electrodes and a life-support system that can keep a person alive for at least what would be a normal
lifetime. During that entire period users of the machine would feel
nothing but a continuous feeling of pleasure and contentment—no
traumas, no depressions, no bad days or Monday morning blues, no
failures, no unhappy love affairs, no fears of impotence or going
broke or losing face or watching a teenage son smash the fender of
the new car. Use of the machine is entirely voluntary, and a person
can decide to get out of the box at any time, even after a few minutes.
But no one who gets into the box has ever decided to get out of it.
They all stay in for the duration of their lifetimes, smiling content-
edly, their bodies going out of shape like a beanbag, eventually forgotten by old friends and relatives, though they couldn't care less.
They are happy. Or are they? Perhaps they only feel happy; perhaps
they have not found the good life at all, but only sleep pleasantly
through life. Would you get in the box? Why or why not?

D. THE SEARCH FOR PERFECTION: THE PURITAN ETHIC

> . . . And he must have a business. Worshipping the Lord in
> prayer and hymn is not enough. Contemplation of the good
> means nothing without the accomplishment of the good. A
> man must not only be pious; he must be useful.
>
> —Alfred Whitney Griswold,
> Three Puritans on Prosperity

What we have said so far about wealth, success, and pleasure in the good life may
seem obvious enough, but what is missing from our account is the *moral* quality

that pertains to American business life. Morality is typically considered to consist of a set of rather rigid rules, which tell us what we can do and what we are forbidden from doing (as in "thou shalt not steal.") But morality is, first of all, a matter of *character,* a question of self-discipline and *wanting* to do the right thing. In America, this emphasis on morals and character has nowhere been more influential than in the "puritan ethic," which at the same time has been historically responsible for the respectability and success of business as a social enterprise.

Morality ——

Morality is the special set of values that mark off the more or less absolute limitations on behavior. It includes such basic rules as "don't kill innocent people" and "don't steal" as well as a general system of *duties* and *obligations* in society. Morality is sometimes summarized as the list of those actions that people *ought* to do or refrain from doing. Morality is only a small part of ethics, however, and the rules and rituals that define society and living well within it are far more extensive than the limitations of morality. Morality may set the guidelines and, especially, mark off what actions are utterly forbidden, but it is ethics more generally that sets positive goals and defines the meaning of life.

Benjamin Franklin summarized the American ethic as well as anyone. His virtues were distinctively social virtues, and his idea of success was as much a matter of abstinence and self-control as achievement. "Temperance, silence, order, resolution, frugality, industry, sincerity, justice, moderation, cleanliness, tranquility, chastity and humility" were hardly the virtues of the woodsman, the explorer, or the prospector. This set of virtues, which we call "the puritan ethic," was derived from a part of religion; but these are nevertheless secular values, separable from religious commitment. In one form or another, they are still very much a part of our conception of success and the good life. They are also emphatically and distinctively *social* virtues, character traits which are aimed at making people's behavior as conducive as possible to the *community's* harmony and peace. They also increase the likelihood of financial success in a "puritan" society. They emphasize hard work, abstaining from excessive pleasures and balancing success with humility—thus making a person work even harder.

We typically tend to think of the good life in terms of individual achievement and satisfaction, sometimes renewing the archaic notion of American "rugged individualism" as a self-congratulatory way of characterizing our independent ideals. Even in the eighteenth century, this notion was out of date for most Americans, except for those who dared to push westward into what was (again, self-congratulatorily) called "uncivilized wilderness." Even then, no sooner did a small number of people arrive in one place than they formed a good Christian middle-class town, in which community solidarity was considered more important than individual "ruggedness." Hard work is not a product of our "rugged individualism" nearly so much as it is a part of our urbanized "puritan ethic." It is not our "pioneer spirit" so much as our desire to be civilized, and it is not just a matter of individual advancement, but a desire for a good society too.

Around the turn of the century, Andrew Carnegie also proclaimed this "puritan ethic"—that success and wealth were worth nothing without the self-control that makes a person a good citizen as well as makes success possible. For example, he once warned a group of young businessmen of "three grave dangers" that would beset the aspiring businessperson on the path to success. "The first and most seductive, and the destroyer of most young men, is the drinking of liquor." Such horrifying loss of control is intolerable to the puritan ethic. The next danger, he added, was "speculation," the appeal to luck ("fortune") instead of hard work and good business sense. Hard work is the key to success; indeed, it is a puritan virtue even without success. The third danger is "the perilous habit of *indorsing,*" that is helping out a friend in debt at the risk of your own financial stake. The puritan ethic may emphasize pleasantness and sociability, but it is not particularly friendly. Foolish sacrifices on a friend's behalf are just as damnable as foolish actions entirely one's own. Saying "make the firm's interest your own," Carnegie stresses loyalty as one of the virtues and then adds, "put all your eggs in one basket and watch that basket." Single-minded concentration and consolidation are also virtues. Finally, he says, "be not impatient, for as Emerson says, 'No one can cheat you out of ultimate success but yourself.'"

Carnegie's basic message, then, stresses the power of self-control in winning financial success; but the aim of acquiring such success in the first place is *to do good* and, ultimately, to prove one's *worthiness* to gain the rewards of success. More than anything else, this concept of self-worth and *deserving* such rewards is the key to the puritan ethic. And deserving, here, means not just *what* has been achieved but also the *moral* concern for being a certain kind of virtuous *character,* whatever a person's background or origins.

Much American thinking is still dominated by the puritan ethic and its emphasis on discipline and good character. Success is the consequence of good character, but good character itself is the mark of living well and the goal of the good life. Pleasure is but passing enjoyment, never an end in itself and often a danger or a distraction. Wealth is the measure of success but, again, not in any way to be mistaken for a goal of its own. Whatever we think of it on reflection, the puritan ethic has provided the fundamental and, to European eyes, for example, the peculiar moral emphasis of American business life. Hard work, wealth, and success are not only means to enjoy life; they are *proof* of a person's good character, and the reasons for respect from fellow citizens.

E.   REJECTING IT ALL: ASCETICISM

You think that I am impoverishing myself by withdrawing from men, but in my solitude I have woven for myself a silken web or chrysalis, and, nymph-like, shall ere long burst forth a more perfect creature, fitted for a higher society. By simplicity, commonly called poverty, my life is concentrated and so becomes organized, which was before inorganic and lumpish.
                                                    —Henry David Thoreau, Walden

In the context of a discussion of business and the good life, perhaps no conception of the good life would seem more out of place than that ancient vision called *"asceticism."* Asceticism is the wholesale rejection of the values of wealth and success. Not surprisingly, asceticism is a view sometimes found among people who have tried but failed to be successful. As a kind of compensation, even a mode of resentment, they may say "all that work and money just makes a person neurotic" or "the rich lose touch with the simple pleasures of life."

Over two thousand years ago, a group of Greek philosophers called *cynics* defended the ascetic life, gave away everything they owned, and sought only the simplest and more basic things in life. One of them, Diogenes, lived in a bathtub and owned nothing but a lantern with which he is said to have searched the faces of everyone, looking for "one honest person." When Alexander the Great came to visit Diogenes in his bathtub, he asked the cynical philosopher, "What can I do for you, wise man?" Diogenes turned to the ruler of most of the known world and replied, "Move over, you're blocking the sun."

By no means a view confined to the unsuccessful or the resentful, asceticism has even been accepted, at least vicariously, by some of the wealthiest and most powerful people in history, who have advocated the "simple" life in the midst of their millions. The puritan ethic is in part derived from its warnings against overindulgence and intemperance. Marie Antoinette had a little peasant hut built for herself on the grounds of the palace at Versailles so she and her friends could enjoy the simple pleasures of life (catered by servants, of course) and then being promoted by the philosopher Jean Jacques Rousseau. Indeed, asceticism has most powerfully been preached not by those who have failed, but by those who have succeeded and have had the opportunity to "see through" the vanities of ambition and success. These people turn in the opposite direction, even demanding poverty and the lack of all possessions as avidly as they once sought wealth and possessions.

The "Noble Savage": Jean Jacques Rousseau

Savage man and civilized man differ so much at the bottom of their hearts and in their inclinations, that what constitutes the supreme happiness of the one would reduce the other to despair. The first sighs for nothing but repose and liberty; he desires only to live, and to be exempt from labor. . . . Civilized man, on the other hand, is always in motion, perpetually sweating and toiling, and racking his brains to find out occupations still more laborious; he continues a drudge to his last minute; nay, he courts death to be able to live, or renounces life to acquire immortality. He pays court to men in power whom he hates, and to rich men whom he despises . . . proud of his slavery, he speaks with disdain of those who have not the honor of sharing it. . . . The savage lives within himself, whereas social man, constantly outside himself, knows only how to live in the opinion of others; and it is, if I may say so, merely from their judgment of him that he derives the consciousness of his own existence.

From *A Discourse on the Origins of Inequality*

American ethics is torn on this matter, as are the ethics of virtually all Christian industrialized nations. On the one hand, our conception of the good life includes the good things in life, most of which cost money. But on the other hand, we think of some of our folk heroes wandering off into the wilderness not to "make their fortunes," but to cast off the burdens of city and social life and to be self-sufficient. In the past few decades, a distinctive trend has developed among many Americans to move to the country to pursue the simple life of growing food and making what is needed. It has turned out not to be such a simple life after all, as many of these modern ascetics have found out. The ideal, in any case, remains the same: in such a life, the concepts of success and wealth have no literal application, unless we want to play with the words, as in Shakespeare's *Othello,* "poor and content is rich, and rich enough." (III, i, 172)

The ascetic life most familiar to us is the religious life of the Christian ascetics, the monks of the late Middle Ages and the various continuing orders that accept the ascetic way of life as a way to salvation or "purification." But it is important to distinguish between the asceticism of the cynics who saw the life of simplicity itself as the good life, and that of the monks who viewed the life of simplicity as a *means* to a further goal, salvation. Again, the distinction between ends and means will be of crucial importance to our discussion of business ethics, for the search for the good life is first of all a question of ends, only secondarily a question of means. Thus, the ascetic life might well be attempted by a jaded hedonist who, having exhausted the more elaborate and urbane pleasures of life, finally tries to find pleasure in the simplicities of life. Some businesspeople live very much by the tradition of the "puritan ethic," trying to maximize success in business by denying themselves a great many pleasures, luxuries, and material goods. Despite considerable wealth and success, there are businesspeople who, nevertheless, insist on living a sparse and frugal life with the aescetic ideal as their end.

F.   DIMENSIONS OF THE GOOD LIFE: WHAT MONEY CAN'T BUY

> "A living, or money," Lee said excitedly. "Money's easy to make if it's money you want. But with a few exceptions people don't want money. They want luxury and they want love and they want admiration."
>
> —John Steinbeck, East of Eden

We have, of course, only scratched the surface in our investigation of the good life. We can agree, perhaps, that it includes at least good health, financial security, success, self-esteem, and at least a reasonable amount of pleasure and enjoyment—including a person's "work" as enjoyable too. We can agree, too, with the puritan ethic—at least insofar as it insists that money, pleasure, and success aren't everything—that a person ultimately must be a *good person,* even if we don't agree with the ascetic that money, pleasure, and worldly success aren't worth anything at all. And we can agree that the good life is a full life, filled with variety and extended far beyond the limited scope of personal problems, whether or not we agree on what sorts of variety and what sorts of extensions are most desirable. Indeed, the good life is most often contrasted not with the "bad life" but rather with the too-limited and narrow life, the life not fully lived, the life too caught up in the petty concerns and personal problems of a too-restricted and too unimaginative vision. In such a narrow life, the scope of the world in humanity, culture, love, friendship, and the larger concerns of society are blocked out or neglected. People living such a life may well be "successful," in a limited sense; and they may even become enormously wealthy, as the history of misers and misanthropes displays rather convincingly. But no one would call such a life "good," or such living "living well." However flexible we may be in our conceptions of

A Day at the Races ———

We'll call him Charlie Robinson, a vice president for a consumer-goods firm. He heads up the brand group and makes $147,000 a year [1993 dollars]. That's salary. In addition there are the bonuses, and of course there is the stock. Robinson has 500 shares. It's not paid for, but the company arranges for the loan.

Robinson is 44 years old. He has a house and an acre of land assessed at $380,000. A nice place, clean air, good schools and yet only 40 minutes from the office.

It's 7:15. Robinson has been home for half an hour. He thinks he'll have another drink—his third—before dinner. Then what? A movie? No, too tired. Besides, brought some work home from the office. Get to it after dinner, then watch some TV, then to bed early. A tough day tomorrow.

Mrs. Robinson wants to know when they are going to be able to take that long weekend and go upstate to see her mother and father. Robinson: "How the hell do I know? I work my head off all day and I have a briefcase full of stuff. I'm not sure when we can get away. Things are rough at the office right now." Mrs. Robinson doesn't bring up the subject again. Debbie, who is in high school, goes up to her room. It's best to stay away from Daddy. He's had a tough day.

O. William Battaglia and John J. Tarrant, *The Corporate Eunuch*

life and our willingness to allow that different people may be happy doing different things, such a life resists our attempt to think of it as "happy."

These other values—not just pleasure, money, and success, but love, friendship, and the less tangible "finer things in life"—are particularly important for business ethics. They have often been left out of any discussion of business life, and the traditional image of the businessperson in America has capitalized on the apparent absence of these values as reason for a general condemnation of the business world and its participants. Some of these values are so important that we will devote entire chapters to them—notably, love and friendship, as well as the more general values of community membership. Here, however, a more neglected set of values will briefly take our attention—those intangible virtues that involve knowledge and culture, whose "practical" expression can be identified in something as simple as good conversation.

American literature and social criticism have long represented the wealthy businessman as a bore. "Suppose 'stocks' to be ruled out," challenged a newspaper editor many years ago, "where would the topics of conversation be found?" Charles Adams, Jr., a railroad president himself, once said:

> I have known, and known tolerably well, a good many 'Successful' men. . . . A less interesting crowd I do not care to encounter. Not one that I have ever known would I care to meet again, either in this world or the next; nor is one of them associated in my mind with the idea of humor, thought or refinement.*

Heilbroner also quotes President Theodore Roosevelt, who remarked disdainfully:

> I am simply unable to make myself take the attitude of respect toward the very wealthy men which such an enormous number of people evidently feel. I am delighted to show any courtesy to Pierpont Morgan or Andrew Carnegie or James J. Hill, but as for regarding any one of them as, for instance, I regard Professor Bury, or Peary the Arctic explorer, or Rhodes the historian—why, I could not force myself to do it, even if I wanted to, which I don't.†

The message here is clear: success in business, no matter how indisputable, even combined with the "puritan" virtues that make a person respectable as well, is not enough for the good life, or, for that matter, to make him or her "successful" in a larger sense of that term. Of course, no one expects a person who has spent most of his or her life in business to be an expert on classical music and modern art at the same time, or to have read all of the classics and the criticism written about them as well as the popular potboilers that are read on airplanes and talked about at parties. Nevertheless, there is a difference between expertise and

---

Mr. Pickwick on the Good Life

"I shall never regret," said Mr. Pickwick in a low voice, "I shall never regret having devoted the greater part of two years to mixing with different varieties and shades of human character: frivolous as my pursuit of novelty may have appeared to many. Nearly the whole of my previous life having been devoted to business and the pursuit of wealth, numerous scenes of which I had no previous conception have dawned upon me—I hope to the enlargement of my mind, and the improvement of my understanding."

Charles Dickens, *Pickwick Papers*

---

*Quoted by Robert Heilbroner, *The Quest for Wealth* (New York: Simon & Schuster, 1956), p. 189.
†*Ibid.*

literacy, between trying to outdo a college professor at his subject and just "keeping up," and between knowing what defines a society's culture and what does not. The same argument applies to current events and politics, which may or may not touch on the business world. "Knowing what is going on" is not simply a matter of good business; it is a question of being a part of the larger world, a citizen, and member of humanity rather than a bore in a business suit. The good life is not a life lived in voluntary exclusion from the problems of the world; it is a life that is inseparably a part of that world, identifying with it and seeing itself as an intrinsic part of it. With the problems of the world, of course, come the pleasures of world citizenship too: the special enjoyment of history and the greatest achievements of human beings that, even as they dwarf our own abilities and accomplishments, make us feel part of something much greater by sharing in the genius of our species.

■ SUMMARY AND CONCLUSION

Ethics is the quest for, and the attempt to understand, "the good life," the life we consider most desirable for "living well." Business ethics is therefore the quest for and the understanding of the good life in business, of what is important to it and what is not, and what is more important and what is most important of all. Wealth is often a necessary means for attaining many pleasures but therefore not an end itself, and there are many pleasures and values in life that are not dependent on wealth. Many people consider the pursuit of pleasure, or *hedonism,* to be the most important ingredient of the good life, but many of our pleasures tend to be long-term and based on achievement. Success is a value that summarizes our emphasis on achievement and also emphasizes the *social* element of the good life. But any adequate understanding of the ethics of business life must also include those many values that are not particular to business, including friendship and love, and a sense of being a valued member of the community, as well as the even less tangible comforts of religion and the arts.

Business is part of society, and business life is inseparably part of the culture and fate of its supportive society; business ethics, therefore, also addresses the role of business and businesspeople in education and the arts. It involves knowledge of history and politics and the sense of having a place in the world. Indeed, the good life is so readily available in business just because, in our society, these other values are so much a part of business life.

■ STUDY QUESTIONS

1. Rank the following values, in terms of your own interests and goals:

   wealth__   excitement__

success___   power___
respectability___   friendship___
freedom___   admiration___
religious salvation___   family life___
creativity___   hobbies, sports, recreation___

Explain your rankings.

2. Is it possible to think that you are happy without actually *being* happy? What does this imply about the nature of happiness?

3. In your own words, what is "success"? What kinds of achievements do you envision for yourself that would give you success?

4. Describe the "puritan ethic." In what ways do your values conform to this ethic? In what ways do they not?

5. What is meant by "individualism"? To what extent are your career goals strictly aimed at your own personal enrichment and achievement? To what extent do your goals explicitly or implicitly include other people (who and how)?

6. Benjamin Franklin and the puritans constantly stressed the importance of "self-discipline." What does this mean? What are its advantages?

7. Quite a few MBA graduates accept *lower* paying jobs than their highest offers. What reasons would prompt you to accept a job whose salary was significantly lower than another?

FOR CLASS DISCUSSION

Three Job Offers

Upon graduation from college or business school, you get three job offers, all of which are for very different jobs. Each job has its own attractions and drawbacks. Discuss your choice among them, stressing what you perceive to be advantages and disadvantages.

Job 1: Working at a small bank in your home town. You already know everyone in the town, and in fact, everyone who is working at the bank. You like the people and know that if you took the job, the stress would be very low and the hours fairly short. But in return for these shorter hours, the pay would be moderate, compared with the other two jobs. The bank has been established for a long time, and there is very little chance that you would ever lose your job. The bank is locally owned so there is no pressure from any parent company, You would have a real opportunity to find your place in the bank, but there is little chance that you would ever get a spectacular promotion.

Job 2: You have been offered a job with Humongous, Inc. You have heard what it is like to work for Humongous: longer hours than you've ever even heard of, report after report after detailed report, and a grueling annual corporate meeting. At these meetings, not only are you expected to have submitted a detailed 50-page report on your own business area for review, but you are expected to have studied the other 120 managers' 50-page reports. The meetings last from 9:30 in the morning until midnight, for four days. As everyone picks over the reports, it is not uncommon for managers to be fired on the spot. In Humongous, Inc., there is little job security and there is little room for a family life or even friends outside the job. The pay, however, is spectacular, and Humongous is famous for taking young managers and promoting them quickly, so that they are soon running business segments with $400 million in sales, while their colleagues in other companies are still just junior executives. The job is more exciting than anything you ever dreamed of, and extremely challenging.

Job 3: An acquaintance from the computer section of your school has just offered you a job. He is trying to start his own company, making robotics, and needs someone to take care of the everyday operating functions. He and his colleagues have all the creativity the company will need, and, in fact, have already come up with several new products they think they can market successfully. All that is left now is to put the firm together, incorporate, get bank financing, and actually start production. As you can see, if the firm takes off, things would be spectacular, and you would be rich, but if it flops, you would be out of a job. The starting pay would be higher than the bank pay, yet far below the pay of Humongous. You would have a free hand in running the whole business, and the computer people would not interfere. The job would require living in the suburbs of a large metropolitan area.

The Opportunist*
James Fenimore Cooper

The service at Mr. Effingham's table was made in the quiet but thorough manner that distinguishes a French dinner. Every dish was removed, carved by the domestics, and handed in turn to each guest. But there were a delay and a finish in this arrangement that suited neither Aristabulus' go-ahead-ism, nor his organ of acquisitiveness. Instead of waiting, therefore, for the more graduated movements of the domestics, he began to take care of himself, an office that he performed with a certain dexterity that he had acquired by frequenting ordinaries—a school, by the way, in which he had obtained most of his notion of the proprieties of the table. One or two slices were obtained in the usual manner, or by means of

---

*From James Fenimore Cooper, *Home as Found* (New York: G. P. Putnam's Sons, 1838) pp. 18–19.

the regular service; and then, like one who had laid the foundation of a fortune by some lucky windfall in the commencement of his career, he began to make accessions, right and left, as opportunity offered. Sundry *entremets,* or light dishes that had a peculiarly tempting appearance, came first under his grasp. Of these he soon accumulated all within his reach, by taxing his neighbors, when he ventured to send his plate here and there, or wherever he saw a dish that promised to reward his trouble. By such means, which were resorted to, however, with a quiet and unobtrusive assiduity that escaped much observation, Mr. Bragg contrived to make his own plate a sample epitome of the first course. It contained in the centre, fish, beef, and ham; and around these staple articles he had arranged croquettes, rognons, ragouts, vegetables, and other light things, until not only was the plate completely covered, but it was actually covered in double and triple layers; mustard, cold butter, salt, and even pepper garnishing its edges. These different accumulations were the work of time and address, and most of the company had repeatedly changed their plates before Aristabulus had eaten a mouthful, the soup excepted. The happy moment when his ingenuity was to be rewarded had now arrived, and the land agent was about to commence the process of mastication, or of deglutition rather, for he troubled himself very little with the first operation, when the report of a cork drew his attention towards the champagne. To Aristabulus this wine never came amiss, for, relishing its piquancy he had never gone far enough into the science of the table to learn which were the proper moments for using it. As respected all the others at table, this moment had in truth arrived, though, as respected himself, he was no nearer to it, according to regulated taste, than when he first took his seat. Perceiving that Pierre was serving it, however, he offered his own glass, and enjoyed a delicious instant as he swallowed a beverage that much surpassed anything he had ever known to issue out of the waxed and leaded nozzles that, pointed like so many enemies' batteries loaded with headaches and disordered stomachs, garnished sundry village bars of his acquaintance.

Aristabulus finished his glass at a draught, and when he took breath he fairly smacked his lips. That was an unlucky instant; his plate, burdened with all its treasures, being removed at this unguarded moment; the man who performed this unkind office fancying that a dislike to the dishes could alone have given rise to such an *omniumgatherum.*

It was necessary to commence *de novo,* but this could no longer be done with the first course, which was removed, and Aristabulus set to with zeal forthwith on the game. Necessity compelled him to eat, as the different dishes were offered; and such was his ordinary assiduity with the knife and fork, that, at the end of the second remove, he had actually disposed of more food than any other person at table.

What is the analogy that Cooper is entertaining here? What is the business lesson implicit in Cooper's making fun of Aristabulus?

HISTORICAL INTERLUDE

BUSINESS AND IDEOLOGY:
AN INTRODUCTION TO MACROETHICS

> It is hardly an exaggeration to say that, with increasing afflu-
> ence, economics has moved into the very centre of public con-
> cern, and economic performance, economic growth, economic
> expansion, and so forth have become the abiding interest, if
> not the obsession, of all modern societies. In the current
> vocabulary of condemnation there are few words as final and
> conclusive as the word "uneconomic." . . . Anything that is
> found to be an impediment to economic growth is a shameful
> thing.
>
> —E. F. Schumaker, Small Is Beautiful

B usiness is a distinctively modern activity, circumscribed and defined by a
set of ideas—what one might call an *ideology*. Many of the concepts we
take most for granted, as entirely "natural," are concepts that would be unintelligible, or would have a very negative significance, in many other societies. For
example, our general sense that most things, including human time and talents,
have a "price" would strike many societies as meaningless or vulgar. The general
importance we place on economic concerns, on how much people earn instead of
how much they enjoy the effort or actually contribute to the community, for
instance, is peculiar to modern times and certain societies. Our notion of individual success would not be understood in a society in which all efforts are team
efforts. The idea of a "bargain" would not be understood in a society that had no
concept of the market. The idea that making a profit is a legitimate activity
would have horrified most people until very recently.

The study of these ideas and the institutions that give them substance in society is the province of what we call *"macroethics."* From a more personal or
"microethical" point of view, these ideas and institutions provide the framework
for the good life and provide our goals and roles in society. But from the larger,
macroethical perspective, these ideas and institutions define the business world
itself; it could not exist without them. Without an ideology that placed so much
emphasis on material well-being, on the significance of consumer desires, and on
the legitimacy of making a profit, there could be no business enterprise.

Macroethics is the study and evaluation of business activity as such. The scientific study of the working of the business world is the province of economics,

but the examination of the *values* of business is the business of macroethics. It takes these values as given and tries to clarify and understand them. It evaluates the values themselves and asks, essentially, do these activities and institutions called "business" in fact serve the good of society? We might say that microethics is a reflection on a person's participation in the practice of business, while macroethics questions the nature and purpose of the practice itself, the ideology that defines and justifies it.

The very word *"ideology"* requires some explanation. It is a term that has suffered from well-known negative connotations throughout recent history; in fact, it has had negative connotations virtually since its inception at the hands of a Frenchman, Antoine Destutt de Tracy, at the beginning of the nineteenth century, during the reign of Napoleon. But Napoleon himself abused ideology as "sinister metaphysics" (and blamed his military losses in Russia on the interference of the "ideologues"). Karl Marx used it as a term of abuse against the liberal and conservative German thinkers he opposed, and in this century "ideology" is in turn often used against Marx and the ideas. In his history of the term, ideology is often confused with *dangerous* ideas and with *distortions* of reality as mere illusions and rationalizations. But the term is wholly neutral and quite innocent. The blandest ideas of everyday life are part of an ideology just as much as the revolutionary's call for the overthrow of governments. The most ordinary visions of ourselves and our world are perceived and conceived through the lenses of ideology just as much as the most grotesque distortions of demagogues and ideological madmen. For example, feeling good about selling your car at a profit, instead of at the going "blue book" rate, is a complex product of our whole system of market-oriented values, however "natural" it might seem to us at the time. Ideologies may be illusory, but more often, they simply refer to our values, the way we see the world and our place within it. Ideologies are sometimes rationalizations, but they are also the very structure of what we believe, how we think of ourselves and what we do. An ideology, properly conceived, is nothing but the way we conceive of and perceive our world, through the *ideas* we have about it.

In a large sense, our ideologies include such broad philosophical concepts as our notion of "human nature" and "the good society" including the origins of the universe, the existence and nature of God, the origins and legitimacy of society and the state, the nature of the self, the possibility of freedom, and other cosmic questions. In a more limited context we can also consider our views about the nature of ourselves in society and in the world of business—our individual places in that world, the relationship between business and society, the working of the marketplace and its ultimate potential for good and for evil. Foremost in our inquiry, therefore, will be questions about the nature of the business world itself, not just as an already established world into which we enter as individuals, but as a historical, rapidly changing and still developing world for which we still need to find its proper place in our society as a whole.

To make the importance of the notion of ideology in business clear, consider the following two examples. First, suppose we accept the idea that business is a matter of "dog eat dog," or, in more sophisticated language, a matter of Darwinian "survival of the fittest." On an individual level, it is clear that this idea will dictate a great deal about what we do in our everyday dealings, how much we will trust one another, what kinds of plots and conspiracies may be necessary in order to "come out on top," or what kind of loyalty we owe to our friends or employer. But at the same time, this brutal idea will have the same kind of consequences in the business world as a whole; corporations as well as individuals will see their situations as a life-and-death battle for profits, which in business life mean survival. With such a vision, we can only expect that the business world will be strewn with casualties—failed businesses, executives out of work, workers unemployed, and consumers bilked without guilt or regrets. The attitude towards the government, in such a model, will most likely be to see it as a kind of referee that on occasion prevents the slaughter from being too excessive and, for the most part, cleans up some of the damage, keeping itself out of the battle so as not to interfere with the "natural selection" of the winners or their ability to compete with one another. This is an extreme picture, of course, but such extreme pictures are often useful for throwing into relief our own more modest views of business and the business world. And insofar as we tend to look at business essentially as a form of competition, a game with its own rules and with winners and losers, some of the features of this extreme ideology will apply.

Second, consider someone who believes that business is rather a cooperative national enterprise, and that what we do for ourselves and our corporations is in turn good for the country as a whole. "What's good for General Motors is good for the U.S.A." we used to hear: but notice that an entire ideology is presupposed in that simple slogan, that business and its success in turn improves the well-being of everyone else. On an individual level, such a benign and optimistic attitude tends to turn business into a team effort, and we see other businesspeople, even competitors—as teammates with the same goal in mind. On the macroethical level, corporations also tend to see themselves more as collaborators towards some grand goal rather than competitors for whom "beating the competition" is by itself a worthwhile goal. Casualties of competition will be viewed with sympathy, as injured team members rather than fallen foes. The expectation will be that a person's successes will be followed by the increased welfare of everyone else and so greeted by their praise as well.

This, too, is an extreme and exaggerated case, but again it serves to throw into relief the more modest optimism shared by most business people today, which is that business, allowed to be successful in its own terms and without interference, will in turn make the nation as a whole wealthier, more prosperous and powerful, and its citizens happier and healthier. Sometimes, we find these two extreme ideologies promoted together, for example, in some of the pronouncements of John D. Rockefeller; more often, economists and businesspeople take a more cautious view towards both positions realizing that business, like most human endeavors, consists of a complex balance between individual competition and mutual effort, between individual survival and success and the survival and well-being of the society in which they play their part. But how this complex balance is achieved is itself a matter of protracted debate and analysis, and forms the core of the writings of virtually every great economist from ancient times until today.

■ FOR CLASS DISCUSSION

The "Ideologies" of Business

Evaluate, in your own terms, the following "ideological" views of business in American society:

a. "It's a jungle out there, a dog-eat-dog world. You do whatever you have to do to survive."

b. "If each of us works hard to maximize our own profits and rewards, society as a whole will definitely be improved."

c. "Nothing happens by itself; if we want to improve society as a whole—correct the problems of racism and unemployment, help the poor and the disabled—then we will have to work at it, and not assume that it will happen as a miraculous side effect of our own selfish efforts."

d. "If a man becomes rich, it is because God intended for him to become rich."

e. "People are basically selfish, so the best we can do is to motivate them with their own selfishness to do some good for others (or at least not do too much harm)."

f. "Business is like a battle. You need teamwork, leadership, obedience, and a sense of ruthlessness toward the competition. You do whatever it takes to win."

g. "Business is really the desire to provide quality products and services for your fellow citizens (and others) at the lowest possible price. The rewards of doing so are a sense of doing good for others as well as doing well for oneself. Profits are important but they are secondary."

Business Life, Law, and Ethics

Remember that time is money. He that can earn ten shillings a day by his labour, and goes abroad, or sits idle, one half of that day, though he spends but sixpence during his diversion or idleness, ought not to reckon that the only expense; he has spent, or rather thrown away, five shillings besides.
—Benjamin Franklin, Autobiography

The peculiarity of this philosophy of avarice appears to be the ideal of the honest man of recognized credit, and above all the idea of the duty of an individual toward the increase of his capital, which is assumed to be an end in itself. Truly what is preached here is not simply a means of making one's way in the world, but a peculiar ethic. . . . It is not mere business astuteness (that sort of thing is common enough), it is an ethos.
—Max Weber, The Protestant Ethic and the Spirit of Capitalism
(discussing Franklin's work)

Business life is obviously concerned with the pursuit of money, both in profits and in growth, whether in the size of the company or in a person's own status and position. Of course, everyone, in every walk of life, pursues money to a certain extent as a matter of mere survival. Artists need money, but they would never describe their work as in itself the pursuit of money. "Do good work," they hope, "and the money will come." Physicians make a lot of money, but do not openly announce that the "end" of their professional life is to make money, with saving lives just the means to do so. But for people who enter the life of business, the pronouncement that their ambition is to make money is considered par for the course; it is what is expected and what is demanded of that life itself. But as we stressed so often in the preceding chapter, this single-minded goal is not, despite appearances, an "end in itself" or a goal that excludes all other goals. It is part of a life that has other dimensions, other rules, and other concerns. Nevertheless, it is a kind of life that is quite distinct.

A.   BUSINESS LIFE: THE HISTORICAL CONTEXT

Perhaps the first point to be made about business life is that it is not the universal human activity it is sometimes thought to be. It is, instead, a remarkably modern and culturally peculiar phenomenon. People have been growing, using, and acquiring material goods for many thousands of years, of course, ever since the first man or woman put together two sticks or planted a seed. People have been trading goods and services since long before the beginning of recorded history, and, in fact, the earliest samples of writing we have are inventories and primitive promissory notes. The Phoenicians were active traders before the time of Homer (800 B.C.), and Baghdad was a fabulous center for merchants and international commerce in the epoch of the Old Testament. In Europe city life in the Middle Ages was largely defined by the trade guilds, and in the East (not only China but Byzantium and eastern Italy) commercial life had been bustling with activity and money making long before anyone in Western Europe ever even thought about "making money" or "increasing productivity" or "making a profit" as such.

What *we* call "business"—defined in terms of mass markets and giant corporations—was not found anywhere on earth until the eighteenth century when it was only in its infancy. It really begins only towards the end of the nineteenth century, perhaps foremost in America, where the novel modern theories about "free enterprise"—the idea that individual greed *alone* would maximize the good of all—were taken seriously. Our subject is therefore a relatively recent innovation, not a description of a universal human phenomenon.

The contemporary commercial enterprise is the product of our society at a certain point in its history. We also must be careful not to assume that business is the same in other cultures. Japanese business, as we shall see, has a very different set of rules and structures than our own. And much of what some countries find odious about "colonialism" has been our assumption of the universality of our market society, the idea that our values of consumerism, individual enterprise, and material wealth are common to all societies. But these values are indigenous in only certain societies, societies that have developed certain factors that make business life—unknown in much of the world and throughout most of history—a dominant institution in American life.

What are the factors which make business life *as we know it* possible? There are geographical and technical factors, of course:

1. The growth of cities.

2. The *industrial revolution* of the eighteenth century, which provided markets and mass-produced goods.

3. An exceedingly long period of world peace, from the fall of Napoleon in 1815 to the outbreak of World War I in 1914.

4. The establishment of banks and other institutions of commerce.

5. The shift from purely physical exchange of goods and services to a largely abstract system of transactions by way of money and paper—the *monetization* of society.

Olde Business ——

If today's business student were to be transported back in time to visit a counterpart in Shakespeare's England in the early seventeenth century, the experience would be disconcerting, to say the least. There would be little cash, and wealth would be calculated mainly by the sheer accumulation of gold, jewels, and precious commodities, most of them taken by force in war or acts of piracy. Indeed, one historian of the business world describes the world of commerce in England as mainly "war and robbery," in contrast to the "vulgar production of useful articles." Piracy was often sponsored by the government. The pirate Sir Walter Raleigh was the right-hand man of Queen Elizabeth I, and one of the leading monopolists in England. Such routine business activities as bookkeeping were scarcely known, and new foreign words such as "bankruptcy" were just beginning to creep into the English language. Consumer demand, and the law of supply and demand, would have been all but unrecognized; what was recognized was the assumed value of precious commodities such as gold, silver, and jewelry, most of it hoarded by the government as national treasure. There were no corporations as such, although huge "trading companies" preserved absolute monopolies, free from all competition in foreign trade. A loss was a loss, and it could not be made up by insurance or higher prices, which were often forbidden by law.

The idea of accumulating capital for future production would not have been considered. Interest charges were generally forbidden and "going to the office" could not have arisen, since business transactions mainly took place on ships, in battle, in the palace, or on the road. Of course, there were few secretaries, no copy machines, and an unfamiliar absence of file cabinets. An information retrieval system was usually a young boy. Prices were fixed and competition minimal. Contracts were awarded by the king, usually on the sole basis of favoritism.

Occasionally, a man (rarely a woman) might get rich through business, but he would never become respectable or powerful. Even those shrewd merchants who, at the end of the Middle Ages, managed to make fortunes and buy castles and titles still suffered the indignities of their vulgar origins. Kings and princes used their wealth, but no businessman in Shakespeare's England would have expected to enjoy the status and power enjoyed by a Henry Ford or Bernard Baruch in this country. A businessman might aspire to luxury, but not much more. The idea of his being "the pillar of the community" would have been as foreign to him a mere three hundred years ago as it was to a Babylonian in Athens in the fifth century B.C.

These changes all presupposed something far more basic: a change in *ideas*. The possibility and the rapid growth of business life in Europe depended on a new set of theories about business, about society, and about human life and social interaction.

Some of these new ideas can be summarized in a phrase, "the market society." The new ideas were, first of all, revisions in Christian theology, since the most powerful ideas not only in the Middle Ages but in early modern times were unquestionably the doctrines of the Christian church(es). The Bible frequently warns against the most basic business ventures: making a profit, charging interest ("usury"), or taking advantage of what, in our terms, "the market will bear." The change in Christian theology came primarily with John Calvin (1509–64), who proclaimed that secular wealth was not opposed to, but rather a sign of, a person's eventual salvation. With Calvin, money making and the wise acquisition of wealth ("thrift") became a far more respectable and legitimate activity than it ever had been. And over the next two centuries, concepts that we now take for granted (as part of "human nature") emerged for the first time—the idea of the *"profit motive"* as a guide to human economic behavior, the concept of general social mobility according to the market and the idea of "making a fortune," the theory of supply and demand, and the concept of "the consumer" as the ultimate determinant of price.

Before, seeking a profit was roundly condemned by both religion and social mores as "avarice"; jobs tended to be inherited from the family or apportioned by the king, regardless of personal advantage or the possibility of better luck elsewhere; the idea of rising "above" a person's station in life was considered dangerous and disruptive to the social fabric as a whole; and prices were generally fixed, both in the Bible and by the secular authorities, as nothing more than "a fair

---

"The Sin of Avarice" ——

"He who has enough to satisfy his wants," wrote a Schoolman of the fourteenth century, "and nevertheless ceaselessly labors to acquire riches, either in order to obtain a higher social position, or that subsequently he may have enough to live without labor, or that his sons may become men of wealth and importance—all such are incited by a damnable avarice, sensuality, or pride."

R. H. Tawney, *Religion and the Rise of Capitalism*

---

price," which meant precisely wages for labor, and nothing more—no interest, no profits, no bargains, no adjustments for supply and demand, and no attempts to create a consumer market for goods where there was not one already. By the seventeenth century, however, the new ideas had eclipsed these older notions and what we call "the business world," or more properly, "the market society," was becoming a reality.

On Lending Money: "Usury" ——

No individual or society, under pain of excommunication, was to let houses to usurers, but was to expel them (had they been admitted) within three months. They were to be refused confession, absolution and Christian burial until they had made restitution, and their wills were to be invalid.

R. H. Tawney, *Religion and the Rise of Capitalism*
(quoting usury laws from France in the twelfth century)

The idea of the market society, however, presupposes another set of ideas even more basic to our conceptions of ourselves, which, again, we tend to take for granted as applicable to everyone and for all times. This is the idea of **individualism,** a cluster of ideas about the importance and legitimacy of individual interests (as distinct from, even opposed to, community and society interests), of individual initiative (as opposed to simply "doing your preordained job"), and of individual identity (that is, the individual person as a self-defining unit, instead of a set of roles and relations within a given and fixed social network). The concept of the individual did not emerge until the eleventh and twelfth centuries, but for centuries the individual was still secondary and subservient to the community, which had priority in almost all matters. Some concept of "selfishness" can be found in Greek philosophy and in the Bible; that in itself is not new. But "selfishness" was always a decidedly negative concept, and so it remained until very recently. The assumption was that individuals working for their own interests, rather than for the interests of the community or society in general, would be bound to be damaging to the general welfare, or, in any case, probably not very helpful to it.

The new assumption of individualism became gospel with the publication of a single book, Adam Smith's *Wealth of Nations,* published in 1776, the same year as the American Declaration of Independence. The theory Smith defended, generally referred to as "the free enterprise system," is that individual members of society, left alone to pursue their own economic interests, will ultimately benefit not only themselves but society as a whole. As Smith imaginatively put it, "an invisible hand" would guide apparently chaotic individualism to collective good. More generally, the theory suggests that what now could be called "the market" could and should be allowed to operate independently of social and governmental interference and control. In doing so, the whole society would greatly improve, become wealthier and better off not only materially but spiritually as well.

The Invisible Hand: Adam Smith ——

As every individual, therefore, endeavours as much as he can both to employ his capital in the support of domestic industry, and so to direct that industry that its produce may be of the greatest value; every individual necessarily labours to render the annual revenue of the society as great as he can. He generally, indeed, neither intends to promote the public interest, nor knows how much he is promoting it. By preferring the support of domestic to that of foreign industry, he intends only his own security; and by directing that industry in such a manner as its produce may be of the greatest value, he intends only his own gain, and he is in this, as in many other cases, led by an invisible hand to promote an end which was no part of his intention. Nor is it always the worse for the society that it was no part of his intention. By pursuing his own interest he frequently promotes that of the society more effectually than when he really intends to promote it.

From *Wealth of Nations*

Thus, the same motives and goals that were so roundly condemned in the Bible and unheard of in most ancient societies now became virtues of the highest order. This is the context in which every person now entering life in business simply assumes as a matter of fact, but it is still only an experiment that has changed considerably since its initiation. Indeed, the theory that the pursuit of individual business advantages and the market left on its own are the ultimate social benefactor is still undergoing its most crucial tests. One assumption will have to be brought out again and again in our discussion of business ethics, whether we are talking about the career of an individual person, the operation of a giant corporation, an entire industry or even the market as a whole: *business is to be considered as an autonomous and independent activity* **because** *it will then serve society.* The concept of "serving society" is still primary, even in the slogan, "what's good for General Motors is good for the U.S.A." Business ethics, then, can be restated as how the individual, and how business in general, best serves society and best serves individuals in that society. To separate business and society, or to separate the interests of the individual and the interests of society, is a difficult and most unrewarding effort. Indeed, it is their interrelation that makes what we are talking about even possible, and without that, the very notion of "business," not just "business ethics," would not make any sense at all.

The Benefits of Capitalism: Adam Smith ——

If we examine, I say, all those things . . . we shall be sensible that without the assistance and cooperation of many thousands, the very meanest person in a civilized country could not be provided, even according to what we very falsely imagine, the easy and simple manner in which he is commonly accommodated. Compared indeed with the more extravagant luxury of the great, his accommodation must no doubt appear extremely simple and easy; and yet it may be true, perhaps, that the accommodation of a European prince does not always so much exceed that of an industrious and frugal peasant, as the accommodation of the latter exceeds that of many an African king, the absolute master of the lives and liberties of ten thousand naked savages.

From *Wealth of Nations*

B.   FREEDOM AND THE MARKET

The most obvious value in business life is material wealth, both for the individual and for society as a whole (or what Smith called "the wealth of the nation"). But a second value may be just as important to business life and ethics, and that is *freedom*. It is the freedom of "the free enterprise system" that allows capitalism to work, according to the classic doctrine, but freedom is also one of the *ends* of the business world, as well as a means to prosperity. (If a country or a company could be run more efficiently and productively by a dictator, would this be acceptable to you, as a citizen or an employee of the firm?) There is a difference, however, between the freedom of business in general (from government regulation, for example) and the freedom of individuals to enter (and leave) the market and do what they want within it. And there is a distinction too between *economic* freedom—the freedom to run a business or seek a career—and other freedoms, for example, political and religious freedoms.

It is often argued that other freedoms depend upon economic freedom as their foundation. (For example, this has recently been argued by Milton Friedman and the "neo-conservative" Norman Podhoretz.) But the opposite is at least as true, if not much more so: freedom of the market is not possible unless there is also freedom of speech, freedom of assembly, freedom of association, and the freedom to pursue our own material happiness. It is because we value the freedom of the individual that "free" markets are allowed to exist at all, whether or not the market then furthers (as advocates argue) or threatens (as critics claim) these other freedoms.

"Alienated Labor": Karl Marx ———

What constitutes the alienation of labour? First, that the work is *external* to the worker, that it is not part of his nature; and that, consequently, he does not fulfill himself in his work but denies himself, has a feeling of misery rather than well-being, does not develop freely his mental and physical energies but is physically exhausted and mentally debased. The worker, therefore, feels himself at home only during his leisure time, whereas at work he feels homeless. His work is not voluntary but imposed, *forced labour.* It is not the satisfaction of a need, but only a *means* for satisfying other needs. Its alien character is clearly shown by the fact that as soon as there is no physical or other compulsion it is avoided like the plague. External labour, labour in which man alienates himself, is a labour of self-sacrifice, of mortification. Finally the external character of work for the worker is shown by the fact that it is not his own work but work for someone else, that in work he does not belong to himself but to another person. . . .

We arrive at the result that man (the worker) feels himself to be freely active only in his animal functions—eating, drinking and procreating, or at most also in his dwelling and in personal adornment—while in his human functions he is reduced to an animal. The animal becomes human and the human becomes animal.

From his manuscript of 1844

But, to make matters more complicated, it has also been argued that economic freedom is not freedom at all and contradicts, rather than supports, these other freedoms. Karl Marx, who is no friend of the business world, also takes freedom to be the most important value in any social system; but, for him, it is the freedom *from* the pressures and inequities of capitalism that is most important, and freedom from the "alienation" of work in which the only goal is "making a living." Freedom to choose, he would say, is not freedom at all; the consumer's ability to choose between twenty brands of soap powders, for example, is not freedom, and the employee's ability to "choose" whether to work or starve— always facing the fear of being fired—is not freedom either. Nevertheless, American business is in agreement with Marx on this, at least: freedom is a most important value, whatever it may be. Indeed, we cannot even imagine the American business system without this emphasis on individual freedom, and the notion of "free enterprise" cannot be separated from the value of freedom as a pervasive feature of American life.

To make this distinctive set of assumptions dramatically clear, let's look briefly at an alternative business world, equally successful (by our standards), which has a very different set of assumptions. In Japanese business, being "independent" and "individualistic" are considered serious *flaws* in a managerial candidate. Students with foreign degrees are generally avoided, and skills in foreign languages and familiarity with American or French or German lifestyles are considered more a danger than a virtue and disruptive to the established ways of behavior in Japan. A student guidance teacher at Tokyo International University, for example, tells her students, "You must conform to Japanese ways. You cannot be forceful or independent or outspoken. Such traits, which highlight individualism, are not highly regarded in Japan." Indeed, the same teacher often punctuates her advice with the old Japanese aphorism, "The nail that sticks out is the one that gets hammered down." How different this is from our American individualist

> The American model is predicated on frequent job changes, fast promotional tracks, highly specialized jobs, well defined corporate control mechanisms, solely made decisions, a high degree of individual responsibility (and culpability), and a looking-out-for-number-one type of concern.
>
> In contrast, the Japanese firm encourages lifetime employment, promotions which are gradual and occur only when the candidate is fully competent, a more generalized career path, control mechanisms founded on common sense and mutual respect, a group orientation toward decision making, the responsibility for both individual and corporate welfare.
>
> Jack Rochester, *The Boston Globe*, review of Theory Z by William Ouchi

ethic, which prizes individual initiative and "speaking out" and independence in general. The contrast can be overdrawn, of course. But the differences are most pronounced precisely when we try to evolve what we are calling "business ethics," for it is there that we find some rather radical differences between business life in Japan and business life in America. There is no presumption in Japanese business ethics that the unrestricted ambitions of the individual will ultimately benefit either the corporation or the large society; indeed, the assumption is quite the opposite, that individual initiative and independence will be harmful both to the company and to the established ways of society. (One writer recently found that the phrase "nice guys finish last" couldn't be translated into Japanese.)

The basic presumption of Japanese business ethics is that the corporation is similar to a large family, with lifelong obligations to its employees even when they are no longer capable of doing their jobs efficiently and even when such obligations threaten the financial well-being of the company itself. On our own market assumptions, of course, such obligations—if they exist at all—are highly controversial, and, in any case, considerations of employee loyalty and corporate duties would be wholly based upon questions of efficiency and success, not assumptions held to be valid regardless of these factors. For example, a Japanese corporation hires a manager for life; it is the responsibility of the company to see that *it* can provide him with useful and rewarding work. In an American firm, on the other hand, it is clearly understood that it is the burden of the manager to prove that she continues to be useful to the company. Needless to say, this difference has dramatic consequences for our views of success and failure, of ambition and personal goals, and of loyalty to the company versus looking out for our own interests, rather than security, which would be considered far more important to a Japanese businessperson.

C.   ETHICS AND THE LAW

The freedom of the market obviously has its limitations, for both the individual and the corporation. "Freedom" does not mean "anything goes." The free market does not permit murder. The free market does not condone stealing, cheating, or extortion. Indeed, the free market depends on respect for private property (and not just one's own), respect for contracts, and the rules of fair play. It demands restraint from brute force and coercion and it forbids fraud. Without such respect and restraint, the free market would not be free; in fact, it could not operate as a "market" at all. Ideally, it could be assumed that every participant in the market, like every player in a friendly football game, agrees to some basic rules and will respect the integrity of the game. Unfortunately, a free market that is open (by its very nature) to all producers and participants cannot make this assumption. Therefore the market, if it is to be free, requires protection from rule breakers, those who would take advantage of its freedoms and commit fraud or extortion. It requires rules and sanctions. In short, the market and its participants must be constrained by *law*. It is the law which ultimately decides and defends the legitimacy of contracts, and prohibits theft, force, and fraud. The first obligation of any business and every businessperson, accordingly, is to obey the law. Without law, there would be no business, and business law thus becomes central to the study of business life.

This is not to say, however, that law is all there is to ethics, or that business ethics ultimately comes down to business law. In our friendly football game, there are all sorts of mutual understandings and expectations that need not be spelled out in the rules of the game. So, too, in business there are all sorts of mutual understandings and expectations that may not be spelled out in the law. The most important of these is mutual *trust*. This does not mean that in business it is obligatory to trust everyone. That would be downright stupid. The expression "never trust anyone," however, is without doubt an exaggeration, a perverse reminder to be very cautious in business dealings. Trust, in fact a remarkably high level of trust, is built into most business dealings, from "self-serve" stations where you pay for your gas after you've already put it in your tank to international agreements between giant multinational corporations. Of course, the law is usually there to back up such agreements, but it is a misunderstanding of both law and ethics to suppose that it is the law as such that is the crucial element here. Indeed, if a businessperson or corporation makes a practice of just remaining on "this side of the law," narrowly avoiding indictments and lawsuits, it is virtually certain that he, she, or it is unethical. Talking an elderly person out of his or her life savings to make a risky investment (and taking a substantial brokerage fee off the top) may be perfectly legal but it is repulsively unethical. The law sets the limits of tolerable behavior, but it does not define ethics as such. It is often said, "You cannot legislate morality." But this is not so much a plea for tolerance as it is a deep insight into the nature of the law. Respect and obedience for law have to first be embodied in practice, in the way people actually behave. The law can successfully circumscribe and sanction only that which is already accepted—no matter how grudgingly—by the people and practices it governs.

The preponderance of law relating to business takes the form of *regulation*. It is a matter of some curiosity and concern that "regulation" is considered a dirty word by most people in business. Regulation is decried as contrary to the free market and destructive of competitiveness. Regulation is said to "tie the hands" of business. And, of course, there are an absurd number of regulations in virtually every industry. Many of these are archaic, residues of a problem long resolved or a period of past abuses. Some of them are simply stupid and the product of a partisan political opportunity. Too much regulation signifies lack of trust in business, in the integrity of businesspeople, in the intelligence of consumers, in the efficiency of the market itself to make a success of good quality and punish poor quality. Too much regulation is a residue of the old intrusiveness of government (the origins of the traditional free market cry, *laissez faire,* "leave us alone"). Too much regulation is still reminiscent of the authoritarianism of the medieval guild ("exactly 1408 stitches per fabric"). In general, it is probably fair to say that most business is over-regulated, which has the unfortunate consequence of shifting the emphasis on the preconditions of the free market away from self-restraint, respect for the rules of fair play, and the public good to mere compliance with the law.

The ultimate purpose of regulation, however, is to protect the market as such, to guarantee the conditions within which an industry can thrive and survive, and, of course, to protect the public good and to provide safeguards for those consumers who could not possibly assess the dangers of some of the products they use (for example, pharmaceuticals and various household chemicals). Regulation is essential to business and it is, or should be, aimed at the public well-being, whatever the private motives of certain politicians or special interests may be. Ideally, of course, *self*-regulation would do the job, if every industry and profession took great care to weed out those of its members who abused their position and compromised its standards. But too often, industries and professionals in particular are reticent about punishing their own kin, politicians and government agencies often legislate regulations erratically and opportunistically, and what is sometimes designated as self-regulation is in fact just an excuse to put a maverick competitor out of business. Accordingly, there will always be regulations, and they will continue to be an irritant to many already ethical as well as law-abiding businesses. But regulation alone does not spell out business ethics, and for the sake of business ethics as well as efficiency, a good deal of our current regulation may well be superfluous.

D.   REGULATION AND TAXATION: THE ROLE OF GOVERNMENT

"Laissez faire," cried the late eighteenth century merchants. "Get the government off our backs," cry our late-twentieth-century corporate leaders. But what is the proper role of government in business? Those eighteenth-century merchants depended upon the king's navy to protect their trade routes, the king's soldiers to protect their factories, the king's courts to protect their contracts. Today's executive enjoys enormous government subsidies, for example, in the support of air travel, not to mention an occasional multi-billion dollar bail-out and the various special benefits and loopholes built into the law for the advantage of this or that industry. Japan's tremendous success over the past several decades has demonstrably been due in part to the national partnership between government and business, and Germany too has succeeded in part because of government sponsorship and cooperation. Today's politicians may still insist that "the government cannot and should not pick winners and losers in business," but the truth is that it can, and many governments do. Our government, too, supports one industry or another in any number of ways, if only by keeping its hands off or looking the other way.

Many regulations are of the form "you must do so-and-so" or "you cannot do such-and-such," but there are other, only slightly more subtle forms of regulation. The most obvious of these is taxation. Taxes, of course, are first and foremost a medium of financial support for the government, the primary source from which it pays for national defense, the interstate highway system, the justice system, many state services, the luxurious lunches enjoyed by some of our elected and non-elected officials, and so on. But taxation is by no means uniform, and taxation in fact functions as something more than a source of support for the government. Taxation is also a form of redistribution, in which money is taken from some people and given, usually in the form of benefits and services, to others. Accordingly, taxation always raises questions of justice: Is it fair to take this much money away from this person or corporation? Is it fair for Mr. A to pay for this or that service which benefits Mr. B? Indeed, libertarians in particular are now asking, is it fair for the government to take away anyone's money, hard-earned or not, for virtually any purpose whatsoever, except, perhaps, for mutual defense? Taxation also serves as a social sanction, encouraging some forms of behavior, discouraging others. If one examines our standard tax forms, it becomes evident that our tax code encourages having children, for example. (In China, where the government is coping with severe over-population, taxes are more, not less, for families with more than one child.) Giving to charity is encouraged and therefore permits a tax deduction. Gambling is discouraged and so gambling debts are not deductible. And so on.

So, too, governments give all sorts of tax breaks to business in order to encourage various activities, such as establishing factories in poor neighborhoods with high unemployment (called "enterprise zones"). Additional taxes, on the other hand, make a product more expensive, which is one way of discouraging its use. High taxes on cigarettes and alcohol are intended not only as government revenue but as a "sin tax," intended to punish and deter people who use these products. Lowered taxes on some industries, for example, oil depletion allowances for oil companies, are supposed to act as incentives. Thus the hands of government regulate business not only through prohibitions and requirements but through the instrument of taxation. A government can be quite "laissez faire" and still exercise considerable control over business through the tax system.

Not all taxes are as obvious as an income tax, however, and corporations as well as private citizens find themselves paying all sorts of taxes which may not present themselves as such. The corporate income tax is almost always a source of great controversy, and needless to say, the combined weight of virtually the whole of the business community is against it. There are also user fees, for example, for access to essential information, for the use of federal highways, the use of airports, for assessments, and for registration and commission costs (for instance, the Securities and Exchange and Commodities Futures Trading commissions both charge a fee on every transaction). Energy taxes, especially taxes on oil, are becoming increasingly popular with government as a way of both raising revenue and trimming energy use. There are various payroll taxes, which fund social security, health care programs, and unemployment compensation. In the past twenty-five years, while corporate income taxes have actually fallen as a percentage of the Gross National Product, payroll taxes have virtually doubled. Then there are excise taxes: on telephone service, for example, and on various air and water pollutants, which serve (supposedly) to cut down the amount of noxious emissions and help clean up the environment. Steep taxes on ozone-depleting chemicals and carbon emissions now serve as a form of environmental regulation. Tariffs are taxes imposed for the importation of goods, and in our complex global economy these affect a great many goods and, again, signify a particular kind of regulation that is often called "protectionism;" that is, it discourages companies and consumers from buying foreign goods and accordingly encourages them to buy local products. This does not usually encourage an improvement in quality, however. For many years, Canada placed extremely high tariffs on all imported wine, making only Canadian wine affordable for most families. Canadian wine became, even in Canada, something of a joke, and, not surprisingly, when Canada opened itself up to international competition its own wines improved considerably.

There is also an extremely subtle form of taxation, not always in the control of the government, which has to do with the value of the currency itself. The value of a country's currency has a great deal to do with the nation's success in exporting its goods, as well as determining the price of foreign goods in the country. The extent to which a country can control the value of its own currency depends on many things, in particular its strength in the world's financial markets. No country is now in a position (as some of the great nineteenth-century European powers were) to simply dictate exchange rates. There are, nevertheless, a number of maneuvers governments can and do exercise in order to manage the value of money.

Sales taxes are, of course, a familiar form of taxation, and such taxes are often highest in states where the income taxes are the lowest. (Texas, which refuses to have an income tax, has some of the highest state sales taxes.) It is worth noting, however, that sales taxes may also discourage consumerism, in effect regulating the market in a very general way, given that almost all goods will cost up to 9 percent more than their stated price. There are also special "luxury taxes" on certain very expensive items—yachts, certain automobiles, fur coats—and many countries in the world employ a value-added tax (or VAT) as a source of revenue. The difference between a VAT and a sales tax or a luxury tax is that a VAT increases the cost of a product at every stage of production. Thus the VAT on manufactured goods can be 20 to 30 percent on top of the actual cost of the product, which would certainly have some dampening effect on consumer enthusiasm. Moreover, the VAT requires much more record-keeping and tax information on the part of businesses; by comparison, a simple corporate income tax begins to look rather attractive.

Taxes are a form of regulation, in the sense that they are a form of government control over business and consumption. By way of taxes and tax reductions, the government can encourage and discourage various activities by making them more or less affordable. This is not the hard and fast regulation of the "Thou shalt not" variety, but it can sometimes be just as effective. Pollution control, for example, is now becoming a matter of taxation rather than prohibitive regulation. But wherever government enters into business life, there are ethical questions and implications, questions of fairness, matters of adequate representation, and consequences concerning the public good. One might say that business ethics is that realm of concern that takes place *within* the bounds set by the government, within the rules of regulation, fair play, and the sanctions set up by the state. But that means that business ethics always depends on good government, and nothing is as destructive to both business ethics and the free market as government that does not play by or enforce the rules of fair play and freedom.

> The U.S. government and industry combined still spend more than any other nation on R & D [research and development]. The problem is many of the projects are impractical. For example, the bulk of the $7 billion in Energy Department research is done in the department's labs, largely isolated from U.S. industry. What's needed is an approach more like Japan's. Tokyo invites industry to help design research for maximum market impact. Companies share in the discoveries, then compete in product development.
>
> —*Business Week*
> April 1, 1991

E. BUSINESS LIFE: MAKING MONEY AND MORE

Business is concerned with making money. But it does not follow from this that every money-making activity is a business, nor does it follow that business is concerned *only* with making money. "Being in business" is in part the pursuit of profit but it is also a great many other things. It is also a distinctive way of life. Business is essentially involved with the production and/or distribution of goods and the provision of services. Business provides jobs and (more or less) meaningful work for millions of people. Business life is a social activity that involves a good deal of interpersonal activity and which depends upon the value of one's enterprise and one's reputation. Indeed, business life defines for many people their role in life, their values, their social status, the people they will meet, the friends they will make, and the way they will raise their families.

1. Most obviously, business life is centrally concerned with the making of money. But this by itself is clearly neither necessary nor sufficient as a characterization. It is making money in a certain way according to certain rules. Physical

laborers work hard in order to make money, but that is not, in our sense, an example of business life. Gangsters make money too, but it is only with the sneer of an extreme cynicism that we describe their money-making activities as "business." There are rules in business (there are rules in the Mafia too, but they do not concern us here): certain ways of making money which count, others which do not. In particular, business buying and selling, whether it be products and consumer services directly or in the enormous variety of investment and management functions, operate between or behind these transactions. Investment banking, for example, is a long way from making, selling, or buying a tube of toothpaste. Nevertheless, it is an activity that is ultimately comprehensible only in terms of, and as a function of, such mundane business transactions, and the money made in banking ultimately comes, one way or another, from the sale of that tube of toothpaste.

2. Business life is not necessarily part of the process of production itself. A businessperson might sell widgets or airplanes, but she is not primarily concerned with their production or, for that matter, their operation—hers is "knowledge work" (as management guru Peter Drucker calls it). These businesspeople are "the new class," according to social critic Alvin Gouldner, neither laborers nor entrepreneurs but rather managers, organizers, conduits, matchmakers, negotiators, mediators. In a small shop (an antiques shop, for example) a proprietor may do the searching, the fixing, the pick-up and delivery, as well as the actual buying and selling, but it is important to distinguish business from activities. Business is transaction, not production as such.

The essential concern of the businessperson is net financial gain within a rather stringent set of rules of fair and proper play. Of course, there are other concerns too—pride of connoisseurship, good craftsmanship, charming salesmanship, and so on—but these are better viewed as means. A carpenter or an entertainer may be a good businessperson too, but the craft of carpentry or a career on the stage is not itself business. Indeed, the daily artifacts of business life in general do not include any hint of products or production or individual customers but rather contracts, agents, brokers, sales representatives, advertising and legal firms, numbers, and paper and more paper. Indeed, certain key positions in business do not even include people or paper, but rather a series of very abstract decisions and verbal instructions that have only the most remote (but ultimately, of course, essential) ties to the goods or services on which the fate of the company ultimately resides. The point is that an accountant or financial director who enters into the corporate level of the fertilizer business need never in his career touch or even see a bag of fertilizer, need know nothing of its use, manufacture, or origins. Such a person, of course, would be extremely limited in curiosity if not also in job flexibility, but the point is that business life, as we currently define it, may be quite removed from products and the customers who buy them, except where "the customer" is also an abstraction or a number.

3. Business life must be distinguished from skilled labor and professional work, whether it be the work of a welder, the semiprofessionally trained drafts-

man, or the highly trained surgeon. This is not to say that business life does not require skills and knowledge; in fact, these skills and the knowledge required for business are of a special sort. And as is well known in business circles, these are not skills and this is not knowledge that can easily be reduced to a series of steps or principles (as in a "how to weld" pamphlet, or, for that matter, as in teaching medical students a delicate surgical technique). It is a profession that is first of all *dealing with people,* not primarily a skill. It is concerned with products, but not primarily with production so much as with sales and distribution, publicity, advertising, and so on.

There is a powerful movement these days to reconsider the central position in the business world—the manager—as a professional, even as a scientist. Thus the literature on "managerial science" has exploded in the past few years, and Peter Drucker has become something of a patron saint to managers, for his arguments and advice. But although Drucker is undoubtedly correct in his evaluation of the new *status* of the manager in large modern institutions, he is perhaps misleading on the issue of "professionalism." Management is not, like medicine or music, a set of specific skills, a body of specific knowledge for sale. It is not a job or role with clear and autonomous goals, but rather a job to do that takes the shape and goals of its context and conforms to the pressures and organization of the situation. At the same time, managerial skills, unlike the skills of most profes-

Drucker on Management ——

Management is work, and as such it has its own skills, its own tools, its own techniques. . . . But the stress is not on skills, tools, and techniques. It is not even on the work of management. It is on the tasks.

For management is the organ, the life-giving, acting, dynamic organ of the institution it manages. Without the institution, e.g., the business enterprise, there would be no management. But without management there would also be only a mob rather than an institution. The institution, in turn, is itself an organ of society and exists only to contribute a needed result to society, the economy, and the individual. Organs, however, are never defined by what they do, let alone by how they do it. They are defined by their contribution.

Management is tasks. Management is a discipline. But management is also people. Every achievement of management is the achievement of a manager. Every failure is a failure of a manager. People manage rather than "forces" or "facts." The vision, dedication, and integrity of managers determine whether there is management or mismanagement.

From *Management: Tasks, Practices, Responsibilities*

sionals, are readily transferable from context to context, and a successful manager in business will very likely be successful in running a hospital, a university, or a government office as well. The manager's skills are primarily social skills— fitting into a situation and motivating others, carrying on effective conversations and communications, and seeing the particular organization in its own context and in terms of its own needs and goals. These are skills, to be sure, but they are very different from the scientific skills of a surgeon or laboratory researcher. And yet, insofar as the businessperson applies his or her skills for the benefit of others, as well as to make a profit, it may make perfectly good sense to describe life in business as a profession.

4. Business life is a communicative practice. It is defined, and its goals are set, by a special language. Virtually every realm of life has its special language, its own verbal coinages and technical terms. Sports, for example, are defined by special terms; in baseball, the word "strike" defines something unique to that game, and knowledge of that term used elsewhere (for example in a union going on strike or one person striking another) would not help a person at all. The term, in other words, helps to define the game itself. So too, in business, the term "profit" helps to define the very enterprise. We could not imagine business without it, or without another word with the same function and meaning. But the special language of business does not consist only of such essential words that define the enterprise but an entire vocabulary of code words, neologisms, and current

On the Language of Business ——

In any discipline the man who comes up with a new concept or a new approach to things first surrounds the concept with a defensive network of jargon. While this makes it difficult for rivals to steal the idea, it also makes it equally difficult for anyone else to grasp the idea too readily. If this is not done—if the concept is instead transmitted in plain English—there is real danger that the acolyte will quickly see the whole thing (the Gestalt) and exclaim, "but that's just common sense!" Worse, he might even observe that the emperor has no clothes on and cry out, "But that doesn't mean anything!" The latter reaction is of course worse than the former, but neither is welcomed by the progenitor of a new management concept.

So management man must be up on all the latest terms and be abreast of all the newest enthusiasms. When someone uses the latest catch phrase over the lunch table or at a conference, he must recognize it and be able to respond in kind. However, response need not imply understanding.

O. William Battaglia and John J. Tarrant, *The Corporate Eunuch* coinages whose primary function is to identify other participants in the enterprise and provide them with their own language. In baseball, for example, there are phrases such as "batting slump" and such acronyms as "ERA" (earned run average). In business, such terms as "fast track," "impact," and "tradeoffs" substitute for everyday phrases like "high potential," "effect," and "compromise." Simple ideas are summarized by larger phrases that are then made into acronyms; businesspeople can tell who is on top of the latest theories by throwing out "MBO" (managing by objectives) or "OD" (organizational development) and "LIFO" (last-in-first-out accounting). Many of these terms seem meaningless to the person outside of the business world. Business life in general, like almost every other enterprise from sports to philosophy to literary criticism, is circumscribed and defined by the language of its essential concepts, as well as its inessential jargon.

5. Business life is defined by a certain *community,* which is defined by certain shared interests (making money), by special language, and by any number of other mores and customs including dress, office locations, lunch habits, and, not least but not most important either, employers. A community is *not* to be thought of as a definite group of people, any more than a town or a city is to be defined by a definite set of buildings or a definite group of people. (If we did so, we would have to rename the town every time someone left, or died, or was born, every time a building was razed or a new one built.) A community is an *indeterminate* group, in which individuals are always entering and leaving. At one time, the community might consist of A, B, C; later of B, C, D; later still of D, E, F. Only on the rarest occasions would all of the personnel of a community change at once, but equally rare would be the community that retained throughout its history a single individual or one family. Sometimes, a corporation forms its own community, in Japan, for example; more often, the business community is far wider reaching and includes not only a large number of people from a certain industry or a given city but a far larger population across several industries and many cities. We might, perhaps, talk about "the American business community" in general, but this is probably stretching the notion so far that we lose all of the essential features of a community—a large degree of interfamiliarity and sense of mutual belonging, a shared language and shared interests, shared customs and a somewhat fixed number of employers and locations. Used car salesmen and antiques dealers may have much less in common with investment bankers and personnel directors of large corporations than they have with people outside of business life altogether. Managers in international corporations may have few concerns in common with local domestic "captains of industry," and financial wizards may have few words to say to directors of sales. What we sometimes call "the American business community," is in fact an overlapping family of communities—a community of communities—each of the particular communities in turn composed of various sub-communities and cliques and more limited career groups. Only in rare cases can a business community be defined with some precision (for example, the relatively small and isolated business communities that have been transported to otherwise "underdeveloped" foreign countries).

But the same point—namely that it is almost always impossible to distinguish one particular business community from others—applies to the delineation of business communities in general and distinguishes them from the larger society. Critics of business often write as if businesspeople were a distinctive cult, who belonged to a world all their own, only occasionally stepping outside to join their families for a weekend or to have lunch with an old (nonbusiness) college roommate. Business communities are, in fact, intertwined in the most intimate and thorough ways with other communities, despite the fact that it is necessary to discuss business life as such in terms of its more or less distinctive community. To be successful in business, in general, is to be successful in that community, and the prime ingredients in that success, accordingly, are to be defined in terms of interpersonal evaluation and acceptance, not on purely financial criteria alone.

6. Because business life takes place in a certain community, it is defined not just by interpersonal contacts and concerns (that is, friendships and shared worries, deals, dissatisfactions) but by a more impersonal set of ties called, in general, "duties and obligations." As a member of the community, a businessperson is expected to take the community itself and its well-being seriously. By virtue of a certain position in that community—whether as one of its leaders or merely one of its aspiring young members—that person is expected to deal with other members in a certain way, obey certain rules, follow certain guidelines—and expects the same of them.

Sometimes, such duties and obligations are spelled out formally, by way of rules or regulations or as part of the instructions for a certain position. More often, however, they are the merely implicit but generally recognized and unquestioned (or only occasionally questioned) manners and mores that keep the community functioning harmoniously together. This is why too much talk about "legal obligations" and "moral behavior" in business and business ethics is so often beside the point. The most important elements of the ethics of the business community and success within it are not formulated as moral principles, much less legislated as legal guidelines, but are part of that enormously complex but essential network of mutual understandings and responsibilities that make up any community, including—most importantly—the obligation not to behave in any way that will cast a moral shadow on the community in general. Of course, there is bound to be tension and intrigue in any competitive organization, but even this must be understood within certain rules and limits *within* which such competition is possible.

■ SUMMARY AND CONCLUSION

Business life is the explicit pursuit of profits (presumably like all jobs and careers). But it is a mistake to think of business solely this way; it is also a community with communal values, as well as an instrument for the productivity and distribution of goods that will benefit the entire society. This sense of the value of business and the business community is a recent development in Western civilization, however. Business practices were scorned by most societies until modern times (indeed, the rise of business might be said to be part of the definition of "modern times"). The expansion of business required the growth of cities and the revolution in industry; it required a protracted period of peace and international exchange, the establishment of banks and other institutions of commerce, and the introduction of an abstract system of exchange. Most of all, it required a new set of ideas about the legitimacy of business enterprises and the value of money; and it required a new emphasis on individualism, individual economic freedom, and the ability of the individual to contribute to the wealth of society through his own, often selfish, ambitions. But all of these values are found, not in business alone, but throughout the whole of society.

What distinguishes business is not so much a distinctive set of values as a distinctive set of activities, having to do with *exchange,* which involves social skills, the use of a special language, and membership in the business community.

■ Study Questions

1. What is meant by "economic freedom"? Does economic freedom derive from other forms of freedom, such as freedom of speech or freedom of religion? Could we have one without the other? Give some concrete examples.

2. Why has Christianity, for most of its history, been so strongly against business? Why do you think it has more recently accepted, even encouraged, business as a way of life?

3. Marxists have long claimed that it is the worker or workers who make a product who should enjoy *all* of the profits. In response, capitalists have claimed that the investor who takes a financial risk deserves the profits in return for that risk. What does each of their arguments assume about the source of value and its fair distribution?

4. What are the major differences between the life of a person in business and an electrical engineer, an academic economist, and a lawyer?

5. Should *competition* be listed as one of the distinctive features of business life? Companies and corporations compete for markets; people compete for jobs. Is competition one of the *general* features of life in most business positions?

6. What justifies government taxation? (It is not sufficient that government has the power to tax. It must also have the *authority* to demand money from its citizens.) What warrants the state's demand for some of the earnings of an individual? For what purposes do you consider the individual taxes you pay legitimate? For what purposes are they not? What warrants

the state's demand for some of the earnings of a corporation? For what purposes do you consider such taxes legitimate? For what purposes do you not?

7. Should there or could there be laws requiring people to keep their promises, to trust or to respect one another, to strive to produce the highest quality products, or do their best? Why or why not? What sorts of business activities can and should the law govern? On what should such laws be based? Where do we find the limits of the law?

8. What is meant by the "fair market value" of an object or activity? How is the fair market value determined? How do you think it *ought* to be determined? Is it possible to make *too much* money on a transaction, assuming the other parties are knowledgeable and willing? (See Historical Interlude, pp. 56–62.)

■ For Class Discussion

1. To what extent do you see your business life and the rest of your life as intertwined, and to what extent do you see yourself "working nine-to-five"? To what extent do you plan or want your family life to be tied up with your business activities? To what extent is this inevitable? Do you plan to travel on business with or without your husband or wife? Do you want or expect most of your friends to be in business too? If offered a house in the "corporate ghetto" of your company, what would be the attractions and the disadvantages to you?

2. A true story: A graduate business student, raised in a family of investment bankers and on his way into investment banking himself, complained about the amount of production management, marketing, and labor relations courses he was required to take for his business degree. "Business," he argued, "is big, international financial deals; all this stuff is irrelevant." Is he correct? What does such an attitude suggest about business values and their relationship with the rest of society? What would be the function of business, so conceived, in our society?

3. One of the wittiest and widest read critics of American business today is *New York Times* columnist Russell Baker. The following is one of his (edited) essays:

As everybody knows, the most important thing in America—after freedom and paying your income tax—is business. "Business is what made America what it is today," somebody once said, and you can bet this month's mortgage payment that the somebody who once said it was a businessman.

Business is no career for sissies. It demands courage, because the businessman never knows when competition may break out. Worse. If he meets with his competitors to make an agreement to keep competition from breaking out, he never can be sure the Justice Department will not catch him.

In today's fiercely noncompetitive world, business also demands an extraordinary degree of incompetence. Oldtimers in the business world, men old enough to remember what it was like a generation or two ago, are often astonished at the amount of sheer incompetence required to get ahead in business today.

Because of free enterprise every American can own two cars, both of which will probably be recalled by the factory for safety defects.

Another characteristic of the American businessman is his daring. If he has a Government contract to make a new weapon, and his costs are running $200 million over estimates, and he still hasn't produced a weapon, and his company is about to go bankrupt, he must be daring. He must be nervy enough to go to the Government and demand that the Treasury bail out his company.

"The business of America is business," Calvin Coolidge said. That was fifty years ago when businessmen still wasted their energies worrying about making railroads run. Nowadays the business of America is government, and the business of government is business.

Somewhere, there is probably still a business or two that makes something good that works, but don't bet this month's mortgage payment on it.

Write a letter to the *Times* in response to Baker's column.

Historical Interlude

A Philosophical Look at Business History

There is a broad sense in which "business" has always been an essential part of human society. People have always traded goods, and, in so doing, conceived of some idea of a fair trade, unfair trade, a sense of sharing, and a sense of the fruits of one's own labor. But the "free market system" and business life as we know it is a very modern innovation, and the very idea of business and working for a profit was condemned throughout most of history. To understand this, let us take a brief tour back to ancient times to take a look at the days when business was not even a respectable, much less powerful, profession.

Ancient Times

Evidence of extensive trading exists in the Middle East as far back as the Sumerian civilization, which flourished almost three thousand years before Christ. They traded weapons, jewels, household goods, and slaves. They even kept some clay records of their transactions. Many of the dazzling finds now in our museums are from the hills of ancient Egypt; large blocks of stone carved with intricate hieroglyphics, or "picture writing," in fact turn out to be inventories or other records of wealth and commerce.

Even in ancient times we can see the prejudice against business that would be found in almost every society for the next twenty centuries. In ancient Athens, Aristotle, a very practical-minded philosopher and student of Plato, theorized about the rules of trade and the nature of "distributive justice" (that is, who should get what), thus becoming the first economist. In his *Ethics* (300 B.C.) he insisted on the "equality" of transactions and tried to formulate some principle by which diverse work (for example, that of a farmer and that of a doctor) might be fairly exchanged. He defends the notion of money as a means for such exchange and, in surprisingly modern terms, insists that "for this reason money measures all things" that can be exchanged. What is decidedly absent from Aristotle's account is any semblance of the law of supply and demand, the idea that "fair price" might be dependent on the nature of trade itself rather than the already established value of the things traded. Money is a mere convenience, a means of exchange. Moreover, Aristotle defines injustice as an unequal trade, which is wholly at odds with some of our basic business notions, such as the idea of a "bargain," or the idea of "getting a good deal." We may not want to think of such competitive victories as the essence of business, but we certainly would not think of them as "immoral" either. Indeed, as we shall see, the prohibition against such bargaining and unequal exchanges, whether mutual or not, becomes increasingly powerful over the following centuries.

It is worth noting that Aristotle distinguishes two distinctly different types of trade, of very different value as well. First of all, there is *"oecinomicus,"* from which we get our word "economics," which refers to household trading—buying shoes, foods, slaves, and the house itself. This is a respectable enterprise, according to Aristotle, for in any society of divided labor and specialization such trading is essential to the life of everyone. Not everyone can build a house or make a shoe; and, in contrast to most societies before his, not everyone was in a position to grow his own food. "Economics," therefore, is a practical necessity. It is by no means a lofty activity; it is not worth much concern and it is certainly not one of the honorable activities that Aristotle and the Greeks called "virtues" (such as courage in battle, magnificence in giving parties, and temperance in food, sex, and drink). It is part of the practical details of life; and though Aristotle talks at great length about the importance of "doing well" when making products (the shoemaker who makes excellent shoes, the physician who prescribes the best cures), he does not talk at all about "doing well" regarding trading itself. A person trades fairly to get what he needs. The idea of business as we know it—trading for the best price possible and perhaps even getting people to buy what they don't need—had not yet arisen.

Aristotle's second notion of trade is *"chrematisike."* This is trading with the idea of making a profit, while not actually producing any product. Such activity is wholly devoid of virtue, according to Aristotle, and people who do such a thing are despicable parasites on society. They are devoid of social sense and only want personal gain. They add nothing to society's welfare and survive by manipulating an intrinsically worthless substance, money, whose purpose is only to be a means of trade. To make a profit, just by manipulating money, is not socially productive, according to Aristotle. It is even, he suggests, "unnatural."

Although Aristotle's Greece was then, in our view, the most "advanced" civilization in history, it was based upon conditions and assumptions so far removed from our own that it is essential to see the differences. Although Aristotle lived in a relatively large and distinguished city, his society was still primarily an agrarian and military society in which the basis of value was still to be found on the farm and the bulk of expenditures still aimed at defense. In the cities, most labor was provided by slaves, and this, not "labor" in our sense, was the basis of the urban economy, which was in turn dependent on the agrarian economy. Although Aristotle talks about money, his society in fact had only minimal reliance on cash as such, and thus the basic features of what we call business life were not present. Merchants could hardly be called businessmen. In the *Republic,* by Aristotle's great teacher Plato, merchants and traders are classed with farmers and wage earners as the most primitive components of society, just above slaves.

Furthermore, the nature of wealth itself was revealingly different in Aristotle's time. We take as a matter of basic principle the idea that the person who *produces* the wealth should *have* the wealth, and much of the debate between capitalists and communists has to do with who actually contributes more—the capitalist who invests money (but by risking it makes production possible) or the worker who actually produces goods. But in Aristotle's time this principle would be considered nonsense. Those who produced the wealth—farmers, tradesmen, ordinary soldiers who captured the riches of a defeated enemy—would never expect to keep or receive back the bulk of what they had produced. The wealth would go to the powerful statesmen and the military generals, to religious leaders, and to others who, in ordinary terms, did not "produce" anything at all. (Virtually no money, furthermore, would be put back into production for the sake of increased productivity and growth.) As economist Robert Heilbroner put the matter, wealth tended to follow power. Rarely if ever could a person become powerful by accumulating wealth. And so it would be for thousands of years. Even in

Rome, the largest economic state of the ancient world, the philosopher Cicero proclaimed the ignobility of merchants. Wealth was one thing; getting it was quite another. Those who toiled were rarely those who reaped. The idea that "the wealth of nations" might in fact best be tied to the personal ambitions of those who actually did the work and—more shocking—those who merely acted as "middle men" had yet a long time to come.

The Middles Ages

In the Middle Ages, from the fall of the Roman Empire to the discovery of the New World, the ancient prejudice against business became not only a matter of "ignobility" but a question of religion and one's very salvation. R. H. Tawney, a noted historian of business history and its relation to religion, comments that there were two assumptions that were underlying the whole history of business in the Middle Ages: (1) economic interests are always subordinate to the real business of life, which is salvation of the soul, and business itself is almost always a

A Medieval Marketplace: Business in a Pre-Business Era ——

Here, in the Mercato Vecchio, the Old Market, were the shops of the drapers and the second-hand-clothes dealers, the booths of the fish-mongers, the bakers and the fruit and vegetable merchants, the houses of the feather merchants and the stationers, and of the candle-makers where, in rooms smoky with incense to smother the smell of wax, prostitutes entertained their customers. On open counters in the market, bales of silk and barrels of grain, corn and leather goods were exposed for sale, shielded by awnings from the burning sun. Here also out in the open barbers shaved beards and clipped hair; tai-lors stitched cloth in shaded doorways; servants and housewives gathered round the booths of the cooked-food merchants; bakers pushed platters of dough into the communal oven; and furniture makers and goldsmiths displayed their wares. Town-criers marched about calling out the news of the day and broadcasting advertise-ments, ragged beggars held out their wooden bowls; children played dice on the flagstones and in winter patted the snow into the shape of lions, the heraldic emblem of the city. Animals roamed everywhere: dogs wearing silver collars; pigs and geese rooting about in door-ways.

Christopher Hibbert, *The House of the Medici: Its Rise and Fall* danger, if not a liability, to salvation; and (2) economics are part of personal conduct in which the rules of everyday morality are absolutely binding, and most of these rules, in effect, exclude the standard practice of every business transaction, other than a simple and equal trade of goods.

Not only the assumptions, but even the medieval vocabulary showed the moral disdain with which all business activities were viewed. What we call "business sense" was called "greed," and what we call "ambition" was "avarice," both sins. Trade, of course, was acceptable as a means of exchanging necessities, but any attempt to make a profit, more than the slight increase due a person for the work put into production, was the deadly sin of "usury." Private property was allowable, but largely in deference to the frailty of human motives and, in any case, not as an "investment." (If a person was lucky enough to own land—either by inheritance or by virtue of a gift from some great lord or king—the idea that he might someday *sell* that land for a profit would have been unimaginable. Land might have been "owned" in some sense, but it was not one of the things that could be traded or exchanged or sold. Indeed, ownership referred far more to duties and responsibilities than to title and assets.) Work, of course, was acceptable, and so too the reasonable wage that a person could claim for it; but what we call "business," selling products for *more* than that wage, at a profit, was considered by virtually every major thinker of the age to be sordid and disreputable. The little business that was transacted in those times, accordingly, was carried out by outsiders whose souls were already in ill repute: Jews, Turks, and other pagans.

The theologian St. Thomas Aquinas, a follower of Aristotle, applauded the idea of a society that had no need of merchants. Like most medieval thinkers, he allowed that, life being as it was, some means of trade was necessary. But even that was an embarrassment and a moral liability. Given the choice, the theorists of medieval society would have done away with business altogether.

These medieval attitudes towards business were formed, first of all, by Christianity. But behind the spiritual suspicion of business activities, a series of more physical and social concerns were also definitive. Unlike the coherent city-state of the Greeks or the enormous empire of the Romans, the isolated, fortified castle-towns that made up the majority of medieval society did not leave much room for "free enterprise." Feudal communities were built up around the fortified manors of powerful lords. In return for their labor on the manor, workers received land and protection. In the absence of a general legal apparatus, tradition was the only dependable guide to social position, and so sons of lords became lords, sons and daughters of serfs became serfs. Society was static and closed. There was little trade as such, since most feudal communities were self-sufficient in most of their needs. Yearly fairs were the rare opportunity to buy luxury goods not produced within the manor itself.

In the fortified towns, however, Aquinas' fears were better founded, for trade was a matter of daily necessity and the possibility of profit-taking was inevitable. But even so, the structure of trade in the medieval towns was highly regulated and

Medieval Guilds in Florence ——

There were twenty-one guilds in all, seven major ones and fourteen minor. Of the seven major guilds, that of the lawyers enjoyed the highest prestige; next in importance were the guilds of the wool, silk and cloth merchants. Emerging as a rival to these in riches and consequence was the bankers' guild, though bankers still suffered from the condemnation of the Church as usurers and felt obliged to adopt certain customs and euphemisms in an attempt to disguise the true nature of their transactions. [There] was the guild of the doctors, the apothecaries and the shopkeepers, of merchants who sold spices, dyes and medicines, and of certain artists and craftsmen, like painters who, buying those colours from members of the guild, were themselves admitted to it. The minor guilds were those of such relatively humble tradesmen as butchers, tanners, leatherworkers, smiths, cooks, stonemasons, joiners, vintners and innkeepers, tailors, armorers and bakers.

Christopher Hibbert, *The House of the Medici: Its Rise and Fall*

quite different from business in our sense. For the most part, production of goods was controlled by the *guilds,* which were, in a very crude comparison, something like the unions of our own day. But unlike unions, they were not concerned with maximizing wages for work or negotiating contracts; they were more like paternalistic *moral* or *ethical* institutions. They set their own rules and determined who would enter and who would not. They set prices and punished unethical behavior. They prevented competition both within the guild and without, not in order to fix high prices, but—quite in line with Aquinas' religious doctrines—in

In France there has been entirely too much initiative displayed of late by the weaving industry, and a *règlement* has been promulgated by Colbert in 1666 to get away from this dangerous and disruptive tendency. Henceforth the fabrics of Dijon and Selangey are to contain 1,408 threads including selvages, neither more nor less. At Auxerre, Avallon, and two other manufacturing towns, the threads are to number 1,376; at Chatillon, 1,216. Any cloth found to be objectionable is to be pilloried. If it is found three times to be objectionable, the merchant is to be pilloried instead.

Robert Heilbroner, *Worldly Philosophers*

order to prevent the sin of usury among the members. In no sense were the guilds dedicated to the growth or the improvement of their professions. Indeed, the primary purpose of the guilds might well be described as keeping things just as they were. They were not primarily concerned with money making; the guilds were much more concerned with morals and the image of their trade as well as assuring themselves a monopoly. They assured quality in their products—indeed they had regulations (on the number of stitches per inch of cloth, for example) that would make the modern businessperson, plagued by government regulations, appalled.

The history of business is filled with anecdotes and stories about men who invented a way of improving production—by developing a new loom for weaving, for example—who were severely punished and even threatened with death for threatening the status quo of their profession. As late as 1666, no innovations in the weaving industry were allowed *by law*. (Heilbroner also reports that about the same time the importing of printed cloth, threatening local industry in France, resulted in the death of 16,000 people executed by hanging and others sent to the galleys for dealing in forbidden wares.)

In the medieval guilds as well as in Aristotle's Greece, any notion of "progress" was not only out of the question, it was viewed as detrimental, if not disastrous, to the structure and security of society. The idea of "growth" as an essential and desirable feature of business was not even a topic fit for discussion. Business as a necessity was bad enough, but the very idea of a *growing* business would have been viewed as sheer insanity, a cancer that would inevitably corrupt and destroy the whole of society.

Given the power of these prejudices and the force of tradition in society, we can only wonder with a keen fascination how our modern business world, which we take so much for granted, ever came into existence. We argue vehemently about "free enterprise" and the need to keep government regulation out of business. But during a surprisingly short, extremely troubled period of time, the idea of the free market did indeed emerge with such force that it has made us all but forget the centuries of anti-business disdain that preceded it.

■ For Class Discussion

The Very Idea of a "Free Market System"

In his *Making of Economic Society,* Robert Heilbroner asks us to imagine ourselves as consultants to a "developing" country:

> We could imagine the leaders of such a nation saying. "We have always experienced a highly tradition-bound way of life. Our men hunt and cultivate the fields and perform their tasks as they are

brought up to do by the force of example and the instruction of their elders. We know, too, something of what can be done by economic command. We are prepared, if necessary, to sign an edict making it compulsory for many of our men to work on community projects for our national development. Tell us, is there any other way we can organize our society so that it will function successfully—or better yet, more successfully?"

Suppose we answered, "Yes, there is another way. Organize your society along the lines of a market economy."

"Very well," say the leaders. "What do we then tell people to do? How do we assign them to their various tasks?"

"That's the very point," we would answer. "In a market economy, no one is assigned to any task. In fact, the main idea of a market society is that each person is allowed to decide for himself what to do."

There is consternation among the leaders. "You mean there is no assignment of some men to mining and others to cattle raising? No manner of designating some for transportation and others for weaving? You leave this to people to decide for themselves? But what happens if they do not decide correctly? What happens if no one volunteers to go into the mines, or if no one offers himself as a railway engineer?"

"You may rest assured," we tell the leaders, "none of that will happen. In a market society, all the jobs will be filled because it will be to people's advantage to fill them."

Our respondents accept this with uncertain expressions. "Now look," one of them finally says, "let us suppose that we take your advice and allow our people to do as they please. Let's talk about something specific, like cloth production. Just how do we fix the right level of cloth output in this 'market society' of yours?"

"But you don't," we reply.

"We don't! Then how do we know there will be enough cloth produced?"

"There will be," we tell him. "The market will see to that."

"Then how do we know there won't be *too much* cloth produced?" he asks triumphantly.

"Ah, but the market will see to that too!"

"But what is this market that will do these wonderful things? Who runs it?"

"Oh, nobody runs the market," we answer. "It runs itself. In fact there really isn't any such *thing* as 'the market.' It's just a word we use to describe the way people behave."

"But I thought people behaved the way they wanted to!"

"And so they do," we say. "But never fear. They will want to behave the way you want them to behave."

"I am afraid," says the chief of the delegation, "that we are wasting our time. We thought you had in mind a serious proposal. What you suggest is inconceivable. Good day, sir."*

How would you further explain "the market idea" to the delegation?

*Robert L. Heilbroner, *The Making of Economic Society,* 4th ed., © 1972, pp. 26–27. Reprinted by permission of Prentice-Hall, Inc., Englewood Cliffs, N.J.

Corporations
and Cultures

*Most of our guys are having fun. They are the kind of people
who would rather be in the Marines than in the Army.*

—Pepsi-Cola spokesperson

A dam Smith described what we might call "classic capitalism" as the complex interaction, cooperation, and competition of a great many individuals, a few of whom were entrepreneurs and owners, most of whom were skilled or unskilled workers, and all of whom were consumers. The dynamics of the market, accordingly, could be described as a microcosm of individual desires, intentions and activities, needing, wanting, making, selling, bargaining, and buying. But the basic unit of the business world today, in both legal and practical terms, is the *corporation.* This is not to deny that the business world is still populated by people, nor is it in any way to deny the importance of the individual. But those now sometimes giant organizations that Adam Smith called "joint stock companies" and dismissed as an unfortunate aberration in the business world are now the institutions around which our business culture is organized. Indeed, some of the largest multinational and global corporations come as close as anyone ever has to dictating policy to the world. There are still small businesses, millions of them, but they all (for the most part) operate in the shadow of the giant corporation. There are still individual entrepreneurs, tens of thousands of them (plus several hundred thousand others who like to think of themselves as such), but when they are successful, they quickly turn into a corporation and may themselves become dispensable to that corporation. It is perhaps the lesson of our times that Steven Jobs, the co-inventor of the personal computer and one of the founders of Apple Computer Company, was unceremoniously fired by Apple's new chief executive officer, John Scully, just a few years after Apple had become a corporation of international proportions.

It is tempting to think of the world of capitalism and the free market as simply an expanded version of Adam Smith's individualistic model, except that in place of individual entrepreneurs, workers, and consumers, we have a competitive dynamic of corporations. Indeed, for the purpose of economic analysis, it is often fruitful to talk this way. But the corporation is not an individual person. It is an institution, an organization that may be made up of hundreds or even hundreds of thousands of individuals. Indeed, even when the corporation is made up of a single individual, as is the case of many professionals, it is a mistake to think of the corporation in the same terms that we use to describe and talk about individuals. In the eyes of the law, corporations and individuals have different responsibilities, are covered by different tax codes, and have different liabilities. And in more personal terms, there is quite a difference between the desires and decisions of a single individual and the demands and decision making of a complex organization. Individuals make up the corporation, but those individuals are not, even all together, the corporation. And how individuals behave within the corporation, as well as how the corporation behaves, is one of the essential ingredients in business ethics.

A.   WHAT IS A CORPORATION?

Most people, and in fact most business writers, simply take the nature of the corporation for granted. It is an organization. It is an institution. It is a collection of individuals with a shared purpose. Or else it is an impersonal monolith known primarily by its products and its corporate logo. Those who live where the corporation (or one of its branches) is located might think of it in terms of a particular building, as the place where a great many of their friends and neighbors hold jobs, and as a source of income for local businesses. Those who work there, of course, think of the corporation in far more complex and personal terms, focusing on their job and their duties, their friends and colleagues at work, their supervisors and their supervisors' bosses in turn, the top executives of the organization, and the very particular paths they walk in their day-to-day activities. But the very nature of the corporation is one of the most perplexing and important issues in business ethics. To what extent is a corporation an abstraction? To what extent is it a collection or a community of individuals? To what extent is a corporation as such a living, moral being? To what extent, in short, is a corporation responsible? When "it" does wrong, who, if anyone, should be punished?

In law, a corporation is conceived as a "fictional person," that is, a creature created by the law but not a "real" person. The purpose of this creation is to consolidate resources, to limit liability, to establish certain obligations, to formalize certain arrangements. A group of investors form a corporation (rather than a partnership, for example) in order to pool their capital and protect themselves against certain sorts of lawsuits that would be ruinous to them personally. An entrepreneur builds a corporation in order to organize a complex manufacturing and marketing system to produce and sell a product that no single individual or small number of individuals could possibly produce, much less market on an appropriate scale. An individual, say, an inventor or a physician, "incorporates" himself or herself in order to enjoy certain tax advantages. But in each of these very different instances, the formation of a corporation *creates* a new entity, a fictitious person, standing (so to speak) apart from any individual or individuals.

There are many reasons for this strictly legal view of the corporation, but it is not our purpose to pursue them here. What is important for us to understand about the nature of a corporation is its responsibilities and obligations, and the various roles and responsibilities of the people who work for and in it. With that in mind, it is essential to begin with the idea that the law alone does not create a corporation but only formalizes or provides the legal framework for an organization or a set of activities that have their own extralegal existence. For example, one can readily view a corporation as a community of people joined together with a single purpose in mind, to make a certain product (or a line of products) and sell them to the consumer. Or one could view the corporation as a system of organizing many different people and many different tasks to serve a single objective or small number of objectives. In either case, however, it is not the particular collection of people who make up the corporation. The company might double the number of its executives and employees, for example, and yet remain "the same" company. Indeed, over a number of years, every single executive and employee might leave or retire and be replaced by someone new, and yet it remains "the same" company. But we should not view the organization as static either. The organization may change, the company may be "restructured," indeed it may grow and be transformed virtually beyond recognition, but in an important sense, it will remain "the same" company. A corporation is something more than the sum of its people, but this need not mean that it is some sort of mysterious or abstract entity whose existence rests with the law alone. A corporation is a community with a structure, an organization. Whether or not that structure, that organization is efficient or successful is another, albeit important, question, as is the happiness and well-being of the corporate community. But the corporation is more than its parts, and the complexity of its structure explains its problematic place in the ethics as well as the sociology of business.

What does it mean to hold a corporation responsible? We praise and condemn corporations and corporate activities, and most of us do so without having any idea who the decision makers in the corporation are or how they make their decisions or what they are thinking about. Indeed, even within the corporation, the exact focus of praise or blame may be a matter of mystery or happenstance, although we might well note that there are usually many more people who are happy and willing to take credit and praise for a corporation's accomplishments than there are people who are willing to accept responsibility for a company's failures and misdeeds. Consider a disastrous decision or mishap of moderate proportions. A middle manager insists that he was "just doing what he was told," and his supervisor claims that she was "just following orders." Her boss in turn was only doing what he thought the top executives wanted done and the executives themselves, even the chief executive of the company, insist that they had no such intention and place the blame squarely on those to whom they had delegated such responsibilities. The board of directors, which is supposedly the overseer of the entire operation, claims to have had no knowledge of what was going on. And the stockholders, who in theory "own" the company, find themselves out of the loop where such decisions are made. Where is the responsibility to be laid? Inevitably, some already beleaguered soul in upper management will be held up as a sacrificial lamb and fired with great fanfare and moral chest-thumping. But such "scapegoating" only hides rather than resolves the difficult problem of assigning responsibility within the corporation.

B.   Corporate Cultures

> Culture: "the total way of life for a people," "the social legacy an individual acquires from his group," "a way of thinking, feeling and believing," "a mechanism for the regulation of behavior."
>
> —C. Kluckhorn, Mirror for Man

"Culture" is a quasi-technical term used by anthropologists to summarize the various structures and values in a society. It is a culture—an *ethos*—that gives any style of life its ethics, including business. Although there is a popular image of corporations and business in general as an unusually homogeneous and interchangeable set of roles and positions, corporations have cultures too. The corporate culture in which we work is as important in determining the style and quality of our lives as the social culture into which we are born. "Business is business," we hear, a statement giving the false impression that business transactions are pretty much all the same. But the truth is quite different; some businesses are more businesslike than others, and some businesses seem hardly like businesses at all.

It is often said, for instance, that "publishing isn't really a business." Of course, commercial publishers aim to make profits and usually do. In fact, they make a reasonable rate of return on their investments and have all the facilities and perquisites of large corporations—impressive buildings, substantial expense accounts, large and efficient accounting departments, corporate hierarchies, corporate suites, tax lawyers, government lobbyists and so on. But the dominant sense in the publishing industry—at least as a matter of shared ideology if not always as a matter of fact—is that their purpose in society is something more than the production of consumer goods with the aim to make a profit; it is also part of that historical tradition that has kept literacy alive since the days when "publishing" consisted of slaves scratching out poetry on pieces of papyrus. This means, among other things, that profit, though essential for survival, is not to be considered the most important aim of commercial publishing, or business life in general, but having a good literary reputation is. Moreover, executives in publishing, because of their products as well as their duties and social responsibilities, are expected to be well-read and admirably literate themselves; this is considered crucial to making the important judgments in the business itself. Publishing is also a relatively conservative industry; brand-new innovations are relatively rare. All these qualities make up the culture of the publishing industry.

A quite different example would be the corporate culture of IBM. IBM has an extremely self-conscious corporate culture and a reputation for social conservatism, particularly in the dress and behavior of its employees. For example, until recently, all employees were expected to wear white shirts and dark suits, a policy that has now been slightly relaxed. But what is much more important is the corporate sensibility itself, which includes an unusually high level of sensitivity towards service and excellence of products as well as an equally unusual emphasis on corporate loyalty and, in return, corporate rewards for the loyal.

On Corporate Size: The Tendency to Bigness ——

In many kinds of industry it has become increasingly difficult for small companies to compete. Entrepreneurs continue to surface and survive, even prosper, but the world belongs more to the Fortune 500 and more and more to the Fortune 50. The reasons for the concentration of industry are not difficult to divine. The cost of entry in most industries is now virtually prohibitive: a billion dollars will not start a major oil company or build a steel mill capable of competing with U.S. Steel, nor can one hope to compete with General Motors, ITT, DuPont, AT&T, IBM, or Boeing with such a small investment of capital. Government regulation exacts a high cost from large companies, but some environmental and health and safety regulations are all but prohibitive for smaller companies. Foreign competitors are often government-owned or subsidized, enabling them to enjoy economies of scale, availability of capital, and efficiencies of stability that can be matched only by the largest U.S. corporations. Despite the complaints on both the left and right that business has grown too big, the point of no return keeps pushing farther and farther out and the prospect of a nation of small, fiercely competitive businesses now suggests economic suicide.

Earl Shorris, *The Oppressed Middle*

Corporate Tribes ——

Anthony Jay, in his *Corporation Man,* suggests that the ideal size for any group organization, allowing maximum interpersonal exchange but at the same time having maximum flexibility and group solidarity, is the primitive "hunting group" of ten people. In fact, there are few businesses that can afford to operate at this scale. This, however, brings us to another feature of corporate cultures that size alone does not tell us: the nature of the groups within the corporation.

Some years ago, Robert Spillman wrote:

> Whatever the formal organizations, people develop an informal organization, which may or may not coincide with the formal organization, and within which certain of their needs are satisfied. The basic unit of informal organization is the work group; and this may consist of from three to eighteen persons carrying out a common task or engaged in linked operations. Each person in that group reacts or responds to the other persons in that group, and the result is that each group tends to act as a cell or unit with characteristics and needs of its own. Members of a social group will tend to subordinate their individual needs to the needs of the group as a whole; but in return the work group protects and shields its members.

Jay concludes:

> The tendency to form "hunting band" groups of around ten people, nearly always men, is a part of our nature. . . . these groups have been the instrument of our survival for up to fifteen million years; and . . . the modern corporation, or any large modern organization, still depends on these groups for its survival. I call it a premise because I cannot prove it; but there is a great deal of evidence to suggest that it is so, and most people who have worked in large organizations will know it in their hearts; they too will have an intuitive knowledge that if you want something done you form a project group, and that somewhere around ten is about the optimum to start working on it. Indeed, the project group is a quite common instrument of management: what the New Biology proves is that it is a great deal more than an instrument of

> management. The hunting band, the ten-group, is the
> foundation of every corporation, the base which supports
> the whole corporate culture. No organization theory that
> does not rest on this base can ever make sense.
>
> Anthony Jay, *Corporation Man*

Every promotion at IBM is accompanied by a trip to the corporate center in Armonk, New York, for a review in the "company philosophy," and continuous education is an intrinsic part of every job. IBM sees itself as having to inspire the loyalty of both its employees and its customers. Everything in the company is aimed at those ends. "Loyalty is something you have to win," says a vice-president at IBM. The credo of IBM summarizes its ideals and, accordingly, its standards of behavior in three short phrases:

> Dignity and respect for the individual. Pursuit of excellence. Dedication to service.

Living in IBM's world is accepting those ideals and standards, as well as the considerable rewards of high pay and security that go along with them.

Corporate loyalty as such summarizes many of the most important features of some corporate cultures. Consider, for example, two rival firms in Minneapolis, General Mills and Pillsbury. General Mills stresses loyalty and corporate unity, and accordingly boasts an emphasis on informality and mutual good will. Promotions are virtually always within the company. Employees generally stay on for many years, feeling that they are part of the company. At Pillsbury, on the other hand, executive defections are so frequent that some have started to call it "the executive finishing school." Within such a culture, quite naturally, people are valued not so much for what they do for the company, much less how long they've been with it, but rather in terms of their marketability and mobility. Size is not in itself a dimension of corporate culture, but it is certainly one of the major determinants of the style, standards, and overall attitudes within a business. The difference between ITT and 3M, for example, may not be easily recognized in terms of mere numbers, but the size of ITT (305,000 employees) dictates a much more rigorous emphasis on the importance of hierarchies of power and responsibilities, while 3M (80,000 employees) is much more concerned with keeping itself together and promoting loyalty as such, with virtually all of its promotions from the inside and maximum mobility within the organization. Smaller businesses (conventionally defined by the U.S. government as fewer than 500 employees) inevitably involve an increase in personal responsibilities, an increase in awareness of what else is going on in the company, and accordingly, more dependability in rewards (and punishments) for successes (and failures).

The small, independently owned corporations and businesses, in classical economic theory, are what the world of business and the free enterprise system is all about. "Small business," so defined, constitutes 60 percent of the American work force. This is the world of "entrepreneurs," who put together their life savings to pursue a novel idea single-mindedly and build a company, perhaps from an office in the garage. Clearly the cultural differences between this case and the corporation are astounding, not least of all the fact that such individuals are in most senses entirely their "own boss." The rewards and punishments are all self-ascribed, and so are the production quotas, expectations for the future, plans for growth, and security. An independent building contractor or independent oil-well driller, for example, enjoys the benefits of freedom and autonomy that virtually no one in the large corporation could even imagine. At the same time, the risks and liabilities are all their own, and the very smallness that provides freedom and increased maneuverability also means extreme vulnerability to elements beyond their control—interest rates and building demands for the contractor and the amount of oil under the ground and its price for the driller.

Another crucial dimension of corporate cultures includes the clientele of the corporation, the kinds of pressures within the organization, and the "openness"

The greeter at a Wal-Mart store might be surprised to know he is living proof of one of the oldest laws of management theory. Instilled by the late Sam Walton, Wal-Mart's deeply ingrained corporate culture of frugality, hard work, service to customers and paternalism towards employees has contributed as much to its success as its slick distribution system and "everyday low prices."

Management thinkers have long associated a strong corporate culture—the beliefs, goals and values that guide the behaviour of a firm's employees—with superior long-term performance. The theory is that strong cultures can help workers march to the same drummer; create high levels of employee loyalty and motivation; and provide the company with structure and controls, without the need for an innovation-stifling bureaucracy.

One snag is that the right corporate culture, reckon the authors, often takes decades to evolve. The best way to speed this up, they say, may be to appoint a boss who is either unconventional (they cite General Electric's Jack Welch, SAS's Jan Carlzon and Nissan's Yutaka Kume) or an outsider (like British Airways' Lord King): and preferably both. Nonconformists and outsiders are good at shaking up, or creating, corporate cultures. Just don't expect any results this century.

The Economist, June 6, 1992

and mutual concern of both peers and superiors. Quite obviously, a business that caters primarily to other businesses (for instance, IBM) will promote quite a different image for itself and its role in the community than a business that caters to the youth entertainment market (such as record companies or film producers). A transportation company that services the more well-to-do (airline companies or limousine services) will quite naturally evolve a different image for itself and a different set of demands for its employees than a transportation company whose main concern is cheap, reliable transportation for those who cannot afford luxury travel accommodations (bus companies or "rent-a-wreck").

A company that believes in getting results through excessive and even impossible demands on its employees rather than by encouraging employees to

---

THINK: IBM ——

"We want manufacturing men to feel that they are executives in the company," said Watson. "The farther we keep away from the 'boss' proposition—of being the 'boss' of the men under us—the more successful we are going to be." Part of the IBM spirit was that no man was to have thoughts of being a boss. It was the equivalent of sin, something like inducing carnal fantasy in a state of grace, to set oneself thus apart. One could be a leader; leadership was encouraged, but only in a one-to-one relationship, one man offering guidance to another. The leader was instructed not to tell people what to do but to help them to do it. . . . Watson said: "The man who utilizes every minute of every hour becomes a bigger, better being every minute."

The IBM man was not a visible part of the roaring twenties and the dissolute life that distinguished them. First of all because he was a serious fellow, intent on making something of himself, but also because Mr. Watson would fire him in a minute if word of excessive frivolity, and any drinking whatsoever, or unacceptable incidents of boisterous or embarrassing conduct got back to the leader. . . .

There were no specific rules about decorum, grooming, and apparel, but a certain style was expected because Mr. Watson approved of it.

Every office had a THINK sign, and every desk was supposed to have one on it, within unobstructed view of its occupant. . . . There was a never-ending emphasis on THINK and company loyalty. The word loyalty was not visually exalted to the status of THINK, but it was second only to the capitalized directive in continuing significance. THINK was what all were required to do; loyalty was the inevitable result of thought, if it was correctly undertaken.

William Rogers, *Think*

improve at their own pace establishes a distinctive work atmosphere. ITT, for example, has a reputation for strict discipline and rigid demands on employees. Pepsi-Cola, in the heat of its perennial battle with Coca-Cola for the lead in the international soft drink war, makes enormous demands on its employees, often pits them against one another, and gives "the golden handshake" to managers who, no matter how hard-working, fail to win the battles. Similarly, Chrysler, in its desperate days following the much-publicized loan guarantee from the federal government when it faced enormous demands to quickly "turn the company around," placed inordinate pressures on its dealers (in fact, scores went bankrupt) and salesmen, as well as on everyone else in the company from top to bottom. On the other hand, Digital Equipment Corporation is one that allows workers to set their own hours and establish their own working conditions, with the expectation that they will periodically report on their progress. Perhaps the most extreme version of this creative laxity is Commodities Corporation in Princeton, New Jersey, which consists mainly of a group of academic economists and financial analysts who work not only their own hours but their own weeks and months, creating their own models of economic behavior and trying them out in the market with company funds. Indeed, the rules are so flexible that an employee is expected to show up at the office only once every few months, though such protracted absences are by no means the rule. How employees think of their own behavior and performance in such a company is obviously quite different from the way someone in the hierarchy at ITT conceives of himself, or from someone who faces the national spotlight at Chrysler.

There are some companies that pride themselves on being tough, if not ruthless; on the other hand, there are corporations such as J. C. Penney where it is corporate creed "not to take unfair advantage of anyone," including customers (who can return any merchandise, no questions asked) or suppliers and employees. Much like the contemporary Japanese corporation, Penney's makes every effort to keep its employees and keep them happy, even by finding easier jobs for those who fall behind or cannot handle their current responsibilities. (Not surprisingly, the *average* executive tenure at Penney's is *thirty-three years.*) Some corporations survive on short-term investments with an emphasis on current returns; others depend on long-term investments with long-term rewards and long-term survival.

The established culture of a large corporation is typically so entrenched, so much a part of the organization, structure, and personality of the company, that changing it is almost always risky. Indeed, a top executive who is given the job of not just "turning the company around" but altering its culture as well (from passive to aggressive, from service to marketing, from free creativity to hard-headed practicality) has been given what is without a doubt the most difficult job in the business world. Far from being merely the superficial rituals and the façade of business, corporate cultures in fact provide what "structuralist" anthropologists call its "deep structure," the conceptual foundation on which it builds, the self-images from which all else begins.

C.   CORPORATE CODES OF ETHICS

The values inherent in a corporate culture can be formalized and spelled out in what has come to be known as **the corporate code of ethics.** In one sense, only the name is new, for virtually every company had some statement of policies long before ethics became a center of focus in the business world. But the idea that values are important to not only a company's identity but to its way of doing business is an idea that has been remarkably slow in coming, and the impetus to formulate these values in the form of a code only started to become commonplace after the Watergate scandal of the early 1970s. At its best, the publication and distribution of a corporate code is an explicit expression of a set of values that has in fact governed a company and its employees for quite some time. At its worst, the publication and distribution of a corporate code of ethics is a desperate attempt to persuade or threaten employees into compliance with a set of principles which do not play a significant role in the day-to-day behavior of its employees. Sometimes the code as stated is nothing but a hypocritical attempt at public relations.

Corporate codes can be short and very general, or they may be very specific and detailed about particular kinds of behavior. At its most general, a corporate code may simply assert the company's commitment to quality in its products and integrity in its dealings with the public, or it may simply remind everyone from salesperson to CEO that "the customer always comes first." Such assertions may indeed be valuable as a constant reminder of the purpose or mission of the company and act as a moral glue to hold the different parts of a complex company together. The best codes, however, take some care in spelling out specific prohibitions and obligations, for example, the limitation on gifts that may be accepted by any employee or manager. Such detailed information in the company code serves as something more than a mere reminder. It gives employees and managers concrete and extremely useful advice in situations that may otherwise be extremely uncomfortable and ambiguous. An inexperienced employee who is on a team assigned to decide between contractors for an office addition is given a pair of very expensive football or opera tickets by one of the applicants for the contract. Should he or she accept these with thanks, or turn them down? A specific rule, "No employee shall accept gifts with a value of more than fifty dollars" answers the question. (Of course, there will always be borderline or "gray" areas, for example, if the tickets cost $25.50 apiece. Serious infractions, however, do not happen on the borderline and the occasional differences in judgment between those who insist on following the code to the letter and those who adhere to its "spirit" are not likely to cause serious disruptions in the company.) In addition to providing concrete guidance, such explicit prohibitions serve another, equally important, function. Our inexperienced employee might find it difficult to rebuff the offer of a smooth-talking, experienced salesperson. How does one say no gracefully when being so cajoled and pressured? But by pointing to the code of ethics, our inexperienced employee can easily explain his position by citing company policy. In other words, the point of a code of ethics is not just to inform and

---

More Companies Enact Ethics Codes ——

The Conference Board surveyed ethics practices at 264 corporations in the United States, Europe, Mexico, and Canada.

• Among firms with ethics codes, 45 percent have enacted their most current statement since 1987.

• Some 84 percent of U.S. companies that responded had an ethics code. The figure for non-American firms was 58 percent.

• Financial firms were less likely to have ethics codes than companies in other industries (57 percent versus 82 percent).

• Some 16 percent of American companies said new legislation prompted revisions or additions to their ethics codes.

• One-fourth of the responding companies said they had established new ethics training programs, ethics committees, or ombudsperson's offices during the last three years.

The Conference Board 1991 (reported in *Business & Society Review*)

---

prompt those who work for the company, but to provide them with an instrument that will actually help them adhere to the values of the company.

Do corporate codes of ethics work? The answer to that often-asked question depends on what is meant by "work," and what kind of a company, as well as what kind of a code, we are talking about. If one believes that the purpose of a corporate code is to hammer employees and managers into shape, thereby converting cynical, disloyal, borderline criminals into God-fearing, moral men and women, then the answer, of course, is that no code—not even a fully sanctioned criminal code—will succeed. If, on the other hand, one accepts the company code as an expression of the actual day-to-day working values of the employees and managers of the company, then it is not entirely clear what it means for the company code to "work," although it does accurately portray the company in its best light and reminds everyone what they are there to do. Of the most critical importance, however, is the example set by the executives at the top. If they are seen to ignore the principles and provisions of the code, there is no chance that anyone else who works for the company is going to take the code seriously. One can and should, of course, back up the specifics of the code with punishments—demotions and firings being the extreme. But having a code "with teeth," although essential if the code is to be taken seriously, does not mean that the success of the code should be measured by the number of violations that are punished (the prosecutor's accounting measure). Indeed, although there will always be a few "bad apples" and a few new employees who do not yet understand the corporate culture, a working code of ethics should be such an accurate portrayal of the company's ideals and behavior that both violations and punishments should be few and far between. And in those cases where the code of ethics is created in order to make radical changes in the behavior of a company and its

Live Long and Profit ——

Life and health insurers have made the following "declaration of interdependence" between the industry and its communities:

The primary responsibility of our business is to operate in the best interests of policyholders, stockholders, and employees. At the same time, we are acutely aware of the needs of our communities. Indeed, responding to their needs serves the long-term interests of our business constituents.

Therefore, we affirm the interdependence of our companies and our communities. Resolving social and economic problems enhances, directly and indirectly, the strength and stability of our business.

Our industry cannot profit if society fails.

Thus, we pledge that, to the best of our ability, our companies, of whatever size and location, will use available resources—including financial, time, talent, and leadership—to improve the social and economic conditions that bear on the quality of life in our communities.

employees, it is not just the content of the code that must be carefully considered, but also the restructuring of the entire company.

J. C. Penney (Corporate Code) ——

1. To serve the public, as nearly as we can, to its complete satisfaction.

2. To expect for the service we render a fair remuneration and not all the profit the traffic will bear.

3. To do all in our power to pack the customer's dollar full of value, quality, and satisfaction.

4. To continue to train ourselves and our associates so that the service we give will be more and more intelligently performed.

5. To improve constantly the human factor in our business.

6. To reward men and women in our organization through participation in what the business produces.

7. To test our every policy, method, and act in this wise: "Does it square with what is right and just?"

BHP (the largest steel and mining company in Australia) ——

Statements of Policy
Standards of Business Conduct

Policy

It is BHP Group policy that the affairs of the Company and its sub-sidiaries be conducted at all times in accordance with the law and, as well, in accordance with high ethical standards. It is the responsibil-ity of all directors and employees of all companies in the Group to ensure, that for their part, this policy is carried out.

Compliance with Law

There is an increasing body of law in Australia which relates to busi-ness conduct. Examples of laws recently enacted deal with agree-ments and practices in restraint of trade and with dealings in the securities of companies. The effect of some aspects of these laws will be to limit and constrain the freedom of companies and their directors and employees to act, in some circumstances, in ways which those directors or employees may think desirable.

It is BHP Group policy that letter and also, where this is clear, the spirit of all laws in force in Australia or overseas, affecting the business conduct of companies and their directors and employees be complied with. Where there is any doubt advice should be sought.

Inside Information

In some circumstances the use of inside information for personal gain is specifically prohibited by legislation. This is the case, for example, in regard to dealings with company securities.

It is BHP Group policy that information which is not public con-cerning the activities or plans of the Company, or any subsidiary or associated company, shall not be used for the purposes of the Group or the company concerned, and shall not be used for personal gain for directors, employees or anyone associated with them.

Conflicts of Interest

It is BHP Group policy that directors and employees should not engage in activities or hold property which would involve a material conflict of interest and which might thus inhibit or appear to inhibit impartial business judgment.

Approval should be sought through appropriate channels from the Chief General Manager in all cases where any appointment, acquisition of property or any business relationship might result in a breach by an employee of this policy or might expose his actions to risk of challenge on this score.

Improper Payments

It is BHP Group policy that any payment made to a third party such as an agent or a consultant, in connection with the obtaining of any order or benefit for the Company or a subsidiary shall be no more than an amount which by normal commercial standards would be properly and openly payable for the services rendered by the third party.

Any payment in the nature of a bribe or kick-back is contrary to policy and is prohibited.

Gifts and Gratuities

It is contrary to BHP Group policy for employees to give or receive monetary or other gifts, personal favors or gratuities in connection with the business of the Group, except, in appropriate cases, items of nominal value and reasonable and authorized business related expenditure for entertainment.

Accounts and Records

All transactions of the Company and its subsidiaries shall be properly entered in the corporate records and accounts and no false, misleading or artificial entries shall be made for any reason.

D.   MERGERS AND ACQUISITIONS: THE ETHICAL DIMENSION

Corporations, like individuals, are dynamic. They grow, they change, they compete, they cooperate, and sometimes they even get "married." Marriage, in corporate terms, is a merger, and as in human marriages, there can be mergers of convenience as well as mergers of necessity. There are happy but also unhappy mergers. There are mergers made in stockholders' heaven as well as mergers seemingly made by the devil. Among the latter, first and foremost are those that are known as **hostile mergers,** the corporate equivalent of the shotgun wedding or, perhaps, a kidnapping. In a hostile merger, the acquiring corporation "takes over" the acquired company against the latter's will, often at the end of a protracted, very expensive, exhausting and dramatic battle. And the first action of the acquiring company may be to physically dismantle the company acquired, selling off the best parts at a considerable profit, engulfing others, and abandoning those that are of no use or commercial value. But like many bad marriages, the "winning" partner of the merger often suffers its own comeuppance. In the last several years several enormously successful take-over companies have found themselves in bankruptcy court for literally biting off more than they could chew. In many cases the debt incurred in the winning take-over bid put the company in an impossible financial position.

But these are the worst marriages, and in any discussion of mergers it is only right and proper that we also provide the happy case scenario. Two companies find themselves competing in a small or diminishing market. One or the other will soon find itself in serious trouble. But instead of competing they decide to cooperate, joining their resources, cutting their operating costs, sharing their expenses, unifying their product lines, and becoming a single profitable company instead of two competing and perhaps unprofitable companies. Or, two companies find that they complement each other. One, perhaps, makes rubber tires. The other manufactures wheels. They deal with each other all the time. Their various sales and manufacturing people often discuss their mutual needs. They often sell their products in tandem and, not surprisingly, they begin to think of themselves as partners. They decide to formalize their already established relationship, merging to form a single company. Again, they pool their resources, probably save a good deal on reduced operating and administrative costs, and very likely make their production and marketing methods much more efficient.

Mergers make sense for many reasons. A national or global business that is served by many different small enterprises finds that it could serve more people more efficiently and give them a much wider variety of services if they joined together as a single operation. Banking, for example, is undergoing such a change in the United States, where interstate banking was until very recently forbidden by law. But anyone who has tried to cash an out-of-state check while traveling knows the disadvantages of such a system, and legislative and other regulative moves are under way to allow more banks to make branches of small local banks and allow them to consolidate their operations and extend to all their customers services that are not now available. Of course, there are dangers to this, for some small local banks will be forced to close (rather than allow themselves to be taken over) and the comforts and advantages of neighborhood banking may be jeopardized. And as several large national and international banks gain an increasing share of the banking business there is always the threat of increasing monopoly and the diminution of competition. But in the current situation, in which everyone seems to admit that there are too many banks and too much confusion, the mergers of major banks and the consolidation of now independent banking systems seems to be the inevitable trend of the immediate future.

Mergers have the particular advantage of putting all of the ingredients of a product under one roof. Automobile manufacturers, for example, depend less and less on outside contractors and producers of parts and raw materials. Why negotiate in the market for goods whose value might fluctuate considerably when you can produce it yourself under more controlled conditions? Suppliers of giant corporations are often in the position of virtual captivity anyway, if a large percentage of their business depends on that one source of sales. (Some large corporations insist on spreading their business around for just that reason, in order to avoid making dependents of their clients.) Mergers are often major steps towards efficiency and competitiveness, and as such it must be said that they are good for business.

Bigger is not always better, however, and mergers are not always good for business, nor are they always in the public interest. The most obvious danger of a merger is the creation of virtual monopolies and the loss of competition in an already limited market. A more immediate catastrophe, the direct consequence of consolidation, may be the elimination of many jobs and the shutting down of factories and offices. People are put out of work and whole communities may be destroyed. When the takeover is "hostile," that is, against the wishes of the current management and often the result of a long expensive court battle, the consequences can be even worse. If the takeover has as its object the "liquidation" of the company and the sell-off of its most valuable assets, for instance, the dimensions of the resulting unemployment and destruction can be disastrous. Not all hostile takeovers have this conclusion. Occasionally, a hostile takeover actually does improve efficiency and pay off for the employees, the stockholders, and the surrounding community. Unfortunately, these are the exception rather than the rule. There is a special class of cases, for example, in which the conclusion of a purported takeover is not control of the company, but the possibility is so threatening to the current management that it "buys out" its own company, incurs great debt, and subsequently has to lay off thousands of its employees and penalize the stockholders as well. When the intended result of the threat is such a pay-off, usually by way of the repurchase of the stock at an inflated price, it is called "greenmail," and is tantamount to a legal form of extortion. The actors in such a drama are often handsomely rewarded, but the inevitable result is a wounding, fatal, of the targeted company, the endangerment or loss of jobs, and the weakening of the industry as a whole. "Greenmail" is not the aim of most takeover attempts, but it is a form of abuse that illuminates some of the dangers of an economy that allows itself to get over-excited about mergers and acquisitions and too complacent with the essential routines of business as usual.

Perhaps the most subtle and certainly the most interesting consequence of most mergers, even the friendliest and most convenient, is the mixing of corporate cultures. Sometimes, as in bicultural (or multicultural) societies, the mix is mutually invigorating; a source of strength rather than a weakness. The energy of one corporate culture invigorates the other, while the other's congeniality makes the whole company a better place to work. But often cultures do not get along, if only because each is accustomed to doing business its own established way. After a merger, there is virtually always a struggle for cultural dominance, sometimes augmented by a personnel battle as well. If one corporate culture has gotten used to a hierarchical, authoritarian structure while the other is a relaxed, consensus-minded egalitarian culture, the immediate results are sure to be marked by mutual resentment. Communication and cooperation will be compromised. "Corporate culture" is not just another cute way of talking about life in the corporation. Culture defines the corporation, and it often determines whether it will be congenial and successful or a hot-bed of ultimately self-destructive hostility.

Mergers and Impositions ——

Out in Bartlesville, Oklahoma, the citizens were having prayer meetings in their churches. The Bartlesville citizens prayed that the board of directors of Phillips Petroleum be granted the wisdom to know what to do about [T. Boone] Pickens, since Pickens was threatening to take over Bartlesville's largest employer. "Those people had things on backwards, [said Pickens]. They thought the *town* owned the *company.* The town didn't own the company, the *shareholders* owned the company, and the shareholder is the forgotten man. That Phillips management didn't even own one tenth of one percent of their own company."

With or without the aid of God, the board of Phillips Petroleum decided to "restructure" the company. It issued more debt, offered some of its assets for sale, bought back the block of stock Pickens had acquired, and, in effect, paid him $89 million to go away.

Pickens scooped up his chips and tried the next company, Unocal, the Union Oil Company of California. Since 1982, Pickens's own company, Mesa, has made investments in—and attempted takeovers of—a number of oil companies far larger than Mesa, with results gratifying to Pickens. On its stock in Cities Service, Mesa made $31.5 million; on General American Oil, $43.6 million; and on Gulf Oil, $404 million. The grateful Mesa directors, all picked by Pickens, voted their chief more than $24.1 million in deferred bonuses since last November. That is a respectable figure even in the state of Texas. It was said around the oil patch that Pickens had found more oil in other people's balance sheets than the great wildcatters had found in the ground.

When Pickens started Mesa, it was a tiny one-horse oil company scratching for funds. Now bankers fall all over themselves to lend to it so it can do its "paper drilling."

"All the companies that we invested in have things in common," said Pickens. "One, the market price of the stock wasn't where it should have been. It was selling at too big a discount in relation to the assets of the company. You need to go through the assets, the reserves in the ground, the refineries, whatever, and determine the value. We believe the stock price ought to sell, per share, close to that. But their stock didn't. Why? The management just didn't care about the shareholder. They cared about their hunting trips in Spain and Norway, that's what they cared about, and if you ask about the stockholder, they say, 'Well, we pay him a dividend, don't we?' "

Actually, it is not unusual for asset-rich companies to sell stock in the marketplace that is worth less than their assets. They tend to sell on the basis of the current earnings, or their current cash flow. To liquidate or sell a company's assets—the only way to realize the full value—takes time, and once it's done, of course, there *is* no more company. That is exactly what the raiders threaten: to sell off all the assets, and thus realize the present worth of the company. Managements oppose this not only because their jobs are at stake but because they are thinking—eptly or ineptly, as the case may be—about the future of the company.

But there is something that bothers me in this mania of raiding and restructuring. The whole focus is on the *present* price of company stock—even at the cost of the *future* price of the stock, should the company continue to exist. For example, one recent defense against take-overs is for the target company to take on more debt; it buys in some of its own stock, or pays out a higher dividend, or buys another company. Interest on all that new debt has to be paid. The money that goes into paying interest and amortization can't go into the growth of the company. It's true that debt used to be considered a good thing to have in periods of high inflation—you could pay back with cheaper dollars—but now the lenders are wise and the interest goes up faster than inflation. Going into debt as a kicker to the stock price, rather than as a source for future earnings, is ultimately a crippling defense.

Eventually some of the bank loans and the "junk bonds" that financed the takeover mania will turn sour, and the takeover phase will be over, just as previous fads have died away. But at present the concern with the fast buck—the next quarter, rather than the next ten years—is paramount. The demand is for instant gratification on a macroeconomic scale. It reflects a shortsighted attitude that is not new in America, that extends even wider than T. Boone and his friends, and that remains one of the weakest aspects of our business society.

Adam Smith, Esquire, Sept. 1985

In Praise of Boone ――――

Let us now praise the Boone Pickenses of the world.

They're parodied as capitalism's juvenile delinquents: corporate "raiders" engaged in "hostile" takeovers financed by "junk" bonds. In fact, hostile takeovers are not simply a giant Monopoly game played for private gain and social loss. They represent a crude check on the power of corporate managers to waste wealth and create inefficiency. I doubt those in Congress who condemn Pickens and want to regulate takeovers understand the distinction.

The ultimate social role of business is to enhance national living standards and competitiveness. Mismanagement has social consequences. In Britain, investment as a proportion of national output has been higher than in the United States. But our investment is 60 percent more productive because American companies invest more wisely and use their investments more efficiently. I am not arguing, therefore, that most management is incompetent or that most investment is made whimsically.

But hostile takeovers represent a healthy reaction to flaws in our business system. When corporate managers are not the major owners of their companies—as most are not—their loyalties become confused. They may be less interested in maximizing profits than in preserving and expanding their corporate domain. By contrast, society's interest lies in maximizing efficiency and living standards; profitability—which means companies producing what people want and doing so efficiently—is a social, not just a business, indicator.

Mature Markets: As long as a company's primary business is thriving, the conflict may lie dormant. Managers can maximize profits and expand simultaneously. But this happy marriage rarely lasts forever. Almost all products have life cycles. Markets mature, and traditional products often generate more cash than can profitably be reinvested in the same product. Corporate management then faces a dilemma: to overinvest in a mature business, or to diversify into a new business, where the company may have no special knowledge or talent.

Hostile takeovers arise mainly to exploit profit opportunities created when corporations cannot cope with their growth dilemmas. Some firms can diversify successfully, others cannot. In some, the force of habit compels them to invest in declining businesses. Given the impulse for survival, managements only grudgingly react to a paucity of internal investment opportunities by paying more of their cash flow to shareholders, who would then reinvest for themselves.

Robert J. Samuelson, *Newsweek,* May 6, 1985

The drama of the hostile takeover, played out on the stage of the business press and involving powerful entrepreneurs, whole teams of highly paid legaland financial advisors, defensive and ambitious managers, anxious stockholders, and thousands of terrified employees, has become part of corporate life. But it can have terrible costs. It elevates insecurity, paralyzes industry, and often rewards outrageous and irresponsible financial behavior. (One recent extremely hostile and well-publicized takeover battle involved high-interest loans of more than twenty billion dollars, not to mention the banking, legal, and consulting fees.) But although such high-stakes financial theater may pay off in entertinment value for the observers and a few of the high-powered participants, there is very little evidence that it is good for business. Mergers as opposed to takeovers, however, can be beneficial and rewarding. One of the more recent and now more important questions of business ethics, and of business law too, is how can we distinguish the good from the bad and encourage the former, not the latter? The free enterprise system allows all of this, with some stringent qualifications, but it is improbable that the hostile takeover is what Adam Smith (or any other serious economist) had in mind. The business of business is production, prosperity, and exchange and not a high-risk game of poker.

E.   WHO RUNS THE CORPORATION? MANAGERS, DIRECTORS, STOCKHOLDERS

Who runs the corporation? In many small companies, there is no question who is boss and who is responsible. There may be but a single person, the owner and perhaps founder of the company, who continues to call all the shots. Or, in some cases, it is the son or daughter of the original owner, or one of the original top employees, or perhaps a family or a small group of executives. Such corporations can grow very large indeed, without ever losing their family sensibility. One notable example is IBM, which continues to think of itself as a family despite the fact that it has well over a hundred thousand employees. The company founder, Thomas Watson, ran his growing corporation with the stern guidance of a caring father, a tradition carried on by his son Tom, Jr. Some very small corporations, on the other hand, seem to run with virtually no one in charge. Decisions are made by consensus in group meetings and everyone seems to take responsibility for everything. But corporate control and responsibility have become major issues in many corporations. The formal lines of authority do not always indicate where the actual power and control of the company lies, and those who are nominally in charge are sometimes less than knowledgeable about what goes on in the company they supposedly run.

In most large public corporations, "ownership" is itself a delicate and often complicated issue. Technically, the stockholders collectively own the corporation, and it is they who choose a board of directors which in turn decides on the top executives who will run the company. But the problem, as Adam Smith anticipated in his brief critical comments about "joint stock companies," is that the management of a corporation cannot always be depended on to run the company in the best interests of the owners. Indeed, a common criticism of today's corporations, across the spectrum of political views, is that management tends to satisfy its own needs and interests at the expense of the stockholders, the customers, and even the employees. To be sure, not all executives are guilty of such behavior. In fact, relatively few executives actually aim to manipulate or "milk" the com-

---

The average chief executive pulls down as much as twenty to thirty times the amount that managers in their companies think the CEO should be paid, according to an *Industry Week* magazine survey. If 51 percent of the managers surveyed had their way, the CEO of the company in which they work would be paid only $100,000 to $300,000 annually, the magazine reports. . . . While the typical executive of a midsize-to-large U.S. firm now makes ninety-five to 150 times more than the average U.S. production worker, the ratio in Japan is about fifteen-to-one and in Europe about twenty-to-one.

—*Business & Society Review*

But, the good news is . . .
Top executives are getting fewer and slimmer perks this year as companies cut costs in the recession.

The biggest decline, according to a survey by the National Institute of Business Management, has been in company cars. Only 59 percent of 367 executives surveyed have a car owned or leased by their employer, down from 64 percent last year and 71 percent in 1985.

Just 21 percent of executives get dining and social club memberships, down from 27 percent last year and 47 percent six years ago. The number of telephone credit cards fell also, to 59 percent from 71 percent.

But a few perks are on the rise, particularly those that enable executives to keep working when they're out of the office. Some 45 percent of those surveyed can have car phones this year, up from 36 percent last year. Similarly, 21 percent have personal computers for home use, up from 14 percent.

—*The Wall Street Journal*
June 13, 1991

pany for their own personal advantage. But recent corporate behavior shows that at least a few executives have been willing to save their own jobs at enormous expense to the company, for example, by incurring enormous debt to buy controlling interest in the company for themselves, by giving themselves huge salaries even as the company is failing and workers are being laid off, by creating "poison pills" (intolerable debts or restrictions) to fend off possible takeovers (which end up damaging the very company supposedly defended), or by giving themselves "golden parachutes"—enormous compensation packages presented when they leave the company, even if the reason for their leaving is their own mismanagement and the ruination of the company. Such behavior may be exceptional, but it is a shocking reminder that foxes cannot be trusted to guard the chickens, and though the top management may run the company, it does not always follow that this will be for the benefit of those who have hired them to do so.

The stockholders are the ultimate owners of the company, but both their power and their responsibility are subject to question. Stockholders are owners because the original owners sold the business to the original buyers of the stock, many of whom then sold their shares to other buyers, and so on through many transactions. Some of those buyers, however, held on to the stock for a very short time, perhaps just long enough to take advantage of a predicted upsweep in the market—perhaps even, in special circumstances, for only a few hours. Such speculators can only be called "owners" in the most attenuated sense, and in any case they obviously have no durable interest in the health and fortune of the company. Indeed, many stockholders do not even know the products or services provided by the companies they "own," and very few have ever set foot on the corporate premises, read anything more about the company than the glossy annual report, or expressed concern or gained any knowledge of the safety conditions in the workplace, the fairness with which employees are treated, or the problems posed by the company's presence in a community. Moreover, a large corporation may have as many as tens or even hundreds of thousands of "owners," many of whom hold only a tiny fraction of the stock, do not go to stockholder meetings or even fill out proxy forms, and have no idea who directs the company or how the company is run. A few large stockholders may, of course, be in a particularly powerful position, and a single stockholder who has gained or retained more than 50 percent of the stock is in the unique position of virtually running the company himself, herself, or itself (if the stockholder is in fact another institution, perhaps even another corporation). But even then, it is by no means assured that the board of directors hired to oversee the corporation or the top management hired to run the company will perform solely or primarily for the benefit of that singularly powerful stockholder. And if the company fails, one can predict that here as well as in the cases where the power is more diffuse, there will be a great deal of finger-pointing and not a great deal of taking responsibility. (A number of recent airline takeovers and subsequent bankruptcies are cases in point.)

The board of directors is a curious institution that has lately come under increased scrutiny. In theory, the board of directors is in charge of the company, and although they do not run the company on a day-to-day basis they are responsible for hiring and overseeing those who do. In fact, many boards of directors are composed of corporate officers who are friends of the company CEO, public celebrities, ex-politicians, university presidents, and other people who may be in no position to understand, much less supervise, the workings of the company in question. Their briefings of the policies and problems of the corporation are indeed brief, and their contact with the company may be limited to a single board meeting every month or so. Their approval often amounts to a "rubber stamping" of executive decisions, and, when something goes wrong, the "directors" may be among the first to express shock and surprise, denying any knowledge or responsibility for wrongdoing. Sometimes, the relationship between top management and the board may be anything but supervisory. In recent scandals regarding the extravagant paychecks chief executives were getting, it became quite clear in a number of corporations that these excesses were granted by the board in exchange for proportionally extravagant salaries for their own (sometimes minimal) contributions. Again, one should view such behavior as the exception rather than the rule, but the number of merely perfunctory boards of directors forces us to think again about who really runs the corporation. A very recent development, however, subjecting members of the board to lawsuits for their responsibility for the company, may well change the role of these directors (though it has also been suggested that they should be protected against such lawsuits). Another suggestion is that they be paid to actually direct the company, with all the work and responsibility that entails.

F. THE SMALL-BUSINESS ALTERNATIVE: SELF-EMPLOYMENT AND THE ENTREPRENEUR

Thus far we have been talking as if the business world were made up primarily, if not exclusively, of large, complex corporations. This is not, of course, an accurate picture of the business world, which includes Mom-and-Pop groceries, sidewalk vendors, independent contractors of all kinds, hundreds of thousands of small and not-so-small shops, restaurants, stores, and services. The United States Department of Commerce estimates that there are about one hundred thousand "small" businesses in the country, a "small business" being defined as one with fewer than five hundred employees. One could add to this, of course, the many hundreds of thousands of people who are one way or another "in business for themselves," whether making and selling crafts, running a restaurant or an antique shop, fixing things, helping people paint their houses or do their income taxes, teaching them tennis or golf, giving art or dance lessons, or reading palms or tarot cards.

Many small businesses are made up of individuals, a family, or a few friends who share a talent, an idea, and some sense of the market. Many if not most small businesses are local. They serve the community in which they are located and depend on a good reputation and a steady stream of satisfied customers and repeat business. Before this century, many small businesses were simply handed down from generation to generation. Today, however, the trend is toward innovation rather than continuity, and it is no longer surprising to see shops proudly advertising themselves as "In business since 1987," less than a decade old and already one of the most established businesses on the block. Indeed, many small-business owners are refugees from the corporate world who grew tired of corporate politics. They wanted a more direct role in the design and development of the product, or more direct contact with the customer. They wanted to work at home, or they tired of the corporate regimen, "dressing for success," and the meetings and memos. In short, they wanted to be their own boss. Indeed, one of the leading motives in the move from the corporation to the street-corner shop or the living room office is the desire to work for oneself. We should not be surprised that most people who go into business for themselves end up working harder than they did in the corporation. After all, they are doing it for themselves, and they know that the responsibility for success or failure is now entirely their own.

One of the dangers of success in small business is the temptation to expand and enlarge; in other words, to no longer remain small. The headlines of the past few decades have been full of successful, even brilliant companies that decided to expand, usually too quickly, and failed. They were drowned in debt, or they could not organize a larger company to run as efficiently as the smaller one. A successful restaurant, for instance, decides to open a second location, loses its sense of uniqueness, and finds that its total sales and number of customers has actually fallen. Or an upstart airline decides to expand its routes, buy more planes, and lease more airport gates, only to fall out of the skies into bankruptcy. An increase in size doesn't just mean additional staff and a bit more of the same. It means more management, more complexity, more distance between operations. It involves the delegation of duties that were, at the beginning, all in one pair of hands. It means more paperwork, more red tape, more worries about withholding taxes, employee benefits, perhaps a new building, and a bank or investors looking over your shoulder. Financing a new or growing business is almost always a problem, whether getting the loan or paying for it. Small businesses and their expansion are often supported by venture capital, but for those who had the urge to "be their own boss" (which was what got them into business in the first place), the idea of strangers overseeing and supervising their enterprise is not very attractive. Moreover, the skills involved in running a successful one-person business or small partnership may be utterly inadequate when facing the demands of running a company. Small businesses are often "one-man bands." A company is an entire orchestra, and the ability to simultaneously play several instruments oneself is no assurance that one can competently lead and coordinate others. A successful entrepreneur may be a terrible manager. Thomas Edison, a great genius of an inventor, was an atrocious manager whose successes were possible only through the efforts of others. Those who create successful, even brilliant, small businesses are often incapable or unwilling when it comes to running a large one.

One of the benefits of running a small business is that business ethics is usually straightforward: make the best product you can, treat your customers (and your employees, if you have any) fairly, be honest, and pay your taxes. There is

The Small Business Alternative: The Entrepreneur ——

He is twenty-six. He is the president of four corporations: American Motorcycle Mechanics School, Evel Kinevel's Electrocycle Service Centers, Triple-A Motorcycle Leasing, and AMS Productions.

My interest in motorcycles was for the money originally. I saw this was going to be a big field. Later, business becomes a game. Money is the kind of way you keep score. How else you gonna see yourself go up? If you're successful in business, it means you're making money. It gets to the point where you've done all the things you want to do. There's nothing else you want to buy anymore. You get your thrill out of seeing the business grow. Just building it bigger and bigger. . . .

The world is full of people who don't have the guts or the balls to go out on their own. People want to be in business for themselves, but they don't want to take the chance. That's what separates me from the majority of people. If I've got an idea, I'll go ahead and put everything on the line.

People say to me, "Gee! You work so damn hard, how can you ever enjoy it?" I'm enjoying it every day. I don't have to get away for a weekend to enjoy it. Eventually I'll move to Arizona and make that my headquarters. I'm young enough. I'll only be thirty-one in five years. I can still do these things—horseback riding, looking after animals. I like animals. But I'll never retire. I'll take it a little bit easier. I'll have to. I had an ulcer since I was eighteen.

I guess people get different thrills out of business in different ways. There's a lot of satisfaction in showing up people who thought you'd never amount to anything. If I died tomorrow, I'd really feel I enjoyed myself. How would I like to be remembered? I don't know if I really care about being remembered. I just want to be known while I'm here. That's enough. I didn't like history, anyway.

Studs Terkel, *Working*

little of the pressure from above that forces managers and employees of large corporations to compromise. There are no stockholders demanding profits at the expense of quality or community. And unless the business is particularly messy or controversial, there is little worry about ruining the environment or disrupting the community. The responsibility is equally straightforward. If the business succeeds, that means you succeeded. If the business fails, you failed. There is none of that "passing the buck" that so confuses such matters in large corporations.

This is not to say that there is not a great deal of luck involved. One quarter of the small businesses started in America fail within two years, and half fail within four years. For a small business, slight shifts in fashion or a downturn in the market can be ruinous. A single bad sale (an instance of food poisoning at a restaurant, a bungled repair job at a fix-it shop) can jeopardize several years of good work and a solid reputation. But failure is part of the business process, a matter not often enough stressed in business classes. One often learns by one's mistakes. You fall, but then you get up and start again. Most successful entrepreneurs have a number of failures behind them, which in retrospect, they are likely to admit contributed to their current success.

Entrepreneurship came into fashion only a few years ago, although the term has been around since the last century, referring to anyone who opened up and owned a business. Today, however, it seems as if everyone is supposed to be an entrepreneur, even middle managers in a giant corporation. One should be suspicious of such fashions, and it is important to be critical about what such terms really mean. Until a few years ago, entrepreneurs were simply small-business owners. Now, with the availability of venture capital and the promise of global markets, the entrepreneur has become a distinctive personality, celebrated in politics and on television as well as in the business community, and, according to the current lore, the hope and salvation of the economic community. The truth is, however, there are not that many truly talented entrepreneurs, and most people would be better off participating in established enterprises than dashing off on their own and often squandering their hard-earned savings and their self-esteem. Many, if not most, people do their best work in jobs and programs that are

An entrepreneur is someone who creates jobs in significant numbers as opposed to buying himself or herself a job, which is what the small businessperson does. Entrepreneurs rarely have any intention of being small-business people forever. The nature of entrepreneurship is almost obsessive. It's not a goal for money, but rather a need—a need to prove something and to be in control. . . . Virtually every entrepreneur I've ever met . . . is a control freak.

Jon P. Goodman, *The Wall Street Journal,* Oct. 16, 1992

already laid out for them. Few people have the swashbuckling nerve or the ability to withstand wholesale failure that characterizes the new entrepreneur. To be sure, we need to encourage innovation and risk-taking, but an entire nation of entrepreneurs and commercial adventurers will not lead to economic success. It will more likely result in financial chaos, in which no one remembers how to cooperate, work together, or work for anyone else.

■ SUMMARY AND CONCLUSION

Business life is defined by the roles people in business play; these roles in turn are determined by the overall practice of business, by the particular structure and goals of particular corporations and businesses, by the "corporate culture" of the particular institution, and by the personalities and goals of the individuals themselves. Corporate culture is that general sense of values and identity shared by virtually everyone in a corporation. The size of a corporation has a great deal to do with its culture, as does its location, the product or service it produces, and the hierarchy of authority and its demands and expectations.

But just as important are the more personal aspects of the organization, including dress codes, friendliness, sense of security and "belonging," expectations of corporate loyalty, and what the company does to earn that loyalty.

The primary decision of all business students (others too), the one that may affect the rest of their lives (which is not to say that it is always irreversible), is that initial choice of jobs. This establishes the skills that are required, the friends and associates, and the sense of self that slowly forms. Eventually these make one way of life seem "natural" for us and others unfamiliar, or at least uncomfortable. A person who enters the "fast track" of corporate life will soon feel that all other corporate lives are dull and unchallenging. A person who enters a job in which patience and long-term development are essential will come to see the "fast tracker" as irresponsible. Another who develops a special skill in finance may soon find that her primary identity lies in the field, not in any particular company or industry. Someone who runs a small business with a relatively small number of employees and eventually comes to know or at least recognize all of them becomes so used to the familiarity and personality of the business that large corporate life seems intolerably impersonal and restrictive. An individual who enjoys the enormous power and opportunities of large corporations, in part because of their size and impersonality, may well find small-business life a bore. Of course, there are the opposite reactions, "the carpet is greener in the other office" syndrome, in which people want whatever they do not have: personality instead of impersonality, large instead of small, fast instead of slow, slow instead of fast. But this is not yet the place to talk about *dis*satisfaction; we are first of all interested in what makes business life satisfying. Choosing the right corporate culture—or no corporate culture, going into business for oneself—is the first and, for most of us, the most important decision of our careers.

■ STUDY QUESTIONS

1. Choose a single company (preferably one you have worked for or investi- gated yourself) and outline its "corporate culture." Include a description of its size and organization, location and physical environment, sense of authority and hierarchy, centralization, scope (local, national, multina- tional), importance of conformity and formality, friendliness, product or service orientation, emphasis on skill and personal-social abilities, sense of aggressiveness, sense of its own public image, concern for the well- being of its employees, sense of security in various levels of responsibil- ity, reward systems and recruitment, and promotion policies.

2. Make a list of those features of a corporate culture that you personally find most appealing and important. In your own role as manager in such a corporation, what managerial roles do you most prefer? What roles do you expect to play the most? In what roles would you best perform?

3. What sort of business personality do you admire and aspire to emulate? Give and explain what you find so appealing and desirable about that person.

■ FOR CLASS DISCUSSION

Is This Any Way to Run a Company?

At ITT, the central ordeal of every executive is the meeting with the chairman, *Harold Geneen.* One by one, the executives must stand before a large interna- tional group of peers, explaining in excruciating detail every figure and, espe- cially, every loss and failure. Geneen says he doesn't want to see just the figures; he wants to see the man and his expression as he presents the figures. Anthony Sampson, writing about the ITT experience in his book *The Sovereign State of ITT,* says:

> For a newly joined manager—and especially from a company newly acquired by ITT—the ordeal can be terrifying; there are stories of one man fainting as he walked in and of another rushing out to get blind drunk for two days. For the hardened ITT man, it is no more

than a routine test of sangfroid. "You have to be prepared," said one of them, "to have your balls screwed off in public and then joke afterward as if nothing had happened."

Is this any way to run a company? Discuss.

HISTORICAL INTERLUDE

AMERICA AS A CORPORATE CULTURE: AN INTERVIEW WITH MARGARET MEAD (CONDUCTED BY PAUL LONDON)*

London: Dr. Mead, the American economy is incredibly rich compared to other countries. What is it about the American character that has produced this kind of wealth?

Mead: Our wealth was mainly produced by open space and by the fact that North America was so sparsely inhabited and so rich. The great plains are extraordinarily fertile for agriculture, and the country is rich in almost every type of mineral resource. Other countries have been dealing with limited space for centuries. But this country was colonized by people who came to escape from all sorts of pressure—the plague, religious wars, political persecution, social disorganization in Europe—and they found all this space.

    There's pretty good data on who the early immigrants were, at least those who came from England. We used to think they were all second sons, disinherited nephews, indentured servants, people from pauper prisons, and so on. There were plenty of those, but it looks as if the bulk were enterprising people from every part of England. From most countries, in fact, the majority of the people who decided to come here did so because they were moving toward opportunity.

London: And the American personality that exists now? In comparison to other countries, how would you say Americans view work?

Mead: In this country today, if you've got one job you tend to have a second one. The typical American is never satisfied. This is partly because in a young country with limitless opportunity there was always pressure

---

*From *Business and Society Review,* #23, with thanks to Robert Bruce Slater.

to do better. Children did better than their parents, grandchildren did better than their grandparents. And then there was, and still is, a very large portion of the American people who work hard because they can think of something else to want. They don't sit down and say, "I'm contented." On the other hand, in a class-based society like that of Western Europe there are clear standard ways of living for each class. If people achieve that standard—the right kind of house, money enough for other pleasures, weddings, etc.—then they'll be satisfied and stay there. This has been extremely clear in the British working class. It's been impossible to increase production in England because the workers have everything they ever thought they would get; they've achieved their class standard. They've got as good housing as they can get. They've got their beer and cigarettes, their holidays, their medical care, and education for their children. So they won't do extra work. Now, an American in the same situation can always think of something else he wants. If he has one car, he wants two, or he could travel, or he could build a different kind of house.

London: You imply that Americans work only for material gain. What of this notion I hold (which may never have been true) of craftsmen in days past, plying their trade with love and care, taking pride in their work?

Mead: We've never really had many craftsmen in this country. They've always been foreigners, Englishmen and Europeans who had a very high division of labor at the time America was settled. You look at farming in England, and you'll find there were shepherds, there were ditchers, there were hedgers, etc. In towns, there were glovemakers and hatmakers. But once they came over here, they cleared land and built log cabins and learned to do everything, none of it very well. They lost their specialization. Europe continued to produce craftsmen, but America produced generalists—people who think they can do anything. If you interview an American for a job, you find out he's already had twenty other jobs.

London: Is there no place where work is a satisfying process on its own?

Mead: It can be satisfying to some people. It's satisfying to the people who are really doing what they want, like artists or professional people. It's satisfying to people who build harpsichords. And you find some people—the Germans are a pretty good example—who use work as a kind of outlet for anxiety; as long as they can work hard, they feel comfortable. In this country, there are many businessmen for whom work has been their whole lives.

London: And they enjoy their work, they find it fulfilling?

Mead: It doesn't mean they enjoy it. It means they would be unhappier not working. By and large, I think business people don't expect to get a lot of joy out of work. They get their pleasure from how much money they make, and whether they're mobile, and whether they're being promoted or not. That isn't exactly the same thing as a craftsman's joy, but it is similar in that it's fully and intensely occupying. A lot of businessmen, especially top businessmen, retire with great regret. Sometimes they're kicked upstairs to the chairman of the board, and they don't enjoy it. Work has been their life and they feel deprived without it. Early retirement can make a top executive die fairly soon. What are you going to do with an admiral when he retires? What are you going to give him as a substitute for a fleet? . . .

London: We also have a relatively new phenomenon where more and more women are taking career-type work seriously. To what do you attribute this?

Mead: There are really two factors. As a result of the population explosion, the whole world wants a lower birth rate. So now we permit people to have abortions and contraceptives. When we start wars and want a large population to use as cannon fodder, we don't encourage any type of birth control. But now we've relaxed our attitudes. We don't force people to get married, we don't have a fit about homosexuality, we permit abortion. Also, while the standard of living has been rising, it often requires two salaries to support it. Scandinavia is an outstanding example: A decent living costs so much there that women have to work in order to pay the taxes, get housing, and pay for day-care centers. They don't have any choice.

London: How about the proposition that women feel work is necessary for their own personal fulfillment?

Mead: Personal fulfillment was invented by people who wanted women to work cheaply. You see, back in the late 1950s it was pretty clear that women were our last source of cheap skilled labor. Here they were, college graduates and high school graduates, and so many of them not working. Suddenly there was a great interest in women "fulfilling" themselves: college courses for women and shows on television with the husband saying, "she must have her chance."

London: Do you think there is any difference in temperament between men and women that affects their qualifications for being the president of a Fortune 500 company?

Mead: Not materially. I think, though, that on the whole women have enjoyed having children. Producing a whole child is a lot more exciting than producing a plastic pitcher. . . .

London: What toll is increased mobility, job relocating, uprooting from one location to another taking on the American family?

Mead: We have always been a very mobile society. After World War II 30 million people moved in this country. It isn't moving alone that does the harm, it's moving from one friendless neighborhood to another.

London: And this raises the tension level in American society?

Mead: The thing that raises the tension level is our town planning. I mean, people who are in the army or the navy move every two years, but they move into an established structure. They know where they are, the kind

of house they're going to have, where the children are going to play tennis, and who's going to call on whom. Their children aren't necessarily
disoriented. The same applies to the children of the big oil companies.
But they are in the minority. Most people go from one place to another
and find no structure in the places where they live. It's not the moving
that's the problem; it's having no structure where they live. . . .

London: You say that women are not temperamentally unsuited to top-
level jobs in industry. Yet they don't often hold down those jobs. Nor do
minorities, such as blacks. Why is it that we have such difficulty providing for equal opportunity and equal access to income and power?

Mead: Because just as some group gains access some other group comes
along. Generation after generation of this country has been made up of
immigrants, and each group of arrivals has looked down on the next. The
minute you have contrasts in a population, religion or education or race,
you're very likely to have some groups more favored than others.

London: But in the U.S., the difficulty of assimilating blacks into power
persists after many, many years, beyond the time an immigrant group
would have been assimilated.

Mead: We've been pretty bad with Asians, too; it used to be necessary to
pass an act of Congress to naturalize a single Chinese. But I agree, the
problem with blacks does persist, and I believe the only way this country
can realize its own ideals is through affirmative action programs. . . .

London: A great deal is being written these days about multinational corporations. What effect do you think they are having on people around the
world? Would you say that American companies are exporting American
values?

Mead: I don't notice them exporting any values at all.

London: Exporting the capitalistic ethic perhaps?

Mead: I don't think they are exporting a "capitalistic ethic." They are
exploiting the labor and cheaper labor or cheaper resources somewhere
else. . . .

London: Is this bad?

Mead: It is bad when we extract raw materials from some other country,
manufacture the products, and then sell them back to people at enormous
profits.

London: Speaking as a capitalist, I would say this is good business. If I
could buy materials in one place, work on them in a second, and sell the
product at a profit, I'm not doing anything illegal.

Mead: I'm talking about ethics. Legalities are irrelevant.

London: Then you think capitalism is unethical.

Mead: No, I think that exploitation is unethical, no matter who does it. The
Soviet Union exploits just as much as we do; it exploits its European
satellites heavily. Exploitation is not limited to capitalists. It applies to
differences in power between rich countries and poor countries.

London: If a corporation changes raw materials into products that people want, it deserves a profit for the value it has added. Is it the size of the profit that you find unethical?

Mead: No, it is that we've not encouraged the poor country's making it itself. It's that we've encouraged keeping raw-material countries and labor-intensive countries dependent on foreign capital. It would be much better if the people there learned to make the products themselves and weren't so dependent. Also, the whole situation has altered enormously since the energy crisis. Carting things around the world takes a tremendous amount of energy, and things now may go around the world two or three times before they reach the ultimate consumer. This is true of food, and it's true of manufactured goods. We aren't going to be able to do this in the future. We're going to need a different ethic to fit the shortage of energy.

London: What of the charge that American corporations disrupt cultures of developing nations through their promotion of products and advertising?

Mead: What this advertising does is make people believe that we live in a way in which we don't, that we all have Cadillacs and they ought to have them, too. American movies and American advertising both give a very distorted picture of American life. Just as the notion spreads to every poor home in this country that everyone except they themselves has a $20,000 bathroom, the same thing is even worse overseas.

London: Might not this spur rising expectations, rising hopes, and make ultimately for more productive societies?

Mead: No, it makes societies more miserable. The developing society does not yet have the resources in labor or technology to produce an airline— one of the first things they always want is an airline—which is very expensive—or a city with tall buildings. So a very small segment of the population gets "show" things, such as Cadillacs, and the rest stay poor. In fact, the problem is getting worse. Populations are increasing rapidly as modern medicine spreads and fewer babies die. There are more children and fewer people to look after them. People are miserable, and they feel that they're being deprived. . . .

London: Do you consider yourself a socialist? A capitalist?

Mead: No! No! No! They're all out of date, the whole lot. They were all developed before the electronic age, before we had any notion of how to handle energy, before we'd gone into space. Socialism, capitalism, and communism are all nineteenth-century ideologies. They are completely out of date.

London: What are you?

Mead: Well, I'm not anything that is. I'm interested in building a future world that has something to do with real conditions.

London: What is the single most important business advice you could give to business executives?

Mead: I think it would be to develop a greater sense of relationship to the whole. Relationship to the planet, in terms of resources and production, a relationship to the community in which they exist, a relationship between all the different echelons within an industry. Less segmentation, less fractionation, less narrowness of approach. As things are set up today, businesses are there to make a profit right now, and it's very difficult for them to take a long-term point of view. I'd like to see them be able to take a fifty-year point of view. Some do try—the du Ponts, for example, have been famous for planning ahead. But, in general, industry is set up to be very shortsighted.

London: But short-term gain is one of the features of the capitalist system. People who invest do so in order . . .

Mead: You have to make a profit, but one of the troubles with the present situation is that the big companies don't care as much about profit as they do about power. I'd like to see them taking more responsibility for the long-term well-being of this planet and the people on it.

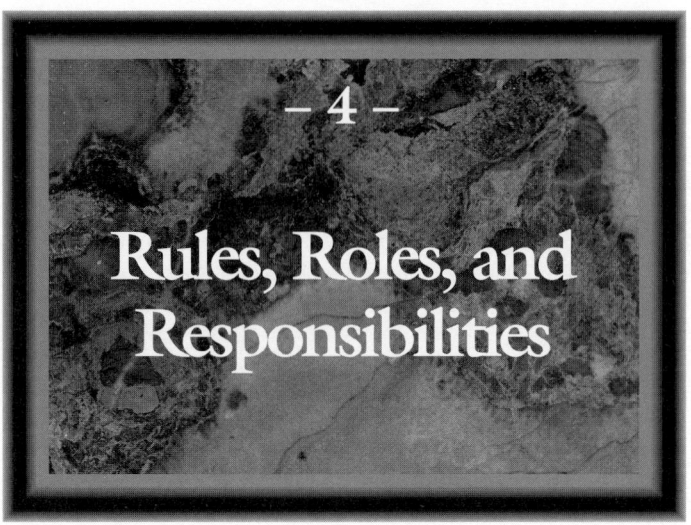

Rules, Roles, and Responsibilities

There was a time when a man's word was his bond. Today, he doesn't even consider his bond to be his bond.
—Mike Royko, Chicago Sun Times, Aug. 1981
(on the air controller's strike)

Much of what there is to say about business ethics can be summarized in a word, namely, *practice*. It is an ordinary word, of course; we often speak of "the practice of law" or "practicing the piano." But recently, in philosophy and the social sciences, the word has been given a more general and, at the same time, a more precise meaning. A practice is an established system of behavior, defined by certain rules and goals. More precisely, the social philosopher John Rawls defines a practice as:

> Any association of definitely patterned human behavior wherein the description and meaning of the kinds of behavior involved and the kinds of expectations involved are dependent upon those rules which define the practice.*

Most games, for example, can be viewed as concisely defined practices. (This is not to say that business is a game, but more on that later.)

In baseball, the game is defined by certain kinds of behavior: "pitching" the ball in a certain way to another; trying to hit the ball with a certain well-defined implement, "the bat"; running a certain sequence of "bases" in a particular order

---

*"Two Concepts of Rules," *Philosophical Review,* Vol. 64 (1955).

subject to certain restrictions, such as not being "tagged" by another person holding the ball; and so on. These actions and their meanings are defined by the rules of the game, and the special terms of the game—especially "hit," "foul," "strike," "out," and "run"—give significance to actions that might well have no meaning outside of the practice. (Imagine a man on the street who suddenly ran towards a sandbag lying on the sidewalk, slid skillfully into it, and declared himself "safe.") Moreover, there are any number of actions that have *no* significance because they are not ruled into the game. For example, there is no rule in baseball regarding spitting, except for spitting on the ball. The rules of etiquette, though they might be deemed desirable even in sports matches, are not themselves part of the practice, but define a practice of their own. The goal of the game, of course, is to score "runs," defined as a particular sequence of actions and achievements that, when successfully completed, give a score of one point for each run. This goal, again, is defined only within the practice, and makes no sense without it. A team playing lacrosse on the baseball field cannot claim to have scored a run, even if one of their players successfully runs around the infield, for they are part of a different practice. Even a member of a baseball team cannot score a run except at a very particular time in the game—when his team is at bat, when he is one of the batters, and so on. It counts for nothing in baseball if a member of the fielding team steals a bat, runs to the home plate, and hits the ball before the proper batter has a chance at it. In a practice, in other words, the significance of actions and their success is defined only within the game itself, and these definitions may be extremely precise.

The practice of a game is not entirely self-defined. The public who sees the games may, for one reason or another, insist on a change of the rules. A commission on sports may declare certain rules invalid. And the very practice of the game itself is circumscribed by a network of more general rules about what kinds of acts may or may not be part of *any* game (murder, for example, is excluded except in a metaphorical sense—as in "killing the ump" or "murdering the other team"). A game must be sufficiently circumscribed to enable both players and observers to determine what is part of the game and what is not, and to keep the practice in perspective, as in "it's only a game." A game is embodied in a more encompassing set of game-playing practices (which allow games to exist at all) that include the general demand that play is always according to the rules, whatever they happen to be. There is also the general overriding rule, for all games (though not always consistently applied to professional sports), that every player must be "a good sport," obey the rules, and not take winning *too* seriously.

A. RULES

The rules of a practice are usually understood as defining the legitimate means of reaching the goal of a practice—for example, scoring a run. But the rules of a practice also define and create the goals themselves, and thus provide the rewards of the practice. The rewards of a practice are both internal and external, just as there are both internal and external rules. The internal rewards might be generally described as "doing well," which would include feeling successful and being skilled, enjoying the praise and esteem of others in the practice, and, where most games are concerned, the concept of winning. The external rewards of a practice would include fame and sometimes fortune, and the opportunity to make television commercials and appearances. Some rewards seem to be both internal and external—for example, the enjoyment itself. But here we should emphasize that the enjoyment of a practice is only possible from *within* the practice, even if a person's participation is limited to that of spectator or "fan." We can enjoy the game of baseball, for example, only if we know what is going on, are able to appreciate acts of skill (as opposed to errors), and know and appreciate the goals of the game.

Business, too, is a practice, and so allows for understanding of much the same kind that we have just applied to the game of baseball. Business, too, has its rules and its roles, and business, too, has both its internal and external rewards, only some of which have anything to do with profit. But business is not a game, despite the popularity of that metaphor and despite the predominance of many gamelike practices within the general practice of business. Games are closely circumscribed; business, however, is a sufficiently general practice, making its outer boundaries much more difficult to outline. Of course, a person can enter into business as a game, particularly if that person's main concern is some other field. Casual investors, for example, play the stock market like a game, but for those who make their living investing in stocks it is not a game. Games tend to be placed in a diminutive perspective, as not entirely serious and certainly not the key to life itself. No businessperson who has just lost an entire fortune will cheerfully agree that "it's just a game," nor should he do so. The internal rewards of business life—success, respect, and certain skills and relationships—are so important to us that they largely determine, and are determined by, the external rewards. Success in business and success in life are not two goals but one.

Business is not merely a game, with specific rules that can be changed in an instant and goals and activities that are clearly insulated from the rest of life. Business is a way of life, an all-embracing career in which its rules and definitions depend on the whole tradition and the overall values and rules of our culture. When a president says, "The business of America is business," he is saying just how central the practice of business is to our way of life in general. But if business is not a game, we still have to look a bit further to see what defines it as a practice, in what ways it is like a game, and in what ways it is emphatically not like a game.

Business as a practice is defined by its rules, by the roles it establishes, by the responsibilities it engenders, by the burdens it creates, and by the rewards it provides. Some of the rather obvious rules of business are, accordingly, the less interesting ones. One such rule, for example, would be "Do not intentionally lose money." However, there are more subtle rules—some of them rarely stated—

Business as a Public Service ——

Business and industry are first and foremost a public service. We are organized to do as much good as we can everywhere for everybody concerned. I do not believe we should make such an awful profit on our cars. A reasonable profit is right, but not too much. So, it has been my policy to force the price of the car down as fast as production would permit and give the benefit to the users and laborers with . . . surprisingly enormous profits to ourselves.

Henry Ford, letter to a stockholder

about the legitimate ways of losing money. "Throwing it away" is considered a clear breach in the rules of the game (thus the confusion and outrage when a group of "Yippies" threw cash over the railings of the New York Stock Exchange several years ago). "Philanthropy" and "support of the arts" are, within the rules of the practice, "throwing money away," but they are rarely judged harshly because the larger practices of social participation overrule the more specific practices of the business world. Losing money as the result of a calculated gamble, a "risk," is considered part of the business practice, although which risks are wise and which are foolish is itself a question answered depending on the circumstances. Brokers involved in the commodities market accept rather unpredictable risks as a part of their job. A manager of a college trust fund would accept quite different risks, in part, due to pressures and expectations coming from outside the business practice itself.

Investment in the future is now defined as the essence of "capitalism." However, only a few centuries ago (as in many "underdeveloped societies" today), this might have been considered "throwing money away," that is, not utilizing it for social needs or enjoyments *here and now*. In other words, how a person dispenses with money, wisely or foolishly, justly or unjustly, is to a large extent built into the rules of the business practice, and these rules are changing. Such essential questions as the size of salaries for upper management, the size of the dividends paid to the stockholders, or the amount of money to be spent for public relations, for legal defense, for foreign investment, or for employee benefits, are defined by the established practices of business. To see this rich network of rules as nothing but strategies for increasing profit is as simple minded as viewing the whole fabric of the baseball practice as a means for scoring runs. Some rules in business are intended to maximize profits, just as some of the rules of baseball are intended to make runs possible and ensure that someone will win the game.

Nevertheless, most of the rules of business define the system of legitimate behavior *within* which such goals are to be pursued, the roles the various participants are to take up in this pursuit, the responsibilities and rewards of each, and the restrictions that limit the pursuit. For example, it is an accepted rule of limitation in American business that competitors should not violate contracts. This is not, as some beleaguered businesspeople sometimes complain, an extraneous moral rule imposed upon business practices by society at large (though, needless to say, society at large does approve of and insist upon such rules). It is part of the essential rules of the business practice itself, part of the restrictions that make it a practice worth encouraging, not only by the society at large but by the businesspeople themselves. To be sure, a corporation could reap much greater profits, at least in the short run, if it totally neglected all quality controls or acquiesced in policies that would eventually cause considerable public harm. But the world of business would not thereby continue to be a rewarding source of livelihood for most people; it would collapse as a practice because its own internal rules had been violated and because it no longer served any positive social purpose. To understand the practice of business, therefore, is to appreciate *all* of its goals, rules, and limitations, not just those few simpleminded propositions about the "bottom line."

B. ROLES

A practice is defined not only by its rules but also by the *roles* it creates for its participants. Just as baseball, as part of its essential structure, creates the roles of "pitcher" and "batter" and "coach" and "umpire," the practice of business defines its roles too. Nothing in the natural order of human society dictates that there should be "managers." In fact, managers were only recently invented to facilitate communication between various components of increasingly large organizations.

There is nothing in nature that identifies certain people as "workers," although most people have to exert some considerable effort to keep themselves alive. "Worker," however, is a specialized term that, for the most part, takes on its current significance only in the nineteenth century with the industrial revolution and modern specialization of skills. It is quite different, for example, from the class of laborers defined by Plato in his *Republic*. With the creation of the "worker," it was prudent also to invent "supervisors." With the dramatic increases in the size of companies, personnel directors were invented to choose workers from an ever-larger pool of unknown applicants, "unions" were created for the protection of the workers in an ever-more overpopulated market, and so on up the corporate ladder. Furthermore, graduate business schools and the "MBA" were created to produce, define, and select the most ambitious and promising executives from an enormous field of bright but indistinguishable aspirants. Indeed, the practice *creates* these new roles; it does not simply employ them. But the roles in turn constitute the practice; there could not be one without the other.

These roles created within the business practice have become increasingly specialized. While a nineteenth-century entrepreneur insisted on knowing every facet of his business from top to bottom, many of today's young executives might know only about a single branch of the business, possibly finance, and a single "ladder" of promotion. At the same time specialization has made roles less specific and the people who occupy them increasingly homogeneous. One recent critic of the MBA programs, for instance, complained that the graduates "all look, act, and think the same." Given such impersonality, the qualifying characteristics that distinguish one manager from another become more extraneous to the actual job at hand and incidental to the role itself. Success and promotion, therefore, become increasingly based on personal appearances and connections.

Role mobility raises serious questions about the nature of success, the reality of "merit," and the question of company loyalty. Because many successful executives are promoted every couple of years, long-term projects and accomplishments become harder to recognize and reward. To the extent that many a managerial position can be filled by any of a large number of eager and bright applicants, only a few people in the business world can claim to be truly irreplaceable. Insecurity, then, is built into the business world; it is no longer the case—as it would have been in Aristotle's Greece or medieval society—that people are more or less uniquely suited to their roles. In order to survive, businesspeople need to be aware of openings elsewhere in case their jobs become redundant through a merger or their company decides to replace them with someone who is younger, more aggressive, or just different. "Blind" company loyalty thus becomes foolish because it is not reciprocal. If taken to its natural conclusions, however, this turn of events could signal the end of business practice altogether with a universal scramble for personal security.

Therefore, to combat the anonymity of rules and the consequent replaceability of the role holders, and to prevent the wholesale breakdown of corporate loyalty, a number of subsidiary rules have become essential. In America, the most common of these is *seniority,* which adds to the various virtues and skills of a role-holder the feature of job tenure, that is, how long a person stays in the job. In Japan, seniority is taken even further, to the point of guaranteeing every employee lifetime employment. The result increases company loyalty enormously and, at the same time, reduces individual opportunity-seeking to a minimum. The American system holds more of a tenuous balance between these two, leaving enough insecurity and flexibility in the seniority system to encourage mobility and personal ambitiousness, but providing at least enough security to allay the abstract fear that, no matter how well a person does a job, a replacement can always be found.

We sometimes say, as a matter of pride, that we create the roles we play. In the theater, for example, it is sometimes said that Sir Laurence Olivier "*created* the role of Hamlet" or, in the movies, that "Sean Connery gave life to James Bond." In both cases, of course, this is untrue: Shakespeare created Hamlet (though even he was dependent upon a set of historical circumstances and arrangements, including the various laws of accession to the throne), and Ian Fleming created James Bond. We rarely if ever create a role; most often, we inherit a role (even if recently or just created) and fill it (more or less) with a few eccentric flourishes of our own. Some people fill roles better than others, of course. Often, people are miscast in their roles; sometimes they find their "true" roles, often they do not. Sometimes people fill a role so well, so brilliantly, that it can be said of them (as it was of Olivier and Connery) that they are "irreplaceable." But, even so, a role only slightly different soon evolves to serve similar functions. What this points to is the nature of a role in general; it is not ever defined by reference to a particular person and his skills and attributes, but rather *impersonally* and abstractly by reference to the skills, responsibilities, duties, and interrelations within the practice. The role receives its meaning from the practice and within the community, not from the person who fills that role. It is true, on a rare occasion, that a person "gives new meaning" to a role, but even this is usually secondary to the meanings already residing in the role itself.

In *Men and Women of the Corporation,* Rosabeth Moss Kantor argues that people do not determine their jobs, but rather, jobs determine the persons that fulfill them. This is true in several senses. First, the role precedes the employee. This is so even when the role is, on a rare occasion, created specifically for that person; the context of the role, the need for it, the place for it, indeed usually everything but the particular title for it, is already there. Second, it is too often thought, mostly by people just entering business (or any practice), that they have identities that they will retain, stepping into and out of their roles in business with the same ease that they step on and off an elevator. But this is hardly ever the case. The job helps make the person; what we do "for a living" molds and shapes us, providing us with friends and social expectations and images of ourselves, as well as specific office duties and responsibilities. We *become* largely the roles we play, whether or not we originally wanted to fit this certain image. Aristotle said it long ago and the French existentialists said it recently: *"You are what you do."* It is no small part of the American work ethic that, given the importance of a job in our overall sense of self and accomplishment, the choice of a particular job is at the same time a choice of *self.* And, not surprisingly, we retain older friends and interests only at the margins, especially if they are at odds with the friends and interests and self-image engendered by our roles in business. To change roles is often to change selves as well, and thus to throw into uncertainty many of our most important relationships.

With all of this talk of "roles" it may well sound as if there is no room in business (or in any practice) for the individual, for the aspirant who is not satisfied with the present role and ambitiously works toward another. But, of course, these are roles too. What we loosely call "the individual" is in fact a fairly common set of roles in business life, from the "fast tracker" who is hired precisely because he is expected to move quickly up the ladder of corporate management to the entrepreneur around whom much of American business originally evolved in the first place. There is, in every company, some place for the maverick, the "wise guy," or the eccentric who, while playing by some of the rules, routinely neglects others. "The aspirant Chief Executive Officer" is just as much an established role in most American corporations as is the CEO itself. The role of aspirant, however, is usually occupied by several people at once. Indeed, we might say that there is even an established role—though by necessity an ill-defined one—for the "outsider" who comes crashing through on occasion with a new idea and great success. The point is, that a practice defines roles for *all* of its participants, and the individual is defined through a network of rules and relationships which together define *who that person is* within the world of business, if not in the larger social world as well. Even the genius who creates a new role (or an entire new industry) does so on the basis of roles established in the past.

C. THE MANAGERIAL REVOLUTION

By far the dominant role in today's corporation (and, in fact, in virtually all American institutions) is the *manager.* Managerial studies have all but taken over most

---

Cultural Heroes ——

America's boardrooms need heroes more than Hollywood's box offices need them. Heroism is a leadership component that is all but forgotten by modern management. Since the 1920's, the corporate world has been powered by managers who are rationalists, who do strategic planning, write memos and devise flow charts. But we are not talking about good "scientific" managers here. Managers run institutions; heroes create them. . . .

Companies with strong cultures are quite adept at recognizing and creating situational heroes. Many place their potential candidates in bellwether jobs—certain critical positions that epitomize what the core of the culture is all about.

When people know what the hero-making jobs are, they're energized. They know what's expected of them; they're free to be innovative. And over a period of time, the company becomes more innovative.

Employees don't have to be leaders or young Turks to win the rewards of heroism. Strong-culture companies create heroes throughout the corporation. The following line from IBM's house organ, "Think," is a case in point: "All those happy faces, you'd think he was the Prince carrying the glass slipper to Cinderella, when in fact he's dropping off a Selectric that the customer recently ordered." Yet this line anoints salesman Joe McClosky a hero for being a 30-year member of the company's highly honored Hundred Percent Club. The trick? IBM deliberately sets their sales quotas so that roughly 80 percent of the force makes the club.

Terrence E. Deal and Allan A. Kennedy, *Corporate Cultures*

business schools, and managerial positions are generally considered the definitive hierarchy in almost every company. Managers, accordingly, are also the linchpin of corporate business ethics. Their decisions set the tone and secure the policy, and their sense of responsibility establishes the moral and social concerns of the business. But "management" is a vague and ambiguous term. "Middle management," now defines virtually the whole of a corporate culture, ranging from the skilled employees at the bottom to the chief executive officer at the top. There is some confusion and considerable controversy about what managers actually do, whether the role is defined by power over other people or, in Peter Drucker's now established view, by virtue of their contributions to the firm and their achievement of certain "objectives." But the fact is that there are many different kinds of managers, and for some of them, power over other people—whether through fear or respect and admiration—is absolutely essential. For others, what they "manage" is more confined to the itineraries of thousands of pieces of paper—letters, memos, transmissions, and a hundred other bits of information—that form the circulatory system of every business. "Manager" very rarely defines a single role; the manager has as many roles and as many faces as the various responsibilities of the job. With each face, too, comes a different set of ethical concerns.

Henry Mintzberg has attacked the classic idea that the manager is a single all-important role-player, like the orchestra leader who controls the parts of the entire organization and brings them into perfect harmony.* Instead, Mintzberg argues that managers play a large variety of roles, most of them not nearly so all-important and powerful as the "orchestra leader" metaphor suggests. Managers are far less reflective and systematic and far more spontaneous and scattered in their performance. ("Half of the activities engaged in by the chief executives in my study lasted less than nine minutes and only 10% exceeded one hour.") Contrary to the view of the managerial role as a single role, Mintzberg found that most effective managers had no regular duties to perform, but rather spent almost all of their time taking care of emergencies, meeting with clients and subordinates, attending to "ceremonial duties" (meeting visiting dignitaries, giving out gold watches, presiding over company-related dinners), and simply passing on information from one office to another. Indeed, most of the work was not, as generally advertised, systematic information processing—as if the manager were some superhuman computer—but rather talking on the phone and attending meetings (66–80 percent total time at the job). Mintzberg reports that few executives ever read the important reports they received, preferring to skim them and pass them on. In general, Mintzberg rejected Drucker's now widely accepted view that management is a distinctive profession, even a "science." Most executives operated on such unscientific notions as "intuition" and "snap judgments," depended almost entirely on personal contacts and bits of information passed to them from above and below, and displayed little time or inclination for that reflective role that contemporary management engineers sometimes describe.

*"The Manager's Job: Folklore and Fact," *Harvard Business Review,* July–Aug. 1975.

The Manager and the Orchestra Leader: Two Models ——

From Peter Drucker, *The Practice of Management:*

> The manager has the task of creating a true whole that is larger than the sum of its parts, a productive entity that turns out more than the sum of the resources put into it. One analogy is the conductor of a symphony orchestra, through whose effort, vision and leadership individual instrumental parts that are so much noise by themselves become the living whole of music. But the conductor has the composer's score; he is only the interpreter. The manager is both composer and conductor.

From Leonard R. Sayles:

> [The manager] is like a symphony orchestra conductor, endeavoring to maintain a melodious performance in which the contributions of the various instruments are coordinated and sequences are patterned and paced, while the orchestra members are having various personal difficulties, stage hands are moving music stands, alternating excessive heat and cold are creating audience and instrument problems, and the sponsor of the concert is insisting on irrational changes in the program.*

> *Quoted by Henry Mintzberg, *Harvard Business Review,* July–Aug. 1975.

None of Mintzberg's discussion diminishes the importance or the success of managers in American business; it is only to present a more realistic picture of what they do and what the role of manager actually represents. In fact, Mintzberg goes on to list no fewer than ten distinctive roles played by the average corporate manager, and with each of these comes a different sense of identity and a different sense of "belonging" within the organization.

1. The *figurehead* role representing the company at important occasions, taking a politician or an important customer to lunch.

2. The *leader* role—hiring and training his own staff, motivating employees, and handing out approval and disapproval whether in words, in writing, or by way of substantial rewards and punishments.

3. The *liaison* role—making contracts beyond his own immediate chain of command, particularly with peers and subordinates.

4.   The *monitor* role—scanning the environment for information, interrogating contacts and subordinates, and editing gossip and speculation.

5.   The *disseminator* role—passing on a select amount of information to subordinates.

6.   The *spokesman* role—giving information to outside groups, including "making a case" for the company; advising shareholders and directors of the company and government investigators and committees.

7.   The *entrepreneurial* role—improving and changing the company; often taken to *the* role of the manager, but in fact a relatively rare and difficult role.

8.   The *disturbance handler* role—confronting disgruntled employees, averting a strike, handling a major customer who is irate, and talking to an essential supplier who has reneged on a contract.

9.   The *resource allocation* role—deciding who will get what.

10. The *negotiator* role—working out acceptable deals with customers, suppliers, unions, and so on.

Sometimes these roles can be split up and distributed to several managers, but they can never be separated entirely. At the same time, no one person ever combines them equally, with equal interest and equal skill, thus making the managerial style and the supposedly singular managerial role as varied as the individuals who might possibly manage and the organizations that require managers. These roles define the person who accepts them, just as the people who play the roles in turn define them and the company culture as a whole. Nothing is more inspiring, in business or in any other practice, than to see people who "naturally" fill a role with ease, as if they were "born into it." At the same time, nothing is more devastating for a person, or harmful to an organization, than to be forced into the wrong role. An expert defensive lineman cannot fill the role of a shortstop.

D.   CORPORATE CHARACTERS

> A man has as many social selves as there are individuals who recognize him and carry an image of him in their mind. . . . But as the individuals who carry the images form naturally into classes, we may practically say that he has as many different social selves as there are distinct groups of persons about whose opinions he cares.
>
> —William James, The Principles of Psychology

We have been discussing roles, but roles are only half of the picture. Different people fill the same role in different ways, and what they bring to the role says as much about it and determines its ethics and its success as the organization that defines the role. A role may be broadly defined, leaving ample opportunity for individuals to mold it to their own personality, abilities, and needs. Even a rigidly defined role, however, allows room for variation and even some bending of the rigidity; indeed, the most surprisingly effective people in business are those who enter a constricted and sometimes inefficient or ineffective role in the corporation and, with a little ingenuity or initiative, enlarge it or turn it into some new employment.

In one well-known effort at business taxonomy, psychoanalyst Michael Maccoby has defined four basic types of corporate personality. The taxonomy is crude but it gives us a good picture of very different sets of personal values and ethical models of success. Not everyone sees the same traits as virtues; one sees ambition as essential while another sees it as "pushy." Most people perceive their role in the corporation in a different way also; some see themselves as citizens and members of a team, while others see themselves as simply "using" the organization for furthering independent ambitions. Maccoby rejects the simple stereotype of the "organization man" of the 1950s (as in William Whyte's classic *The Organization Man*) as a conforming bureaucrat who was typically "other-directed" and security-seeking. Maccoby's basic types offer us four familiar corporate personalities, only one of whom fits Whyte's classic stereotype and all of whom contradict it in one way or another. Maccoby identifies (1) the craftsman, (2) the jungle fighter, (3) the company man, and (4) the gamesman. Let's look at each one.

THE CRAFTSMAN

The craftsman is the person traditionally celebrated by the Protestant work ethic—hard working, dedicated to quality, concerned with the product, and conscientiously respectable and practical. Benjamin Franklin and John Calvin had the craftsman mainly in mind, and so do those who still think of business in terms of the inventive and industrious individuals who make their way in the world by making something that everyone else wants, taking pride in the quality of the product, and selling it, as much out of pride as profit.

The craftsman is often the skilled worker in the corporation, whether this be so tangible as an engineer or as abstract as a researcher. The skills are precise; the work easily measurable in terms of quality. Everyone knows who did it, and there is the source of pride. Most craftsmen, according to Maccoby, tend to be "quiet, sincere, modest, and practical" although there is a difference between those who are more receptive and democratic versus those who are more authoritarian and intolerant. The craftsman enjoys admiration, but "self-containment and perfectionism do not allow him to lead a complex and changing organization . . . he tends to do his own thing and go along."

THE JUNGLE FIGHTER

Jungle fighters have little need for particular skills, and if they have skills it is only as a way of starting out or using them at strategic points to get ahead. Unlike the craftsman, the jungle fighter is out for one thing—power. He views life, as the title indicates, as a Darwinian struggle for survival, eat or be eaten, kill or be killed. Jungle fighters are not self-contained but wholly concerned with other people, whether as allies or as enemies, as a means to get ahead or as part of the competition or as an obstacle to be removed.

The jungle fighter has little corporate loyalty, needless to say, but uses the corporation, as he uses other people, simply as a convenience for his own ambitions. Maccoby distinguishes two kinds of jungle fighters, two "sub-types": there are *lions* who are the conquerors, and there are *foxes* who "move ahead by stealth and politicking." But the successful corporate jungle fighter, says Maccoby, "like the Godfather, is fast becoming a figure of the past."

THE COMPANY MAN

The company man is the standard "organization man," whose identity, unlike that of the craftsman or the jungle fighter, is wholly tied up with the company itself, rather than the particular job he does or any particular responsibilities. The company man may not be admired but he is generally well-liked, concerned for the well-being of other people in the company as well as for the reputation and the integrity of the company as a whole. It is often said that this type of employee is becoming increasingly rare. More likely, however, the business world itself is paying less attention to him and the number of company men remains as high as ever.

Company people may be, as Maccoby says, occasionally "fearful and submissive, concerned with security more than success"; but, at the same time, it is the company people who maintain the standards of the corporation, who are most concerned with its integrity, and are therefore the primary defenders of "business ethics." For every instance of a company led astray, with its employees intimidated into submission or at least into silence, there are another hundred corporations whose ethics remain firm and honest, because of the stabilizing force of company people, who always have more to lose than to gain from a corporation that forgets its reputation to gain profits.

THE GAMESMAN

The leading character in Maccoby's typology is the gamesman, who is a new entry into the corporate game. The gamesman is interested in a challenge. He is not ruthless, like the jungle fighter; winning isn't everything. The gamesman tends to be ambitious, impatient with those who are more cautious like the company people (even though they provide the board and many of the pieces with which the gamesman can proceed). The gamesman is willing to take risks; he may at times be a constructive and even inspiring corporate "player." New ideas and strategies are often his contribution, and he sees the business world in general, perhaps even life itself, as a "game."

Gamesmen may be excellent team players too, for not all games are played alone. Indeed, Maccoby insists that "the new corporate top executive combines many gamesman traits with aspects of the company man. He is a team player whose center is the corporation." He now merges individual career goals with those of the corporation, at least temporarily and sometimes indefinitely. The gamesman often tends to be a "worrier, constantly on the lookout for what might go wrong." He is "self-protective and sees other people in terms of their use for the larger organization. He even uses himself in this way, fine tuning his sensitivity." Indeed, there is little doubt that Maccoby sees the future of the American business enterprise in terms of "the gamesman's capacity for mature development."

It is the gamesman, not the businessperson in general, who is imbued with the "spirit of competition." For the company person, competition is more likely to be the tension that is sometimes required to test his loyalty, but hardly desirable or enjoyable in itself. For the jungle fighter, competition means only an unusually large challenge to his ambitions, and it is not the battle itself that is desired, but only the resultant victory. And the craftsman, of course, couldn't really care less, unless the competitor somehow reflects on his skill or the quality of work. The gamesman, however, has the desire to win and to be in control, and so, like the jungle fighter, may be a disruptive and disharmonious element in an organization as well as its stimulation. He wants a high salary, Maccoby insists, "because this is how the game is scored." But this in turn means "staying ahead of his peer group," which inevitably causes friction and resentment within the corporation. Not surprisingly, therefore, as Maccoby points out, "many gamesmen operate well while young middle managers, but fail to resolve middle-age and middle-management crises." In other words, the "gamesman" personality is largely a young person's role, thus easily overemphasized by business students and by social critics lamenting what they perceive as a "me-generation," a generation of students "out for themselves." But not only is this unfair and untrue of most students, it is a misleading and self-destructive strategy for the "gamesman" as well. It is not just a matter of personality but of age, that most gamesmen, if they are to survive and do at all well, eventually find themselves company people instead. They may still maintain their youthful love of challenge and competition, but these become occasional diversions, certainly not the essence of everyday life.

These personality types are roughly hewn and are by no means exact, exhaustive, or exclusive. There is a bit of each type in everyone, and differences in personalities might well be seen as differences in proportion. But to this limited personality list we should undoubtedly add dozens more dimensions, for instance, the "adult-parent-child" trinity of transactional analysis, which asks such questions as how much people need to be told what to do and given challenges by others; how much they need to give orders and advice, unwilling to take orders themselves; how much they treat others as equals rather than as inferiors or superiors; how much they need and like to work with other people and seek their approval; and how much they prefer to work alone and according to their own standards and goals. There are the neo-Freudian measures of self-esteem of "inferiority" and "superiority" ("complexes") and the multiple psychological measurements of trust (How much do you trust? Whom do you trust?), compulsiveness, cleanliness, efficiency, and so on. Ultimately, all of these categories provide us with the ability to better understand ourselves and others, and help to explain how some people fit some roles so well while others do not.

The "Outlaw" ——

Perhaps no other situational hero fires the imagination of employees more than the outlaw or maverick: Billy the Kid, Patton, bad boys with a heart of gold. This hero is necessary when the company needs some degree of creativity for a challenge to existing values. Outlaws can symbolize the darker side of an organization, yet their bizarre behavior will release the pent-up tension everyone feels, and, for savvy companies, help identify areas where change is necessary.

One recent outlaw at IBM was famous for driving his big Harley-Davidson motorcycle inside the research center, which is normally quieter than a morgue. While the scientists were working busily, he would come roaring down the corridors. Yet IBM didn't fire him, and not just because he was extremely good at what he did. More important, he was useful to the corporation because he was a lightning rod for releasing people's tension—not at the corporation but at himself.

As outlandish as it may sound, smart managers actually cultivate certain of these mutineers. Even IBM, a bastion of conservatism, recruits outlaw heroes. It all began when top management worried that the company was too strait-laced, that maybe there were too many white shirts around. They created an IBM Fellows Program and even advertised for outlaws. Ads in *Fortune* called for "Dreamers, Gadflies, Heretics . . . "

Terrence E. Deal and Allan A. Kennedy, *Corporate Cultures*

E.   RESPONSIBILITY: MY JOB AND ITS DUTIES

Responsibility is the cornerstone of ethics. Responsibility does not come into question only in those dramatic cases in which blame for a catastrophe must be laid, or at the top of the organizational hierarchy where responsibility can be shuffled no further. ("The buck stops here" stated the famous placard on President Truman's desk in the oval office.) Responsibilities, however, are part of *every* position, and accrue for every role in a practice; we might say that responsibilities are what define a role. The shortstop on a baseball team is defined by the duty to field balls within a specified range of the infield, just as the umpire is defined by the responsibility to fairly judge and "call" pitches as "balls" or

> *Responsibility* is accountability, answerability, sometimes liability but also rewardability. It is a position of trust, in which others depend on your skills and abilities. Typically it includes authority, built-in "perks," and a set of relationships (subordinates and superiors) as well.

"strikes." An individual might well enter into a certain role in business without knowing what its rewards might be, but that person only rarely would enter into a role without (for very long) knowing its responsibilities. Indeed, until then, we could quite properly say that she had not yet started the job, no matter how long she had been paid or had her name on the masthead. A job *is* its responsibilities.

Responsibilities need not be awesome and they need not be tied to blame. Responsibilities might include saying a cheery hello to the file clerk as well as seeing to it that paychecks are properly issued or that the proposed paper plant will not pollute the Washington wilderness. Responsibility to the company also includes acts *not* to be committed, such as not giving away company strategies or secrets.

Responsibilities are not entirely fixed and rigid, however. Some responsibilities consist of specific tasks, but in every role there is also the open-ended responsibility that might be summarized as "taking advantage of unforeseen opportunities" or "using initiative." A football player is expected to fall on a "free ball," for example, whatever his role or position on the field. A person in business is expected to use some initiative when a new possibility presents itself to the firm, if only by quickly informing those who ought to know about it.

Responsibility goes hand in hand with authority. Authority is not to be found only at the "top," any more than responsibility is to be found only there. Like responsibility, authority is inherent in every role and in every position. In fact, it is authority that makes responsibility both possible and necessary, and it is responsibility that gives direction to authority. Sometimes, a practice will delegate responsibility without simultaneously delegating authority; this is often a disaster. In business, for example, it is wise never to accept a position or a promotion that doesn't provide sufficient authority to carry out its responsibilities. Similarly, authority without sufficient responsibility too easily turns "authoritarian," not necessarily out of any personal fault of character, but rather because the roles are ill-defined; there may be nothing more to a position than power over others, without any job to do.

How do we identify responsibility if everyone is responsible? The answer to this important question is blurred by the examples often used, which all have to do with the identification of *the culprit* in the wake of some disaster. The Edsel proved to be a failure; whose fault was it? A company finds itself in the red, even with a product that sells well; whose fault is that? An electric power company takes every precaution to protect a city's source of power, but an "act of God" intervenes and the precautions are inadequate. Who is responsible? But the reason these questions are often so frustrating is not because of any difficulty in the nature of responsibility; the problem is rather in our unreasonable expectation that every disaster must have a single (or at most a few) identifiable cause(s). Sometimes, this is indeed the case. But most of the time, the responsibility in question is a wholly *shared* responsibility, whose components are the responsibilities of each individual in each position in the entire organization. There are differences, of course; those with more responsibility pertaining to the project, that is, those people who are most directly concerned with its planning and execution, naturally must accept most of the credit or blame for its success or failure. But it is also true that those in authority, who may not be directly in touch with the project at all, may be even more responsible and, consequently, receive more of the credit or blame. The top executives of a company may have only minimal contact with a low-level concern; nevertheless, they will very likely take much of the blame if something goes seriously wrong, just as they are rewarded (by high

The Quality Circle: Shared Responsibilities ——

So much of our emphasis on responsibility is on *individual* roles and responsibilities that we sometimes ignore the importance and benefits of *shared* responsibilities. In the post-war years of the 1940s, some American industries experimented with the idea of creating small teams of labor and management people in a group without the usual hierarchy of power—the "Quality Circle" or "QC." Their task was to jointly suggest ways of increasing productivity and efficiency, and it worked very well. But, ironically, the idea did not catch on in America but traveled instead to Japan, where it contributed significantly to that country's remarkable economic success during the past two decades. Today, Ford, Northrop, General Motors, Westinghouse, and Bethlehem Steel have all initiated QCs, with significant results. Some of the companies pass on a percentage of any savings to the QC that comes up with the suggestion, but virtually all of the companies attribute the success of the QC to the simple feeling of involvement and responsibility among the circle members. "What we are appealing to is people's desire for recognition by their peers," claims a QC coordinator at Northrop.

salaries, for instance) for taking the responsibility in the first place. On the other hand, such responsibilities even include cases in which subordinates directly contradict an explicit instruction without the executives' knowledge.

Responsibility runs throughout an organization, just as it defines particular roles and jobs. It is not diluted by being shared; it is rather multiplied and given resonance. Responsibility for failure or for success lies in the particular responsibilities of each and every role, no matter how small, and in how those responsibilities are fulfilled. And more often than not, the responsibility for a disaster and almost always for a success will be found not just in one failure or a few failures but only in the aggregate failure, which for each individual may mean only the tiniest shade of blame.

Where corporate decisions are involved, it is no easier to assign blame or credit. The problem of assigning responsibility rarely rises in cases of success; the problem, if there should be one, is singling out a small number of people for praise among the many who clamor for it. When the results of a project are a failure or catastrophe, however, it is only occasionally that a person or a group will readily admit responsibility, and it is therefore difficult to point to the link in the chain of decisions or operations where the project was distinctively misconceived or the operation particularly bungled. More often than not, it seems that projects fail in increments, one error compounding another or one decision erring by way of following or sometimes attempting to correct another. Not infrequently, therefore, the assignment of blame to a single person or department, particularly the person "in charge," is to be explained more within the realm of public relations or internal morale rather than within the realm of business ethics. But responsibility is rarely so easily assigned, and the locus of responsibility is a far more subtle question than it often appears to be in such cases.

Responsibility defines a role; virtually every job in the business world is defined by its responsibilities. But we must add to this simple statement the complication that there are many roles that most people play, even within a corporation, and so many levels of responsibility too. Many times these may not always be in harmony. A person may be an assistant manager for new product development in a corporation, with that role defined by a fairly precise list of duties and responsibilities. But the same person has responsibilities concerning the department as a whole, responsibilities to the vice-president in charge (who, to make matters a bit more complicated, also got him the job). He also has responsibilities to the company as a whole, perhaps even to the larger conglomerate of which that company is a part. Between these various levels of responsibility, particularly in times of trouble, sometimes there arise conflicts in duties. Let us say the vice-president in charge has committed a fairly innocent, but at the same time, costly and foolish mistake. The person in our example has a duty to the company to correct the mistake, but this would entail "blowing the whistle" on the person to whom he also has both personal and professional responsibilities. The welfare of the department may be at stake. There is no quantifying of responsibilities in such cases, and there may be no easy answer to the question "What should I do?"

Within a given role, it may be that the responsibilities are clear and the priorities between them if they conflict, are clear too. If a person is responsible both for making sure that there are cups in the paper-cup dispenser in the lounge water cooler and for making sure that the final analysis of the Thurgood acquisition is ready for the three o'clock board meeting, there is no question about which ought to be done first. Within a role, there will very likely be irreconcilable conflicts too; suppose two such analyses are required for the board meeting, and there is

Antigone; Or, Either Way You've Had It ———

In the original story of *Antigone,* retold in the classic play by Sophocles, Antigone is the daughter of Oedipus (and thus already fated to suffer for the sins of her parents). Her brother, Polynices, takes part in a revolt against his brother Eteocles, the King, and they kill each other in battle. The new King, Creon, their uncle, declares that Polynices must not be buried, thus violating one of the ancient Greeks' most fundamental religious rules. Antigone, however, has the sisterly obligation to her brother to see to it that he receives the dignities of burial. Thus she is torn between two incompatible alternatives: to bury her brother and disobey the king or to obey the king and violate her divine family duties. She finally decides to bury her brother, and is executed for doing so.

The conflict between two systems of responsibilities is a common occurrence in everyone's life, and it is particularly familiar in business situations. The following case may lack the dramatic impact of *Antigone,* but it represents the kind of conflict that virtually every businessperson may encounter sometime.

John Harris is the vice-president of a small textile factory owned by a large national conglomerate, for which Harris has worked for almost twenty years. The plant is inefficient and out of date, and no longer competitive in the marketplace. The national office wants to shut the plant down, and Harris knows that—in terms of economics—it is the only sound decision. On the other hand, Harris knows that the factory is essential to the community, in which he is an established and trusted citizen. Shutting down the factory will mean the loss of a tragic number of jobs, which will not be soon replaced by any other industry. Moreover, most of Harris' friends and some of his family are employed by or dependent on the factory. If he vigorously protests the closing, Harris will most certainly be fired by the national office (which will no doubt close the factory anyway). But if he doesn't do everything in his power to protect the plant and the jobs it provides, he is most certainly betraying his community. What should he do?

only the possibility of completing one. Between various roles, particularly at different levels of corporate participation in times of stress, there is a great likelihood that there will be conflicts of duties. Writers in ethics have tried to formulate precise principles for the resolution of such conflicts of duties. (The philosopher Immanuel Kant, for example, tried such a scheme in the 1790s, and several generations of British "utilitarians," in a very different way, tried it too.) But perhaps we should maintain a very different perspective on such conflicts, one embraced by Aristotle and his society long ago; ideally, he said, the various levels of society (or, we can say, a corporation) function in harmony, their principles in unison and their demands in concert. But when things go awry, when principles diverge and commands contradict one another, *there may not be any best or "right" solution,* and it is folly to pretend there is one. Indeed, it is the nature of *tragedy,* a conflict of principles where there is no resolution. For example, in the Greek tragedy *Antigone,* Antigone is torn between the King's decreed law that her brother shall remain unburied and the divine law that she has a duty to bury him. Whichever she chooses, she is damned and it would be of no point for a philosophical ethicist to formulate some abstract principle to choose her strategy for her.

Within the somewhat safer situation in the corporation a person can also be caught in an impossible choice. A manager might need to decide between firing a friend, for example, and undermining the morale of the entire company. There is sometimes no "right" choice, and no happy answer. Yet he must choose. Business ethics does not promise an easy or a painless solution; choices are not always easy, cannot always be made easy, and cannot, as we would wish, always make everything "work out all right."

What we have just said about conflicts between levels of corporate responsibilities becomes even more complex and confusing when *roles* within and without the corporation come into conflict. Even if our identity is largely formed by our jobs in this society, it is surely not the case, for virtually anyone, that it wholly consists of this corporate identity. We are also the members of political groups, sporting clubs, and religious groups, and not all of these, presumably, are attached to the company we work for. We have friends, relatives, and neighbors as well as family and career. We live in a neighborhood that is not wholly dominated (usually) by company concerns, and in a city or town, and in a state and a nation with which we identify. In addition, each of us has a role as simply a human being, part of humanity, and this too is a role with responsibilities, not only towards people we know, but to some we may never even see.

F.   CORPORATE LOYALTY

> "We're not a captive employer, but after training someone, we expect a little service in return."
>
> —A Coca-Cola executive

An essential part of playing a role and taking on its responsibilities is *loyalty.* It is an old-fashioned word, thought by many to be irrelevant to today's business world, in which mobility and opportunity have taken the place of the old emphasis on staying with the company for forty years, rising slowly up the corporate ladder, and retiring with a banquet and a gold watch. But though the responsibilities of a role may for the most part be precisely designated in terms of particular duties, obligations, and goals, any position that is more than merely an explicit consultantship carries with it another set of responsibilities that are not so precise. A football player may have as his precisely defined duties those which are definitive of his position, as tackle, guard, running back, as well as the open-ended responsibility to "take advantage of opportunities." But in addition, he has a more general responsibility to "have team spirit," to speak favorably of his team and its players in public, to support the efforts of other team members as well as further his own career, to stay with the team at least for a reasonable amount of time and not routinely accept any other offer that comes along "just for a change." But, of course, what counts as a "reasonable amount of time" is open to some dispute; in football, this usually means at least a full season, or several (forgetting for the moment about the legalities of contracts). In business, it used to be that anyone who switched jobs more than a few times in a lifetime was considered "unstable"; today, it is not uncommon to find young executives who change jobs every two or three years. Turnover of younger managers has *quintupled* in the past twenty years, and, according to a recent study, most corporations can assume that they will lose more than half of their younger recruits within five years.*

In this context, does the notion of "loyalty" and the general concept of "responsibility to the company" make sense? The answer is still "yes," but with qualifications that would have been neither necessary nor available twenty years ago. Loyalty is a two-way affair. It is the responsibility of a company to *inspire* and *deserve* loyalty just as much as it is the responsibility of the employee to be loyal. The changes in the concept and status of loyalty in recent years affect both sides of the corporate relationship. Changes in the conception of loyalty and its obligations are most obvious on the side of the younger employee. The sociological fact is that young executives (under 45 years of age) never experienced, and were too far away from, the monstrous depression of the 1930s to have their parents' fears about the tenuousness of employment. Young executives were not as worried about job security, opportunity, and challenge. But now, with a protracted recession, those old fears are coming back again.

In addition to this, the nature of corporate training and corporate work has changed. It used to be that people learned their jobs while working in them, and their responsibilities tended to be relatively unspecialized. Today, most employers expect some prior experience if not even an advanced degree (usually an MBA or a bachelor's degree in accounting or finance). These specialized skills are easily saleable to other companies. Individuals may feel bound to a *profession*

*Sterling Robert, *Fortune,* Feb. 9, 1981.

rather than a company and may not feel the same responsibility that people used to feel toward the company that originally trained them and "gave them a break." Indeed, corporations themselves instill this attitude too; managers are often hired specifically to instill new policies or "turn around" a sluggish operation, more or less with the understanding (sometimes quite explicit) that they will be in that position for only a few years, or until the job is done. An entirely new industry, nicknamed "headhunting," has been supported by the corporate world as a means to find new executive talent. Also the game of "executive raiding"—buying top executives from competing organizations—has reached a new and dramatic extent encompassing virtually the whole business (and government) world. In other words, lack of loyalty, as well as loyalty, is made part of the ethics of business, by businesses themselves.

The current concept of loyalty comes not just with the encouragement and support of the corporate world; it is also due to corporate lack of attention, and this bears directly on business ethics. Not only do corporations reward people who move, they punish people who stay. Firms that systematically purge themselves of "dead wood" usually without providing any fair alternative; companies that become so large that it is virtually impossible for a young executive to ever meet, much less to get to know and respect, the chief executives; companies that display their own lack of responsibilities or corporate ruthlessness in their policies; companies that fire employees en masse, often without bothering to see who is at fault and who is not; companies that hire senior executives who are themselves anonymous and uninspiring—these send a clear message to young executives that *this company is not to be trusted, only used.**

High salaries and promises of opportunity may encourage people to stay, but this is not the same as loyalty. A company can't *buy* loyalty, though it can keep people there by paying enough. "Loyalty is something you have to win," insists W. E. Burdick of IBM, and from the corporate side that means offering young executives not only competitive salaries and opportunities now, but providing them with a sense of personal attachment and even gratitude, and sense of identity and concern for the company. It means bestowing rewards and recognition as a routine part of the running of the corporation, making employees feel that they "belong," and, consequently, that they would not feel so "at home" elsewhere, even with a higher salary and more impressive title. Of course, there will always be opportunities that are so enticing that anyone with any ambition would leave for them, and there will always be those who, in the words of one young Harvard graduate, "wouldn't stay in the same job even if I loved it." But loyalty is as much the creation of the company as it is the sense of responsibility and attachment of the employee.

Why loyalty? Why encourage it? Why have it? From the corporate side, the answer is obvious. Even a well-trained person takes time to adjust to new

---

*Simeon Touretsky, "Changing Attitudes: A question of Loyalty," *The Personnel Administrator,* April 1979.

surroundings, to win the trust and the cooperation of colleagues, and to get down to actually running things rather than finding out what's going on. Even someone who knows exactly what needs to be done needs training time in this sense, and that costs money. Someone who is "just passing through," although doing a perfectly competent or even brilliant job, does not lend the additional support of team spirit and corporate morale. Indeed, such a person often lowers morale even while, technically speaking, doing a perfect job. Inspiring loyalty, in other words, may be good business.

From the employee side, loyalty has an obvious disadvantage; it tends to close off other opportunities that might well lead to better pay and faster promotion. But to offset this, there is a positive advantage of much greater weight, though much harder to measure or quantify. Consider two employees, one of whom considers herself a loyal member of the firm and personally committed to its interests, the other who sees himself as just "doing a job" and getting paid for it, all the while begrudging the company every bit of work it gets out of him. The first is not only more likely to succeed, but also much more likely to be happy. Since ancient times, philosophers have pointed out that nothing is more important to the good life than to enjoy what we are doing, even if it is also what we *must* do. And that means not just doing the specific tasks and assignments that go along with a job; it means accepting the position itself and the entire organization in which it plays an essential part. (The ancient philosophers were mainly concerned with the city-state; the modern business example would again be the company or corporation.) Loyalty is not just doing what we have to do; it is also that satisfying feeling that what we do is important and right, because we approve of the larger context and feel an essential part of it.

What Ever Happened to Good Old Loyalty?

Loyalty is on the minds of many corporate executives. They express the opinion that employee loyalty is vanishing—at least the variety that they remember from an earlier era. Yesterday's loyalty seemed to be a personal characteristic reflected in the attitudes and behaviors of most people. People were faithful to the organizations in good times and bad, exhibiting what now appears to have been blind loyalty—a loyalty based on obligation.

Blind to Earned Loyalty
The concept of loyalty has changed from one of "blind and obligated" to one of "insightful and earned". Several generations ago, if a person worked hard and kept his nose to the grindstone, he could pretty well be assured of work for a lifetime. People were loyal to organizations because they believed organizations would be loyal to them.

The passage of "good old loyalty" may be lamented by many, but there is some good news. It has been replaced by a strong new type—namely, earned loyalty.

So, rather than lament the loss of "good old loyalty," let's focus on a loyalty that may well provide a stronger motivational force for both management and the managed. I have identified five basic elements of the new loyalty.

1. Values and Standards. Loyalty tends to be more easily earned in those organizations that have clearly-defined values and challenging standards. People are likely to be loyal to values that lead to outstanding achievements in products, services and relationships.

2. Clear Expectations. A willingness to be specific and forthright in terms of expected behaviors does a great deal toward developing a feeling of loyalty on the part of those who will follow. It is easier for people to be loyal to what they clearly understand.

3. Frequent Feedback. People need to know where they stand and how well or poorly they have performed when evaluated against the expectations, standards, and values. People need to hear good news as well as bad. Frequent feedback is a way of increasing meaningful involvement.

4. Respect for the Individual. The new loyalty will have to be earned on the basis of respect for the individual. Respect requires trust, based on consistency in personal and interpersonal relationships; a willingness to be open with expectations and requirements; to really listen and engage in honest exchange.

5. Long-Term Commitments. This last element is probably most difficult to achieve. In what appears to many to be an atmosphere of layoffs, terminations, forced resignations and retirements, it is difficult to convince people that long-term commitments are realistic or possible.

The New Days

The new loyalty is predicated upon doing the right thing for people. When people feel they are having the right thing done for them, they will probably give the organization this new loyalty. The old loyalty was role-centered; new loyalty is person-centered. Person-centered actions will establish new loyalty as a moral motivator—not through obligation—but through choice and earned respect.

The new loyalty is possible, but it will take more work on the part of committed leaders. Excellence in leadership brings loyalty in followership.

Alexander B. Horniman, University of Virginia Business School,
reprinted from *Ethics Digest*

Working for a company is not just a job for a salary; success is not just a position and power. Being in business is playing a role in a certain practice, being a participant in a certain world; but playing a role gets reduced to mere mechanism, a "job"—no matter how interesting its tasks or goals—if it does not also include some sense of identity, some sense of "belonging" and being tied to a larger entity. Such a sense of belonging, of course, is not absolute, and it is not beyond reconsideration. The football player in our earlier example may well switch teams every few years (voluntarily or not), but it is essential that while he is on a particular team he shares that team's "spirit" and sense of identity. A bright young executive may well find it advantageous to switch companies every few years, but that is far different from entering each job with the intention of switching and with the sense that no ties or attachments will come from working for a particular firm. Loyalty no longer means spending forty years and retiring with a gold watch, but it still essentially means what it has always meant—feeling some sense of identity and concern with the company and not just doing a "job" but performing a role and accepting responsibilities. This imprecise sense of mutual support and concern we call, in old-fashioned parlance, "loyalty."

G. The System Problem

In any company of any complexity and public impact, there is a very special danger that, even if all employees of the organization do their jobs and fulfill their responsibilities, the results may still be disastrous. This is *the system problem,* an ethical dilemma in which the whole is much more than the sum of its parts.

Several recent examples of the system problem can be found in major pharmaceutical companies. In such cases, the companies perceived real needs for safe drugs of a certain sort (effective pain killers, like Darvon; non-addictive sleeping pills, such as Quaalude; and safe tranquilizers, like Valium). They developed the drugs in question according to the most rigorous standards available and tested them extensively, indeed, much more extensively than would be required in almost any other country in the world. Having developed and established the safety and effectiveness of such drugs, the company then turned the project over to the marketing department, who effectively promoted the product among doctors and pharmacists and, consequently, the public. The problem in each case turned out to be that the products were too good, the marketing too effective, the sense of acceptance and safety too thorough. The result in each case was massive abuse—from excessive use to suicide, mixing with alcohol, and notorious "recreational" use leading to extensive illegal traffic and mob involvement. Lawsuits followed, government regulation became extensive, and the companies sometimes suffered a loss in reputation as well as substantial financial losses. Who is responsible for the results of such unforeseen complications? Probably no one, or everyone. When everyone does exactly what is supposed to be done, the system problem can still arise.

The system problem can also lead to problems of a specifically ethical nature, despite the fact that everyone in the company acts perfectly correctly. An executive in the recent Lockheed bribery scandal, in which the company pleaded guilty to paying off Japanese government officials, confided, "None of us would bribe anyone, but once the thousand decisions had been made, once everyone had put all their effort into the project, it seemed at the top as if there was nothing else to do." Once the company had bet everything on the success of a single product, there was no backing out. The system problem, in other words, can be a problem of accumulated pressure throughout the system; it is as if the momentum of a larger company were so great that, once all of its employees were working towards a certain goal or in a certain direction, very little could stop it, including, especially, the chief executives at the top.

The system problem affects every large organization. It is, first of all, one of the problems of large size, the other side of the various advantages attached to so much collected power and capital. Decisions, once implemented, cannot be turned around quickly; goals, once agreed upon, cannot be immediately forgotten or replaced. What we call "the corporate culture," like the culture of a nation or a society, has deep roots and relatively rigid rules that cannot simply be canceled or easily changed. Most of the time, the business world is sufficiently stable, and the internal concern for propriety sufficiently great, so that the next result of the company's efforts are pretty much what everyone expected and worked for. (There is always good luck and unfortunate circumstances, of course, but that is not what concerns us here.) However, when large companies face sudden reversals or unexpected changes in their situation, the system problem can become a very real problem for everyone involved. Corporate loyalty at that point becomes vague: is loyalty to the company as important as concern for what is right, or perhaps, as important as the concern for people outside the company who are going to be adversely affected?

The system problem presents us with the dilemma that, even if people are just doing their jobs, the overall result may nonetheless be bad. In the most dramatic imaginable cases, of course, there are the moral dilemmas such as the lieutenant in the military who is ordered to do what he knows to be wrong. But the system problem is present in every large enterprise—university teaching, working in a large hospital, running even a medium-sized city—as well as in every business that is more than "small" (500 employees). Watching out for the system problem is the ultimate job—and ultimate dilemma—of every manager, who, on the one hand, has particular responsibilities to carry out on a day-to-day basis, but, on the other hand, has or ought to have the well-being of the company as a whole in mind. Sometimes, however, the everyday responsibilities and the well-being of the company, or the company and its surrounding community, are not harmonious, and that is when the larger perspective, the basic aim of "business ethics," becomes of crucial importance.

■ Summary and Conclusion

Business is a form of *practice*. It is an activity with shared and established goals and rules and its own internal as well as external rewards. The most obvious and explicit goal of business practices is to make a profit, but it is evident from even a routine study of business practices that this is only one of its primary goals, at least from the point of view of its participants. Some of the rules of business are fully explicit, and some are even written into law. But many of the most important rules and regulations of business life may be unwritten, even, for the most part, unspoken. Much of business practice is established by tradition and by example, including a general and usually unchallenged sense that "we don't do things that way."

The heart of business practice, and the defining characteristics of every role in business, is *responsibilities,* including both responsibilities within and to the company, and responsibilities outside the firm. One of these responsibilities, though by no means absolute, is summarized as *loyalty* to the company. But loyalty (like a great many other responsibilities) must be defined in two directions at once, the loyalty expected of an employee, on the one hand, and the encouragement of loyalty on the part of the company, on the other. Loyalty, however, should be deserved by the company. If the overall result of a company's activities are harmful or unethical, for example, the loyalty of its employees is not a virtue. This is *the system problem:* an organization may be structured such that everyone who works in it may be doing a perfectly proper job, but the net result is nevertheless improper. The resulting conflict between loyalty to the company and the larger responsibilities to society present one of the most difficult dilemmas in business ethics. Such conflicts in general, in which there are ethical imperatives on each side of two (or more) conflicting courses of action, are called *ethical dilemmas.*

■ Study Questions

1. List three familiar activities (not just sports) that are *practices* and briefly describe their rules, goals, and implicit regulations. Pick one familiar activity that is *not* a practice and decide why it is not a practice.

2. What features of business are definitively part of the practice of business, that is, without which business would no longer be business as we know it? Name some familiar features of business that are not essential or definitive aspects of business. Is the making of profits an essential part of business? Are company social gatherings an essential part of business? Are business lunches an essential part of business? Why or why not?

3. Is a salary one of the internal rewards of business, or an external reward, or both? Why?

4. Looking at business as a practice, make a list of rules and regulations *within* business. Which of these are typically explicit (for example, the sorts of rules that appear in a corporate "code of ethics")? Which are merely implicit, but recognized and accepted by at least a large majority of businesspeople?

5. Pick a single business position (a job you have already held or investigated or know rather well at least secondhand) and define its role in the company and in the larger community, as well as the particular responsibilities that define that position. Can you define that particular role without mentioning those responsibilities?

6. Should seniority determine the salary and security of an office manager (as it does typically for a factory worker in a union, for example)? What arguments are there for the importance of seniority? What arguments are against it?

7. What considerations are relevant when you are deciding whether or not to accept an offer from a competing firm? Assume that salary, status, and promotional opportunities are appropriate considerations. What sorts of considerations would be relevant to your sense of feeling you ought—or ought not—to stay with the firm that hired you in the first place?

8. With which of Maccoby's four "corporate types" did you identify? Do you think that your actual personality and abilities are in accordance with the type you picked?

■ FOR CLASS DISCUSSION

Fitting In

The Algo Company is a moderately sized corporation that makes a wide range of household products. It has nearly a dozen plants scattered around the country, whose manufacturing and purchasing procedures had never been adequately coordinated. The various plants operated independently—as they had for decades—but the result was a certain confusion and inefficiency, a duplication of work, and more expensive purchases of raw materials. Accordingly, Mr. Sampson, the Algo Company president, appointed a Mr. Postal as vice-president in charge of coordinating the activities of the various plants. He gave Postal wide latitude and a great deal of discretionary power. The appointment was announced through a formal notice sent out to the directors of the plants and published in the company newsletter.

Postal's first decision was to centralize Algo's purchasing procedures by forcing all purchases of over $1,000 to be approved by his office. The paperwork involved was considerable, and the extra time between the plant decision and company approval kept increasing. The plant directors, consequently, began purchasing smaller amounts of material—though more often—in order to keep the amounts of each order below the $1,000 limit. Postal eventually noticed that purchasing costs were increasing, though slightly, and so revised his demand such that *all* purchasing orders would come through his office. The plant directors did not express their resentment, but they did relegate most of the responsibility for purchase decisions to the head office, resulting in an even larger backlog of paperwork and decision making in Postal's office and even more expense and inefficiency. A sensitive assistant suggested to Postal that he travel to the various plants and discuss the needs with the directors, but Postal insisted that he was much too busy with the work in his office. The work load continued to increase and, at the same time, the productivity of the individual plants began to drop.

Sampson fired Postal, and appoints *you* to take his place. What essential decisions about the nature of responsibility must you make immediately? What responsibilities do you have in your new position? What are the first moves you would make to reverse Algo's disastrous trends?

Case Study: The Space Shuttle Challenger ——

On 28 January 1986, the Space Shuttle Challenger exploded approximately seventy-three seconds after lift-off. The seven-member crew included Christa McAuliffe, the first teacher in space. All were killed. The explosion was virtually certainly caused by a burn-through of the O-rings sealing two sections of Challenger's right solid rocket booster (SRB). The SRB was designed and produced by Morton Thiokol, Inc.

The night before the disaster, engineers at Morton Thiokol were unanimously opposed to launching. The Thiokol engineers were concerned that the abnormally low temperatures would cause a failure of the O-ring seals on Challenger's SRBs. The coldest previous launch had been at fifty-three degrees, and even at that temperature, hot gases had blown past and charred the primary seals in two of the SRB joints as well as one of the secondary seals. The O-ring seals had generated a long history of concern among Thiokol engineers. William L. Ray, an engineer who had worked on the initial design of the SRB, had written memos as far back as 1971 complaining about the inadequate design for the seal. Another Thiokol engineer, Roger M. Biosjoly, had written a memorandum in the summer of 1985 warning that there "could be [a] catastrophe of the highest order" if the company did not improve the SRB's safety seals. Another engineer said, "We all knew if the seals failed, the shuttle would blow up." Another Thiokol engineer recalled watching the launch, thinking, "Oh God, we made it. We made it. . . . Then . . . the shuttle blew up. . . . And we all knew exactly what happened."

Despite the objection from the Thiokol engineers, NASA wanted to go ahead with the launch. Robert Lund, a vice president of Morton Thiokol, said of the attempt to persuade NASA not to launch: "We got ourselves in a thought process where we were trying to prove it wouldn't work and we couldn't do that." The Thiokol engineers were overruled by their managers, and Thiokol signed off for a launch. The temperature at lift-off was in the thirties. Upper managers at NASA subsequently denied that they had known about the Thiokol protest and said that, had they known about it, they would have halted the launch.

Suppose that you are a team of middle managers at M.T. It is ten hours before the launch and you are at a meeting to decide what (if anything) you should do.

*Adapted from J. Callahan, *Ethical Issues in Professional Life*
(Oxford University Press)

HISTORICAL INTERLUDE

THE RISE OF CAPITALISM AND THE PROTESTANT ETHIC

During the eighteenth century in England and in the rest of Europe, there was a momentous change in attitude toward business and money. As populations began to increase and towns grew into cities and territories into states, the need for large-scale trade and professional traders increased. As demand for goods increased, pressure on the guilds to step up production increased, and with the industrial revolution beginning, for the first time large-scale mass production became possible. Increased centralized power in the growing nation states decreased the power of the lords of the manor, and in the most "progressive" countries like England and France, for example, feudalism broke down very quickly as the life of society moved from the manors to the royal courts and the cities. The number of merchants increased to serve these new urban societies, and in order to handle the increased interchange of money and goods and civil matters of various kinds, a new class of people emerged in the cities, a "middle class" (between the serfs and manual workers on the bottom of the class scale and the lords and kings on the top), called the *"bourgeoisie"* (after "burgher," meaning "of the city"). This new class no longer toiled in the fields or actually "produced" things; they were primarily organizers and functionaries—clerks, accountants, lawyers, and, most important here, *businessmen* in our modern sense. They organized the activities of small armies of merchants who did the actual road work, the buying and selling, the collecting and the bargaining.

We have already pointed out that in order for such a world to emerge, much more was necessary than increased population and a new class of people to organize its material transactions; a new set of ideas was necessary as well. First of all, trade and profit making had to be seen not just as necessary evils (as in Aquinas) but as respectable enterprises. This was hinted at by some late medieval thinkers, such as the philosopher Duns Scotus, but took its primary source of support from a quite different religious impetus; it followed from the Reformation of Martin Luther in the first half of the sixteenth century and, most significantly, from the work of his Swiss successor in the next century, John Calvin. The reformation in general brought together the realm of the secular and the realm of the religious, and so tended to integrate the everyday necessities of life—including trade and its motives—with the more noble virtues of morality and religion. Luther himself, it is important to note, retaining the medieval attitude towards business and profit making, considered any charge more than "just price" of an item usury, a mortal sin. He too considered the merchant "an abomination before God" and despised the newly forming middle class. Luther's attack on the authority of the Catholic Church, it should be remembered, was not an attack on its authority and severity but, to the contrary, an attack on its laxness and corruption. Yet he insisted on the two medieval assumptions, that economic interests were wholly subordinate to the main interest of life, salvation, and that economics was to be wholly constrained by the rules of morality and "the Law of God."

John Calvin, on the other hand, was truly an advocate of what we now consider "good business." He thought work a virtue, not only the work of production (so admired by Aristotle, Aquinas, and Luther too) but also the work of the merchant and the work of the new man of the "middle class," who helped organize trade. Moreover, because Calvin believed in the rather harsh doctrine of "predestination" (that is, that an individual's salvation or damnation was already settled before birth and there was nothing he could do about it), he did not believe that life had to be dedicated to the salvation of the soul. Therefore, people could pursue wealth and success, and, indeed, these might even be viewed as some tenuous indication of their destiny in the hereafter as well. Moreover, Calvin taught the somewhat novel virtue of thrift, thereby using newly accumulated riches wisely rather than simply squandering them. And with thrift came capital, savings that could be used for future production. Calvin provided the theological support for the concept of investment; money should be put back to work to make more money. So too he became an early supporter of economic growth.

With Calvin, individual ambition and initiative took on new importance. It was no longer so clear, as it had been to Aristotle, that the individual ought to subsume his own interests to the interests of the good of society as a whole. Nor was it clear, as it had been to Aquinas and even to Luther, that the life of business and the pursuit of individual wealth would be "perilous to one's soul." Accordingly, the two medieval assumptions that made economics subservient if not suppressed by religion and morality could now be turned upside down. Could it be that success in business might be the mark of a person's salvation? And could it be that the new world of business, rather than being wholly constrained by morality, is itself an essential determinant of morality and an asset, rather than a threat, to the overall well-being of society?

It is with Calvin that we find ourselves on the edge of our concept of what is technically defined as "the market society," a society in which business is no longer an occasional source of luxury or an unfortunate necessity; business now becomes the primary determinant of value as such. It is with Calvin that we find ourselves ready to understand the modern move from a conception of human nature in terms of society ("man is a social animal" says Aristotle) or in terms of his soul (as in Aquinas and Luther) to our conception of human nature in primarily economic terms, or as homo economicus ("economic man"). This is the image of men and women as maximizers of their own interests, who are primarily concerned with getting what they pay for and getting paid for what they do. We sometimes talk as if this is itself "human nature," but it is always important to appreciate the fact that, right or wrong, it is but one of a large variety of conceptions of human nature that have paraded through philosophy and theology over the past four or five millennia. But with this conception of the individual as maximizer of his own interests, we are ready to entertain the outrageous idea of the free market society, a society in which people are bound neither by tradition nor by force but only by their own economic interests, unafraid for their salvation and unrestricted by official regulations whose primary purpose is to minimize competition and regulate fair exchange. Out of this scramble for personal advantage, so the theory goes, will emerge a better society.

But before we complete this picture and introduce the one man who provided it with a philosophical structure and defense, Adam Smith, it is necessary to see very quickly just how this picture could have emerged and why it strikes us as so powerful. We have already seen the enormous changes in society and its ideas that were required before the idea of a free market society could even be suggested and before business and life in business could even be tolerated as a respectable enterprise in society. There had to be new respect for wealth (which has almost always been praised in one way or another) and for the making of wealth as well. There had to be a new emphasis on the individual, in addition to his role in society. There had to be both an appreciation for the need to make a profit as the motive of trade and exchange and the positive value of the profit motive itself. Cleverness in business had to be seen as something more than deception and avarice, and progress had to be understood as something more than a disruption and a danger to the stability of life. But our present way of thinking goes far beyond all of this. Indeed, the central debate in our society today concerns not whether government should allow business (which would seem to us absurd) but whether government and social concerns should have any control over business whatsoever. The economist Milton Friedman, for example, says that they should not, that business is business and that the business of business is profit, nothing else. How could this extreme turn of events have been possible? To see this, it is necessary to look very briefly at an intermediary step between medieval traditional trade, in which profit and progress played no role whatever, and modern market society, in which the pursuit of profit and the idea of progress are definitive of our entire society. That intermediary step is called mercantilism, and it is in reaction to it that we can understand the feverish opposition to regulation that defines the modern business world.

Mercantilism is considered by many economists to be a pre-capitalist stage of economic development in which emerging nations (for example, seventeenth-century France under Louis XIV) hoarded up gold and other valuable commodities, searched the world for new wealth and plundered it from others, and encouraged exports of goods for sale but severely discouraged imports of any kind. Such a policy will quite obviously act as a spur to production and usually result in a rapid accumulation of national wealth, but what is clearly missing from this picture of dynamic economic growth and the encouragement of production and profit is the concept of "freedom." Because business was so strictly controlled by the state, the competition of the marketplace did not set prices and encourage innovation and production; but the explicit demands of the government regulated the flow of goods through a sometimes bewildering network of tariffs, treaties, and laws. There was competition, but between nations not individuals. The idea of growth pertained more to the nation than to individual businesses, and the wealth accumulated was primarily accrued to the king; only secondarily, and then solely through the king's gratitude and generosity, was wealth transferred to the businessman. In Louis XIV's France, for example, the "web of regulations, tariffs and ordinances . . . suffocated the entrepreneurial impulse at the same time that it sought to foster it," writes Robert Heilbroner. And against this largely inefficient and strangling set of government regulations came a protest. "How can we help you?" asked the French finance minister Colbert of a businessman named Gourany. *"Nous laissez faire"* (leave us alone) came the answer. With that came the rallying cry of the modern business society: "Leave us alone." But to understand a reaction is not yet to take it at face value. To demand an end to unreasonable and suffocating restrictions may be totally reasonable, but to think that this means an end not only to all government regulation but to all social concern about business is quite another matter. "The dove finds it so much easier to fly in the lighter air," writes the philosopher Immanuel

Kant, "that it mistakenly believes that it would be easier yet to fly if there were no air at all." Excessive social intrusion may well be bad for business, but the heart of free enterprise is still the concept of the good society, just as it was for Aristotle, and just as it was for Aquinas and Luther, in their more secular moods.

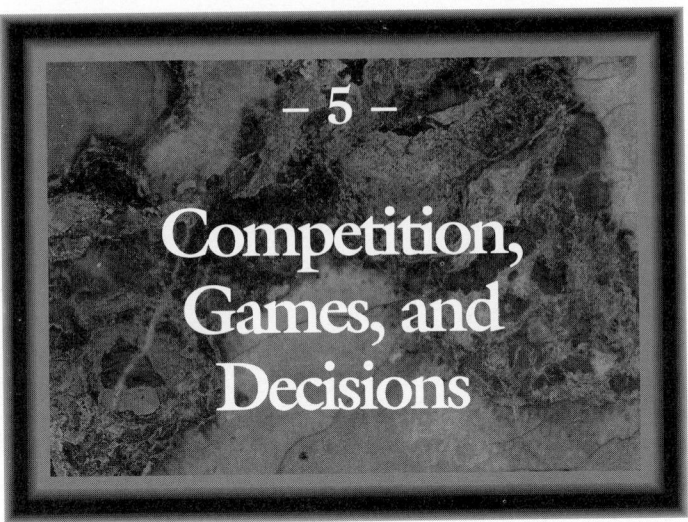

– 5 –
Competition, Games, and Decisions

Pleasure is in the race, not the goal alone. Success is the reward of exertion, yet we play the game of life (serious play!) as we do the game of chess—for conquest; the pleasure is in the conquest, the stroke by which victory is obtained.

—Louisa Tuthill, 1850

E thics is life; business ethics is business life; and business, more than any other way of life except sports, is *competition,* whether between individuals or corporations. In Adam Smith's classic *Wealth of Nations,* competition makes the market "work" and assures the lowest prices, the proper supply, enough jobs and reasonable wages, as well as the wealth of the society. But the ethics of competition is itself a matter of controversy; is competition a means, or is it an end in itself? Do the results of competition—rewarding those who win, punishing those who lose—actually succeed in encouraging good work and fair play, or do they make people desperate and negligent of both the rules and each other's interests? And where do the rules of "fair play" enter in, or is business the Darwinian jungle of "survival of the fittest" that some of its more pessimistic or brutal analysts have suggested?

A.   THE GAME OF BUSINESS

The centrality of competition in the business world lends itself to a metaphor, particularly in sports-loving America. It is the metaphor of business as a *game.*

We tend to view not only business as a game but also politics, sex, conversation, war, and even life itself—all understood in terms of playing well or poorly, winning or losing, having fun or being a bad sport. Accordingly, our views of life tend to have a certain levity—unknown throughout most of the world—that tends to leave us particularly vulnerable to the tragedies, inconveniences, and unsportsmanlike conduct of both nature and the rest of the human race. Military strategists play "war games" in which the actual effects of war, in terms of human suffering, are carefully eliminated. In business we tend to see the skill and cleverness (and some luck) of the players determining winners and losers. But in doing so, we also ignore or neglect other aspects of business, especially the effects on nonplayers.

The connections between competition, games, and the practice of business in the free market system seem obvious. Competition moves the market and making a profit or winning is its motive. Both businesses and games involve planning and strategy, and a certain amount of gambling in the face of uncertainty and risk. As practices, both businesses and games are defined by their own rules, their own language and goals, their own specifiable skills and possible "plays." To the participants both seem wholly self-contained and autonomous activities. They are alerted only occasionally to the impact of their activity for anyone else and belligerently protective of the sanctity of the game itself. Baseball players may be only occasionally aware of the social and psychological value of the game or the effects of their winning. So too in business: when competition becomes an end in itself, it is the game itself that seems to be everything, at least while it is being played. "Outside" considerations, whether from absentee stockholders or environmental protection groups, from dissatisfied consumers or government regulatory committees, are most unwelcome.

In our discussion of practices in Chapter 3, we not surprisingly used games as our examples because they are well-defined, clearly self-contained practices and obviously bound by a certain set of rules, though made up of traditions and conventions as well. The metaphor of business as a game also lends itself to a useful mode of analysis called *game theory*—that is, the theory of policies and planning, and making rational decisions in the face of the uncertainties and risks of the market. Furthermore, the game metaphor gives us a valuable view of business in terms of our "microethical" perspective. It views business first of all as an *activity of individual participants,* not as a "system" or as a mechanism. We often forget that some of the classic macroeconomic theories (for example, those of Adam Smith and Karl Marx) view business (or capitalism, more properly) as a huge machine, in which individual human choice and activity simply fit into predetermined roles and mechanisms, which are wholly predictable if not actually predestined. But people *play* games, and business is first of all people making decisions and taking the consequences. Business life is not simply a system or a mechanism, even if it is made up of roles in an already well-established social institution. It is an activity performed well or badly in searching for certain "payoffs" and taking certain responsibilities, as in a game.

Business as a Poker Game ——

We can learn a good deal about the nature of business by comparing it with poker. While both have a large element of chance, in the long run the winner is the man who plays with steady skill. In both games ultimate victory requires intimate knowledge of the rules, insight into the psychology of the other players, a bold front, a considerable amount of self-discipline, and the ability to respond swiftly and effectively to opportunities provided by chance.

No one expects poker to be played on the ethical principles preached in churches. In poker it is right and proper to bluff a friend out of the rewards of being dealt a good hand. A player feels no more than a slight twinge of sympathy, if that, when—with nothing better than a single ace in his hand—he strips a heavy loser, who holds a pair, of the rest of his chips. It was up to the other fellow to protect himself. In the words of an excellent poker player, former President Harry Truman, "If you can't stand the heat, stay out of the kitchen." If one shows mercy to a loser in poker, it is a personal gesture, divorced from the rules of the game.

Poker has its special ethics, and here I am not referring to rules against cheating. The man who keeps an ace up his sleeve or who marks the cards is more than unethical: he is a crook, and can be punished as such—kicked out of the game or, in the Old West, shot.

In contrast to the cheat, the unethical poker player is one who, abiding by the letter of the rules, finds ways to put the other player at an unfair disadvantage. Perhaps he unnerves them with loud talk. Or he tries to get them drunk. Or he plays in cahoots with someone else at the table. Ethical poker players frown on such tactics.

Poker's own brand of ethics is different from the ethical ideals of civilized human relationships. The game calls for distrust of the other fellow. It ignores the claim of friendship. Cunning deception and concealment of one's strength and intentions, not kindness and open-heartedness, are vital in poker. No one thinks any the worse of poker on that account. And no one should think any the worse of the game of business because its standards of right and wrong differ from the prevailing traditions of morality in our society. . . .

Alfred Carr, "Is Business Bluffing Ethical?"
Harvard Business Review, Jan.–Feb. 1968

B.   HOW BUSINESS IS NOT A GAME

Despite the virtues of modeling business on game theory, which we will discuss later in this chapter, the metaphor has its limitations. Business is not a game but both business and games are *practices.* The practice of business has its obvious gamelike *components,* which may well be a primary source of inspiration for ambitious business graduates; but the practice of business is much more than these components, no matter how exciting and noticeable they may be. Competition is indeed essential to the practice of business in the free market system, but it doesn't follow either that business is simply competitive, or that business, as competition, is a game.

Reactions to Carr on Business as Poker ──

"All of us in business know that 'playing the game' yields only short-term rewards. We'll admit our faults, but we'll not endorse them as part of our philosophy. To do so would bring the house of business down on itself." (John Valiant, New Product Manager, William H. Rorer, Inc., Fort Washington, Pennsylvania)

"My own experience in dealing with hundreds of companies has led me to believe that sharp dealing or the slightest prevarication on the part of a businessman usually results in information excommunication to the back alleys of the business world or to obscurity." (Mark Rollinson, President, Greater Washington Industrial Investments, Inc., Washington, D.C.)

"I think a better strategy in business is to work hard, be honest, and be smarter than anyone else." (L. D. Barre, Vice President—Marketing, RTE Corporation, Waukesha, Wisconsin) . . .

"But it is not at all the case that businessmen do not expect the truth to be spoken. On the contrary, almost all day-to-day business is conducted verbally or on the basis of nonlegal documents. The economic system would collapse without mutual trust on a practically universal scale among business executives.

"Mr. Carr apparently assumes that 'not telling the whole truth' is synonymous with 'telling a lie.' Businessmen know that it would be ridiculous to expect anything more than a straight answer to a straight question. Moreover, it is perfectly acceptable to withhold the truth by saying, 'I am sorry, I am not willing to discuss that subject.' There are many reasons of self-interest or discretion which would justify a refusal to answer any questions, and businessmen do not expect that those reasons need be given. . . .

"Mr. Carr's argument would be sound if business functioned in a vacuum. Because business is an integral part of society, however, it will always be judged by societal criteria.

"But it is surely the function of what we call conscience to extend the area where truth is used, and to 'play games' only on recognized playing fields."

Implicit or stated in many letters is the idea that Mr. Carr approved of what he called "game strategy" (a notion to which he vigorously objects). . . . The stricture of F. W. Henrici, Systems Analyst for Schering Corporation, Bloomfield, New Jersey, is typical:

"What really bothers me is Mr. Carr's attempt to give businessmen something with which to salve their consciences. Almost everyone knows that one doesn't reach a position of power in business, or even in the church, without a little hanky-panky. So be it. But if you lust for power, or money, or success, so that you are willing to put up with hanky-panky, then at least suffer those pangs of conscience. Know that other men scorn you in some small way for the things you condone."

Harvard Business Review, May–June 1968

The considerable confusion between games, competition, and the practice of business comes from our tendency to see so many activities in terms of the game metaphor. First, not all competition is gamelike. The Darwinian struggle for survival is the ultimate competition, but it surely is not a game. So too, business may be essentially competitive though it is not a game. Second, both games and competition presuppose more general practices that define and circumscribe them, and provide the criteria for "fairness" as well as the ultimate goals that justify them (whether just entertainment or the wealth of nations). A game is played only in a culture that provides the context for that game. Competition also presupposes noncompetitive practices with shared goals and rules; furthermore, no practice can consist entirely of competition, because the very idea of a practice presupposes shared assumptions, agreements, mutual interests, and goals. (Thus the Darwinian struggle is not a practice, and two businesses fighting a life-or-death battle for survival may well give up their rule-governed behavior in the business world too.) Of course, while playing a game, we tend to focus wholly on the competition, taking the context for granted; and in business competition, the rules of fairness and "good sportsmanship" are often obscured. However, those rules are always there, making our enterprise possible. What's more, they are not imposed from the outside or constrictions on free trade; they are the definitions that make the free enterprise system possible. These rules are the parameters that make it all possible.

Games are by their nature limited, restricted, carefully defined, and isolated from the rest of our lives. Life itself is not a game; games are short vacations from the rigors and uncertainties of life. In games, conditions are controlled; the

Pepsi Claims Coke Hired Its Executives to Discover Secrets ——

Coca-Cola Co., the soft-drink market leader, always has derided No. 2 PepsiCo Inc. as a copycat.

Now the shoe is on the other foot.

Pepsi is accusing top-selling Coke of running scared—luring away Pepsi executives to learn that company's trade secrets.

Meanwhile, Coca-Cola is so enraged by Pepsi's statements and media coverage that it's threatening to scuttle a preliminary agreement to end the flap.

In Atlanta, Coke said Friday that Pepsi is "disseminating false information," and vowed to "reassess" last week's "informal" settlement. Especially irksome to the proud company was a *New York Times* headline indicating that Pepsi had "won a legal battle" over Coke.

In Purchase, N.Y., Pepsi was telling the media that Coke "has attempted to halt the erosion of its U.S. sales by hiring executives knowledgeable about the 'nuts and bolts' of Pepsi-Cola's marketing strategy." Until this year, analysts said, Pepsi's domestic market share was rising faster than Coke's. But Emanuel Goldman, an analyst with Sanford C. Bernstein & Co., said that this year their U.S. market share growth rates are about the same, with Pepsi having 24% of the market and Coke 35% . . . .

Coke said there's nothing new about switching jobs in the soft-drink industry. It said Pepsi has made off with more than 15 of its own employees during the past 10 years.

Coke also insisted that it "doesn't need" unethical methods to beat Pepsi. In a statement, the company said it "has never hired employees of any other company for the purpose of obtaining trade secrets or confidential documents of any kind."

The Wall Street Journal, Oct. 6, 1980

circumstances that determine the fate of the players are carefully defined. Rules are exact, or as exact as need be. Games have distinct beginnings, and distinct ends. They can be cancelled because of rain or because one of the players no longer feels like playing. No one loses the baseball game cancelled by rain; but a businessperson can lose when a business arrangement is cancelled or postponed. Tennis buffs or football fans may display no limits to their enthusiasm just before a game, but this unbridled enthusiasm has its clear and definite limits. A player who fails to respect the clear and distinct end of a game is a "bad sport." But business life has no such well-defined limits. A particular negotiation may last just so long, but the manufacturing job goes on; a company may win the race to market its newest product, but that is not the end of the business. And people wholly devoted to their careers may work more than normal hours. We do talk about people who "work too much," but we do not put strictures on the allowable involvement of people in their careers as we do in mere games. We might say that this difference between the scope of games and the scope of business life is merely a "matter of degree." And so it is. But the difference between taking a hot bath and being boiled alive is simply a difference in "degree" too.

In general, games involve competition, but they also presuppose cooperation. We focus on the former, but the latter is even more essential. In a basketball game, competition may develop between two players of the same team for scoring the most points. It need not even be a "friendly" competition. But this competition is tolerable *only* insofar as it improves the overall performance of the team. The competition may spur both players to play better. Then again, it may inspire them to interfere with each other and jeopardize team cooperation. Here, the competition between *individual* players is clearly secondary to competition between teams. But here too, competition is by no means absolute. In the name of competition, an ice hockey player might well put another player out of the game with such brutality that the game itself comes to get a bad name and disillusions its spectators. Not only the brutality, but the sense of competition that inspires it, has gone beyond the bounds, for, even in hockey, the point of the practice is not ultimately to win but to play and to play for the edification of others. In other words, the competition between teams is bounded by the integrity of the sport, which essentially requires cooperation.

In business, the idea of competition is so familiar that we fail to ask "competition with whom" and within what constraints. Sometimes, the picture that emerges is a kind of shoddy Darwinism, in which everyone is in competition with everyone else, every employee with every other employee who has or wants a similar job, every applicant or potential applicant for a vacancy, every business student with every other student, and every firm with every other firm. If this were so, it would not be the survival of the fittest but rather a jungle of mutually defensive barbarians uninhabitable by almost anyone but a few "jungle fighters." But, of course, it is generally not like this at all. Most people who go into business, including bright and ambitious fast-trackers, see it as an extremely hospitable and pleasant environment, filled with people helping one another, working together, and competing together rather than just against one another. Rivalries frequently appear but always *within* the context of a shared and more or less harmonious enterprise, and then they are noteworthy competitions, not the normal state of affairs. Even in business school, where an artificially high state of competitiveness dominates, the Darwinian metaphor is at every point punctured by friendships and study groups, by alliances against a particularly harsh teacher, and mutual good will. Competition is a shared set of goals and rules and concerns as well as an antagonism, albeit, a limited antagonism that only seems in the heat of the moment to be an all-or-nothing affair. There is good reason why we confine our fiercest competitions to the carefully controlled arena of sports events;

we might as a people love competition and find our greatest sense of achievement and success in "the good fight." But such competition can be endured only briefly by most people, and few people can tolerate more than an occasional battle in their work. Competition may be the spice, but it is not the substance, of business life.

Games presume more or less voluntary participation. One is a player *by choice,* whether on a team of five basketball players or one of the millions in a national lottery. If someone wants to play football, he has no right to complain of being tackled (assuming the game is tackle football, that he in fact has the ball, that the ball is in play, that the tackler is on the other team, and so on). But competition does not always presume voluntary participation and, again, business competition is not always to be thought of in the voluntaristic imagery of gamesmanship. Sometimes, it is much more like the Darwinian struggle, imposed upon those in business who have no desire whatever to play games. But more important still is that, while games include *only* those who play more or less voluntarily, business clearly includes and involves any number of people who in no sense choose to be included or involved. The fans and the residents of a particular community may well benefit from a local sports event, but this is more or less clearly delineated from the game itself. The people served or threatened by a local corporation, on the other hand, quite properly object to a rigid distinction between "competition" and its consequences, especially if they involuntarily have to bear the brunt of those consequences.

One familiar modern argument—and it is noteworthy how modern and how distinctly American it is—says, in effect, that business is a self-enclosed game that deviates when it chooses from the ethics of society in general. The classic article here is Alfred Carr's essay on business bluffing in which he argues that business is like poker, and bluffing—which he says is essentially a form of lying—is allowable as part of its basic rules. He concludes that business has its own rules, just as a game has its own rules. But however much investment banking may resemble poker or chess, and however much commodities markets may resemble blackjack or the shell game, the game metaphor quickly breaks down as soon as we ask those elementary questions that lie beyond the immediate "game" itself—who is sponsoring this game and who is affected by it? We can understand a price war between two rival corner service stations in this way, but competition between major oil companies affects not only the owners but the entire economy and possibly international politics too. *There is too much at stake* in business to consider its activities—even when they are gamelike—as mere games. Business *is* serious business.

C.   THE RULES OF THE GAME

Society appears no longer to want industry to allocate the social costs of production to society at large. Not being a player in this game at the economic level, society can only

> *seek political solutions. That means a rule change—a new game. Business, too, is going the political route to obtain some influence over what the new game is to be.*
> —John MacDonald, Fortune, Feb. 11, 1980

As a practice, business is circumscribed by rules; but, like any practice, business does not just consist of rules. Most of its guidelines are implicit, tacitly understood by all players, with certain minimal allowable deviations (bluffing in negotiations, or surprise plays in football) and, equally important though rarely said, an indefinitely long list of understandings about what a businessperson or player does *not* do (forge contracts, or deflate the football to hide it under a jersey). But in addition to these many, many tacit understandings, there are the explicit rules, spelled out in OSHA* guidelines or printed on the top of a board game box. It is simply false to think, as "bad sports" sometimes do, that what is not explicitly prevented by the rules of the game is thereby acceptable; indeed, if that were the case there could be no game, for the list of rules itself would be so long that players would never finish reading the initial instructions. Most practices, in other words, including games and business and games in business, are built upon an accretion of activities and "plays" that are paradigmatically acceptable, with some deviations and an inarticulate understanding that no serious deviation from those practices will be acceptable, whether or not anyone has ever challenged them and put them in a rule.

For example, for many years, people played golf with nondescript golf balls of approximately a certain size and certain composition. These became more or less standardized and soon there was an "official ball." However the deviations became more ingenuous, until, finally, some manufacturers made balls that traveled much farther than usual, just on the basis of their composition. No one had ever specified before that the ball must be so and so, but when a certain advantage was obvious and the competition became more a matter of equipment than skill, a new rule had to be written. The "official" ball was now not just a "golf" ball, but a specific type. When the established nature of the practice was changed in this way, a new rule had to be formulated.

There are certain rules, of course, that are required just to start the game. When a group of children make up a game, they don't begin by making up the rule book; they begin with a general description that serves as a set of rules: "You take the (ball, coin, rock) and try to (get it in the hole, over the fence, up the tree)." Explicit rules are added as needed: "No, you aren't allowed to get that close." What is presupposed even before the rules—perhaps the ultimate tacit understanding—is the purpose or function of the game, for instance, entertainment ("Let's keep from getting bored by playing this game") or to make some chore more enjoyable ("Cleaning up this place would be much more fun if . . . "). *All* of the rules of the game, and all of its tacit understandings, will be directed

---

*Occupational Safety and Health Administration.

towards—or at least will not oppose—this ultimate purpose, even though this need never be said.

The gamelike components of business must be understood in much the same way as components of entertaining sports. The explicit rules—for example, those that have become laws or government regulations and those that have been stated (usually vaguely) as an industry-wide "code of ethics"—are mostly attempts to settle disputes and deviations that are too far from the established practice and its tacit rules or, in extreme cases, antagonistic to its ultimate purpose. Consumer safety laws and environmental protection regulation standards, for example, are quite obviously reactions to *excessive* deviations of business. Though critics of industry often claim that there was no concern for consumer safety or environmental protection before such laws or regulations existed, this is not the case. Instead most of the deviations were not sufficiently harmful or noticeable within the general social fabric, or for some other reason were not considered worthy of attention and regulation, so no rule was required. Laws against monopoly and trusts had to be passed only when it became quite obvious that the "market mechanism" discussed by Adam Smith did not in fact guarantee the free competition he said it would. It is particularly important, in this light, to view government regulation not just as a restriction or imposition on business competition and games but rather as protective and constitutive of them. Without such regulations the practice would be ruined of its own accord, even by its own progress in competition.

Some rules and regulations, of course, are punitive, restrictive, and interfere with competition. It is an open question whether this is good or bad, so long as we do not consider competition as an end in itself. But it never is; even in the most competitive games, the question of the purpose or the function of the game serves to frame the limits and purposes of the competition too. Some competitions need to be interfered with—like a fist fight in the middle of a baseball game; other competitions are deemed valuable and essential to the practice—like the competition between teams. Of course, it is essential that the rule makers (legislators or regulators) can tell which is which and what is what, but the point is always that rules, laws, and regulations do not as such restrict competition; they also encourage it, protect it, define it, and make it possible. A game without rules is not a game; a game without limits is nothing at all.

The hottest topic of our day, perhaps, is whether government should regulate business or whether business should regulate itself; in game talk, we ask should the rules be made up by government or within the practice itself? But this way of putting it also shows the senselessness of the government—business antagonism that seems to be the organizing principle of so much theory. Wherever the explicit rule or law comes from, it can only be based on established practice. It is possible, of course, for a government to legislate a practice out of existence; this is what happens when a foreign government "nationalizes" an industry, for example. It is also possible for a business practice to rule itself out of existence, for instance, if it passes a rule (or refuses to make a rule) limiting some aspect of itself that runs contrary to its reason for existence. Thus, when Henry Ford refused to bend to consumers' desire for variations in automobiles, he virtually destroyed his entire market by maintaining a practice that no longer served the public. In any case, the purpose of rules is to protect and define the practice, not to limit it or interfere with its competitive aspects and gamelike components. Every game is embedded in a larger social context and defined *within* a larger noncompetitive practice. And that larger practice, which is by no means just a game, is business.

D. AN INTRODUCTION TO GAME THEORY

What kind of games do we find in business? Too often, we think only of a single kind of game, the competitive "zero-sum" game in which one player wins and the others lose. But before we discuss such games, it is important to appreciate the range of games and the fact that competition is not essential to all of them.

We play games alone or with others; games involve competition, and coalitions with others. Games are cooperative as well as competitive, and there are games in which everyone wins as well as games in which everyone loses. Every game has an essential assumption—that every player is trying to maximize what game theorists call "utility," simply summarized as what we want out of it, or the "payoff." This assumption of a kind of rationality—that people will try to get what they most want—is by no means always the case. People are sometimes confused about what they want, or ineffective about getting it (for example, preferring that no one should win rather than the chance that they might lose). Game theory in business, as in every other game, is a kind of idealization, an abstraction from the less than wholly rational ways in which people actually play games. But for the most part, game theory in business has a relatively simple and familiar payoff—*profit*. But profits, we shall later see, are not the only goal of business games, even in the most classic games.

Among the variables theorists use to understand games, the most essential are these:

1. Number of persons playing:
   a. One person: no competition, a bet that *x* will happen
   b. Two persons: a true game, mutual strategies must be taken into account
   c. Three persons: allows for coalitions as well as competition, grouping together in competition
2. Solutions:
   a. Noncooperative: competitive, one person's loss tends to be the other's gain
   b. Cooperative: noncompetitive, mutual gain, or minimal mutual loss

3. Outcomes:

   a. Constant (zero) sum: if some win, others must lose

   b. Non-zero-sum: possible that everyone wins or everyone loses

4. Knowledge:

   a. Certainty: knowing all possible moves

   b. Risk: know probabilities, odds, chances

   c. Uncertainty: don't even know the odds

Consider a single-person game played under conditions of uncertainty.* Suppose you have just broken five eggs into a bowl to make an omelet, and now find yourself (for some odd reason) worried that the sixth might be bad. Suppose that there are only three possibilities: (1) break the egg in the bowl, (2) break the egg in a saucer, or (3) throw it away. The uncertainty is that you have no way of knowing whether the egg is good or bad, before breaking it. Now, given your three choices and your complete lack of knowledge, here are the following outcomes:

If you	*then if*	
	egg is good	*egg is bad*
break egg in bowl	6 egg omelet	no omelet, 5 good eggs destroyed
break egg in saucer	6 egg omelet but you have to wash saucer	5 egg omelet and a saucer to wash
throw away	5 egg omelet and wasted egg	5 egg omelet

The example may be trivial, but only because the comparative utility of wasting an egg and washing a saucer seem relatively unimportant to us. But if the eggs in question are, for instance, thousands of investment dollars, the question is very significant and practical—given a rather large investment already, how much more should be invested, especially if further investment might even *jeopardize* the overall soundness of the enterprise?

In fact, such business games are extremely common, but what is equally common is the supposition that, because the game is played under uncertainty, it is simply a matter of "luck." But the point is that canons of rationality, and questions of wisdom and foolishness enter in just as much when there is uncertainty as when there is certainty. Strategy, rationality, and seeing the rational—and irrational—solutions mark the main distinction between the good players and the

---

*Luce and Raiffa, *Games and Decision* (New York: Wiley, 1957), p. 276.

losers. (There is such a thing as being "too rational," but this usually means failure to make a decision, or irrationally focusing on just one set of outcomes and
ignoring the others, rather than being, literally, too rational.) There is a point in
every game where a player must make a decision, and there are almost always
considerations bearing on the outcome of a game that cannot be captured in ratio-

Fine Wine: Game Theory at Work ——

In decision theory, a decision maker can actually come up with an
answer to what he should do, based on the weighted average of the
value of the outcome multiplied by the probability of it happening.
This is called an Expected Monetary Value, or EMV.

At Buddha Brothers' Winery, Fred Zen is faced with a dilemma.
The grapes are almost ready for harvest but a storm is coming. Fred
could harvest the grapes now; however, his wine would be worth
only $3.60 a bottle wholesale, because the grapes are not quite ripe.
He could leave the grapes on the vine, and if the storm doesn't come
his grapes would ripen normally, and his wine would sell for $3.90.

The dilemma facing Fred Zen is the storm. If the storm comes (a
50/50 chance), the grapes would absorb water through the root system, and the grapes would be so diluted that Fred couldn't risk the
harm to Buddha Brothers' reputation by making wine from them. He
would rather sell the grapes to someone else for the equivalent of
$1.50 a bottle. But, if it is a warm storm, then there is a 30 percent
chance that a special mold, called botrytis, will strike the grapes and
lead to a high quality bottle of wine that would sell for $12 a bottle.
There would be a reduced output of only 60 percent of what would
normally be produced, but to produce such a premium wine would
be a real boost to Buddha Brothers. Using decision theory, should
Fred harvest the grapes right now and not chance what a storm, if it
comes, might do? He could now bottle wine worth $3.60 a bottle.
Based on the Expected Monetary Value method, if he does not harvest, he should expect a bottle worth only $3.55. (The Expected
Monetary Value if there is a storm would be $12.00 × .6 reduced vol-
ume × .3 chance of the botrytis forming + $1.50 × .7 chance of no
botrytis = $3.21. But there is only a 50 percent chance of a storm.
The Expected Monetary Value of not harvesting if there is no storm
would be $3.21 × .5 + $3.90 for a regular bottle × .5 chance of no
storm = $3.55.)

What decision trees cannot take into account, though, are various *nonmonetary consequences,* which very often overturn these
types of analysis. For example, Buddha Brothers has a big loan
repayment due this year, and not much cash in the bank. Fred proba-

bly should not risk the 35 percent chance (5 × .7) that the storm might come but the botrytis not form and he would have to sell the grapes for $1.50 a bottle. He might lose his vineyard and his life's work if this happened. On the other hand, Fred now has a 15 percent chance (5 × .3) to really improve the reputation of Buddha Brothers if the storm comes and the botrytis forms.

Fred decided to wait. The storm did come and the botrytis did form. Buddha Brothers is now known as one of the premium California vineyards.

Based on a case from Harvard University School of Business

nal ideals of game theory—for instance, the impatience of people, their fear of failure, the love of taking an occasional reckless chance.

Consider the following spectacular example of a two-player game. Two of the financial giants of the turn of the century were Cornelius Vanderbilt and Jay Gould. Vanderbilt owned the railroad from Buffalo to Chicago; Gould had just

Basic Reference Lottery Tickets ——

In decision theory, Basic Reference Lottery Tickets, or BRLTs, are used to determine when you personally are indifferent to varying amounts of risk.

Suppose you had a 50/50 chance at $100,000, and someone offered you $50,000 to buy the chance from you. If you were willing to accept the $50,000 (as decision theory would say that you should do on an EMV basis), then you would be willing to take a $50,000 BRLT. In other words, that person would be willing to pay you $50,000 for a 50/50 lottery on $100,000. Now, suppose someone offered you $40,000 as a sure thing, against the same 50/50 chance at $100,000. Would you take it? Decision theory would say you shouldn't, because the one outcome would still be worth $50,000 on an EMV basis, and the other only $40,000. But at least for most of us, we would still prefer the $40,000 sure thing to the chance at walking away with nothing. Would you take $30,000? $20,000? $10,000? Or maybe it is a particularly tight month, and you desperately need $100, so you'd even take that if it were a sure thing.

The amount you'd be willing to take on this bet is an indication of your own personal attitude towards risk based on your own situation. We could go through and do a series of 50/50 bets, and come up with your *risk preference curve,* and it would tell you at what point you personally would be indifferent to any two options.

bought a competing railroad. To force Vanderbilt out of the market, Gould dropped the price for shipping a car load of cattle from $150 to $125. Vanderbilt retaliated by dropping the price on his railroad to $100; in return Gould dropped his price to $75 and Vanderbilt dropped his to $50. The competition by then had become a test of wills, and when Gould dropped his price to $25, only a sixth of the original price, Vanderbilt spitefully, and triumphantly, dropped his price to $1. Gould apparently conceded defeat and raised his price back up to $175, even more than the original $150, yielding the railroad business to Vanderbilt. What Vanderbilt did not know, however, was that Gould began buying up enormous numbers of cattle in Chicago and shipping them to Buffalo on Vanderbilt's line for $1 a carload, then selling them at an immense profit in Buffalo. Vanderbilt, though the "winner" of the railroad competition, swore once and for all he would never again try to compete with Gould.

E.   Zero-Sum Games

Zero-sum noncooperative games are the classic examples of games in business; they are the most dramatic, and the difference between winning and losing is most obvious. They involve that toe-to-toe, face-to-face shootout competition that has been a staple of American mythology for most of us since we saw our first Western movie.

   A zero-sum game is defined as a game in which there must be winners and losers (unless there's an "even draw"). It is, therefore, necessarily competitive and, in a game of only two people, a classic case of trying to "outsmart" the other. As soon as there is a third player, the possibility of coalitions and behind-the-scenes cooperation comes into play. In a zero-sum game, the crucial factor in strategy is trying to figure out not only your own possible moves but the other person's possible and probable moves as well. In two-person poker—to cite the classic nonbusiness example—each player must decide not only what he will do first, but try to decide what the other person will do, and what the other person will do in response, and so on. This involves a good deal of psychological insight as well as some knowledge about odds of possible outcomes. In business as well as in poker, such keen insight and knowledge only rarely come from mere "hunches" or "intuition." They more usually come from thought, study, and practice.

   Consider the following example of a two-person, noncooperative zero-sum game that took place in the 1920s between the two leaders of the American auto industry, Ford and General Motors.* It is a zero-sum game because the auto market at the time was an inelastic market, with a predictable number of potential car buyers and little potential of growth. It can be considered a two-*person* game (despite the fact that it is, at least on paper, a battle between two corporations)

---

*Reported by John MacDonald, *The Game of Business* (New York: Doubleday, 1975).

because it was in fact a battle between two auto industry wizards, Henry Ford and Alfred Sloan of GM. It was a non-cooperative game because GM was trying to invade Ford's territory and take away its absolute domination of the auto industry. It could have been a cooperative game only if GM had agreed to be satisfied with its current share of the market or if Ford had been willing to give up some of its market in return for stability. Ford was then by far the largest auto manufacturer in the U.S.—more than twice the size of GM at that time.

When the game began in 1921, Ford's classic Model T completely dominated the low-priced automobile market. Ford's volume was so large, and hence his costs so low, that it was virtually impossible to introduce a car of similar quality for as low a price, and Ford, with his low manufacturing costs, had an enormous cushion with which he could lower prices quickly to bankrupt a competitor before it could get even a foothold in the low-priced market. On the other hand, Sloan figured that if GM could produce a somewhat more elaborate car (the "Chevrolet"), but at only a slightly higher price than the Model T, it could capture a significant portion of the Model T market, the segment that was willing to pay a slightly higher price for much more car. The aim of the game was clear on both sides: GM had to gain a large enough foothold in the low-priced car market to establish sufficient volume. With large volume, unit cost would fall, allowing GM to then lower its unit price enough to compete more or less directly with Ford. Ford had to stop GM from doing so.

Using MacDonald's analysis, Ford had four possible strategies, once he learned about GM's plans: (1) wait to see how GM does in its new market, (2) cut his price immediately to boost Model T sales even more, (3) produce another car to compete directly with the GM Chevrolet, or (4) both choices (2) and (3). Complicating the game, as in most games, were unpredictable conditions beyond the control of either player. In particular, there was the question of the economy; if it improved, more people would be willing to buy a slightly more expensive car. If it declined, fewer people would be willing to spend any more money than necessary. Accordingly, a poor economy would help Ford; a good economy would help GM. (In fact, there was a booming economy in the mid-1920s, but neither player could have predicted this.)

Given the uncertain condition of the economy, Ford's strategies would be these: (1) waiting would be too risky, for if the economy improved at all, GM would win; (2) cutting prices also would be risky, for if the economy improved, people would be willing to spend more for the GM car, and Ford's cuts would have negligible effect; (3) developing a new car would allow Ford to compete directly with GM whatever the turn of the economy, but the sales of a new car would cut into the sales of the Model T; and (4) both cutting price and developing a new car would therefore be the optimal strategy, competing directly with GM if the economy improved but also guaranteeing a victory if the economy declined. In fact, the psychology of the players had more to do with the outcome than the rationality of the strategies. Ford, confident of his leadership in the low-priced market, waited too long. He did not start production on a new car, and as GM prospered he did the only thing he could: he cut the price of the Model T. But it was too late: GM won the game and got a foothold in the market.

But business, unlike games, is continuous; when the game was over, Ford and GM were still competitors. Soon, in 1923, a new game began, this time, with a new move and a new variable—the development of closed cars and the unknown question of how the public would like them. Chevrolet went for it, Ford did not, sticking with the Model T. It was at this point that Chevrolet took over the low-priced car market from Ford. (Ford then closed down production and shifted over to the Model A, a closed car.)

Zero-sum games in business often involve not a single utility, namely profit, but two or more. Risk, for example, is a factor in the game; avoidance of risk may also be one of the goals of the game. When a large number of oil company executives were asked whether they would make a very large investment, with a 50/50 chance of earning five times the profit or being broke as the outcome, most said "no," despite the fact that such a gamble is obviously wholly rational, from a purely theoretical game stance. When the amount of the investment was quartered, on the other hand, with the same odds and payoff, almost all said "yes."

An example of a zero-sum game with two sets of goals is the classic confrontation MacDonald provides for us from the liquor industry, between the two giants, Seagram's and Schenley, in 1948. Again, the two corporations were in fact represented by two powerful game players, Samuel Bronfman of Seagram's and Lewis Rosensteil of Schenley. And, as in the previous example, we have a fixed and relatively inelastic market, resulting in a zero-sum game in which one player's loss is the other's gain. In this case, however, there are two distinctive goals; one is profit, the other, less tangible, is the reputation of the brand names of certain whiskies. This alters the nature of a zero-sum game in an essential way; since there are in effect two zero-sum games, it is possible that the two players will cooperate, each accepting one win and one loss. For instance, Seagram's, with its prestigious brand sales, could sacrifice its profits to buy more inventory from Schenley at a high price, but at the same time maintain its status in the industry. Schenley, at the same time, could have sold its small inventory of whiskey to Seagram's, made a large profit, and also maintained its own small market share of blended whiskey sales, but sacrifice its ambition to rival Seagram's in the market share of prestigious brand labels. In other words, each had two choices: Seagram's could pay a high price for inventory and keep brand sales but at a lower profit, or let its brand share decline while maintaining high profit on blended whiskey; Schenley could sell its inventory at a high profit but lose brand sales, or could keep its inventory and establish its own prestige in brand sales but lose high profit. If both corporations had chosen their first alternative, the game would in effect become a complex cooperative game; in fact, Rosensteil of Schenley decided *not* to sell the inventory, and so it became a noncooperative game. Such games in fact are extremely common, underscoring the fact that even most noncooperative zero-sum games have solutions that are nevertheless cooperative and to both players' *mutual* benefit.

in America.) This is your big chance to shift into the high quality sector of the computer market.

Submit a sealed bid.

Classic Danish Ham*

November 7, 951. Something was rotten in the state of Denmark. The air bit shrewdly on the bitter cold morning as Antonio Venezia (Harvard M.B.A., '25) rushed to keep his appointment with a high official in the Danish monarchy.

Hamlet, prince of Denmark, had contacted Antonio with an air of urgency. He had indicated that an important problem was before him but, for political reasons, he preferred to speak with an outside consultant rather than with his own advisors. Antonio saw this as the prologue to the omen coming on, and agreed to speak with Hamlet.

Antonio was quickly ushered into the private office of Hamlet by the prince's executive courtiers Messrs. Rosencrantz & Guildenstern. The prince's too-too solid flesh pressed tightly against his light grey business doublet as he rose to shake Antonio's hand.

> "What's on your mind?" asked Antonio.
> "To be, or not to be," said Hamlet. "That is the question.
> Whether 'tis nobler in the mind to suffer
> The slings and arrows of outrageous fortune
> Or to take arms against a sea of troubles,
> And by opposing end them. To die—to sleep—
> No more; and by a sleep to say we end
> The heartache, and the thousand natural shocks
> That flesh is heir to. 'Tis a consummation
> Devoutly to be wished. To die—to sleep.
> To sleep—perchance to dream: ay, there's the rub!
> For in that sleep of death what dreams may come
> When we have shuffled off this mortal coil,
> Must give us pause. There's the respect
> That makes calamity of so long life.
> For who would bear the whips and scorns of time,
> The oppressor's wrong, the proud man's contumely,
> The pangs of despised love, the law's delay,
> The insolence of office, and the spurns
> That patient merit of the unworthy takes,
> When he himself might his quietus make

---

*This case was prepared by Research Associate W. Shakespeare, under the supervision of Assistant Professors E. Lander and R. Stone as a basis for class discussion rather than to illustrate either effective or ineffective handling of an administrative situation.
Reprinted with the permission of Eric Lander.

With a bare bodkin? Who would fardels bear,
To grunt and sweat under a weary life,
But that the dread of something after death—
The undiscovered country, from whose bourn
No traveller returns—puzzles the will,
And makes us rather bear those ills we have
Than fly to others that we know not of?
Thus conscience does make cowards of us all,
And thus the native hue of resolution
Is sicklied o'er with the pale cast of thought,
And enterprises of great pitch and moment
With this regard their currents turn awry
And lose the name of action."

What are Hamlet's options?

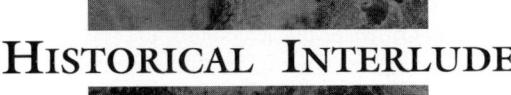

HISTORICAL INTERLUDE

ADAM SMITH AND THE GOSPEL OF CAPITALISM

He intends only his own gain, and he is, in this, as in many other cases, led by an invisible hand to promote an end which was no part of his intention. . . . By pursuing his own interest he frequently promotes that of society more effectively than when he really intends to promote it.

—Adam Smith, Wealth of Nations

When I teach the history of economic thought, I usually make an offer on the first day of class that I will give an "A" to the student who can find a single favorable reference to a businessman anywhere in the 900 pages of Wealth of Nations by Adam Smith. No student has ever gotten an "A" that way. Few have gotten them any other way. You will find more denunciations of businessmen in Wealth of Nations than you will find in any other book that I know of, with the possible—and I say this advisedly—exception of Das Kapital by Karl Marx.

—Thomas Sowell, appearing on "Face the Nation"

T here is little competition for the title, "the father of capitalism"; that contest was won long ago, in 1776, by Adam Smith of Glasgow. In that year, the year of the American Declaration of Independence and the beginning of the Revolutionary War, Smith published his epoch-making book *Wealth of Nations.* It was a mammoth book, very much bound to its times, taking on the dominant but already outmoded economic theories of the eighteenth century and virtually inventing the field that we know as "economics." But the book did not just describe the conditions of mid-eighteenth century England; it set in motion an ideology that has ruled "free enterprise" discussions ever since. Proponents and antagonists of capitalism both trace themselves back to Adam Smith and declare themselves his "true" spokesmen. The book was not, as it is usually taught, just a classic treatise in economics; it is also a great work of "macroethics," a redefinition of the concepts of the good life. In this, it is a part of that long moral tradition that stretches back to Plato's *Republic* and Aristotle's *Politics.* Its subject matter is justice and the good society, not just the mechanisms of the market.

Adam Smith was born in Scotland in 1723, attended the University of Glasgow and then Balliol College, Oxford, in 1740. In 1748 he returned to Edinburgh and became a professor at the University of Glasgow, where he remained for the next decade. During that time, he published his first great book, *The Theory of Moral Sentiments* (1759), which made him well known and respected in the intellectual world. A wealthy duke hired him to be tutor to his stepson. This position allowed him to retire with a pension for life. It was during this time that he wrote *Wealth of Nations,* in quiet retirement in Kirkcaldly, Scotland. He died one of the most prominent men in Britain in 1790.

Most people know of Smith mainly through *Wealth of Nations,* but *The Theory of Moral Sentiments* is equally important for an understanding of his ethical views. The key to that work is the notion of *sympathy,* the compassionate feeling that ties us emotionally with other people and enables us to care for their well-being as well as for our own. It is sympathy that usually moves us to take sides in disputes, and it is sympathy, not a list of general moral principles, that allows us to know, in most cases, what is right and what is wrong. It is sympathy, too, that explains our sense of gratitude to others, which in turn determines our sense of justice and merit. Furthermore, quite the contrary of the rule of self-interest that so dominates *Wealth of Nations, The Theory of Moral Sentiments* places our sense of sympathy at the origins of our judgments of ourselves. "Conscience" is the voice of this reflective sense within us, and Smith assumes throughout his discussion the general acceptance of the social virtues of justice and concern for the well-being of others. Every individual can and should be ruled by this sense of sympathy and its consequent sense of virtue. Indeed, even the pursuit of our own "selfish" interests ought to be and usually is ruled by this same sense of virtue (called "prudence"). For Smith, as for so many other British moralists of his time, self-interest and interest in the well-being of others were not to be thought of as antagonistic but as complementary and mutually reinforcing. It was an ancient ideal, prominent, for example, in Plato and Aristotle: the good of the individual and the good of the community were one and the same.

It is in this amiable context that we should view the macroethical and economic theories of *Wealth of Nations.* Smith does not presume that all people are selfish, and he does not assume that the good society will result from individual pursuit of profits alone. Yet economic life, according to Smith, does indeed proceed on the principle of self-interest, namely that the general welfare will be served best if individuals are allowed to pursue their own financial well-being. Sympathy does not play a role in *Wealth of Nations.* And yet, what Smith means by "wealth" is itself a radical redefinition of that term as it was understood by the leaders of his time; and his redefinition, though not stated in terms of sympathy, nevertheless has his own virtues of justice and benevolence built into it.

Wealth, according to the reigning economic theorists of the day, was to be measured by the amount of precious metals—mainly gold and silver—locked away within the borders of the country, or, on an individual level, locked within a personal strongbox. This made some sense in the days of expansionist nationalism, when Louis XIV and the other kings of great nations needed gold to hire and equip armies to protect their countries. In place of this *mercantilist* definition of wealth, however, Smith proposed a sense of wealth in terms of consumer goods, and the wealth of the nation was not to be measured simply by the amount of gold and silver in its treasury but by the amount of consumer goods available to its citizens—*all* of its citizens. Thus, *Wealth of Nations* is already a powerful treatise on justice and the good society, even without saying so. The basic premise, so familiar to us that we do not even debate it, is already there; wealth is a function of the general well-being, not merely an economic function of the state, and not merely a function of the amount of gold. (Nor was it just a function of *land,* which was once the key to wealth in agricultural societies, but less so in urban industrialized societies, which England was just becoming.)

Much of *Wealth of Nations* is an attack on existing economic theories, and so of little interest to the modern reader. And many of its arguments are too specific to the times and industrial magnitude of early industrialized society, and so are dangerous examples, if not wholly irrelevant, to modern society. And yet again, the greatness of Adam Smith was that he also transcended his times, and came up with a vision of order and harmony in the already terrifying, dirty, and sometimes cruel industrial world, which was just beginning. Even those who reject major aspects of Smith's theories often do so by appeal to that same sense of order and harmony, and the revolutionary egalitarian view that wealth is a function of *everybody's* well-being.

The basic principles of Smith's economics, which are the basis of his ethical optimism as well as that of his ethical concern for the general well-being, are well known: central to his theory is the all-important **law of supply and demand,** which serves as the self-controlling device of society, preventing the greedy from getting too much and the poor from becoming poorer. It assures the adequate supply of consumer goods in society as well as an adequate pool of workers to produce them and capital to sponsor them. This law, in effect, supplies the "invisible hand" that is so often quoted from Smith's works. One powerful person's interests may well go unchecked to the destruction of the entire society; but a whole nation of competing self-interests will necessarily lead to prudence, to a balance of interests, and to the interplay of competitive forces that we refer to as "the free enterprise system."

It is absolutely essential to such a system, however, that no one person's or group's interests are capable of dominating all of the others. This starting point is familiar to readers of British philosophy; Thomas Hobbes, a century earlier, began his *Leviathan* with the stipulation that every man, being more or less vulnerable to the murderous ambitions of other men, would be equally willing to join in a "social contract" that would benefit everyone and, in effect, provide the foundations of a cooperative society. So too, in his time, Smith could safely assume that no manufacturer or industrialist could possibly take over an entire market. No one was big enough, and any overture to price-fixing or other dampers on competition would soon enough give new competitive advantages to one or another clever entrepreneur with a new idea or a more efficient technique. ("People of the same trade rarely meet together, but the conversation ends in a conspiracy against the public.") And there were too many of them. In that "nation of shopkeepers" (Smith's original phrase) there were so many people producing the basic implements of domestic usage that competition between them, and the impossibility of successful collusion, seemed to be one of those obvious facts of life. And of corporations, then, in their infancy, Smith had little to fear or say.

Competition is not itself a *moral virtue* for Smith, as so many of his successors would interpret it. Human nature was not inherently competitive, and competition was not considered the "proof" of manhood. Darwinism was still a century away (*Origin of Species* wasn't published until 1859) and the idea of the business world as a "jungle" was not yet even plausible. Indeed, beneath the bewildering confusion of thousands of cottage industries and before the smoke-filled cities that would so appall Friedrich Engels a century later, Smith perceived the world of British business as a civilized, respectable hive of busy bourgeoisie and laborers, in which all individuals doing their tasks and pursuing their own interests added up to the overall good of the whole. Competition was not itself a virtue; it provided the incentive for hard work and productivity, which were virtues. People supplied demands, and they demanded in turn. It was not a world of corporations and unimaginable luxuries; it was a world of small manufacturers, workers, and shopkeepers, supplying themselves and each other with the basics of a civilized existence: cloth, pins, kitchen utensils, and the necessities and comforts of life.

There was, however, one source of competition for these small manufacturers so powerful that, with a stroke of the pen or the sword, they could be put out of business or hampered in some less fatal way. That was the government, which in the era of nationalism and mercantilism, had indeed proven to be the single most disruptive and dampening element in business competition. In fact, much of the government interference in business was by way of *encouraging* enterprise and competition. (One of Louis XIV's ministers complained that he had to push the local industrialists toward making profits, even against their will.) But the fact remained that if Smith was right, if competition *alone* between the small businesses would optimize the well-being of the nation, then government must be kept out of business. Thus the French cry, *laissez faire,* was quickly taken from Smith's own views, though he had continuously warned against "the mean rapacity and monopolizing spirit" of merchants and manufacturers. But it was government alone that, in those days, provided the source of the greatest threat to the smooth working of the competitive enterprise system. It is with that in mind that we must understand Smith's insistence that the government should leave the market alone. Though this is now considered a "conservative" position, then it was thought of as a radical and "liberal" view.*

In his *Theory of Moral Sentiments,* Smith stated clearly his confidence in the reality of human sympathy and benevolence. On a person-to-person level, perhaps, this is the key to our behavior, however quickly some cynics will point out the exceptions. But from the viewpoint of the wealth of the society as a whole, Smith was not in the least inclined to trust sympathy as the motive or mechanism; there he cited self-interest. "It is not from the benevolence of the butcher, the brewer or the baker that we expect our dinner, but from regard to their self-interest. We address ourselves not to their humanity, but to their self-love, and never talk to them of our necessities, but of their advantages." And yet, whether the language is one of "our necessities" or "their advantages," it is clear to everyone that both are involved by way of a competitive game, requiring both strategy and cooperation. In such simple economic confrontation, the microethics of the situation are as simple as the microeconomics; don't cheat or steal, but buy as cheaply as you can, sell as dearly as you can. And in a world of dozens or perhaps hundreds of other shopkeepers, where the customer can easily bargain, the butcher, the brewer, and the baker cannot afford to simply charge whatever they would like. But so too in a world filled with customers, the shopkeepers and the manufacturers know that they are also in a bargaining position. This is supply and demand; in a nation of shopkeepers and small manufacturers, it explains a great deal. And it explains not only the amount of goods available and the prices charged for them; it also explains, and in just the same terms, the supply of workers and the demand for their labor, as well as the prices that they can charge for their labor and their willingness to take one job or another.

The ethics of Adam Smith are not so mechanical as his economics, however. Underlying his theory of competition is a *utilitarian* acceptance of human material desires as the ultimate good of society and the proper aim of an economy. It was not always so; whole economies have been geared to war or to the funeral preparations of the pharaoh or king, and whole societies have dismissed individual desires as vulgar and profane. But notice, too, that the idea of a self-regulating economic system was not of ethical importance to Adam Smith, except as a

---

*It is worth noting that the word "liberal" traditionally refers to the "free market" proponent, who is now considered a "conservative."

means to promote the overall good of society. Indeed, if it had proven to him that individual people would be best off and happiest under a dictatorial society, or with extensive government regulation of industry, he probably would have accepted that, as he did accept all kinds of government interference in private lives and business when the national interests or the interests of justice were involved. The value of the autonomous businessman or the autonomy of business was not part of his philosophy; in fact, he had little confidence in the personal beneficence of businessmen, and had nothing flattering to say about them throughout *Wealth of Nations*. But what he did believe was that small-business men, left to pursue their own interests without even a hint of concern for the public interest, much less speeches about their "social responsibility," would improve the wealth of the society immensely, provide consumer goods efficiently at a reasonable price, and provide work for the laborers, including modest comforts for many. The ethical justification of his system was not that business is in itself good or exhilarating or the proper way for a person to spend his time, but that it would provide "universal opulence even to the lowest ranks of people." Today, this is looked upon with suspicion as "the trickle-down effect," but in 1776, it was an attempt to recognize that the needs and desires of the poor were also to be measured into the wealth of the nation, and so to be included in the justification of business economics as well.

Smith's macroethics, accordingly, can be simply stated: the justification of the business world is the fact that it can, through the law of supply and demand and by assuring competition, best ensure the improvement of society, including the bettering of the condition of those who are the worst off. If it does not have that effect, then it fails the ethical test, whatever might be said about the wisdom of its economic mechanism. Individual well-being is "the bottom line" of Smith's philosophy, and though businesspeople throughout the world may still pay homage to him as the first and foremost defender of the free enterprise system, Ralph Nader and the American consumer owe him at least an equal debt of gratitude. As Robert Heilbroner sums it up, "For the first time in the philosophy of everyday life, the consumer is king."

GREAT LINES FROM *WEALTH OF NATIONS*

ADAM SMITH

The property which every man has in his own labour, as it is the original foundation of all other property, so it is the most sacred and inviolable.

People of the same trade seldom meet together, even for merriment and diversion, but the conversation ends in a conspiracy against the public, or in some contrivance to raise prices.

The desire for food is limited in every man by the narrow capacity of the human stomach; but the desire for the conveniences and ornaments of building, dress, equipage, and household furniture, seem to have no limit or certain boundary.

With the greater part of rich people, the chief enjoyment of riches consists in the parade of riches, which in their eyes is never so complete as when they appear to possess those decisive marks of opulence which nobody can possess but themselves.

To widen the market and to narrow the competition is always the interest of the dealers. . . . The proposal of any new law or regulation of commerce which comes from this order, ought always to be listened to with great precaution, and ought never to be adopted, till after having been long and carefully examined, not only with the most scrupulous, but with the most suspicious attention. It comes from an order of men, whose interest is never exactly the same with that of the public, who have generally an interest to deceive and even to oppress the public, and who accordingly have, upon many occasions, both deceived and oppressed it.

The division of labour . . . is the necessary, though very slow and gradual, consequence of a certain propensity in human nature . . . to truck, barter, and exchange one thing for another.

Nobody ever saw a dog make a fair and deliberate exchange of one bone for another with another dog.

It is not from the benevolence of the butcher, the brewer, or the baker that we expect our dinner, but from their regard to their own interest. We address ourselves, not to their humanity but to their self-love, and never talk to them of our own necessities but of their advantages.

If among a nation of hunters . . . it usually costs twice the labour to kill a beaver which it does to kill a deer, one beaver should naturally exchange for or be worth two deer.

We rarely hear, it has been said, of the combinations of the masters; though frequently of those of workmen. But whoever imagines, upon this account, that masters rarely combine, is as ignorant of the world as of the subject. Masters are always and everywhere in a sort of tacit, but constant and uniform combination, not to raise the wages of labour above its natural rate.

No society can surely be flourishing and happy, of which the far greater part of the members are poor and miserable.

Wherever there is great property, there is great inequality. For one very rich man, there must be at least five hundred poor, and the affluence of the few supposes the indigence of the many.

Bankruptcy is perhaps the greatest and most humiliating calamity which can befall an innocent man.

The uniform, constant, and uninterrupted effort of every man to better his condition, the principle from which public and national, as well as private opulence is originally derived, is frequently powerful enough to maintain the natural progress of things toward improvement, in spite of both the extravagance of government, and of the greatest errors of administration.

It is the highest impertinence and presumption . . . in kings and ministers, to pretend to watch over the economy of private people, and to restrain their expence, either by sumptuary laws, or by prohibiting the importation of foreign luxuries. They are themselves always, and without exception, the greatest spend-thrifts in society. . . . If their own extravagance does not ruin the state, that of their subjects never will.

[Every individual generally] neither intends to promote the public interest, nor knows how much he is promoting it. . . . [H]e is in this case, as in many cases, led by an invisible hand to promote an end which was no part of his intention. Nor is it always the worse for society that it was no part of it. By pursuing his own interest he frequently promotes that of society more effectually than when he really intends to promote it. I have never known much good done by those who affected to trade for the public good. It is an affectation, indeed, not very common among merchants, and very few words need be employed in dissuading them from it.

The violence and injustice of the rulers of mankind is an ancient evil, for which, I am afraid, the nature of human affairs can scarce admit of a remedy. But the mean rapacity, the monopolizing spirit of merchants and manufacturers, who neither are, nor ought to be the rulers of mankind, though it cannot perhaps be corrected, may very easily be prevented from disturbing the tranquillity of any-body but themselves.

The natural effort of every individual to better his own condition, when suffered to exert itself with freedom and security, is so powerful, that it is alone, and without any assistance, not only capable of carrying on the society to wealth and prosperity, but of surmounting a hundred impertinent obstructions with which the folly of human laws too often encumbers its operations.

To found a great empire for the sole purpose of raising up a people of customers may at first appear a project fit only for a nation of shopkeepers.

Consumption is the sole end and purpose of all production; and the interest of the producer ought to be attended to, only so far as it may be necessary for promoting that of the consumer.

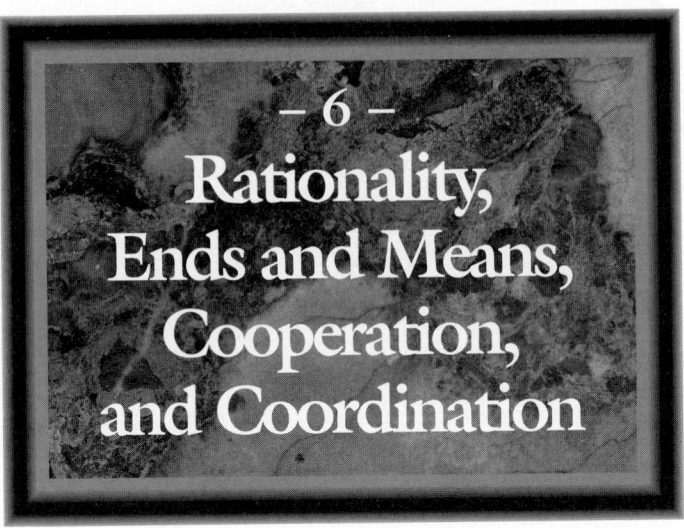

– 6 –
Rationality, Ends and Means, Cooperation, and Coordination

The day might not be far off when everyone will be rich. Then we will once again value ends above means.
—J. M. Keynes, "Economic Possibilities for Our Children"

E very business decision can be made well or badly, wisely or foolishly, with a high probability of good results or the likelihood of failure. Knowing what the goal is, choosing the best means to that goal, recognizing the optimal strategy—all these are involved, in addition to a little luck, in getting what we want. This is just as true of our pursuit of happiness and the good life as it is in the more tangible negotiations of a business deal. In both ethics and game theory, this recognition of ends and means is summarized in an all-important ideal—*rationality*. Indeed, the ancient Greek philosophers, and many contemporary philosophers too, simply sum up the good life itself as the life of rationality. It consists of a kind of clarity, a kind of self-knowledge—knowing who we are, what we want, and what we ought to do to get it.

Rationality begins with our ability to reflect and understand, our ability to weigh alternatives, and recognize the best ways to do things. But it also consists of our recognition of how we fit into the scheme of things, our place in our own society, the effects of our actions on other people, and the rules and expectations within which we act as social beings. To be rational is to act according to rules and expectations not merely our own, as well as to act in such a way as to get what we want and live well. Happily, these two dimensions of rationality usually coincide, and the way to social acceptance and the way to happiness are one and the same.

In business life, we can discern the same two dimensions of rationality at work in virtually every decision we make. There is the necessity of knowing what the goals of the company are and how our own tasks fit into them. There is the necessity to weigh alternative courses of action with an eye to those goals and, at the same time, weigh the more personal advantages and disadvantages of the various options. But equally important is knowing the rules and expectations—both explicit and merely implicit—that govern the range of possible decisions and courses of action. A strategy that is completely common and legitimate in one form of business might be totally unacceptable in another. Rationality consists *both* of the recognition of the best means to the right end and the recognition of the social and ethical context within which those ends and means are acceptable.

We must distinguish rationality, in the sense that we are concerned with here, from its more restricted sense in contrast with passion and emotion. We often distinguish rationality and reason from passions and emotions, the former being "cool" and "reasonable," the latter explosive, disruptive, "blind," and unreasonable (*ir*rational). But if rationality in the sense we mean it here has to do with recognizing the good life and living it, there is no reason to suppose that emotions and "being emotional" might not be just as crucial to that recognition and that life as the calmer deliberations of reason. Indeed, we could argue forcefully that the emotions make the good life so good, render life meaningful, and put the sparkle in our actions, our cares, and our concerns. Two hundred years ago, the Scotch philosopher David Hume summed up this view by saying, "Reason is, and ought to be, the slave of the passions." So when we stress the importance of rationality, we are by no means insisting that the good life is without emotion, without its loves, hates, indignations, perhaps even its envy and contempt. The good life includes spontaneity, passion, "losing your temper," and "falling in love." Emotions too are rational or irrational—just as reason is—insofar as they contribute to, or interfere with, the good life. A rational decision is not always calm and deliberative; sometimes our best decisions are made in "the heat of the moment," by "intuition," or "on a hunch."

Rationality is also to be contrasted not so much with nonrationality, that is, the unthinking life of plants and most animals, but rather with *irrationality,* picking the *wrong* strategy, the wrong ends or means, *not* knowing who or what we are and not understanding our place in the general scheme of things. Irrationality may be simple self-destructiveness; for example, an employee in a fit of rage and resentment may tell the boss what he thinks of her and systematically dump out the content of his files onto the office floor. But irrationality may also be the more subtle and less emotional mistakes of a decision not sufficiently thought through or adequately researched. Irrationality may be being blinded by the promise of some immediate reward at the expense of future possibilities or in the face of future disaster. It may be differing in opinion so much with colleagues or companions that what is said no longer has any foundation in shared beliefs and values, even if these differences do not lead to any tangible tragedy or faulty decision.

Rational Management: A Bit Irrational ——

Why do so many managers who appear crisp, logical, and determined at the conference table frequently accomplish little or nothing when they return to their offices? But why do other managers work effectively both within and outside the organizations and produce a string of significant accomplishments in a short time . . . ?

Our analysis suggests a reasonable, but perhaps surprising, conclusion: managers who consistently accomplish a lot are notably inconsistent in their manner of attacking problems. They continually change their focus, their priorities, their behavior patterns with superiors and subordinates, and indeed their own "executive styles." In contrast, managers who consistently accomplish little are usually predictably constant in what they concentrate on and how they go at their work. Consistency, if our study is correct, is indeed the hobgoblin of small and inconsequential accomplishment. . . .

In other words, low accomplishers tend to develop a set style or approach, and, when they err, it is always in the same particular direction. Consistency is their downfall, not only a general consistency of style, but also a tendency to persist in using a limited number of tools and techniques, based on a small assortment of managerial premises which they use over and over again.

In contrast, each outstanding achiever in our cases not only had a different executive style, but was inconsistent in personal style. Paradoxically, successful implementors have many styles. They are regularly inconsistent.

Wickham Skinner and W. Earl Sasser, "Managers with Impact,
Versatility and Inconsistency,"
Harvard Business Review, Nov.–Dec. 1977

Rationality, and irrationality too, are tied up with a shared way of looking at things, an agreed-upon framework of values and strategies. Sometimes, within that framework, a new value or a new strategy may be recognized as superior to all the others. But most of the time, values and strategies that may well be accepted and effective in some other context will simply seem irrational and not make any sense at all. The management procedures of some other cultures, as in Theory Z communal effort in Japan, to take a simple technical example, may appear to be utter nonsense to our business culture; yet, in that context, such procedures may work just as well. The life of a Benedictine monk, to take a more ethical and philosophical example, may well have been one of the most rational options for a religious person in the twelfth century, but that life may seem utterly irrational now, for instance, if chosen by a successful executive who decides to "drop out" and seek a better life.

A. RATIONALITY: ENDS AND MEANS

Rationality is not a simple or singular concept. We have already pointed out two different dimensions of rationality that can sometimes point in opposite directions, as when a person's or company's interests conflict with the acceptable courses of action within a social context. Furthermore, there is the very important difference between long-term and short-term rationality; what may be of enormous profit in the short run (for example, selling the machines that are essential to your industry) may be disastrous in the longer run. (What counts as short and long term, of course, depends on the context; in the commodity market, long-term may be a matter of weeks, while in the automobile business it is a matter of years if not decades.) But even in the simple distinction between means and ends, there may be (and almost always is) a complex hierarchy or continuum of means and ends, making the rational course of action more complex in turn.

To begin with, we might be rational in the recognition of goals (ends) but irrational in the choice of means; or we might be irrational in the choice of ends but perfectly rational in obtaining them. An example of the first case would be a person in business who knows, rightly, that her goal in life is power; but instead of working her way up the corporate ladder to a position of power, she bullies everyone, making enemies and virtually guaranteeing that she will never be promoted to any position of power at all. An example of the second would be an executive who believes that the only way to the good life is to ruthlessly pursue the largest profits, at whatever cost in terms of good will, friendship, and public relations. But, in fact, he proves himself to be a perfect business game player, bluffing out the opposition, overbidding and underbidding with calculated precision, winning every confrontation with the most rational strategy and the best planned tactics. And yet, he might be the first to admit that, though he loves the thrill of the game, every victory leaves him feeling empty and unfulfilled. Thus, we can see two quite distinct sources of rationality and irrationality; one concerning the recognition of the ends of the good life, the other concerning the means for obtaining those ends.

This conception of rationality is further complicated, however, by the fact that we often talk of ends, means, and rationality within carefully confined contexts. For example, in playing poker the odds against any given hand are calculable and players should have some rough idea what they are. The psychology of the opponents is also, at least to some extent, knowable, and even if they were strangers before the game, a player will learn a great deal by watching them even through the first few hands. The end of poker is clearly *winning,* and that means walking away from the table with as much money as possible. Rationality, in one obvious sense, is recognizing this end.

In our second sense, rationality is playing the best strategy, playing the odds, taking only *calculated* risks. Playing poker rationally is, in the words of the Kenny Rogers song, the ability to "know when to hold 'em, know when to fold 'em, know when to walk away, know when to run." Psychological strategies

Long Term, Short Term ——

In Japan . . . people are not judged on performance during a short period of time, under pressure, say, to produce an increase in earnings. Executives can take a longer perspective in guiding the organization, which is considered perpetual.

—Toshio Ozeki, Nikko Securities Corp., Tokyo

One common criticism of contemporary business ethics is that it is too concentrated on the short term, on results within the year or even within the quarter, rather than the decade or longer. In some industries, long-term planning is absolutely essential, for example, in heavy industry (automobiles or steel). And yet, chief executives of those same companies are often measured by company performance within a period of a few years, or less. What effect will this have on the longer-term health of the company and the industry as a whole? What kinds of strategy would be personally advantageous to an executive in such a position? What steps would you suggest to optimize the company's long-term interest?

A Tool That Starves the Golden Goose

To most people, "discounted cash flow" is just a puzzling piece of jargon. To business, however, it is a basic tool, as common as an attache case, as influential as the computers. Few factories are built, new ventures launched, or other expensive commitments made unless they satisfy the test of discounted cash flow. And according to Robert H. Hayes of Harvard, this basic yardstick is badly warped.

In simplest terms, discounted cash flow merely reflects the fact that a dollar in hand today is worth more than a dollar later. A dollar in hand can be put to work—invested at a profit. The discounted cash flow technique is an effort to express the value, in today's dollars, of projects that will throw off cash 10 or 20 years down the road. As an example, it would take $100,000 ten years from now to equal $24,718 today, if interest rates are assumed to remain at 15 percent. Thus, investing more than $24,718 to earn $100,000 ten years later would be losing money.

According to Mr. Hayes, the tool as applied, has an inherent bias against capital spending that leads companies to under-invest in their businesses. He contends the tool has led to severe disinvestment in American industry, enough to threaten the economy's future. "Present value calculations support a decision to operate on the goose and remove some of its golden eggs prematurely," Mr. Hayes writes in the current *Harvard Business Review,* "even though doing so impairs its future egg-laying ability. . . . "

Most telling, Mr. Hayes says, the tool allows managers to avoid hard decisions. "Managers can all too easily hide behind the apparent rationality of such financial analyses while sidestepping the hard decisions necessary to keep their companies competitive," he asserts.

The New York Times, May 12, 1982

make this notion of rationality more complicated, but they do not change the notion of rationality itself. The aim is still to win and the most rational strategy is still the strategy that allows a player to win. Rationality, in short, basically amounts to being good at the game.

But now, we can ask a quite different question: is playing poker itself rational? In asking this, we are in effect asking what the end of playing the game is, as opposed to the end of the game itself. We are asking whether playing poker is the best means to this other end. Sometimes, this question can be easily answered; sometimes, it cannot be. For instance, if two executives on a long cross-country flight play poker to enjoy themselves and "kill time," it is fairly easy to evaluate both the end and the means. Their end is rational if, for instance, neither has urgent work to do, or is really too tired and ought to be sleeping. The means (playing poker) is rational insofar as they do thereby enjoy themselves, instead of, for example, getting so furious with each other that they do not enjoy themselves at all and finally land at their destination with the strong mutual feeling that they would both be far better off if they had spent their time reading magazines or talking to the other passengers. But this pair of questions about rationality is virtually independent of the question of the rationality of their actual poker playing. It might be quite irrational for them to play the game (since both of them have urgent reports to dictate and neither of them actually enjoys playing the game), yet their poker playing itself might be perfectly rational. Or, they might be perfectly rational by playing poker (for it is indeed the best way to "kill time," allowing them to enjoy themselves and arrive at their destination relatively relaxed and refreshed) but their playing itself may be perfectly abysmal (much to the chagrin of the professional poker player sitting across the aisle from them).

This difference between "levels" or contexts of rationality can sometimes be captured by our earlier distinction between **intrinsic** and **extrinsic** goals or ends, with a corollary sense of intrinsic and extrinsic rationality. We might teach a child a game or a skill by offering a reward, for instance, encouraging a child to learn to play the piano by offering him candy for playing. This is extrinsic motivation and involves an extrinsic goal, not at all related to the activity itself. But once the child has learned to play, the activity itself—playing well—is its own reward.

The Ethics of Saving: Long-Term and Short-Term Goals ——

The maturing baby-boomers, twenty-five to forty-four years old, don't really know what it means to save. And they have their corporate counterparts. The corporate treasurer who borrowed to the hilt ten years ago at a long-term fixed rate of 8 percent is a hero and probably insured his corporate career. The corporate treasurer who kept the nickels intact is a chump. . . . Nevertheless, we now have a problem with our corporations: they have piled up so much debt that their balance sheets are askew and they have lost much of the liquidity that comes with savings. This means that they must go to the marketplace to borrow more frequently.

Whom do they meet in the marketplace, bidding for the savings? First of all, the government, which is living beyond its means to the tune of $100 billion or so this year. Second, the millions of individuals who borrow through their banks and with credit cards. And yet we are surprised when all these bidders push interest rates up to new highs!

We have, rather belatedly, a Congress and an administration that have tried to do something about saving. It makes sense to encourage people to save with expanded Individual Retirement Accounts and Keogh plans, because that retirement money will stay put for a long time. It made very little sense in terms of saving to permit tax-exempt All-Savers Certificates, because that money is around for only a year at a time, not long enough to loan out for long-term projects. But at least there is a sense in Washington that something ought to be done to encourage saving; the results of the Japanese practice of saving four or five times the percentage of earnings that we save are now apparent.

This is more than a financial problem. There is a very deep-seated instinct in mature people and in productive societies to build things, to leave something for the next generation. A hundred years ago in this country that might have meant leaving a farm in good working order or participating in the development of one's town or community. It takes a generation to grow good trees (even in this country of instant gratification, no one has produced an instant tree). A farm that consumed its seed corn was out of business. Nationally, we have been living on our seed corn.

"Adam Smith," *Esquire,* April 1982

This is intrinsic motivation, the goal of the activity itself. In poker, we have to make a more subtle distinction; the aim of the game is to win. This is the intrinsic goal. One reason for playing the game, however, is also to make money (as opposed, for example, to "killing time" and enjoying oneself, though presumably a rather good player could pursue both ends at once). This is the extrinsic goal. The two ends look the same, but in fact they are not. The intrinsic goal of winning might be served just as well by pieces of paper or poker chips rather than actual money (or its substitutes); the extrinsic goal of making money requires actual cash with real purchasing power, and this is the reason for playing the game. Intrinsic goals and intrinsic rationality concern the goals and best strategies within the game; extrinsic goals and extrinsic rationality concern the reasons for playing the game in the first place.

This distinction has one particularly practical application. One way of describing rationality, in more routine and everyday terms, is to talk about **efficiency.** To do something efficiently is to do it in the most rational way. But efficiency only measures the most rational way of doing a particular activity; it is an open question whether that activity is itself appropriate or conducive to realizing overall goals. That is, the most *efficient* way of doing something might not be the most *effective* way. For example, it is not uncommon for managers to be highly efficient around the office, in fact getting a great deal of work accomplished in a minimum of time. But, if it is the *wrong work* or if it takes up time from other activities that might better serve the goals of the department, it may nevertheless be ineffective.

There are people who are extremely efficient in their personal lives too. They make lists and establish priorities; they are demanding that things are done correctly and intolerant of waste and scornful of inefficiency. The problem is that they thus reduce their lives to lists and demands, devoid of relaxation and the sheer enjoyment of wasting time and taking it easy. They may impose expectations on themselves and others that are so precise that interpersonal relations become more like negotiating sessions than companionship and sharing. And in the end, they may be less effective in their goals because of their efficiency. The good life, we may say, is not always the most efficient way of living. Indeed, it might be persuasively argued that taking care of details and trying to tie up all the loose ends in the rather chaotic tapestry of life is a sure way of *not* living the good life, by trying to make it more precise and predictable than it could possibly be.

We could pursue this idea of levels of rationality further by asking what the purpose of "enjoyment" might be, or for what reason the poker player wants to make money. In the first case enjoyment is an end in itself, not a strategy for anything else. When someone wants to make money, however, it is clear that, in addition to asking whether a certain activity is the best way to make money, we can also ask: Why should the player want money? The answer is not obvious. The player may be extremely rich already. And if playing poker also involves nonfinancial risks that the player can ill afford (such as the risk of heart attack

Efficiency and Effectiveness ———

The key to success in business management, we are often told, is **efficiency.** Efficiency means doing most rationally what is already being done, getting the most production with the least cost. **Effectiveness,** however, may be more critical to a company's success than efficiency. Effectiveness is the focus on overall results, rather than just the most efficient means to an already established end. If the overall results are inadequately conceived, all of the efficiency in the world will not produce success. As Peter Drucker comments, "No amount of efficiency would have enabled the manufacturer of buggy whips to survive."

Efficiency is essential to good business, of course; a business will go bankrupt without it. But efficiency always requires a framework of effectiveness, that is, efficiency *at the right projects, aimed towards the right goals.* Quoting Drucker again: "Effectiveness is the foundation of success—efficiency is a minimum condition for survival *after* success has been achieved. Efficiency is concerned with doing things right. Effectiveness is doing the right things."

from the tension or the risk of being seen in an "immoral" game by others), the extrinsic end (making money) as well as the means (playing poker) might be seen to be irrational.

B.   PROFIT: ENDS OR MEANS

In talking about business ethics, I hope that it is obvious why the concepts of rationality, ends and means, and intrinsic-extrinsic goals might be valuable to us. For example, it is often said that the end of business activities is to make profits. But a corporate president, though interested in company profits, usually sees these profits as a means to personal goals of money, power within the company, and a future with the company. But are profits intrinsic or extrinsic goals of business? Are all means of making profits equally rational? With reference to what further goals are we to judge this? To what extent are profits the goal of business itself (that is, the whole world of business)? To what extent are they the goal of particular businesses? To what extent are they the goals of people in business? And if we decide that profits are the *intrinsic* goals of business activity, what are the *extrinsic* goals that making profits serve? For individuals, the extrinsic goal, at least up to a certain income level, is presumably purchasing power, but it is not at all clear what the comparable intrinsic goal might be for corporations or for business as such. Some profits, of course, go into further capital investment; others go to the stockholders. But what is the purpose of this except to make

The Bridge on the River Kwai ——

In the movie *Bridge on the River Kwai,* the British officer (played by Alec Guinness) is assigned by his Japanese captors to build a bridge of enormous strategic importance for the Japanese. To keep himself and his men in good spirits and to fill the desperate time of their captivity, the officer throws himself and his men into the project. But the bridge, of course, is strategic to the enemy, and thus directly against the British interest, which is winning the war. The irony of the movie is that the British officer gets so caught up in his task, and is so proud of its results, that he actually resists the Allied attempt to destroy his handiwork.

This is a classic illustration of irrationality, in the sense that a subordinate goal has come to obstruct the ultimate goal. The building of the bridge is the end of the captives' activity, but it is certainly not the ultimate end; indeed, it is directly opposed to their ultimate goal of winning the war against the Japanese. Even assuming that they were perfectly rational in building the bridge, therefore, we would have to say that, insofar as they resisted or resented its destruction, they were irrational.

more profits, spur more investment to buy more capital to make further profits and so on? Somewhere, the question has to be answered, What are the profits for?

The classic economic answer, though sometimes buried under the rhetoric of "free enterprise," is "for the overall well-being of society" or, in Adam Smith's classic phrase, "for the wealth of the nation." But this raises an all-important point, namely, that the whole of business activity, the whole of the business world, the whole world of profits, capital, and investment can and must be viewed as itself subservient to a further goal, which accordingly serves as the justification for that world. The business world exists because in fact, or at least by way of promise, it best serves the well-being of society as a whole. The intrinsic motivation may be the maximization of profits, just as the intrinsic motivation of poker is winning as much money as possible (within the rules of the game). But any number of intrinsic constraints can determine what the most rational means to do this might be. Also an overriding system of social goals that are extrinsic goals, and therefore extrinsic constraints, determine to what extent the free enterprise system is itself a rational system and to what extent it must be modified, limited, or expanded to serve those external goals. It is all so easy within that world—as within a poker game—to take our efforts so seriously that we lose sight of the extrinsic and overriding goals of the activity itself.

We can, on occasion, complain that certain efforts to protect the extrinsic goals unduly interfere with the intrinsic goals and rationality of the activity, thereby jeopardizing the success of the activity in realizing the extrinsic goals.

For example, playing poker "for fun" does not mean that someone shout continuously, "Remember, it's only a game." That may be true, but the enjoyment of playing the game nevertheless requires taking it seriously and, at least for a while, not thinking of it as "only a game." Similarly, it may be that society attempts to protect its interests by regulating or monitoring business in such a way that it actually interferes with business' efforts to promote the good for society. But on the other hand, it may also be the case that government or public pressure groups quite rightly restrict the activities of business, if in fact business is not fulfilling its extrinsic goal of serving society. This is to say that business itself is not the ultimate context and so does not itself determine what is rational and what is not rational. Business is part of and is to be judged in terms of a larger context that enables it to exist and flourish in the first place. That larger context is society.

In Chapter 9 we will discuss in some detail the much debated question of the "social responsibilities" of business. But for now, it is only necessary to point out that the standards of rationality for business—not only in terms of acceptable means to make a profit but also in terms of the ultimate ends of profit as such—is both an intrinsic matter and an extrinsic question concerning how business fits into the rest of society. Profits undoubtedly motivate much of business activity and have as their consequence the invention and production of beneficial and even life-saving products and devices. But the connection between the motivation to profit and the desired effects of that motivation are essential here, and the rationality not only of particular business decisions but of business itself depends upon this connection.

"The profit motive" is said to be the sole aim of business enterprise. The businessperson, of course, wants to make a profit. Profits guarantee the survival and the growth of the company. Profits prove the ability of the employees in the business; profits keep investors investing. Profits allow for a wide range of activities (many of which may only marginally be business related, or not at all). But, if we were to think of business as a gigantic game, we would still have to say that its intrinsic goal, to make profits, is still subservient to further goals (the well-being of society and the success or survival of the individual businesspeople within that corporation and in the business world more generally) and that it is by no means the only goal in business. We might even argue that making profits is more like a *condition* for continuing business life than its goal. We need only look at the most routine forms of office life, as opposed to the abstract figures on the financial pages, to see that business has many goals that are far more important than profits.

Making profits is obviously one of the ends of business. It is also the most common and plausible justification for the free market system in providing a supply of quality products to meet consumer demand and enrich the lives of people not themselves in business. One of the arguments for profit, in fact, is that profits make possible expansion and research in order to provide more and better products to meet existing and increasing demands. And yet, in the arguments about "the profit motive," this all-important goal of quality and supply is often left out, as if the pursuit of profit were an end in itself. But the "social responsibilities" of business are nowhere more in evidence and undebatable than in the imperative to do what the free market system is supposed to do: supply and satisfy consumer demand and produce the best products possible to do so. Is this an extrinsic goal for business or an intrinsic goal? Defenders of the profit motive would say it is the former, but we can easily see why it might better be considered as the latter. Serving society with its products and satisfying the demand for goods is not just a function we would like the business world to play in society, it is also the intrinsic goal of the business world itself, indeed one of the primary ends that the means of "the profit motive" is meant to serve.

It is surprising, from this perspective, that the question, Does business have social responsibilities? should still be asked by anyone. Indeed, the question prompts another question: What would it possibly mean to say that business does not have social responsibilities? No activity—particularly no activity with so many energetic players, so many rules, and so many consequences—is performed for no purpose at all. We might suggest that business is one of those few activities that might plausibly be said to be performed "for its own sake." But this is demonstrably false, both in terms of the motives of almost everyone in the business world (how many people would accept their jobs without salary, "just for its own sake"?) and in terms of the actual deliberations and decisions of business. (Is there any company in the world that has no *reason* to make profits, no purpose to put them to, no concern what happens to them once they are made, so long as they produce in turn more profits?) We need not use the loaded term "responsibility" to make the point, but the very existence of business as a legitimate activity rests on the theory that our "free market" business system is the most rational way of maximizing the general social well-being. If it does not do this, it loses its reason for existence, and no amount of pleasure or desire to simply manufacture widgets will warrant its continued existence if it fails to serve this end.

This argument is sometimes presented in a subtle way, classically by Adam Smith, currently by Milton Friedman. In distinguishing between intrinsic and extrinsic goals and rationality, we mentioned that, *within* the scope of an activity or a game, a person may well lose sight of the extrinsic goals that performing the activity or playing the game is supposed to serve. This is natural enough. But Adam Smith's theory is that, even if all of the participants in business are ignorant or neglectful of the overriding social goals of their activity, nevertheless, those goals will be served, as if, to use his eloquent image, "an invisible hand" will guide all of our independent selfish pursuits and lead them in the direction of the common good. Of course, this theory had a complex and sophisticated argument behind it, with economic presuppositions—and problems—that we will not explore now. However, the conclusion of his argument is that business ought to be allowed (with certain qualifications) "free" rein of its activities, including making money, whether or not individual businesspeople are aware of the fact that their activities aim collectively towards the common good.

Does Management Mean Efficiency? ——

The problem is one we do not like to face. American government may be bureaucratic and inefficient, but American industry is just as bureaucratic and inefficient.

Who works for a firm that has not added some new layers of management in the last ten years? Who works for a firm that does not generate huge amounts of paper reports—most of which do not get read, much less acted upon? Who works for a firm that has fired secretaries and insisted that managers do their own typing since the introduction of word processors?

What firm has taken the ruthless steps to raise office productivity that it would take without hesitancy to raise factory productivity? What firm does not now have a bigger legal staff? What firm has really used computers to get that much prophesied office revolution under way? What private managers are trying to improve decision-making so that they can fire managers?

The answer: almost none. Those 5.5 million new white-collar workers prove it.

America is becoming a white-collar bureaucratic nation partly because our education system is supplying vast numbers of new workers who are trained to be bureaucrats. And as is now the fashion in supply-side economics, supply creates its own demand.

Lester Thurow, *Newsweek,* Aug. 24, 1981

Adam Smith's image alters our picture in a psychologically confusing way. On the one hand, serving the common good is still essential to the justification of business life, but on the other hand, this need not in any sense be the *motive* of actual business participants, who may be looking only after their own profits and interests. What Smith's theory means, therefore, is that we have to distinguish further between the intrinsic and extrinsic goals and rationality *of the activity itself,* and the goals and rationality of the individual players (including individual companies and corporations). This does not in any way undermine the essential claim—that business owes its continued existence to its satisfying of the extrinsic goals concerning the well-being of society. What it does introduce is the danger that businesspeople and their economic defenders, looking only at the intrinsic goals of business and looking only askance at the extrinsic social goals, will defend their activities solely in terms of intrinsic goals, thus giving the rest of society the unavoidable impression that profits are indeed their only concern, whether or not society *might* benefit from business' profit-making activities.

Just as a rational activity might have irrational goals, or as a rational end might be served by irrational means, so, too, we have to understand that "rationality" is an ideal we can only approximate by various means (for example, by computing the exact probabilities in a poker game). But when what is at stake is as vague and open to individual nuances and interpretations as "the good life," our concept of rationality must be accordingly loosened and made less precise. It is not clear that there is any single set of goals that will serve everyone as the ends of the good life, nor is it probable that any single set of goals—apart from the provision of the basic necessities of life to everyone—will serve as the undebatable ends of what we are calling "the common good" or "social well-being."

Even Adam Smith was ultimately uncertain whether consumer goods alone should count as "the wealth of nations," and we, too, can and do debate endlessly the importance of material comforts and luxuries over more spiritual and aesthetic riches, the advantages of labor-saving devices over the discipline of hard work, the value of a person's time versus the pay for that time, the importance of leisure time versus work time, family ties versus business success, public works and spaces versus privacy and private possession of property. But what this introduces into our consideration is a highly *subjective* element: different viewpoints and different values, none of which are clearly superior or inferior, some of which suit some people and some of which suit others. Given a fairly precise goal—for instance, how to maximize profit in a certain business venture—it might be possible to give a precise *objective* account of the rational course of action. To say that there is an objective account is to say that there is a single account that all people will agree to, once they have understood it. To say that some of our considerations are subjective, therefore, particularly regarding our choice of ultimate ends, is to say that there is no single account that virtually all people will agree to, even if they understand it. We are *not* saying that the account is merely arbitrary or whimsical, that it cannot be defended or justified, that it is irrational or contrary to rationality. We must allow for flexibility where flexibility is required and insist that there may be various conceptions of the good life and various ways of living well, all of which can be articulated and defended as rational and shown to be livable in a consistent, satisfactory way in a given community with given (even if debated or confused) cultural standards.

C.   RATIONALITY AND INTERSUBJECTIVITY

In a somewhat ascetic religious society, it would be quite clear that wealth and merit would not be evaluated primarily on material gains; indeed, to place the value of possessions above the value of the soul would be considered the height of irrationality. On the other hand, in a particularly materialistic consumer community, a person who abstained from ownership of any comfort or luxury would be considered eccentric, at least. Rationality thus has a social component—it presupposes an appeal to socially accepted values and priorities. Of course, most people will quickly add that their priorities are the *correct* priorities and that the others are quaint diversions or curiosities (or worse). Nevertheless, without entering into the difficult question of whether all values are indeed "relative" (that is, relative to a particular community, a particular place, a particular time), we can see that one of the determinants of rationality is going to be the social context.

In a society that has so many conflicting values affecting us all at once, however, this "relative" nature of rationality takes on an individual importance as well. Each of us must choose between conflicting priorities or, in more dramatic (and misleading) language, we must choose our own values. Ethics and rationality, therefore, involve a certain amount of uncertainty and choice. Sometimes, rationality amounts to simply *making* a choice. Sometimes, rather than making the *correct* choice or in many cases, what is "correct" depends far more on how we see our decision through than which alternative we choose in the first place.

This fact of subjectivity, however, should not be overemphasized or misunderstood. The choices we make, both in business and in the rest of our lives, may well have a personal dimension—a matter of taste or personal preference that no general rule would decide for us. Nevertheless, the range of alternatives within which we choose (whether the options for buying and selling or the flavor of ice cream in the freezer) are not a subjective matter, but rather presented to us by the world in which we find ourselves. Furthermore, although our choices may be personal, the standards for those choices typically are not. The rules of choice are delimited as "objective" by society and the range of choices, no matter how wide it may seem to us at the time, is virtually always restricted severely by concerns that are themselves not our choice at all.

Even insofar as rationality, and consequently ethics, is a subjective matter, a question of each individual having to evaluate goals and priorities and the means to achieve them, rationality remains a *public* concern and a question of what philosophers call *intersubjectivity:* it necessarily involves other people and their goals and priorities too. In the most obvious way, what people do and want affects and is affected by other people; one person cannot have the ambition to be president of Megolith, Inc. in a vacuum. It requires coordination with other people, political alliances, power over some, subservience to some, and competition with others. It means proving ourself in a business setting in which other people's goals and expectations play a definitive role in success or failure. Furthermore, it is almost as obvious that most of our goals themselves, except perhaps some of our basic biological needs such as food and sleep, are largely determined by our influences from other people—parents, peers, teachers, and various role models we meet and have observed since childhood.

Less obvious but just as important, the very nature of most of our goals and values is to be shared in a social context, as we have indicated throughout this book. They do not even make sense, much less become realizable, except in a certain kind of context. Businesspeople, no matter how shrewd, could not become successful in a society that had no place for them to display skills or talents. Indeed, many businesspeople feel that, even within business society, they are sufficiently misplaced in the hierarchy or in the wrong company so as to make their skills and even their goals unintelligible to the people they work with and work for. Rationality is not just an individual matter; it also, perhaps even primarily, must fit our goals and priorities, our ends and means, to a context in which they are appropriate.

The fact that most goals and priorities are shared means that *cooperative* solutions to most human conflicts exist. Rationality, in the larger sense, is an attempt to find those cooperative solutions. Thus, a risk-averse person earning a satisfactory but not maximum return on an investment may leave room for high risk but greater returns for others, while the maximum return for one person may mean that everyone else is quite unsatisfied and resentful. Indeed, the increment of satisfaction to the person who maximizes investment may well be considerably less than the dissatisfaction and resentment of those who are left without a reasonable return, and if their action in turn is to make it impossible for the first investor to enjoy or even keep the return (by extensive litigation or by pushing through government regulation) the net result may well be that no one is satisfied. Rationality is thus the need not only to satisfy our own goals in the context of other people, but to satisfy their goals as well, if only for the purely self-interested reasons that have to do with our own satisfaction.

D. THE COORDINATION PROBLEM

Rationality often means cooperation and coordination. An essential part of game theory, though not nearly so dramatic as zero-sum competitive games, is the realm of cooperative solutions to complex combinations of goals among many players. The problem is to maximize everyone's outcome, taking every player into account. In business, the simplest example is the direct two-party buyer and seller relationship. The solution to the coordination problem is the price that both allows the buyer to feel she got a "good deal" and allows the seller to feel he made a reasonable return. If we add more buyers and sellers—essentially creating the ideal free market—the coordination problem becomes systematically more complex; the question of supply and demand becomes crucial, whereas in the simple buyer–seller case the question was rather one of how much each was willing to pay or take, respectively.

In the much more complex context of the corporation, we have an extremely formidable coordination problem between the directors and managers and many employees, the stockholders and the consumers, and the community in general. To say that the goal of the corporation is only to make a profit becomes a form of idiocy, something like saying the aim of football is to get the ball over the line (no matter whether during a play or not, whether during a game or not). We might even go on to suggest what Adam Smith would not have considered, that the modern corporation *is* essentially an answer to the coordination problem, an attempt to centralize and organize decisions and activities of the marketplace in order to maximize satisfaction for as many people as possible—both inside and outside the corporation. Of course, with the power to coordinate also comes the power to control and monopolize. But perhaps it is a mistake to think of the modern-day corporation as a continuation of Adam Smith's free enterprise system; instead, it should be seen, as John Kenneth Galbraith has long suggested, as an alternative to it, an alternative whose justification is, in general, that it is a more *rational* means of coordinating the complex ends of an enormously complicated society, than the more anarchistic model of unorganized individuals competing for the best prices in the marketplace.

Coordination problems arise in game theory when the cooperative outcome of a game is considered more important than its competitive outcome; in most of life, however, coordination problems are nothing less than arranging our world so that we can get along with one another. Language, for example, is a coordination problem, according to philosopher David K. Lewis, not only in the obvious sense that we will be able to have a conversation only if we both speak the same language, but in the more profound sense that language itself exists primarily as a set of *conventions,* and all conventions Lewis argues, are coordination problems.*

Even our simplest interpersonal actions presuppose solutions to coordination problems. For example, according to Lewis, if we decide to meet for lunch, it is obviously necessary, if we are to do so successfully, that we pick the same place and time, and this place and time must be mutually agreeable to both of us. That is a coordination problem—hardly a trauma for most people, but it is a simple example of the kind of rational solutions we make almost every hour of the day. Indeed, even walking to lunch involves a coordination problem. Suppose you are tall and have a long stride, while I am short and slower. If we are to walk together, I must go faster, and you must conscientiously slow down. It is a simple, rational solution to a problem that barely deserves mention, but to speak of winners and losers in such a situation, or to think of this case as one more case of "dog-eat-dog competition in the business world," is surely to misunderstand the nature of human relationships entirely.

The free market, despite the one-sided rhetoric of competition, is actually a coordinating mechanism, and the "freedom" is far more the freedom to participate and negotiate and to try to maximize our interests than it is simply the freedom to compete. Suppose we are established producers in the computer market, varying our prices with the fluctuations in the cost of labor and raw materials, but otherwise satisfied with our profits and our share of the market. If any producer in this market should suddenly lower its prices, that would immediately set all the other manufacturers against it, begin a price war, lower profits for everyone, and,

---

*Basic theory and examples in this section are from David K. Lewis, *Convention* (Cambridge: Harvard University Press, 1969).

obviously, hurt everyone at least a little and probably someone disastrously. If any producer raises prices, of course, it simply loses a share of the market unless everyone follows suit. So even apart from cartels and price-fixing and other illegalities, the rational solution to this basic coordination problem of the market is that all competitors set their prices within the range of everyone else's prices. The competition of the market provides the necessity for doing so, but it is the coordination of the market that allows it to function at all.

The operation of the market itself, in determining what is to be produced as well as the price at which it will be sold is a coordinating mechanism. Consumers must make known what they want and will buy; producers must make known what they can and will produce. There must be some medium of exchange of value to all parties (the essential rational function of money), and there must be the physical coordination of distribution and delivery to the markets. We could say that within a company, organization and management consists of coordination problems and their solutions: coordination of the company with the consumer and the market in general, and coordination of the employees with each other both in their roles and responsibilities and in their personal interests and relationships (for example, by adjusting salaries so that employees feel that they are more or less fair).

The rational solution to every coordination problem is what is sometimes called an *equilibrium combination.* The equilibrium combination is the outcome that renders all participants better off than if they had simply acted alone. The best equilibrium combinations also maximize everyone's outcome, vis-à-vis everyone else's. But this is not always the case, and it is not always possible. Given the actions of everyone else, an equilibrium combination provides the solution to the coordination problem because, given the actions of everyone else, it allows for an individual's best interests. There may be better outcomes for some; there may even be better outcomes for everyone, if a better combination is used. But what is always the case is that the equilibrium-type solution provides for everyone's interests better than no solution at all.* It is therefore in everyone's interest to be rational in the sense of agreeing to solve the coordination problem in *some* mutually agreeable way, rather than not solving it at all and acting independently. In most business situations, *negotiating* a settlement, even if it is not the best one that could be hoped for, is more rational (more in a person's own best interests) than simply fighting it out in a zero-sum game. Again, competition may be the spur of the market, but cooperation and coordination are the essense of the market; there could be no market without them.

---

*The role of government regulation enters into this question of rationality at this point. We might look at regulation as the attempt to provide a set of ground rules or limits within which all participants (including the public) are better off than if there were no such rules. Regulation itself is not irrational, but essential. There can be irrational regulation, however, since bad or inefficient regulation may not benefit everyone and may even leave some worse off than if it had not existed at all.

If Richard Saunders had been willing to negotiate with the men from OSHA, his Wichita, Kan., foundry and its 60 employees probably would still be making wing flaps for Boeing 747 jets, control columns for Gates Learjet planes, and other aircraft parts.

But the Saunders Inc. foundry is closed because of a confrontation between Mr. Saunders and the Occupational Safety and Health Administration. Mr. Saunders, a 62-year-old Texan who designed World War II planes for Howard Hughes, "approaches genius," an aviation executive says.

The Labor Department's OSHA, on the other hand, thrives on give-and-take. Its inspectors often make tough demands that later are negotiated into more lenient compliance measures. "The general practice is to work out some sort of compromise," says Douglas Stratton, a Kansas lawyer who represents a number of companies in OSHA matters.

Despite the differences in style, Mr. Saunders had little to fear from OSHA last February when two of the agency's inspectors entered his modern, all-electric foundry. "It was the most outstanding foundry in the U.S.," an aircraft executive says. In an industry of notoriously dirty, dangerous workplaces, Saunders' plant was a paragon. "It undoubtedly was the cleanest damn foundry I've ever been in, and I've been in over a hundred," a Boeing executive says.

The inspection could have been as routine as it was in 1975, when OSHA complimented Mr. Saunders on his foundry. But this time, according to a worker who was there, Mr. Saunders called an OSHA man "a stupid SOB" because he was showing employees how they could get hurt on the job. "That's the stupidest damn thing," says a still-angry Mr. Saunders, who chewed out the OSHA inspector. "Showing someone how to stick his arm in something is just stupid."

Soon after the incident, four OSHA inspectors studied the 42,000-square-foot foundry. Eventually they wrote citations for 23 alleged "serious violations" of federal job-safety laws. Serious violations supposedly "can cause serious physical harm or death" to employees.

Businesses normally can negotiate with local OSHA officials to soften the demands. "What you do is you sit down and work out something," says an aircraft executive. "You do the minimum for compliance. That's the way it works." For his big company, that means sending three or four industrial engineers and a few lawyers to deal with OSHA.

But Mr. Saunders refused to negotiate. . . . He figured he couldn't devote the time to a court case because he was the only one doing the engineering and metallurgical work for the $3 million to $5 million worth of castings the company made each year.

E.   THE INTERPERSONAL ART OF RATIONALITY: NEGOTIATION

The crucial element in the most basic zero-sum competitive games (apart from the ultimate aim of winning) is keeping strategy a secret from the opponent. In poker, for example, not betraying the strength of a player's hand is absolutely essential; in football, the secrecy of a team's plays is almost always essential to its success. But in cooperative games and in solving the coordination problem, exactly the opposite is the case; it is one of the most important parts of the solution that the various participants let it be known what they have and what they want. Indeed, even in competitive situations as in business, we may keep some of our strengths and weaknesses hidden. But just as important is the extent to which we make clear what we demand, what we would be willing to accept, and what we would be willing to do for it. This discussion is called *negotiation,* and it is the key to rationality in business.

In every business encounter, certain matters are taken for granted. It can be assumed, for instance, that every participant wants to do as well as possible financially within the bounds of legality and fair play and without sacrificing personal or professional integrity. Where this is not assumed, as sometimes it cannot be, the game changes considerably—if there is a game at all—and negotiation itself becomes less central as a solution and more an aspect of competition. Just think of this situation: an acquaintance you do not trust promises to pay you back a small loan by the middle of next month. You listen to his promise not as a statement of fact or intention but rather as a ploy, which you must deal with in one way or another. But where fairness and honesty is taken as the starting point—as it certainly is in most business situations—negotiation can be considered primarily as a solution to the coordination problem, a way of maximizing everyone's interests, some of which, at least, will be the realization of financial interests. This in itself is not negotiable. (Imagine a business meeting that began with one party asking the others, and not as a joke, whether they would like to make any money out of the deal.) But given the obvious goals and guidelines, negotiation then becomes an art, in which the talents of the professional poker player are often overestimated and the skills of the counselor are often neglected.

We sometimes think of negotiation, as we do of games in general, as a zero-sum process of confrontation, intimidation, and manipulation. But negotiation, as most games, begins far more with "we" rather than with "me against you," with shared values and compatible solutions rather than with winners and losers. Roger Fisher and William Ury summarize the coordination problem of negotiation as getting to a "win-win" solution.* "Conflict is a growth industry," they write, and the standard ways of meeting conflict, both in business and in personal life, are deeply inadequate. Either we rigidify our position to turn the situation into a zero-sum competitive game, which Fisher calls "Soviet style—I must win, you must lose," or we try to "be nice" by making an appeasing gesture, "the hostess phenomenon," in which we give up our own demands much too easily, with inevitable regret and resentment later on.

Negotiation, according to Fisher and Ury, is first of all a matter of separating "the people from the problem." "The basic point," they remind us, "is you can be decent to people and very tough on the problem." Developing a working relationship, even with an adversary, is essential to negotiation (just the ingredient that is so clearly missing in poker and football). Second, recognition and understanding of the other person's or people's position is just as important as recognizing and understanding our own. This means not just recognizing the actual demands that are made, but understanding the interests behind them. A company may demand a certain price for its products, but what it really wants is an assured and continuing market, in return for which it will gladly yield on the price. Employees may demand a raise or a promotion, when what they really want is a clear and public statement of appreciation for certain accomplishments. A manager may insist on more efficiency in an office and less socializing, but what he actually wants is more visible respect and cooperation from employees. Understanding real interests and distinguishing them from stated demands—which may be very different—is essential to successful negotiation. What often begins as a head-on confrontation of demands and refusals is in fact a screen for interests that may be perfectly compatible. To react only to the confrontation without looking at the underlying real interests is to lose a situation that might readily be a "win-win" outcome for everyone.

"No matter what the conflict, there are always shared interests," write Fisher and Ury. Indeed, even where there are real conflicts, these too can be made part of a mutually satisfactory negotiated settlement, through a series of "trade-offs" for example. But what is always crucial is the mutual recognition of respective interests, the realization that sometimes a certain point cannot be negotiated as such but might well be used as leverage for another concession, more easily gained. Indeed, there is always what Fisher and Ury call "negotiation jujitsu": using the strength of another party's demands to motivate an agreement, instead of the usually disastrous reaction of trying to stand up to and reject a nonnegotiable and crucial demand. We should ask questions instead of making demands and invite criticism of our own position instead of insisting that all our demands are reasonable and all others irrational.

Getting to Yes: Negotiating Agreement Without Giving In (New York: Houghton Mifflin, 1981).

Standing Firm: Don't Compromise ——

Compromise is usually bad. It should be a last resort. If two departments or divisions have a problem they can't solve and it comes up to
you, listen to both sides and then, unlike Solomon, pick one or the
other. This places solid accountability on the winner to make it work.

Condition your people to avoid compromise. Teach them to win
some battles, lose others gracefully. Work on the people who try to
win them all. For the sake of the organization, others must have a fair
share of victories.

When you give in, give in all the way. And when you win, try to
win all the way so the responsibility to make it work rests squarely
on you.

Robert Townsend, *Up the Organization*

In a zero-sum game, the size of the pie is fixed; the only question is who gets
the bigger piece. But in negotiations, it is virtually always the case that the number of options and alternatives can be expanded; an employer might well be
unable to increase an employee's demand for more salary, but there may be other
means of compensation—use of a company car or increased insurance benefits—
that will satisfy both. But even so, one key to successful negotiation is always to
have a clear acceptable alternative, a "Best Alternative to a Negotiated Agreement" or "batna." A seller knows the best negotiating position is to have an alternative buyer; a buyer knows that the best negotiating position is to have an
alternative seller. The heart of the free enterprise system turns on the ready avail-
abilities of alternatives—"batnas." But in the corporate world too, negotiation
without options is negotiation without leverage. The alternative need not be
wholly opposed to the negotiations; it must consist of an acceptable position that
is more or less independent of the various solutions being negotiated. At the same
time, however, if the alternatives were that wholly acceptable, negotiation would
not be necessary in the first place. Rationality, therefore, suggests that negotiation
is almost always the best route to maximizing our interests, assuming, that is, that
we know realistically what they are and what they are ultimately worth.

■ SUMMARY AND CONCLUSION

Rationality is an ideal governing most of human behavior. In its simplest definition, rationality means getting what we want in the best way possible. This
includes wanting what is best, however, for it is possible to rationally obtain an
irrational *end,* and the net result is still irrational. Rationality also depends upon

some agreed-upon framework of values, as well as some more or less established rules or guidelines concerning acceptable *means. Irrationality,* therefore, may consist of (1) not choosing an effective way of obtaining our goals or (2) choosing the wrong goals, or both. Our goals, however, are often means to some further ends, and rationality—and irrationality—are therefore typically involved in a sequence of ends and means, in which broad perspective of what we *really* want is always necessary. Profit, for example, may be a goal of business activity, but it is also a means to other ends—the growth and survival of the business; the well-being of the company, its employees, and stockholders; and, ultimately, the overall good of society. Rationality is often a matter of *cooperation* and *coordination,* giving maximum satisfaction to as many participants as possible. This in turn requires *negotiation,* which may be called from an *intersubjective* point of view, the *art* of rationality.

■ STUDY QUESTIONS

1. Is being "calm and cool" always the most rational approach to a business decision? Is "getting emotional" always irrational?

2. Describe an incident in your own life in which you worked hard and long towards the wrong end. What makes it the "wrong end"?

3. Some managers consider consistency of style and approach essential to good and "scientific" management. What danger does this consistency raise? In what sense is it sometimes more rational to be inconsistent?

4. Describe three situations in business in which it would be clearly irrational to try to make a profit.

5. In a business with which you are familiar, what is the purpose(s) of making a profit? What would happen if it did not make a profit (but didn't lose money either)? What particular restrictions—which are not matters of law—limit the profits you are willing to make in that business?

6. How much money (given current currency values) would you like to be making in ten years? Why?

7. What is the difference between an *efficient* manager and an *effective* manager? Do you handle your class schedule efficiently? Effectively? Both? Neither?

8. When should you *refuse* to negotiate your position?

9. Name two of your own business values that you would consider somewhat "subjective." Does this mean that there is nothing that you can say in their defense? Name two values that you consider more or less "objective." What makes them so?

10. Using "The Bridge on the River Kwai" box (p. 177) as an example, give an example in your own life in which the excessive pursuit of a subordinate goal (getting an "A" in a difficult class, getting into a fraternity or sorority that didn't seem to want you) obstructed your achievement of a much more important goal.

■ FOR CLASS DISCUSSION

"When in Rome . . . " *

The Italian federal corporate tax system has an official legal tax structure and tax rates just as the U.S. system does. However, all similarity between the two systems ends there.

The Italian tax authorities assume that no Italian corporation would ever submit a tax return which shows its true profits but rather would submit a return which understates actual profits by anywhere between 30 percent and 70 percent; their assumption is essentially correct. Therefore, about six months after the annual deadline for filing corporate tax returns, the tax authorities issue to each corporation an "invitation to discuss" its tax return. The purpose of this notice is to arrange a personal meeting between them and representatives of the corporation. At this meeting, the Italian revenue service states the amount of corporate income tax that it believes is due. Its position is developed from both prior years' taxes actually paid and the current year's return; the amount which the tax authorities claim is due is generally several times that shown on the corporation's return for the current year. In short, the corporation's tax return and the revenue service's stated position are the opening offers for the several rounds of bargaining that will follow.

The Italian corporation is typically represented in such negotiations by its *commercialista,* a position that exists in Italian society for the primary purpose of negotiating corporate (and individual) tax payments with the Italian tax authorities; thus, the management of an Italian corporation seldom, if ever, has to meet directly with the Italian revenue service and probably has a minimum awareness of the details of the negotiation other than the final settlement.

Both the final settlement and the negotiation are extremely important to the corporation, the tax authorities, and the *commercialista.* Since the tax authorities assume that a corporation *always* earned more money this year than last year and

---

*"Case Study—Italian Tax Mores" was prepared by Arthur L. Kelly (a private investor and member of the board of directors of several international corporations) and based on actual facts. It was originally presented at Loyola University of Chicago in April 1977 at a Mellon Foundation symposium entitled, "Foundations of Corporate Responsibility to Society." Printed with permission of the author, all rights reserved.

never has a loss, the amount of the final settlement, in other words, corporate taxes that will actually be paid, becomes, for all practical purposes, the floor for the start of next year's negotiations. The final settlement also represents the amount of revenue the Italian government will collect in taxes to help finance the cost of running the country. However, since large amounts of money are involved and two individuals having vested personal interests are conducting the negotiations, the amount of *bustarella*—typically a substantial cash payment "requested" by the Italian revenue agent from the *commercialista*—usually determines whether the final settlement is closer to the corporation's original tax return or to the fiscal authority's original negotiating position.

Whatever *bustarella* is paid during the negotiation is usually included by the *commercialista* in his lump-sum fee "for services rendered" to his corporate client. If the final settlement is favorable to the corporation, and it is the *commercialista's* job to see that it is, then the corporation is not likely to complain about the amount of its *commercialista's* fee, nor will it ever know how much of that fee was represented by *bustarella* and how much remained for the *commercialista* as payment for his negotiating services. In any case, the tax authorities will recognize the full amount of the fee as a tax deductible expense on the corporation's tax return for the following year.

About ten years ago, a leading American bank opened a banking subsidiary in a major Italian city. At the end of its first year of operation, the bank was advised by its local lawyers and tax accountants, both from branches of U.S. companies, to file its tax return "Italian-style," in other words, to understate its actual profits by a significant amount. The American general manager of the bank, who was on his first overseas assignment, refused to do so both because he considered it dishonest and because it was inconsistent with the practices of his parent company in the United States.

About six months after filing its "American-style" tax return, the bank received an "invitation to discuss" notice from the Italian tax authorities. The bank's general manager consulted with his lawyers and tax accountants who suggested he hire a *commercialista*. He rejected this advice and instead wrote a letter to the Italian revenue service not only stating that his firm's corporate return was correct as filed but also requesting that they inform him of any specific items about which they had questions. His letter was never answered.

About sixty days after receiving the initial "invitation to discuss" notice, the bank received a formal tax assessment notice calling for a tax of approximately three times that shown on the bank's corporate tax return; the tax authorities simply assumed the bank's original return had been based on generally accepted Italian practices, and they reacted accordingly. The bank's general manager again consulted with his lawyers and tax accountants who again suggested he hire a *commercialista* who knew how to handle these matters. Upon learning that the *commercialista* would probably have to pay *bustarella* to his revenue service counterpart in order to reach a settlement, the general manager again chose to ignore his advisers. Instead, he responded by sending the Italian revenue service a check for the full amount of taxes due according to the bank's American-style tax return even though the due date for the payment was almost six months hence; he made no reference to the amount of corporate taxes shown on the formal tax assessment notice.

Ninety days after paying its taxes, the bank received a third notice from the fiscal authorities. This one contained the statement, "We have reviewed your corporate tax return for 19___ and have determined that (the lira equivalent of) $6,000,000 of interest paid on deposits is not an allowable expense for federal tax purposes. Accordingly, the total tax due for 19___ is lira _____." Since interest paid on deposits is any bank's largest single expense item, the new tax assessment was for an amount many times larger than that shown in the initial tax assessment notice and almost fifteen times larger than the taxes which the bank had actually paid.

The bank's general manager was understandably very upset. He immediately arranged an appointment to meet personally with the manager of the Italian revenue service's local office. Shortly after the start of their meeting, the general manager said, "You can't really be serious about disallowing interest paid on deposits as a tax deductible expense." To this the Italian revenue service representative replied, "Perhaps. However, we thought it would get your attention. Now that you're here, shall we begin our negotiations?"

If you were the American bank manager, what would you have done?

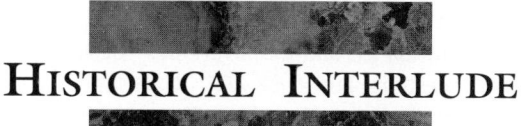

Historical Interlude

Five Challenges for Free Enterprise

If the free market system worked as well as Adam Smith said it would, as an ideal self-regulating mechanism with perfect competition and consumer sovereignty, there would probably be no field of "economics," and "business ethics" would be little more than a list of employment opportunities and their advantages and disadvantages. But the fact is that there has never been "perfect" competition, and the world assumed by Adam Smith is very different from the realities of the present. The separation of business, government, and the public interest is no longer possible even in theory; indeed, that separation was possible only in a society in which business was an unimportant and generally peripheral activity. But we live in a business society in which corporate cultures and the

---

The Stability of the Free Economy
"Stockmarket Plummets 508 Points" ——

NEW YORK The stock market plunged out of control Monday in a selling panic that rivaled the Great Crash of 1929, pushing the Dow Jones average down more than 500 points, draining more than $500 billion from the value of stocks and sending shock waves around the world.

"Whether today was a financial melt-down or not . . . I wouldn't want to be around for one worse than this," said John Phelan, chairman of the New York Stock Exchange.

The Dow's plunge to 1738.74 left it 22.6 percent below Friday's level, a one-day loss far larger than the 12.8 percent drop on Oct. 28, 1929, known as Black Friday, or Oct. 29, 1929, when it fell an additional 11.7 percent.

—Associated Press, Oct. 20, 1987

"businesslike" approach to most aspects of our lives are taken for granted, even by many of those critics who attack them hardest. Indeed, we might argue that even the world of Adam Smith was not the world he envisioned in his book; but he, at least, lacked the retrospective advantage that we have and had no chance to see how his great experiment—and that is what it still is, a great experiment—fared in the course of history.

The following five challenges to free enterprise are something more than mere questions of performance and the "workings" of capitalism; they are not primarily economic questions but *macroethical* questions, questions about the values of the free enterprise system as such. They are the questions most often repeated by the critics of business, and anyone in business who acts as a spokesperson for business must be familiar with them.

IS TRUE COMPETITION POSSIBLE?

Competition as the mechanism of self-regulation has turned out to be more mythical than actual; sometimes, competition becomes so keen, then so vicious, that many, and on occasion all, of the competitors are forced out of business, doing no good either for them or for the society they serve. To avoid cutthroat competition, businesses often get together and fix prices, form cartels, and establish monopolies, all of which undermine the whole idea of free enterprise. Can a free enterprise system, without regulation, in fact maintain the competition that is at the basis of the theory? Is this a flaw in the theory itself, or is it that the system is still not free enough, as some modern critics (Stigler, Friedman) maintain? Or is competition itself an archaic feature of capitalism, as some economists (Robert Heilbroner) have argued?

Does Capitalism Require a Divorce Between Work and Life? ("Alienated Labor")

Impersonality is the key to the modern business world, and not just an unfortunate feature to be complained about. The impersonality of large markets, abstract bookkeeping procedures, the enormity of markets, and the uniformity of products make the system possible. The legal vehicle of the corporation is not just an unfortunate outgrowth of what may once have been a personal competition between small numbers of entrepreneurs; it is a legal necessity, limiting liability, increasing stability, and making life in business more orderly and less risky than it would be otherwise. Impersonality is the heart of the system, but it also fosters a sometimes tragic separation between what a person does "for a living" and the rest of life, a distinction between friends and business, a feeling of anonymity. Psychiatrists are now arguing that loneliness and "alienation" are the leading psychological problems in America—and the cause of serious physical illness too. Can this be corrected (as for instance, the Japanese seem to be doing) by incorporating many of the personal features of feudal life into the structure of the corporation itself? Or is it, as the Marxists insist, that impersonality and "alienation" is intrinsic to the free enterprise system itself?

Does Capitalism Create, Rather Than Just Supply, Its Own Demand?

The basic law of the free enterprise system is the law of supply and demand. But with the advent of modern advertising and media techniques, the sovereignty of consumer demand is no longer a reality, if it ever was. Demands are created, sometimes against the interests of the consumer. (The free enterprise system in the illegal drug market is the most extreme and shocking example, but a hundred more palatable examples make the same point, from Saturday morning advertising of sweet breakfast cereals for children to ego-inspiring advertisements for gas-guzzling cars for adults.) A different way of stating this set of objections might be to challenge the basic assumption of *homo economicus,* that we are all rational creatures maximizing our own interests. Sometimes, we do not know our own interests, and even when we do, we are not always rational about them. Can this be incorporated into the free enterprise system without giving up the ultimate confidence in the ability of the system to increase the welfare of society? Or will we eventually end up with the cynical dismissal of misfortunes of all kinds, from exploding cars to poisonous process foods, on the grounds that "caveat emptor" or "you pays your money and you takes your chances"?

DOES CAPITALISM IN FACT SERVE THOSE WHO ARE LEAST WELL OFF IN SOCIETY?

The social promise of the free enterprise system has always been that it will benefit those who are not its successful entrepreneurs as well as those who most directly profit from it. But even in eighteenth-century England, the *increase* in poverty was one of the most striking accompaniments of the industrial revolution and the new capitalism. Some of this (the wretchedness of factory workers as described by Dickens, for instance) has been corrected through a series of government interventions and social outcries. (Could the circumstances have been corrected by the self-regulation of business? What "free market" mechanism would motivate this?) But even in our present society, the numbers of people who are unemployed and have no real opportunities of even getting into the world of success and wealth are ominous. Is this a product of the system? Or is it also to be explained on the basis of some other feature of modern-day society? Such debates define the direction of our society and the nature of business in the near future. And they are essentially, whatever else they are, debates about the very *idea* of business, debates about the nature of business life and the rules and responsibilities that define it. There is no such thing as "business is business"; however, there is the very idea of business and what it is supposed to be, and to do business is—thinkingly or unthinkingly—to live with and redefine that idea.

CAN BUSINESS REGULATE ITSELF? IS GOVERNMENT REGULATION A NECESSITY?

Finally, and once again, the overall assumption of the separation of business and society—the "freedom" of "free enterprise"—has to be thrown into question. Whether or not it is true that business will regulate itself, the goals and responsibilities of business remain beyond its confines in the arena of society as a whole. Would most of us question the right of government to interfere in the free enterprise of a business that was selling strategic arms to an enemy with whom we were currently at war? We might say, "such practices will eventually prove bad for business," but are we willing to wait so long or take that chance? If a business enterprise causes sickness or suffering or destroys public lands, are we willing to maintain our faith in the self-correcting properties of the system? Or are we not, at least sometimes, wholly justified in imposing on business the strictest regulations and the harshest penalties without waiting for the world of business to correct itself, perhaps after the damage is done? But such arguments, as we have discussed, tend to be too easy and pit social and moral concerns against business interests in too crude and clumsy a way. In fact, the interrelation between the business world and the rest of society—insofar as they are distinguishable at all—is much more intricate than such familiar examples would indicate. Business is part of society; its rules are for the most part society's rules, and that is just as true now as it was in the days of Aristotle and Aquinas. We still hear a great deal of talk about business-government "interface" and friction, but it is also time to ask whether "free" enterprise (free from government control)—even among our giant corporations—can any longer compete with the national government-supported enterprises of our foreign competitors, especially Germany and "Japan, Inc." Is the whole discussion about "regulation" just another relic from the past?

Does the free enterprise system in fact maximize the well-being of society in general? Can it continue to be "free" and still succeed? Are there alternative economic-ethical systems that are worthy of our attention (leaving aside the horror stories about "communism" and "socialism" that are too often presented as the *only* possible alternative to the free market system)? Have we moved beyond the days of classical capitalism altogether? Two hundred years after Adam Smith, it is essential that people in business now go beyond Smith's theoretical faith in the market and actually point to the benefits and improvements that business has made possible. (The wonders of modern technology alone are certainly not enough. The Nazis were remarkably inventive without a hint of "freedom.") And it is just as essential that people in business now look at their world with that rational self-scrutiny that has always signaled the maturity of every human enterprise, and say with some clarity what still needs to be done, what values have become eclipsed, and what aspects of Adam Smith's theory are real, which were only a dream, and which can still be made into a living social reality.

Robert L. Heilbroner: Does Capitalism Have a Future? ——

What lies ahead for capitalism? That's a question that makes people nervous. It conjures up visions and specters. It paralyzes thought.

Nevertheless, it is a question that ought to be thought about now, while most of us are concentrating only on the present and the immediate future, worrying about the depression and whether it will get worse. For I believe we are not only in a depression but also in a crisis—a period of change for capitalism. Hence to the question "Does capitalism have a future?" my answer would be, "Yes, but not the future most people expect." Sooner or later, the depression will mend and we will be back to where we were, more or less. But the crisis will not mend in the same way. When it has run its course, we will be on new ground, in unfamiliar territory.

From *The New York Times,* Aug. 15, 1982

Largest Layoffs ——

The largest layoffs announced by major American companies in the first quarter of 1991:

Sears, Roebuck	33,000
IBM	14,000
General Dynamics	7,000
General Motors	6,000
Citicorp	4,400
Pan Am	4,000
Chrysler	3,990
Digital Equipment	3,500
Hills Department Stores	3,000
USF&G	2,800
Aetna Life & Casualty	2,600
Trans World Airlines	2,500
Boeing	2,000
Grumman	1,900
Inland Steel	1,370

—*The New York Times*
April 15, 1991

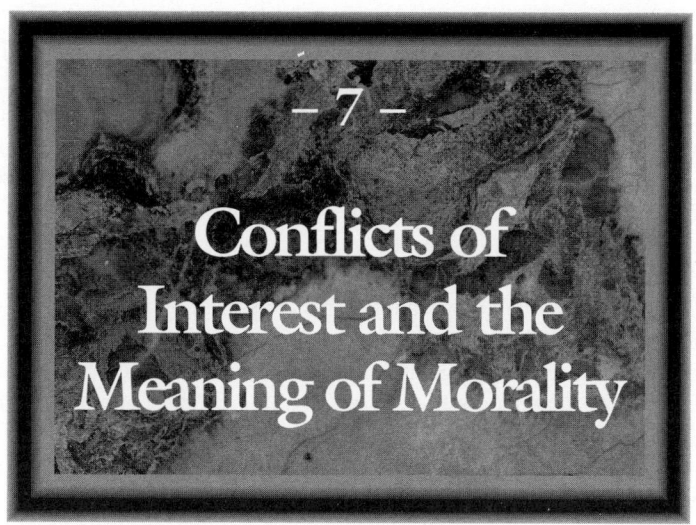

– 7 –
Conflicts of Interest and the Meaning of Morality

Every year thousands of Americans are killed or injured where they work. . . . The OSHA (Occupational Safety and Health Administration) recently calculated that the steel industry could annually save the lives of several hundred of its coke workers if it invested in equipment to control coke fumes. The cost per life saved would be $4.5 million. Is this too much money?

—Leonard H. Orr, Business and Society Review, #22

W e could imagine a world, perhaps, in which there would be no conflicts of interest, no hard choices, no tragedies, and in which people could fulfill both their desires and their responsibilities without adversely affecting anyone else. But that would be just an imaginary world; this is not such a world. One person's gain is often another person's loss. One desire conflicts with another, and one responsibility contradicts another. Sometimes, conflicts of interest can be negotiated. Sometimes, they cannot be. Sometimes, one side (or both sides) of a conflict is not merely a matter of interest but a matter of *morality*. And, sometimes, there are only losses and wrong answers—"damned if you do and damned if you don't"—the stuff of tragedy.

The most obvious conflicts of interest in business are the built-in conflicts of competition; that is, competition considered as a (more or less) zero-sum, noncooperative game. But even in non-competitive practices, there can be conflicts of interest, and the practice as a whole can conflict with larger interests, such as the good of society as a whole, or with particular, undeniable moral interests, such as the right of an innocent person not to be killed. The profits of a corporation sometimes conflict with the interests of employees, of consumers, of "the public," as well as with the profits of their competitors. The careers of two middle managers, angling for the same promotion, are in conflict; a number of contractors, bidding for a single contract, are in conflict, too. In every case, the question of who will win has to be supplemented by the more crucial question of who *ought* to win. The strongest is not always the best; "might" does not make "right." Conflicts of interest are not just contests of power, they are also questions about priorities. When is one person's gain worth another person's loss? When is it worth risking, or sacrificing, human lives?

Conflicts of interest emerge as a problem not only between people and companies, but *within* a person's life. In any position of any complexity, roles can conflict, personal interests and aspirations can conflict with obligations, or responsibilities can confront opposing responsibilities. Because all of us play several roles in our jobs as well as in the rest of our lives, and because the roles in our jobs cannot always be wholly in harmony with our other roles in life, there are bound to be conflicts of interest, whether they be within a particular job (Do I have a primary obligation to my immediate boss, or to the company as a whole, when they are at odds?), between one job and other job opportunities (Should I leave the company for a better job elsewhere, or do I have an obligation to stay and contribute what I can?), or between job and extra-career relationships (How can I fire this person, as I am supposed to, even though he is my friend?).

A.   THE NATURE OF CONFLICT AND ITS LIMITS

> War is father of all and king of all. . . .
>
> —Heraclitus

Understanding ethical conflict begins with an image of human nature. Some theorists—for example, Konrad Lorenz—have suggested that human beings are essentially aggressive animals; in other words, the urge to conflict is built into our genes, whether or not we in fact have anything to be in conflict about. Using this theory, we might say that the origin of competition and private enterprise was spite and belligerence rather than the more noble motives espoused by the classic free enterprise theorists. Philosophically, the most powerful proponent of this kind of basic conflict theory was the seventeenth-century British philosopher Thomas Hobbes. He suggested that every one of us is essentially selfish, out for ourselves, and, consequently, at odds with everyone else. He wrote that human life is "naturally" a "war of all against all," and it is "nasty, brutish and short." This image has been reinforced by popular expositions of Darwin's theory of "survival of the fittest," and is all too prevalent in current American "self-help" psychology as well as in the common business metaphors, "it's a jungle out there," "the battle for survival," and "looking out for number one." In this view, conflict between us is basic; cooperation is a matter of prudence or necessity, but always as a bastion against the forces of natural conflict that are in us all.

An alternative vision, however, has its foundations just as firmly in biology and the theory of evolution. It is the view that people are basically cooperative, not competitive. The French philosopher Jean Jacques Rousseau, for instance, suggested that human beings in nature are not selfish but basically compassionate. The anthropologist Richard Leakey has argued that the basis of human society has always been cooperation, and that this, not selfishness, is built right into our biological inheritance. Indeed, the Darwinian argument, which is applicable not only to humans but to "social" animals from ants to gorillas, is that cooperation is itself one of the most advantageous evolutionary traits, assuring the survival of the species in addition to the survival of more individuals of that species. In modern philosophy, this same sense of a cooperative context, *within* which particular conflicts arise, has been argued by the German philosopher G. W. F. Hegel and the American philosopher Josiah Royce. Conflicts, on this second account, always take place within a context of shared interests.

In the midst of conflict, it often seems as if nothing else matters. Too easily, we imagine ourselves in a basic struggle for survival, an image appropriate to two people stranded in the desert, perhaps, but hardly appropriate in the average corporate context. Two assistant managers may battle ferociously and even "ruthlessly" for promotion, but both are interested in the survival of the company in

Macbeth Lands Top Scotland Job; Wife Viewed as Motivating Force ——

Shakespearean purists will wince at how [Professor Gregory] Barnes rewrites "Macbeth," the 400-year-old tale of the bloody struggle for the Scottish throne. Duncan, the aging, incompetent chief executive of Scotland Corp., promotes his inexperienced son Malcolm, thus passing over his ambitious executive vice president, Macbeth.

Macbeth had thought he was in line for the job, having heard hints from three consultants (the witches). Pushed by Lady Macbeth ("The epitome of the corporate wife," says Mr. Barnes), Macbeth abandons his principles and stops at nothing to supplant Duncan. Eventually his guilt and inadequacies get the best of him, and control of Scotland Corp. passes to another of Duncan's sons. . . . "There's an individual who will stop at nothing in any company," he says. Knowing that such power-hungry people exist, he adds, "teaches you to cover your own rear end; the real world isn't all management by objectives and theory X and theory Y."

Sandy Graham, *The Wall Street Journal,* March 26, 1981

which they are competing. They are also interested in the survival of the system in which they are competing. In the absence of a business world, there would be no arena in which people could employ their business skills and reap the benefits. As one prominent executive has recently written, "Business has to assure the health of the society in which competition and profits are possible." To focus simply on the conflicts and competitions and ignore the larger context, turns the question of conflict and conflict resolution into nonsense, or worse, a brutal question of winners and losers and nothing else. But within the larger context, all kinds of limits and considerations and possibilities for negotiation become possible. Indeed, we could even argue that, where shared interests in a shared context exist, there are virtually always negotiable solutions, optimal for all concerned— so long as we don't think that "optimal" means "satisfying everyone's interest." As long as conflicts of interest exist, there must also be sacrifices of interests too, if any interests are going to be satisfied. Indeed, "conflict resolution" often means just that—not the satisfaction of everyone's interests or demands but simply being able to move on.

There are, however, genuine conflicts within these shared interests that are not mere matters of misunderstanding. Life is sometimes a very real zero-sum, noncooperative game, particularly for the poor and disadvantaged, who usually have little motivation or reason to cooperate with other groups in society, compromising for "the interests of society." Competition is not always up for negotiation to reach a position of mutual advantage. (It is sometimes dictated by law.) Not all competition is the gamelike, mutually agreeable sort of competition that we sometimes idealize when we think only of already wealthy and successful steel magnates, real estate brokers, or investment bankers. Sometimes indeed it is a cut-throat fight for survival in which the overall interests of society or the good name of business are all but forgotten and the Hobbesian picture of "war of all against all" does seem to fit appropriately. In such cases, the "reasonable" notions of compromise and negotiation may be impossible to apply, however much philosophers and others have tried to assure us that there are rational principles that will solve all problems.

Some situations are not "reasonable" or prone to the impersonal solutions of reason. The sought-after principles are more often than not so limp or vague as to be useless ("act as you would like the other person to act," "try to maximize happiness for all parties," "do not knowingly do harm"). But this is not to say that there are never any solutions, never "reasonable" ways of making decisions or settling conflicts. Indeed, there are usually reasonable solutions. That is why we entertain the false hope that perhaps there *always* are such reasonable resolutions.

B.   PRIORITIES

Not all conflicts are evenly matched, but even where they are not, if their interests are complementary a ready solution is at hand. For example, in classical eco-

The Ethics of Self-Preservation ——

The ethics movement couldn't be more timely. Given the looming threat of layoffs and enormous pressure to turn a profit these days, managers are sometimes understandably tempted to engage in a bit of dodgy behavior. "People are so desperate to keep their jobs that they act inappropriately," says Michael Josephson, who heads the Joseph & Edna Josephson Institute of Ethics in Marina Del Rey, California.

—Business Week
September 23, 1991

nomic theory, an initial conflict between buyer and seller is presumed; it is in the buyer's interest to buy as cheaply as possible and it is in the seller's interest to charge as much as possible. This is a straightforward conflict between interests. But, of course, the seller comes down in price while the buyer is willing to pay a bit more, and although neither gets what was ideally wanted, both recognize that they got the best deal possible and both are satisfied. Or, if they can't agree on a price, both feel that the best deal available was no deal. We can complicate this picture enormously with competing buyers, competing sellers, problems of supply, coalitions between buyers or between sellers, government price controls and product regulations, and so on. However, the basic principle remains the same: where conflicts of interest are purely quantitative and measurable on a single scale (in this case, price), they are resolvable through negotiation and compromise, such that all parties involved can know "objectively" what the best deal they should expect will be. The rationality and mastery of such quantitative competition is the subject matter of classical economics; it is not at all the province of business ethics. But it is the paradigm case of a conflict that is easily and rationally solved, however complex it may be.

The problem for business ethics begins to emerge when nonquantitative variables enter the picture, or when the values in conflict are on different and incommensurable scales. When psychological variables such as the emotional significance of an object complicate the picture, classical economic theory breaks down as a solution. For example, when a person in desperation pawns a watch that is an heirloom, the negotiations cannot be measured in the terms of worth as such, even if the end result must of necessity be selling the watch for an agreed-upon price. In this case the seller cannot feel that it was "a good deal," whether or not the price was fair. The conflict is the priority of financial need over sentiment, and though the priority seems clear in this case, the conflict is more complex than the buyer-seller conflict of classical economics. Two scales of value are involved, one the objectively measurable scale of worth and fair price, the other the subjective scale of emotion and sentiment (subjective value), for which there can be no readily acceptable measure of price.

Profit and Selfishness ———

In the summer of '72 the *Times* of London reported that Archbishop Camara of Brazil had asked for a meeting of members of both Houses of Parliament. "Why do you not help lay bare the serious distortions of socialism such as they exist in Russia and China? And why do you not denounce, once and for all, the intrinsic selfishness and heartlessness of capitalism? . . . "

The fundamental mistake here is that of identifying the interested with the selfish. This is wrong. For, though selfish actions are perhaps always interested, only some interested actions are also selfish. To say that a piece of conduct was selfish is to say more than that it was interested, if it was. The point is that selfishness is always and necessarily out of order. Interestedness is not, and scarcely could be.

For example: when my daughters eagerly eat their dinners they are, I suppose, pursuing their own interests. But it would be monstrous to denounce them as selfish hussies, simply on that account. The time for denunciation could come only after one of them had, for instance, eaten someone else's dinner too; or refused to make some sacrifice which she ought to have made. Again, even when my success can be won only at the price of someone else's failure, it is not always and necessarily selfish for me to pursue my own interests. The rival candidates competing for some coveted job are not selfish just because they do not all withdraw in order to clear the way for the others.

The upshot, therefore, is that it will not do to dismiss any one economic system as "intrinsically selfish and heartless" simply because that system depends upon and engages interested motives, or even simply because it allows or encourages people to pursue their own interests in certain situations of zero-sum conflict.

From Anthony Flew, "The Profit Motive," *Ethics,* July 1976

The most dramatic examples of such conflicts of value scales can be found in those industries that make products whose reliability often means the difference between life and death. In the notorious memo from the engineer at General Dynamics to the board of directors informing them of the possibility of a DC-10 mishap in the air, we can see a brutal conflict between the purely economic question of the price of investigating and fixing the cargo doors and the noneconomic concern, which is "the value of human life." What offends most people in such cases is the effort to convert the latter value into a function of economics, asking the "cost" of losing an airplane full of people. Such reasoning misses the point of the conflict altogether. Of course, a consumer (or the family) can sue a company

There was the engineering director at General Dynamics who sent the following memorandum to his superior a few years ago: "It seems to me inevitable that, in the 20 years ahead of us, DC-10 cargo doors will come open and cargo compartments will experience decompression for other reasons and I expect this to usually result in loss of the airplane"; he added that floor changes would be costly, but "may well be less expensive than the cost of damages resulting from the loss of one plane-load of people." This advice was ignored, and two years later a Turkish Airlines DC-10 crashed in France after its cargo door blew open, killing all 346 passengers.

Ralph Nader, *Taming the Giant Corporation*

for making a product that is fatally faulty; and the settlement, most of the time, consists of a financial payment. But though this may solve the legal conflict it does not solve the conflict between economics and "the value of human life." Here there is no such thing as "a good deal" for the victim's family even if the settlement is generous. Two different values are at stake, financial value on the one side and what we can cautiously call "ethical" value on the other. It is important not to infer from this that business will inevitably be on the side of "financial value" and society will be on the side of "ethical value"; the reverse is often the case, and conflicts between the two sets of values are just as prevalent *within* business.

Comparing two different value scales is often impossible, for there is usually no way of converting one to the other and no clear way of measuring them both against any third scale. For example, we cannot tell who is a better athlete by measuring the lifetime scores of, let us say, Joe Namath and Wilt Chamberlain because the points earned in football and the points earned in basketball represent very different skills and accomplishments. We cannot measure the quality of art by comparing prices either, though great works of art are frequently bought, sold, and traded. We cannot thereby compare artistic worth (as opposed to their market value, which is a function of supply and demand and fashion).

It is sometimes suggested that conflicts in the business world between financial interests and noneconomic interests ought always to be resolved in favor of the financial interests (that is, maximizing profit), since business consists of financial institutions with financial obligations. Thus, a manager who faces a choice between laying off workers or increasing pollution on the one hand and losing a profit on the other is bound by his obligation to the former alternatives. Some noneconomic interests, even within the corporation (worker safety, the good will of the company, pride in the quality or usefulness of the product), clearly outweigh the financial interest at least most of the time. When they do not, some nonfinancial explanation is almost always available. (Indeed, woe to the company that is philistine enough to allow its spokesperson to say in public that a decision involving safety, or even reputation or quality, was made for the sake of profit, rather than some other noneconomic concern, such as the autonomy of the workers or the health of industry competition.)

It is equally absurd to say, as some critics of business do, that conflicts in business between financial interests and noneconomic interests should always be resolved in favor of the noneconomic interests. There are a great many trivial and insignificant noneconomic interests just as there are petty financial concerns that are not worth thinking or worrying about, much less proving a source of real conflict. Conflicts may exist between pride and finance, for example, in which it is clearly pride that should be swallowed rather than a significant financial gain sacrificed. A business doesn't like to sell out to a superior competitor, for instance, but sometimes it is foolish not to. Business has fashions also, but it is an imprudent businessperson who sacrifices profits just for the sake of temporary fashion. Few companies can afford aesthetic extravagance, for example, when building a new factory. Business or a businessperson might make any number of sacrifices for the sake of some good other than business that, nevertheless, would not be reasonable to expect.

When two different value scales conflict, whether an economic scale and a noneconomic scale or two noneconomic scales, we would like to think that there is some rational way of resolving disputes. One possibility is the dominance of one whole scale over another. The conflict between different value scales cannot always be settled so obviously. What about our interest in the survival of plants and lower animals? At what point does our taste in food (as opposed to our need to eat to survive) justify killing? At what point does our defense of freedom justify declaring war, with considerable sacrifice of human life? Is it *ever* justified to risk a human life in return for purely financial gain?

The most important part of the answer to this last question is the fact that, wherever possible, risk of life must be a *voluntary* act. Thus we do not think it immoral when people risk their own lives for profit, whether in the dangerous but necessary jobs of firefighting, gold mining, or working for the CIA in foreign countries having anti-American sentiments. We are also willing to tolerate an enormous risk of life when other values are at stake, for example, the values of individual freedom and convenience in driving an automobile despite the always present danger of accidents. The sense of voluntariness becomes more questionable, however, when we are talking about employees who risk their lives for the corporation. Are they fully aware of the risks they face? If people accept a job jumping out of helicopters, we assume that they are aware of the risks involved, but if an unknowing worker accepts a job in an industry in which certain health hazards cause long-term disability, it is not at all clear that the risk taking is voluntary. Indeed, the question whether risks are voluntary continues to be one of the most difficult concrete questions in business ethics and is by no means decidable simply by the fact that a consumer "chose" to buy a certain product or an employee "chose" to take a certain job.

> ## Do Workers Choose Danger? ——
>
> Many of our commentators, acknowledging that some jobs are dangerous, state that the assumption of such risks ought to be voluntary, for no employee should be forced to take risks. This might be called a "free market" approach to the job market. Manuel Gomez, a safety and health expert for the research organization Inform, points out that most workers may not have sufficient information or flexibility to exercise free market freedom. Workers in dangerous occupations are very often tied to their jobs. Gomez doubts, for example, that many coal miners would want their children to become miners also. He believes that men like Red Adair, the highly paid Texan who puts out oil well fires, are unusual in that they actually choose to do risky jobs.
>
> From *Business and Society Review,* #22

We do, however, put a price on human life. Although the scale of value of human life will never be convertible to the scale of financial values, nevertheless, we do consider certain exchanges fair, especially if they are agreed to *voluntarily* by the person whose life is in question. Life insurance does this as a matter of routine; civil liability suits do too. "Life is cheap in Casablanca," says Sidney Greenstreet in the movie named after that city. And, unpleasant as such thoughts may be, kidnappers and the family of the kidnapped have to put a price on a human life too. Sometimes, the price is not financial; for instance, we tolerate the enormous number of road deaths in America by appeal to the value of individual freedom and convenience. We accept an extraordinarily high murder rate because we appeal to the value of the right to own firearms and the desirability of keeping police surveillance of private citizens to a minimum. Many people obviously consider the risk of death by lung cancer less undesirable than giving up the value they gain by smoking. We might say without hesitation that the value of human life transcends all other values, but our actions show quite clearly that we do not entirely believe this. Even that scale of values on occasion yields to others and, though we do not like to think of it this way, sometimes life yields to other scales, at least if the gain is great enough.

It would be false, however, to conclude that there is no rational way of adjudicating conflicts of interest involving different scales of value, and that such decisions are merely "subjective" or "a matter of individual decision." When an executive has to choose between a course of action that risks the lives of many people and an alternative that involves only the sacrifice of a certain aesthetic, for example, building an architecturally beautiful but wholly unsafe new factory, there is no question what the rational choice must be. Some decisions are indeed "subjective" and "a matter of individual choice," like the case in which a person

Two Faces of Business Ethics: Talk and Action ——

Ironically, the biggest purveyor of sex on daytime TV is not ABC, as is commonly thought, but Procter & Gamble, which owns six out of the 13 soaps. Last June, in a widely publicized speech, P&G chairman Owen B. Butler, allied his company with the Coalition for Better Television which has the backing of the Moral Majority. The chairman warned that P&G was listening "very carefully" to conservative critics of television and said such groups were "expressing some very important and broadly held views about gratuitous sex, violence and profanity."

Despite these pious words, however, in the face of its crumbling daytime empire, P&G has been, and continues to be, in the forefront of pushing sex and occasionally resorting to cheap thrills. For example, last year "As the World Turns," a P&G show, featured an absurd dream sequence in which Joyce Hughes performed a striptease to seduce Oakdale's stodgy lawyer Grant Colman. . . .

On "The Guiding Light," another P&G soap, Morgan Richards had sex with Kelly Nelson at the tender age of 17. (So much for P&G's glorification of traditional family values.) The poor girl then ran away from home, got involved with a bunch of pimps from Chicago and later was raped and kidnapped. . . .

"Another World" could be renamed "Another Bed" at times. In one week alone during the month of July, the P&G soap featured no less than five bedroom scenes, each with a different couple. . . . But how ironic that P&G should have scored a breakthrough in the area of sex.

Terry Ann Kropf, *The Boston Globe*

is forced to sell a family heirloom or in which a person faces the possibility of selling the family business. But in most cases of conflict, there are fairly clear priorities even if, in difficult cases, these balance each other and the decision seems arbitrary as a result.

Different scales, even if not clearly and absolutely ranked such that the values of one *always* override the values of the other, still can be given *general* priorities, even if this does not dictate all the values on the scale and even if the relative priorities of some scales would be highly controversial. In general, life-and-death issues take priority over financial concerns; ethical values take precedence over aesthetic values; questions of integrity are more important than questions of personal interest. At the extreme ends of the scales, it is possible that a decision may go the other way, but in general, we may *prima facie* presume that the one kind of value takes priority over the other.

> ***Prima facie:*** an essential concept in moral philosophy, and in law, which allows us a middle term between absolutes and merely relative claims. A *prima facie* priority is accepted at face value *except* for cases in which there is an unusually strong counterclaim. For example, a company has a *prima facie* obligation to honor its contracts to foreign governments, and it would be assumed to do so, but the obligation is not absolute (that is, assumed in *any* circumstance). In case of war with that other country, the obligation would probably be overridden by other moral obligations. Similarly, people have a *prima facie* right to the rewards of their labors. Nevertheless, there are circumstances—a national emergency, for example—in which this right might be overridden. In the absence of such unusual conditions, however, *prima facie* claims are assumed to be valid.

There is an old joke in which one person asks another, "Would you sacrifice your integrity for a billion dollars?"

"Sure," says the other.

"How about $20?"

"What do you think I am?"

"We've established that; now we're just haggling over the price."

The joke is crude, but it summarizes an essential ethical point: at the extremes of any scale of values, the usual priorities of the scale break down. If a work of art is sufficiently "priceless," no amount of money can do it justice. If the amount of money is great enough, the integrity of most people becomes sufficiently shaky to be undependable. We might well lament this fact and wish it were not so; however, in a society in which money rather than birthright, political connections, intelligence, taste, charm, integrity, and friendship determines so much about our success and happiness, it would be utterly stupid not to take this fact into account in any discussion of ethics. Does this mean that we are all "just haggling over the price"? Certainly not, but it does mean, as the old prospector (Walter Huston) insists in *The Treasure of the Sierra Madre,* that people tend to go more than a little crazy when the financial stakes are excessive. But as much as we might talk of the "limitless possibilities" in our society, the fact of the matter is that, for most people, the possibilities are relatively modest. And it is a good thing that they are, for at the extremes of the scale our priorities—and consequently our chances at the good life—often go awry.

C.   ETHICAL DILEMMAS

In every job with even a modicum of responsibility—in other words, in virtually every job, career, and profession—there is the very real, perhaps inevitable possibility of finding oneself confronting an ethical dilemma. An ethical dilemma is a practical conflict of more or less equally compelling obligations. For example, an employee may find himself or herself torn between an already made promise to a subordinate and a new demand from the boss, or one might encounter a conflict between the responsibilities of one's job and other obligations to one's friends, family, or community. One may have already promised a bonus to an assistant when the administration sends down an order to cut back on expenses, or one might find oneself in the awkward position of having to fire the favorite cousin of a best friend. Some ethical dilemmas emerge when two more or less equally established rules contradict one another. Some of the most painful dilemmas occur when there is a conflict of loyalties to two different organizations, to two friendly colleagues, or to one's co-worker and one's company. An ethical dilemma might best be contrasted with an ordinary, nonethical dilemma, say, a conflict of two desires ("I love the chicken *cacciatore,* but I am also in the mood for steak tonight") or between a desire and an obligation ("I know I promised him I would study with him tonight, but then I'll miss that great movie").

Responsibilities often involve obligations, and obligations sometimes conflict. Ideally, an organization will try to minimize such conflicts, either by carefully structuring the organization such that priorities are clear or by providing a set of proceduress—whether democratic or by appeal to a single authority. In an organization that is not so structured or that is rife with politics, however, such conflicts tend to be far more common. There may be no established priorities between conflicting rules. There may be no possibility of consensus or no single authority who will accept ultimate responsibility for resolution of conflicts. Most serious of all (but not at all uncommon), there may be pressures from the top to perform—"solve this problem," "meet this deadline," or "meet this financial goal"—but no guidelines or court of appeal should these pressures turn out to be unreasonable. Knowing how to handle ethical dilemmas is therefore essential to everyone's job, career, or profession, whether or not this is an official part of one's job description or an explicit part of one's duties.

The first and most important skill that is required in handling an ethical dilemma is recognizing the dilemma and recognizing it as an ethical dilemma. This sounds more self-evident than it often appears to be in practice. By their very nature, ethical dilemmas are typically painful affairs, in which there may be no satisfactory solution (either hurt X or hurt Y, disappoint P or let down Q). It is all too tempting, therefore, to misread an ethical dilemma as something else. For example, in business situations, people often try to translate an ethical dilemma into a straightforward business decision, perhaps by way of "cost/benefit analysis" in which only dollar amounts are weighed into the decision. The results are often disastrous. The engineers and senior vice presidents of one of the most successful automobile companies once decided to save a few dollars per car in return for an expected several hundred violent but avoidable deaths, calculating that the total cost of anticipated lawsuits and settlements would be less than the engineering costs of repairs. On a more personal level, people often try to make ethical dilemmas "easy" (by making them no longer "ethical") but looking simply at dollars and cents instead of taking care to consider the feelings of those people affected and those obligations which escape any dollar and cents quantification. Or, people reinterpret ethical dilemmas as nothing more than "personal differences," or they refuse responsibility by blaming the institution or system in which such dilemmas occur. But conflicts of obligation or loyalties, while undeniably "personal," are always much more than that as well, and while institutions and systems may well be blameworthy for fostering ethical dilemmas or making their resolution more difficult, it is an inescapable part of one's job, in even the best organization, to recognize and resolve ethical dilemmas.

How does one recognize such a dilemma? Ethical dilemmas are not all of a single kind, and so there are a number of different ingredients that should give us fair warning. The first is the conflicted and seemingly irresolvable nature of the situation. Whatever one decides, there are compelling arguments on the other side as well. Second, it is an ethical dilemma, which means that it is not simply one's own wishes, desires, or ambitions that are in question. Other people are involved, or larger principles, or perhaps even the well-being of an entire community. Ethics is often signified by such words as "ought" and "should," and ethical dilemmas are typically indicated by a conflict of such "oughts": on the one hand I ought to do X (because it is part of my new job description), but on the other hand I ought to do Y (because I promised that I would do so before I was promoted). Conflicts of loyalties are among the most common ethical dilemmas on the job, and these are not to be construed as merely "personal" issues. The question is, which loyalty takes priority? What are the sources of these loyalties and are the loyalties justified? What are the consequences of following one loyalty rather than the other? Conflicts of duties on the job are also common, particularly if the job is complex, or if it was created as an amalgam of two (or more) different jobs, or if the duties involved shift with shifting circumstances or changing personnel. Again, one must evaluate the priority of these conflicting duties, trace and evaluate their origins, their continuing significance and the consequences of one breach of duty rather than the other.

Once recognized as an ethical dilemma, the most important feature in its resolution is the thoroughness with which it is pursued. By its very nature, an ethical dilemma always leaves loose ends, leaves something undone or someone unsatisfied. It is therefore the conscientiousness of the resolution, rather than the resolution itself, that may be the test by which a person is measured. To have considered two (or more) difficult options and their consequences and chosen with difficulty between them is almost always the best that one can do. To have chosen a single conclusion without considering the alternatives, without considering the plight of the various people involved, and without considering the various possible consequences may be unforgivable, even if one were to choose (by chance) the best of the alternatives.

Under pressure, the temptation is to make as speedy a decision as possible, to get the whole matter out of the way. But the test of one's handling of an ethical dilemma typically comes afterwards (sometimes long afterwards, perhaps in a year-end review or a lawsuit), and it is the detail and explicitness of one's considerations that makes the difference between a wise and well-considered decision and an irresponsible "cover-up." One should take the time, therefore, to make sure that one has considered all the options and evaluated all the probable consequences for everyone involved. And above all, an ethical dilemma should not be kept secret or considered a private matter to be hidden from one's superiors. In an ethical dilemma, it is essential to know where to go for advice, for help, for legal assistance, for moral support. Living through an ethical dilemma is never a pleasant part of one's work, but handling one well is often the ultimate proof that one is suited to the career that one has chosen.

Survey Question	Percent who agree	
	1990	1980
1. Most people will tell a lie if they can gain from it.	66	60
2. People claim to have standards of honesty and morality but few stick to them when money is at stake.	67	62
3. People pretend to care more about one another than they really do.	58	58
4. An unselfish person is taken advantage of in today's world.	55	53
5. Most people are just out for themselves.	51	46
6. People inwardly dislike putting themselves out to help people.	54	46
7. Most people are not really honest by nature.	40	34

Business & Society Review

D. MORALITY

One set of values, more than any other, almost always takes priority over others. These are the most basic values of our society, those without which life as we know it would be impossible. Such a moral rule as "don't kill people you don't like" is absolutely essential; indeed, it is taken for granted as we ponder the various options facing us, for example, when dealing with a disagreeable client. "Don't steal" is not only one of the rules of competition in business, it is one of the foundations of the private property system. If everyone stole freely, it is hardly imaginable what it would mean to "own" something. Moral rules are fore-most among our *prima facie* duties and obligations.

Moral rules are usually not, however, absolute. We would think a friend fool-ish, if not downright idiotic, if he refused to break a minor promise to pick us up at the office after work instead of making a fortune in a late-breaking deal by staying a little late at his office. If a great artist requests in her will that her work be burned, our moral obligation is to do so. But if the aesthetic value of the work is sufficiently great and we override her request and our obligation, we feel per-fectly justified in refusing to burn the work. We might rightly blame an automo-bile manufacturer for building cars that are more dangerous than expected or necessary, but we do not blame the automobile companies for continuing to pro-duce what might be instruments of murder and self-destruction for thousands of people. Every business that was ever built on the basis of exploration or innova-tion has run the risk of killing some of its employees in the effort. Again, it is not clear that we could defend our way of life and at the same time consider moral values in fact as absolute. But yet, this much is true: Moral values do have *prima facie* status. Indeed, that is what we mean when we say that people have a *moral* responsibility, that they *ought* to do that action rather than any other, even if there is some considerable personal sacrifice involved. In general, moral obligations take priority over virtually all other interests and responsibilities; the prohibition against killing innocent people is more important than any financial concern. And yet any financial concern might possibly have fatal consequences, so while we might agree that morality always takes priority, we might nonetheless insist that the question of risk is not absolute, and that even in such cases, possible circum-stances can exist in which we might reconsider our moral priorities.

E. What Is Morality?

We have suggested that morality is a specific set of *prima facie* principles that we all accept without qualification, for example, the Ten Commandments. But not all ten of the commandments are generally considered "moral" ("keeping the Sab-bath" is not usually so considered, nor is "honor thy parents," however important that may be). Furthermore, many moral precepts are not included in them. Differ-ent groups in our society have strikingly different moral demands, as evidenced again by attitudes towards sex and marriage, for example. When we look at other societies, we see a bewildering array of different values that are proclaimed "moral." Some cultures, for instance, do not recognize stealing as immoral or, for that matter, killing either, depending upon who is killed and why. Adultery is considered by many people in America, if our novels, films, and television serials are taken as evidence, not to be immoral but rather to be exciting, a challenge, even "cool," or part of the good life. Indeed, even if we take such a general pre-cept as "knowingly do no harm" (*primum non nocere*), we find so much variation in terms of what counts as "harm" (physical hurt, psychological insult, financial

---

The Unimportance of Being Earnest ——

Good resolutions are useless attempts to interfere with scientific laws. Their origin is pure vanity. Their result is absolutely nothing. They give us, now and then, some of those luxurious sterile emotions that have a certain charm for the weak. That is all that can be said of them. They are simply checks that men draw on a bank where they have no account.

Oscar Wilde, *The Portrait of Dorian Gray*

---

loss, spiritual condemnation, public humiliation, loss of freedom, deprivation of pleasure, deprivation of interesting information, death, or damnation) and so many qualifications and exceptions to the rule of *who* shouldn't be harmed (our fellow human beings, fellow countrymen, people who are judged to be "good," people with the right religious beliefs, people who don't try to harm others, people who aren't too repulsive, or people we personally like) that it is easy to give

---

"We Don't Make the Laws" ——

Among the most respected of our business institutions are the insurance companies. A group of insurance executives meeting recently in New England was startled when their guest speaker, social critic Daniel Patrick Moynihan, roundly berated them for "unethical" practices. They had been guilty, Moynihan alleged, of using outdated actuarial tables to obtain unfairly high premiums. They habitually delayed the hearings of lawsuits against them in order to tire out the plaintiffs and win cheap settlements. In their employment policies they used ingenious devices to discriminate against certain minority groups.

It was difficult for the audience to deny the validity of these charges. But these men were business game players. Their reaction to Moynihan's attack was much the same as that of the automobile manufacturers to Nader, of the utilities to Senator Metcalf, and of the food processors to Senator Hart. If the laws governing their businesses change, or if public opinion becomes clamorous, they will make the necessary adjustments. But morally they have in their view done nothing wrong. As long as they comply with the letter of the law, they are within their rights to operate their businesses as they see fit.

A. Carr, "Is Business Bluffing Ethical?" *Harvard Business Review,* Jan.–Feb. 1968

---

up in desperation and conclude that anything might count as "moral" for some people and "immoral" for others.

It will not do, however, to say simply that *whatever* a person or a people hold as their highest values—that is, those that override all others—are moral. If there are people who actually do hold their financial interests in highest esteem, for example, and will actually do absolutely anything for financial gain—it does not follow that their pursuit of wealth is thereby moral. We would rather say that they are amoral (without morality). Not all values can be moral values; in fact, very few values can count as moral values, no matter how much they might mean to us and even if, on occasion, they might override moral values. Money isn't moral, no matter how much it matters, and making money cannot in itself be a moral responsibility, whatever we might say about "the social responsibility of business is maximizing profits."

Morality is a set of principles, or rules, that guide us in our actions. Moral rules tell us what to do—for example, "tell the truth," "treat others as you would like to be treated yourself"—and what not to do—for instance, "do not cheat," "do not kill," and "do not steal." The Ten Commandments, from the Old Testament, and the injunction to love one another, from the New Testament, form the core of much of our morality, which can therefore appropriately be called Judeo-Christian morality. Moral rules typically take the form of commandments, or orders, often with the words "ought" or "ought not" (or "thou shalt" or "thou shalt not"). Morality and moral rules—whether stated as law or not—form the basic structure of every society, defining the limits of what is permitted, and defining what is expected, too.

The image of morality as coming "from above" is appropriate. First, it is often said, and not only in our society, that moral laws come from God. Second, we learn these laws from our parents, who do indeed stand over us and indoctrinate us with them through their commands, examples, threats, and gestures. Finally, and most important, morality itself is above any given individual or individuals, whether it is canonized in the laws of society or not. Morality is not just another aid in getting us what we want; it is entirely concerned with right and wrong. These ethical considerations are above tampering by any individual, no matter how powerful, as if they have a life of their own.

That characteristic of morality as independent of individual desires and ambitions has led many people to characterize morality simply in terms of some absolute and independent agency. Most often, this absolute and independent agency is God.

But whether or not we believe in God, it is clear that something further is needed to help us define morality. Even assuming that there is a God, we need a way of determining what His moral commands must be. One might say that He has given these commands to various individuals, but the fact is that different people seem to have very different ideas about the morality that God has given them. Some, for example, would say that it explicitly rules out abortion and infanticide. Others would argue that God does not rule these out, but makes it clear that they are, like other forms of killing (a "holy war," for example), justifiable only in certain circumstances. And in view of such disagreements, we cannot simply appeal to God but must, with reasons that we can formulate and defend, define our morality for ourselves. There is the further question of whether we should follow God's laws just because they are His or rather, whether God is good because His laws are good. If the latter, then we have to decide what is good in order to know that God is good. If the former, then we have to decide whether or not to believe in God precisely on the basis of whether we can accept those laws. Either way, we have to decide for ourselves what laws of morality we are willing to accept.

Similar considerations hold true of that familiar appeal to conscience in determining what we ought to do or not do. Even if we believe that conscience is God-given, the same problems emerge again. Should we follow our conscience just because "conscience tells us to"? Or do we follow our conscience just because we know that what our conscience commands is good? And if we believe that conscience is simply the internalization of the moral teaching of our parents and society, then the question takes an extra dimension: should we accept or reject what we have been taught? Since our consciences often disagree, we must still decide which rules of conscience one ought to obey. Conscience doesn't determine what we ought to do, it only reminds us of rules we have already accepted.

If morality is a set of rules or principles which may sometimes go against an individual's interests, why, we must ask, should anyone be moral? Why would a person go against his best interests? Why do we accept such principles? How do we justify them? These are the questions that define the work of moral philosophy. Most of us would agree with at least the central principles of Judeo-Christian morality: don't kill, don't steal, honor your parents, and so on. We might well disagree about what counts as killing, of course. But what we might also disagree about is the reason behind the principle in the first place. Should we not kill because, ultimately, not killing is in our own best interests? Should we not kill because morality or being moral is desirable for its own sake, whether or not it is in our interests? Or is this principle perhaps just one of the curiosities of our own society, a rule that we consider extremely important but that other societies may not?

Theories of morality are formulated in order to answer these questions of interpretation. To know what is meant by a moral commandment, it is necessary to know why it should be a moral commandment in the first place. Is it in order to make us happier and healthier? In order to guarantee a more orderly society? In order to please God and not have our city destroyed, like Sodom or Gomorrah? For example, if the commandment not to kill is interpreted according to the theory that morality is a set of principles imposed upon us by God, then the interpretation of that principle is to be filled out, presumably, by looking for further information about God's intentions, whether in the Scriptures or by appealing to the current authorities in whom such opinions are vested (the Pope, religious scholars). If, on the other hand, moral principles are taken to be efficient guides to promoting human happiness and the general welfare, then the law against killing has to be interpreted and defended by showing that obedience to such a law does indeed make more people happier and fewer people miserable than they would be if there were no such law. Abstract moral theories, therefore, and the substantial principles and activities of morality are intimately connected. We often talk as if moral principles appear from nowhere. But in fact, all of our morals are embedded in a complex social network of theory and practical observations, and that network allows us to interpret and make sense of what otherwise would be empty commands that might be interpreted any way anyone wanted to interpret them. (It was clear to the Hebrews, for example, how the Ten Commandments were to be interpreted, since those were the key principles of a morality that they had more or less been following for centuries already.)

In the twenty-five hundred years or so in which scholars, preachers, and philosophers of all kinds have been formulating their moral theories, it has become evident that theories of morality tend to fall into a number of precise but overlapping categories. Most generally, we might classify moral theories into two groups: **moralities of principles** and **goal-oriented moralities.**

F.   MORALITIES OF PRINCIPLES

The least complicated example of a morality of principles would be the Ten Commandments, which simply give us a list of orders. Such orders were called by Immanuel Kant **categorical imperatives**—an "imperative" simply being an order or a commandment, "categorical" meaning "without qualification." They are categorical, or without qualification, because they offer no reasons or conditions; they just tell us what it is that we must do or not do. It is the authority of the principle itself—or the authority by which it is given to us—that is the sole reason needed to obey it. In addition, of course, obeying the principle might in fact be good for us; indeed, it might even be the preconditions for the stability of our society. But a morality of principles insists that it is the status of the principle itself, apart from its consequences and whatever personal reasons we might find for obeying it, that is its justification for us.

Moralities of principles may appeal to a number of authorities, and these authorities may be either within us or outside of us. The traditional Judeo-Christian moral theory makes the authority and the source of morality (God) wholly outside of us (although there may be some inner reminder as well, such as conscience). But moralities of principles may be secular as well as religious, and the king, the president, the state in general, or the local oracle or prophet may serve as source and authority of moral principles. When people say, "you must obey it, it's the law," they are tacitly appealing to the state (or the "law") as an authority to be obeyed, even if the consequences of the law in question are such that we might all be better off if there were no such law. And within the family, it is often the case that, without understanding the purpose or the consequences of an order, young children are expected to obey their parents, just because they are, in that context, the authorities.

KANT AND THE AUTHORITY OF REASON

The most complex and sophisticated theories of moralities of principles, however, are the ones that make the authority *internal* to us. According to such theories, moral rules and principles are not imposed upon us by God or by society. Rather, they are to be found within us, as *conscience,* for example, or the voice of *reason.* Kant developed this type of moral theory and insisted that morality, whatever else it might be, is first of all a matter of reason and rationality, and that the source of moral principles—however we might learn them as children—is ultimately in ourselves. He called this *autonomy,* which means that every one of us is capable of figuring out what is right or wrong on his or her own, without appeal to external authority, just by using the faculty of reason. It is the authority of reason that justifies moral principles, and Kant added the intriguing suggestion that the laws of God are justified because they too are clearly rational, whereas the traditional view is that the laws of God are justified just because they are from God. (Kant believed devoutly in God, but he also believed that morality has to be a matter of autonomy for us, which means that God cannot give us laws; He can only tell us what our reason is already capable of justifying.)

Kant's morality of principles theory begins with the insistence that it is always the rationality of the principles, not the consequences of our actions, that is morally relevant. Accordingly, he said, it is not so much our actions themselves which are of moral interest (since any number of circumstances or events can interfere with them) but rather our *intentions,* which are completely within our control. (Kant called this a "good will.") A people are moral insofar as they try to be moral, to obey moral principles, to do their *duty.* And though obeying these moral principles and trying to do our duty will, in most cases, benefit both us and other people, this is in no way relevant to their justification. The justification for being moral is simply that it is the rational thing to do. Nothing else. (See the Historical Interlude to this chapter.)

If, as Kant maintained, consequences themselves are irrelevant, how are we to decide what the moral thing to do *is?* First of all, Kant didn't say that consequences are in no way to be considered; what he said was that we are not concerned with the *actual* consequences (which, as in the case of an accident, may have little or nothing to do with our intentions). But we are concerned with the *intended* consequences, and, more important, we are concerned with the overall rationality of a particular *type* of action. For example, suppose we want to know whether it would be moral to tell a lie in certain circumstances. Suppose I need fifteen dollars immediately, but I know that I cannot pay it back. I now consider, "Should I lie to you and tell you that I will pay you back when I know very well that I won't?" But since what concerns us here is the rationality of such action,

Kant ——

Nothing can possibly be conceived in the world, or even out of it, which can be called good without qualification, except a good will.

To secure one's own happiness is a duty, at least indirectly; for discontent with one's condition, under a pressure of many anxieties and amidst unsatisfied wants, might easily become a great temptation to transgression of duty.

Kant's formulations of the categorical imperative:

1. Act only on the maxim *[intention]* whereby you can at the same time will that it should become a universal law.

2. Act as if the maxim of your action were to become by your will a universal law of nature.

3. Always act so as to treat humanity, whether in yourself or in others, as an end in itself, never merely as a means.

4. Always act as if to bring about, and as a member of, a Kingdom of Ends *[that is, an ideal community in which everyone is always moral].*

—Fundamental Principles of the Metaphysics of Morals

rather than the consequences of this particular transaction, what I must ask myself, according to Kant, is whether such action could be carried out *generally* by everyone in similar circumstances. Thus I ask myself, "What if everyone were to borrow money under false pretenses, by lying about being able to pay it back?" Kant's answer is clear: if everyone were to lie about paying back money, it would be a very short time until no one would believe anyone else who promised to pay back money. If someone said to you, "Could you lend me five dollars? I'll pay you back tomorrow," you would simply laugh and consider it some kind of a joke. This, Kant argued, is enough to show that the intended action is immoral and irrational. If it's not possible for everyone to act similarly, then the action in question is immoral and should not be taken.

Now we get a clear view of what is perhaps the most important feature of Kant's morality of principles theory. The test of a moral principle's rationality its *universalizability*—that is, its capacity to be generalized for everyone, everywhere. What this also means is that one and the same *set* of moral principles will apply to every person, in every society, at every time in history, regardless of the particular circumstances and interests of individuals or different societies. Of course, this is also sometimes said to be true of God-given moralities (though not, usually, of moralities whose authority resides within a particular society). Customs may differ, of course, but morality must be the same everywhere. Thus the authority of reason, for Kant, was as powerful and as universal as the authority of God in His giving us the Ten Commandments. Indeed, Kant said, they are one and the same authority.

G.   GOAL-ORIENTED MORAL THEORIES

Goal-oriented moralities do not place such an emphasis on authority or on the source or status of principles. Indeed, it is possible to have a goal-oriented morality that contains few if any principles as such. Aristotle's *Ethics* was somewhat like this, insofar as the emphasis was on how people behaved and on their fitting into the practices of the community rather than obeying principles for their own sakes. But even where there are principles in goal-oriented moralities (and Aristotle's Greece was full of principles too) they are not taken as absolutes in themselves, but rather only as guidelines, as instruments to achieving the ideal society and the best life for everyone.

> **John Stuart Mill** was born in London in 1806. His father was also a famous philosopher, and the young man was subjected to a rigorous education in virtually every field of knowledge. He became the leading logician, social scientist, and moral theorist of nineteenth-century England. His view of individual liberty (as the right not to be interfered with so long as you do no harm to others) is still the basis of much of our own thinking about civil liberties, and his theory of morals—utilitarianism—is still taken to be the dominant moral theory, according to many contemporary philosophers. He died in 1873.

UTILITARIANISM: BENTHAM AND MILL

The clearest case of a goal-oriented moral theory in modern times is a still-dominant view called **utilitarianism,** which was formulated in the eighteenth and nineteenth centuries by a number of British philosophers and social thinkers, including Jeremy Bentham (1748–1832) and John Stuart Mill (1806–1873). Utilitarianism is clearly a goal-oriented moral theory because it places all of its emphasis on the actual consequences of moral rules and principles, and insists that they be justified only by appeal to how happy they make us. The morality of principles theories, on the other hand, do not ask whether being moral will make us happier; they insist that we ought to be moral for the sake of being moral. Of course, morality of principles theorists also want to be happy and want us all to

> **The utility principle:** Always act for the greatest good for the greatest number of people.

be happy too, but they separate, as the utilitarians do not, moral questions of what is *right* from merely practical questions of what will benefit or harm us.

For the utilitarian, however, questions of what will benefit or harm us count as everything, as Mill said succinctly, "The sole evidence it is possible to produce that anything is desirable is that people actually do desire it." The goal of morality, according to Mill, Bentham, and almost all other utilitarians, is to make people happy, to give them pleasure, and spare them pain. Indeed, Bentham developed a "happiness calculus" precisely in order to calculate, for any action or law, what the consequences in terms of pleasure and pain would be. Thus, in the previous section, if we wanted to evaluate the action that Kant rejected as "immoral" and "irrational," we would not ask, "What if everyone were to lie?" but rather, "What would be the actual consequences of my lying in this situation?" Bentham would essentially add up the benefits of the action, using a quantitative point system, subtract the painful consequences from this, and see whether the action was therefore desirable or not.

John Stuart Mill qualified Bentham's calculus considerably. Mill insisted, for example, that there were different *qualities* of pleasure and pain as well as differences in *quantity*. It is better to be only slightly satisfied with a "higher" pleasure than to be very satisfied with a lower pleasure—or, as Mill phrased it metaphorically in his work *Utilitarianism:*

> *It is better to be a human being dissatisfied than a pig satisfied; better to be Socrates dissatisfied than a fool satisfied.*

Mill's qualification makes the calculations virtually impossible, but the basic principle is still the same: the greatest good for the greatest number of people, the most happiness and the least pain for as many people as possible, for every act and every law or principle. (See Historical Interlude.)

H.   SOME MINIMAL CONDITIONS OF MORALITY

This book is not the forum to debate the correct conception of morality or to enter into the sometimes virulent polemics regarding its application outside of business life. For most people most of the time, however, it is not the conception or morality that is important, but simply its acceptance, that is, we all want to *be* moral. To be moral, minimally, is to accept the following six guidelines in our behavior as a means of sorting out the conflicts in which we are daily involved.

1. *Morality means consistency.* It means treating similar cases similarly. If two employees work equally hard for equally long, and the only difference between them is that you occasionally enjoy a drink after work with one, morality means that you should, in your position as their superior, treat them the same, give them equal raises, and give them equal consideration for promotion.

2. *Morality means universality.* It means applying to ourselves the same considerations we apply to others, and vice versa. If it is wrong for someone else to hold clandestine meetings to get a new client or an account, it is wrong for us too. If it is correct to lubricate a deal with an extravagant dinner party, it is correct for our competitor too. Universality also means that the same considerations must apply to *anyone* involved (or not involved). Indeed, one of the basic meanings of morality is that, as a universal consideration, it transcends all roles and other responsibilities and applies to all individuals, just as a matter of their belonging to a certain society. (Let us leave open the difficult question about whether it also extends to all peoples at all times. Then we must also leave open the very difficult questions about morals in international cross-cultural business, in which moral rules might be very different in different cultures.)

3. *Morality means reasons.* Much of what we do in life is a matter of personal taste, spontaneity, or "whim"; it is nobody's business but our own. Morality, however, means the willingness to give reasons, to back up our actions with justifications, sometimes with a principle ("I would never lie to a client"), sometimes just with an explanation ("I thought this would be best for everyone involved"). The reasons too, however, must fit the first two conditions; that is, they must be consistent (contrary reasons for similar acts or the same reason for very different actions are contradictory), and they must be universal, applying to *anyone* who might be or might have been involved in a similar position. Reasons must also fit the next standard, which is the key to the content of all morality.

4. *Morality means concern for others.* Rigid principles alone, however consistent, universal, and backed by reasons, are not moral unless they are essentially concerned with other people's (as well as our own) well-being. This is the "utilitarian" component of morality. Principles may be excellent rules of thumb for the best thing to do or not to do most of the time, but the reasons behind the

A Test for Morals ——

In the course of teaching business classes through the semesters, I have been the butt of a great many accusations about the unethical behavior of American entrepreneurs, the deceptive advertising of Madison Avenue silver tongues, and even the rolling back of odometers by the local used-car dealers. I have not been personally involved in any of the activity, I hasten to add, I have simply been held accountable for it. All of it. By business students.

Enough, I said one day. I have done nothing wrong. I am not a crook. I vowed to bring the issue to the surface.

I set about my plan by inviting comments from my business students . . . about the structure of the system. The real question, as I saw it, was whether our business activity is inherently unethical or whether business persons are simply a product of our social system and therefore a reflection of our collective social values. Hogwash, they said. . . .

In pressing for more substance in their arguments, each semester I posed the same question to them at least once on written exams. I asked for detailed discussion. And on those very exams, I deliberately made grading mistakes on the numerous other questions, giving my students the advantage by two to five points. In short, I gave them grades which clearly were too high.

I turned back their papers, smugly awaiting the rush of feet to my desk to point out my error and to bring their unquestionably ethical behavior to a shining apex. I was confident of my students' motives. When none of them rushed forward, I pointed out the need for them to review my grading lest I had made a mistake on their papers. Still no comment. . . . Not one student, in my seven years of teaching, has ever come forward to point out my error in their favor. . . .

My game usually ends each semester when I nonchalantly explain my own dirty trick on the last class day, thus giving them every opportunity to come clean before final exam day. . . . "Surely, it is a hoax," they say. "For shame," I mumble under my breath, enunciating clearly so they can hear me. I had caught them. Even set the trap. They were furious.

After years of refinement of my game of "values clarification," I have arrived at several conclusions:

1.   It is . . . too late to reach business students with ethics courses.

2.   One dirty trick in the hand is worth two fists of mud in the bush when the entire system is under attack.

3.   Our economic system is closely tied to our social system.

4.   Some of our business students, particularly those I have observed after they were exposed in my little test, would make terrific drama coaches.

Pat L. Burr, *Business and Society Review,* #19

principles are always essential, namely, that such actions as dictated by the principle are most often conducive to other people's (and our own) best interests. "Do not lie" is usually a trustworthy guideline, but the reason behind the principle is that lying usually causes trouble, foments distrust, forces the liar to remember a tangled and time-consuming web of fabrications that follow from the original lie, and so on. Concern with others' well-being can be a matter of principle, but much more likely (and likably) for most of us, it is a matter of compassion and concern of a more direct and emotional variety. We know what it *feels* like to be in their situation more or less. (We may never have starved, but we know what it's like to be hungry; we may never have been bankrupted, but we know failure.) But concern for others' well-being goes beyond concern for their health and material welfare; it also includes respect for their own sense of what's right and wrong, their own ability to make decisions for themselves, and, what we have yet to discuss in detail, a respect for their *rights*. (This is the topic of subsequent chapters.)

5. *Morality means responsibility.* Morality is moral action; it is not our fine moral posture; it is not the principles we freely pronounce to anyone who will listen; it is not willingness to criticize the moral behavior of other people; it is not, after the immoral fact, lamenting our past actions or announcing our regrets or confessing tearfully on television or apologetically to the press. Morality means taking responsibility for what we *do,* acting in accordance with other people's concerns and rights, not only in abstaining from action that violates their rights but in actively pursuing the welfare and rights of other people (as well as our own). Morality means *acting* on principles, not merely believing in them. Indeed, we have a special term of abuse for those who do not "do as they say"; we call it *hypocrisy.*

6. *Morality means character.* We have stressed throughout that moral behavior is not to be thought of as antagonistic to our own self-interests. Attention to the rights and well-being of others is only occasionally at odds with our own interests; this is where we find the most common kind of conflicts, and this is where morality comes into play as a resolution of those conflicts. But where morality does its job best is not when it is forced to come in as an external reminder about what we ought to do; morality works best when it has actually been absorbed as a matter of our character, so that we see possibilities and opportunities in a moral light, with other people's interests and rights as much a part of the picture as our own. A person of moral character actually prefers to prove that moral goodness instead of winning some competitions, knowing full well that such a self-conception and an image for other people is more reward than the winning. (A simple example of this attitude is familiar, for instance, when we sometimes let a weaker opponent win a tennis game or a chess match; indeed, it is also one of the fundamental rules of fair competition, "pick on someone your own size.") When we see our own interests in terms of such a moral self-conception, the sting is pulled out of all but the most fatal conflicts, for our own interests and the interests and rights of others virtually always turn up on the same side.

A Very Different View of Morality: Nietzsche ———

Wandering through the many subtler and coarser moralities which have so far been prevalent on earth, I found that certain features recurred regularly together and were closely associated—until I finally discovered two basic types. . . . Master morality and slave morality. . . . The noble human being separates from himself those in whom the opposite of such exalted, proud states finds expression: he despises them. It should be noted immediately that in this first type of morality the opposition of "good" and "bad" means approximately the same as "noble" and "contemptible." (The opposition of "good" and "evil" has a different origin.) One feels contempt for the cowardly, the anxious, the petty, those intent on narrow utility; also for the suspicious with their unfree glances, those who humble themselves, the doglike people who allow themselves to be maltreated, the begging flatterers, above all the liars. . . .

It is different with the second type of morality, slave morality. Suppose the violated, oppressed, suffering, unfree, who are uncertain of themselves and weary, moralize: what will their moral valuations have in common? Probably, a pessimistic suspicion about the whole condition of man will find expression, perhaps a condemnation of man along with his condition. The slave's eye is not favorable to the virtues of the powerful: he is skeptical and suspicious, subtly suspicious, of all the "good" that is honored there—he would like to persuade himself that even their happiness is not genuine. Conversely, those qualities are brought out and flooded with light which serve to ease existence for those who suffer: here pity, the complaisant and obliging hand, the warm heart, patience, industry, humility, and friendliness are honored—for here these are the most useful qualities and almost the only means for enduring the pressure of existence. Slave morality is essentially a morality of utility.

Here is the place of the origin of that famous opposition of "good" and "evil": into evil one's feelings project power and dangerousness, a certain terribleness, subtlety, and strength that does not permit contempt to develop. According to slave morality, those who are "evil" thus inspire fear; according to master morality it is precisely those who are "good" that inspire, and wish to inspire, fear, while the "bad" are felt to be contemptible.

Friedrich Nietzsche, *Beyond Good and Evil*

Only the person who ignores such concerns, in pursuit of self-interest, finds inconveniently or disastrously that morality eventually intrudes into what seemed to be a set of well-laid plans and ruins them. In a sense, then, developing a moral character is an excellent strategy to maximizing our own self-interest and conflicts of interest too.

"Bribery": A Question of Context? ——

The new "business ethics" denies to business the adaptation to cultural mores which has always been considered a moral duty in the traditional approach to ethics. It is now considered "grossly unethical"—indeed it may even be a "questionable practice" if not criminal offense—for an American business operating in Japan to retain as a "counsellor" the distinguished civil servant who retires from his official position in the Japanese government. Yet the business that does not do this is considered in Japan to behave antisocially and to violate its clear ethical duties. Business taking care of retired senior civil servants, the Japanese hold, makes possible two practices they consider essential to the public interest: that a civil servant past age 45 must retire as soon as he is outranked by anyone younger than he, and that governmental salaries and retirement pensions—and with them the burden of the bureaucracy on the taxpayer—be kept low, with the difference between what a first-rate man gets in government service and what he might earn in private employment made up after his retirement through his "counsellor's fees." The Japanese maintain that the expectation of later on being a "counsellor" encourages a civil servant to remain incorruptible, impartial, and objective, and thus to serve only the public good; his counsellorships are obtained for him by his former ministry and its recommendation depends on his rating by his colleagues as a public servant. The Germans, who follow a somewhat similar practice—with senior civil servants expected to be "taken care of" through appointment as industry-association executives—share this conviction. Yet, despite the fact that both the Japanese and the German systems seem to serve their respective societies well and indeed honorably, and even despite the fact that it is considered perfectly "ethical" for American civil servants of equal rank and caliber to move into well-paid executive jobs in business and foundations and into even more lucrative law practices, the American company in Japan that abides by a practice the Japanese consider the very essence of "social responsibility," is pilloried in the present discussion of "business ethics" as a horrible example of "unethical practices."

Peter Drucker, "Business Ethics," *Public Interest,* 1981

This leaves open the hard questions about the precise arena of moral concern, how the "well-being of others" is to be interpreted and restricted, how we resolve clashes between a sense of other people's autonomy and right to make their own decisions and our own sense of their best interests (this is an important and common conflict in the relationship between producers and consumers, for example). It provides no simple answer to the troublesome and sometimes tragic questions that arise when two *moral* interests collide, for example, an employee's moral responsibility to speak out against high level illegality in the company and the same employee's moral responsibility not to sabotage the company. But in such cases again, the sorts of reasons we muster on both sides of the argument and the strategy to finding a solution must be based on an estimation of how each alternative would affect the well-being of everyone involved (which might include the whole of the country) as well as the effects on ourselves, and how each alternative would affect the rights of other people, as well as fulfill our own sense of responsibility and priorities. It does not give us the magic "answer" to such troublesome questions as when a pre-negotiation sweetener (such as a very fancy lunch or a weekend in the company hunting lodge) becomes a bribe, or whether, and if so, bribes are moral moves in the business game (also whether or not they are illegal). It does not tell the businessperson when to pursue profits and when to sacrifice profits to social demands, consumer interests, and dubiously moral demands or conditions.

However, all this is not to say that "there are no answers in ethics"; it is to say that morality is, first of all, a certain way of dealing with the world, which begins with the equal recognition of other people's well-being and rights as well as our own. It pursues these in a morally complex world in which there are so many countervailing currents of concern that almost every decision, if we were to think about it long enough, becomes almost impossibly convoluted. But then, the purpose of morality is not to make us think ourselves into indecision; it is rather, precisely, to force us to *make* decisions, sometimes precipitously, sometimes the result of extensive consultation and thought, but always within the guidelines listed above and with a *shared* world of interests and rights as the central focus of our dealings with the world.

■ Summary and Conclusion

Business ethics is necessary because our interests and our principles often conflict; sometimes, our interests conflict with *moral* principles, which have a *prima facie* priority. In general, our conflicts can be resolved only if we are clear about our priorities, not only in the sense of what is more valuable (in the easy to measure matter of cost, for example) but also in the sense of what *kind* of value and what *scale* of value is at stake. Although business is primarily defined in terms of financial values, financial values do not always take priority in business. But neither do moral values always take priority. This is not to say that the resolution of conflicts is "arbitrary" or merely "subjective." It is only to say that there are not usually simple, universal principles that will solve our problems and resolve our conflicts. Morality, whatever else it may be, is first of all sensitivity to the complexities of a problem and to the variety of different people and interests involved in it.

■ STUDY QUESTIONS

1. You find yourself competing with several classmates (who are not good friends) for a job that you want very much. Draw up a "code of ethics" in which you clearly state the kinds of activities which you consider immoral in that competition. (We can assume from the start that illegal activities will be out of bounds.)

2. "People are basically selfish." "People are basically cooperative." Evaluate both of those positions. Which do you find yourself assuming when you talk about business life?

3. Is there a "Macbeth" in your life? How do you handle him or her?

4. Under what circumstances would you risk your life for your job? Under what circumstances would you *not* risk your life? What conditions would make you feel as if such risks were no longer voluntary on your part?

5. Is "the profit motive" essentially selfish? Does that make it *immoral?* Explain your answer.

6. What is it that defines (most of) the Ten Commandments as *moral* imperatives? On that basis, how do you recognize other moral principles that are not on that list? For example, is "do not cheat on federal income taxes" a moral principle? How about "no sex before marriage" or "do not take or give bribes"?

7. Is lying immoral? Under what circumstances?

8. Is keeping a contract a *moral* duty? Why or why not?

9. What is wrong with Procter & Gamble's sponsoring the very shows on television that it publically denounces? Is there any situation in which your behavior is analogous?

10. Kant insists that "nothing . . . can be called good without qualification except a good will." What does he mean by this? Why is it so important to our conception of morals?

11. What is wrong with "act for the greatest good for the greatest number of people"? What sort of circumstance can you describe in which doing so would be clearly *im*moral?

■ For Class Discussion

A Matter of Morals?

Hoyt P. Steele, a retired vice president of General Electric Co., acknowledges that he once authorized a payoff of as much as $1 million to a government official of Puerto Rico.*

The payoff, an amount identified in a General Electric document as "one big one," ranks among the largest by any U.S. corporation to an individual in many years. The slim, 70-year-old Mr. Steele is the first businessman, and GE is the first company, to stand trial on criminal charges stemming from the Justice Department's investigation of corporate bribery overseas.

Testifying in a dingy federal courtroom here, Mr. Steele said he authorized the payment in response to extortion demands by Carlos Velasquez Toro, an official of the Puerto Rico Water Resources Authority. Mr. Velasquez was influential in evaluating bids for a $93 million power project submitted by GE, Westinghouse Electric Corp. and other competitors. GE got the contract.

"I authorized a payment, yes; not a bribe," Mr. Steele testified under questioning from Joseph Covington, government prosecutor. "The objective was to avoid being cheated out of a contract . . . that I thought we had probably already won." . . . Instead of reporting the alleged extortion to law-enforcement authorities, Mr. Covington contends, GE took elaborate steps to conceal the $1 million payoff (Mr. Velasquez apparently turned down $300,000, describing it as an "insult"). . . .

What makes the case particularly interesting is all the scurrying that went on in GE's executive suites when revelations about the Caribbean payoff reached corporate headquarters in Fairfield, Conn. Depending on how the testimony is viewed, GE appears to be either one of the most forthright companies to be caught in payoff scandals or one of the shrewdest.

Walter A. Schlotterbeck, GE's senior vice president and general counsel, testified that he learned of a "possible" improper payment in the summer of 1975, just before the September deadline for filing the company's federal income tax return. Mr. Schlotterbeck said he instructed his subordinates to investigate, and he promptly informed GE chairman Reginald H. Jones. Mr. Jones was "quite distressed at this unhappy message I was bringing him," Mr. Schlotterbeck testified.

With the chairman's approval, Mr. Schlotterbeck testified, GE determined that it wouldn't deduct the payment as a business expense. Instead, GE listed $1,250,000 (along with $26.4 million in other nondeductible business expenses) on Schedule M of the corporate return. Schedule M identified expenses that have been taken on a company's books but not claimed on its tax return. In this way, Mr. Schlotterbeck continued, GE guarded against committing tax fraud. . . .

---

*From "Trail Reveals Tangled Tale of GE Payoff," *The Wall Street Journal,* Feb. 10, 1981. Reprinted by permission of *The Wall Street Journal,* © Dow Jones & Company, Inc. 1981. All Rights Reserved.

[GE's lead lawyer, Henry S. Ruth, thinks that] GE should be commended rather than indicted. "General Electric acted like a guy who walks into a police station to disclose a crime, and the officer says, 'Fine. You're under arrest,'" Mr. Ruth contends.

HISTORICAL INTERLUDE

IMMANUEL KANT*

Nothing can possibly be conceived in the world, or even out of it, which can be called good without qualification, except a *good will.* Intelligence, wit, judgment, and other *talents* of the mind, however they may be named, or courage, resolution, perseverance, as qualities of temperament, are undoubtedly good and desirable in many respects; but these gifts of nature may also become extremely bad and mischievous if the will which is to make use of them, and which, there-fore, constitutes what is called *character,* is not good. It is the same with the *gifts of fortune.* Power, riches, honor, even health, and the general well-being and con-tentment with one's condition which is called *happiness,* inspire pride and often presumption, if there is not a good will to correct the influence of these on the mind, and with this also to rectify the whole principle of acting, and adapt it to its end. The sight of a being who is not adorned with a single feature of a pure and good will, enjoying unbroken prosperity, can never give pleasure to an impartial rational spectator. Thus a good will appears to constitute the indispensable condi-tion even of being worthy of happiness.

A good will is good not because of what it performs or effects, not by its apt-ness for the attainment of some proposed end, but simply by virtue of the voli-tion—that is, it is good in itself, and considered by itself is to be esteemed much higher than all that can be brought about by it in favor of any inclination, nay, even of the sum-total of all inclinations. Even if it should happen that, owing to special disfavor of fortune, or the niggardly provision of a stepmother nature, this will should wholly lack power to accomplish its purpose, if with its greatest efforts it should yet achieve nothing, and there should remain only the good will (not, to be sure, a mere wish, but the summoning of all means in our power), then, like a jewel, it would still shine by its own light, as a thing which has its whole value in itself. Its usefulness or fruitlessness can neither add to nor take

---

*From Immanuel Kant, *Fundamental Principles of the Metaphysics of Morals,* trans. T. K. Abbot (New York: Longmans, Green, 1898).

away anything from this value. It would be, as it were, only the setting to enable us to handle it the more conveniently in common commerce, or to attract to it the attention of those who are not yet connoisseurs, but not to recommend it to true connoisseurs, or to determine its value.

There is, however, something so strange in this idea of the absolute value of the mere will, in which no account is taken of its utility, that notwithstanding the thorough assent of even common reason to the idea, yet a suspicion must arise that it may perhaps really be the product of mere high-flown fancy, and that we may have misunderstood the purpose of nature in assigning reason as the governor of our will. Therefore we will examine this idea from this point of view.

I omit here all actions which are already recognized as inconsistent with duty, although they may be useful for this or that purpose, for with these the question whether they are done *from duty* cannot arise at all, since they even conflict with it. I also set aside those actions which really conform to duty, but to which men have no direct *inclination,* performing them because they are impelled thereto by some other inclination. For in this case we can readily distinguish whether the action which agrees with duty is done *from duty* or from a selfish view. It is much harder to make this distinction when the action accords with duty, and the subject has besides a *direct* inclination to it. For example, it is always a matter of duty that a dealer should not overcharge an inexperienced purchaser; and wherever there is much commerce the prudent tradesman does not overcharge, but keeps a fixed price for everyone, so that a child buys of him as well as any other. Men are thus *honestly* served; but this is not enough to make us believe that the tradesman has so acted from duty and from principles of honesty; his own advantage required it; it is out of the question in this case to suppose that he might besides have a direct inclination in favor of the buyers, so that, as it were, from love he should give no advantage to one over another. Accordingly the action was done neither from duty nor from direct inclination, but merely with a selfish view.

On the other hand, it is a duty to maintain one's life; and, in addition, everyone has also a direct inclination to do so. But on this account the often anxious care which most men take for it has no intrinsic worth, and their maxim has no moral import. They preserve their life *as duty requires,* no doubt, but not *because duty requires.* On the other hand, if adversity and hopeless sorrow have completely taken away the relish for life, if the unfortunate one, strong in mind, indignant at his fate rather than desponding or dejected, wishes for death, and yet preserves his life without living it—not from inclination or fear, but from duty— then his maxim has a moral worth.

To be beneficent when we can is a duty; and besides this, there are many minds so sympathetically constituted that, without any other motive of vanity or self-interest, they find a pleasure in spreading joy around them, and can take delight in the satisfaction of others so far as it is their own work. But I maintain that in such a case an action of this kind, however proper, however amiable it may be, has nevertheless no true moral worth, but is on a level with other inclinations, for example, the inclination to honor, which, if it is happily directed to that which is in fact of public utility and accordant with duty, and consequently honorable, deserves praise and encouragement, but not esteem. For the maxim lacks the moral import, namely, that such actions be done *from duty,* not from inclination. Put the case that the mind of that philanthropist was clouded by sorrow of his own extinguishing all sympathy with the lot of others, and that while he still has the power to benefit others in distress, he is not touched by their trouble because he is absorbed with his own; and now suppose that he tears himself out of this dead insensibility and performs the action without any inclination to it, but simply from duty, then first has his action its genuine moral worth. Further still, if nature has put little sympathy in the heart of this or that man, if he, supposed to be an upright man, is by temperament cold and indifferent to the sufferings of others, perhaps because in respect of his own he is provided with the special gift of patience and fortitude, and supposes, or even requires, that others should have the same—and such a man would certainly not be the meanest product of nature—but if nature had not specially framed him for a philanthropist, would he not still find in himself a source from whence to give himself a far higher worth than that of a good-natured temperament could be? Unquestionably. It is just in this that the moral worth of the character is brought out which is incomparably the highest of all, namely, that he is beneficent, not from inclination, but from duty. . . .

The second proposition is: That an action done from duty derives its moral worth, *not from the purpose* which is to be attained by it, but from the maxim by which it is determined, and therefore does not depend on the realization of the object of the action, but merely on the *principle of volition* by which the action has taken place, without regard to any object of desire. It is clear from what precedes that the purposes which we may have in view in our actions, or their effects regarded as ends and springs of the will cannot give to actions any unconditional or moral worth. In what, then, can their worth lie if it is not to consist in the will and in reference to its expected effect? It cannot lie anywhere but in the *principle of the will* without regard to the ends which can be attained by the action. For the will stands between its *a priori* principle, which is formal, and its *a posteriori* spring which is material, as between two roads, and as it must be determined by something, it follows that it must be determined by the formal principle of volition when an action is done from duty, in which case every material principle has been withdrawn from it.

The third proposition, which is a consequence of the two preceding, I would express thus: *Duty is the necessity of acting from respect for the law.* I may have *inclination* for an object as the effect of my proposed action, but I cannot have *respect* for it just for this reason that it is an effect and not an energy of will. Similarly, I cannot have respect for inclination, whether my own or another's; I can at most, if my own, approve it; if another's, sometimes even love it, that is, look on it as favorable to my own interest. It is only what is connected with my will as a principle, by no means as an effect—what does not subserve my inclination; but overpowers it, or at least in case of choice excludes it from its calculation—in other words, simply the law of itself, which can be an object of respect, and hence a command. Now an action done from duty must wholly exclude the influence of inclination, and with it every object of the will, so that nothing remains which can determine the will except objectively the *law,* and subjectively *pure respect* for this practical law, and consequently the maxim that I should follow this law even to the thwarting of all my inclinations.

Thus the moral worth of an action does not lie in the effect expected from it, nor in any principle of action which requires to borrow its motive from this expected effect. For all these effects—agreeableness of one's condition, and even the promotion of the happiness of others—could have been also brought about by other causes, so that for this there would have been no need of the will of a rational being; whereas it is in this alone that the supreme and unconditional good can be found. The pre-eminent good which we call moral can therefore consist in nothing else than *the conception of law* in itself, *which certainly is only possible in a rational being,* in so far as this conception, and not the expected effect, determines the will. This is a good which is already present in the person who acts accordingly, and we have not to wait for it to appear first in the result.

But what sort of law can that be the conception of which must determine the will, even without paying any regard to the effect expected from it, in order that this will may be called good absolutely and without qualification? As I have deprived the will of every impulse which could arise to it from obedience to any law, there remains nothing but the universal conformity of its actions to law in general, which alone is to serve the will as a principle. . . .

I am never to act otherwise than so *that I could also will that my maxim should become a universal law.* Here, now, it is the simple conformity to law in general, without assuming any particular law applicable to certain actions, that serves the will as its principle, and must so serve it if duty is not to be a vain delusion and a chimerical notion. The common reason of men in its practical judgments perfectly coincides with this, and always has in view the principle here suggested. Let the question be, for example, May I when in distress make a promise with the intention not to keep it? I readily distinguish here between the two significations which the question may have: whether it is prudent or whether it is right to make a false promise? The former may undoubtedly often be the case. I see clearly indeed that it is not enough to extricate myself from a present difficulty by means of this subterfuge, but it must be well considered whether there may not hereafter spring from this lie much greater inconvenience than that from which I now free myself, and as, with all my supposed *cunning,* the consequences cannot be so easily foreseen but that credit once lost may be much more injurious to me than any mischief which I seek to avoid at present, it should be considered whether it would not be more *prudent* to act herein according to a universal maxim, and to make it a habit to promise nothing except with the intention of keeping it. But it is soon clear to me that such a maxim will still only be based on the fear of consequences. Now it is a wholly different thing to be truthful from duty, and to be so from apprehension of injurious consequences. In the first case, the very notion of the action implies a law for me; in the second case, I must first look about elsewhere to see what results may be combined with it which would affect myself. For to deviate from the principle of duty is beyond all doubt wicked; but to be unfaithful to my maxim of prudence may often be very advantageous to me, although to abide by it is certainly safer. The shortest way, however, and an unerring one, to discover the answer to this question whether a lying promise is consistent with duty, is to ask myself, Should I be content that my maxim (to extricate myself from difficulty by a false promise) should hold good as a universal law, for myself as well as for others; and should I be able to say to myself, "Every one may make a deceitful promise when he finds himself in a difficulty from which he cannot otherwise extricate himself?" Then I presently become aware that, while I can will the lie, I can by no means will that lying should be a universal law. For with such a law there would be no promises at all, since it would be in vain to allege my intention in regard to my future actions to those who would not believe this allegation, or if they over-hastily did so, would pay me back in my own coin. Hence my maxim, as soon as it should be made a universal law, would necessarily destroy itself.

There is therefore but one categorical imperative, namely, this: *Act only on that maxim whereby thou canst at the same time will that it should become a universal law.*

Now if all imperatives of duty can be deduced from this one imperative as from their principle, then, although it should remain undecided whether what is called duty is not merely a vain notion, yet at least we shall be able to show what we understand by it and what this notion means.

Since the universality of the law according to which effects are produced constitutes what is properly called *nature* in the most general sense (as to form)—that is, the existence of things so far as it is determined by general laws— the imperative of duty may be expressed thus: *Act as if the maxim of thy action were to become by thy will a universal law of nature.*

We will now enumerate a few duties, adopting the usual division of them into duties to ourselves and to others, and into perfect and imperfect duties.

1.   A man reduced to despair by a series of misfortunes feels wearied of life, but is still so far in possession of his reason that he can ask himself whether it would not be contrary to his duty to himself to take his own life. Now he inquires whether the maxim of his action could become a universal law of nature. His maxim is: From self-love I adopt it as a principle to shorten my life when its longer duration is likely to bring more evil than satisfaction. It is asked then simply whether this principle founded on self-love can become a universal law of nature. Now we see at once that a system of nature of which it should be a law to destroy life by means of the very feeling whose special nature it is to impel to the improvement of life would contradict itself, and therefore could not exist as a system of nature; hence that maxim cannot possibly exist as a universal law of nature, and consequently would be wholly inconsistent with the supreme principle of all duty.

2.   Another finds himself forced by necessity to borrow money. He knows that he will not be able to repay it, but sees also that nothing will be lent to him unless he promises stoutly to repay it in a definite time. He desires to make this promise, but he has still so much conscience as to ask himself: Is it not unlawful and inconsistent with duty to get out of a difficulty in this way? Suppose, however, that he resolves to do so, then the maxim of his action would be expressed thus: When I think myself in want of money, I will borrow money and promise to repay it, although I know that I never can do so. Now this principle of self-love or of one's own advantage may perhaps be consistent with my whole future welfare; but the question now is, Is it right? I change then the suggestion of self-love into a universal law, and state the question thus: How would it be if my maxim were a universal law? Then I see at once that it could never hold as a universal law of nature, but would necessarily contradict itself. For supposing it to be a universal law that everyone when he thinks himself in a difficulty should be able to promise whatever he pleases, with the purpose of not keeping his promise, the promise itself would become impossible, as well as the end that one might have in view in it, since no one would consider that anything was promised to him, but would ridicule all such statements as vain pretenses.

3.   A third finds in himself a talent which with the help of some culture might make him a useful man in many respects. But he finds himself in comfortable circumstances and prefers to indulge in pleasure rather than to take pains in enlarging and improving his happy natural capacities. He asks, however, whether his maxim of neglect of his natural gifts, besides agreeing with his inclination to indulgence, agrees also with what is called duty. He sees then that a system of nature could indeed subsist with such a universal law, although men (like the South Sea islanders) should let their talents rest and resolve to devote their lives merely to idleness, amusement, and propagation of their species—in a word to enjoyment; but he can not possibly *will* that this should be a universal law of nature, or be implanted in us as such by a natural instinct. For, as a rational being, he necessarily wills that his faculties be developed, since they serve him, and have been given him, for all sorts of possible purposes.

4.   A fourth, who is in prosperity, while he sees that others have to contend with great wretchedness and that he could help them, thinks: What concern is it of mine? Let everyone be as happy as Heaven pleases, or as he can make himself; I will take nothing from him nor even envy him, only I do not wish to contribute anything to his welfare or to his assistance in distress! Now no doubt, if such a mode of thinking were a universal law, the human race might very well subsist, and doubtless even better than in a state in which everyone talks of sympathy and good will, or even takes care occasionally to put it into practice, but, on the other side, also cheats when he can, betrays the rights of men, or otherwise violates them. But although it is possible that a universal law of nature might exist in accordance with that maxim, it is impossible to *will* that such a principle should have the universal validity of a law of nature. For a will which resolved this would contradict itself, inasmuch as many cases might occur in which one would have need of the love and sympathy of others, and in which, by such a law of

nature, spring from his own will, he would deprive himself of all hope of the aid he desires.

These are a few of the many actual duties, or at least what we regard as such, which obviously fall into two classes on the one principle that we have laid down. We must be *able to will* that a maxim of our action should be a universal law. This is the canon of the moral appreciation of the action generally. Some actions are of such a character that their maxim cannot without contradiction be even conceived as a universal law of nature, far from it being possible that we should *will that it should* be so. In others, this intrinsic impossibility is not found, but still it is impossible to *will* that their maxim should be raised to the universality of a law of nature, since such a will would contradict itself. It is easily seen that the former violate strict or rigorous (inflexible) duty; the latter only laxer (meritorious) duty. Thus it has been completely shown by these examples how all duties depend as regards the nature of the obligation (not the object of the action) on the same principle.

Now I say, man and generally any rational being *exists* as an end in himself, *not merely as a means* to be arbitrarily used by this or that will, but in all his actions, whether they concern himself or other rational beings, must be always regarded at the same time as an end. All objects of the inclinations have only a conditional worth; for if the inclinations and the wants founded on them did not exist, then their object would be without value. But the inclinations themselves, being sources of want are so far from having an absolute worth for which they should be desired that, on the contrary, it must be the universal wish of every rational being to be wholly free from them. Thus the worth of any object which is to *be acquired* by our action is always conditional. Beings whose existence depends not on our will but on nature's, have nevertheless, if they are not rational beings, only a relative value as means and are therefore called *things;* rational beings, on the contrary, are called *persons,* because the very nature points them out as ends in themselves, that is, as something which must not be used merely as means, and so far therefore restricts freedom of action (and is an object of respect). These, therefore, are not merely subjective ends whose existence has a worth *for us* as an effect of our action, but *objective ends,* that is, things whose existence is an end in itself—an end, moreover, for which no other can be substituted, which they should subserve *merely* as means, for otherwise nothing whatever would possess *absolute worth;* but if all worth were conditioned and therefore contingent, then there would be no supreme practical principle of reason whatever.

If then there is a supreme practical principle or, in respect of the human will, a categorical imperative, it must be one which, being drawn from the conception of that which is necessarily an end for everyone because it is *an end in itself,* constitutes an *objective* principle of will, and can therefore serve as a universal practical law. The foundation of this principle is: *rational nature exists as an end in itself.* Man necessarily conceives his own existence as being so; so far then this is a *subjective* principle of human actions. But every other rational being regards its existence similarly, just on the same rational principle that holds for me; so that it is at the same time an objective principle form which as a supreme practical law all laws of the will must be capable of being deduced. Accordingly the practical imperative will be as follows: *So act as to treat humanity, whether in thine own person or in that of any other, in every case as an end withal, never as means only.*

JOHN STUART MILL*

O n the present occasion, I shall, without further discussion of the other theories, attempt to contribute something towards the understanding and appreciation of the "utilitarian" or "happiness" theory, and towards such proof as it is susceptible of. It is evident that this cannot be proof in the ordinary and popular meaning of the term. Questions of ultimate ends are not amenable to direct proof. Whatever can be proved to be good must be so by being shown to be a means to something admitted to be good without proof. The medical art is proved to be good by its conducing to health; but how is it possible to prove that health is good? The art of music is good, for the reason, among others, that it produces pleasure; but what proof is it possible to give that pleasure is good? If then, it is asserted that there is a comprehensive formula, including all things which are in themselves good, and that whatever else is good is not so as an end but as a means, the formula may be accepted or rejected, but is not a subject of what is commonly understood by proof. We are not, however, to infer that its acceptance or rejection must depend on blind impulse, or arbitrary choice. There is a larger meaning of the word "proof," in which this question is as amenable to it as any other of the disputed questions of philosophy. The subject is within the cognizance of the rational faculty; and neither does that faculty deal with it solely in the way of intuition. Considerations may be presented capable of determining the intellect either to give or withhold its assent to the doctrine; and this is equivalent to proof.

What Utilitarianism Is

A passing remark is all that needs be given to the ignorant blunder of supposing that those who stand up for utility as the test of right and wrong use the term in that restricted and merely colloquial sense in which utility is opposed to pleasure. An apology is due to the philosophical opponents of utilitarianism, for even the momentary appearance of confounding them with anyone capable of so absurd a misconception; which is the more extraordinary, inasmuch as the contrary accusation, of referring everything to pleasure, and that, too, in its grossest form, is another of the common charges against utilitarianism: and, as has been pointedly

---

*From John Stuart Mill, *Utilitarianism* (New York: Longmans, Green, 1861).

remarked by an able writer, the same sort of persons, and often the very same persons, denounce the theory "as impracticably dry when the word 'utility' precedes the word 'pleasure,' and as too practicably voluptuous when the word 'pleasure' precedes the word 'utility'." Those who know anything about the matter are aware that every writer, from Epicurus to Bentham, who maintained the theory of utility, meant by it, not something to be contradistinguished from pleasure, but pleasure itself, together with exemption from pain; and instead of opposing the useful to the agreeable or the ornamental, have always declared that the useful means these, among other things. Yet the common herd, including the herd of writers, not only in newspapers and periodicals, but in books of weight and pretension, are perpetually falling into this shallow mistake. Having caught up the word "utilitarian," while knowing nothing whatever about it but its sound, they habitually express by it the rejection or the neglect of pleasure in some of its forms: of beauty, of ornament, or of amusement. Nor is the term thus ignorantly misapplied solely in disparagement, but occasionally in compliment, as though it implied superiority to frivolity and the mere pleasures of the moment. And this perverted use is the only one in which the word is popularly known, and the one from which the new generation is acquiring its sole notion of its meaning. Those who introduced the word, but who had for many years discontinued it as a distinctive appellation, may well feel themselves called upon to resume it if by doing so they can hope to contribute anything towards rescuing it from this utter degradation.

The creed which accepts as the foundation of morals "utility" or the "greatest happiness principle" holds that actions are right in proportion as they tend to promote happiness, wrong as they tend to produce the reverse of happiness. By happiness is intended pleasure, and the absence of pain; by unhappiness, pain, and the privation of pleasure. To give a clear view of the moral standard set up by the theory, much more requires to be said; in particular, what things it includes in the ideas of pain and pleasure; and to what extent this is left an open question. But these supplementary explanations do not affect the theory of life on which this theory of morality is grounded—namely, that pleasure and freedom from pain are the only things desirable as ends, and that all desirable things (which are as numerous in the utilitarian as in any other scheme) are desirable either for the pleasure inherent in themselves, or as means to the promotion of pleasure and the prevention of pain.

Now such a theory of life excites in many minds, and among them in some of the most estimable in feeling and purpose, inveterate dislike. To suppose that life has (as they express it) no higher end than pleasure—no better and nobler object of desire and pursuit—they designate as utterly mean and groveling; as a doctrine worthy only of swine, to whom the followers of Epicurus were, at a very early period, contemptuously likened, and modern holders of the doctrine are occasionally made the subject of equally polite comparisons by its German, French, and English assailants.

When thus attacked, the Epicureans have always answered that it is not they, but their accusers, who represent human nature in a degrading light, since the accusation supposes human beings to be capable of no pleasures except those of which swine are capable. If this supposition were true, the charge could not be gainsaid, but would then be no longer an imputation; for if the sources of pleasure were precisely the same to human beings and to swine, the rule of life which is good enough for the one would be good enough for the other. The comparison of the Epicurean life to that of beasts is felt as degrading, precisely because a beast's pleasures do not satisfy a human being's conceptions of happiness. Human beings have faculties more elevated than the animal appetites and, when once made conscious of them, do not regard anything as happiness which does not include their gratification. I do not, indeed, consider the Epicureans to have been by any means faultless in drawing out their scheme of consequences from the utilitarian principle. To do this in any sufficient manner, many Stoic, as well as Christian, elements require to be included. But there is no known Epicurean theory of life which does not assign to the pleasures of the intellect, of the feelings and imagination, and of the moral sentiments, a much higher value of pleasures than to those of mere sensation. It must be admitted, however, that utilitarian writers in general have placed the superiority of mental over bodily pleasures chiefly in the greater permanency, safety, uncostliness, etc., of the former—that is, in their circumstantial advantages rather than in their intrinsic nature. And on all these points utilitarians have fully proved their case; but they might have taken the other and, as it may be called, higher ground with entire consistency. It is quite compatible with the principle of utility to recognize the fact that some kinds of pleasure are more desirable and more valuable than others. It would be absurd that, while, in estimating all other things, quality is considered as well as quantity, the estimation of pleasures should be supposed to depend on quantity alone.

If I am asked what I mean by difference of quality in pleasures, or what makes one pleasure more valuable than another, merely as a pleasure, except its being greater in amount, there is but one possible answer. Of two pleasures, if there be one to which all or almost all who have experience of both give a decided preference, irrespective of a feeling of moral obligation to prefer it, that is the more desirable pleasure. If one of the two is, by those who are competently acquainted with both, placed so far above the other that they prefer it, even though knowing it to be attended with a greater amount of discontent, and would not resign it for any quantity of the other pleasure which their nature is capable of, we are justified in ascribing to the preferred enjoyment a superiority in quality so far outweighing quantity as to render it, in comparison, of small account.

Now it is an unquestionable fact that those who are equally acquainted with and equally capable of appreciating and enjoying both, do give a most marked preference to the manner of existence which employs their higher faculties. Few human creatures would consent to be changed into any of the lower animals for a promise of the fullest allowance of a beast's pleasures; no intelligent human being would consent to be a fool, no instructed person would be an ignoramus, no person of feeling and conscience would be selfish and base, even though they should be persuaded that the fool, the dunce, or the rascal is better satisfied with his lot than they are with theirs. They would not resign what they possess more than he for the most complete satisfaction of all the desires which they have in common with him. If they ever fancy they would, it is only in cases of unhappiness so extreme that to escape from it they would exchange their lot for almost any other, however undesirable in their own eyes. A being of higher faculties requires more to make him happy, is capable probably of more acute suffering, and certainly accessible to it at more points, than one of an inferior type; but in spite of these liabilities, he can never really wish to sink into what he feels to be a lower grade of existence. We may give what explanation we please of this unwillingness; we may attribute it to pride, a name which is given indiscriminately to some of the most and to some of the least estimable feelings of which mankind are capable; we may refer it to the love of liberty and personal independence, an appeal to which was with the Stoics one of the most effective means for the inculcation of it; to the love of power or to the love of excitement, both of which do really enter into and contribute to it; but its most appropriate appellation is a sense of dignity, which all human beings possess in one form or other, and in some, though by no means in exact, proportion to their higher faculties, and which is so essential a part of the happiness of those in whom it is strong that nothing which conflicts with it could be otherwise than momentarily an object of desire to them. Whoever supposes that this preference takes place at a sacrifice of happiness—that the superior being, in anything like equal circumstances, is not happier than the inferior—confounds the two very different ideas of happiness and content. It is indisputable that the being whose capacities of enjoyment are low has the greatest chance of having them fully satisfied; and a highly endowed being will always feel that any happiness which he can look for, as the world is constituted, is imperfect. But he can learn to bear its imperfections, if they are at all bearable; and they will not make him envy the being who is indeed unconscious of the imperfections, but only because he feels not at all the good which those imperfections qualify. It is better to be a human being dissatisfied than a pig satisfied; better to be Socrates dissatisfied than a fool satisfied. And if the fool, or the pig, are of a different opinion, it is because they only know their own side of the question. The other party to the comparison knows both sides.

It may be objected that many who are capable of the higher pleasures occasionally, under the influence of temptation, postpone them to the lower. But this is quite compatible with a full appreciation of the intrinsic superiority of the higher. Men often, from infirmity of character, make their election for the nearer good, though they know it to be the less valuable; and this no less when the choice is between two bodily pleasures than when it is between bodily and mental. They pursue sensual indulgences to the injury of health, though perfectly aware that health is the greater good. It may be further objected that many who begin with youthful enthusiasm for everything noble, as they advance in years, sink into indolence and selfishness. But I do not believe that those who undergo this very common change voluntarily choose the lower description of pleasures in preference to the higher. I believe that, before they devote themselves exclusively to the one, they have already become incapable of the other. Capacity for the nobler feelings is in most natures a very tender plant, easily killed, not only by hostile influences, but by mere want of sustenance; and in the majority of young persons it speedily dies away if the occupations to which their position in life has devoted them, and the society into which it has thrown them, are not favorable to keeping that higher capacity in exercise. Men lose their high aspirations as they lose their intellectual tastes, because they have not time or opportunity for indulging them; and they addict themselves to inferior pleasures, not because they deliberately prefer them, but because they are either the only ones to which they have access, or the only ones which they are any longer capable of enjoying. It may be questioned whether any one who has remained equally susceptible to both classes of pleasures, ever knowingly and calmly preferred the lower, though many, in all ages, have broken down in an ineffectual attempt to combine both.

I have dwelt on this point, as being a necessary part of a perfectly just conception of utility or happiness considered as the directive rule of human conduct. But it is by no means an indispensable condition to the acceptance of the utilitarian standard; for that standard is not the agent's own greatest happiness, but the greatest amount of happiness altogether; and if it may possibly be doubted whether a noble character is always the happier for its nobleness, there can be no doubt that it makes other people happier, and that the world in general is immensely a gainer by it. Utilitarianism, therefore, could only attain its end by the general cultivation of nobleness of character, even if each individual were only benefited by the nobleness of others, and his own, so far as happiness is concerned, were a sheer deduction from the benefit. But the bare enunciation of such an absurdity as this last renders refutation superfluous.

According to the greatest happiness principle, as above explained, the ultimate end, with reference to and for the sake of which all other things are desirable—whether we are considering our own good or that of other people—is an existence exempt as far as possible from pain, and as rich as possible in enjoyments, both in point of quantity and quality; the test of quality and the rule for measuring it against quantity being the preference felt by those who, in their opportunities of experience, to which must be added their habits of self-consciousness and self-observation, are best furnished with the means of comparison. This, being, according to the utilitarian opinion, the end of human action, is necessarily also the standard of morality, which may accordingly be defined as "the rules and precepts for human conduct," by the observance of which an existence such as has been described might be, to the greatest extent possible, secured to all mankind; and not to them only, but, so far as the nature of things admits, to the whole sentient creation.

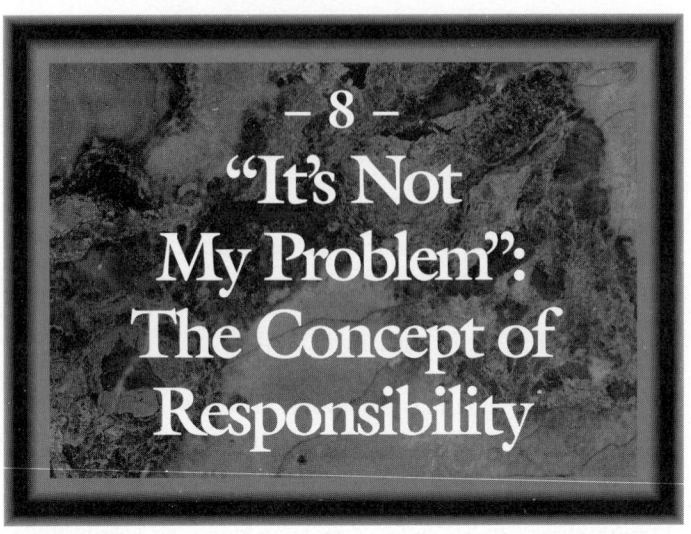

– 8 –
"It's Not My Problem": The Concept of Responsibility

Responsibility, n. A detachable burden easily shifted to the shoulders of God, Fate or Fortune, Luck or one's neighbor.
—Ambrose Bierce, The Devil's Dictionary

Living well is not living alone; it is participating in society, being part of institutions and practices, and finding ourselves in positions of responsibility with obligations to others and duties to be performed. These are not detractions from the good life, but an essential part of its nature. To be a participant in a practice is to have responsibilities, and to be a member of a society, by virtue of being a participant in certain practices, is to have *social responsibilities* as both an individual citizen and as a participant in those practices.

Being in the business world is to have responsibilities, both duties and authority within business and obligations and expectations in society more generally. Responsibilities within business might be as weighty as the fiduciary responsibility to thousands of stockholders or the responsibility of developing a new weapon in war before the enemy does; they might be as petty as being responsible for checking to make sure the lights are out or the doors are locked; they might be as personally difficult as having to fire other employees; or they might be assumed responsibilities such as dressing appropriately, not throwing garbage in the hallway, or not allowing the plants by the window to wither and die. And yet, this obvious point has been so overladen with puzzles and problems and insurmountable difficulties, and, consequently, strategies for "passing the buck," that it has all but been forgotten. Within a corporation of even modest size, the lines of responsibility have become so complex and the delegation of authority so ambiguous that virtually no one seems to be able or willing to claim responsibility, not even the chief executive officer, who can always claim that any particular responsibility was in the hands of some subordinate or another, thus passing the "buck" back down the line.

Whatever the myth of the "power of the corporation," a far more common feeling within the organization is often *impotence*—"there's nothing I can do about it," or simply, "I'm just doing my job." The slogan on everyone's desk becomes "it's not my problem," instead of the classic, "the buck stops here." No one will take responsibility because "responsibility" is very difficult to define clearly and delegate absolutely, even in the simplest institutions.

But if no one person in particular is responsible, then at least, we would think, the corporation itself is responsible. But there we hit a different problem: As a financial institution, it has been argued recently, the corporation does not have social responsibilities, except perhaps financial responsibilities for damages it has actually caused in carrying out its other financial duties. In fact, as a legally created fiction, it can be argued that corporations cannot have responsibilities or be held responsible at all. A corporation cannot be sent to jail; we can fine a corporation or legislate it out of existence, but it is a matter of somewhat scholastic argument whether this constitutes "punishment." (What or who exactly is punished if the investors get their capital out in time and can simply reinvest next week?) But employees of the corporation, even the CEO, naturally tend to pass much responsibility on to this legal fiction, in part to explain their own feelings of powerlessness and in part to point up the *collective* nature of their responsibility. But the argument too often moves from "everyone is responsible," to "no one is responsible." Indeed, corporations were originally formed to legally limit the liability of the individuals within the corporation. But, once again, the locus of responsibility has shifted, has been obscured, has passed into oblivion. The corporation itself is not literally responsible, and the natural conclusion for many of the critics of business is that American business as such is *irresponsible;* corporations refuse to accept responsibilities that, everyone else agrees, are quite obviously theirs.

Irresponsibility entails responsibility; irresponsibility is the failure to live up to responsibilities. We all do have responsibilities, by virtue of our positions in business and in society in the first place. What we find in so much of the current discussion of "the social responsibilities of business" is a hopeless tangle of confusions. The crucial question is not "who is responsible?" (however preferable it may be to single out a person or group when heads are to roll or a criminal prosecution is about to take place) but "what are everyone's responsibilities?" We must begin with the assumption that *everyone* who is in the case has responsibilities. We must understand the precise nature of these responsibilities and design some fair system of reward and punishment in general, but especially in cases of crisis and accomplishment.

A. Responsibility: Fallacies, Obscurities, and Escapism

The market is the institutionalization of non-responsibility.
—E. F. Schumacher

"The Burden of Responsibility"

In the late 1800s the philosopher F. H. Bradley defined responsibility by claiming, "For practical purposes, we need make no distinction between responsibility and liability to punishment." Ever since, philosophers and social theorists have joined with police, lynch mobs, and criminologists in equating responsibility with blame for wrongdoing and thus "liability to punishment." But responsibility is not necessarily an accusation. It is not essentially a burden. It is not usually a question of who is to be blamed. Responsibilities are positive as well as negative; responsibility means "liability to praise" as well as to blame and punishment. However, responsibility as such is not so much a matter of either praise or blame (which are its consequences) so much as a matter of the everyday demands and expectations of any person who plays virtually any role in virtually any practice. In other words, it is a mistake to think of responsibility as a "burden" or as a "liability." Our responsibilities are that set of duties and activities that constitute our jobs, our roles in the organization, and our citizenship in society. Sometimes, if we perform well enough, we may be put up for promotion or given a significant bonus; sometimes, if we perform badly enough, we may be blamed, fined, demoted, fired, or indicted. But for the most part, most of the time, and for most of us, our responsibilities and the activities that fulfill them are so routine, so familiar, indeed so often dull or not even noticed, that we do not think of them as responsibilities at all, unless we are asked or challenged ("who is in charge of . . . ?"). Our responsibilities give us "something to do"; they make our work significant by fulfilling demands and expectations; and they make us "somebody" by fitting us into the larger scheme of things, whether it be the day-to-day workings of a small department or the life-and-death demands of a society in crisis. They make us useful, valuable, important. To have responsibilities is, ultimately, to *belong.* There is nothing negative or burdensome about them, at least, most of the time.

"Moral" Responsibility

It is necessary to distinguish *moral* responsibility, which is responsibility of a very specific sort, from responsibility more generally, including most of our responsibilities within business and within society too. Moral responsibilities are those duties and obligations that are based on the rules and expectations of *morality.* Keeping promises is often cited as an example of a moral responsibility (though fulfilling contracts may be more of a borderline case). Watching out for the well-being of children is clearly a moral responsibility. Many moral responsibilities consist of responsibilities *not* to commit certain actions—not to cheat, lie, or steal from our employer, employees, or customers. Moral responsibilities, unlike the responsibilities that define a particular role or position, apply to everyone, in every role or position; in other words, they are not part of any particular practice or profession, but shared by everyone in society.

Moral responsibilities, like moral rules, have at least an initial "trump" status; they override non-moral responsibilities. Thus, if we have made a promise that conflicts with the ordinary responsibilities of our job, the moral responsibility of keeping the promise takes priority. If doing our job will result in grievous harm to innocent people, then we have a moral responsibility not to do the job. But though every job is performed only within the context of such moral responsibilities, the job itself is not defined by these. Not all responsibilities are moral responsibilities, and it is important to appreciate the importance of both moral and non-moral job-related responsibilities, without confusing them or dismissing either one of them.

Responsibility and the Law

Responsibility must also be sharply distinguished from *legal* responsibility, which requires a law or statute that can be broken and for which legal apparatus is available for indictment, conviction, and punishment. Indeed, in discussions of responsibility there is far too much attention to legal responsibility and laws, as opposed to the established responsibilities and customs of practices. It is true, of course, that every citizen has at least a *prima facie* obligation to obey the law. (Many authors have argued that this is itself a moral responsibility.) But the law by itself does not determine all responsibilities, and responsibilities often exist independently of the law. To be negligent may not be illegal; it is still irresponsible. Laws are made when confusion or chaos threatens and when responsibility needs reinforcements, but it does not define responsibility as such.

Ten years ago, executives of the Lockheed Corporation were indicted for bribing Japanese officials in order to assure the purchase of one of their new planes. The Lockheed executives insisted that they "had no choice" and that, in any case, the laws were not clear. In fact, the practice itself was extremely unclear, for it was not entirely evident that giving financial "assurances" in Japan—a more established custom—was the same as bribery in the United States (though several high Japanese government officials resigned after the scandal). In the congressional committee hearings on the matter, Dan Haughton went on record insisting:

> At the present time there is great confusion over what is legal under
> U.S. law and what is not, over what has to be reported in financial
> statements and what does not. Certainly there is a great need to have

> *the laws and regulations clarified at the earliest possible time. It is*
> *my hope that this can be done without causing undue harm to Ameri-*
> *can companies, American workers, and American shareholders. As*
> *far as Lockheed is concerned, it is my hope that the actions of our*
> *Government in this regard can be accomplished without causing the*
> *maximum amount of damage to my company.*

But social responsibility is by no means limited to legal and politically enforced obligations. Such legalistic thinking reduces all good will to duty and all kindness to obligation; the notion of "fairness" is sacrificed to mere obedience and the customs and cultures of ethics are reduced to a skeleton of legalities. But this is to miss the idea of responsibility altogether. Responsibility must first be understood in terms of the whole context of our everyday activities, satisfactions, successes, and failures. Legal responsibilities are only the limiting obligations within which our responsibilities define what we are and what we do. In the words of business ethicist Tom Donaldson, legal guidelines provide a "floor," not a "ceiling," to our ethical responsibilities.

The Ultimate Responsibility

People, not corporations, have responsibilities. It is convenient for the press, for example, to simply summarize and say "the responsibilities of the oil companies," and it is necessary legally for the courts to deal with *X* and *Y* corporation and not the people within it, at least for civil suits. It is also understandable that a person within the corporation, feeling powerless and not even knowing what decisions are being made "upstairs," will refer to "the company" as an entity unto itself. But responsibility is ultimately the responsibility of individual people within the corporation; add up those responsibilities (no matter how difficult it may be to figure out their proper delegation) and there need be none left over for the corporation to assume. *People* are responsible, not just corporations, and only rarely the business world as a whole.

Milton Friedman makes this point succinctly in *The Social Responsibility of Business:*

> *What does it mean to say that "business" has responsibilities? Only*
> *people can have responsibilities. A corporation is an artificial person*
> *and in this sense can be said to have artificial responsibilities, but*
> *"business" as a whole cannot be said to have responsibilities, even*
> *in this vague sense.*

Of course, what does *not* follow is that businesses, or even "'business' as a whole," cannot be ascribed responsibilities in another sense, namely, as the *collective* responsibilities of all the people who make up businesses and business. This, unfortunately, is what Friedman goes on to argue by way of continuing his general strategy of cutting business life and responsibilities off from the more general ethics and interests of society. But Friedman is correct at least in this: "business" as such is not responsible; *people* in business are responsible. Thus "the buck," no matter how passed around within the corporation, cannot be passed to the corporation itself, and cannot so easily be gotten rid of.

A more cynical and forceful way of making the same point can be found in a much older polemic, this one largely antagonistic to the business world, by Edward Alswortz Ross in *Sin and Society* (1907). Of the corporation, he wrote*:

> *It feels not the restraints that conscience and public sentiment lay on the business man. It fears the law no more, and public indignation far less, than does the individual. You can hiss the bad man, egg him, lampoon him, caricature him, ostracize him and his. Not so with the bad corporation. The corporation, moreover, is not in dread of hell fire. You cannot Christianize it. You may convert its stockholders, animate them with patriotism or public spirit or love of social service; but this will have little or no effect on the tenor of their corporation. In short, it is an entity that transmits the greed of investors, but not their conscience; that returns them profits but not unpopularity.*

Ross compared "passing the buck" to the pea-in-the-shell game, in which the public

> *allows itself to be kept guessing which shell the pea is under, whether the accountability is with the foreman, or the local manager, or the general manager, or the directors. How easily the public wrath is lost in the maze! Public indignation meets a cuirass of divided responsibility that scatters a shock that would have stretched iniquity prone.*

Fining the corporation, Ross argues, is no more than a "fleabite"; fining the officers of the corporation, who are then indemnified by the board of directors, is no more effective, perhaps even "encouragement to do it again." Not to be taken in, Ross argues in fire-and-brimstone style:

> *Never will the brake of the law grip these slippery wheels until prison doors yawn for the convicted officers of lawless corporations. . . . The directors of a company ought to be individually accountable for every case of misconduct of which the company receives the benefit, for every preventable deficiency or abuse that regularly goes on in the course of the business. Hold them blameless if they prove the inefficiency or disobedience of underlings, but not if they plead ignorance.*

---

*Quoted in Mintz, Morton and Jerry S. Cohen, *Power Inc.* New York: Viking, 1976.

B.   Corporate Responsibility

Individual responsibility may be the bottom line, perhaps, but there is, neverthe-less, plenty of room for blame and praise at the level of the corporation. It is not just figurative speaking that allows us to criticize or compliment a corporation for its behavior, and that is not just shorthand for commenting on the individual offi-cers and employees of the company, individually or collectively. But in what sense can a corporation, which is, after all, a fictitious entity created by law for a limited set of business objectives, be responsible? In a case in which a corpora-tion causes serious harm, for example, it is very likely that the majority of the population of the company did not have any idea what was going on, had nothing directly to do with the harm, and could probably not have done anything about it even if they had known about it. Indeed, sometimes the most serious corporation wrongdoing seems to be no more than the misbehavior or incompetence of a sin-gle individual.

A short time ago, the *Exxon Valdez* went off course and hit a reef, polluting miles and miles of pristine Alaskan wilderness, killing wildlife, ruining the local fishing industry, spoiling the coastline, and costing the Alaskan economy billions in losses and clean-up costs. The fault seemed to lie with one man, the captain of the *Valdez,* who had been drinking heavily and had left the bridge. But, then, that means that he wasn't in charge of the ship, so how could he be responsible? The actual navigation was in the not entirely competent hands of the first mate, who evidently had not been adequately trained for such an enormous responsibility. The ship did not have a pilot, who presumably would have been in the proper posi-tion to take over from the captain. It turned out, on investigation immediately after the accident, that the captain had a prior arrest record for drunken driving. Should the personnel people at Exxon have known about that? Should they have done something about it? In any case, shouldn't company policy have required that there be more than one person aboard capable of handling the tanker? Moreover, the ship was not triple-hulled, as many tankers now are, and this would have pro-vided the vessel with protection which, in all likelihood, would have minimized if not prevented the damage to both the ship and the environment. Indeed, the more we look at the case, the more diffuse the question of responsibility becomes.

In such cases, we find ourselves asking all sorts of "what-if?" questions. What if the human resources department had been more scrupulous about the driving records and personal habits of all shipping personnel? What if the naviga-tors and map makers had been more explicit about setting out the charted path of the tanker and marking the path to prevent error? What if there had been stronger regulations concerning the impact resistance of tanker hulls, or if it had been required that at least two fully qualified pilots be aboard? What if such ships were made to bypass such wilderness areas as Prince Edward Sound? (Where would they be routed then? What about a more extensive use of overland pipelines?) What if America were to cut down on its demand for oil? All of these questions were asked and debated in the months following the disaster.

The captain, who had quickly "disappeared" after the accident, was put on trial. He was found innocent of the charges. But the hard question was exactly where the blame should rest. The captain, after all, was not actually steering the vessel. The mate who was steering the ship was not held responsible although he physically caused the accident by going so far off course. Nevertheless, he was not found to be negligent or blameworthy for his actions. There were any number of people within the organization, from those in charge of ship maintenance to those in charge of personnel, who might have done more to prevent such a disaster, but it is not clear that by not doing so they were not fulfilling their duties. Ultimately, one supposes, the diffused blame all comes together in the office of the person who is in charge of the company and, therefore, all of its "actions"— the chief executive officer, the CEO. But the CEO rightly claimed that he could not possibly have known what was happening with a single captain of a single tanker in a corporation that employs hundreds of thousands of people. Should he, nevertheless, be held responsible? On what grounds? Some philosophers and legal theorists introduce the notion of *regulative* responsibility, that is, a sort of responsibility that results not from one's direct or "proximate" contact with the case at hand nor does it even suppose knowledge of the harm in question. It is responsibility that results from one's "position of overall responsibility," from being "in charge." That is, after all, what those extremely high-paid (millions of dollars) executives are supposedly paid so much money for—for taking responsibility for the company, its decisions, and mistakes.

Nevertheless, whether or not we hold the chief executive ultimately responsible, it is clear that *the company* must also be held responsible. But, again, what is it to hold a company responsible? One cannot send Exxon, as one might have done with the irresponsible captain, to prison. A court can fine Exxon, and the Alaska citizens can sue Exxon for their losses in civil court, but where does that money come from? From the stockholders, who were farther away from the mishap and much less in a position to know the situation than the chairman or the people in human resources. Why should they be penalized? And, of course, if the fines and settlements are large enough, the cost will be passed on to the consumers at the gas pump. So who is really being punished? And who is really responsible in the first place?

One reply, of course, is that no one is responsible. Or, perhaps, a few people are partly responsible, but no blame is forthcoming, and the idea that the company is responsible is simply ludicrous. Responsibility, the argument continues, belongs to individual agents. Responsibility can be shared, and several persons may be equally and fully responsible for a misdeed they performed together, such as commiting a crime, or standing by negligently while some easily preventable disaster was unfolding. (For example, consider four night watchmen playing cards and not paying attention as thieves steal the entire contents of the warehouse they are supposedly watching.) But a corporation, this argument goes, does not "act" at all. Its "actions" are nothing but the decisions and implementations of individuals within the organization. This may include virtually all of them—as in the production of their products and the collected corporate gift to the United Way at the end of the year. It may be a single individual, most likely the chairman, who makes a decision, or it may be a few individuals in the middle of the organization, acting on behalf of the corporation but nevertheless acting alone. But what does this mean, "acting on behalf of the organization"? How do we tell the difference between an employee who does wrong simply as a private citizen, one who does wrong as an employee of the company, and one who does wrong on behalf of the company? Individual responsibility is part of the answer to any question of responsibility, but it is not the whole answer. Individuals can be held responsible not only alone but in groups, as groups, and as organizations that transcend the individuals who are members.

Any large corporation is constantly in flux. People join, people leave. They retire. They are fired. They take a leave of absence. They are temporarily replaced. The identity of the corporation, in other words, cannot possibly be reduced to the collective identity of all of its employees and managers. It continues despite the change and replacement of its employees. Indeed, over a ten- or twenty-year period, any organization will experience a near total change in its personnel, and yet it remains "the same corporation." How is this possible? Well, first of all, and least interesting, it retains the same legal status, the same name, the same trademark. More interesting, it may retain the same corporate culture, the same basic form of organization, and the same way of doing things and making decisions, even though all of the decision-making slots are now filled with other people. In many instances, the people who run the corporation when scandal or disaster hit were not even there when the seeds of the scandal or the original mishaps occurred. Most drug companies, for instance, face lawsuits that stem from chemicals sold and taken ten, twenty, even thirty years earlier. It may take that long for the disastrous side effects or dangers to be known. But when the company is held responsible, the executives who ran the company and approved the sale of the drug, perhaps even knowing the dangers but not telling the public, have long since moved on or retired. And yet, we have no hesitation, at least before we think about it, in blaming *the company,* over and above any particular individuals whom we might blame as well. But then the question of corporate agency comes back to us. What is it for a corporation to act as an agent? What is the difference between a corporation and simply a mob of people, who may act together but only for the moment and without any actual organization? What does it mean to blame a corporation, and what does it mean to punish a corporation?

The agency of a corporation is determined, according to business ethicist Peter French, by the structure of its "corporate internal decision" (CID) structure.* A corporation, unlike a mob or a random collection of people (say, at a

---

*French, Peter, Jeffrey Nesteruk, and David Risser, *Corporations in the Moral Community.* Fort Worth: Harcourt Brace Jovanovich, 1992.

football game), has a formal organization, filled by people who understand not only that they are engaged in a cooperative enterprise, but that each has certain specified duties and responsibilities. The corporation can be said to have made a decision when that decision is made by the right people or passes through the designated channels of the "corporate internal decision" structure. Thus corporate responsibility is something more than collective responsibility. It depends on a structure, on a formal organization, and though the individuals who fill the positions in that organization may come and go, the structure itself remains essentially the same. A corporation is responsible for a decision and its implementation if it properly passes through the "corporate internal decision" structure. (An interesting question: how much must that structure change in a corporate "restructuring" or in the merger of two very different companies before we insist that it has become a different corporation?)

The idea of a "corporate internal decision" structure as the key to corporate responsibility allows us to answer a number of troubling questions. First of all, we can understand how it is possible for an employee of the company to do wrong *as an individual,* not as an employee of the company. He or she acts outside of the corporate internal decision procedure, not going through proper channels, not notifying the proper people of what he or she is doing, and not fulfilling the explicit or merely understood duties and responsibilities of his or her job. Of course, the corporation may be responsible for hiring such a person, and in some instances should be held responsible for his or her supervision, but if, for example, an employee takes a bribe from a customer in exchange for "looking the other way" during an obviously illegitimate transaction, the responsibility lies with the employee, not the corporation. Bank tellers, for example, are often in a position to do wrong in this way, but unless it becomes a common practice and the bank does not implement more secure safeguards, we usually do not blame the bank for such individual malfeasance. Of course, paying bribes may enter into the corporate internal decision process, if, for example, it is the chairman of the company (or someone with delegated authority) who negotiates a bribe in the name of the company, as in the famous case of the Lockheed corporation in Japan a decade ago. The idea of a corporate internal decision structure also explains how it is that corporations can be held liable for negligence. It is one thing if a designated employee fails to take responsibility or act competently concerning some event that is under his or her control. But it is possible that *no one* in the corporation has some particular duty or responsibility, and so no one is responsible when there is a disaster in that area. But nevertheless, the corporation is responsible. It is responsible for that gap in its internal decision structure. To be sure, the uppermost executives will no doubt take most of the heat, but the charge of negligence is not for them alone. The corporation has a responsibility, even if the responsibility in question is part of no one's job.

Matters are not usually so innocent, however. Disasters usually have their forewarnings, and scandals almost always leak some preliminary stink, noticeable to anyone who is paying attention and cares what is going on. More often than not, the information that might have prevented the problem is available well beforehand, and the gap in the structure is obvious in lesser matters as well. Most corporate wrongdoing is a combination of self–interest, risk taking and negligence. It is looking after profits first of all; passing the buck on a decision, thereby ensuring that disaster won't occur on one's own watch but not doing anything to actually prevent it from happening; figuring that one will probably get away with it anyway; hoping that no one will notice or the lawyers will take care of it; and rationalizing that "it's not so bad" or "we'll fix it before it becomes a serious problem." In every such instance, it seems, someone must be at fault and to blame, but all too often it seems to be no particular individual or individuals who are. It is the corporate internal decision structure itself that is to blame, or the abuse of that structure by executives who are by no means acting outside of it. Or perhaps it is the corporate culture, which cultivates toleration for certain sorts of vices and quashes certain sorts of virtues. In any case, corporate malfeasance is virtually never clearly attributable to individuals alone. Nevertheless, there is a party to blame, even if all of the individuals in the organization are faultless and have conscientiously done their jobs. But it does not follow, as some "anti-business litigators" seem to think, that every corporation is therefore at fault whenever it is involved in misfortune or tragedy. The fact that corporations can properly be held responsible does not mean that they always ought to be held responsible, and the fact that they are sometimes at fault does not mean that it can be presumed that they are in every case. The issue of responsibility has to do with fulfilling one's responsibilities as well as neglecting to do so, and if some corporations should be held more accountable than they have been, others should be more readily recognized as the good citizens that they are.

The corporation is, by its very nature, a liability shield. It protects the owners—the stockholders—against ruinous personal claims, and it protects the executives, managers, and employees of the company against most charges that might be laid against them because of wrongs properly charged to the company. Of course, in the case of gross negligence, some heads will roll, and in the face of a major scandal, expensive fines and civil judgments may result, stock prices and dividends will fall, and indeed, on occasion, the company may go bankrupt, wiping out the investments of the stockholders and putting the employees out of work. But in the most ordinary case, the people who work for and run the company are not seriously harmed by a liability suit, apart from the annoyance and aggravation of depositions and testimony. A key figure—usually the present CEO—may lose his or her job as a way of demonstrating the fact that the company takes such matters very seriously (even if that person was not in charge when the malfeasance itself took place). On some occasions, there may be structural shake-ups that will adversely affect people but, all in all, the cost of a liability lawsuit rebounds around the abstract financial structure of the corporation and has usually a minor (and only temporary) effect on the stockholders and an even more subtle (yet durable) effect on consumers in the prices they pay for the product.

C.   How to Misunderstand Responsibility

Responsibilities as Impositions

From the fact that responsibilities precede us in the jobs we do and then define the roles we are to play in them, it is easy to make an enormous mistake—one that too often muddies the discussions of business ethics—namely, thinking of responsibilities in business as *external* constraints on our activities. These could be impositions applied to business and often interfering with business enterprises by government regulations or consumer pressure groups. Responsibilities, by their very nature, are *intrinsic* to roles and to participation in practices. They are not foisted upon us but rather we accept them as part of, as definitive of, our roles. Of course, we also have responsibilities to people outside of our business, including stockholders, government, the surrounding community, customers, suppliers, and the people who service the business (custodians, plumbers, the Xerox representative), but the responsibilities themselves are part of our job. The manager of the corporation has obligations to the stockholders, but these are not imposed upon the manager; indeed, such obligations define that job. The assistant manager is told to straighten out the XYZ account, and this becomes his responsibility; but his job as assistant manager *is* to bear such responsibilities, however much he may grumble that this particular task "isn't my problem."

"But That's Not Part of My Job": The Limits of Responsibility

Certain responsibilities define a job, but others do not. A woman who is an executive assistant in charge of organizing a production team has every right to be indignant if her male superior demands that she make his morning coffee. This is not because he does not have the power to give her orders (which he does) but because, by implication at least, that particular task signifies that she is considered to have the responsibilities and, consequently, the status of a very different kind of role, one that interferes with and confuses her business roles and responsibilities. Similarly, a manager has a certain responsibility to please the stockholders, but this does not include the responsibility to please them in every way, to agree with their political opinions, to break or bend the law, or, for that matter, to *maximize* profits above a "reasonable return" at the sacrifice of other values, including the morale of the employees, the good will of the community, or other non-profit-oriented functions of the corporation. Such refusals may cost people their jobs, but an essential part of ethics is knowing where to draw the line between pleasing and prostitution.

Responsibility, Freedom, and Autonomy

It is a philosophical cliché that responsibility and freedom go hand in hand; indeed, it is said that we are responsible only for those states of affairs that we are free to change (or not change). "Ought implies can," summarized Immanuel Kant. But it is a popular platitude that responsibility *limits* freedom, perhaps even makes freedom impossible. If managers have a responsibility to give the stockholders a reasonable return for their investment, for example, they are not then free to give all of that money to charity. But this view of responsibility as a limitation of freedom is one-sided and misleading; the other side is that responsibility presupposes freedom, not only in the philosophical sense summarized by Kant but in a purely practical sense too. Responsibility requires a certain amount of *autonomy,* that is, the presumption of independence in decision making, the trust that this person can and will do the job without excessive supervision or commandeering. Peter Drucker, for example, defines "management" in just these terms, not in terms of "power over other people" but as "productive efficiency" when left to do the job. We should add, however, that virtually all jobs, with only a few exceptions, carry at least some of that same sense of autonomy. It is an autonomy or a freedom within distinctive limits, it is true; it is an autonomy defined by certain goals, by certain permissible means, by the limitations of our own abilities, and the limitations of our resources. Nevertheless, it is an essential kind of freedom without which most of our careers, including in particular the many careers in the free enterprise system, would not even be possible. The reason for this freedom is to allow for responsibility that will get jobs done. Without autonomy, there would be little responsibility; but without responsibility, autonomy wouldn't mean much either.

Responsibility versus Self–Interest: The Disastrous Dichotomy

> Management has the responsibility to earn a profit for its shareholders, but also to help preserve an environment in which profit is possible.
> —Philip T. Drotning, Business and Society Review, Spring 1978

Perhaps the most insidious fallacy of all, presupposed by too many defenders of business autonomy and presumed alike by many of those who seek to refute it, is the view that acting responsibly is inevitably acting contrary to our own best interests. The model here, in many cases, is that rather occasional incident in which, contrary to all our desires and ambitions, we are painfully reminded of some responsibility—perhaps a promise made long ago. But again, responsibilities more often define our roles and our positions rather than undermine them, and in that sense we might say that they provide and define many of our advantages as well. Yet we often see responsibility even defined as the need to act against our own interests for the benefit of others. Nothing could be more contrary to the truth.

The popular philosopher of "the virtue of selfishness," Ayn Rand, made her reputation with this dubious dichotomy between "selfishness" on the one hand—acting in your own interest—and what she defined as "altruism"—acting against

Profits and Social Responsibility: A Cost/Benefit Analysis ——

One of the most common arguments for social awareness and responsiveness on the part of business is that, in the long run, it is good business. From an ethical point of view, such an argument still lacks a basic sense of moral, as opposed to merely self–interested, values. But every argument, if it is sound, reinforces a position; is this particular argument sound?

In 1977, two researchers, Frederick D. Sturdivant and James L. Ginter, studied the relationship between social and economic performance and reported in the Spring 1977 issue of *California Management Review* that "while the findings will certainly not support the argument that socially responsive companies will *always* outperform less responsive firms in the long run, there is evidence that, in general, the responsively managed firms will enjoy better economic performance."

Sturdivant and Ginter studied sixty-seven firms that had been previously ranked by *Business and Society* as the best and the worst in their responses to social issues and problems. They measured both the attitudes of top management and the actual social performance of these firms. They demonstrated that the managers of the "best" firms were systematically more concerned with minority problems and other social issues, and the "worst" were typically more negative in their attitudes. Over a ten-year period, they concluded that "it would appear that a case can be made between responsiveness to social issues and the ability to respond effectively to traditional business challenges."

In 1992, John Kotter and James Haskett, two professors at Harvard Business School, once again studied the link between strong ethical culture in a company and economic performance. Among those firms who took seriously their responsibilities to the customers and the employees (as well as the stockholders), revenues were on average four times as much as those companies that did not take these responsibilities seriously. These companies also expanded on average four times as much and increased their profits by an average of 750 percent and their stock prices by as much as 900 percent.

Figures from *Management Review,* Dec. 1977, and *The Economist,* June 6, 1992

your own interests for the benefit of others. More recently and more respectably, Milton Friedman tacitly assumes the same sort of dubious definition of "social responsibility" in which an act of being socially responsible is distinguished from an act of self–interest (that is, for a corporation to improve its profits), even if the latter has beneficial social effects. But usually those acts that are in our own best interests are *also* acts that fulfill our responsibilities. Or, turning that around, fulfilling our responsibilities, whether as individual citizens *or* as members of the business world, is almost always to maximize our self–interest, often including our financial self–interest as well.

CONFLICTS OF RESPONSIBILITY

We ought to fulfill our responsibilities, that goes without saying. But it does not follow that because we have a responsibility we should fulfill it, no matter what. There may be other responsibilities, including other responsibilities pertaining to exactly the same job, that compete with or contradict it. We may have the responsibility of turning off the lights when the last employee has gone home, but in the face of a fire in the accounting department it is not hard to see that the latter responsibility overrides the first.

Within virtually every job in business (and almost everything else), a person may play a variety of roles. In any corporation of even modest size, an individual will inevitably be a member of a department as well as an employee of the company as a whole, may have special allegiances to others and strong ties to certain people outside the company, and obligations to fellow workers that are not strictly job responsibilities. Sometimes, these various roles and their responsibilities conflict. Sometimes, one role seems to subvert another, and one responsibility seems to contradict another. Loyalty to the company may conflict with loyalty to the department; loyalty to a particular subordinate may contradict the responsibilities of a manager. Such conflicts are the stuff of life; often, there is no clear resolution to them. But the one line of escape that will not work—short of simply quitting the job—is to deny one responsibility in the name of the other, to pretend that one cancels out the other. Of course, we must always make a decision. Of course, we must in fact decide to fulfill one responsibility and forgo the other. But both remain responsibilities, and we bear the consequences. Indeed, a third responsibility enters here as a result of the conflict between the first two. We are responsible for making a proper decision between them. For example, an employee might rightly argue that she has a responsibility to hold weekly meetings with the accounting staff, but during a crisis when the CEO calls an emergency meeting that happens to conflict with the weekly meeting, the responsibility of the employee is clear. The first responsibility does not simply disappear; it is overridden. It is the responsibility of the employee, too, to see priorities.

Conflicts of responsibilities are most dramatic, however, when the two roles involved are not both within business but rather, one within business (say, a manager's fiduciary responsibility to the stockholders) and the other the result of a nonbusiness role (to family or friends, to community or country). Again, it is not that one responsibility cancels out the other, but yet there may on occasion be a conflict for which there is no clear solution, perhaps even no solution at all. However, a prevalent argument today says, or at least assumes, that the one responsibility cancels out the other and that business responsibilities, because they typically consist of actual contracts and obligations, take priority over social responsibilities. But it is simply not true that business automatically takes priority, nor is it true that contracts and obligations always take precedence over what is sometimes referred to slightingly as "good will."

One professor of management said that in the choice between fulfilling a contractual obligation to stockholders (no matter how minor an obligation) and saving twenty-five thousand jobs, the foremost responsibility of the manager is the contractual obligation; in fact, he added, saving jobs is not essentially the manager's responsibility at all. It is rather a sign of his "good will," assuming, of course, that it doesn't interfere with his obligations. Even though this manager seemed extremely concerned about saving jobs and with social concerns in general, when the question became one of "responsibility," he too quickly gave in to what is surely a fallacious as well as inhumane argument. What such arguments tend to show is that some people in business still do not take the concept of business responsibility seriously, despite indisputably good intentions and social concern on their part. It also shows, perhaps, the bloated importance of a certain notion of "obligation" (in particular, "contractual obligation") in our current thinking about ethics. (Contracts create responsibilities, but not the *only* responsibilities.)

"It's His Responsibility, Not Mine": Denying Responsibility

Nothing in the logic of responsibility supports the familiar inference, "if X is responsible, then Y is not." Responsibilities can be *shared,* indeed, shared very widely. Responsibility is not a fixed commodity, such that the more of it one person has, the less someone else has. There is such a thing as *collective* responsibility, whether or not it is possible (for example, in order to praise or punish) to identify the precise amount of responsibility belonging to each of the various individuals who are collectively responsible. (What is often called "corporate responsibility" is better understood as *collective* responsibility.) If a director of planning seems clearly responsible for an error of calculation that cost the company thousands of dollars, it may well be the case that his assistants, who did not catch the error, and his superiors, who trusted him and passed on his reports without recalculating, are all responsible as well. So, too, it may be that dozens or hundreds of people who had early access to the plans but failed to look hard enough to catch the error are responsible. Of course, all are not equally responsible. In fact, only the director will probably be punished directly. But it does not follow that only the director is responsible either; reward and punishment are not the test of responsibility, only its more tangible (and somewhat arbitrary) consequences.

The same point prevails when we are talking about a feature of a whole society. It may well be that a particular practice or attitude existed long before we were born. Nevertheless, insofar as we continue to participate in it, it is our responsibility. As always, this is not hard to admit when the practice and its consequences are admirable. We all take pride in the American institutions of freedom and enterprise (however much we may disagree about some of the details and effects); we all accept responsibility, though abstractly, for our country's performance in World War II and for the benign and not insignificant progress made after the war in race relations and the standard of living for minorities. Indeed, the "we" of our casual speech and emotions such as pride (which presume a sense of responsibility, however vicarious) point quite clearly to our assumption of shared and collective responsibility—when the results are good. But when it comes to the question of racism or treatment of Native Americans or the abuses of power and wars of dubious merit, we are all quick to absolve ourselves of responsibility, pointing out quite rightly that these conflicts existed before we were born and that we as mere individuals could not possibly have altered them. But laying the responsibility elsewhere—on institutions and government policies, on the country's past history, and on other factors beyond our control—does not cancel out the fact that we, too, are responsible. We can always protest; the exercise of responsibility does not guarantee or require actual results. We always have the power to do *something*, however (in the world picture) insignificant. The personal cost of complaining (for example, in a company that practices blatant discrimination or is making inferior and dangerous products) may be too great. But the responsibility remains nonetheless and that is a fact we must live with and, quite possibly, atone for. What constitutes our responsibilities cannot be decided by seeing how much of our responsibility can be passed on to someone or something else. Our responsibility is our responsibility, regardless of who else might be responsible too.

"There's Nothing I Can Do About It"

The above point about collective responsibility applies as well to the question of power and impotence. We have already said that responsibility presumes a certain authority, a certain amount of power. But it is not true that we are responsible only for what we can actually change or do. A person who plays a small role in a large corporation is most likely incapable of changing its policies. The corporation that is singled out as a "polluter" may be incapable of even beginning to clean up the mess it has made. But the person and the corporation are nevertheless responsible, responsible at least for making an honest effort, for doing what can reasonably be done, and for mobilizing a larger effort to do what cannot be done alone.

Of these last points, we might say the underlying point is that unclarity and inability do not undermine claims of responsibility but may confuse them. There are always the twin questions, "What could I have done?" and "What can I do?" And there is always a positive answer to both of them, for something always could have been done and, more importantly, something always can be done now.

D. CONSUMER RESPONSIBILITY

In fact, the people responsible for pollution are consumers, not producers. They create, as it were, demand for pollution. People who use electricity are responsible for the smoke that comes out of the stacks of generating plants.

—Milton Friedman

One element in the argument concerning responsibility of business is often lacking, namely, the responsibilities of the consumer. Industry pollutes, but in many cases, consumers could refuse to support those industries or express willingness to pay more in return for more pollution control. The classic argument, of course, is that the consumer is "sovereign"; and with this argument, the consumer and not

---

An Example of Consumer Responsibility ——

On August 7, 1981, *The Washington Star* stopped publishing. It had been circulating in the nation's capital since 1852, providing Washington readers with an alternative and competition to the more liberal *Washington Post.* Losses had been running at $20 million a year.

In the interviews with employees and management following the close of the *Star,* one theme was repeated by virtually everyone: "If one tenth of the people who were now moaning the *Star's* loss and the consequent decline of newspaper competition in Washington had actually subscribed," complained one bitter editor, "the *Star* would still be printing today." One of the managers pointed out that advertising revenues had dropped disastrously, but, again, that the same advertisers who now felt sorry for the *Star* were the ones who could have kept her afloat.

The *Star* example is one of many; consumers complain about the low quality fare on television, but then watch the programs and buy the products—and keep on complaining. Consumers complain about low quality merchandise but don't complain to the store, the manufacturer, or the Better Business Bureau. They eat unacceptable dinners at restaurants without sending them back to the kitchen or otherwise telling the management; they just don't show up again. Book-lovers complain about the high price of books, but don't buy them; an editor once said that most of the people who lament the expense and difficulty of publishing poetry themselves buy less than an average of *one book per year!* Consumers lament the fact that there is no this or no that, but then don't support either this or that when it is made commercially available to them.

the industry itself is responsible for not only products but also unwanted by-products. In fact, few consumers, even collectively, are so powerful or so knowledgeable as all that, and consumers are rarely collective. Yet, there is an important truth in the observation that consumers, in a sense, "vote" with their money about the products that should be available and the costs (including nonmonetary costs) that will be included in their production. Consumer boycotts, though surprisingly rare, are powerful instruments of control. Even unorganized, large groups of consumers can turn an industry around, eliminate obnoxious advertising, keep a competitor in business, or give all of an industry to a single company, just by the collective weight of their purchases. Yet consumers often complain about a product that they continue to buy, without desperately needing it. What we "need," of course, is an important issue; but by any criterion, a great many of our purchases could be eliminated, especially if we thought there were an issue worth making by not purchasing them.

E.   STOCKHOLDER RESPONSIBILITY

The stockholder is often treated as an anonymous investor, a mere *"homo economicus"* who has no other interests besides protecting his or her investment and maximizing returns. But investors are people, first and foremost, and as stockholders—"owners" of a publicly held company—are responsible for evaluating their investments not only in terms of financial security and expected return but also in terms of the quality of the company, the way it treats its employees, its impact on the surrounding community, and its attitudes toward the world. The biggest tobacco companies have shown considerable growth and profits in recent years, in part because of diversification and acquisitions, but also in part because of a vigorous campaign to spread the smoking habit to large parts of the so-called Third World, Asia in particular. An investor ought to think carefully and conscientiously about whether he or she wants to make money from the success of such a campaign. (Cancer and other lung diseases have shown increased frequency in these areas, although some of this can also be attributed to severe pollution.) Some manufacturing companies have considerably increased their profits by moving their factories out of the United States (costing American workers their jobs) and into countries where the wages are much, much less, and sometimes, due to widespread unemployment, clearly exploitative as well. Should investors endorse such a move, and reap their profits from exploited foreigners? Surely this is in part an ethical and political decision and not just an economic one. Should one support local companies, encouraging corporations to keep jobs in America? That is a decision that stockholders help make, by voting not only "with their dollars" but with their votes as well. Some successful oil and mining companies similarly exploit foreign workers and also seriously damage the environment. Again, there is a moral decision to be made here on the part of the stockholders. Of course, one can always invest in the company hoping, as an "owner," to help change company policy. And one can invest in such companies knowing full well that one is, in fact, supporting the practices in question. But what one cannot do, as a stockholder, is claim utter ignorance or indifference. Even if one's knowledge of the company is limited to reading the annual or quarterly report and watching CNN or the evening news, it is usually obvious enough what one is supporting and, alternatively, what one is not. Nor can a moral person claim indifference or abstain from moral thinking when it is "only finances" that are in question. To be a stockholder is to have certain privileges and opportunities and, with them, certain responsibilities, even if one invests not directly but through mutual funds or a money manager. The stockholder is (or ought to be) still in charge. Thus the number of "socially responsible" and "environmentally sensitive" funds have proliferated in the past decade or so, and, perhaps not surprisingly, they have tended to do rather well. The stockholder, after all, is no mere *homo economicus*. He or she is a responsible individual (or institution) who should keep the public good in mind, as well as the size of his or her own bank account.

■ SUMMARY AND CONCLUSION

Responsibility should be viewed, first of all, in terms of the positive roles and expectations that define the jobs we do and our place in society. The key question of responsibility is not so much *who* is responsible but rather *what* are the responsibilities that *each* person has. This applies just as much to the consumer as it does to the chief executive officer of a large corporation. They all have their own responsibilities, and with those responsibilities a certain amount of freedom and power to carry them out. Where moral issues are involved, the responsibilities thereby become moral responsibilities and *prima facie* obligations. But there is nothing in the notion of responsibility that renders responsibilities a "burden" or against our individual self-interest. Quite to the contrary, our responsibilities often define our self-interest and the framework within which we are able to pursue the good life for ourselves.

Beneath all of the confusion about "who is responsible" in the complex anonymity of the giant corporation, the question of responsibility always, ultimately, comes down to the individual. The individual's power and influence may be limited or may be torn between conflicting loyalties and responsibilities. But the hallmark of responsibility is always the questions, "What can *I* do?" and "What *must* I do?" But sometimes the answers to these questions are not to be found in the limited context of our job or company. Especially when (but not only when) the responsibilities in question are moral responsibilities, the question of "higher" obligations, not to our job or company but to society as a whole, comes into focus. That much debated arena of "social responsibilities," accordingly, is our next chapter.

■ STUDY QUESTIONS

1. Can a corporation be responsible for its actions? What does this mean? In what sense can we *punish* a corporation?

2. Find an example of a corporation or institution that suffers from "the system problem" (chapter 3), in which employees are all doing their jobs but the net results are either destructive to the community or immoral (or both). If you were working for such a company, in a position of limited power, what would you do? What *should* you do?

3. Pick a particular job with which you are familiar (preferably one you have held yourself) and make a list of the responsibilities defined by (and which define) that job. Which of those responsibilities do you consider essential for the successful operation of the company? Which do you consider inessential but, nevertheless, desirable and valuable? Which do you find basically pointless? Why?

4. Is it every employee's responsibility to maximize the company's profits? List a few positions whose responsibilities have nothing to do with profits or that actually can go against the profit making of the company.

5. Can a person have freedom within a company without having responsibilities too? Give an example. Can a person have responsibilities without having the authority to carry them out? Give an example. What are the dangers of such a situation?

6. What distinguishes a *moral* responsibility? Are all responsibilities moral responsibilities?

7. What distinguishes a *legal* responsibility? Are all legal responsibilities moral responsibilities?

8. Is a sense of social obligation in business an aspect of "socialism," as Milton Friedman charges? Why or why not?

9. Is there ever a situation in which an employee has *no* responsibility for his company's behavior? What are the mitigating circumstances that would prompt us to say that an employee is not at all responsible? Is it ever the case that there is *nothing* an employee can do about his company's behavior?

10. What are the responsibilities of a consumer? Make a list of "The Consumer's Code of Ethics." To what extent do you consider yourself a responsible consumer? Choose one of the consumer products you have recently purchased and write up an analysis of the overall effects on society of the product whose continued production and use you have just supported.

■ FOR CLASS DISCUSSION

International Business Responsibilities:
The Nestlé Baby Formula Case

For several years, a number of American companies enjoyed an enormous market in Africa and Asia for their baby formula products. The dominant firm was Nestlé, a Swiss-based company, but Abbott Laboratories, American Home Products, and Bristol-Myers shared a considerable portion of the market too. It soon became clear, however, that the use of the baby formulas overseas was doing enormous damage and killing babies, perhaps thousands of them. Illiterate mothers could not read the directions; the water with which they mixed the formula was often contaminated. The formula was not nearly as nutritious as natural mother's milk and many of the babies suffered severe malnutrition. Moreover, the formula tended to be addictive, since once the babies were weaned to the bottle, the mother lost her capacity to produce milk of her own.

Marketing practices were sometimes questionable. Employees of the formula companies would visit villages dressed as medical personnel, promoting the products. New mothers were given free samples while still in clinics or hospitals. Worldwide sales climbed to $2 billion, but the death toll climbed, too. In 1981, the World Health Organization (WHO) proposed an international restriction on the marketing of infant formula. The final vote was 118 to 1, with only the United States voting against it. The principle invoked was free trade and, more dubiously, free speech. (The code would have restricted advertising.) The American officials of WHO resigned. There was a worldwide protest. International reaction was that America put business profits ahead of even the health and lives of babies.

When the evidence of widespread malnutrition was starting to come in, what should the infant formula manufacturers have done? Who is responsible for what in this case? What should the United States government have done, in your opinion? What should Nestlé and the other companies have done?

HISTORICAL INTERLUDE

THE CRITIQUE OF CAPITALISM: KARL MARX

The less you eat, drink, buy books, go to the theater, go dancing, go drinking, think, love, theorize, sing, paint, play sports,

> etc., the more you save and the greater will become . . . your
> capital. The less you are, the less you give expression to your
> life, the more you have, the greater is your alienated life. . . .
> So all passions and all activity are submerged in greed.
> —Karl Marx, Early Writings (1844)

> Man exploits man, and sometimes, the other way around.
> —Woody Allen

In any book on business, the name Karl Marx is bound to strike the reader as—pardon the expression—a red flag. But although Marx will go down in history as *the* classic antagonist of capitalism just as surely as Adam Smith will go down as its classic defender, he is a more complex and sympathetic figure than most textbooks would have us believe. Marx did not spring into the world fully bearded and bristling with anticapitalist dogmas; he was, first of all, a humanist who grew out of the same traditions and concerns as Adam Smith, and in particular the "liberal" tradition that put individual freedom and well-being at the very basis of any acceptable ethical system.

Where he disagreed with Smith—and he was not the only classical economist to do so—was in his economics. Where Smith saw a future of progress through business competition, Marx saw a bleak vision of increasing distance between rich and poor, monopoly of the few instead of competition among the many, and, eventually, an inevitable explosion of resentment, a revolution of the poor against the rich in which capitalism would disappear. But instead of focusing on that supposedly "inevitable" revolution, Marx spent most of his effort developing a set of criticisms of capitalism. To dismiss them as "outdated" is to shut our eyes to the world, and, in any case, is no more justified than dismissing Adam Smith's version of "free enterprise" as equally "outdated." But Marx, like Smith, has transcended his times. Whatever has been made of his views by tyrants and opportunists, he presented us with the single most powerful critique of capitalism, with which every person in business ought to be familiar.

Marx was born in 1818, in Germany near the French border. His father was Jewish but had converted to Christianity for political reasons. Marx was raised on the great thinkers of the Enlightenment, and as a young man he was, like his father, a liberal. In fact, even in his more radical days in Berlin—but before he began the revolutionary analyses of *Das Kapital* in the 1860s—his social views included quite a few features that are acceptable today (freedom of the press, for example). Even *The Communist Manifesto* of 1848, *the* most famous revolutionary pamphlet in history, suggests reforms that have been generally accepted by American business, for instance, a shorter work week. But before he had entered politics in any sense, Marx was, according to his own stated ambitions, a romantic poet. While at the university in Berlin (1837–41) he wrote poetry, fell in love, drank a lot, and by all accounts was a likable fellow (though not a very good poet). He also became interested in philosophy, read a great deal of the idealist philosopher Hegel—who was the most popular thinker of the time—and decided to get a doctorate in philosophy. His "liberal" views got him in trouble, however. (His most radical article was an essay criticizing government censorship of the press.) He found himself incapable of getting a university teaching job and worked as a journalist. Unable to cope with the harsh censorship of the Prussian government, he left Germany once and for all and moved to Paris. There he had two encounters that would change his life: he met the young "socialists" hanging around the Left Bank, who encouraged him to read the new British political economists—Adam Smith in particular—and he met Friedrich Engels, who had also been a student in Berlin.

Prompted by his reading of the British economists, Marx left behind his German romantic idealism, which placed *ideas* at the basis of human reality and accepted instead a doctrine of *materialism,* according to which the primary (but not the only) determinants of human life were the physical necessities, their production, and distribution. Like Adam Smith, Marx believed that the ultimate values of any ethical or economic system had to be human desires, but unlike Smith, he did not believe that *consumer* desires were or should be sovereign. Germany, for one thing, was not a "nation of shopkeepers" but rather a nation of pious and hard-working peasants and craftsmen. But by 1850 or so, when Marx finally moved to London, England was not a nation of shopkeepers either. Marx, in an important sense, held the Protestant work ethic as dearly as Smith; for Marx, a person's work was his identity, and to deprive a person of the fruits of labor was, in a crucial way, to rob him of his selfhood and self-esteem. This is what Marx called "the alienation of labor," that is, the frustration of what Marx took to be everyone's most basic desires—to be a productive and creative member of society.

It is important here to neither exaggerate nor ignore the differences between Smith and Marx. Both accept what is generally called "the labor theory of value," the view that the value of any object is the work that it takes to produce it. But where Smith places his emphasis on the commercial value of the product (through supply and demand in the market system), Marx places his emphasis on *the process of production itself.* It is the *impersonality* of the market system that so troubles Marx, and the fact that it robs us of what is most personally important to us. On this basis, we can easily surmise that, no matter how much Marx might dislike the impersonality of modern corporate America, he would much more despise the cold anonymity of the means of production under modern-day communism, which operates in his name.

For Adam Smith, the mechanism of the market and the values of our personal lives were kept quite separate; Smith simply assumed that the increased satisfaction of our material needs and desires would allow more room for pursuit of "the finer things in life." But Marx sees that the pursuit of profit can too easily become an end in itself, that he who controls the means of production also has the ultimate power in a society and, consequently, that capitalism too quickly reduces *everything* to a commodity to be bought and sold. Marx's ultimate objection to capitalism, therefore, is a question of ethical values, but a question that turns on the mechanism of the market itself, its tendency to devour everything else. Indeed, this somewhat cannibalistic metaphor pervades all of Marx's later writings, and provides the dominant image of his philosophy just as surely as the polite two-person bargaining game provides the dominant image for Adam Smith. In capitalism, the emphasis on buying and selling ("commodity fetishism") overwhelms all other values. Impersonality overwhelms everything personal, turning life itself into a mechanism in which each of us is merely an involuntary "cog." And quite the contrary of Adam Smith's optimistic picture of continuing competition, eased by mutual sympathy, or at least kept safe by mutual impotence, Marx saw that a few powerful producers could rather quickly overwhelm everyone else and work the market strictly to their own advantage. And finally, Marx suggested that capitalism, having devoured everything else in our lives, would turn on itself and devour itself as well. It is a brutal image, but in the mid-nineteenth century, it was also a brutal industrial world, no longer the modest world of cottage industries and manufacturers of pins described by Adam Smith.

The rejection of capitalism because it tended to turn all values into commercial values was one part of the Marxian critique; rejection of capitalism because it was so impersonal and robbed us of the personal satisfaction of our own productivity—the satisfaction so familiar to anyone who has ever built a table, painted a picture, built a house, or fixed a boat—was another. But as his work progressed, and as the industrial revolution progressed too, a new source of criticism entered into Marx's writings, one that would come to dominate his later theories almost totally. Adam Smith's promise was that free enterprise would benefit *everyone* in society, and, by contrast to the economic systems preceding his, that may well have been true. But one hundred years later, when the sufferings of the working people were worse than ever before—the subject of so many social novels by Dickens and Zola, for instance—it was no longer apparent that capitalism was in any way improving the life of the working people who made industry run. Indeed, it seemed brutally apparent that capitalism, in its treatment of workers as anonymous factors in the market that was subject only to the law of supply and demand, was proving as heartless as any of the cruel systems of the past. And so the ultimate criticism of Marxism, the one that more than any other has so struck millions of people around the world, is the charge of *indifference and injustice:* indifference to the plight of individual people who are victims rather than beneficiaries of the free enterprise system, and injustice in that the treatment of work as itself a market phenomenon actually encourages unemployment and low wages as a means for keeping the prices of commodities down.

It is with the recognition of what he called the **proletariat,** or working class, that Marxism emerges in Marx's writings. But it is important to note that Marx did not believe that such a class already existed, for the workers of the world did not yet *think* of themselves as a class, and it was one of the aims of his more popular works to bring this "class consciousness" about. Taking the labor theory of value to its logical conclusion, Marx argued that those who did the work produced the value and, consequently, deserved the products of their labors for themselves. In other words, his emphasis on the actual activity of production instead of the commercial value of the end products led him to a conclusion that would have not been tolerable to Adam Smith—that the work itself was everything and the operations of the market were only a systematized form of theft. Marx, in other words, is very much in the line of ancient and religious thinkers who rejected the activity of business as parasitic on the honest labor of the working man.

We no longer believe, as Aristotle and Aquinas did, that there is something immoral about making a profit from another person's labor or about making a gain simply from the manipulation of paper rather than the actual physical production of some goods. But this is not all there is to Marx's argument, and it is important to understand that it turns on one of the most powerful ethical concepts in the world today. That concept is **exploitation,** and it is the sense of being exploited that did, in fact, create the class consciousness Marx urged (for example, in the American labor union movement) and that continues to appeal so powerfully to so many people in Third World countries, especially former colonies of the great industrial empires.

Exploitation, simply stated, is getting a lot less back than what was put in. A businessman exploits the energies of a young business graduate, for example, by giving him a great deal of work to do for very little pay, perhaps motivating him with phony promises of future promotions that he has no intention of keeping. A manager exploits a group of workers by paying them far less than the job is worth, perhaps because unemployment is so high that the workers have little choice if they want to work at all. What counts as "exploitation," of course, is one of the most difficult questions of business ethics, and turns, ultimately, on the idea of an *unjust* exchange. Hiring the child next door to shovel the snow from your driveway for fifteen cents might well be considered (for example, by the child's parents) to be exploitation. Many people consider what is called "the minimum wage" exploitation, but many executives earning $40,000 a year might feel exploited too, if they feel that they are giving far more of themselves to the company than such salaries would indicate. But Marx, needless to say, was not particularly interested in the executive manager who felt exploited with his five-figure salary. He was worried about the *systematic* exploitation of workers that he saw as built right into the free market system. Some cases of exploitation (the case of the young business graduate) may be based on a kind of deception; most exploitation, however (like the manager who underpays desperate workers), is a matter of taking unfair advantage of the central feature of capitalism itself—the law of supply and demand with regard to the work force. Treating work as a commodity and making sure that there is always a pool of unemployed workers willing to take jobs at an ever lower wage guarantees the exploitation of workers in general. But what makes the argument all the more powerful, once again, is the labor theory of value—the idea that it is the workers themselves, and the workers *alone,* who have a right to the products they produce.

The Marxist argument, then, can be formulated quite simply. The premise is the labor theory of value:

> *In capitalist societies, labor creates all economic values.**

Then, the simple fact, that

> *labor gets back only part of the value created, the remainder going to capital as profits or as interest.*

Therefore,

> *in capitalist society, labor gets back much less than it has contributed, and this, by definition, is exploitation.*

The counterargument offered up by the defenders of capitalism, in turn, can take two now-standard tactics. One is to reject the labor theory of value altogether. The other is to modify the theory to allow for the role of investment and risk as necessary parts of the overall business picture on the grounds that there would be no work at all (in industrial society) without capital, and no capital without incentive to invest. But to see how these counterarguments work, it will be necessary to take a look at the concept of *justice* itself, and this we will do in a later chapter.

Marx's ethical arguments against capitalism, then, must be appreciated and met on a number of fronts; if the classic claims of Adam Smith are to be justified, it is necessary to show how capitalism does not tend to turn everything into its "cash value" or convert personal values into the impersonal factors of supply and demand, or at least, how capitalism is compatible with cultural and spiritual values that we believe ought to be immune from mere economic determination. And it is necessary to show that capitalism and the free market do in fact improve the lot of the worst off among us or, alternatively, that capitalism and the free market will not hinder other concerns, whether government or religious organizations or the corporations themselves, from serving the general public good, which is, in both Smith and Marx, business' justification. The difference is, Smith thinks it succeeds, and Marx thinks it fails. And it is doing the world of business no favor to simply dismiss Marx's criticisms out of hand, for it is on their refutation—not in academic arguments but in the workings of the business world itself—that the future of business in the world will depend.

---

*This formulation of the argument is from Bernard Gendron, "The Marxist Theory of Exploitation."

A PRIMER ON MARXIAN ECONOMICS*

Paul M. Sweezy

I am a Marxist, and I am firmly convinced that only Marxism allows us to understand the functioning of capitalist societies. The essence of capitalism, as explained in the short second part of the first volume of Marx's *Capital,* is the accumulation of capital; which means continuous and perpetual expansion. To be healthy a capitalist enterprise must grow and grow and grow. The alternative is stagnation and eventual death. And individual enterprises can grow only if the economy as a whole grows. This process has been going on in the United States ever since the first Europeans set foot on these shores.

The mechanism of growth is that society's surplus product—what is left over after a conventional and always relatively low level of subsistence is provided to the actual worker-producers—is appropriated and controlled by a small class of owners, in our day corporations and their stock- and bond-holders. Out of this surplus the owning class consumes enough to live well and in many cases in great luxury, but it cannot begin to consume the whole surplus, nor does it desire to do so. By far the larger part is accumulated, i.e., invested with a view to making profits and hence increasing the surplus still further in the future.

But this process can continue only so long as profitable markets grow in proportion to capital, and this is far from being guaranteed. If markets do not grow sufficiently, the result is an interruption of the process—crisis, depression, stagnation. It follows with iron logic that a high-priority pre-occupation of everyone in business and government is and must be the expansion of existing markets and the creation of new ones. And the means used, private and government alike, will be the most varied, the most ingenious, and, if need be, the most violent and ruthless imaginable. The list would be endless. I will mention only a few of the most important and commonly used: invention of new or seemingly new products, territorial expansion, penetration of rivals' markets, conquest of foreign peoples, credit creation and expansion, deficit financing, advertising, armaments, and wars. But despite all these methods to create and expand markets, periodic breakdowns of the accumulation process have occurred since the earliest days of capitalism and, as everyone now knows, continue to occur every few years. Right now we are in the worst period of stagnation since the Great Depression of the 1930s, with no signs of an early return to anything remotely approaching prosperity.

Let us now look at American capitalism against this background:

(1) American capitalism in its roughly three centuries of existence has expanded enormously, has greatly increased the productivity of human labor, and has raised the per capita consumption of goods and services severalfold. The cost

---

*From *Business and Society Review,* #23.

of these achievements, however, has been formidable. The system has exploited and often violently repressed not only its own work force (slave and free) but also vast numbers of people around the world whose economies and societies have been subordinated to the needs of American capitalism. The increased productivity of labor has been at the expense of dehumanizing the work process which absorbs the best part of the lives of most people. And in the long run perhaps the greatest, and ultimately fatal, flaw in capitalism is that an infinitely expanding system in a finite environment is a living contradiction, a time bomb bound sooner or later to explode with shattering and death-dealing ecological consequences. From the beginning, capitalism has always recklessly polluted and destroyed its environment, but until recently this did not seem to matter much. Now, however, the signs of overstrain are everywhere visible, and it is getting to be a commonplace that economic growth in the developed countries, and especially the United States, must be brought under control and decisively checked in the historically near future. What is unfortunately not so widely understood is that this implies the end of capitalism and its replacement by a planned system of production for use, rather than a market system of production for profit.

(2) What about "equity" in American society? I suggest that there are two basic aspects to any meaningful concept of "equity." The first is that everyone without exception should have a sufficiency of the things needed to live a decent life: employment at useful work in humane conditions, adequate housing, a healthy diet, good health care, security for the young, the old, and the infirm. The second is that inequalities in the provision of these necessities should be both small and declining over time. Judged by these criteria the American economy has obviously failed miserably in terms of equity.

(3) The fact that income in the United States is distributed extremely unequally—that there is a small stratum of super-rich millionaires at the top and literally tens of millions of poverty-stricken at the bottom—is sufficient proof that some groups have profited inordinately while others have suffered because of the character and development of the American economic system. But it is necessary to add that in a society of exploiters and exploited, oppressors and oppressed, everyone, whether rich or poor, suffers from the alienation and dehumanization which are inherent in such a society.

■ Study Questions

Marxist Paul Sweezy sums up the Marxist criticism of capitalism in three basic points:

1. In its rapid expansion over the past three centuries, American capitalism may have increased productivity and raised the per capita consumption of goods enormously, but it did so only at the cost of *exploiting* its work force and *dehumanizing* the work process itself.

2. In that same period of time, the distribution of goods has not become more but rather less equal.

3. In that same period of time, income has not tended to become equal but rather has divided even more, creating a class of super-rich and tens of millions of poor.

How would you respond to each of these criticisms? (What kinds of information—"hard" empirical data—would you need to make your case?)

– 9 –

Social Responsibility and the Stakeholder

We either have a social fabric that embraces us all, or we're in real trouble. . . .

—Chairman of the Ford Foundation, 1981

The debate over the question, "Does business have social responsibilities?" has now gone on for decades. It reached a pinnacle in 1970 when Milton Friedman published his polemic in which he flatly denied such responsibilities, indeed even argued that it would be *ir*responsible for businesses to interfere in such public matters. He wrote:

> In a free enterprise, private property system, a corporate executive is an employee of the owners of the business. He has direct responsibility to his employers. That responsibility is to conduct the business in accordance with their desires, which generally will be to make as much money as possible while conforming to the basic rules of society, both those embodied in law and those embodied in ethical custom.
>
> Of course, the corporate executive is also a person in his own right. As a person he may have many other responsibilities . . . if we wish, we can refer to some of these responsibilities as "social responsibilities." But in these respects he is acting as a principle, not an agent. . . . If these are "social responsibilities," they are the social responsibilities of individuals, not of business.
>
> —Milton Friedman, The New York Times Magazine, Sept. 13, 1970

The idea that social responsibilities belong to individuals, not businesses or business, is distinctively unclear. If people have considerable power, prestige, and wealth by virtue of their business roles and positions, it is not clear what it means to say that they have social responsibilities only as "an individual," distinct from those business roles. On the other hand, why suppose that people are members of society—and thus have social responsibilities—*solely* by virtue of their individual citizenship, rather than by virtue of all roles and positions—including in their jobs in business—that make them each a distinctive member of a particular society?

The idea that businesses and business have no social responsibilities is, in several senses, nonsensical. In terms of sheer existence, it is the responsibility of business to sell decent products at affordable prices. In any sense of responsibility, it is the responsibility of business not to destroy the society it serves, whether this is to be couched in terms of self-interest ("management has the responsibility to earn a profit for its shareholders, but also to preserve an environment in which profit is possible") or in terms of social concern as such ("either we have a social fabric that embraces us all or we're in real trouble") or responsibility in the simplest and most basic sense ("you clean up the mess you make"). There are several kinds of responsibilities, and some of them obviously pertain to business just as much as to any other enterprise, institution, group, or person. For example, there is the strictly *causal* responsibility for what we have done; to say that a business or a businessperson is responsible for a situation in this sense is to say nothing

---

The Social Responsibility of Business Is to Increase Its Profits ——

When I hear businessmen speak eloquently about the "social responsibilities of business in a free-enterprise system," I am reminded of the wonderful line about the Frenchman who discovered at the age of 70 that he had been speaking prose all his life. The businessmen believe that they are defending free enterprise when they declaim that business is not concerned "merely" with profit but also with promoting desirable "social" ends; that business has a "social conscience" and takes seriously its responsibilities for providing employment, eliminating discrimination, avoiding pollution and whatever else may be the catchwords of the contemporary crop of reformers. In fact they are—or would be if they or anyone else took them seriously—preaching pure and unadulterated socialism. Businessmen who talk this way are unwitting puppets of the intellectual forces that have been undermining the basis of a free society these past decades.

Milton Friedman, *The New York Times Magazine,* Sept. 13, 1970

other than the fact that he, she, or it *did* it. There are contractual responsibilities, that is, the responsibility of fulfilling contracts; business has such responsibilities and indeed, most of the American system of business has its foundation in contracts. There is the broad and universal responsibility shared by every member of

Henry Ford II, chairman of the Ford Motor Company, points out that the corporation is not designed to solve social problems:

It would be easier to respond to these questions if we could all agree on what is meant by the term "social responsibility." In my view, it is a subject that has been misunderstood and very much overworked.

It has always seemed to me that the social responsibility of a corporation is not something different from its business responsibilities. There cannot for long be one without the other. Good management recognizes this and conducts the affairs of the corporation accordingly.

A business firm's fundamental responsibility to society is the same as it has always been: to produce and market products that consumers want and to accomplish that task efficiently. It has a corollary responsibility, of course, to conduct its business in such a way as to avoid harming the interests of third parties or the society at large. Air and water pollution, for example, must be reduced to the lowest possible levels. In that sense, corporate social responsibility is very much alive and should, where necessary, be reinforced by appropriate laws.

To go a step further, a corporation cannot, for example, hire people merely because they need work. But a responsible corporation will hire and promote employees purely on the basis of their ability to do the corporation's work, will pay and treat them fairly, and will provide safe and healthy working conditions. A corporation cannot assure that its products will all be perfect. But a responsible corporation will do its best to remedy defects promptly when they occur.

What should be better understood, however, is that the corporation is not an all-purpose mechanism. It is a specialized instrument designed to serve the economic needs of society and is not well equipped to serve social needs unrelated to its business operations. I would guess that this is essentially what Milton Friedman meant to convey in his statement, and I would readily agree with that view.

I believe that the great majority of corporations will continue, without added pressure from society, to carry out their business functions in a socially responsible manner.

From "Is Social Responsibility a Dead Issue?"
Business and Society Review, Spring 1978

society, including every enterprise or institution, not to do harm willfully to others (given certain qualifications, such as the prevention of a greater harm or the production of some greater good). And there is the general sense of responsibility, again shared by enterprises and institutions as well as by all individuals, that if we cause harm, we are bound to try to correct it, or at least compensate for it, one way or another.

Few people object to these senses of social responsibility. But Friedman, for example, objects to a quite different kind of social responsibility that is concerned not so much with what a company has done, or, indeed, with what it will do in the course of its normal business operations. It is the kind of social responsibility that usually goes under the name of "doing good." It is over and above the contributions to society provided by the products, services, and jobs the company offers. It presupposes no fault on the part of the person or business doing good; it supposes no personal or financial interest in doing good either. This social responsibility requires us to help the poor, hire the unemployed, support the arts and education; in short, to make the society in which we live a better place to live. These may be less than moral obligations but they are, nonetheless, essential responsibilities.

Why should we do such a thing? To ask the question is virtually to answer it: to make our society a better place to live is at the same time to improve our own lives. But the action and its effect are not always so obvious. We might benefit some other part of society that is sufficiently remote from our own lives so that its effects will not be felt. We might give to the arts we enjoy, but why should we feel the least bit obliged to support the other arts that we do not enjoy? And suppose we find, as is often the case, that the workings of society or the performances of the arts keep on going without our own support, because other people and institutions are already supporting them anyway?

Such questions do not apply so much to persons as members of institutions: it is as an individual citizen that we enjoy the opera or the art museum, not as an employee or a manager. The business itself, on the other hand, obviously does not enjoy either opera or art at all. Does this mean that it is not the business of business, or of people in business (*as* businesspeople) to support the arts? And can the same arguments be extended to social problems—the problems of racism, hardcore unemployment, poverty, the elderly, and the need to support education? What are the social responsibilities here, and what is merely a matter of personal preference and the competition of the market, but not a responsibility at all? Several arguments, while often persuasive, are not of particular relevance to the question of social responsibility. One much debated question is whether "doing good" is, in the long run, profitable for business. Perhaps it is, but the argument concerning responsibility is whether we ought to "do good" (as a business or as a businessperson) even if it is not, in the short or long run, profitable. But it is a mistake to think that this means such actions are *opposed* to our self-interest in terms of profit. Indeed, the most telling response to Friedman comes from the corporate boardrooms of America. Here is Philip T. Drotning, director of corporate social policy at Amoco:

The flaw in Dr. Friedman's statement, rejecting corporate expenditures for social purposes, is the fact that while decrying such action he also acknowledged the right of management to exercise discretion in making some such expenditures (i.e., philanthropy) because it is in the economic self-interest of shareholders to do so. At that point the argument became one of degree rather than principle, and management would seem free to exercise its discretion to make any social expenditures which could be justified on the basis of the long-term economic self-interest of its shareholders.

It is on this basis, in fact, that most such expenditures are made. Management recognizes that its growth and prosperity, and perhaps its survival, is dependent on a healthy society, and it commits corporate resources to help insure a healthy society. . . .

The other flaw inherent in Dr. Friedman's position is the underlying assumption that socially responsible behavior by a corporation must, of necessity, have a negative impact on the bottom line. I do not

The "Business Roundtable"

"The Business Roundtable issues this statement out of a strong conviction that the future of this nation depends upon the existence of strong and responsive business enterprises and that, in turn, the long-term viability of the business sector is linked to its responsibility to the society of which it is a part. . . ."

We recognized that corporations have a responsibility, first of all, to make available to the public quality goods and services at fair prices, thereby earning a profit that attracts investment to continue and enhance the enterprise, provide jobs and build the economy. And we said that all sides must recognize the fundamental importance of profits and their contribution to the long-term viability of the enterprise: "If the bottom line is a minus, there is no plus for society."

Perhaps Samuel Gompers, father of the American labor movement, put it better when he said, "The worst crime against the working people is a company that fails to make a profit."

As shareholders make the corporation possible by providing funds for corporate birth, growth and development, we said that the interest of shareholders must be considered in all important corporate activities.

But the character of shareholders has changed. At one time most of them were long-term, personally involved individual investors. Now large numbers of them are grouped in institutions as unidentified short-term buyers most interested in maximum near-term gain.

Such interest must be balanced with a long-term perspective. The simple theory that management can get along by considering only the shareholder has been left behind in old economic dissertations.

Chief executive officers who have been out there facing reality know that corporations are surrounded by a complicated pattern of economic, social, ethical, and political ideas and expectations. They know that they have to be concerned not only about shareholders but about such constituent groups as customers, employees, communities, suppliers and society at large. And they believe a corporation best serves its shareholders by carefully balancing the legitimate interests of all constituents.

Reginald H. Jones, former chairman of the General Electric Company, put it well: "Public policy and social issues are no longer adjuncts to business planning and management. They are in the mainstream of it. The concern must be pervasive in companies today, from boardroom to factory floor."

Carefully weighing the effects of decisions and balancing different constituent interests must be an integral part of the corporation's decision-making and management process. A corporation's economic responsibility is by no means incompatible with other corporate responsibilities.

The specifics of how a corporation addresses these responsibilities will vary from one company to another. Each corporation has an individual character, related to its products, markets, facilities, manufacturing processes and other aspects of its business. Some theorists may long for a total operational strategy or even a statute to dictate corporate responsibility, but only the naive or contentious would seek to fashion such a document.

It is true that business enterprises are not designed to be either political or cultural institutions, but the business community will be well-served by habit of mind that stays alert to social currents. That fundamental point carried through to the conclusion of our statement: "A corporation's responsibilities include how the whole business is conducted every day. It must be a thoughtful institution which rises above the bottom line to consider the impact of its action on all, from shareholders to the society at large. Its business activities must make social sense just as its social activities must make business sense."

We think that's good business.

Andrew C. Sigler, *The New York Times,* Feb. 29, 1981.
© 1981 by the New York Times Company. Reprinted by permission.

believe that this is a valid assumption, or that corporate experience indicates that this is the case.

Another argument, again often convincing but not essential here, is the argument that what are called the social responsibilities of business are merely a matter of mutual interest, not in terms of profit, perhaps, but in the simple sense that the people who work for a company have to live in society too; therefore, their well-being and the community's well-being are one and the same. This would certainly be the case in such matters as crime control, environmental issues, and the quality of education, as well as more general concerns for the aesthetics of the town or city and the accessibility of the arts. This usually provides an overwhelming argument for social action, since whether or not the abstraction "the company" cares very much about living conditions, the employees of the company will care. But the question of social responsibility goes beyond this question of mutual interest too. Should businesses and businesspeople contribute to soci-

Creating Stakeholder Value ——

Businesses are facing changes more extensive, more far-reaching in their implications, and more fundamental in their transforming quality than anything since the modern industrial system was established.

In every area, the pace of change is dizzying: corporate restructuring through mergers and takeovers, globalization of markets, new technology and high-speed obsolescence of technology-based products, intensified competition as customers enjoy more choices, escalating customer demands for quality and service, and ever-higher employee expectations. Increasingly, what distinguishes the winners from the losers is the ability to anticipate and influence these kinds of changes—to be masters, not victims, of change.

Those corporations that will succeed and flourish in the times ahead will be those that create a climate encouraging exploration of new business possibilities, encouraging responsiveness to signals that external directions are shifting, and encouraging active listening to new ideas.

They will work in partnership with all their stakeholders to continue to create new value. Stakeholders are those groups on whom a company depends—the people who can help it achieve its goals or can stop it dead in its tracks. This includes shareholders and members of the financial community, customers, employees, suppliers, governments and other communities.

Rosabeth M. Kanter, *Harvard Business Review,* 1989

ety even when it is not so evidently in their mutual interest, granting that these other motives may well provide considerable incentive for them to do so?

In response to the debate over the social responsibilities of business, business ethicists have introduced the concept of a **stakeholder.** The word is something of a pun on "stockholder," and the point is precisely to replace the over-emphasis on the rights and demands of the stockholders with a more general regard for all of those constituencies which are involved with and affected by the corporation. Among the various stakeholders of the corporation are its customers, its employees, its various suppliers and external contractors and consultants, the surrounding community, the larger society (and, we might add, that often "silent" stakeholder, the environment), as well as the stockholder. The stockholder is indeed a stakeholder and the company does have obligations and fiduciary responsibilities towards its stockholders. But the stockholders are but one constituency among many, and there is no fair argument, for example, that employees must always be sacrificed to the interests of the stockholders, or that customers, not the stockholders, must foot the bill for increased taxes or the cost of a liability judgment against the company. But increased attention to the stakeholders of the corporation is not just a matter of morals and social responsibility. It is also good business. Recent research has shown rather conclusively (though not in all cases) that attention to customers and employees and demonstrated concern for the community and environment tends to "pay off" in terms of increased sales, better community relations, improved financial status in the markets, and increased workplace morale and stability.

A.   TWO KINDS OF SOCIAL RESPONSIBILITIES

It is now customary, but possibly misleading, to divide up what are generally called "the social responsibilities of business" into two categories, one rather uncontroversial, the other the subject of intense and often bitter moral debate. The first involves what is referred to as *impact,* the actual causal influence of an industry or a business on the surrounding community, the environment, the political situation, and its own consumers.

Unfortunately, the most common examples of impact are examples of the negative impact of certain by-products of industry, and such examples have the inevitable effect of putting business on the defensive and giving the very phrase "social responsibilities" a bad name. But, although there is less to say about them here, let us begin by insisting that the first examples of business impact ought to be the *positive* contributions of business to American society through the invention of live-saving pharmaceuticals and labor-saving devices and through the mass availability of relatively cheap transportation and communication facilities. It is ironic that some critics of business can make a career out of attacking negative business impact without ever noting the extent to which their criticism is made possible by business. So, the first examples of impact should be the quality products that business has made available, and it is on the basis of such impact that business has commanded and largely deserved the privileged place it now occupies in American society.

There are also positive by-products of business activity—impact not as part of the product of a business but as a part of its activity. Providing jobs to the community is the most single important positive by-product of most business activities. Enriching the community and enlarging the tax base, thus providing better living for all residents of the area, is another. "Impact" is, thus, not to be construed as a negative term; it refers to the effects of business on the community in general. On the whole, we should probably argue that the overall impact of most businesses on most communities is very positive, both in terms of the goods it produces and in terms of the benefits of business activity itself.

The Good Guys ⸺

Here are the firms that the Council on Economic Priorities has rated among the most socially responsible in 1992:

Alexandra Avery	General Mills
Autumn-Harp	Giant Food
Aveda	Hershey
Avon	Johnson & Johnson
Ben & Jerry's	S.C. Johnson
Body Love Natural	Kellogg
Cosmetics	Newman's Own
Church & Dwight	Procter & Gamble
Clientele	Quaker Oats
Colgate-Palmolive	Supermarkets
Earth's Best	General
Earthrise	Tom's of Maine
Eden Foods	Upjohn

Not So Good

American Cyanamid	Mobil
Archer-Daniels-Midland	Perdue Farms
Bayer USA	Pfizer
Chevron	Texaco
Conagra	Tyson Foods
General Electric	USX
Kimberly-Clark	

The Council on Economic Priorities

Then, however, there is negative impact, bad products and the harm caused by business activity. Examples of negative impact would be a large company settling in a small town, thereby instantly causing overcrowding in the schools, massive traffic congestion, and overloaded public services; a business creating pollution from manufacturing processes in the local river or the air; a multinational corporation's activity in a foreign country that destabilizes the legitimate government there; and a faulty product that injures or kills people who have bought it.

We must further distinguish this kind of responsibility according to the familiar concerns of foresight, ability to prevent the negative situation in advance, and the degree to which correction of the situation is within someone's control. Some disasters and accidents cannot be foreseen; a producer surely cannot be held responsible for *any* detrimental activity involving its products, just as a corporation cannot be held liable for all of the most distant consequences of its activities. A producer of industrial alcohol should not be held responsible for the illness of a group of teenagers, who ignore the clearly marked poison label and drink the stuff anyway. The electronics industry is not responsible for the deterioration of social relations and literacy levels in a society subsequent to the invention of television, nor is the inventor of a new can opener responsible for the fact that, possibly sometime in the future, someone may ingeniously invent a way to make a deadly weapon out of it. It is still being debated to what extent the chemical producers who were responsible for the Love Canal tragedy could have known of the danger, should have been more cautious about possible dangers, might have been able to prevent the tragedy through a more thorough protective processing of the waste material, and, now that the damage is done, whether or to what extent they are capable of correcting or paying for the situation. (See "For Class Discussion" at the end of this chapter.)

However, though the details of every case can and probably will be so debated, the general business stance regarding their social responsibilities in which such negative impacts are concerned seems clear: a business is responsible for taking *reasonable* precautions regarding the influence and effects of its activities and correcting mistakes that are due to its not taking such reasonable precautions. What is "reasonable" of course depends on the context and the cost. The harder questions concern the extent of a business' responsibilities when it clearly has taken such precautions. Surely it cannot dismiss the issue by saying "we did all that we could at the time," but neither does it seem reasonable to say that there is no difference between a company that knowingly causes a disaster and one that unknowingly and against its efforts causes a similar disaster. Indeed, there seems to be no question in most people's minds about the liability of a business that knowingly or willfully causes harm to the community or its customers: they are to be punished severely, and forced to make ample restitution.

The second category of "social responsibilities" ascribed to business consists of activities that business *could do* with considerable benefit to the community, but that do not suppose any prior wrongdoing or destructive activities on its part.

Business Helping Business ——

Chemical Bank is providing $250,000 in no-interest loans and grants to support small businesses in the New York area. The funding is part of Chemical's new Microbusiness Initiative Program.

The New York bank is earmarking $182,000 for local projects of two internationally recognized nonprofit organizations, Accion International and the Council for Economic Action. The bank will also provide a total of $67,000 to sixteen local groups.

The money will fund a loan pool for small businesses in New York, a loan-loss reserve, and a study of the feasibility of a program to train and provide financing for small-business owners.

—*The American Banker*
June 1991

These are the areas in which businesses most often protest that these are not their responsibilities, or are beyond the bounds of their competence.

One way of distinguishing this second class of social responsibilities is by noting that nothing in them is intrinsically tied to the actual operations of a business. They do not (or need not) in any way involve the actual products of the company, nor do they involve the workings of the company or its by-products, such as increasing the working population and wealth of a town or, negatively, causing pollution or congestion. (Sometimes, the way a company treats its employees is included under the heading of "social responsibilities," but this is better considered as part of the intrinsic rules of fairness within the business enterprise.) A related way of describing this set of social responsibilities is to describe them as *responsibilities that every member of a society, whether individual or institutional, has equally, just by virtue of being a member of that society.* Of course, different people, and different institutions, will have differing capacities for fulfilling those responsibilities. A millionaire has more money to contribute to good causes than a subsistence-level working family, and most corporations have much more money to contribute, and power to change things, than most small businesses and almost all individuals.

Responsibilities belonging to businesspeople *as people* in business may also apply to them as individuals. ("I gave at the office" is not always sufficient.) It may be that business and businesses have special responsibilities by virtue of their power and their wealth and influence, but the same responsibilities are not shared by others, including individuals, proportionate to their power, wealth, and influence. Some critics of business, for example, chastise corporations for not doing more for the arts or education or for the cure of social ills, even while these critics do not themselves give an equal proportion of their own wealth and effort. Insisting on the social responsibilities of business, in other words, in no way replaces or displaces the social responsibilities of individuals, the government, or enterprises in other parts of society.

B.   THE PRIORITY OF SOCIAL RESPONSIBILITIES

One primary concern of business, its intrinsic goal, is to produce a profit, although, as discussed earlier, this should never be thought to be its only intrinsic goal. Accordingly, a natural response to almost all problems in many business situations is going to be couched in terms of "cost" and "benefits," and questions of social responsibility will be couched in that language too. This is not unreasonable, but making a profit is not necessarily the ultimate concern of business or businesspeople. In playing poker the ultimate aim is to win the hand, but in poker, or in anything else, "winning isn't everything." Playing poker for entertainment, for instance, can be more important than winning. Even if business is out to make a profit, social responsibility, which is not intrinsic to business life as such, may be more important; indeed, it may even be the reason for the existence of business and business life in the first place.

What this means is that, first of all, questions about business responsibilities are not answered solely by cost and benefit considerations; neither are such questions simply to be brushed aside. Suppose, for example, a firm could solve the

---

The Ultimate Responsibility ——

Socrates is in prison, about to be executed for trumped-up "crimes against the state." His friend Crito offers to rescue him by arranging his escape. This is Socrates' answer:

Socrates: My dear Crito, I appreciate your warm feelings very much—that is, assuming that they have some justification; if not, the stronger they are, the harder they will be to deal with. Very well, then: we must consider whether we ought to follow your advice or not. . . . At the same time I should like you to consider whether we are still satisfied on this point: that the really important thing is not to live, but to live well.

Crito: Why, yes.

Socrates: And that to live well means the same thing as to live honourably or rightly?

Crito: Yes.

Socrates: Then in the light of this agreement we must consider whether or not it is right for me to try to get away without an official discharge. If it turns out to be right, we must make the attempt: if not, we must let it drop. If it becomes clear that such conduct is wrong, I cannot help thinking that the question whether we are sure to die, or to suffer any other ill effect for that matter, if we stand our ground and take no action, ought not to weigh with us at all in comparison with the risk of doing what is wrong. . . . Ought one to fulfill all one's agreements, provided that they are right, or break them?

Crito: One ought to fulfill them.

Socrates: Then consider the logical consequence. If we leave this place without first persuading the State to let us go, are we or are we not doing an injury, and doing it in a quarter where it is least justifiable? Are we or are we not abiding by our just agreements?

Crito: I can't answer your question, Socrates; I am not clear in my mind.

Socrates: Look at it in this way. Suppose that while we were preparing to run away from here (or however one should describe it) the Laws and Constitution of Athens were to come and confront us and ask this question: "Now, Socrates, what are your proposing to do? Can you deny that by this act which you are contemplating you intend, so far as you have the power, to destroy us, the laws, and the whole State as well? Do you imagine that a city can continue to exist and not be turned upside down, if the legal judgments which are pronounced in it have no force but are nullified and destroyed by private persons?"—how shall we answer this question, Crito, and others of the same kind? There is much that could be said, especially by a professional advocate, to protest against the invalidation of this law which enacts the judgments once pronounced shall be binding. Shall we say, "Yes, I do intend to destroy the laws, because the State wronged me by passing a faulty judgment at my trial?" Is this to be our answer, or what?

Crito: What you have just said, by all means, Socrates.

Socrates: Then what supposing the Laws say, "Was there provision for this in the agreement between you and us, Socrates? Or did you undertake to abide by whatever judgments the State pronounced?" [Notice that here and in what follows it is "the Laws" talking to Socrates.] "Now first answer this question: Are we or are we not speaking the truth when we say that you have undertaken, in deed if not in word, to live your life as a citizen in obedience to us?" What are we to say to that, Crito? Are we not bound to admit it?

Crito: We cannot help it, Socrates.

Socrates: "It is a fact, then," they would say, "that you are breaking covenants and undertakings made with us, although you made them under no compulsion or misunderstanding, and were not compelled to decide in a limited time; you had seventy years in which you could have left the country, if you were not satisfied with us or felt that the agreements were unfair. You did not choose Sparta or Crete—your favorite models of good government—or any other Greek or foreign state; you could not have absented yourself from the city less if you had been lame or blind or decrepit in some other way. It is quite obvious that you stand by yourself above all other Athenians in your affection for this city and for us its Laws:—who would care for a city without laws? And now, after all this, are you going to stand by your agreements? Yes, you are, Socrates, if you will take our advice; and then you will at least escape being laughed at for leaving the city. . . . Do not take Crito's advice, but follows ours."

That, my dear friend Crito, I do assure you, is what I seem to hear them saying, just as a mystic seems to hear the strains of music; and the sound of their arguments rings so loudly in my head that I cannot hear the other side. I warn you that, as my opinion stands at present, it will be useless to urge a different view. However, if you think that you will do any good by it, say what you like.

Crito: No, Socrates, I have nothing to say.

Socrates: Then give it up, Crito, and let us follow this course, since God points out the way.

From Plato's Dialogue, *Crito*

local minority unemployment problem at minimal cost to itself. Does it have a social obligation to do so? Most people would say "yes," and in most cases the figures would show that the company would actually benefit, financially as well as in public esteem. But suppose another company could also solve the local unemployment problem but only at a disastrous cost, perhaps sufficient to put it out of business and all of its employees out of work. Does it have an obligation to solve the same problem? It is difficult to imagine an affirmative argument. Cost and benefit, therefore, are not irrelevant. But it is surely wrong to suppose, for this reason, that a business has a social responsibility *only* when it benefits financially in solving it and does not have a responsibility if it loses money, no matter how little. Social responsibilities have a certain priority, but not to the exclusion of economic interests, except, perhaps, in the most extreme situations.

Some responsibilities, including responsibilities aimed at benefiting the public, are part of our job, or even define our job. Therefore, we accept those responsibilities as part of, as definitive of, the job; but we can quit the job and thereby give up those responsibilities. Social responsibilities cannot be tossed aside, especially when they are not specific to any particular role in society but belong to everyone in society in whatever role. They are part of *those roles* as well as part of every individual.

One set of social responsibilities, clearly, is the recognition that we all are members of a certain society and are thereby bound to obey its laws, even when these turn to our disadvantage; in fact the ultimate recognition of social responsibility is the right of society to demand, by virtue of its laws, that an individual give up his life. Furthermore, a businessperson has social responsibilities not *only as an individual,* but as businessperson also. Business, too, is a part of society, and it is society that gives meaning and significance (not to mention the rewards) to positions in business as well as to individual citizenship. To be in business, therefore, is already to accept social responsibilities as a member of the business world. We may not be asked to give up our lives, but we can be sure that our responsibilities in the job do not stop at the limits of the job and its responsibilities.

What are these responsibilities that transcend any particular position or role? The name alone tells us that they are responsibilities concerned with the "social," with the good of society and all members in it, with the reputation and enrichment of that society culturally, spiritually, and intellectually, as well as materially. It is the concern with the good life, not now primarily as an individual aspiration but, so far as possible, available, if in varying degrees, to everyone in society. As always, the scope of the term "society" is in question; does this refer to our immediate community of friends and colleagues, the city, state, nation, or all of humanity? Whatever the answer to this question (which of course has no single answer), the notion of social responsibility is the tie that binds us to any number of other people, many of whom we may not know, may never meet, or may personally despise, but whose interests, in some abstract and not very personal way, concern us, if only because their well-being affects us too. For instance, concern for crime in the streets is not, by the nature of the problem, just the concern that only we should be safe, it is inevitably a *mutual* concern, and it is each of our responsibilities to do what we can about it (something more than not "mugging" anyone ourselves).

We have often viewed the suggestion that protection from crime should be left to individual resources (whether burglar alarms or private firearms) as a kind of barbarianism. We take this stance, first, because such means leave the poor entirely defenseless and, second, because it signals the breakdown of society as such—the abandonment of one of the most basic concerns that marks the emergence of "civilization" from the primal state of nature envisioned by some philosophers as a "war of all against all." The presupposition of the notion of social responsibility is simply that we are not alone in the world. We are dependent, both positively and negatively—positively in the sense that most of the rewards of the good life are produced by, given significance by, and remain possible only in a coherent and relatively harmonious society, and negatively, in that life would be extremely unpleasant, if not dangerous, without some mutual

Queens Plant Opens Job Market to Nine Dropouts ——

The graduation took place without pomp in the most modest of circumstances.

But to the nine high school dropouts receiving technical diplomas last week—certification they were trained to operate machinery that makes leather goods—it was a moment of pride. And for the owners of the Queens factory in which the ceremony took place, it was proof that unemployed and untrained youths could be given a trade and a job without a penny of government money. . . .

One evening a week over a four-week period, the students worked with Campbell Bosworth employees learning the intricacies of skivers and lockstitch, beveling and embossing machines. They received no stipend, and their teachers, Mr. Schiller said, asked for no pay. If the students showed a commitment to learn, attending every class and by the end of the course demonstrated competence, they were told the program would find them jobs.

All nine students succeeded. They are scheduled to begin work this week, and the company plans to train three more groups of students before Christmas. The Chamber of Commerce and the Vocational Foundation plan to use the example to persuade other businesses in the city to begin similar programs.

At the end of the last class, the students, clad in blue smocks, stepped forward in the machinery workshop as their names were called. They were each awarded a diploma and a pair of scissors, a symbol of their entry into the trade.

"To have a trade means a chance of a career, no more 'Sorry, we're looking for somebody who's done this before,'" said 20-year-old Todd Williams, who has had "from here to there odd jobs" since he dropped out of Boys and Girls High School in Brooklyn three years ago.

"Someday I'd like to have a house, raise a family away from my neighborhood," he said. "I don't want my kids to see what I've seen."

The New York Times, Oct. 11, 1981

respect and sense of shared belonging. (Even if there were laws and sanctions for protecting life and property, think how unpleasant life would be—and sometimes is—if people casually insulted you in the street, treated you with wholesale suspicion, and refused to deal with you—all within the law.)

Consider the perennially important question of unemployment, particularly minority unemployment, one of our more serious social ills. The first thing to say, perhaps, is that unemployment is *everybody's* problem. It is not just the problem of the unemployed workers themselves. It is not just the problem of those businesses (as well as government and public institutions) that are in the most obvious position to do something about it by hiring more workers. Moreover, the fact that businesses have the need and resources to hire, whereas most private citizens do not, is not itself a valid argument to prove that only business has that responsibility. It is a problem that affects or should affect all of us, not just in the cost of unemployment compensation (through taxes) and increased crime rates, but in the very texture of the society in which we live, even if we never actually have to look the problem in the face.

If the disastrous consequences of mass unemployment are not merely an economic issue, neither is the solution. Indeed, one of the crucial and cruelest aspects of Adam Smith's "free enterprise" doctrine is that labor itself is a "market," defined by competition and supply and demand. According to the classical theory, given a large pool of unemployed workers, competition increases among them, thus increasing competition for jobs, lowering wages, and thereby lowering prices and raising profits. Economists are almost weekly publishing new arguments about how full employment will benefit rather than hamper the economy. But the more important point is that the argument against unemployment is an ethical, not economic, argument. The social responsibility to eliminate unemployment is not a matter of cost/benefit analysis but of concern for others. In Adam Smith's time, the existence of considerable numbers of hopelessly poor people was taken for granted, and no one even would have suggested that the problem of poverty and unemployment was solvable. But in our society, where we so freely moralize about the importance of work and the rewards of achievement, there is something hypocritical about the existence of people willing to work who cannot find jobs. The social responsibility falls to business not because (as a Marxist would argue) it is the business world that is responsible for their plight, but rather because it is everyone's responsibility to solve such problems and some businesses are in a good position to do so.

C. CAUTIONARY TALES

One of the deterents to socially responsible action is the circulation of horror stories, many of them apocryphal, about companies that have gotten into serious trouble by over-extending their domain of responsibilities to include social responsibilities. Peter Drucker, for instance, offers us two "cautionary tales" of "good intentions and high responsibility—gone wrong."*

First, he tells the saga of Union Carbide, which benignly moved one of its plants into the worst of the depressed areas of West Virginia, where there was near total unemployment and no opportunities for jobs whatsoever. The problem was that the only plant that was viable in the area employed a process that was

---

*Management, pp. 320–25.

In 1983, I was transferred to Durham, North Carolina, where Mitsubishi Electric was establishing its first overseas semiconductor base, Mitsubishi Semiconductor America. As president, I oversaw everything from site acquisition and factory construction to employee hiring and sales. Moreover, U.S.–Japan friction over semiconductors was heating up, and in the midst of worsening relations, I had to integrate my company into its new community.

In the United States, a company cannot succeed without interacting with the local community. In Durham, where the traditional American community survives, people do not rely on government; the community has been built on individuals' sense of solidarity. This same spirit can be seen in many U.S. cities and towns, where, for example, volunteers rather than fire departments handle firefighting. Knowing community feeling was strong, I shuddered to consider what would happen if the people took a dislike to our company.

At first, I did not know the words "philanthropy" and "corporate citizenship." One day, however, a game was held commemorating the Durham baseball league's entry into the national Little League. Since our company donated the new league's scoreboard, I was invited to the commemoration ceremony. To my surprise, I was taken onto the field, handed a microphone, and asked to sing the U.S. national anthem. When I began, the entire crowd stood up and joined in. An American told me: "This is philanthropy."

—Kazuo Watanabe, in *Look Japan*
February 1992

already obsolete and very costly, requiring large amounts of quality coal, not readily available. When the plant opened, explicitly for the sake of its social effects and despite the questionable economics, it did indeed provide several thousand jobs, but it also created a serious air pollution hazard. After opening as a public hero in 1951, Union Carbide soon became the enemy when, ten years later, a mayor was elected on the campaign slogan "fight Union Carbide." Even *Business Week* (Feb. 1971) chastised the company in the article "A Corporate Polluter Learns the Hard Way." Drucker concludes that "Union Carbide's management did not behave very intelligently." They decided to help out a suffering part of society, but committed themselves to an obsolescent process and a losing economic proposition to do so. In the end, it helped the community very little (though short memory and ingratitude also played a role). Furthermore, it was forced to outlay large sums of money to try to correct the pollution problem.

The second "cautionary tale" is the most poignant, for it seems to strike at the heart of the insistence that business do its part in aggressively supporting

America's Corporate Conscience Awards ——

Charitable Contributions
- 1992   US West
- 1991   H.B. Fuller, Foldcraft
- 1990   Cummins Engine
- 1989   Dayton Hudson
- 1988   Ben & Jerry's Homemade
- 1987   General Mills, Polaroid, Sara Lee

Community Action
- 1992   Prudential Insurance
          Supermarkets General
- 1991   Time Warner
- 1990   Xerox
- 1989   Digital Equipment Corp.
- 1988   Best Western International, South
          Shore Bank
- 1987   IBM, Amoco

Environment
- 1992   Church & Dwight; Conservatree
- 1991   Herman Miller, Smith & Hawken
- 1990   AT&T
- 1989   Applied Energy Services
- 1988   3M

Employer Responsiveness
- 1992   Donnelly Corp.
- 1991   Kellogg
- 1990   Pitney Bowes
- 1989   Federal Express
- 1988   IBM
- 1987   Procter & Gamble

Equal Employment Opportunity
- 1992   General Mills
- 1991   Hallmark Cards
- 1990   US West
- 1989   Eastman Kodak
- 1988   Xerox, Gannett,
          General Mills
- 1987   Avon

Council on Economic Priorities

American ideals, even in opposition to—if need be—local public sentiment. In the late 1940s, a major steel company hired a northern Quaker civil rights advocate to manage a southern division of its industry, explicitly, as he was told on his hiring, in order to speed up the hiring and promotion of blacks. He spent a year establishing himself and then, when a new extension of the mill was opened, he hired a small but significant number of black workers for the new crews. Their skill was not in question, and no white seniority rights were violated. Nevertheless, the union responded immediately and threatened to go on strike. Drucker accounts with both irony and sympathy the plight of the poor manager, as in desperation he approached an old Quaker civil rights friend, only to be chastised by him too for being "immoral," despite the unquestioned morality of his civil rights goals. His "immorality" was "using the economic muscle of a big company to impose your mores and values on the community in which you operate. . . . Using the economic power of a business, the power of the employer, and the authority of your office to dictate to the community . . . is 'economic imperialism' and cannot be condoned no matter how good the cause." The manager resigned and moved back north. The company reverted to its old ways, only to be bitterly attacked, a few years later, for its racism and illegal and immoral practices.

Drucker summarily concludes by saying that "the demand for social responsibility is not as simple as most books, articles, and speeches make it out to be." But other critics take such cases much further. Friedman, for example, uses them not as "cautionary tales" but as doomsday warnings about what inevitably happens when business goes beyond its proper bounds and inteferes in social concerns under the guise of "social responsibility." But this, surely, is not the proper or even a plausible conclusion to Drucker's two tales. What stands out is the economic foolishness of the first instance. The moral *should* be, "don't try to do good when the means to do so involve possibly fatal financial risks and side effects that might well be more socially harmful than the evil you intend to cure." On the other hand, social responsibilities and economic survival are not essentially in conflict, and it is a scare tactic to point out those few cases in which a company irresponsibly jeopardized the latter for the sake of the former (assuming that to be the proper description of their own calculations in the matter).

In the second case, we are struck first by the oddity of the Quaker activist friend's remarks, and second by the timidity of the company who hired and supposedly supported the northern manager in the first place. The company should have realized full well that the immediate reaction to even token desegregation of the plant work force would be hostile. The company could have been a national model and the local bigoted union a national buffoon. The company didn't pursue its lofty goal, didn't support its own manager, and didn't stand up to the union. The moral is not that "social responsibility isn't so simple," but that fighting the evils of society takes some tact and persistence, not half-hearted attempts.

Social responsibility and corporate self-interest are not always antagonistic. Deep down, they are essentially one and the same concern, for, as Drucker comments elsewhere, a healthy business is hardly possible in an unhealthy social environment. There will always be occasional but dramatic stories of business failure or serious setbacks because of socially motivated (rather than simply economically motivated) enterprises. But these are not to be taken so seriously, any more than the large number of business failures and setbacks due to straightforward economic investments are to be taken as a "warning" against risk and investment in general. Indeed, perhaps the problem with such "cautionary tales" is that there are not nearly enough of them, for not enough corporations have taken risks for the sake of society for us to clearly see what is effective and what is not, what succeeds in benefiting the corporation as well as society. Indeed, for all of the talk about "risk" and "investment," the score on social experimentation shows the business world to be extremely conservative.

D.   THE QUESTION OF COMPETENCE

Is a corporation *competent* to attempt to fulfill such social responsibilities? The quick but not very informative answer is that they would not be responsibilities if there were no competence, since, in Kant's brief phrase, "ought implies can." Neither a business nor a person can be responsible for what he, she, or it *cannot* do. The other side of that equation, however, is that *if* there is a responsibility that all of us share (including corporations) then competence, too, is presumed. In other words, in such issues, *competence itself becomes one of our responsibilities.* We are responsible for being competent to carry out our responsibilities.

What are the special competencies needed to try to alleviate racial tensions, or at least not add to them? And if some special sensitivity must be learned, we should not say, whether of ourselves or a corporation, that we or it is not competent; we and it have a responsibility to become competent in racially charged situations, if indeed we live and work in a community that is racially charged. We may need special competence to handle a violently racial riot, but we do not need special competence to hire minority workers or to promote without reference to race, sex, or religion. As another example, we may need special competence to be an art critic but not to buy art and support the arts. Of course, what we do need is some knowledge and sensitivity in order to avoid the charge (now made as an explanation why business should not support the arts at all) that businesspeople are not in general competent to make aesthetic judgments, and so should not be expected to. This is nonsense. Businesspeople do make aesthetic judgments, even in the purchases they make to decorate their buildings and offices. In fact, they now provide a large segment of support for many artists and house some of the more significant art collections in America.

Knowledge of the arts, as well as knowledge of contemporary racial problems, can be learned by anyone in a position of responsibility. The argument is not that businesspeople do not have special competence in such social or

Social Responsibility Funds: How Did They Do (in 1991)? ——

Stock and Bond Fund	Assets (millions)	Gain or loss
Calvert - Ariel Appreciation	$90.0	+32.7%
Calvert - Ariel Growth Fund	262.0	+33.1
Calvert Social Investment Funds		
• Managed Growth	365.0	+17.8
• Bond	38.0	+15.8
• Equity	51.0	+21.9
Domini Social Index Trust	3.6	+8.5*
Dreyfus Third Century	359.0	+38.1
New Alternatives	24.0	+25.6
Parnassus Fund	32.0	+51.9
Pax World Fund	270.0	+20.8
S&P 500		**+30.4**
Shield Progressive Environment	3.8	−1.9
Rightime Social Awareness	6.1	+23.4

Money Market Fund	Assets (millions)	Yield (1/3/91)
Calvert Money Market	$187.0	4.7%
Working Assets	236.0	4.3

*Fourth quarter, 1991
Investing for a Better World

aesthetic matters and therefore do not have responsibilities. It is rather that, because they have such responsibilities (as everyone does), they have the responsibility to educate themselves appropriately. If nothing else, this might be solved simply by hiring a part-time consultant in race relations or art. But competence itself is only sometimes a limitation of responsibility; much of the time, it is rather an *additional* responsibility, to be gained as quickly and as efficiently as possible as a way of discharging other responsibilities.

E. NOBLESSE OBLIGE

One of the presumptions of every civilized society in history (whatever its economic system and its views of "free enterprise") is to have had a generally understood sense of the responsibility of those in society who are better off than everyone else; this is sometimes called *noblesse oblige,* the obligations of the nobility. This is rarely a matter of law; sometimes, it is a matter of charity and philanthropy, but this captures only the fringe of the idea, rather than its essence. It is the responsibility of those who have more, to contribute more for the good of society. Of course, we are talking, at least in our society, of a matter of degree and proportion, not a simple matter of class. Everyone has the responsibility to contribute, but some can contribute more than others. It is a simple matter of historical fact that business in America today, and people *in their positions in business,* have far more money, power, and influence than almost anyone else. It is not a question of special responsibilities for business alone. In earlier ages and other societies, these responsibilities belonged to the aristocracy, or the hereditary monarchy, or the best hunters, or the priesthood. It is a matter of *noblesse oblige,* and this, throughout history, has always been considered argument enough.

It has been taken for granted since ancient times that it is the obligation of the powerful and the wealthy (these are often, if not always, the same) to support the arts, to glorify society, and to enrich everyone's everyday life with works of magnificence, spiritual power, and so on. This has never been considered a burden, but rather a privilege, and a chance for self-aggrandizement. The pharaohs and the ancient kings supported the arts, and the Catholic Church supported the arts to a tremendous degree. The great kings of Europe prided themselves on the art they sponsored; indeed, many of them are remembered today only because of the art they commissioned. The aristocracy of every country of every period defined itself by its artistic taste and sponsorship (no matter how much of it was awful). Even in America, the business tycoons of the nineteenth century are known today not for their railroads or their oil rigs but for their art collections and sponsorship of the arts, which now define so much of cultural life in America.

The argument, simply, is that the responsibility of supporting the arts in America, and, consequently, having a major say in their direction and health, has always fallen to the wealthy—*whether institutions or individuals.* By virtue of their money and prominence in contemporary American society, business in general and businesses in particular have a special responsibility to support the arts. Again, this is not because it is an obligation peculiar to business; any other institutions in our society would have a similar responsibility if they had similar resources. Indeed, we all do have such responsibilities now, proportional to our abilities to pay. But, as things are, business has the money, so business has the responsibility. If it is complained that such powerful business influence will surely corrupt the arts, then it is the further responsibility of businesspeople to educate themselves such that they will not do so. The responsibility now passes to them: *noblesse oblige,* "the obligations of the nobility."

The essence of the social responsibility doctrine is that many of the most significant activities and decisions of businesses are not solely business activities and decisions. Consider the owner of a professional urban sports team, for example; suppose he receives a generous offer from a buyer in another state. The team

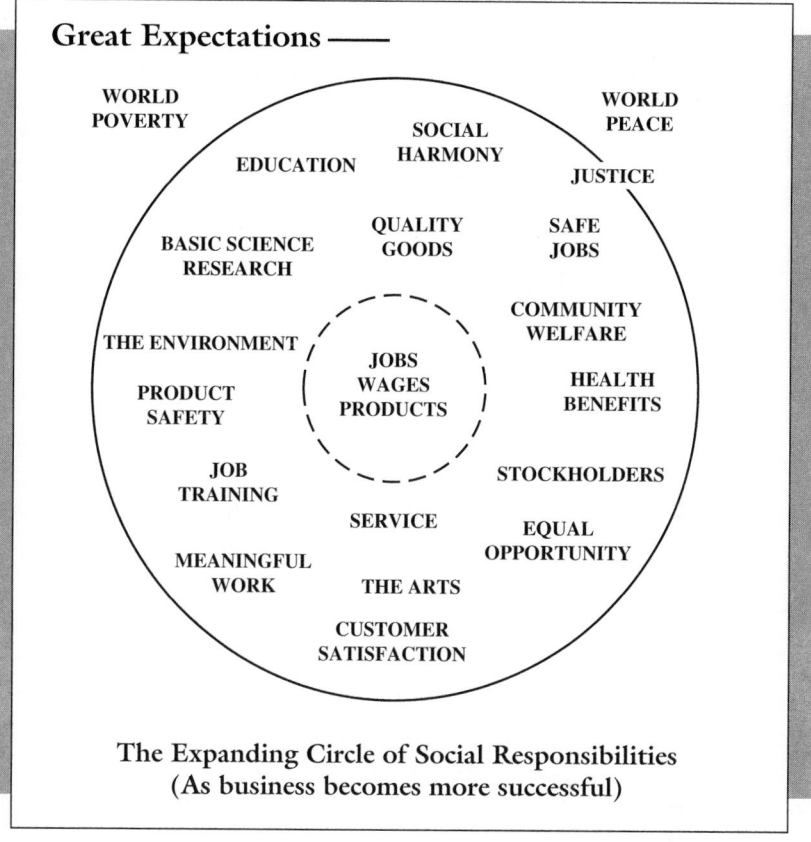

Great Expectations ——

WORLD
POVERTY

WORLD
PEACE

SOCIAL
HARMONY

EDUCATION

JUSTICE

QUALITY
GOODS

SAFE
JOBS

BASIC SCIENCE
RESEARCH

COMMUNITY
WELFARE

THE ENVIRONMENT

JOBS
WAGES
PRODUCTS

HEALTH
BENEFITS

PRODUCT
SAFETY

JOB
TRAINING

STOCKHOLDERS

SERVICE

EQUAL
OPPORTUNITY

MEANINGFUL
WORK

THE ARTS

CUSTOMER
SATISFACTION

The Expanding Circle of Social Responsibilities
(As business becomes more successful)

has near-fanatic local loyalty and has for years been the pride and focus of shared identity in the city. As a business decision, the only considerations would be those of price and profit, but it is obvious that the context of the decision requires something more. It is not that the owner has no right to sell, of course, but his right must be weighed against a quite different set of responsibilities to the community. This is also a question of social responsibility and an instance of *noblesse oblige*. In nations where sports teams are sponsored by the government, the idea of moving a team from one place to another does not arise. But in a country that leaves its sporting life up to the free enterprise system, there is a responsibility on the part of those who have the resources to "own" such teams to respect the very important social role their "property" plays in the life of the community.

Does business have an *obligation* to support the arts and local cultural activities? In the strong moral sense, probably not. But consider people who have rather lucrative resources at their command, who never give anything to the community, who treat the social and cultural life of the city as quite removed from

Ten Top Corporate Givers

1)	IBM	$135.0
2)	Hewlett-Packard	74.5
3)	General Motors	62.2
4)	Exxon	55.8
5)	General Electric	38.8
6)	Merck & Co.	38.5
7)	AT&T	36.1
8)	Dayton Hudson	33.9
9)	Ford Motor Co.	32.7
10)	Digital Equipment	32.6

(in millions)

Source: Public Management Institute

On their home turf, Japanese corporations are not known for their philanthropy. However, since coming to the United States, they have picked up on this practice, emulating American companies. Here are some signs of this activity:

• Toyota gave $2 million to the National Center for Family Literacy to fund new literacy programs across the nation. It's the largest grant ever given by a business to a family literacy program under which parents who have not completed high school return to school with their children.

• Twenty Japanese companies have set up foundations in the United States. The largest is the Hitachi Foundation, which gave grants of $2.5 million last year (up from $900,000 in 1988).

• Honda's foundation will give away $1.2 million this year to youth and science programs.

their own interests. These people might well fulfill all of the obligations imposed upon them, break no rules of law or morality, but yet be judged almost universally as unlikably mean-spirited. Suppose they care nothing about giving to charity or friends and never support any cultural function not strictly necessary for survival. Such people might be not at all morally reprehensible; indeed not even irresponsible. But nevertheless, our feeling would rightly be that such people are only minimally members of society.

So too, corporations and business in general might well define their "social responsibilities" so narrowly as to include only the requirement of preventing harm and the fulfillment of actual contracts and obligations. If they do not support the community, they will not benefit from the well-being of the community. Many times, they happen to be the wealthiest "citizens" so to speak, of the community, in command of more resources and therefore in a better position to influence—for better or worse—the life of the community.

F.   The Problem of Paternalism

Social responsibility presumes as well as aims for a harmonious community, with mutual interests and shared goals and the well-being of every member of that community. But as we make the effort to fulfill the positive social responsibilities to improve society, help others, and support the arts and education, an accusation may emerge of a very different kind than the charge of "irresponsibility." It may be argued that some people are taking too much authority in society, thereby stripping others of their self-esteem and their autonomy in making their own decisions. Sometimes, a double bind traps businesspeople and corporations: whatever they do they are doing either too much, too little, or both. Either they are taking too much authority (and, as we argued in the last chapter, there is no responsibility without authority too) or they are not contributing enough and are therefore irresponsible. The unacceptable solution sometimes suggested is that business confine its role to simply donating its money, with no say in how it is to be used. But there is a difference between mere charity, which may come with no strings attached, and *support* in the important sense, which means participation as well as financing. But there is also the charge of participating *too much.*

Sometimes, when businesses step in to fulfill their social responsibilities—by supporting the arts, by encouraging a certain public policy, by shifting the established practices of a community—they are accused of **paternalism,** taking on an overly "fatherly" role towards others and thus taking away citizens' own sense of responsibility and autonomy. Sometimes, of course, the charge is warranted. In our individualistic society we generally object whenever anyone or any institution—including the government—forces upon us policies—no matter how wise or beneficial—that we feel we ought rather to impose on ourselves. We object to highway speed limits, not because we don't believe that controlled speed is necessary but because we think we can judge for ourselves what constitutes a safe speed. We object to the restrictions on some pharmaceuticals on the grounds that we ourselves ought to be able to decide, on the basis of available information, whether to take the risks of using them and not abusing them. Paternalism is depriving a person of that autonomy and ability to make a rational, personal decision, against his or her consent.

Most of the classic arguments regarding paternalism are concerned, naturally enough, with government, and the extent to which government is entitled or obliged to step in and "protect us from ourselves." But the issue of paternalism enters into the concern for the social responsibilities of business as well. On the one hand, because the free enterprise system is based on the assumption that consumers are "sovereign," they have the ability and the right to make their own decisions. This may break down in certain cases (for example, where advertising for young children is in question), but, nevertheless, the premise of free enterprise is that individuals know what they want and what is good for them without the supervision of any regulatory agency to decide for them. This premise also applies to the role of business, which is to supply what the consumers want. But if consumers decide that they are unwilling to pay for safety belts in cars, does the auto industry nevertheless have an obligation to install them? If consumers decide to generally abuse a dangerous drug, does the manufacturer have any responsibility other than to make its risks clear, perhaps with a warning label? On the assumption of consumer sovereignty, any effort on the part of the manufacturer to take steps beyond the production of quality products and honest representation of the nature of its products would be paternalistic.

On the other hand, it is clear that, given the complexity of many modern products and the proven incompetence and irresponsibility of many consumers, merely to "let the consumer beware" is not enough. It is possible to idealize the ability and right of people to decide for themselves, but it is also necessary to recognize that most people are far from ideally rational agents. They can be sometimes illiterate and unwilling to indulge in a protracted study of the effects and side effects of the products they buy.

Furthermore, to make matters even more complicated, the ideal of consumer sovereignty leaves out one crucial ingredient—namely, the fact that consumer demand is often *created* by the manufacturer through advertising. Thus the problem of paternalism shifts considerably. It is not just a question of the manufacturer deciding whether or not to satisfy some consumer demand; it is rather a question of deciding whether or not to *create* that demand. In some cases, such as the creation of mass hysteria about body odors, this is only obnoxious but not particularly harmful. In others, however—the portrayal of smoking as a sexually sensual or behaviorally and aesthetically desirable accoutrement, for example— the question of paternalism becomes much more difficult. In the case of the tobacco industry, the question of consumer sovereignty may boil down to whether it has the obligation to put itself out of business. The idea that smokers consume tobacco products voluntarily is an appeal to the ideal autonomy of the consumer, but the inherent danger of the product would point rather to the inability of consumers to know what is good for them. To what extent is business responsible for the well-being of consumers, when the consumers' own choice is involved? And if business will not take this responsibility, to what extent is the government then responsible for restricting business activities, and thus acting paternalistically both towards the consumer and business?

G. THE SILENT STAKEHOLDER: THE ENVIRONMENT

There is one stakeholder, however, that both invites and demands our attention, although it is not a member of the community or an employee or customer of the corporation. That stakeholder is nature, and though the environment does not have a voice or a vote in the running of our society, it nevertheless provides the atmosphere, the very ground and climate, within which all business and all human activity takes place. For many centuries, the impact on nature by relatively small and not-yet-industrialized human activity was not sufficient enough to notice, except, perhaps, in towns with very concentrated populations. To be sure, there was some air pollution that resulted from the many fires that were used to cook food and warm houses, and there was always a problem of waste disposal, which was not always delicately handled and whose importance for community health was slow to be appreciated. But it is only recently that we have had to worry about the problems of massive carbon monoxide poisoning of the air due to the millions of internal combustion engines in automobiles and toxic chemicals spewed into the air by thousands of factories, not to mention the particularly deadly wastes of nuclear plants. It is only recently that we have managed to pollute not only local streams and rivers, but literally kill entire lakes and poison the oceans. We are also guilty of releasing enough dangerous chemicals into the air and damaging the surface of the earth to such an extent that we have endangered the atmosphere and the climate of the planet. And as the population of the planet continues to grow—from two to five billion in only a few decades—there will be more pollution, more environmental damage, more mouths to feed, and more vehicles to power. More and more of the earth's resources will be devoured, and much of what will be returned will be waste and pollution rather than replenishment.

The United States is, in fact, well ahead of most other countries in its efforts to fight pollution, conserve resources, and clean up the planet. Nearly a third of the trees in Germany's romantic Black Forest are dead from the pollution along the Autobahn. Most of eastern Europe's rivers, including the historic Danube (which hasn't been "blue" for decades), have become cesspools of chemical waste. The air in Tokyo and Mexico City is so bad so much of the time that citizens are warned not to go outside, or to wear gas masks if they do. We still do not know how extensive and long lasting the damage may be from the breakdown of Russia's Chernobyl reactor. And the intentional damage done to the Red Sea and the entire atmosphere of the Middle East by Saddam Hussein during the Persian Gulf War of 1991 has still not been fully evaluated, much less cleaned up. But, of course, we are not innocent in this regard, and much of our own apparent good fortune has to do with the fact that our messiest industries are often shipped overseas, where environmental restrictions and protection laws are far more lenient. A chemical pesticide factory owned and operated by the American company Union Carbide leaked its deadly contents one night a few years ago and killed thousands of people in Bhopal, India, leaving many more thousands with chronic ailments and illnesses. It is, perhaps, a matter of luck that our nuclear mishaps due to negligence or faulty design have thus far had little impact. And, of course, the *Exxon Valdez* disaster is not far behind us, and there have already been similar disasters with comparable environmental damage.

It is the nature of environmental pollution that, unlike most mistaken policies or ill-designed products, the results cannot be simply revised or recalled. Resources depleted are often resources gone forever, and environmental damage is often irreversible. What's more, environmental damage often cannot be contained, and the damage caused in one part of the world may quickly and unstoppably affect another. For example, the production of "acid rain" does not recognize international boundaries, say, between the United States and Canada or between Germany and Switzerland. Similarly, the damage that is being done to the atmosphere by way of depletion of the ozone layer and the "greenhouse effect" does not just affect the countries most responsible for causing it. The smoke and pollution from Iraq's oil fires spread beyond the Persian Gulf to much of the planet within a few months. The destruction of the rain forests in South America and Southeast Asia are felt in the industrialized countries of Europe and North America, and the cultivation of cattle for the beef industry, according to environmentalist Jeremy Rifkin, is destroying the planet.

Where does business enter into the environmental question? Our industries produce millions of tons of potentially harmful substances, some seventy thousand different compounds, and at least several hundred of these can be seriously argued to present serious health or environmental risks. To complicate matters, substances that seem to be harmless at first can later be shown to pose serious dangers. For example, asbestos—which only a few decades ago was being celebrated as a fibrous wonder that could (and did) reduce and eliminate the danger of fire—proved to be extremely toxic and has been blamed for many deaths. So, too, have the elements lead and mercury, and radium and the compounds dioxin and benzene. But often the damaging effects of such substances, in addition to not being predicted beforehand, may take decades to appear. Even smoking tobacco, (which comes as close as possible) to cumulative or delayed causation of fatal damage to the human body, takes decades to develop and leaves enough room for argument about the specific mechanism of the cause for industry defenders to insist that "the connection has not been proved." Even where the damage is immediate and visible, there may be good arguments of the cost/benefit variety that conclude that the product in question is worth the cost to the environment or the human body—but worth it to whom? And who will ultimately pay the cost?

Virtually every industrial product has some pollution, some noxious or seemingly unusable substance as its by-product. Some industries are relatively clean, of course—the computer software business, for example. Others are notoriously "dirty," in fact, so polluting that it has become a real question whether we

Japanese Green Acres ——

Once the bane of environmentalists as a major importer of goods from endangered animal species, Japan has begun to rack up green points with its changing attitude toward wildlife trade, albeit slowly and at some times inconsistently.

While most countries have environmental agencies to monitor trade in wildlife, Japan chose its Ministry of International Trade and Industry for that role. . . . "[W]e have gradually understood the importance of protecting the environment," says Tadashi Sagisaka, director of MITI's import division and one of Japan's point men on wildlife trade.

Environmentalists who long saw Japan as their biggest enemy now offer praise. In many ways, "the situation seems to have been ameliorated," says Hideomi Tokunaga, an activist working on the endangered species issue. "The attitude of the government officials has changed."

—*The Wall Street Journal*
February 27, 1992

are willing to tolerate them on our soil, even at the cost of becoming dependent on foreign-made products. The steel industry is a prime example, and it should not be surprising that many of our largest and once most successful steel companies have been diversifying in part in order to avoid the enormous costs it would take to clean up their industry. The result: an increase in our dependence on steel from abroad—not a healthy alternative.

The production of paper is a particularly messy business, as is the recycling of paper, we should add. But only a few extremists have seriously suggested that we should give up paper and its manufacture, although the cost of paper production is pollution. But pollution can be controlled, and there are continual developments in technology that will help decrease and limit pollution in the paper business. The problem is technology can be very expensive. If a paper company buys and installs the new technology, its costs of production increase significantly. That means, presumably, that it will have to charge more for its product. But now suppose, just for the sake of simplicity, that there are ten paper manufacturers competing with the same product in the same market. If one of them installs the new technology, but the others do not, that one environmentalist hero will soon find itself unable to compete with the others. Its product will be the most expensive. Now suppose that all but one of the companies go for the new technology. That one environmentally irresponsible holdout will in fact capture much of the market, assuming that people will tend to buy the least expensive product. One might like the ten companies to get together and agree that they will all install the new technology and all raise prices together, but, first of all, this is illegal. It is called "collusion." And, second, what is to prevent one or more of the ten from cheating on the agreement, refusing to install the new technology, thus beating the others on prices? This suggests two answers.

The first and most preferable is that the consumers take control of the situation by refusing to buy paper from companies that pollute more than is necessary, but that also means that they must be willing (and not just say that they would be willing) to pay higher prices for "cleaner" products and their production. This is becoming a real market phenomenon in certain industries. But, unfortunately, it does not happen in all industries, either because consumers remain more concerned about low prices than they are about the effects on the environment, or because the information about production and pollution is not readily available to the consumers. Consumers can only find out so much, and in many cases, the details of production and the chemistry of the process may well be beyond the grasp of any but the most educated scientist or industrialist. And most consumers buy and use many hundreds, if not thousands, of products in a few months or years, and they cannot possibly be expected to keep abreast of the production processes of them all.

This leads to our second answer. Where consumer pressure is inadequate or consumers are not well-enough informed to pressure companies into adopting pollution-free technologies, combined, specialized consumer pressure must be brought into play. Occasionally for some special, well-publicized concerns—for example, the killing of dolphins in the harvesting of tuna—media attention may be sufficient. But more often another route is required, and that is government regulation. Most people would probably not voluntarily spend the extra several hundred dollars it costs to reduce the exhaust emissions on their automobile, and many people would not buy fuel-efficient cars if the price of gasoline remains cheap enough. And so the government steps in, for the common good, to require of the producers that they all conform to a uniform standard. Thus the ten paper companies will legally have to install the new pollution-reducing technology, grumbling no doubt about government interference, and each of them will raise their prices knowing that the others must do so as well. The consumers will pay the difference because, if they want paper, they have no choice. But they will also have a cleaner environment, whether or not they notice the difference. So, too, when the government mandates emission standards and fuel efficiency, the industry growls and automobiles get more expensive, but the air also gets cleaner. The difference in the density and frequency of the "smog" (smoke + fog) in Los Angeles over the past twenty years has been truly remarkable to those who have lived (or visited) there.

Perhaps, given the choice, some people would prefer cheaper, bigger, more polluting cars. But aren't future generations, who have no voice in the matter, entitled to clean air? Should all of those who do not want bigger cars and are willing to pay the price for a (relatively) pollution-free environment have to suffer in deference to the preferences and choices of a few? The question of choice here is critical, because it is on the basis of free choice that the very idea of the free market is founded. What if people do not care about the environment or worry about pollution? But here the hard-to-calculate question of future generations and other non-consumers (such as infants) comes into play, and here we need a larger vision, which it is the job of government to provide, to see beyond the sometimes narrow focus of individual consumers. This is a touchy point. People may well say, indeed insist, that the environment be protected and the air be cleaned up, but when left to their own personal choice they prefer to leave that burden to others. Here the government acts on the basis of one choice and frustrates another. But where the environment is concerned, this split willfulness (the demand for a healthy environment on the one hand and the demand for a dubious individual freedom to pollute on the other) is all too common.

From these examples, and many more like them, we can appreciate the fact that much of the pollution in the air and water caused by industry must be blamed not on business alone but shared with the consumer and the citizenry at large. And it is the government—so often maligned for its role in regulation—which must sometimes come to the rescue. In the 1950s and '60s, the Detroit automobile industry (then unchallenged by foreign manufacturers) designed and built enormous and unnecessarily overpowered cars because the consumers demanded them. With the growing awareness of the environmental problem and stiffened emissions standards, consumers began to change their tastes, but it must be said that Detroit was disastrously slow in responding. Japan and Germany, however, were quicker off the mark, and by the 1980s the demand for small, fuel-efficient cars was such that it was not just the environment that was at stake, it was the American auto industry. Given the new awareness of the fragility of the planet, consumer and citizen demand for cleaner, healthier procedures and processes, even at somewhat greater cost, will continue to have a strong voice in the market. Indeed, one of the growth industries of the 1990s, it seems, is the environmental protection industry—hazardous waste and trash disposal, clean-up processes, and anti-pollution devices.

Concern for the environment raises deep questions that go far beyond the scope of a book in business ethics, but perhaps we can mention at least one of the most tantalizing issues here. The argument we have been following so far has been in many ways a cost/benefit or utilitarian-type argument, namely, that the harm done to all of us through environmental pollution is much worse than the small gains we might make in cheaper prices or in the joy of driving a tank-sized car. But there is another kind of argument that makes the environment into a true stakeholder rather than just a resource that we can use and abuse at will. This argument is one of the most intriguing aspects of the current "deep" ecological movement and maintains that the environment and the planet are not to be treated merely as means but as ends in themselves. To justify our actions purely by reference to nature's usefulness to us is somehow offensive and entirely invalid. Suppose, for example, that a beautiful lake in northern Alaska, which is virtually inaccessible to almost all visitors, could be destroyed for some minimal gain in resources. An analyst who looked only at the costs and the benefits might well conclude that its destruction does not matter. But surely it does matter, and that suggests that we see the beauty of nature as significant in itself, not just for our use or enjoyment. So, too, one might argue, "What does it matter if a certain species of fish or bird goes extinct?" But it does matter, though the question "to whom?" is, of course, the tricky part. Quite apart from the still utilitarian argument that the loss of any creature in the ecology might have dire though unforeseen effects on our interests (for example, it might someday supply some valuable medical ingredient), it can be argued that every creature in the ecology has its place, and its loss is something other than merely "our" loss. Thus nature has been elevated, as it has often been in other cultures and at other times, to an object of respect and even reverence in its own right. Hard-headed business executives and students might find this view a bit sentimental, but it is surely a healthy antidote to the overly callous and ultimately self-defeating attitude towards nature as an inexhaustible resource that has held sway at least since the industrial revolution.

The concern for the environment, like so many public issues, has too often taken an unjustified toll by way of increased attacks on and suspicions of business. But, again, one should be cautious about leveling blame and assigning responsibility and instead focus the accusations where they are deserved. Many companies are conscientious about the environment and the effects of their production methods. Others are not. And, in any case, the fate of the environment is ultimately in the hands of not only business but consumers as well. Environmental protection is not just the responsibility of big business. The environment is a stakeholder for all of us.

While 88 percent of Americans say they are taking some steps to protect the environment, only 21 percent would be willing to pay a 15 percent premium for environmentally friendly products and only 29 percent of us feel guilty when using products that are harmful to the environment. Perhaps this ambivalence has to do with Americans' dim view of corporate America. Only 7 percent believe companies are taking appropriate steps to protect the environment, and fully 58 percent are unable to name a single company they consider "environmentally conscious."

—*Franklin's Social Ticker*
July 1991

■ SUMMARY AND CONCLUSION

"Social responsibilities" are those roles and responsibilities belonging to individuals and business by virtue of their membership in society. Social responsibilities can be distinguished from responsibilities within the corporation or within the business world, but it is important to appreciate the extent to which the fulfillment of the social responsibilities of business—in particular the enrichment of society through efficient production and distribution of goods—is identical to the responsibilities of people and corporations within the business world. A corporation has obligations not only to its stockholders but also to its *stakeholders,* all of those people who have a vested interest in or are affected by the activities of the company.

Social responsibilities can be divided into positive and negative responsibilities, responsibilities *to* do certain activities and responsibilities *not* to do others. Social responsibilities can be further divided into those that have an *impact* on the community and those additional activities that business adds to its usual activities for the benefit of the community. Usually, a well-run and successful business will have the good of the community built into its conception of its own successful operation. This includes a sense of its own membership in the community and its obligations to support that community as well as enjoy its advantages. It includes a sense of *noblesse oblige,* appropriate to its power and success, to provide some of the good things for the community that less powerful and successful institutions cannot provide. None of this should be considered as impositions upon the business community, but rather the natural features of an institution that has, by law, been given the unusual benefits of being designated as an independent "person" before the law, and as a member of the community as well.

Of special and recent concern is the "silent" stakeholder, the environment. The environment raises special concerns because it ultimately affects everybody, and because it does not have a voice or a vote as such in the running of either the corporation or the community. And yet, the environment does make claims on us, not only for the sake of our children, but for the sake of the earth as such.

■ STUDY QUESTIONS

1. Milton Friedman argues that "the social responsibility of business is to increase its profits." Do you agree with him? In what sense? Does accepting that argument require that a business not involve itself in community welfare projects and other attempts, not essential to the business as such, to improve life in the surrounding community?

2. To what extent is a company responsible for the pollution caused by its operations? Assuming that the manufacturing process of a company cannot help but alter the environment in some undesirable way by virtue of its essential mode of operation, draw up a list of general guidelines to minimize that negative impact and compensate the community for the inconvenience. (It will help if you choose a particular industry with a specifiable pollution problem.)

3. When Ford first introduced seat belts in cars, the public did not like them and would not pay for them. Should Ford have pursued the issue, knowing how many lives would be saved? Or was it correct in withdrawing seat belts from the market on the grounds of consumer sovereignty?

4. Does a business located in a minority community have a responsibility to hire members of that community in its operations? Does a business located in such a community have an obligation to hire an appropriate *majority* of community members?

5. Does business have a responsibility to support the arts? Who does? If an art form is failing because of lack of public support (for example, not enough people going to the theater), should it be allowed to fail? How would you determine whether an art form is an essential part of culture to be saved even if, for the time being, it does not have sufficient popular support?

6. Does business have a social responsibility to support education? What are the advantages to business in doing so? What are the disadvantages?

7. Choose one of Drucker's "cautionary tales" and describe how it might have been recast to provide more satisfactory results.

8. The great corporations have made significant and very visible contributions to the arts, sponsoring theater on television, great musical performances, and museum exhibitions. But what can a small business with limited resources do to promote the arts in the local community? Name four such contributions that would be readily possible for even the smallest local businesses.

9. Should private enterprise take responsibility for the welfare of the poorest members of society? Should government do so? Should private charity? What are the arguments for business involvement in the problem of poverty, assuming that the business itself is in no way responsible for the plight of these people?

10. A company, in order to assure lifelong loyalty and efficient work from its employees, develops a program of total employee benefits, from providing its employees with a house and an inexpensive place to shop to

recreational facilities, health services, and funeral arrangements. Is the company being "paternalistic"? Should a company take such interest in the private activities of its employees?

11. An American company moves into South America and establishes a production schedule that requires the local employees to adjust themselves to an American business schedule. This means, among other things, not being able to eat lunch with their families, working much longer hours and much harder than the local customs have always dictated, and living and dressing in ways foreign to them. The local employees deeply resent this; absenteeism is extremely high, while the work is often badly performed. To what extent should a company adjust itself to the local customs, and to what extent should it not feel forced to do so? Does a company have an *obligation* to conform to the local customs, or is it, at most, just "good business" to do so?

■ FOR CLASS DISCUSSION

Impact: Love Canal

Love Canal, near Niagara Falls, New York, has become the textbook case of industrial pollution. For 40 years, Hooker Chemical and Plastics Corp. had dumped chemical wastes into their Love Canal dumpsite. Since then, Love Canal residents have suffered from abnormally high rates of pollution-related disorders, including birth defects, miscarriages, and liver disorders. Many of the houses have been boarded up, and whole neighborhoods are now unfit for human habitation.

Hooker Chemical faced prosecution by the Justice Department. It is one thing to be the cause of pollution and damage, but it is something more to know about it in advance. And government officials now say that Hooker clearly knew about the dangers long ago. As *Business Week* reported:*

> One point is startlingly clear: Hooker's claims to the contrary, the company realized that its dumps could endanger public health long before the problems started, according to company documents released by Eckhardt's subcommittee. In the case of Love Canal, where 239 families already have been evacuated, Hooker knew of the danger 20 years ago. In 1958, several children suffered chemical burns as they played near the closed dump. Hooker sent out investigators who found that chemical residues were exposed. The company told the school board, which had purchased the property, but did no more.

*From *Business Week,* June 29, 1979.

Hooker Chemical is probably not an isolated case. Hazardous wastes are an unavoidable by-product of almost every industry. This means that there is and will continue to be a national problem of dumping-caused pollution, which is, in itself, impossible to avoid as long as society also demands and needs the products of industry. The serious problem, however, is not so much finding dumping sites, it is taking responsibility by the companies themselves to make sure that such sites are and continue to be safe. That is not the case, according to the Environmental Protection Agency, with Hooker Chemical:

> Officials of the Environmental Protection Agency and the Justice Dept. . . . are looking for evidence to prove that Hooker's silence during much of that time permitted the problem to grow from that of a troublesome dump to a possible cause of a public health crisis. Experts believe that the damage could have been contained, and in some cases avoided, if Hooker had acted differently. . . . Through the years, documents show, Hooker had uncovered many problems at Love Canal but did nothing. "On hindsight, there is no question but that more could have been done," says Jerome Wilkenfeld, who in 1958 was Hooker's assistant technical director and is now director of health and environment for Occidental Petroleum Corp., which acquired Hooker in 1968. He told the investigators subcommittee that Hooker made no attempt to inform area residents or to publicize the problems.

The Other Side of the Story*

Love Canal has become the replacement for Kepone as the key word in equating chemical industry operations with environmental hazards. The Love Canal experience has focused attention on tightening hazardous-waste disposal practices and helped speed proposed legislation for a \$500-million/year "superfund" to pay for cleanup of spills and old dump sites. And the course of legal action in the waste-disposal field could well be shaped by the manner in which Love Canal's \$2.3-billion worth of filed intents-to-sue are handled.

But the company that is synonymous with Love Canal, Occidental Petroleum's Hooker Chemical subsidiary, claims it has taken a bum rap. Hooker asserts that its waste-disposal practices at Niagara Falls, N.Y., *are no worse than those of others in industry.* The company says it has been cooperating fully with all government agencies to solve remaining environmental problems. (In addition to Niagara Falls, Hooker practices at Montague, Mich., and White Springs, Fla., have been questioned.)

And top company officials feel that Hooker has been maligned by the media.

---

*From *Chemical Week,* June 29, 1979.

"In our opinion, the company acted responsibly from beginning to end. There is not one incident where we didn't come forward to cooperate fully. Love Canal was the ignition for an environmental microscope of the company. Any responsible company would suffer under that kind of scrutiny," according to Baeder.

"They [Hooker] were no more negligent than any other companies," says Merzei. The problem, he believes, is in *"trying to judge yesterday's practices with today's rules."*

And Davis contends disposal at the Love Canal site was "damn good practice even by today's standards."

Baeder's frustration is the "public's inability to get a balanced picture. The picture the public perceives is not true," he says. "Yes, we have had problems; yes, we are working on them; yes, we will be responsible."

The problem, the company says, was not the disposal practices, but rather the *breaking of the seal by construction activities around the site.* On April 25, 1953, Hooker, under pressure from local authorities, deeded the property for $1 to the Board of Education of the School District of the City of Niagara Falls.

The deed clearly states that the property was *filled with chemical-plant wastes.* Hooker says it warned the board against disturbing the site. Nevertheless, the board built a school adjacent to the center of it.

Baeder says the true extent of the health problems at Love Canal are not known yet, but that it is far from the "killing ground" that the media has described. He claims that damage didn't extend beyond the two streets adjacent to the dump site, and that the data on birth defects and miscarriages shows no excesses for the area.

HISTORICAL INTERLUDE

SOCIALISM (AND "COMMUNISM")

T o understand what "socialism" is, we must first get beyond the word, which has become—to use the obvious epithet—a "red flag." It is not the same as "Communism" (with a capital "C"); it entails no particular political system, either democratic or totalitarian, and it is no more to be conflated with eastern European failures and unhappiness than capitalism is to be conceived solely in terms of unemployment and the undeserving rich. To label "socialist" virtually any effort on the part of government to try to promote the well-being of its citizens by way of interfering with the "free market"—whether by regulating markets or by taxation and distribution of income—is a ploy that too often confuses the ethical (as well as political and economic) issue. The issue is, namely, whether and to what extent a society and its government have an *obligation* to interfere with the mechanisms of the free market in order to help those who remain outside of its advantages and opportunities.

Socialism and what was once called "communism" (with a small "c") are ancient arrangements but only very modern ideals or ideologies. "Communism," for example, was for thousands of years not a dogma; it was simply the way of life necessary to enable small tribes to survive. Plato in his *Republic* suggested a clearly socialist ideal of a society, as did Sir Thomas More in his *Utopia* of 1516. But it was only in the late eighteenth and early nineteenth centuries, when the great urban industrialized centers had begun to create that impersonally competitive confusion that we call "the free market," that "communism" and socialism were advanced as radical ideas—or perhaps, as reactionary ideals.

In communism, for example (though communism and socialism were not always clearly distinguished), the idea was the forming of small, personal groups, or "communes," in which the old tribal sense of participation and sharing would be once again established as primary. In England (and then America) experimental communes were formed by visionaries such as Robert Owen (1771–1858), and in France by Saint Simon (1760–1825) and Charles Fourier (1771–1837). They opposed individualism and private property and emphasized the importance of sharing. They emphasized group planning and hard work, and so built in a strong merit-incentive system of rewards, despite their discouraging of individualistic competition. Owen, in fact, did not at all oppose his socialism to capitalism, but he opposed Adam Smith by believing that it was the responsibility of government to cure unemployment instead of the sometimes cruel and impersonal dictates of "the market." He also insisted that it was the responsibility of government to maintain the best possible educational institutions and a good environment for the building of character. Indeed, his early socialism resembles the current conservativism of George F. Will more than it does what was the totalitarian communism of eastern Europe. Today, the closest approximation of an ideal "commune" would be the conservative kibbutz in Israel, again, hardly to be confused with Communism in China or Cuba.

Socialism was never a single theory, and, consequently, never formed the cutting edge of a worldwide movement, as urged by its more enthusiastic proponents, notably Marx and Engels in their *Communist Manifesto* of 1848. Marx and Engels made fun of the French "utopian socialists" (Saint Simon and Fourier in particular), and though it is rarely emphasized by contemporary Marxists, Marx and Engels disagreed rather extensively between themselves. Many of the early socialists were quite conservative in their social beliefs. Others held quite radical and even scandalous views, notably Charles Fourier, for whom "sexual liberation" was a socialist goal far more important than economic organization. Some of the socialists were also anarchists and urged the "withering away of the state" (the phrase came from the German poet-playwright Friedrich Schiller). Others

believed in strong central organization as a way of assuring fairness and efficiency. Some urged taking full advantage of the new technological progress in
Europe; others, notably the Luddites (after Ned Ludd, an eighteenth-century
machinist who believed that technology would cause massive unemployment),
urged an abandonment of technology. Many socialists, although against the idea
of private property and individual ambition, were nevertheless strongly for personal freedom and argued that capitalism, not socialism, threatened that freedom.
(For the French writer Pierre Joseph Proudhon, whose aphorism "property is
theft" was often quoted by Marxists, economic necessity and anonymity were far
more damaging to liberty than the planning required by socialism.) Coercion by
hunger or fear of unemployment, the socialists argued, were far more debilitating
than the interventions of government.

In modern economic theory, "socialism" has a rigorous if restricted definition. It is an economic system that requires public ownership and management of
the means of production and the distribution of goods (though it need not oppose
the institution of private *personal* property, including houses, automobiles, and
other consumer goods). But behind this restricted economic definition, there is,
as always, an ethical viewpoint presupposed. The central idea is equality and fairness, coupled with the sense of urgency: if the free market does not take care of
the needs of the poorest members of the society, then the society as a whole—
especially those who profit most from the market system—have the obligation to
help the poor. The much discussed red herring—whether this should be a public
or a private obligation—is beside the point. If the poor were well served by the
reliable charity of the rich, the question would not arise in the first place. And
while the argument goes on about *who* will help the poor and how, the poor continue to be poor. Socialism, as an ethical viewpoint, is essentially just this impatience with ideology and irresponsibility, though socialism is often thought to be
itself an overly talkative ideology. (Oscar Wilde complained that the trouble with
socialism was "too many meetings.") But the essence of socialism is not to be
confused with its noisy ideological counterparts. Its fundamental ethical views
are largely those of many (though not all) capitalists too—the need for some
management of the economy to minimize unemployment and inflation and for
government action to provide services that the private sector does not provide
(public housing, urban transportation, school lunches, libraries, safeguards
against disasters beyond the means of any individual, and so on) whether these
are to be provided by employers or unions or government. Indeed, the modern
business student might well be surprised to find that many of the "revolutionary"
reforms urged by Marx and Engels in their firebrand *Manifesto* were little different from most Democratic and many Republican election platforms in this
century.

There are more radical versions of socialism, of course, and those that only
borrow the name as an excuse for power and total economic control. The attack
on individualism, for example, may have any number of versions, from the original eighteenth-century idea that individual initiative was no guarantee of the good

of society as a whole to the more romantic idea that an individual has significance only as a member of society. The extreme attack on individualism, which suggests that the individual is nothing and the state everything, which we call "fascism," did not come of age until this century, and then the socialist would have no exclusive claim to it. Indeed, according to a great many socialist arguments, it is the individual—and the basic needs of the individual—that provide the ultimate source of value and concern. (Remember that Marx, as well as Adam Smith, accepted the "labor theory of value.")

If there is a deep ethical difference between the socialists and the capitalists, it often comes down to a not very profound disagreement about the extent to which welfare from the state "demeans" or "degrades" the recipient. But even here, it is worth reminding ourselves that the word "welfare" and the idea of the "welfare state" was introduced as a *positive* term, by the "Fabian" socialists of the late-nineteenth century. The term and the idea, like the idea of socialism itself, took its unabashed aim to be the well-being and the happiness of the individual.

If the basic ethical ends are at least similar, then what is the vehement disagreement between the socialist and the capitalist? First of all, it largely concerns the question of *means* to well-being and happiness: whether capitalism is ultimately (especially in the short run) more efficient and effective in securing the material well-being for all citizens or whether government planning and regulation is indeed necessary. But it is also a question of the priority of values, even if the values themselves are essential to both positions. Both the socialist and the capitalist believe in the importance of human freedom and self-sufficiency, but the socialist is willing to sacrifice these to *some* extent in return for general well-being and security. Both the capitalist and the socialist believe that everyone in the society ought to have a decent standard of living, but the capitalist, unlike the socialist, is willing to sacrifice this general humanitarian goal if it interferes with the freedom of the individual to make a profit. For the socialist, general security and well-being are ultimate goals, and they are more important than the individual freedoms defended by the capitalist. But to say that they are more important is not to say that individual freedom is of no importance to the socialist. It is just less important, and, especially in countries where widespread starvation and extreme poverty are in evidence, we can understand why this should be so.

A related difference between the values of socialism and those of capitalism concern the concept of justice. Socialism places the emphasis on the idea that all people should be able to get what they need. The result is a modified sense of merit, and merit is the heart of the capitalist sense of justice. In American capitalism, for example, the financial rewards for the right idea at the right time might be virtually limitless. Socialism would not allow such limitless rewards in a society in which other people (whether or not they too had ideas) had nothing. Socialism, accordingly, tends to emphasize noneconomic rewards such as honors or status, while capitalism emphasizes financial rewards, often to the exclusion of any other meaningful honors. But this is not at all to say that there is no room for financial rewards and incentives for good work under socialism; it is only that such rewards and incentives should be modest, just sufficient to motivate good work.

Against the socialist, the capitalist might well argue that such modest incentives do not motivate nearly so much as the "shoot for the moon" ambitions of the American entrepreneur, but the debate here may in fact be just as much about "human nature" as it is about values. How much of a reward does a person need to be motivated to have good ideas or do good work? And are financial rewards the most effective in this, or might other kinds of incentives, for instance, knowing that all work is for the good of the community, work just as well? Why isn't *honor* more motivating than money? The socialist would reply that participation and praise in the community is far more "rewarding" than any merely financial reward. Is the socialist right about this? Our answer, probably, is that we would like *both* the sense of honor in the community *and* the financial rewards. But how much is this a reflection of the kind of society we already live in, rather than a universal human truth? And is our own capitalist bias really a good reason to dismiss socialism altogether, and to condemn every step towards government planning or intervention as "a step towards socialism"? Revulsion for a word should not blind us to the very real questions with which socialism confronts us: Can the market really do what its advocates say that it can do? And is it fair, no matter how efficient the market, that some should be so richly rewarded while others starve? These are not questions of ideology, but the basic nagging of the sense of justice of any civilized person, capitalist or socialist.

– 10 –

Free Enterprise and Social Justice

Life is never fair, and perhaps it is a good thing for most of us that it is not.

—Oscar Wilde, "An Ideal Husband"

Most of us work, will work, or have worked for a salary, and most of us have suspected, at one time or another, that we were not being paid quite what we're "worth." All it takes is a quick look at a person down the hall or across the street who is doing the same work for twice the salary, or, in some cases, doing far less for many times more. Needless to say, such examples are readily available, and few of us could honestly admit that we have never had the sense of being underpaid or, much worse, being **exploited** in our work.

But on the other hand, there are examples just as readily available to us of people who do more work for less pay or do jobs we would not even be willing to do, for much less than we make. And, if we are willing just to look, we see that some have perfectly miserable jobs, or no jobs at all, for whom such a question as "Am I being paid what I'm worth?" is an extravagant and unimaginable luxury. As we look, we are quite likely to manufacture some form of rationalization about why we should be so much better off than they, but it usually doesn't work. We accordingly feel compassion, at least perhaps a bit guilty—though most of us manage to put away such feelings fast enough.

These feelings themselves—both the feeling of being underpaid and the feeling that other people are not getting their fair share or opportunity—are the primitive urgings of our sense of **justice.** Ultimately, justice is an abstraction that yields principles and disputations among philosophers and the greatest legal minds of all ages. But first of all, it is that raw "gut feeling" that virtually all of us recognize in ourselves when we see that the world is not as fair as we think it ought to be.

Justice lies at the very heart of morality and the good life; it is our ideal of a fair and harmonious society. Morality consists in part of those principles and traits of character that promote justice, a general concern for other people's interests as well as our own. Justice is not the only requirement of a good society, of course; prosperity, for example, is necessary too, along with peace, good all-around health, and some communal sense of mutual concern and well-being. Indeed, in a sufficiently prosperous society, in which people had what they needed and contributed willingly to the general good, the concern for justice would probably be unnecessary. But in a society in which some people are rich while others are near starvation, and in which there are still many unpleasant jobs to be done, the fair distribution of wealth and work is an essential concern for the very existence of a livable society. We call this concern **social justice.** It means that, in an affluent society, everyone has the right to expect a decent life.

Justice, like morality, is an essentially *impersonal* concern. It goes beyond personal feelings and preferences to general principles that apply to everyone. In this very important sense, we might say that *formal equality* is the basic premise of justice. This is not to say that everyone deserves equal pay or equal treatment regardless of what they do. Social justice does not mean universal equality. But it does insist that, in a very general sense, all people's interests will be considered and that "irrelevant" features such as race, religion, sex, and age will not count for or against them. For example, if two managers are doing the same job with equal efficiency, it is assumed that they deserve equal pay, regardless of the fact that one is a man and one is a woman, one is white and one is black. The question

Equal Work, Equal Pay? ——

Until recently in America, one of the primary reasons for not paying women as much as men in equal jobs was that women, if they were single, had no family to feed, while the man had a wife and family, and if women were married, then their salaries were considered "pin money"—just a bit extra to buy some luxury for the family. If the man the woman was competing against was not married, then the argument was that he needed to save so that he could marry and raise a family in comfort. Presumably a woman was just working until she could find a man with a large enough cushion put aside so that she could marry him. Even if it were true that most women would get married, why is this argument unjust? What conception of justice is being presupposed in this argument?

of what is "relevant" is of course extremely difficult, particularly when such factors as work experience, seniority, and personal congeniality are concerned. Nevertheless, it is the first principle of justice that, in some sense, "all men are created equal," according to our Declaration of Independence of 1776. The rules of fairness apply to all of us in the same way.

In Plato's *Republic,* justice is defined simply as giving every person his *due,* or what is *owed* by other people and by society in general. The same phrase reappears in Roman Law (*"justitia est constans et perpetua voluntas ius suum cuique tribuens"*) and in St. Thomas Aquinas: "Justice is a habit whereby a man renders to everyone his due by a constant and perpetual will." The simplest formulation, perhaps, is to be found in contemporary American philosophy: John Rawls sums it up as "justice is fairness." Justice, in other words, means everyone getting a fair share. The question, of course, is what counts as a "fair share." In Plato's society, a person's fair share of both income and honor depended on his "place" in society. A person's "place" was more or less fixed from birth, and both the rewards and the responsibilities of a person's position were fixed more or less precisely too. Americans believe, however, that people should not have "fixed" positions in society and that no one has a set "place," but rather everyone has or should have "equal opportunity" to gain any position whatever. Moreover, the positions themselves fluctuate in status and value, along with supply and demand, which makes the worth of any particular role in society, as well as its responsibilities, uncertain as well. (Consultants, toxicologists, and solar energy engineers, for example, would not have been in great demand a few years ago.) What this means for us is that justice—everyone's getting a "fair share" of income and social benefits—has now become much less determined, much more negotiable, and far more dependent on successes and failures and changes in business and the market, and so it is far less clear what any given person deserves compared with what other people deserve.

A.   DISTRIBUTIVE JUSTICE

Justice is of particular importance in business and in business ethics because it is one of the most critical claims made for—and against—our "free enterprise" market system (that this is a way of solving the economic problem of producing and distributing goods as fairly as possible throughout the whole society.) Indeed, this is a thesis shared by a great many non-Marxist economists, whether conservative or liberal. The claim, simply stated, is that business can and does this better for most of society in its pursuit of profits and the production of goods. This can be interpreted in two very different ways, however: (1) that the free enterprise system assures justice (which has its own independent standards) and (2) that the free enterprise system itself is essential to justice. The first is a factual claim (assuming we agree what is just) that historians have often tried to prove; the second is a straightforward philosophical claim—a definition of justice—that is essential to many contemporary defenses of capitalism. In either case, however,

Aristotle on Justice ——

This form of the just has a different specific character from the former. For the justice which distributes common possessions is always in accordance with the kind of proportion mentioned above (for in the case also in which the distribution is made from the common funds of a partnership it will be according to the same ratio which the funds put into the business by the partners bear to one another); and the injustice opposed to this kind of justice is that which violates the proportion. But the justice in transactions between man and man is a sort of equality indeed, and the injustice a sort of inequality; not according to that kind of proportion, however, but according to arithmetical proportion. For it makes no difference whether a good man has defrauded a bad man or a bad man a good one, nor whether it is a good or a bad man that has committed adultery; the law looks only to the distinctive character of the injury, and treats the parties as equal, if one is in the wrong and the other is being wronged, and if one inflicted injury and the other has received it. Therefore, this kind of injustice being an inequality, the judge tries to equalize it; for in the case also in which one has received and the other has inflicted a wound, or one has slain and the other been slain, the suffering and the action have been unequally distributed; but the judge tries to equalize things by means of the penalty, taking away from the gain of the assailant. For the term "gain" is applied generally to such cases, even if it be not a term appropriate to certain cases, for example to the person who inflicts a wound—and "loss" to the sufferer; at all events when the suffering has been estimated, the one is called loss and the other gain. Therefore the equal is intermediate between the greater and the less, but the gain and the loss are respectively greater and less in contrary ways; more of the good and less of the evil are gain, and the contrary is loss; intermediate between them is, as we saw, the equal, which we say is just; therefore corrective justice will be the intermediate between loss and gain. This is why, when people dispute, they take refuge in the judge; and to go to the judge is to go to justice; for the nature of the judge is to be a sort of animate justice; and they seek the judge as an intermediate; and in some states they call judges mediators, on the assumption that if they get what is intermediate they will get what is just. The just, then, is an intermediate, since the judge is so. The judge restores equality. . . .

What does Aristotle mean by "equality" here?

Aristotle, *Nicomachean Ethics,* trans. W. D. Ross
(Oxford: Oxford University Press, 1925)

the linkage between business and justice is clear: the one serves the other, and, even if it is greed and avarice that motivate some individuals, business itself is to be defended in loftier terms, as an instrument of justice.

To be in business, in this view, is to enlist in a sizable army of those who secure justice in our society. But notice that we are now talking about a particular kind of justice, which social theorists and philosophers usually call *distributive* justice (as opposed, for instance, to criminal justice, which is primarily concerned with the fair punishment of those who break the law). Distributive justice, as the very name tells us, is concerned with the fair distribution of the goods of society, everything from food, shelter, and health care to diamonds, sports cars, honors, social position, and accessibility to the arts and education; indeed, everything that money can buy, and some things it can't buy. Distributive justice is also concerned with the fair distribution of the hardships and responsibilities of society, from the dangers and inconveniences of military service to the delegation of social responsibilities to all citizens, whatever their occupations or circumstances. It is all too easy to think of distributive justice just in terms of people getting what they deserve; justice also requires a fair distribution of the burdens of society—which are also deserved—including the burdens of the jobs or the risks through which we earn what we deserve by way of salary, reward, or profit.

We might well challenge the idea that business has a primary responsibility for (distributive) justice. Why not the government, since that is one purpose of government? Why not everyone? Why single out business and businesspeople in particular? And indeed, the effort to assure justice is the primary (though not the only) responsibility of government, and the responsibility of all of us in our various ways and according to our means. But in our society business dictates authoritatively what is available and how it is distributed, whether or not it is responding to—or creating—the consumer demand it feeds. Business controls production and marketing and consequently determines distribution, both in terms of the kind and amount of goods available and their general accessibility. American business has dominant control over innovation by sponsoring research and directing talent, time, and money. It also has dominant control over what innovations will be produced, or not.

Of course, government also controls distribution to a large extent, through promotion of its own research and regulations on business and through taxation and various subsidies. Indeed, the primary focus of much of the debate between liberals and conservatives concerns just this role of government in "regulating" business, that is, determining the distribution of not only goods but also opportunities and the *means* of production and distribution. But much of governmental control is itself a part of the business world by way of governmental protection (for example, against foreign competition), guaranteed loans (such as those to Chrysler and Lockheed), and even governmental sponsorship (for example, synthetic fuels and various aerospace development programs). Sometimes, the government is even a competitor.

It is through business, more than through any other organ of our society, that the distribution of wealth and work takes place. It is, in other words, the primary instrument of distributive justice. But this in turn makes the question of governmental regulation and control even more important, unless it can be shown that the internal ethics of business in fact coincide with and effectively satisfy the demands for justice that we share as a society. The question of government regulation, in other words, is not a question of government interference into the free market system. It is rather a question of making sure that the practice of business succeeds in what it sets out to do, which is to maximize "the wealth of the nation" and effect the fair distribution of goods, as well as enrich the lives of a limited number of people who are the most immediate beneficiaries of the market.

B.   THE PROBLEM OF JUSTICE: IS THE FREE MARKET FAIR?

> The law, in its majestic equality, forbids the rich as well as the poor to sleep under bridges, to beg in the streets, and to steal bread.
>
> —Anatole France

The *concept* of justice is easy enough to understand and accept; everyone should get a fair share. The *problem* of justice is defining what counts as "a fair share." Two easy answers present themselves, both of which are wholly unacceptable. The first is that we should all get an *equal* share of the benefits and burdens of society; the second easy answer is that we should get what we can earn, nothing less but nothing more either. The first answer is unacceptable because it makes no allowance whatever for differences in need or differences in effort, skill, talent, or risk. It leaves out what we take to be an essential ingredient in any adequate conception of justice—*merit,* that is, that people *earn* their income. Because some people work harder and more effectively than others, they *deserve* more than others too. But the second answer, that people should get what they earn, no more and no less, ignores what the first answer too easily concludes, that people do deserve equal pay for equal work; and we do not tolerate inequalities without some convincing argument why one person should earn more and another less.

These two easy answers together point out the two poles of our conception of justice, *equality* and *merit.* Like many matters in ethics, they represent two essential ingredients, in a kind of dialectical tension; neither can be ignored so both must be included. The equality ingredient is the insistence that everyone should be presumed an equal member of society and so, in the absence of other reasons, be given or allowed to earn an equal share of its benefits. It is also the insistence that everyone should therefore be presumed to have an equal share of social duties and responsibilities as well. The merit ingredient supplies some of the reasons for not giving everyone an equal share; it is clear, for example, that rewarding people for special skills, harder work, and takings risks is ultimately advantageous to everyone in society, since such skills, effort, and investments make the society as a whole more prosperous. Therefore, even within the demand of the quality requirement, there is a good utilitarian reason to give more of the goods to those who work harder or contribute more, for by so doing we increase the share of those who earn less by providing cheaper, higher quality goods as well as jobs that, because of the general prosperity, can pay more too.

In addition to this consideration of the general welfare, however, there is our additional feeling—an intrinsic part of our "Protestant ethic"—that people who contribute more should get more, whether or not this in fact helps others as well. It is this additional feeling that causes the tension with the equality demand, since it is a matter of plain fact, in every society—socialist as well as capitalist, feudal as well as democratic—that some people end up with *much* more than everyone else, whether they do so by shrewd investments, by virtue of an invention, or by having a genius for management. But even those who wholly agree that some should get more may yet protest, "but so *much* more!?" Thus, the problem of justice is bringing merit and equality into a fair balance.

One of the best known slogans from Marx, still the rallying cry of most communists and many socialists, is "from each according to his abilities, to each according to his needs." Whether we agree with this or not, it is a powerful conception of justice, and it captures the problem of justice in a straightforward, if controversial way. The first phrase, "from each according to his abilities," is a reference to merit, to the extent of a person's contribution to society. But notice that, in the Marxist slogan, merit is not tied to income or reward; it is valued for its own sake. Ideally, the socialist hopes that, out of patriotism or love of society and fellow citizens, all people will work to the best of their abilities. In fact, in socialist as well as non-socialist countries, people's motives are not so selfless; they expect and demand rewards for their efforts. This fact has led even the most orthodox communist societies to add some extra incentives and rewards for better workers and skilled specialists. Nevertheless, the idea here is shared by both socialist and capitalist countries—that justice involves people contributing to the society in some productive way to the best of their abilities.

The second phrase of the Marxist slogan, "to each according to his needs," points to a further ingredient in justice. The demand for equal treatment may be the basic principle of justice, but equality does not always mean equal amounts. A person who is very ill and needs extensive medical care and equipment, for instance, may demand much more of the resources of a society than a person who is in perfect health. Filmmakers need much more money to work their craft than writers or painters, and those with many children need much more than a single person with minimal responsibilities. The emphasis on need thus points to a concern of justice that goes beyond equality and seems to be wholly independent of ability and merit. Indeed, a very sick person may well be incapable of working or contributing anything to the society, and yet that individual, we feel, should not be deprived of society's benefits.

It is in this matter of need that the Marxist position and at least one extreme version of the free market position (often called "libertarianism") conflict head-on. The Marxist position insists that needs should be fulfilled *regardless* of contribution or merit (except, perhaps, in criminal cases): the extreme free market position insists that it is contribution alone that determines what a person should receive, which yields the cruel conclusion that those who cannot contribute get nothing, except, perhaps, the whimsical contributions of charity. Some free enterprise enthusiasts, such as George Gilder (*Wealth and Poverty*), have argued that nothing should be given to these people, since "the spur of poverty," as opposed to the dependency of the welfare state, will inspire them into the market and into wealth of their own. With such views popularly promulgated, supposedly in defense of American business, it is not surprising that, to much of the world, the inadequacies of the Marxist slogan look far more reasonable than the cold cruelty of the free market system. Not only does our society richly reward some people who clearly don't deserve it, but it then pretends through its rhetoric that the people who suffer most in that same system are just not trying hard enough and, perhaps, would be better off if they even suffered a little bit more.

The formulation of an adequate conception of justice is, first of all, the ordering and synthesis of these sometimes conflicting components of justice. The foremost example of a current philosophical theory of justice, for instance, is that of John Rawls. He puts the two components together in two principles: first, an equality principle that insists that everyone is to be considered equal, and second a "difference principle" that allows for inequalities but also insists that such inequalities must be justified by the fact that they ultimately benefit everyone, particularly those people at the bottom of the socioeconomic ladder. For example, it could be argued that giving high salaries and bonuses to executives may cause inequality but nevertheless spurs productivity and efficiency and so promotes the well-being of everyone, including, especially, the workers who are least paid but most dispensable, who thereby keep their jobs and still make more than they would in a less productive company.

What is fair virtually always includes consideration of each person as in some formal sense equal to every other (for example, before the law and irrespective of race or the circumstances of birth) and also includes some consideration of the person's contribution to the well-being of other people. But justice as fairness also includes other considerations too, including, for example, people's abilities and efforts (a very intelligent employee may complete a task quickly but do much less work than another, who takes much longer but works much harder). Another person may deserve a reward not for productiveness or effort but by virtue of morality, for example, for resisting extreme temptation (to go to another company, for instance) or for keeping up the morale of an enterprise.

We also think it just to reward people for the "burden of responsibility," whether or not they themselves are productive in any direct way. It is enough that they are in a position to be blamed if things go wrong, and so, conversely, we think it right that they also share in the rewards when a project is successful. By the same token, we think it just that people receive fair return on useful risks that they are willing to take; return on investment is just insofar as it is reward for taking the risk in the first place. Justice also depends on the completion of contracts and promises, even if a person does not deserve or need the promised amount in

Two Principles of Justice: John Rawls ——

We may think of a human society as a more or less self-sufficient association regulated by a common conception of justice and aimed at advancing the good of its members. As a co-operative venture for mutual advantage, it is characterized by a conflict as well as an identity of interests. There is an identity of interests since social co-operation makes possible a better life for all than any would have if everyone were to try to live by his own efforts; yet at the same time men are not indifferent as to how the greater benefits produced by their joint labours are distributed, for in order to further their own aims each prefers a larger to a lesser share. A conception of justice is a set of principles for choosing between the social arrangements which determine this division and for underwriting a consensus as to the proper distributive shares.

The two principles of justice . . . may be formulated as follows:

First, each person engaged in an institution or affected by it has an equal right to the most extensive liberty compatible with a like liberty for all; and

Second, inequalities as defined by the institutional structure or fostered by it are arbitrary unless it is reasonable to expect that they will work out to everyone's advantage and provided that the positions and offices to which they attach or from which they may be gained are open to all.

These principles regulate the distributive aspects of institutions by controlling the assignment of rights and duties throughout the whole social structure, beginning with the adoption of a political constitution in accordance with which they are then to be applied to legislation. It is upon a correct choice of a basic structure of society, its fundamental system of rights and duties, that the justice of distributive shares depends.

Peter Laslett and W. G. Runciman, eds., *Philosophy, Politics and Society* (Oxford; Oxford University Press, 1967)

any other sense. If I have sincerely promised to pay a local millionaire ten dollars I once borrowed from him, it does not matter that he does not need the money, or that he has not earned it, or that he is a rather vile person. Indeed, having a *right* to what we have earned or been promised is the very heart of private enterprise. (We will discuss this in the next section.)

Finally, and most difficult, there are occasions in which an injustice to an individual may be so overriden by the good of the entire community that it becomes just, paradoxically, to be unjust. For example, in Shakespeare's *The Merchant of Venice,* the usurer Shylock has extracted a promise of "a pound of flesh" from the unhappy Antonio, who has borrowed a substantial amount of money. One of the main themes of the play is the tension between the justice demanded by Shylock in view of his contract, and the dire harm done not only to Antonio but to the entire community if the contract is fulfilled. In less literary but more realistic terms, justice would seem to demand interfering with a company's rights of free trade, for example, in the case of an arms sale to an enemy nation, or the sale of advanced technology to a country that would present our society with a grievous threat to its existence. What is fair, in other words, may go beyond the individual case when the well-being of the whole society is concerned.

C.   The Capitalist Conception of Justice: Entitlement or Merit?

Each different conception of justice weighs the various characteristics of justice differently. The Marxist, for instance, defends working according to a person's abilities and need, but minimizes other ingredients as less important or irrelevant. An extreme egalitarian emphasizes equal shares and equal work for everyone. A more moderate egalitarian might insist that everyone receive a decent standard of living and contribute a minimum of effort, but leave any additional rewards and efforts outside of the concern of justice. A bureaucrat might argue that people should be given work and rewards strictly in accordance with their responsibilities, while a strict contract theorist might argue that work and rewards are to be distributed solely on the basis of contractual agreements between the individual and society, implicit or explicit.

Capitalism is not a single conception, and the capitalist conception of justice is not a single conception. It may be directly opposed to the Marxist and socialist insistence on government ownership and control, but within the capitalist insistence on "free" and "private" enterprise there is nevertheless a spectrum of theories with very different and sometimes opposed emphases. For example, the most prominent and most celebrated conception of the capitalist conception of justice is the notion of *merit,* which we have already discussed. Capitalism is not just an economic system; it is also an ethical framework in which the question of what a person has *earned* or *deserves* plays a particularly important role. But what a person earns is not a single notion either; the sense in which workers earn their wages is very different from the sense in which investors earn their dividends, which is very different again from the sense in which top executives earn large salaries and bonuses. The concept of what a person "deserves" is also not as simple as it seems. John Rawls insists that people do not deserve the advantages (or disadvantages) that they are born with, and so, some have argued, no one deserves the further advantages (or disadvantages) that are made possible thereby (as in "it takes money to make money," etc.). The notion of *luck* thus plays an important role in the capitalist conception of justice, for the wealth and circumstances that people are born into or inherit may be an overwhelming factor in

---

Some Factors of Justice ——

Equality: every person counts as being the same.

Merit: what a person actually contributes.

Effort: the amount of work, regardless of contribution.

Ability: results and effort are weighed by virtue of what this particular person can do.

Moral Virtue: setting an example or being "a good person," whether or not this has any effect on results.

Responsibility: willingness to take the blame or make the critical decisions.

Need: what an individual requires to live decently and to be as productive as possible.

Contractual Obligations: previous contracts or promises that may entitle a person to a share regardless of merit or need.

Benefits to Society: the good of everyone, even if unjust to a few individuals (the "utilitarian" conception of justice).

Return for Risk: incentive and reward for taking chances, in order to support a useful enterprise.

---

their success. This is balanced, on the one hand, by an equally strong emphasis on the notion of *equality,* which we have discussed, such that everyone at least deserves equal *opportunity* to succeed in the marketplace, although equal opportunity is clearly at odds with the prior advantages some people have from birth.

How is it possible to defend both the importance of luck and the need for equal opportunity when the first dictates that people are in very different positions regarding the possibilities for success and the second insists that they all be given the same initial opportunities? Well, first of all, some authors—Robert Nozick, for example—have sharply distinguished what people *deserve* (by virtue of having earned it) from what they are *entitled* to, possibly by virtue of luck or the fortunes of birth or inheritance. Nozick would thus agree with Rawls that no one *deserves* the fortune (good or bad) inherited at birth but he would insist that a person may nonetheless be *entitled* to that fortune. This theory of justice is sometimes called, accordingly, **entitlement theory,** and it forms the basis of one of the most influential capitalist theories today. Adam Smith defended capitalism and its sense of justice by arguing that capitalism was the most effective means of maximizing wealth for everyone—a utilitarian conception of justice according to which business is the means to the general well-being. The entitlement theory, on the other hand, insists that the ethics of capitalism is itself a matter of justice; people have a right to what they (legally) earn, win, or inherit. There may still be an emphasis on equal opportunity, but it is equality of the *rules and procedures* of the market that make us equal (for example, the SEC prohibitions on using "insider information" in investments on the stock market). However, equality of *results* is not only not guaranteed by capitalism, it is almost inevitably prevented.

Entitlement theory has a long history, as old as capitalism itself. The most prominent proponent of this theory was the English philosopher John Locke (who wrote nearly a century before Adam Smith). He argued that private property is a "natural right" ("entitlement" is often used as a synonym for "right") and that people make property their own by "mixing one's labor with it," that is, working or producing something with it (growing crops, building a house or a factory). Entitlement theory is the conception of justice that puts at the core of justice just such a right based on productivity; thus people often justify their wealth by pointing to the investments they have made and the products this has made possible. But entitlement theory is not just the theory that defends possession according to productivity. It is also the theory that defends possession as a right in its own terms (thus, "possession is nine-tenths of the law").

Entitlement theory is crucial to capitalism, therefore, not only because it stands at the basis of our conception of private property—without which there could be no "private enterprise" and no capitalism, but because it also makes con-

Capitalism versus Social Justice? ——

It is fashionable these days to social commentators to ask, "Is capitalism compatible with social justice?" I submit that the only appropriate answer is "No." Indeed, this is the only possible answer. The term "social justice" was invented in order *not* to be compatible with capitalism.

What is the difference between "social justice" and plain, unqualified "justice?" Why can't we ask, "Is capitalism compatible with justice?" We can, and were we to do it, we would then have to explore the idea of justice that is peculiar to the capitalist system, because capitalism certainly does have an idea of justice.

"Social justice," however, was invented and propagated by people who were not much interested in understanding capitalism. These were nineteenth-century critics of capitalism—liberals, radicals, socialists—who invented the term in order to insinuate onto the argument a quite different conception of the good society from the one proposed by liberal capitalism. As it is used today, the term has an irredeemably egalitarian and authoritarian thrust. Since capitalism as a socioeconomic or political system is neither egalitarian or authoritarian, it is in truth incompatible with "social justice."

From Irving Kristol, "A Capitalist Conception of Justice," 1978

Justice: The Entitlement Theory ——

1. A person who acquires a holding in accordance with the principle of justice in acquisition is entitled to that holding.

2. A person who acquires a holding in accordance with the principle of justice in transfer, from someone else entitled to the holding, is entitled to that holding.

3. No one is entitled to a holding except by (repeated) applications of 1 and 2.

What does this seemingly innocuous doctrine entail? What does it imply about the legitimacy of government taxation? What does it suggest about the legitimacy of most historically based claims to ownership of land?

From Robert Nozick, *Anarchy, State and Utopia* (Basic Books, 1974)

---

tracts and the respect for them the core of our notion of justice, such that—if there is a binding contract—our notion of justice tolerates actions that a non-capitalist society would not even consider (for example, evicting old people from apartments for breach of contract or upholding the misfortune of a consumer because he signed a contract accepting the situation).

The Protestant and puritan emphasis on hard work, the egalitarian emphasis on equality and equal opportunity in particular, and the entitlement emphasis on rights and contracts stand in uneasy relation to one another and often conflict. We accept the fact that some people have enormous gains on the basis of little merit and suffer large losses for an unlucky guess or poor judgment, and we defend some people's right to great wealth even if others live in poverty. We celebrate the freedom of every citizen to participate equally in the market, but we also recognize the fact that this equality is to a tragically large extent ideal and unrealistic. Indeed, the emphasis on entitlement and people's rights to what they already have make systematic correction of existing inequalities virtually impossible. Moreover, the capitalist conception of entitlement also makes it unlikely that the poorest members of society will have their needs systematically satisfied, since redistribution of the wealth is insisted to be a private and voluntary matter— through charity and generosity—rather than forced redistribution through taxation and legal obligation. Whether or not this is "fair" depends on how we judge luck and entitlement and how much we also believe in the other ingredients of the capitalist conception of justice—merit and equal opportunity, in particular—as well as those various components more prominent in non-capitalist, more socialistic conceptions of justice.

Is capitalism fair? Does capitalism indeed serve justice? Those are critical questions for everyone in and around the business world. Capitalism as we know it gives far more recognition to the sanctity of private property—whether or not it is earned or productive—than many other ethical systems. Capitalism thrives on the self-image of hard-working, productive individuals, but the fact is that hard work and productivity are not always rewarded by the market, and the difference in fortune between a hard-working line worker in a factory and a clever real estate speculator should be enough to convince us that hard work and productivity are not all that there is to the capitalist ethic. Merit certainly plays a crucial role in the capitalist ethic, but it is not nearly the whole of the story. Entitlement is at least as important, but with this too comes our special emphasis on *risk,* an emphasis on taking chances (and being richly rewarded for it) that, in many societies, is not a virtue at all but rather what Aristotle called "foolhardiness" in his fellow Greeks. The classical capitalist ethic talked about the importance of individual ambition and greed, which "an invisible hand" would turn to everyone's benefit, but that was not very plausible in 1776 among Adam Smith's patriotic and community-minded entrepreneurs, and it is no more convincing today in modern corporate capitalism. Justice, as well as individual gain, remains the ethical cornerstone of the business world; without it "free enterprise" would be an objectionable practice confined once again to the fringes of society. But what justice means—to what extent it emphasizes our entitlement to what we already have, to what extent it emphasizes hard work and what we earn, and to what extent it emphasizes equality for all and concern for the poor—these are questions that are not yet settled, questions on which the future of the business world depends.

D.   THE PROBLEM OF POVERTY: THE UNDERCLASS

> In our time, there exists another form of ownership which is becoming no less important than land: the possession of know-how, technology and skill. . . . The fact is that many people, perhaps the majority today, do not have the means which would enable them to take their place in an effective and humanly dignified way within a productive system in which work is truly central. Marxism has failed, but the realities of exploitation and marginalization remain in the world.
>
> Pope John Paul II

On a national level, the problem of justice comes down to the problem of poverty. What counts as poverty is itself at least as controversial a question as the problem of what to do about it. Poverty is defined in terms of not having enough money to meet basic needs, but what counts as a need—indeed even as a basic need—depends on the expectations of society in general. As Lester Thurow puts it,

"Wants become necessities whenever most of the people in society believe that they are in fact necessities." In our society, we consider people "poor" if they can't afford a car or a refrigerator; in most countries of the world, *not* being poor means having enough rice or beans to eat. And yet, the cross-cultural comparison is not as compelling as the intrasocietal inequalities; it is the *gap* between the best off and the worst off that offends us, and only to some extent can this be rationalized in terms of the fact that some people are harder working, more skilled, and contribute substantially more to the good of society as a whole.

The poverty statistics have been argued vigorously in opposite directions. On the one hand, the gap and proportions between the richest and the poorest have increased in recent years. On the other hand, the level of income of the poor has risen too. Regarding race and poverty, the differences between median black income and median white income is still appalling, but the average black income has risen incredibly—indeed, faster than the average income of almost any minority group anywhere.

There is an obvious economic solution to the problem of poverty in America: extensive redistribution of wealth through taxation and welfare or a negative income tax. Why is this not done? Because this flies in the face of another part of our conception of justice. We accept the fact that people in so rich a country should not be poor, but most Americans also have their doubts about the justice of taxation. Individuals have the right to keep what they have honestly earned. Poverty, in other words, is an ethical problem, not so much an economic problem. It is, consequently, a political problem as well, for those who have money already are naturally tempted to try to keep it, always looking somewhere else for the solutions to social problems. Lester Thurow says it this way in *The Zero Sum Society:*

> To protect our own income, we will fight to stop economic change from occurring or fight to prevent society from imposing public policies that will hurt us. . . . We want a solution to the problem that does not reduce our income, but all solutions reduce someone's income. . . . The problem with zero-sum games is that the essence of problem solving is loss allocation. But this is precisely what our political process is least capable of doing. When there are economic gains to be allocated, our political process can allocate them. When there are large economic losses to be allocated, our political process is paralyzed. And with political paralysis comes economic paralysis.

We might argue against Thurow that ours is not a zero-sum society, that capitalism creates wealth as well as poverty, and that a sufficient increase in the wealth of the nation overall will inevitably benefit the poor as well. This is true, but it is clear that the impoverished family may well not have the luxury of time to wait for the new boom of capitalism and its promised "trickle down" benefits. Nor is it at all clear, even if this counterargument is correct, that the amount of wealth recreated and redistributed will be anything approximating a minimal sense of distributive justice. We might support Thurow's argument in a self-interested way by suggesting that eliminating poverty will also cut down crime. However, first of all, this probably is not true, and second, it misses the point that it is an ethical argument concerning justice that is at stake here, not a precaution against being "mugged." The existence of poverty itself is an embarrassment to our sense of fairness. One of the promises of the free enterprise system is that it will be eliminated, but it has not been. Indeed, the justification of the business world is that it will provide wealth not only for those who are actually "in" business, but for everyone else as well. The capitalist conception of justice, which is based on the freedom to choose and to keep the fruits of our successes, also includes the awareness that the freedom and that right depend upon the value of business for the rest of society as well. Perhaps it is too much to suppose that the solution to poverty be taken up as one of the primary aims of the business enterprise; but if the business world can't solve the problem, then government will, unavoidably at the expense of business. Or in the blunt words of John Kenneth Galbraith:

> The market, none should doubt, continues to render a highly useful service. In economics there are no absolutes. But the only possible policy toward the market, either for conservatives or liberals, right or left, is one of open-minded pragmatism. Where it works, the market should be allowed to work. Where it doesn't, regulation has to be accepted.
> —New York Review of Books, Jan. 22, 1981

It is the promise and ultimately the presupposition of the free market system that everyone gets to play, that needs will thereby be met and work will thereby be stimulated. But the problem of poverty in the context of the free market

---

Ten Worst U.S. Metro Areas for Renters Living in Substandard Housing ——

New Orleans	53%*	Birmingham	26%
San Antonio	39%	Rochester	25%
Houston	32%	Fort Worth-Arlington	20%
New York	29%	Chicago	20%
Philadelphia	27%	*Percentage of low-income	
Atlanta	26%	renters living in physically	
		deficient housing	

Center on Budget and Policy Priorities, based on U.S. Census data, late 1980s

---

The Power of Positive Thinking ———

Chino is a slightly built sixteen-year-old dropout from Evander Childs High School, in the Bronx, who commits as many as five or six muggings a day. He is part of an army of teenage yoke men, push-in robbers, crib men, and purse snatchers roaming the city today who consider violent street crime a career. Last year, youngsters like Chino were responsible for many of the city's 100,550 muggings (275 a day), 27,358 felonious assaults (75 a day), 212,748 burglaries (582 a day), and 147,073 grand larcenies (402 a day). Of the 98,923 people arrested for major felonies in 1980, 44,170 were twenty years old or younger; 12,762 were under sixteen.

"I do it to get money," Chino begins, nudged into a discussion of his habits by a detective who knows—and who frightens—him. "I need money. We be hanging around smoking chiba [marijuana] and drinking beer [Chino is partial to quart-size bottles of Schaefer], and we start thinking about getting money, and we just go and get some."

Do you ever feel sorry for the people you rob?

"Sorry? You mean pity?" Chino has been asked that question many times by detectives and social workers, and he gives the same answer as always: "You need the money. You got to get the money. You can't go worrying about things. You just got to take the opportunity. If you go around worrying, you'll never get any money."

What about getting caught? What about getting shot by some cop?

"You don't think about getting caught," says Chino, frowning in annoyance at the question. "You can't be worrying about getting caught or cops or anything. You think about the money. About getting the money. You got to think positive."

From *The New York Magazine*, March 9, 1981

---

system is not just the existence of deprivation and misfortune in the midst of affluence. It is a problem inherent in the free market system itself. It was the qualified optimism of Adam Smith that even the ordinary worker in modern society could enjoy comfort unknown to many a pre-industrialized king, and, indeed, much of the working class in America today is part of the middle class, with most working families enjoying such luxuries—still rare in much of the world—as automobiles and in-house refrigerators. But many families in America do not have these comforts, indeed, do not even have homes. Some of them work at full-time jobs, but their wages are insufficient to support them, and their education and training are inadequate to help them earn more money. Others do not work or cannot work, and whether or not they are entitled to help from the government in the form of welfare, they comprise a seemingly permanent, immobile core at the very heart of our society, often at the heart of our inner cities. This is the **underclass,** an unfortunate group often condemned to a life of dependency and hopelessness on account of race or by virtue of chronic physical or mental incapacities.

Ideally, business writers and economists suggest, the market should provide a "level playing field." But before one even begins to worry about the state of the playing field, one has to get in the game, and it is the tragic fact about our society today that many people cannot get in the game, cannot get the education or enjoy an environment in which entry into the market by legitimate means is possible. It has been recently argued, with statistics to support the argument, that welfare in fact feeds dependency and what appears to be unemployment is in fact a syndrome of disincentives. And indeed it seems to be tragically true that the ambitious social programs initiated twenty-five years ago have not eliminated the underclass and have not solved the problem of poverty but, apparently, have only aggravated it. It is difficult to separate the various factors at work here given the rather radical changes in America's conception of business and the indisputable shifts in the distribution of wealth (with a drastic increase in the top 1 percent, stagnation or worse in the well-being of more than half of the population) and the entrenchment of a welfare system that was supposed to be temporary but instead seems to be solidified in place. But what is clear, and where business comes into the picture, is the fact that today's jobs require education and training. Thirty years ago, most of the workforce could do a decent job at decent pay with a high school education or even less. Today, even a college education is not always sufficient for a great many "high-tech" jobs, and that rather large proportion of the population who once held decent semi-skilled jobs now find themselves unable to hold anything more than a minimum-wage, short-term job in a parking lot or a fast-food franchise, and even those jobs are becoming scarce. It is not only the failure of industry but the massive failure of education to keep up with industry that have eliminated the jobs that a semi-educated person could once assume to be readily available.

Adam Smith surmised, and future theorists of the "dismal science" of economics confirmed it, that the free market required a pool of unemployed workers at the "bottom" of the economic scale in order to keep wages down. Karl Marx recognized the entrenched nature of this feature of capitalism and referred to what we call the underclass with a dismissive name, the **lumpenproletariat,** and for all that he preached in the name of the working class (or **proletariat**) he seemed to write off the underclass. But in a society that puts ever more emphasis on the importance of self-sufficiency and the importance of a job (if not a career) to maintain basic self-esteem and human dignity, this is intolerable. It is no better to rationalize that the members of the underclass are as they are by choice, that these people could work but do not or will not, when the basic tools (and not just incentives) are lacking. Too often, the irrelevant facts of race, gender, or religion provide systematic reason for despair, loss of self-esteem and self-confidence, and, consequently, an inability to even present oneself as required for even the

A Teenage Jobless Catastrophe ——

On the last working day before the Labor Day weekend, the government acknowledged that 50.7 percent of all black teenagers are unemployed. When you tally jobs for all minority teenagers, it turns out that 45.7 percent of them are looking for work.

These are horrendous statistics that would not be tolerated by any industrial society on earth, save ours. No, the acting White House press secretary said, this issue was not discussed when the President met with the chairman of his economic advisers. And no, nothing specific will be done about it.

The jobless black and Hispanic teenagers are lost among the vast army of unemployed. There are 7.6 million people out of work, more than the population of Massachusetts, New Hampshire and Vermont. The minority teenagers comprise only one out of every 18 people looking for a job.

The August U.S. unemployment figures:

Black teenagers	50.7%	Blacks	15.0%
All minority teenagers	45.7%	Whites	6.1
White teenagers	15.6	Adult men	5.9
All workers, all races	7.2	Adult women	6.7

The teenage minority unemployment catastrophe contributes substantially to the crime problem. It robs a generation, or 45.7 percent of a generation, of the self-respect and satisfaction of working, of buying what they want, of building a stake in this society. We deny them a seat at the table. They see the good life on TV.

What stakes does a black teenager have in a society that condemns more than half his fellows to unemployment? . . .

Bob Marley, the reggae singer whose premature death stilled the most eloquent voice of ghetto youth, sang, "A hungry man is an angry man." Our welfare system, designed to eliminate hunger, has worked. The poor can eat. But they hunger for more than food. They want dignity, self-esteem, a little of the good life, they want what the rest of us want, a little more.

David Nyhan, *The Boston Globe,* Sept. 5, 1981

most menial jobs and services. Those of us who were raised in an environment of hope cannot easily understand what it is like to grow up in an environment of hopelessness, and even those who escaped such an environment will find it hard to remember what it is like to be hopeless. This is where business comes in, with the aid and encouragement of the whole society. Business is where the action is, and business is better than anyone at defining its needs and training those who can satisfy those needs. For example, proposals are moving ahead in several states to provide customized training provided by various companies but financed, in part, by the government and, in particular, by funds drawn from unemployment compensation funds. Too often in the past, so-called training programs at self-proclaimed "career training schools" turned out to be useless or fraudulent, inadequate in their instruction, and unable to deliver promised jobs. The new programs, however, are based on real training in real companies with real jobs. Those who benefit from training and move from hopelessness to hope cease to be drains on an increasingly strained welfare system—not to mention the prison system—and become part of the market. We cannot afford an underclass, and for the sake of the market as well as social justice, the problem of poverty can and must be solved during our lifetime.

E.   EQUAL OPPORTUNITY: REALITY AND MYTH

> What is clear . . . is that earnings inequalities cannot, as some have suggested, be explained by the process of acquiring human skills. According to this argument, many low-earnings individuals are thought to be in the process of investing their human capital through on-the-job training. Being willing to work for low wages is simply the way that they pay their employer for this type of training. . . . Once they complete their training their wages will rise, the distribution of earnings will become more equal, and as a consequence the lifetime distribution of earnings must be more equal than the annual distribution of earnings. But if this were true, we would expect to see a more equal distribution of earnings among older workers who have completed their human capital investments. In fact, however, the income distribution among older workers is more unequal than the distribution of income for males as a whole . . . . Black males earn less than white males for the same degree of work. . . .
>
> —Lester Thurow, Generating Inequality

"Life is not always fair," said Jimmy Carter, a few months before he lost the 1980 presidential election. Indeed, it is not. But there is a difference between the contingencies of life and the social structures that we have built and continue to defend every day. These structures not only serve to our advantage but also appear to us, from our vantage point, as quite "natural and fair." In the eighteenth century before the revolution, the aristocrats of France, for example, were quite pleased to defend the "natural" order of society by pointing out the ultimate fairness of that order as God's design. A white American male, whatever other problems he might have, usually grows up simply assuming he has the option of entering the business world. To him equal opportunity seems obvious; there it is, waiting to be chosen, when and if he wants to choose it. It is hard to think of the

Black Business ——

• The number of black-owned businesses increased 38 percent between 1982 and 1987, compared to the 14 percent increase in all firms. Sales for black-owned firms increased 105 percent in the five-year period (*The Wall Street Journal,* April 3, 1992).

• A *Wall Street Journal* poll of black entrepreneurs found that 39 percent believed their business had been hurt by being minority owned. Some 22 percent said minority ownership was helpful; 35 percent said it made no difference.

• At banks across the country, blacks were turned down for mortgages at a rate 2.4 times higher than whites (Federal Reserve Board).

• Fewer than 2 percent of the partners in law firms in Chicago, Cleveland, Houston, and Baltimore are minorities (*The Wall Street Journal,* January 22, 1992).

option as not being there. However, the skills and options that have been prepared and encouraged in one person's life are not the same as those perceived and developed in another's.

Business ethics *is* the ethics of equal opportunity. Perhaps that is much more the case in modern America than it has often been elsewhere; but here, at least, some sense of "anyone can play" has always been at the very core of both capitalist economics and the capitalist conception of justice. The very notion of the "free market" has a certain built-in blindness to irrelevant personal differences (such as race, religion, sex, and social status), since all that is relevant within the market is the availability of a product or skills and the demand for the same. The limited notion of "economic man," while ethically truncated in many respects, has had the virtue of eliminating many prejudices from the business world. But yet, many prejudices regarding race and sex, especially, remain. Whether or not the market itself is "free," the conditions for entry are far from being equally available to everyone, and some groups are systematically shut out (with a few very visible exceptions) from the higher positions of the business world.

In classical capitalism, equal opportunity was prevented by the division between those who had capital and those who could only offer their time and labor for sale. Adam Smith's free market model incorporated clear distinction between the market for workers and the entrepreneurial class who competed and benefited from the market; the idea of a worker rising from stockboy or livery attendant was not even a matter for speculation. And yet, this is what we consider the absolute essence of not only our sense of economic justice but the heart of free enterprise as well. The story of the "robber barons" would be purely a matter of repulsion if these extraordinarily wealthy and powerful men had not started out "at the bottom and worked their way up." But the workers in Smith's system did not; indeed, it was to the benefit of the market system that they remained as poor as possible. "To make society happy," reports Heilbroner of a moralist in the early eighteenth century, "it is necessary that great numbers be wretched as well as poor." *Lack* of opportunity for many people, not equal opportunity for all, was the presupposition of the free market system. And though minority groups might well enter the market as labor, selling themselves cheaper than others, they would probably never advance any higher in the system, at least, not according to our favorite American myth, the "Horatio Alger rags to riches" story.

And yet, minorities do in fact make it up "from the bottom." Does this prove that the system is "free" after all? As we argued above, the existence of an isolated individual's success does not establish the possibility of equal opportunity. There is, as Lester Thurow has argued in his books *Generating Inequality* and *The Zero-Sum Society,* distribution of jobs and income according to *groups* as well. The system of a market open freely to members of one segment of society but closed (except for occasional, calculated leaks) to members of other groups may not be so regimented as in Adam Smith's original model, but its effects are much the same. Indeed, the effects are far more vicious in one respect: in Smith's society, the poor resigned themselves to being poor (not that they enjoyed it or did not envy the rich), but in our society, the much-advertised promise of equal opportunity and its rewards coupled with the brute fact of inequality leads inevitably to intense resentment as well as envy and, just as inevitably, to crime and violence. Illegal enterprise is not only the result of "the state trying to legislate morality." It is also the creative effort of groups who are systematically excluded from the legal market system, using the same principles of supply and demand to reach the same goal of personal wealth by other means. (Not all illegal market activity consists of illegal goods; the bulk of "the black market" in any country, including this one, consists of otherwise *legal* goods sold illegally.)

Equal opportunity is the heart of our economic-ethical system. The world of business depends on it, for in a world where fortunes can be staggering, justice requires that everyone have accessibility to success. Otherwise, our market system is no longer "free," but rather just an aristocratic playground in which the lucky few—by virtue of birth or circumstances—can play an extravagant game. Equal opportunity is the precondition of the business world, insofar as there can be no justifying "free enterprise" without it.

F. Affirmative Action— or Reverse Discrimination?

> You do not take a person who for years has been hobbled by chains and liberate him, bring him up to the starting line of a race, and say, "You're free to compete" and justly believe that you have been completely fair.
>
> Lyndon Johnson, address to the graduating class, 1965,
> Howard University

At a time when there seems, at least, to be fewer and fewer good jobs and much more competition for them, it is understandable that affirmative action should be a controversial subject. Affirmative action is, in short, a preferential means of giving opportunities to those who belong to a designated class of, in general, disadvantaged individuals. Affirmative action, however, is often accused of really being "reverse discrimination," that is, the unjust preference of some individuals over others just because of their membership in the designated class, regardless of their merit and regardless of whether they, as individuals, have been disadvantaged or not. We all are familiar with both sides of the argument: On the one hand, people who have been systematically deprived for generations are entitled to compensation, and this means being given special opportunities to succeed, admissions and scholarships to colleges that would not be justified on the basis of high school performance alone, and job opportunities that would not exist on the basis of skills and performance alone. On the other hand, say the other candidates, why should *I* be punished and put at a disadvantage because of something I did not do? Let there be fair competition, and may the best man or woman win. There are evasions, such as "all things being equal, we will choose the minority candidate," but the premise of the problem is that all things are *not* equal. There are utilitarian arguments, to the effect that those specially chosen can be justified because they will serve society in much needed ways (for example, black professionals practicing in the black community) or serve as role models for others (rather than in terms of their admittedly inadequate qualifications). There is also the rejoinder, however, that people thus chosen are condemned to be looked upon by their peers as inferior, even if, in fact, they are just as well qualified and accomplished. The debate takes on some problematic and profound concerns of justice, such as the responsibilities of one generation for the deeds of the past, the ultimate meaning of "merit," and the subtle ways in which one may be "advantaged" or "disadvantaged" by a competitive system.

The argument goes on and on in this way, fueled by the inevitable statistics of success and failure rates, but the conclusion of the argument is more often than not foregone, determined by the status and (in)securities of those taking part in the argument. It is all too easy for a well-to-do, well-educated and established professional, for example, to take the side of the disadvantaged, for they do not have to share in the cost of privileging some at the expense of others. (Thus the popular disdain for "limousine liberals.") So, too, it is far more problematic than it may first appear, however moving it may be, when a student who has been working for years to get into business school or a manager who has been bucking for vice-president objects that "it's not fair" when an affirmative action candidate gets the position that he or she so coveted. Occasionally, one does find professionals who are willing to risk or sacrifice their own positions to give way to those who have been disadvantaged, and one sometimes sees students who accept the fact that they have lost out on a much-desired opportunity because of affirmative action, but these are distinctive exceptions, rare concessions to a larger picture of the public good and social justice. Much more often, and understandably, people perceive justice in terms of what most affects them, and their most immediate and emotional responses are to those injustices of which they see themselves as the victims.

It has become more and more difficult to present an account of affirmative action—or reverse discrimination—which does not immediately trigger biased reactions, while allowing students and professionals on both sides of the argument to look at the problem with at least partially disinterested eyes, but a recent study by a philosopher has finally done it. Luc Bovens of the University of Colorado found that his Caucasian students, about to enter the job market, were particularly unsympathetic to affirmative action "under any guise." This being the case, he described for his class an affirmative action situation in which the reactions of most of his students were not at all those so evident in the American context, namely, the preferential treatment of Communist party members in state-run companies under Communist rule. (Bovens actually gave the example to his students *before* they began talking about affirmative action.) When Eastern European communism collapsed a few years ago, the managerial and other positions that had been filled by Communist party members were suddenly up for grabs. The problem was, however, that after so many decades of communism only the Communist party members had had the necessary education, training, and experience to perform the jobs, and so they were the only fully qualified applicants. People who had refused to join the Communist party, often at great disadvantage to themselves and their careers, were not as qualified and were often wholly unqualified, regardless of any potential they might have had to learn the required skills. But, in the backlash against communism, there was an obvious reason to give preference to those who had refused to join the Communist party, rather than continue to reward those who were members of the party and had played a part in the oppression and degradation of everyone else. What reasons could be given for overlooking well-qualified and experienced Communist managers in favor of less qualified or unqualified non-Communists? After discussing this example in class, Bovens then switches the case to American affirmative action.

Should We Hire Communists? ——

There are two consequentialist arguments in support of preferential treatment for candidates who did not work their way into managerial positions through ties with the Communist party. First, it might be argued that it will be beneficial in the long run to give a special edge to candidates who show promise yet have never had the opportunity to develop their talents. Second, there is the danger that old practices of nepotism within an in-group power elite will die hard if managerial positions in private companies are mainly stacked with former members of the Communist party.

Both these arguments play a role in the affirmative action debate in this country as well. As to the first argument, it is a common policy of admission committees in U.S. colleges to scout for talent from poorer school districts that is not reflected in test scores. The same argument could be made in support of giving a special edge to promising women and minorities in admission procedures for educational programs and selection procedures for jobs. The analogue to the second argument in the affirmative action debate is that a concern for more qualified candidates who are denied jobs due to affirmative action is misplaced. For without some affirmative action constraints, the subtle biases and barriers of the good-old-(white)-boys network would remain untouched and a much larger number of more qualified women and minorities would be overlooked for less qualified white male competitors.

Compensation for Past Injustice

One may also present a compensatory argument for not hiring more-qualified former Communist managers. Since former Communist managers built up their qualifications on grounds of exclusionary practices, it is not unreasonable that they be hindered from reaping all the benefits of these qualifications and that they be forced to accept a special edge for their competitors who were victimized by such exclusionary practices. This argument is reflected in the claim that affirmative action in this country is justified on the ground of the right of women and minorities to be compensated for past discrimination. This claim has typically received criticism on two scores.

First, it is argued that those who benefit from affirmative action are not the ones who have suffered most from past discrimination. But in this respect the situation in this country is not any different from the situation in Poland. Among the candidates who meet the minimal standards and did not have any ties with the Communist party, it would hardly be surprising to find proportionately more people whose lives were less deeply affected by the political conditions than people who have genuinely suffered under the Communist repression. I do not believe this observation should block preferential treatment in Poland since this practice provides for at least some means of compensation which may then need to be supplemented by other programs. And if it does not block preferential treatment in Poland for candidates who were not associated with the Communist party, why should it block affirmative action in this country for women and minorities?

Second, it is argued that at least some Caucasian men who are asked to make sacrifices today through affirmative action programs are not themselves responsible for past racist or sexist practices. But again there is a parallel with the Polish situation. Certainly there will be some individuals with successful careers who carried their Communist-party cards with moral integrity and have not themselves partaken in any political corruption. Yet they too have enjoyed the advantages of an unjust political system and this is sufficient to justify that some of these advantages will be neutralized due to a policy of preferential treatment.

Equality of Opportunity

A final argument is that candidates who were not affiliated with the Communist party did not receive an equal opportunity in the past to develop their capacities and that to provide for this opportunity is to give them a special edge on the job-market.

Yet a core argument by opponents of affirmative action in this country is that giving a special edge to women and minorities violates the rights of Caucasian men to equal opportunity. Let us consider how this argument would fare in the Polish context. It would be ironic if the former Communist manager were to claim that discounting some of his or her qualifications were a violation of equality of opportunity considering that these qualifications were built up precisely on grounds of an exclusionary political system. But is an appeal to equality of opportunity by Caucasian men in opposing affirmative action in this country any less ironic? Caucasian men have been able to build up their qualifications on grounds of cultural institutions that are exclusionary of women and minorities in many respects. Hence, the same irony shines through when they demand that the full competitive force of their qualifications be respected in the light of equality of opportunity.

From Luc Bovens, "Affirmative Action: A Polish example?"
in *From the Center,* vol. X, no. 3, Fall, 1991. The University of
Colorado Center for Values and Social Policy.

■ SUMMARY AND CONCLUSION

Justice is central to our conception of morality and the good life, and it is one of the key concepts of business ethics. Distributive justice, in particular, is concerned with the fair distribution of the material goods produced and collected by society, to all members of that society (and, to some extent, outside of that society as well). Complicating questions of justice, however, is the fact that a number of different and often opposed considerations enter into our conception of what is fair and proper in the just distribution of society's goods (and responsibilities, too). There is, first of all, our sense that everyone ought to gain something from society's wealth, at least that minimal support required to keep a person or a family alive. In this sense, we believe that everyone should be treated equally and that no individuals should perish if society has the means to keep them alive.

Second, however, our sense of merit, that a person *deserves* goods from society in return for work, and our sense of equality often disagree. Furthermore, merit and desert may mean very different measures too, the amount of effort, or the amount of actual contribution, for example. Between equality and merit, the notion of equal opportunity provides a middle concept in which equality of opportunity fulfills our sense of equality, while the actual use of that opportunity fulfills our sense that rewards should be based on merit. In a world where so much depends on luck, however, including the luck of having been born into an advantaged family, equal opportunity remains an abstract ideal, towards which we can work only with difficulty. But justice is, first of all, a concern for the well-being of others, and justice is served, if imperfectly, by our sense that there are others in society less fortunate than we are, whom it is our responsibility, if not our obligation, to help.

■ STUDY QUESTIONS

1. What is justice? How does your characterization of justice apply to the actual workings of the business world? What improvements would you suggest in terms of the realization of justice? What would be the probable costs to business of implementing these improvements?

2. What does *luck* have to do with justice? Is it ever fair for a person to win great riches without doing anything to do so? What limitations would you put on the fairness of such lucky occasions? Are lotteries just, in your opinion?

3. The originators of the cartoon *Superman* sold their idea and all rights to their comic character for a modest fee some twenty-five years ago. The comic book, the television show, and a series of movies went on to make many millions of dollars. Should the originators of the character have shared in those subsequent, unexpected royalties?

4. One manager works hard at his job, puts in long hours, and often leaves the office thoroughly exhausted. Another finds her job quite pleasant, spends a few hours a day chatting with subordinates and talking on the phone. The rest of the time, she plays golf and relaxes with friends. Their measurable results are virtually identical. If you were their superior, would you give them identical salaries and bonuses? Would you reward one more than the other? Why?

5. Should a chairman of the board, who does little work and has little actual responsibility in the company, be paid a salary that is many times larger than the salaries of the executives who actually make the company work? Why?

6. Novelist James Baldwin contrasts the attitudes of a European waiter and his American counterpart by noting that the former has the security of knowing that he has his job for life, while the latter, who has aspirations to be something else (the owner of the restaurant, perhaps) also has to worry about keeping his job. Given this choice of mobility and security, how do you see the overall sense of justice of each system? Is it fair to keep a person in the same position, even if he or she is capable of doing much more? What are the advantages and disadvantages of each system?

7. Women used to be paid lower wages, despite equality of work and merit, on the basis that women who worked were either single and didn't have a family to feed, or were married and thus had another income in the family. Was this ever just? Is that same basis a fair assumption today? Are there any reasons for paying some people less than others for equal work and merit?

8. Does a person have an *obligation* to work in this society? If a person can work but, given an unenviable assortment of job opportunities, *refuses* to do so, does he or she thereby give up any claim to a share of the goods that society can provide?

9. Suppose you invest $100 in a particular stock that is supposed to be a long-term steady growth stock. What, given the present market, would you consider a fair return on your investment to be? Dreams aside, what amount of return would you consider to be *more* than a fair return on your money? What amount would you consider to be *un*fair?

10. Does the free enterprise system, overall, improve justice in our society? In what ways does it do so? In what ways does it not do so?

■ FOR CLASS DISCUSSION

The New Horatio Alger?

I think it will be found that the best and the greatest . . . have had a lineage which linked them to honor and public virtue, but almost without exception the lineage of honest poverty— of laborious wage-receiving parents, leading lives of virtuous privation, sacrificing comforts that their sons might be kept at school—lineage from the cottage of poverty, not the palace of hereditary rank and position.
                    —Andrew Carnegie, "The Advantages of Poverty"

Chino (p. 330) did not even apply to Harvard Business School. In fact, he never graduated from high school. His father couldn't get a job at all, while his mother was away so much, doing menial jobs for wealthy families across town, that he rarely saw her. Since he was twelve, he had been more or less the head of the family. He was also a shrewd businessman, with nearly a decade of successful experience in marketing and public policy. His income is well into the six-figure range; he is generous with his money, supporting his family and investing heavily in the neighborhood community without the incentive of a tax deduction to motivate his generosity. Chino is one of Boston's largest nonsyndicated cocaine dealers. He is Puerto Rican and uneducated, or at least he lacks the credentials that would allow his ambitions, skill, and success to be recognized in the business world. What he wants, however, is that same sense of success and significance, along with the material trappings of the good life—a fast car, the clothes he sees advertised, financial security, and enough ready cash to live well—in the very American sense of that phrase.

Chino is the rub in the free enterprise business world. He is smart and ambitious. He, too, believes that the social responsibility of his business is to maximize profit and satisfy consumer demand. He sees the illegality of his enterprise as nothing other than unfair trade restrictions and excessive government regulation over what ought to be a straightforward relationship between consumers and suppliers. He has been told, on frequent occasions, that he should "go straight" and get into the business world in an honest way, display his talents, and "work his way up the ladder." But the only jobs he has ever been qualified or considered for are jobs in stockrooms and parking garages, where it has been quite clear that the possibilities for advancement were slim, and the sense of degradation considerable. As Chino sees it, this is the land of opportunity, and his opportunities are in the streets. He considers the profits worth the risks, and he knows how to manage and minimize them. What could convince him otherwise?

Frederico, one of Chino's childhood friends, *is* in Harvard Business School. He does not return to the old neighborhood, only a fifteen-minute subway ride away. His standing with his old friends became tenuous when he started to spend inordinate amounts of time in high school studying, reading, and expressing his ambitions about "making it in the white world." This was not considered treachery so much as foolishness and antisocial behavior, since "no one ever made it from here." But Frederico did; he was accepted with a full scholarship to Columbia University, worked hard and did well enough to get into Harvard. He is now on the fast track, and, along with a certain pro-racial bias and "affirmative action" pressure in the air, his newly acquired credentials and skills make him a sure success in the business world, or rather, the white middle-class American business world. Not surprisingly, Frederico is now discussed not with admiration but with disdain by his friends, when they speak of him at all.

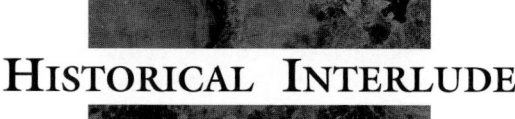

HISTORICAL INTERLUDE

THE GREAT DEPRESSION: JOHN MAYNARD KEYNES AND THE "NEW DEAL"

Let us clear from the ground the metaphysical or general principles upon which, from time to time, laissez-faire has been founded. It is not true that individuals possess a prescriptive 'natural liberty' in their economic activities. There is no 'compact' conferring perpetual rights on those who Have or on those who Acquire. The world is not so governed from above that private and social interest always coincide. It is not so managed here below that in practice they coincide. It is not a correct deduction from the Principles of Economics that enlightened self-interest always operates in the public interest. Nor is it true that self-interest generally is enlightened; more often individuals acting separately to promote their own ends are too ignorant or too weak to attain even these. Experience does not show that individuals, when they make up a social unit, are always less clear-sighted than when they act separately.

—John Maynard Keynes, Essays In Persuasion

Adam Smith viewed the macroeconomics and the ethics of capitalism with optimism. To him, the pursuit of private gain would bring about public wealth, not by individual intent but by "the invisible hand," that self-righting mechanism that would assure fair prices and adequate supply, as well as jobs for everyone. Marx, on the other hand, saw the same mechanism of individual pursuit of wealth as leading, inevitably, to the impoverishment of the working classes, to mass unemployment, and eventually to the destruction of capitalism. But in an important sense, they were both wrong. The mechanisms and the "inevitability" of wealth and poverty were not so automatic as both supposed. The assurances of Adam Smith were refuted once and for all in that dreadful month of October 1929. But the doomsday promises of Karl Marx were not the alternative; capitalism survived, chastened and confused. The ethics of capitalism and the free market had been radically altered, however, along with the economics. The new essential ingredient was *security,* a "safety net" for those for whom capitalism failed. The ethical cost was government intervention.

The crash of 1929 was the most severe of a recurring series of "downturns" in the "business cycle." It brought into focus a number of factors that had plagued the more optimistic accounts of capitalism for decades, indeed, ever since (and before) the writings of Adam Smith. Supply and demand was not the only operative economic law, even in a market free from outside interference. The Great Depression proved that there could be enormous demand without an appropriate supply, and that there could be massive unemployment even while there was an extensive need for production. The Great Depression showed that the safety mechanisms Smith had postulated at the bottom of the free market—such that demand would always require labor, if at greatly reduced wages—and his contention that money would always be available for investment, through profits and savings, had failed. In the early years of the 1930s, the number of unemployed in America was a crippling 14 million; the national income dropped from nearly $90 million in 1930 to less than $40 million only four years later. The grand prosperity of the "Roaring Twenties," although marked by symptoms that, in retrospect, clearly indicated tragic collapse, had prompted then-President Herbert Hoover to announce the end of poverty in America. It was as if the Great Depression was a refutation of everything that Americans and their economic theories believed in.

Into the turmoil of the desperate free market system stepped two giants who would change the course of economics and ethics in this country. In England, the master economist John Maynard Keynes introduced new ideas into free market economics that were no less revolutionary than those once introduced by Smith and Marx. And in America, a new president, Franklin Delano Roosevelt, introduced his countrymen to "a New Deal," which included a dramatic *ethical* change from the ideal of total self-sufficiency and "laissez faire" to a powerful vision of government responsibility, not only to its individual citizens but to the manipulation of the formerly "free" economy as well. In fact, Keynes and Roosevelt had virtually nothing to do with one another. (The president's advisers read Keynes; Roosevelt did not.) But they stepped into the desperate world of the Great Depression at the same critical moment in history, and their views of government intervention and responsibility marked a parallel change in ethics and economics, both in the classical theories of the free market and in the way people in business—in every capacity—would look at themselves and the society in which they plied their skills.

Keynesian Economics

We are all Keynesians now.

—Richard Nixon, 1973

Adam Smith's classical theory had argued that there would always be an equilibrium point in a free market economy. If the supply of shoes is excessive, the price will fall, but only until people see what a bargain shoes are and start buying again. If the price of shoes is too high, people will stop buying new ones and wear their old shoes longer, until the price falls once again. High wages in one job will attract workers from lower-paying jobs, and a glut in the labor force will result in lower wages, a bargain for employers; therefore, employment is guaranteed, if only demand continues and the labor force does not grow too much. In other words, Smith believed that in a free market supply and demand of goods and workers would stabilize prices and wages and assure the greatest prosperity and maximum employment.

During the depression, however, demand for goods was greater than ever before, and so was the demand for jobs, and yet the unemployment rate was tragically high. People were starving all over the country, and yet farmers plowed under fields because they could not get a fair price for food. The need for clothing and shelter did not diminish with the depression, but clothing manufacturers and home builders were idle, their employees were on the streets, and many businesses went bankrupt. The proponents of Adam Smith had no answers. Such massive and irreversible unemployment was not in accordance with their theories. The equilibrium point had not yet been found, or rather, the equilibrium point, if there was one, was intolerably below the level of almost full employment that any civilized society needed to survive, especially in a society where one's personal worth is measured in such a large part by one's work.

Keynes' fundamental discovery was not so dramatic as Smith's revelation of the mechanism of the free market system or Marx's predictions of the inevitability of capitalism's demise. But then, the flaws of the free market system that had brought about the Great Depression were not the most noticeable aspects of economics either. Keynes' great book had none of the theatricality of a revolutionary text, included no calls to the barricades, and had few cries for action in the usual sense. His *Treatise on Money* and his even more formidable *General Theory of Employment, Interest and Money* focus our attention on some of those aspects that had been too easily taken for granted during times of prosperity—the problem of unemployment and the various assumptions linking savings, investment, and loans that had broken down in the boom and crash of the 1920s. The assumption about money had been that money saved was money earned (as Benjamin Franklin had moralized), and also money banked and invested as well. The

Keynes ——

If our poverty were due to famine or earthquake or war—if we lacked material things and the resources to produce them, we could not expect to find the means to prosperity except in hard work, abstinence, and invention. In fact, our predicament is notoriously of another kind. It comes from some failure in the immaterial devices of the mind, in the working of the motives which should lead to the decisions and acts of will, necessary to put in movement the resources and technical means we already have. It is as though two motor-drivers, meeting in the middle of a highway, were unable to pass one another because neither knows the rule of the road. Their own muscles are no use; a motor engineer cannot help them; a better road would not serve. Nothing is required and nothing will avail, except a little clear thinking.

I call attention to the nature of the problem, because it points us to the nature of the remedy. It is appropriate to the case that the remedy should be found in something which can fairly be called a device. Yet there are many who are suspicious of devices, and instinctively doubt their efficacy. There are still people who believe that the way out can only be found by hard work, endurance, frugality, improved business methods, more cautious banking and, above all, the avoidance of devices. But the lorries of these people will never, I fear, get by. They may stay up all night, engage more sober chauffeurs, install new engines, and widen the road; yet they will never get by, unless they stop to think and work out with the driver opposite a small device by which each moves simultaneously a little to his left.

From *The Means to Prosperity*

standard version of the Protestant work ethic required that money be saved, rather than consumed, but with the often highly visible consumption of the newly rich, consumption began to have its adherents. Income, investment, consumption, and savings were all measures of prosperity.

In traditional capitalism, the assumption that separated philanthropy from greed was the assumption that the rich would invest their money in productive assets, which would in turn require productive workers, so that the poor would benefit from increased investment because there would be more jobs, and more jobs meant more incomes. In other words, the assumption was that savings and investment were necessarily linked. And in the age of Adam Smith, when savings ("thrift") generally meant the capital reinvested in new machinery, new projects, and new factories and therefore in new jobs, that may have had some plausibility.

But as the nation in general became more prosperous, it was not just the entrepreneurs who were saving and directly investing their money; the middle class and the working class were also putting some of their money into savings, encouraged by the whole history of the puritan ethic as well as by the government and the general wave of prosperity and money available to save. But much of the new savings were invested only in paper assets, in very inflated stock market prices, driven up through wild speculation by almost everyone. There were wild stories about stock boys who had become overnight millionaires by buying on margin on a tip; if a stock boy could do it, then so could anyone else. There was so much money available to be thrown at the stock market that the law of supply and demand broke down—there was too much supply, despite plummeting interest rates. Companies couldn't use the money. They couldn't spend it fast enough. Banks couldn't give the money away, and the effect was as if all the money in circulation had been stuffed into a strongbox, taking it out of circulation.

The supply of money was unlimited, the demand for goods was unlimited, but the demand for new investment was disastrously low. The result was the depression, and the cure, Keynes insisted, was for government to interfere with the "free" but failed market that Adam Smith had warned against. Government would create the demand through government spending and by creating projects and jobs (useful if possible, but useless if necessary) on the theory that any job is better than none and any increase in purchasing power will stimulate the demand for consumer goods. This in turn would spur business investment, which would lead to more jobs and the end of the depression. Massive government intervention was the answer to the depression; the mechanism of the market was not enough. Keynes was in no way attacking the "freedom" of the market so much as he was insisting that there were limits to its power. Keynes believed in the free market so long as it worked, but when the market so dramatically fails to satisfy even the minimal needs of so many millions of people, then government intervention is both ethically and economically necessary.

Roosevelt's "New Deal"

What does this view do to the ethical basis of capitalism? The ultimate end, of course, remains essentially the same—the greatest well-being of the greatest number of people in the society. But the emphasis on self-sufficiency and saving that had been urged as an ultimate ethical principle by Hoover, for example, now became clearly relegated to second place. It was not eliminated altogether, as critics of the "New Deal" have often argued; the work ethic and the emphasis on productive employment remained the key to the program. But self-reliance now had to be viewed in the context of an overall dependency, a mutual support system. Few participants in the economy could see themselves, as traditional capitalism suggested, as totally autonomous market players who could work or not work, buy or sell as they alone could choose in response to the conditions of the market. "If I read the temper of our people correctly," proclaimed Roosevelt in his 1933

Roosevelt's Inaugural Address, March 4, 1933 ——

The money changers have fled from their high seats in the temple of our civilization. We may now restore that temple to the ancient truths. The measure of the restoration lies in the extent to which we apply social values more noble than mere monetary profit.

Happiness lies not in the mere possession of money; it lies in the joy of achievement, in the thrill of creative effort. The joy and moral stimulation of work no longer must be forgotten in the mad chase of evanescent profits. These dark days will be worth all they cost us if they teach us that our true destiny is not to be ministered unto but to minister to ourselves and to our fellow men.

Recognition of the falsity of material wealth as the standard of success goes hand in hand with the abandonment of the false belief that public office and high political position are to be valued only by the standards of pride of place and personal profit; and there must be an end to a conduct in banking and in business which too often has given to a sacred trust the likeness of callous and selfish wrongdoing. Small wonder that confidence languishes, for it thrives only on honesty, on honor, on the sacredness of obligations, on faithful protection, on unselfish performance; without them it cannot live.

Restoration calls, however, not for changes in ethics alone. This nation asks for action, and action now.

---

inaugural address, "we now realize as we have never realized before our interdependence on each other." But interdependency was an ethical foundation too long ignored—or simply taken for granted—in classical economics. The model of a self-regulation mechanism of autonomous individuals had to be supplemented (but by no means replaced) by a model of an enormous social network in which some people were far worse off than others and in which the functioning of the market had to be the *active* concern of the society as a whole—the government. Trusting the mechanism to work itself out correctly, even with continuing hard work and lots of money, was no longer acceptable.

The rallying cry of classical economics had been "laissez faire"—leave the market alone. But the freedom of the market was not an end in itself; it was defensible only so long as it did provide the prosperity it promised. This was clearly not the case in 1933. Four years of "laissez faire" policies and encouragement of the "self-sufficiency" ethic had had no good effect on the depression. When Roosevelt was elected, he immediately promised a "New Deal" for the American people, and in his inaugural speech proposed as much an ethical manifesto as he did a new economic approach. He attacked "greed" and defended mutual concern for the disadvantaged. He attacked the monopolies and mismanagement as the real enemy of free enterprise and defended government intervention as an antidote. He defended that huge minority in American life, for whom the Hoover slogans of self-sufficiency must have seemed like a cruel joke—the old and chronically ill and the systematically unemployed. He defended a basic belief in welfare services, not as a matter of *noblesse oblige* and Christian charity, but as a basic matter of human rights and, consequently, the responsibility of the entire society. The farmer with crops that couldn't make it to the market, the willing worker who couldn't get a job—they were no longer to be viewed simply as the losers in a nationwide game of business; they were victims of a system in which other people prospered. And the small businessman caught in the destructive spiral of cutthroat competition was also a victim who needed some security and some help. The old puritan virtues of thrift and hard work were no longer enough to assure success. Less self-sufficency, yes—but in return for survival and the possibility of a prosperous life. It is not an ethical choice that most of us would disagree with.

Roosevelt himself was not a Keynesian; however, a powerful member of the Federal Reserve Board under him, Laughlin Currie, had been converted to the Keynesian doctrine of government intervention, in part because of his own perilous experiences as a banker during the depression, in part because of his recognition of the plight of farmers, workers, and businessmen alike. He was the "Washington wedge of Keynes," as J. K. Galbraith described him, and when he moved from the Fed to the White House as Roosevelt's economic adviser, he filled the government with Keynesians. Conservatives viewed this as a conspiracy; Currie saw it just as the necessary thing to do. The result was a wholesale change in the conception of the role of government in economic affairs, which might be summarized in the name of one of its leading programs—*social security*. The actual decrease in unemployment due to the Keynesian "device" is debatable; so too the "device" had its other results—a large deficit ($3.6 billion in 1934, $3.9 billion in 1939) and the seeds of inflation. But whatever the economic results, the shift in attitudes was clear. Making money was no longer the centerpiece of the American ethic.

As an ethical viewpoint, New Deal Keynesian theory replaced the emphasis from self-sufficiency and the puritan pursuit of wealth to concern for security for the "little person" and the welfare of the less advantaged members of society. It insisted on a sense of social responsibility and direct intervention of government in the market to ensure some semblance of fair distribution of the wealth even when the market itself would not provide this. The Great Depression did not in fact end because of the New Deal; it was rather washed away by World War II. The massive spending required by government in wartime provided just the demand that Keynes suggested, though at an enormous cost in human life.

– 11 –

Human Rights and International Business

We hold these Truths to be self-evident, that all Men are created equal, that they are endowed by their Creator with certain inalienable Rights, that among these are Life, Liberty and the Pursuit of Happiness.

—United States Declaration of Independence

O ur discussion of justice, in its survey of contributions and rewards from the top of the career ladder to the bottom, from the very wealthy to the very poor, is nevertheless incomplete. So far, our entire concern has been a concern for mutual well-being, and the demand that the poorest among us should somehow benefit, or at any rate not in any way be further harmed, by furthering the advantages of the wealthy and the well-off. But there is another essential feature of justice that cannot necessarily be measured in terms of "utility" and overall well-being. This is the notion of *rights*.

If the discussion of justice were wholly limited to questions of mutual well-being and fair distribution, the questions we have raised would be difficult enough. But the addition of considerations about *rights* adds not only a complication—because rights, like moral obligations, can conflict—but an entirely new dimension to the argument. Except in extreme circumstances (or if a right is rather trivial) rights take precedence over considerations of utility. Suppose a corporation wants to establish a plant in a community that very much needs the jobs and the new source of wealth; indeed, suppose that *everyone* stands to benefit considerably from the new operation. But there is one hitch. The property that is required for the plant includes the property of one extremely unlikable, miserly, mean-spirited recluse, who, despite the benefits and the pressures of the entire community, refuses to sell. The motives may be purely malicious; the benefits to the recluse may indeed be even greater (given the very high price offered for the property) than the benefits to everyone else. People in the community may feel no positive affection for the recluse, and may have been wishing for years, in fact, that this most unpleasant and troublesome person would move away. The demands of social well-being and utility, in other words, are overwhelmingly against the recluse, and yet, the case is clear. The recluse has *rights*. He has a right to his property, so long as it was legally acquired and is used for legal purposes. And, for whatever reason, he can continue to hold on to that property, by right, against the most overwhelming pressures. Such is the power of claims about rights.

Rights often have something resembling *trump* status, even when other demands of justice would be otherwise. We might argue, of course, that respect for rights should itself be defended in terms of our overall well-being, even if some particular rights, such as the rights of an antisocial recluse, go against our sense of well-being. The precondition of the very existence of a free and "civilized" society is mutual respect for *all* rights, even those that seem questionable. Nevertheless, on a case-by-case basis, rights and general social well-being are different and can on occasion be opposed, with rights taking precedence. In particular, such basic human rights as the right to life are often argued to take priority over *all* other considerations, no matter what profits may be at stake and no matter how much the general well-being might be maximized with the sacrifice of just one or two innocent victims. (See "Not all rights claims . . . are absolute," p. 355.)

Rights provide protection for individual freedom and interests. They allow us to pursue our ambitions and beliefs without undue interference from other people, groups, or governments. They assure us all that our concerns and well-being count regardless of their importance or influence in a community, and they provide a basis upon which we can justify our actions even against the interests of a large majority. Indeed, one of the most general rights—defended by Immanuel Kant, for example, as the basis of all morality—is the right to human dignity and being treated as a person, rather than merely as a means to someone else's ends.

A right is a legitimate demand, an **entitlement.** Most rights entail an obligation on the part of someone else. If I am owed a hundred dollars by virtue of a contract we signed, then I have a **contractual right** to that money, and you have a corresponding obligation to give it to me. It does not matter if I am already very rich and will spend that money on peanuts for the pigeons in the park. It does not matter if you are very poor and will have to give up meat for a month in order to pay me. Because of the contract, I have a right and you have an obligation.

Contractual rights are by no means the only or most important rights. There are also *legal* rights guaranteed by law, at least within a particular country or community. Every adult non-felon American, by law, has the right to vote; no one, including the government, can stop him or her from voting. But most important of all, every person, in every society, no matter what the law and no matter what the circumstances, has certain basic rights, which we call **"natural"** or **human rights.** These do not depend on law, although the just society will recognize them in law; they do not depend on any particular social order, although, again, the just society will build these rights into its social order. We all have these rights simply by virtue of being "a human being." What's more, no society, no law, and no other person can take these rights away from us; our Declaration of Independence calls them "inalienable."

Considerable disagreement exists over what counts as a "natural" or a "human right." The Declaration of Independence insists that three such rights are "life, liberty, and the pursuit of happiness." In an earlier draft of that document, Thomas Jefferson intended to include what many social philosophers also consider a natural right, the right to own property. "The Bill of Rights," the first ten Amendments to our Constitution, adds to this list a great many other rights (though it is not always clear which of these are to be considered human rights as such and which are legal rights specific to citizens of the United States). The right to freedom of speech and freedom of religion, the right to a fair trial by jury and the right to remain silent, and the right to join organizations and demonstrations are all rights guaranteed to us in the Constitution. Other rights of this basic kind of particular importance to the business world are the right to make contracts, the right to work, and the right to sell products at a profit. We would expect a lively debate over the status of some of these rights in arguing with a Marxist, however, or for that matter, with a medieval Christian saint, for the idea that a person has a "natural right" to make a profit would have been sharply disputed throughout most of history. But without entering into such debates here, we can at least say that these are the rights that form the foundations of modern capitalism. The right to private property, the right to make a profit, the right to enter into the (legal) business of our choice, and the right to make contracts—these are the essential conditions of any business environment. But, it is important to add, these rights also entail obligations on the part of every businessperson without which business life would quickly become impossible.

A. Freedom Rights, Positive Rights, and Human Rights

Most of the "natural" or "human" rights protected by law in our Constitution have to do with freedom: the freedom or the right to worship, the freedom or the right to speak our minds, the freedom or the right to sign contracts, the freedom or the right to assemble in groups and form political organizations, the freedom or right not to be tortured or put in jail arbitrarily. Accordingly such rights are **negative** or **freedom rights.** We might summarize such rights as "the right to be left alone," or "the right to keep what we have."

However, another kind of rights claim also exists; there are rights to be provided with something, *even if we cannot or do not get it on our own.* For example, the right to a good education in our democratic society is considered a fundamental right necessary to the good of society. Moreover, we have the right to a decent job and the right to work, given our ethic that insists that our worth and self-esteem are based on our work. There is the right to adequate medical care, even if we cannot pay for it ourselves. These rights are more controversial than freedom rights, we can call these **positive rights**—rights to some commodity or benefit offered by society.

These rights are subject to the argument that such commodities or benefits ought to be earned and are not a matter of right at all. Some have argued that a free education, for example, is not taken as seriously as an education that must be paid for or that free medical care should be considered charity, not a right. The right to work has sometimes been invoked against labor unions by the same people who would otherwise deny that right in favor of the free market mechanism of supply and demand. But whatever the arguments, it is important to appreciate the claim that positive rights demand that society (whether government or business or some other groups or individuals) actively provide services that need not be earned or directly paid for. Such is the intent, however vague, of the United Nations Declaration of 1948 (sects. 22, 25):

> *Everyone, as a member of society, has the right to social security . . .*
> *and a standard of living adequate for health and well-being.*

Whenever a person has a right, we said, other people have an obligation to that person. In the case of freedom rights, that obligation mainly consists of the duty not to interfere, not to stop a person from speaking, not to prevent a group from practicing their religion (assuming that it does not break the law), not to torture a person for information, and not to arrest that person unjustly. These duties apply to everyone, although, to be sure, many of them are directed mainly to governments, which otherwise have more power than individuals and even the largest institutions. But with regard to positive rights, the obligation of others is something more than leaving people alone; it requires providing something for them, usually at considerable expense and effort. Thus there is a question over the right to education and medical services, for example, that is as long-standing as it is inevitable: who will pay? And, not surprisingly, government, private institutions, and individuals constantly battle about who will pay, who will provide the services, what and who should be taxed and how, and what other sacrifices will be required.

The obligations of business to respect freedom rights is quite clear. Even when the well-being of a company is threatened, business has an obligation to respect the rights of others, in particular, its employees and consumers and the community that surrounds it. A company may be profiting mightily by the illegal dumping of toxic chemicals and face disaster if this illegality is exposed. Nevertheless, an employee who chooses to speak out and expose the abuse has a right to do so, and the company has an obligation not to stop him. A company may find that it can maintain current prices and profits only by seriously cutting the quality of its product, which will include the elimination of safeguards and the substantial risk of at least a few fatal accidents. And yet, the consumer has a right not to be faced with such risks, and the company has an obligation to respect this right. Of course, most cases are far more complex than this; the rights in question are not so clear and the trade-off of benefits and damages is far more negotiable. Nonetheless, at least in clear cases, rights take precedence, and freedom rights entail a corresponding obligation on the part of business to respect them.

Positive rights are the rights that most often enter into arguments about "the social responsibilities of business." Businesspeople and economists readily recognize and respect freedom rights, even if on occasion they may argue that such rights are overridden by other rights or by overwhelming concerns of social utility. But positive rights are such that recognition and respect for them also entail the necessity of deciding who will provide for them. Most people are perfectly willing to acknowledge everyone's right to a decent education and at least minimal medical care, but not all who recognize that right also recognize their own obligation to provide that education and medical care. To recognize a right does not necessarily mean taking primary responsibility for it. But here again we see the difficulty in trying to quantify considerations that we discussed under the heading "responsibility." Just because one person is not responsible alone, and just because others have a responsibility too, does not absolve anyone from responsibility. If we recognize that people have a positive right to certain benefits of society, there is a sense in which we thereby accept our part of that responsibility, no matter how minimal that may be.

We can argue that the obligation to provide such benefits belongs to the government, but, in this country, that is only an indirect way of taking care of the obligation ourselves. However, we can take up the responsibilities directly by providing job training or in-house medical care for employees. Indeed it may be that much of the enormity of the national problem could be reduced by such local and private initiatives. Groups or individuals can willingly contribute talent and time to see that such services are provided efficiently and well. But what we cannot do, though such is the temptation, is deny such rights to others while insisting on them for ourselves, or pretending that the responsibility for the realization of such rights lies wholly elsewhere, and not with ourselves at all.

B. ABUSES OF RIGHTS CLAIMS

Because rights claims are so powerful, overriding all but overwhelming considerations of general social well-being, they are also easily abused. We have become tediously used to people claiming their "rights," when what they are actually doing is claiming some special privilege or advantage for themselves. Thus, Jeremy Bentham, the classic utilitarian, dismissed all rights talk as "nonsense on stilts." Indeed, our emphasis on the ultimate importance of rights makes such abuse inevitable. Freedom rights are often invoked to justify the most perverse and abusive behavior; positive rights are sometimes claimed to gain the most extravagant compensations and benefits. For example, bitter ex-employees may stand on the right to free speech to libel and scandalize a former employer, while employers sometimes maintain their right to hire and fire as they choose as an excuse for violating the rights or interests of their employees. But, at the same time, no one wants to violate the rights of others; no employer wants to truly be guilty of violating the rights of employees, of consumers, or of the community. But when customers commonly sue corporations for what is in fact their own irresponsibility and incompetence, when communal pressure groups vow to punish or "tame" the giant corporations, how is a person to distinguish real rights claims from bogus ones? Here are some common abuses:

1. Not all rights claims, in fact very few, are absolute. A rights claim, even if justifiable in itself, must stand up to other rights claims and, at least sometimes, overwhelming cases of social well-being. The classic case of a person who defends yelling "fire!" in a crowded theater as an expression of "freedom of speech" may indeed have that right in general, but not in this case, because the overwhelming interests (as well as the right to life) of the other patrons take priority. A rights claim, even if justified in itself, is therefore not a "non-negotiable demand." All demands are negotiable, even those based on fundamental rights, for the question is always, "who else's rights are involved?" The concept of rights, like the concept of justice, depends on the general application to everyone, and the rights of one person must always be weighed against the rights of others.

2. Rights are not the same as expectations. Americans became so used to buying gasoline at 27¢ per gallon in the late 1960s that we came to think of this as a right rather than the lucky advantage of an epoch. Californians became so used to free university education that they came to think of this as their right, rather than the special benefit of living in a state that so far had a quickly expanding and extremely wealthy population and a highly enlightened view of itself and its possibilities. Corporate executives have gotten so used to expense account lunches that they now consider this to be a right, rather than a fringe bonus from the company and a loophole from the government. Consumers got so used to other people testing and making safe gadgets they used that perfect products came to be expected as a right rather than a rarity that had, through technology and testing, become surprisingly common. We may get spoiled by our advantages and confuse them for rights, or we may enjoy something for so many years that we come to believe that the world owes it to us. However, expectations in themselves, no matter how entrenched, do not constitute rights.

3. Privileges are not rights. Some states print on the bottom of a person's driver's license, "driving in this state is a privilege, not a right." Privileges are gifts,

of a sort, even if almost everyone enjoys them. They can be taken away if they are abused. One essential feature of "human" or "natural rights," we pointed out, is that they are said to be "inalienable"; they cannot be taken away, and they cannot be given up, even under coercion. Privileges, however, are tentative rewards; they can be taken away and they can (and sometimes must) be given up; for example, one person's right to a job may interfere with another person's right to equal opportunity. Most employee benefits are company privileges, not rights. They must be earned and deserved continuously, and they are not matters of right at all.

4. Might is not right. The oldest abuse is the insistence that because we *can* do something we have a right to do it. In other words, "might makes right." But the essential importance of rights is precisely the fact that having rights protects a person (or an institution, even a nation) from being coerced or abused by others more powerful. Because most businesses can sometimes price gouge the consumer, we insist that consumers have rights; because virtually every employee of almost any company is somewhat vulnerable to the power of the company, we insist that employees have rights. Of course, protecting rights is always a problem, because, by the nature of the case, rights claims are usually claims of the weaker against the stronger. That is why it is so important to incorporate all essential rights in law, which then has the power to protect the weak against even the strongest opponent. Might does not make right, but it is essential to society that right has might. Otherwise, there is the danger that rights claims, no matter how obviously justifiable, will be impotent protests against injustices that cannot be prevented.

5. Not all rights are legal rights. As important as it is to embody rights in law, for their own protection, not all rights are so embodied and not all laws in fact protect rights. In an ideal society, perhaps, rights and laws would exactly coincide. (But then, in an ideal society, people would probably not need laws or rights claims either.) Bogus rights claims are sometimes founded on laws, for example, in states that still rely on antiquated constitutions that define rights no longer tolerable or intelligible. This means that judgments about the justifiability of rights claims cannot simply rest on an appeal to the law (though objecting to a bogus rights claim that is protected by law tends to be involved and time consuming). Furthermore, there are bound to be rights claims antecedent to law. For example, until a few years ago, no laws concerned ownership of the heavens. Now, with the exploration of space, there will soon be claims and, subsequently, laws. A current example in some big cities is the claim to air and sun rights, as skyscrapers turn what was once taken for granted into a sought-after rarity. Laws are made as a response to rights claims (real or anticipated). A basic right, such as the right to work, nevertheless has to be constantly redefined in terms of new conditions and new laws. In rights, as in ethical issues in general, there is no easy appeal to principles of law. The law can be confused and incomplete. On occasion the law can even be unjust. Concern for rights ultimately concerns other people and their well-being, and it is on this uncertain ground that even rights claims have to be negotiated.

C. THEORIES OF RIGHTS

Where do rights come from? Some rights, such as contractual rights, are created in our agreements and our promises. When I sign a contract agreeing to pay you ten thousand dollars for painting my house, I thereby incur the obligation to pay you that money and give you the right to it, if you do the job. Other rights are created by law; the right to vote in national elections, for instance, is a legal right. But a more difficult question concerns the origin of "natural" or "human" rights, which are not created by individual agreement or by law. What helps determine this critical question is also the extent to which such rights are indeed to be literally extended to all human beings, or whether they are simply claims that are valid in one place but not in another.

Two theories of rights have dominated our thinking about social justice and the nature of citizenship in a society. One, defended in the past few centuries by such diverse thinkers as John Locke, Jean Jacques Rousseau, Thomas Hobbes, and John Rawls is a "social contract" theory; in other words, it is the attempt to explain even natural and human rights as a kind of contractual right. In this theory, the primary unit of society is the individual; and it presupposes that individuals existed before societies, individuals who agreed to enter into society and could decide—can still decide—to break away from it. This theory speculates that society originates in an agreement entered into by all its members (or, more accurately, it is agreed upon by them as the condition for their entering into society). In this agreement, everyone accepts certain mutual advantages and disadvantages and gives up certain freedoms in return for certain guarantees. Foremost among these guarantees are *rights.* I give up my "freedom" to kill you, for example, and in return I get the right to life, the right not to be killed myself. We both agree to be bound by the contracts we make, and so have the right to make certain demands in return for the obligation to respect other people's similar rights. The "contract" is in fact a metaphor, but it is an important image representing what many theorists take to be the core of concern for rights, the *mutual respect* for one another without which all promises, rights, and obligations would be only so many inconveniences. And indeed, everyone born into or entering such a society would automatically be assumed to enter into a similar agreement, to respect the rights of others in return for respect of his or her own rights. Rights are thus, according to this theory, a matter of mutual agreement.

Why do we accept such an agreement, except when it is to our advantage? We accept the general agreement because we do not know what may befall us in the future. We do not know when we ourselves might become unpopular, or if our religion might become generally disdained, or our beliefs considered subversive, or our lives in jeopardy. We do not know when our jobs could be taken away or if or when we might lose our ability to care for ourselves or educate our children. We might defend the social contract, therefore, on straightforward grounds of *prudence,* and, indeed, this is its most common historical defense. But we could also suggest that another motive is operating here besides long-term

Rights and Utility: John Stuart Mill ——

To have a right, then, is, I conceive, to have something which society ought to defend me in the possession of. If the objector goes on to ask why it ought, I can give him no other reason than general utility. If that expression does not seem to convey a sufficient feeling of the strength of the obligation, or to account for the peculiar energy of the feeling, it is because there goes to the composition of the sentiment, not a rational only but also an animal element—the thirst for retaliation; and this thirst derives its intensity, as well as its moral justification, from the extraordinarily important and impressive kind of utility which is concerned. The interest involved is that of security, to everyone's feelings the most vital of all interests. All other earthly benefits are needed by one person, not needed by another; and many of them can, if necessary, be cheerfully foregone or replaced by something else; but security no human being can possibly do without; on it we depend for all our immunity from evil and for the whole value of all and every good, beyond the passing moment, since nothing but the gratification of the instant could be of any worth to us if we could be deprived of everything the next instant by whoever was momentarily stronger than ourselves.

From Utilitarianism

self-interest—the genuine interest in others' well-being. Contracts, after all, are matters of *mutual* benefit, and we can be moved in part by others' benefits as well as our own.

The second theory has much older origins than the first. Society, in the first theory, consists solely of a collection of individuals, and rights are nothing but contractual agreements among these individuals. The second theory takes society itself to be the primary unit, not created by any collection of individuals but rather prior to individuals both in its origins and in its character. Individuals become what they are by being in a certain society. Individual rights, therefore, are what they are because a person is a citizen of a certain society. In this second theory, rights become more akin to privileges, even if, by the nature of certain societies, it is guaranteed that they will not be taken away except under extreme provocation or emergency.

Moreover, every society recognizes such provocations and emergencies (violent crimes, acts of war or "of God") and so recognizes *its* right to take away or override the rights of its citizens. In the first theory, "emergency provisions" also would be considered part of our mutual agreement; in the second theory, this rather represents the essential nature of rights—society gives them and society can take them away. But it is important to emphasize that the latter theory, though

---

Rights: Hegel ——

The crucial point in the generally accepted definition of right is "the restriction which makes it possible for my freedom to coexist with the freedom of others." On the one hand, this definition is only negative. On the other hand the positive factor—the so-called law of reason—is a familiar notion of abstract identity [that is, that we are all ultimately one]. But the definition we have just quoted, which has been especially popular since Rousseau, takes what is fundamental to be the individual, not the general community. The phenomena this has produced both in men's heads and in the world are frightful.

It is only because right is the embodiment of the absolute concept [that is, our sense of the whole of humanity] that it is something sacrosanct.

From The Philosophy of Right

---

it quite obviously lends itself to abuses not so easily defended in the first, is not intrinsically a "totalitarian" theory or anything of the sort. We can enjoy just as many rights just as securely with the understanding that they are contingent privileges granted by society as we can with the understanding that rights are a matter of mutual agreement.

A third theory, more difficult to expound and equally difficult to prove, is at least as powerful and influential as the two theories preceding. Often it is presented as religious doctrine. It is the theory that rights are created neither by mutual agreement nor by grant from society but rather rights are given by God, not just to the participants in this agreement or to the members of this society but to every human being everywhere, and in whatever circumstances, automatically. The God-given rights theory has one distinct advantage over the other two; it resolves in a stroke a critical problem of all rights theory, namely, how we are to apply our principles to other societies.

D.   THE PROBLEM OF RIGHTS IN INTERNATIONAL BUSINESS

We call rights "human" or "natural" because we believe they belong to all human beings. They are not products of special agreements and not peculiar to particular societies. Whether or not we ascribe this universality to God or human nature or simply to the logical extension of our own beliefs about human beings, our very talk about rights makes some rights basic and universal. Otherwise, we might argue, talk about rights is just a pretentious and misleading way of talking about mutual agreements and advantages or certain privileges granted by some societies to their members. If respect for rights is ultimately meaningful, it must be respect for rights of people everywhere, not just of colleagues and neighbors. But this is often more easily said than practiced.

Suppose slavery (or its near equivalent) is still a thriving practice in an "underdeveloped" country; what are the responsibilities of American business-people doing business there? First, they must respect the rights of everyone not to be a slave, however slavery is to be defined. But then, what if this is not to be an empty ethical gesture? Presumably, they must not use slave labor nor employ contractors who in turn will use slave labor. But the question becomes more diffi-cult because taking advantage of virtually any of the resources of the country will, at least indirectly, involve dependency upon and, therefore, encouragement of the institution of slavery. Should they then abstain from taking *any* advantage of the country by leaving and abandoning all interests there? Or is even this a backward means of support for slavery, if only by leaving it untouched? This was the dilemma, in only slightly muted terms, facing American companies involved in South African industries. Any involvement whatever, under then current con-ditions, involved encouraging if not actually participating in **apartheid,** a racial policy that often lacked even the generosities and few mutual benefits of outright slavery. On the other hand, pulling out of South Africa would have amounted to giving up any position of authority or political power within which enormous effects on the future of those policies might have been possible. At the same time, leaving would have opened the field to other opportunists who might have had much less concern for rights than we do. Apartheid as a formal policy may soon be a thing of the past in South Africa, but its legacy remains. Although they can vote, South African blacks, who make up eighty percent of the population, still have restricted power and limited opportunities. And while the probabilities of a civil war have been somewhat defused, the violence continues, now often between black groups. The problem of whether to do business with South Africa has, accordingly, been somewhat diffused as well, for it is no longer so obviously an "outlaw" regime in violation of the most basic human rights. But the injustice continues, and so international companies must still think of South Africa in the same problematic moral terms that they must view a great many other parts of the world. What is it to be in business in another country? Is it an arrangement that works for the mutual benefit of both the business and the citizens of that other country? Or does it benefit the business and only a few well-placed individuals, perhaps officials? Does it mitigate the injustices to be found in that country or does it aggravate them and make them worse? Indeed, these are the same ques-tions we ask of business in our own country, but where foreign customs and stan-dards of living are so very different from ours, the questions become all the more complicated.

If Americans enter into business with another country where cheap labor offers remarkable advantages but violates our idea of a fair minimum wage—not to mention the conflict of interests with industries and their employees in the same field back home—does our sense of fairness and rights demand that we pay workers abroad what *we* feel they require, rather than the going rate? This raises another problem in that we could totally overthrow the local culture, as people lined up to produce radios and no one chose to continue farming or shop keeping. (The same problem, of course, arises in cases here at home.) In the early days of the auto industry, Henry Ford found that paying his workers a considerably higher wage than the going rate enormously boosted both the quality of work and the reputation of the company. Could similar policies work on an international scale? Do we have the right to take advantage of foreign workers in a way that we would consider unconscionable regarding our own? If we believe that the right to work is a natural right, do we have an obligation to try to add jobs in other countries where we are involved?

This brings us to an extremely important, difficult, and timely topic: the cross-cultural application of ethical standards of business, with particular reference to transnational and global firms. In light of the recent North American Free Trade Agreement, which effectively opens the borders between the United States, Canada, and Mexico, no one needs to be convinced of the urgency of this topic, or of the enormous difficulties it presents to the ethicist or to the international businessperson. Particularly with reference to the United States and Mexico, the problems of fair as well as free trade are a matter of considerable controversy. The two nations have very different standards of living and, consequently, very different expectations. Unemployment in the United States is a serious problem, but the number of unemployed in Mexico, many of whom would like to come to the United States for work, is devastating. That makes the open-border argument extremely problematic.

As difficult as questions of justice and fairness may be at the national level, they are even more difficult at the international level. It is one thing to issue the challenge to train and provide possibilities for millions of unemployed and underemployed American workers. But when we open up the question of training and employment opportunity to the global market and ask the same question of tens or hundreds of millions of workers, what are we to do? How do you extend what is already a serious challenge to a world that is filled with cruel dictatorships, civil wars, starving millions, and more millions of homeless refugees? Indeed, a more modest question is how does one act when one sets up shop there? What are the constraints on international business, and what are the rights of individuals that must be respected and cannot be denied?

In any discussion of the cross-cultural application of ethical standards of business to transnational and global firms, be they academic, anthropological, or practical, what hovers is a specter of deep uncertainty, namely, whether or not there can, in all cases, be some singular set of cross-cultural standards for business practices. It has often been said and it is transparently obvious in the international business world that what is considered just and right in one society may be considered merely optional or even unjust and evil in another. American and Australian corporations getting organized in Indonesia find that the local system of family obligations wreaks havoc on their efforts to recruit on the basis of skill and merit, and firms trying to get a foothold in Japan find themselves forced to take a crash course in the culture before they can even get in the door.

With the current emphasis on "multiculturalism"—for the most part benign despite some segregationist and mutually antagonistic tendencies—it is often correctly said that what we call "morality" is in fact a local concept, not, as Kant famously argued, a matter of "universal and necessary" concern. Across generations and moving from one part of a culture (or subculture) to another, we will find deep differences, not just on particular issues (abortion, welfare, the legitimacy of violence in self-defense), but, in the very conception of "practical reason" upon which we depend to justify our views and resolve our differences. Moving from culture to culture, from West to East or North to South, the difference in customs and values, perhaps even moral values, may be quite different and even incommensurable. Given the differences in circumstances between cultures and nation-states, such as abysmal gaps between living standards, deep disagreements about politics and the nature of society, and the autonomy of the individual versus the legitimacy of authority, it is doubtful whether one and the same set of standards could possibly apply everywhere.

It is in this difficult global context that Tom Donaldson, in his pioneering study *The Ethics of International Business,* attempted to provide a positive answer to the nagging question of cross-cultural ethical standards in international business. Donaldson argues an "ethical algorithm," a decision procedure, for resolving cross-cultural disagreements. He distinguishes two types of conflicts and, accordingly, gives us two alternative sets of suggestions about how to

---

Hard-Headed Reasoning ———

As I have made evident over the years, I am committed to a liberal immigration policy. That [position is based], I think, on hard-headed economic grounds. As Germany, France, Switzerland, and other countries have come to rely on a large number of immigrant workers, or, as they are known in Germany and elsewhere, guest workers, so we must rely for a wide variety of effort on willing and committed workers from our neighboring countries. And beyond that we need the inflow of educated and otherwise highly qualified talent that other countries can provide.

"We all look back with favor on our past immigration policies and what they have done for us. It is deeply inconsistent that we think the future to be different and, indeed, anomalous. Why is it that what contributed so much in the past should be so questioned in the present?

—John Kenneth Galbraith

Dynamic Contribution ———

The major economic effect of immigration is to provide a steady stream of fresh human resources to the economy. Provided immigrants are attracted by the opportunities of the American economy rather than by the welfare provided by the American polity, they contribute greatly to the vitality of the economy. They are highly motivated, willing to work and venture, and bring in fresh insights. Immigrants have made a disproportionate contribution to dynamism of the economy because of these characteristics ever since our forefathers first landed in the New World.

—Milton Friedman

resolve intercultural disputes in which we are the more powerful partner. The two types divide on the basis of the question whether the issue is one of "level of economic development." Where this is the issue, the question is whether people at home would permit the practice being considered were they in a similar economic situation. Where this is not the issue, the question is whether (a) it is possible to conduct business successfully without the practice in question and (b) whether the practice violates a "fundamental international right." It is (b), of course, that raises the most intractable moral questions. The nature of rights demands that we should not violate such rights, but do we always know what they are, or even whether there are any?

It is possible to distinguish four more or less distinct "stances" toward conflict and conflict resolution in the international business and ethical scene:

1. The absolute stance (The "moral" position. Any alternative position is intolerable.)

2. The hypothetical stance (The empathic approach: "What if you were in their position?")

3. The procedural approach (No substantive principles, but a fair process for resolving disputes.)

4. Local agreement (No substantive principles and no systematic procedure, just consensus, preferably through negotiation, by the two or more parties concerned.)

The strong preference of most moral philosophers and religious thinkers would seem to be the first alternative, the absolute stance. It includes the language of "fundamental international rights." But it is this strong moral stance that the international business and ethical scene calls into question. The second stance openly recognizes the differences between one's own situation and those of the other people and attempts to understand this difference and the possible justification for an ethical position other than one's own. One problem is the necessity of some form of empathy through which one can "put oneself in the other's place," although this may not always be possible. The third stance has become the standard ground of social philosophy since John Rawls' *Theory of Justice* (it is also the basic stance of most modern democracies), but only a few writers in business ethics seem content with a wholly procedural justification of business practices. Most established procedures, after all, tend to favor the status quo, and in cases of severe economic inequality such as we find in the realm of international business, it is the status quo that is called into question. It is for this reason that philosophers and social critics often turn to utilitarianism—or at the other extreme, libertarianism—to provide some substantial as well as merely procedural principles appropriate to the absolute stance. But if substantial as well as procedural principles and the very notion of fairness are culture-bound, then the only solution to cross-cultural conflicts, short of force, would be some attempt at local agreement, compromise, and accommodation. Needless to say, few business ethicists find this satisfactory. Indeed, perhaps, even this is too optimistic a strategy, assuming as it does that negotiation and what is often called "reasonable behavior" can be assumed in all cultures. But anyone who has ever been to a business meeting in which harmony rather than frankness is expected, to take a fairly mild example, recognizes the enormity of that assumption. And where religious beliefs or violations of the sacred are involved, as in the recent exploitation of ancient Indian or Aboriginal holy grounds for mining, there is very good reason to doubt the possibility or appropriateness of negotiation or "reasonable" compromise. Where this leaves us, I am not prepared to say, except that it seems that any attempt at a systematic cross-cultural conflict resolution strategy is possibly a mistake. But this is not to say that we are therefore left in a state of potential anarchy or conceptual incommensurability. It is always an open question what can be achieved through negotiation, compromise, and mutual understanding, and the first rule of international business should be that the question be left open and mutual understanding as well as mutual profits remain one of the goals of international business.

It is important to ask, "If I were in this position, what would I do?" But if the position in question is squalor and poverty, it is very difficult to know what one would do. "Would I, if I were so poor, be willing to permit this practice, for example, allowing toxic wastes to be buried in my land?" How would one know? How would one consider the nature of risk, a notoriously culture-relative concept?* And if to this are added the considerable cultural and religious differences that are typically involved, the question of empathy employed becomes virtual nonsense. "What if you, a healthy, educated, middle-class, Protestant, male American business executive with a high-paying, high-power job in a (relatively)

---

*Douglas, M. and B. Wildofsy, *Risk and Culture* (Basic Books, 1989).

When in Jakarta . . . ⸻

You have just opened an automobile dealership in Indonesia, where the practice of paying off officials is commonplace. These pay-offs are typically given as "gifts," and although no one ever actually demands money and no amounts are ever stated, there is a general understanding of their necessity and size. Legally, such pay-offs are not allowed. But they are so widespread and accepted that they amount to a general tax, more or less evenly distributed among businesses. Businesses that do not pay are not subject to violence or harrassment but do nevertheless suffer from the absence of certain basic civic services. Apart from the cost and inconvenience to your business, what are the arguments against such pervasive corruption when, in fact, it is the established practice of the country in question, often dating back centuries to feudal times?

A Fair Day's Pay ⸻

You have been put in charge of a mining operation in Southeast Asia, where the average wage is less than a dollar a day and there is massive unemployment. You are paying your workers two dollars a day. The mine soon proves to be extremely profitable. A delegation of local workers comes into your office and requests a substantial raise in pay, arguing that the minimum wage in the United States is several times more than this. What do you decide to do, and how do you justify your decision?

violence-free city were instead an emphysemic, illiterate, unskilled, pregnant Muslim female in a grossly over-populated city with continual random violence and virtually no employment opportunities?" What could be the meaning of such a question? This is why, perhaps, Donaldson prudently limits his first type of conflict to matters of economic development (as if economic development could be so neatly separated from all other aspects of social and political life). But what this suggests is that the hypothetical approach too is of only limited application, and whatever one wants to say about the possibility of *understanding* the world-view of another people and reconciling our differences and interests, that understanding and reconciliation is not going to succeed by way of an unexamined and extremely problematic notion of empathy. In sufficiently different and desperate circumstances, who knows what we might allow?

In his discussion of the ethics of international business, Donaldson takes the recognition and respect for human rights as primary. In one sense, it is impossible to deny this. To say that people have certain rights is to insist that we find it intolerable to treat them in certain ways. But this emphasis on rights may be problematic, not only because the American focus on rights has become obsessive, to the exclusion of much else in ethics, but also because it is not at all clear that the concept of rights—even in the guise of "human rights"—can serve the purpose intended in the international domain. The concept of rights, at least as it is employed in the amendments to the United States Constitution, is a rather modern concept, which has been rightly argued by many anthropologists and Eastern philosophers to be an extremely ethnocentric concept as well. (This does not mean, of course, that the concept of rights is illegitimate.) In any case, however grandly we and the United Nations might declare our faith in human rights, the fact is that the recognition of such rights is so sufficiently limited in the world that, apart from the whims and sanctions of American foreign aid, it may give us a too limited basis for international business ethics. When Donaldson chooses as one of his criteria the recognition and respect of "fundamental international rights," it is not at all obvious whether we are recognizing the rights of others or projecting an ethnocentric conception of rights onto other people. That may well be a conscionable criterion for proceeding in business—but it does not solve the cross-cultural conflict question at hand. There is always the danger of "ethical imperialism," imposing one's values on others by force, which would include economic coercion.

In our "pluralist," multi-cultural society, it should be clear that most of these international cross-cultural problems are to be found here at home as well. The question of whether we would encourage certain policies or treat workers and the environment fairly and with respect is just as much a question when we are dealing with other states and other communities as with other countries. Indeed, the

---

When an American buys a Pontiac Le Mans from General Motors . . . he or she engages unwittingly in an international transaction. Of the $20,000 paid to GM, about $6,000 goes to South Korea for routine labor and assembly operations, $3,500 to Japan for advanced components (engines, transaxles, and electronics), $1,500 to West Germany for styling and design components, $800 to Taiwan, Singapore, and Japan for small components, $500 to Britain for advertising and marketing services, and about $100 to Ireland and Barbados for data processing. The rest—less than $8,000—goes to strategists in Detroit, lawyers and bankers in New York, lobbyists in Washington, insurance and health-care workers all over the country, and General Motors shareholders—most of whom live in the United States, but an increasing number of whom are foreign nationals.

—From *The Work of Nations,* by Robert B. Reich

The Ten American Companies With the Largest Overseas Business in 1991 ——

1)	Boeing	$11,021,000,000
2)	General Motors	10,185,000,000
3)	Ford Motor	8,602,000,000
4)	General Electric	7,268,000,000
5)	IBM	5,476,000,000
6)	Du Pont	4,844,000,000
7)	Chrysler	4,649,000,000
8)	United Technologies	3,307,000,000
9)	Caterpillar	3,291,000,000
10)	McDonnell Douglas	2,896,000,000

Source: *1991 Top Ten Almanac*
(Workman Publishing)

prudential argument almost always is persuasive—that we do not foul our own nest. That has nothing to do with justice or rights; that is simply the basis of common sense. But whether or not we foul *other people's nests* is no longer a matter of prudence but a matter of their rights and our obligations. How we act and whether we recognize those rights and obligations is the continuous test of our own moral character and humanity, and so the main subject of business ethics as well.

■ SUMMARY AND CONCLUSION

A right is a legitimate claim that a person can make against others, even against the whole of society. A contractual right, for instance, is a claim that one person can make against another, by virtue of a contract. A person has rights as an employee and rights as a citizen of a country; every human being has "human" or "natural" rights, no matter what his or her job, status, or citizenship. "Human" or "natural" rights are sometimes said to be inalienable—they cannot be taken away under any circumstances. Many of our most familiar rights are "freedom" rights, such as the right to freedom of speech, freedom of worship, and freedom of the press. These rights allow us to demand that we not be interfered with by the government, by institutions, or by other citizens. Positive rights pertain to certain goods that society can provide; the right to a decent job, to adequate health care, and to education are among these. In our society, it is generally understood that every person has the right to make contracts, to enter into business, and to make a profit. What is not clear is the limits of these business rights, and whether they should be allowed to conflict with other rights and other concerns, such as the public good. In international business these questions become even more complicated, for it is not clear to what extent this language of rights continues to apply.

■ STUDY QUESTIONS

1. How can a person prove that he has a right to do something? Suppose a friend (or ex-friend) of yours were to claim a right to take your automobile as his own. What sorts of reasons could he plausibly give to convince you of that right? What sorts of counterclaims would you make back to him?

2. Under what circumstances can a contractual right be overriden? Suppose I promised to purchase a minimum of 20,000 widgets from your factory this year. What kinds of considerations would lead you to let me out of our agreement? What kinds of arguments could I use to *force* you to drop the agreement?

3. Do you always have a right to something just because you have a *legal* right to it, that is, because it is yours by law?

4. Original ownership of a property is an overwhelming reason for someone to claim a right to it, under many legal traditions. What problems are there with this "original ownership" consideration?

5. Suppose an elderly recluse refuses to sell her land, on which she and her family have lived for generations, to a development project that would be overwhelmingly good for virtually everybody else in the community. Should a single person have the right to "stand in the way of progress" (assuming, for the sake of the question, that it *is* progress)?

6. Under what circumstances would a consumer *not* have the right to know the ingredients or the effects of a product?

7. An artist, in desperation, sells one of her works for a mere hundred dollars, enough to buy a meal and pay the rent for the week. Five years later, that same work is sold at an auction for $125,000. Should the artist be entitled to some share of those profits? Explain your answer.

8. You are the chief negotiator for your company overseas, and, by the way, you are also a woman. The possibility of a deal comes up in a Middle Eastern country, but when you arrive you are informed that the parties interested in doing business are not willing to deal with a woman. What do you do?

9. An extremely valuable mineral site is discovered on the sacred land of a local tribe, which they now own by treaty. What are the procedures and constraints that should be followed in negotiating the possibility of mining that site with the tribe? How should you proceed?

10. The laws concerning occupational safety precautions are much weaker in a small African country than they are in your own, and the sense of risk—what is considered a reasonable threat to life and limb on the job—among the local workers is considerably more tolerant than you are used to at home. Should your enforcement of safety regulations in the plant you are building in that country be made as strict as they would be if the plant were being built in your home town in the United States? Or is considerable laxity allowable because of local laws and expectations? Explain your answer.

■ FOR CLASS DISCUSSION

Enforcing Civil Rights

Consider the following survey conducted by *Business and Society Review* (#13): Assume that you are president of a firm that provides a substantial portion of the market of one of your suppliers. You find out that this supplier discriminates illegally against minorities although no legal action has been taken. Assume further that this supplier gives you the best price for the material you require, but that the field is competitive.

Do you feel that it is proper to use your economic power over this supplier to make him stop discriminating?

Responses:

Yes, 17 (33%). No, 34 (67%).

Comments:

"It would be in order to bring this matter to the attention of the supplier. It would be improper to use this economic power to bring about the correction of this error. There are other means more appropriate to correct the situation. Two wrongs do not make a right."

"The use of economic power to coerce the supplier to cease employment discrimination would be essentially a reprisal tactic and an unwarranted intrusion into the internal affairs of another company. This kind of leverage amounts to a dictatorial effort to enforce a moral judgment upon a business relationship and ultimately weakens the basic principle of equal rights."

"A company has a responsibility to its customers, employees, and stockholders to use reliable suppliers. The improper conduct of a supplier, if that is known, must, of course, be considered in a final decision concerning the future of the relationship. However, enforcement of society's laws in instances such as that described is the responsibility of regulatory agencies under the constitutional guarantee of 'due process.' Economic power should not be used to circumvent the Constitution or none of us will have anything left. We routinely make all of our suppliers aware of our affirmative-action employment policies."

"I feel it is improper to do business with any firm known to be violating the law."

"No—this action is coercive and illegal."

"No—not without legal proof that the supplier is breaking the law—otherwise we would be acting as judge and jury." (Two people gave this answer.)

"Yes—you not only are entitled to but *should* inquire to be sure suppliers are complying with the law."

"No—the enforcement of the law is for civil authorities. It should not be enforced by economic power plays."

How would you answer, and why?

THE UNITED NATIONS HUMAN RIGHTS DECLARATION (1948)

Whereas disregard and contempt for human rights have resulted in barbarous acts which have outraged the conscience of mankind, and the advent of a world in which human beings shall enjoy freedom of speech and belief and freedom from fear and want has been proclaimed as the highest aspiration of the common people.

Whereas it is essential, if man is not to be compelled to have recourse, as a last resort, to rebellion against tyranny and oppression, that human rights should be protected by the rule of law.

Whereas it is essential to promote the development of friendly relations between nations.

Whereas the peoples of the United Nations have in the Charter reaffirmed their faith in fundamental human rights, in the dignity and worth of the human person and in the equal rights of men and women and have determined to promote social progress and better standards of life in larger freedom.

Whereas Member States have pledged themselves to achieve, in cooperation with the United Nations, the promotion of universal respect for and observance of human rights and fundamental freedoms,

Whereas a common understanding of these rights and freedoms is of the greatest importance for the full realization of this pledge,

Now, Therefore The General Assembly *proclaims*

This Universal Declaration of Human Rights as a common standard of achievement for all peoples and all nations, to the end that every individual and every organ of society, keeping this Declaration constantly in mind, shall strive by teaching and education to promote respect for these rights and freedoms and by progressive measures, national and international, to secure their universal and effective recognition and observance, both among the peoples of Member States themselves and among the peoples of territories under their jurisdiction.

Article 1   All human beings are born free and equal in dignity and rights. They are endowed with reason and conscience and should act towards one another in a spirit of brotherhood.

Article 2   Everyone is entitled to all the rights and freedoms set forth in this Declaration, without distinction of any kind, such as race, colour, sex, language, religion, political or other opinion, national or social origin, property, birth or other status. Furthermore, no distinction shall be made on the basis of the political, jurisdictional or international status of the country or territory to which a person belongs, whether it be independent, trust, non-self-governing or under any other limitation of sovereignty.

Article 3   Everyone has the right to life, liberty and security of person.

Article 4   No one shall be held in slavery or servitude; slavery and the slave trade shall be prohibited in all their forms.

Article 5   No one shall be subjected to torture or to cruel, inhuman or degrading treatment or punishment.

Article 6   Everyone has the right to recognition everywhere as a person before the law.

Article 7   All are equal before the law and are entitled without any discrimination to equal protection of the law. All are entitled to equal protection against any discrimination in violation of this Declaration and against any incitement to such discrimination.

Article 8   Everyone has the right to an effective remedy by the competent national tribunals for acts violating the fundamental rights granted him by the constitution or by law.

Article 9   No one shall be subjected to arbitrary arrest, detention or exile.

Article 10   Everyone is entitled in full equality to a fair and public hearing by an independent and impartial tribunal, in the determination of his rights and obligations and of any criminal charge against him.

Article 11   1. Everyone charged with a penal offence has the right to be presumed innocent until proved guilty according to law in a public trial at which he has had all the guarantees necessary for his defence. 2. No one shall be held guilty of any penal offence on account of any act or omission which did not constitute a penal offence, under national or international law, at the time when it was committed. Nor shall a heavier penalty be imposed than the one that was applicable at the time the penal offence was committed.

Article 12   No one shall be subjected to arbitrary interference with his privacy, family, home or correspondence, nor to attacks upon his honour and reputation. Everyone has the right to the protection of the law against such interference or attacks.

Article 13   1. Everyone has the right to freedom of movement and residence within the borders of each state. 2. Everyone has the right to leave any country, including his own, and to return to his country.

Article 14   1. Everyone has the right to seek and to enjoy in other countries asylum from persecution. 2. This right may not be invoked in the case of prosecutions genuinely arising from non-political crimes or from acts contrary to the purposes and principles of the United Nations.

Article 15   1. Everyone has the right to a nationality. 2. No one shall be arbitrarily deprived of his nationality nor denied the right to change his nationality.

Article 16   1. Men and women of full age, without any limitation due to race, nationality or religion, have the right to marry and to found a family. They are entitled to equal rights as to marriage, during marriage and at its dissolution. 2. Marriage shall be entered into only with the free and full consent of the intending spouses. 3. The family is the natural and fundamental group unit of society and is entitled to protection by society and the State.

Article 17   1. Everyone has the right to own property alone as well as in association with others. 2. No one shall be arbitrarily deprived of his property.

Article 18   Everyone has the right to freedom of thought, conscience and religion; this right includes freedom to change his religion or belief, and freedom, either alone or in community with others and in public or private, to manifest his religion or belief in teaching, practice, worship and observance.

Article 19   Everyone has the right to freedom of opinion and expression; this right includes freedom to hold opinions without interference and to seek, receive and impart information and ideas through any media and regardless of frontiers.

Article 20   1. Everyone has the right to freedom of peaceful assembly and association. 2. No one may be compelled to belong to an association.

Article 21   1. Everyone has the right to take part in the government of his country, directly or through freely chosen representatives. 2. Everyone has the right of equal access to public service in his country. 3. The will of the people shall be the basis of the authority of government; this will shall be expressed in periodic and genuine elections which shall be by universal and equal suffrage and shall be held by secret vote or by equivalent free voting procedures.

Article 22   Everyone, as a member of society, has the right to social security and is entitled to realization through national effort and international cooperation and in accordance with the organization and resources of each State, of the economic, social and cultural rights indispensable for his dignity and the free development of his personality.

Article 23   1. Everyone has the right to work, to free choice of employment, to just and favourable conditions of work and to protection against unemployment. 2. Everyone, without any discrimination, has the right to equal pay for equal work. 3. Everyone who works has the right to just and favourable remuneration ensuring for himself and his family an existence worthy of human dignity, and supplemented, if necessary, by other means of social protection. 4. Everyone has the right to form and to join trade unions for the protection of his interests.

Article 24   Everyone has the right to rest and leisure, including reasonable limitation of working hours and periodic holidays with pay.

Article 25   1. Everyone has the right to a standard of living adequate for the health and well-being of himself and of his family, including food, clothing, housing and medical care and necessary social services, and the right to security in the event of unemployment, sickness, disability, widowhood, old age or other lack of livelihood in circumstances beyond his control. 2. Motherhood and childhood are entitled to special care and assistance. All children, whether born in or out of wedlock, shall enjoy the same social protection.

Article 26   1. Everyone has the right to education. Education shall be free, at least in the elementary and fundamental stages. Elementary education shall be compulsory. Technical and professional education shall be made generally available and higher education shall be equally accessible to all on the basis of merit. 2. Education shall be directed to the full development of the human personality and to the strengthening of respect for human rights and fundamental freedoms. It shall promote understanding, tolerance and friendship among all nations, racial or religious groups, and shall further the activities of the United Nations for the maintenance of peace. 3. Parents have a prior right to choose the kind of education that shall be given to their children.

Article 27   1. Everyone has the right freely to participate in the culture life of the community, to enjoy the arts and to share in scientific advancement and its benefits. 2. Everyone has the right to the protection of the moral and material interests resulting from any scientific, literary or artistic production of which he is the author.

Article 28   Everyone is entitled to a social and international order in which the rights and freedoms set forth in this Declaration can be fully realized.

Article 29   1. Everyone has duties to the community in which alone the free and full development of his personality is possible. 2. In the exercise of his rights and freedoms, everyone shall be subject only to such limitations as are determined by law solely for the purpose of securing due recognition and respect for the rights and freedoms of others and of meeting the just requirements of morality, public order and the general welfare in a democratic society. 3. These rights and freedoms may in no case be exercised contrary to the purposes and principles of the United Nations.

Article 30   Nothing in this Declaration may be interpreted as implying for any State, group or person any right to engage in any activity or to perform any act aimed at the destruction of any of the rights and freedoms set forth herein.

■ For Class Discussion

A Borderline Case

The Third World and the First World meet on Juárez Avenue, a strip of bars, restaurants, and curio shops catering to tourists who spill over the border from El Paso. For Americans who want to photograph, purchase, or eat a bit of Mexicana, Ciudad Juárez is a convenient sally. They drive in, soak up the ambience around the "mariarchi plaza," and go home.

But there is a permanent American presence in Ciudad Juárez, invisible to the sightseers though manifest to the city's inhabitants. To see it, one must take a frustrating drive through streets choked by traffic, bus fumes, and food vendors. On the outskirts of the city, in the barren Chihauhua desert, it rises like a gleaming mirage: row upon row of modern buildings and well-manicured lawns.

The buildings are *maquiladoras,* assembly plants run by foreign-based multinational corporations, most of which are headquartered in the United States. Juárez is home to about 125 foreign-owned factories that employ 45,000 people—a manufacturing nexus larger than Youngstown, Ohio, in its steel-producing heyday. Most of the *maquiladoras* operate within spanking new industrial parks, where security is tight and rent is cheap.

U.S. companies import American parts into Mexico, assemble the parts in *maquiladoras,* and export the products back to the United States. The finished goods are usually stamped, Assembled in Mexico of U.S. Material. A host of U.S. corporate giants—including General Electric, Zenith, RCA, and General Motors—as well as many smaller subcontractors have set up shop along the 2,000-mile Mexican frontier, dominating the economies of such cities as Juárez, Tijuana, and Mexicali.

Maquiladora managers prefer to hire teen-aged women, believing them to be more dexterous and tractable than men. Since electronics assembly must be done in a clean, temperature-controlled environment, the new factories are air-conditioned, to protect the parts, not the workers, from sweltering desert heat that can send the mercury to 114 degrees. Garment manufacturers do not have that concern, so many of their factories are scattered about Juárez in old, uncooled buildings.

The *maquiladoras* are a tremendous boon to the corporations. Labor costs generally run 20 to 25 per cent of what they would be in the United States; the work week is 25 per cent longer; the pace of work is faster, and Mexico's high unemployment rate disciplines the labor force. Richard Michel, who manages General Electric's seven *maquiladoras* in Mexico, boasts of a 2 per cent absentee rate in his factories, compared with 5 to 9 per cent in the United States. Productivity, he adds, is 10 to 15 per cent higher south of the Rio Grande.

Though *maquiladora* wages lag far behind those in the United States and represent a fraction of the workers' productive output, the pay is good by Mexican standards. However, border-zone wages are declining in real terms because of unfavorable exchange rates with the dollar. U.S. prices affect Mexican prices;

moreover, the workers spend between a third and half of their earnings on the U.S. side.

The *maquiladoras* run smoothly, but not because the interests of the workers are protected. Between 1971 and 1978, the government's Board of Arbitration issued 482 judgments involving *maquiladora* employees. Only fourteen were favorable to the workers.

Mexican law requires that senior workers be assured job security, but there are many ways for multinational corporations to get around the requirement. Employers can slash hours or shut the plant down for a period, thereby forcing the employees to seek work elsewhere. Companies have also been known to swap workers, eliminating accrued seniority in the process. High turnover is seen as a key to high productivity, and workers are pressured to leave when they reach their late twenties.

In choosing a Third World outpost, business executives consider three variables: labor costs, freedom of operations, and stability. Even before the Bracero Program ended, Mexico's border cities suffered unemployment rates of 30 to 40 per cent; wages, following the law of supply and demand, were accordingly low. The unemployment rate in the region remains at least 40 per cent [in 1984].

Runaway plants deprive U.S. workers of jobs, and the *maquiladora* competition drives down wages in the United States, particularly along the border, where there is a palpable threat that more shops will flee to Mexico.

The damage north of the border has not been offset by benefits to the south. Unemployment in Mexico's frontier area has not been reduced, and living conditions have remained, at best, unchanged.

James W. Russell, "A Borderline Case: Sweatshops Across the Rio Grande," from *The Progressive,* April 1984.

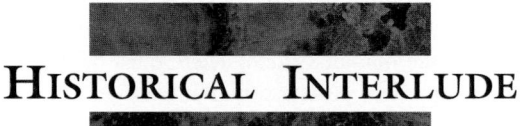

HISTORICAL INTERLUDE

JOHN KENNETH GALBRAITH

Taxes on unearned income and inheritance are good for the work ethic; over time they return the rich and their offspring to useful toil. It is one of the oddities of our time that we think the work ethic to be particularly ethical for those in the lower income brackets.
—J. K. Galbraith, New York Review of Books, Jan. 22, 1981

Since the Great Depression and the New Deal, one of the primary goals in American social and economic policy has been *security,* the establishment of a "safety net" for those who cannot survive on their own. This shift in emphasis from reward to security underscores the fact that justice and the macroethics of an economy as a whole are largely a matter of perspective, that is, a question of which ingredients of justice are given primacy. Adam Smith stressed the overall wealth of the nation; many modern economists stress freedom of choice. But the emphasis of the New Deal was on security and the *rights* of every individual to a decent standard of living. To be sure, this presupposes a high level of national prosperity to begin with, as well as sufficient "incentive" to get people to work. But what is most important in any economic policy, according to this New Deal, neo-Keynesian viewpoint, is social security.

John Kenneth Galbraith is the most elegant and best known spokesman for this ethical position today. He begins with the premise that American society today is already affluent, and that in an affluent society, safety net programs can easily be afforded. He also believes that the incentives in our society are adequate to get people to work and says of people who cry for more incentives, "Lurking behind the word incentive, we must never forget, is always the wish of someone for more income." The essence of his ethics is the emphasis on rights—the right of every person to a safe and clean environment, adequate health care, and equal opportunity to get a worthwhile job and a good education. He constantly reminds us that "conservative backlashes" are merely "the rediscovery that the rich don't want to pay taxes," and have the money to be very vocal about it, and that "despite the revolutionary jargon, the revolutions of the rich are much more easily contained than the riots of the poor and hungry."

Galbraith is wary of a market system so "free" that private affluence leads only to "public squalor," and the looming social problems of our society are ignored because they are not profitable. Where the market works, well and good; where it does not work, some other agency, most likely government, must step in. Balances (or "countervailing powers") are key here, between government regulation and the free dealings of the market, as well as between entrepreneurial critics of government intervention and excess and governmental authorities pointing to failures or injustice in the market system. There must be a balance between the private goods that people can purchase individually and those public comforts and conveniences that can only be developed and maintained through cooperation, such as parks, libraries, education, and safe streets to walk on. These are essential components of the good life in a business society, whether or not they are themselves products of or profitable to the business community. Through its high level of affluence, our society has reached the point where the imbalance between those goods we can consume individually and those we can enjoy only in cooperation with others has become glaring. As we become richer and own more cars, we need more and better roads and parking lots, and more traffic police. As we own more and fancier stereos and expensive electronic gadgetry, we need a more efficient police force to keep others from stealing them. As jobs become increasingly technical, businesses need a better-educated work force, and so society needs better public education.

According to Galbraith, our society can afford to provide these public goods now because it has solved the basic "problem of production." The problem of production is simply the basic question of how to produce enough food and goods to feed, clothe, and house the population, and it has always been the paramount problem in most societies. Our society has solved this problem, primarily through the incredible increases in technology of the last century or so. America has more than enough factories and farms and raw materials to fulfill the basic needs of everyone, and the problem is no longer one of production, it is a problem of distributive justice.

John Kenneth Galbraith is not so much an economic theorist in the tradition of Smith, Marx, or Keynes as he is an economist-social critic, a "gadfly" who enjoys puncturing the pretentions and bad arguments of those in power. Raised in poverty on a farm in northern Canada, he comments in his autobiography that he has ever since been "compulsively against any self-satisfied elite, . . . one never overlooked any righteous opportunity to oppose, or, if opportunity presented, to infuriate." Thus, he has made a career and many enemies challenging "the most pompously exchanged cliches of the corporate executive, the most confidently vacuous voices on military adventure and the most generally admired triteness on foreign policy." Indeed, Galbraith is equal in the ferocity of his attacks on the "too free market" and on government bureaucrats. In his concern for basic rights and the good life, he has learned to be skeptical of those in power who claim to defend the public interest but, in fact, are out for themselves.

The heart of Galbraith's criticisms of the free market system, which he inherits from Keynes, is simply the fact that it does not always work, particularly regarding such problems as poverty and unemployment. Consequently, he has become the foremost defender of government planning to balance out the inequalities of the market. In fact, he argues, government is already well entrenched in business, underwriting, through government-supported research, some of the largest business concerns, such as the airline manufacturers, and some of Galbraith's most scathing sarcasm is directed at those business leaders who cry for more government help for themselves (through reduced taxation or protection from foreign competition) but reject government efforts to regulate as a restriction on business freedom.

Galbraith is not so much against the free market system as he believes that much of what is believed about that system is a myth—a case in which "truths conflict with needed belief." On two crucial issues in particular, Galbraith argues, the classical picture of the free market system is simply wrong (whether or not it may have been correct in earlier times). First of all, the classic image of the independent entrepreneur, in competition with any number of other independent entrepreneurs, has been replaced by the monolithic corporation. Second, the classic ideal of consumer sovereignty has been replaced by mass market advertising and the *creation* of consumer desires.

Businesspeople still talk about the "profit motive," but profit seems to have very little to do with the motivation of most corporations or the people who work in them. What concerns the managers of most corporations is survival, and making (short-term) profits is but a means to keeping their jobs. But, contrasted with the classical picture of the entrepreneur, this makes most corporations highly risk adverse and very conservative, slow to innovate and quick to protect themselves. A large corporation like General Motors becomes a major bureaucracy run by management concerned with its own continuation. Not only the public, but profit too is sacrificed to the internal demands of the bureaucracy. Original ideas are discouraged and competition is eliminated wherever possible. The entrepreneur is replaced by the corporation, and the dynamics of the free enterprise system are replaced by the sluggishness of the institutional bureaucracy.

In part because of the dominance of conservative corporations, the classical flexibility of business in the face of changing demand is no longer possible. American car manufacturers found themselves tied into the equipment for large car manufacture, with seven-year lead times on new equipment for producing small cars, and they were unable to shift their production to small cars even when it became painfully evident that consumers wanted smaller cars. Many companies that make one product would find it very difficult, if not altogether impossible, to change to another product altogether. (Buggy whips were still manufactured many years after the automobile market was in full swing; those manufacturers were incapable of making anything else.) But this means that, for their own security, many corporations cannot depend upon consumer demand matching their products; they must create consumer demand for their products rather than take the chance that consumers will want what they cannot produce.

Consumer sovereignty, which in classical economics determines the market and makes sure that what is needed is produced, is no longer the force that controls production. There is little likelihood that the world would have demanded many of our contemporary hygiene products if corporate advertising campaigns had not convinced consumers of their necessity. And it is unlikely that consumer demand alone would dictate the desirability of a hundred different brands of breakfast cereal, unless advertising, not the product or the needs of the consumer, determined the market. These examples may be harmless in themselves, but what they suggest is the absence of the central feature that is supposed to make the free market work for the public good, namely, that the genuine needs and desires of the consumer determine the direction of business enterprise.

Galbraith's arguments do not undermine business as such, nor are they intended to. The point is rather to put business in its proper place in society, with government, consumers, and the public interest acting as "countervailing powers" against too powerful business interests. It is the pretense of business to always serve the general interest that Galbraith attacks, especially when such claims are couched in the language of the classic free enterprise system. There is no such system, Galbraith argues, and those who argue in its name are more likely furthering their own interests rather than the public interest.

– 12 –
Freedom and Power: Privacy and Pressures in the Workplace

It is by the goodness of God that in our country we have those three unspeakably precious things: Freedom of speech, freedom of conscience, and the prudence never to practice either of them.

—Mark Twain

Freedom is a magical word. In the name of "freedom" people sacrifice their lives in wars, quit well-paying jobs and otherwise happy marriages, or defend policies and programs of all kinds, even those which would seem to jeopardize freedom or cause considerable suffering. "Even the Nazis were for freedom," writes Frithjof Bergmann, underscoring his argument that the word freedom itself is not to be trusted. The question is rather, "What is freedom?" *Why* is it so good and desirable? Within the "free enterprise system," what does it mean for the individual to be free? Is freedom a means to the general well-being of society (in which case we want to know if it is indeed the best means to that end) or is it rather an end in itself, the basis of those *rights* (freedom rights) which everyone has and which demand respect even if they do not lead effectively to improved social well-being?

"Power," on the other hand, is something of a suspicious word. In our egalitarian society, power represents the superiority of one person over another, and, therefore, an apparent infringement of rights. We fully appreciate the importance, particularly in large organizations, of chains of command and authority, but, contradicting ourselves, we also believe in some ill-defined sense that no one ought to have authority over anyone else. Needless to say, this leads to considerable confusion and inefficiency, as well as much unnecessary resentment and apologetics.

Freedom and power present problems both within the corporation and within society about the corporation as a whole. They must be considered together. Even the largest corporations complain, particularly with regard to social issues, that they do not have the freedom and the power to carry out what is sometimes demanded of them. A single textile company, for example, rightly complains that it cannot solve its own pollution problems without going bankrupt unless the entire industry joins together and agrees, or is forced, to adopt similar policies. If one company takes the initiative, it thereby adds considerably to its costs and its prices and will soon go out of business because of the competition.

The logic of freedom and power in such large-scale examples is in fact much the same as the logic of freedom and power on a smaller, more personal scale. A single employee can complain, "What can I do alone?" But there is always a positive answer; we can always do *something,* though this may entail considerable risk. The question then becomes, for the large corporation as well as for the lone individual, *how much risk is reasonable?* At what point is action no longer freedom but foolishness? At what point are we no longer free or exercising power but rather giving in to *coercion,* being forced to comply in the face of threats?

A. Freedom

> There is but one task for us all—
> One life for each to give.
> What stands if Freedom fall?
> —Rudyard Kipling, "For All We Have and Are"

One of the preconditions of the good life, at least for us, is *freedom.* Indeed, without freedom, the very idea of success in business would be unintelligible; in fact, life in the business world, as we know it, would be impossible. Business requires "free" enterprise, free, that is, from total government control, free to buy and sell and make a profit. The good life, in a business society, presupposes the freedom to participate, the freedom to choose what we want and will work for. But freedom can become more than a mere presupposition of the good life; it can be elevated to the primary ingredient in the good life as such. Indeed, a great many Americans work fanatically at their jobs just in order to take early retirement and be free from work and want. This might seem perverse—why don't they just make themselves "free" right now?—but of course our idea of freedom is not quite so simple. When, paradoxically, people make themselves slaves to their work in order to become free, they are sometimes simply deceiving themselves; it is the work itself that they crave. Freedom, when they get it, may well be crushing. But there is another sense of freedom here, another of our American ideals, that we summarize as "being your own boss." In a world increasingly dominated by large corporations, in which virtually everyone is an employee, in which everyone follows orders from others, and makes a product or provides a service for someone else, it is inevitably attractive to consider the ideal of being "the boss" and answering to no one. Of course, in most of the business world, no one is wholly free. The CEO answers to the stockholders; the consultant is ultimately at the mercy of those who hire him for information or advice; and everyone, as part of the "free" enterprise system, has to answer to the market. Indeed, on this view we might suppose that the only people who are free are those who have already made their fortunes and retired, for they need to answer to no boss and no stockholders; they can remain oblivious to the market and, quite literally, be their own boss. But is this so? Even the most superficial review of American history and literature shows us that such people, like John D. Rockefeller, are often "slaves" to their fortunes—worried about its disposition, concerned about its worth, and burdened by its responsibilities. And this in turn often leads to a largely ascetic reaction—that ultimately it is the poor person who is most free. Rockefeller and Carnegie both waxed eloquent on "the virtues of poverty." This, of course, is nonsense. What it shows is only how confused our notion of "freedom" is, no matter how great its importance.

One of the more perennial pieces in business newspapers and magazines is the article on the high-flown "drop-out," the person who has made it in business but decides either to quit a high position in a major corporation for a position in a much smaller one or to quit the business world altogether. Why? The answer is almost always the same—"freedom." For example, an executive recently resigned as president of a $1.6 billion-a-year subsidiary of Exxon to become chief executive of a small firm one-quarter the size but not anyone's subsidiary. The reason he gave, "I'm too damn much of a free spirit." Not long ago, one article on "dropping out" centered on several women who had made it into the higher echelons of the business world only to realize that the confinement and obstacles of the corporate structure failed to satisfy their ambitions, no matter how successful they were. Their reasons, again, were such things as "personal growth, freedom, the opportunity to be one's own boss," and they all began small businesses for themselves. This is worth remembering in the midst of the many clichés about "free enterprise" and "freedom"; the *enterprise* may indeed be more or less "free" but the sense of freedom *for the individual* is yet open to question. It is not clear that corporate success, for some people, will satisfy this important ingredient of the good life.

"Freedom" is often contrasted with "authoritarianism" and, in economic and social matters, with "socialism." But socialists would define "freedom" in part as freedom from the threats and insecurities of the "free" enterprise system. They would argue that security is more important to freedom than choice. Sometimes, we tend to think of freedom as being unrestricted, flouting the rules, or rejecting everything. However, consider this idea from John Barth's novel, *End of the*

Vanderbilt, Gould)—who seem to have had this conception of the good life too. They had so much money already, had so broken through every possible standard of business success, had access to every pleasure they could possibly have imagined, that the one thing left to them was power—an awesome power that not even most politicians could obtain. For example, William Randolph Hearst virtually singlehandedly started the Spanish American War in 1898 with his patriotic and outraged newspaper headlines.

The life of power need not be restricted to such large-scale titans of business, however; it also is found in some office managers and petty bureaucrats, for whom the best thing in life may be their exercise of what little power they do have and attempts to acquire more of it. In fact, the nineteenth-century German philosopher Friedrich Nietzsche developed a theory according to which the quest for power—"the Will to Power"—dominated all of life. This was perhaps excessive, even for the purpose of discussing German politics or American business. But the recognition that power is a legitimate drive and an acceptable goal for the good life is an essential ethical insight. Such an insight is often buried or repressed under our ideological insistence that all people, even in a complex organization, ought to think of themselves as equals and, therefore, accept power over other people only with hesitation and a hint of repulsion. In fact, some people enjoy power and are not even remotely hesitant about accepting it. Power is not to be shunned or rejected as such; it is not power itself that is in question, but what is done with it and how it is exercised.

The problem, however, is that once again we find that too often ends get mixed up with means and that the quest for power might in fact be merely a means to something else, or else a false goal that makes the good life impossible. For example, the newspaper tycoon in Orson Welles' classic film *Citizen Kane* spends his life in pursuit of power, but we learn, at the very end of the movie, that what he really wanted all along were the simple joys and affectations of childhood, which he had been deprived of. Not infrequently, the search for power is a kind of *compensation* for some other virtue that has been lost or lost sight of—for example, love or respect. People thrust into management positions in business sometimes try to convince themselves that they want power, when in fact they do not and never did. Power-seeking people, because they have been told for so long that seeking power is evil, often end up seeking it in the most devious ways, unrecognized even to themselves. As a result, they are often inefficient and defeat themselves.

C. FREEDOM AND SOCIETY

> What I have always believed, and still believe, is this: one is always free to make oneself, no matter what is made of one.
> —Jean-Paul Sartre (1970)

"We want freedom, and we want it now!" What political protest has not begun with that as its banner? But freedom doesn't exist in a vacuum. It does not simply mean being "left alone." We can always find solitude; there are still many thousands of uninhabited but inhabitable square miles of earth to move to if someone is desperate enough to seek them out and willing to do what must be done to survive there. What we want by way of freedom, however, is a distinctively *social* phenomenon, defined in terms of our relationship with other people. We want to be left alone, but not too much and not for very long. We do not want to be hounded by our creditors, but we still want them and their products and services to be accessible. We would like our supervisors to spend less time looking over our shoulders, but, at the same time, we would very much like more compliments and more people to take notice of our accomplishments. We say we want freedom, but in fact what we would prefer is more recognition.

Wanting freedom in the modern business world has very little to do with the sense in which people demand freedom in most political contexts. Indeed, much of the problem in abstract discussions of freedom turns on the unanswered question, "freedom as opposed to what?" If freedom is offered as an alternative to slavery, being beaten daily and getting too little to eat, few if any people in the world would not prefer freedom. But that, surely, is not what we mean by it, when, for example, employees wish they had more freedom in the job, or managers wish they had more freedom to pursue more independent lines of thought. If freedom is opposed to mere mechanism, or, in human terms, being compelled to do *exactly* what we are told, and nothing else, then most of us would prefer freedom. But the choice is rarely so absolute.

Suppose our boss or mentor were perfectly efficient, perfectly knowledgeable, maximally productive, and that, unlike slaves, we were neither beaten nor punished in any other way, but encouraged and rewarded for carrying out our instructions. Is this lack of freedom? If it is, would we really care? How many jobs require freedom and flexibility just because the instructions were unclear, the staff was inefficient, or the odds and expectations were *against* getting the job done? Indeed, how much of what we call "freedom on the job" is in fact rather incompetence and inattention of superiors, time to waste because of inadequate delegation of responsibilities (rather than time for genuine relaxation), and generally bad or inefficient management? If this is freedom, then it is not something so obviously desirable, and certainly not the end towards which we want our whole society and business in particular to strive.

Freedom is often contrasted with "oppression," but for most people this oppression is not a Simon Legree taskmaster, or a tyrant (Caligula, Nero, Stalin), nor the grueling monotony and severe limitations on talk, sex, knowledge, language, and thought depicted in such horror classics as Orwell's *1984*. It is rather a matter of being bored and feeling unappreciated, feeling "exploited," or feeling "forced" to do things we do not want to do ("coerced"). These are hardly the degradations and deprivations other people in the world suffer and try to overcome in their demand for freedom. Some people complain about the lack of freedom just because they can't do *anything* they want to do; others consider themselves unfree or "oppressed" because they can't indulge their fantasies of showing up at work in a bathing suit, or even without a tie. Indeed, we take the essential freedoms that are denied to much of the world so much for granted that the word itself has tended to become obscured. We are already so free, as far as the world is concerned, that we imagine and sometimes demand *total* freedom, which is absurd and unattainable. It is as if, to paraphrase a metaphor from Immanuel Kant, a bird found itself so free in the heights of the atmosphere that it imagined itself even more free if there were no air at all.

Freedom entails a context, an atmosphere, a social situation in which it *means* something. Free speech means nothing on a desert island; free speech means something only if other people can listen, be moved, and disagree. The purpose of free speech, in turn, is not simply the recognition of our right to make noise and express an opinion; it is the recognition that free speech in a democratic society is the best way to keep all of the political alternatives open and in competition, the best way to guarantee the recognition of grievances and differences of opinion, the best way to protect ourselves against the corruption that breeds in silence and in the absence of a free press and concerned, articulate citizens. Free speech, to pick out only one of our freedom rights, is aimed at and presupposes the fulfillment of social responsibilities. It is not just the right to speak our mind; it is the obligation to *have* a mind, to be well informed, and to think out what we are saying. So too, all freedoms entail responsibilities; the freedom to make contracts entails the obligation to honor contracts, the freedom to reap what we sow or keep (most of) what we earn entails the responsibilities of planting, producing, or working in the first place. No freedom is free of responsibilities. No freedom is free of a social context, except perhaps, for an odd weekend in the mountains or alone in a fishing boat. Freedom is not only being left alone. It is also, and always, the freedom *to do* things in society, to fit in a certain way, to have a certain social identity, to have a certain amount of respect, to be able to make decisions about how we will do what we must do and what we will make of ourselves.

Freedom, then, is almost always to be found in a social context. It entails responsibility and power as well as presupposing a social setting and a job to do, in which one is free. Philosophers sometimes describe this as distinction between two kinds of freedom, corresponding to some extent with our distinction between freedom (or negative) rights and positive rights; these are *"positive"* freedom and

> People hardly ever make use of the freedom which they have, for example, freedom of thought; instead they demand freedom of speech as compensation.
>
> Søren Kierkegaard, *Journals*

> ## On negative freedom: ——
>
> The history of liberty is the history of resistance . . . the history of the limitation of government power.
>
> Woodrow Wilson
>
> ## On positive freedom: ——
>
> Whoever refuses to obey the general will [of society] shall be constrained to do so by the whole society; this means nothing else than he shall be forced to be free.
>
> Jean Jacques Rousseau

"negative" freedom. Negative freedom is freedom *from* coercion or threats, freedom from unreasonable government interference or regulation, freedom from unwarranted search and seizure, and freedom from restrictions on what we believe, say, or worship. Positive freedom is the freedom *to do* what we want to do or are supposed to do, the freedom to fulfill as well as to make contracts, the freedom to obey the law as well as the freedom *from* unreasonable laws, the freedom to get a job done, as well as the freedom to say or do or dress as we wish at work. But even this becomes complex when we see that underlying both kinds of freedom is a social setting in which freedom gets its meaning. Freedom is neither positive nor negative, nor can it be understood in isolation from more general considerations about self-identity and the good life.

D. FREEDOM AND SELF-IDENTITY: THE PROBLEM OF PRIVACY

> The actions of man are never free; they are always the necessary consequence of his temperament, of the received ideas, and of the notions, true or false, which he has formed to himself of happiness.
>
> —Baron Paul Henri d'Holbach

What counts as freedom depends on who we are. Creative people are unfree if they cannot create, perhaps because of other people's restrictions, because of a neurotic "block," or because they don't have the materials or resources. People who enjoy working alone are unfree insofar as they are forced to work in teams with others, but others who work well only as team members might just as well be unfree when forced to work alone and deprived of the group context. People who pride themselves on eccentric or particularly fashionable dress will feel

> There were no specific rules about decorum, grooming and apparel [at IBM], but a certain style was expected because Mr. Watson approved of it.
>
> William Rogers, *Think*

unfree working for any company with a stringent dress code, but others who do not particularly care about clothes or individual dress will not be at all unfree in the same circumstances. Managers with innovative ideas are unfree insofar as they cannot follow through and make them work, but managers whose talent consists of helping other people in implementing their ideas would not be unfree even if innovative thinking on their part is discouraged. Freedom is always relative to something that we want to do, to the kind of person we are, and to our responsibilities and place in society.

What is perhaps most distinctive about our "individualist" culture is the fact that so much of what we want to do and be is defined primarily in terms of *ourselves,* our own conceptions of who we are and what we want to do.

This conception of the personal self, a **private** self, is rather peculiar in history and society. All cultures have some sense of privacy—the sex act, for example, is expected to be done in private and not in public in almost all societies—but few societies have such a strong and determined sense of privacy as ours. We treasure our personal lives and our time alone. We prize our personal privacy for its own sake, as something to which every individual is entitled. We often define our virtues in terms of those most intimate with us—a good family man, a good mother—and we often characterize our "true selves" in terms of these most intimate relationships. Just as often, we define our "true selves" in those moments when we are utterly alone, fishing in some isolated stream or hiking up some deserted mountain trail. It is because these relationships and these moments are so important to us that we fight to maintain some sense of privacy, even in the most public situations. Politicians whose lives are devoted to public service and success are nevertheless adamant about their need for privacy, and even the most sociable and public jobs demand some sharp distinction between what is public and what is private. In a study several years ago, social scientist Arlie Hochschild investigated the psychological toll on those whose work is uninterrupted congeniality—flight attendants, professional hosts and hostesses, many salespeople and entertainers. She concluded that the stress in such jobs is considerable, not just because of the difficulty in maintaining a smile in the face of the abusive or offensive behavior of some clients, but because of the deprivation of privacy.

Privacy, in an important sense, is freedom from other people. It is extremely important for us to occasionally separate from others and protect part of ourselves as our own, even in the most intimate circumstances. The German poet Rilke writes that a good marriage is one in which both partners "protect each other's solitude." In our working lives, especially if one works for a corporation or any public institution, this sense of privacy is even more important. Every job has its limits—the limits of the private and the personal—beyond which neither an employer nor a customer can go. The most obvious limit, in most jobs, are the boundaries of a person's body, not just the physical boundaries of his or her skin but the psychological boundaries of his or her "personal space." Except where it is specifically required or expected, no employer is entitled to touch, pinch, or otherwise impinge on an employee's body. Such would be a violation that in certain circumstances would amount to sexual harassment, and is a form of harassment even without any sexual implications or overtones.

It is also a violation of an employee's privacy for an employer to delve into his or her personal life and private habits. Whether a woman is married or single or whether a man is "straight" or "gay" are private matters that are, or should be, of no concern in the office. So, too, one's political opinions and religious convictions are one's own private business (so long, of course, as one does not use his or her position as an advantageous platform to promulgate those views to others who are, in effect, a captive audience). Although they do not explicitly say so, the original amendments to the United States Constitution, the Bill of Rights, often have been argued to have been intended as a guarantee of privacy; indeed, the presumption of privacy has been argued to be the presupposition of virtually all of the amendments. One is free to hold whatever religious beliefs and political opinions he or she will, and, outside of the office, free to promulgate them as well. No employer is allowed to fire a person or even inquire into his or her beliefs or marital status or sexual orientation, unless for some special and specific reason such facts will directly interfere with the job to be done.

A particularly tricky problem relating to the question of privacy and the employee's right to do what he or she wants outside of the office concerns the complex socio-legal problem of drug use and abuse. First of all, such activities are illegal, and there are some serious legal questions about whether an employer or a prospective employer has the right to know if his or her employee is in violation of the law, even outside the workplace. Second, drug use does not affect a person just during the time when he or she is actually ingesting the substance. There may be a lag or a hangover effect that lasts many hours or several days, and surely an employer has the right to know about any such activities that might seriously affect job performance and job safety, including the safety of others. Third, use of some drugs is not just habit-forming but addictive, and it is not always possible to restrain oneself from taking drugs on, as well as off, the job. The use of such "recreational" drugs may therefore threaten to spill over into the job as well, even if it has not already done so. An employer therefore has the right, one could well argue, to know whether or not his employees take such drugs and whether they might be a danger to themselves or others.

Nevertheless, it is a serious and difficult question whether or not an employer has the right to test for drug activity. Drug testing—usually by way of urine or blood samples—is by any measure a violation of the employee's privacy.

The Ultimate Freedom ——

We were never more free than during the German occupation. We had lost all our rights, beginning with the right to talk. Every day we were insulted to our faces and had to take it in silence. . . . And because of all this we were free. Because the Nazi venom seeped into our thoughts, every accurate thought was a conquest. Because an all-powerful police tried to force us to hold our tongues, every word took on the value of a declaration of principles. Because we were hunted down, every one of our gestures had the weight of a solemn commitment.

Jean-Paul Sartre, *Situations III*

Thus there are no accidents in a life; a community event which suddenly bursts forth and involves me in it does not come from the outside. If I am mobilized in a war, this war is my war; it is in my image and I deserve it. I deserve it first because I could always get out of it by suicide or by desertion; these ultimate possibles are those which must always be present for us when there is a question of envisaging a situation. For lack of getting out of it, I have chosen it. This can be due to inertia, to cowardice in the face of public opinion, or because I prefer certain other values to the values of the refusal to join in the war (the good opinion of my relatives, the honor of my family, etc.). Any way you look at it, it is a matter of choice. This choice will be repeated later on again and again without a break until the end of the war.

Jean-Paul Sartre, *Being and Nothingness*

It is one thing to catch an employee taking drugs on the job or behaving irresponsibly. It is something quite different to subject all employees to humiliating, perhaps painful and possibly dangerous, medical tests as well. Furthermore, the established tests are considerably less than reliable, resulting in false negatives and, much more serious, false positives. An employee who tests positively for drugs, perhaps because of perfectly legal prescribed medications, some natural physiological phenomenon, or even a glitch in the test, is put in a highly suspicious and difficult position.

Freedom *from* is not always a good thing. A man who has just been fired might well declare that he has been "set free," but if there is no other role for him besides his job, no new job to take the place of the old one, freedom can be tantamount to exile or torture; it is being stripped of an identity, not being free at all. Freedom, to make a difference, always has a *positive* element, something to do, someone to be. Slavery, the extreme opposite of freedom, literally means the total absence of even the physical ability to leave or do what one wants, or at least, facing terrible punishment if even attempting to do so. But even slavery, most of the time, is made up of psychological attitudes of dependency more than actual physical confinement and threats. What most of us would call "slavery," working in a job we don't like for pay that we consider insufficient, has to be understood just as much in terms of "positive" freedoms—how we see ourselves and how we identify with our jobs and working life—as the "negative" elements of threats and fear of being unemployed or unpaid altogether. In other words, freedom is *always,* except in perhaps the most extreme cases of physical imprisonment or threats, positive as well as negative. It consists of how we see ourselves and what we take to be our identity and goals as well as the lack of power to change our position or the fear of some terrible punishment or alternative.

E.   Autonomy

> *If we now look back upon all previous moral theories, we can see why they had to fail. Man was seen to be bound to laws by his duty, and not yet subject to his own, yet universal, legislation. This principle I call the principle of autonomy.*
>
> —Immanuel Kant

Autonomy is what most of us have in mind when we talk about freedom. Autonomy is the ability and the "room" to think and act for ourselves rather than simply following orders or rules from others. In the business world, autonomy is measured primarily not by whether we are free to do as we want (which is rare

---

Disobedience and Its Necessity ——

A commander in chief [manager] cannot take as an excuse for his mistakes in warfare [business] an order given by his minister [boss] or his sovereign [boss's boss], when the person giving the order is absent from the field of operations and is imperfectly aware or wholly unaware of the latest state of affairs. It follows that any commander in chief [manager] who undertakes to carry out a plan which he considers defective is at fault: he must put forward his reasons, insist on the plan being changed, and finally tender his resignation rather than be the instrument of his army's [organization's] downfall.

Napoleon, *Military Maxims and Thoughts,*
quoted from Robert Townsend, *Up the Corporation*

indeed, and true only of occasional research scientists and a few lucky others), but rather the freedom to do what we *are supposed to do* as we see best. Again, freedom has its meaning only within limitations, within assignments that are not, usually, of our own choosing (except insofar as the all-important choice of continuing to work in a job or not). Autonomy is the freedom to make plans and lay strategies and see through a course of action of our own design. For this we must take responsibility and, consequently, deserve praise (if it is successful) and blame (if it is not).

The lack of autonomy is the delegation of responsibilities without the power to carry them out, without the sense that we can solve problems or fulfill goals without using our own judgment. Sometimes, for example, in a factory assembly line, it may be more efficient to have less autonomy *and follow more narrowly defined rules and routines.* But there is a price to pay here in lack of pride in the final product, because the worker may not feel that it is a personal accomplishment. In addition, the lack of a sense of responsibility and participation inevitably results in lower quality, literally more "routine" work, and an inability to adjust to even minor discrepancies or deviations in the routine. Moreover, the same lack of pride eventually becomes reflected in overall attitudes towards work and the job and lack of loyalty.

Autonomy, on the other hand, provides exactly this sense of responsibility, of pride, and of participation. It has virtues, therefore, that cannot always be measured in the efficiency of routine work. Indeed, in our culture, our sense of self and self-worth is so bound up with this notion of autonomy, our own decisions and activity in doing whatever we are to do, that little self-worth exists without it. In the middle levels of management, where freedom and power are most confusing, that sense of autonomy may mean the difference between a happy life in business and a coherent corporate culture on the one side, and a life that is at least metaphorically compared to slavery and renders corporations ill-organized gangs of disgruntled workers who all feel they are there only because they "have to be."

Autonomy, as the working part of freedom, clearly presupposes a goal, an aim, a role, or a position. We have autonomy only insofar as we have something *to do* and some position with responsibility. Through autonomy we "prove ourselves" by establishing our worth and our identities, our success (or failures), and our capacities and limits. But autonomy, though it can be infringed upon by other people, is not to be understood as opposition to or independence from other people; rather, it presupposes a kind of dependency, at least a joint effort, a role in the midst of others. Moreover, to confuse autonomy with absolute freedom, not only to carry out our goals but to even conceive of these goals or to think, as we sometimes do, that autonomy is everything, is cruel in another way; many people like or even "need" to be told what to do, and leaving them floundering in their own uncertainties is more destructive than supportive. We sometimes overemphasize creativity. We need mentors and guidance and rules; we need roles and goals given to us, *in which* we can be autonomous. We might negatively say this is "paternalistic"; but much of what we call paternalism, in our overemphasis of individual autonomy, freedom, and responsibility, is in fact the simple recognition that very few of us can function in a vacuum, without established roles and goals within which to do what we do.

The concept of autonomy also allows us a new way of looking at corporate loyalty. Too often, loyalty is identified with "commitment" and a consequent *restriction* of freedom and power, but, if our role or roles in life define our freedom and give us our power, then loyalty is just as much a matter of self-identity and having a context in which to be free and exercise power as it is a restriction on freedom and power. Of course, mobility provides a source of freedom and power of its own, but this strictly negative freedom—essentially the freedom to leave—must always be balanced against the freedom to stay, and that means to enjoy those aspects of autonomy that are possible only within a particular context. Complete mobility, after all, ultimately amounts to being nowhere at all.

F.   POWER AND AUTHORITY: THE PRESUPPOSITIONS OF AUTONOMY

Power, in the last analysis, is the ability to get things done. This may necessarily include having influence over other people and being able to mobilize them to act according to our needs and commands, but it does not necessarily include—indeed includes usually only in cases of desperation—having power *over* other people, which is a very different thing. A successful manager more likely impresses employees with abilities and contacts than with threats or promises. Machiavelli wrote that it is safer to be feared than loved, since love is undependable, but fear is not. However, if executives cannot expect to be loved by the

---

Bases of Social Power ——

Social power is not a singular concept; it may have several bases and meanings that are quite different and can contradict as well as reinforce one another. In a recent study, John R. P. French and Bertram Raven distinguished five such bases of social (managerial) power:

1. Reward power: controlling resources that can reward.

2. Coercive power: controlling resources that can punish.

3. Expert power: controlling necessary knowledge or information.

4. Reference power: being personally attractive to other people.

5. Legitimate power: authority invested in a position or role.

people who work under them, they should not plan to instill fear either. Power is not necessarily, or even desirably, power over other people. It is, first and foremost, the ability to get things done, including the ability to mobilize others in your behalf, preferably through inspiration rather than intimidation, through the promise of shared accomplishment rather than the threat of punishment.

Accountability Without Power: Sources of Bureaucratic Powerlessness ——

People who have authority without system power are powerless. People held accountable for the results produced by others, whose formal role gives them the right to command but who lack informal political influence, access to resources, outside status, sponsorship, or mobility prospects are rendered powerless in the organization. They lack control over their own fate and are dependent on others above them—others whom they cannot easily influence—while they are expected by virtue of position to be influential over those parallel or below. Their sense of lack of control above is heightened by its contrast with the demands of an accountable authority position: that they mobilize others in the interests of a task they may have had little part in shaping, to produce results they may have had little part in defining. . . .

Powerlessness [is] the general condition of those people who could not make the kinds of powerful alliances that helped to manage the bureaucracy. People without sponsors, without peer connections, or without promising subordinates remained in the situation of bureaucratic dependency on formal procedures, routine allocations of rewards, communication that flowed through a multi-layered chain of command, and decisions that must penetrate, as Robert Prestlius put it, "innumerable veto barriers." People who reached dead ends in their careers also rapidly lost power, since they could no longer promise gains to those who followed them and no longer had the security of future movement. Powerlessness was also the psychological state of people who, for whatever reason, felt insecure in their functioning as leaders and anticipated resistance rather than cooperation from those whom they were to lead. Indeed, the structural characteristics of modern organizational life tend to produce the symptoms of powerlessness in more and more lower-to-middle managers, supervisors, bureaucrats, and professionals. The chance to engage in the non-routine, to show discretion, to take risks, or to become known, are all less available in the large bureaucracy.

Rosabeth Moss Kantor, *Men and Women of the Corporation*

Rosabeth Kantor in *Men and Women of the Corporation* points out that power in the corporation should not be viewed relative to the people *below* but rather to those above. Indeed, an unfortunate but familiar figure in almost every organization is the stunted manager who, having virtually no contact or influence with those above, reigns as a petty tyrant over those below. Success may be significant enough to impress those above, but not, evidently, enough for promotion or special praise. On the other hand, those who command the most respect and are best able to mobilize their employees are perceived as having precisely this influence above, thus acting as a liaison and representative for everyone else as well.

Power also ties in with responsibility. Indeed, the two are logically linked. Where there is power, there is responsibility; where there is no power, there is no responsibility. But this logical truth might better be construed as a practical warning: it is not at all uncommon for executives to delegate responsibility to more junior managers or employees without the power or authority to carry it out. This is a guaranteed recipe for disaster for the recipients of the assignment, for though the nominal responsibility is theirs—and thus the blame for failure too—the precondition for responsibility and the prerequisite for success has been denied. But then again, it is just as important to appreciate the fact that power and authority need not be *total* in order for us to be responsible, any more than we must have total responsibility in order to be responsible. Indeed, no one has total power, or total responsibility, in any organization of the complexity of the modern corporation. And everyone has at least some power, minimally, the power to quit or to "blow the whistle." The cost may be considerable, but cost does not cancel out freedom or responsibility either.

G.   CORPORATE POISON: RESENTMENT

> The executive suites of thousands of corporations in the United States are filled by men who have become professional eunuchs. The drive and potency they once possessed have been spent. . . . They spend their days doing things that often seem meaningless.
> —O. William Battaglia and John J. Tarrant, The Corporate Eunuch

Within a large company, individual power is as much a matter of appearance as fact. In a best-selling book a few years ago, Michael Korda made a professional survey of power and its techniques and not surprisingly, many of them turned out to be matters of appearance—the corner office, the arrangement of the furniture, and who keeps whom waiting for meetings and appointments. Cultivating the appearance of power often leads to or amounts to the real thing. A person who acts the part of success will quite often gain success by engaging the trust of colleagues and impressing those above who will give more power and authority to the person they see as responsible. All this, in turn, leads to real power, such as it

is. Even real power, in the complex network of actors and efforts in the corporation, is largely appearance, but still quite real. The corporation and its roles define
power and its possibilities; power as well as responsibility is one of the rewards
of a job. Indeed, the just distribution of power and responsibility may be a more
crucial issue in distributive justice, for many people, than the more obvious and
tangible question of salaries and bonuses.

The importance of power and its connection with appearance, however, has a
danger of enormous proportions. Because the company defines power and its
possibilities, and power is largely a matter of appearance, it is all too easy for
employees—even some top employees—to feel that they are entirely *impotent* in
their role in the corporation. Chief executive officers of even the most powerful
organizations complain that their own power is far more appearance than reality.
Virtually anyone facing the obstinacy of a world that does not always yield to our
wishes knows this feeling of impotence. But impotence, like power, is relative to
goals and expectations. People who expect to do very little will not feel impotent,
but others who expect their decisions and efforts to make major changes can very
easily be made to feel impotent, no matter how much they in fact accomplish.
Impotence is a sense of not being able to do what we want and expect to be able
to do. But it is also a sense of our position in an organization, and power, ultimately, comes down to a large organization's doing what we think it should do.
Our actual effect, except in rare cases, is always subject to doubt. But success
usually allays such doubts, and, again, the appearance of effectiveness usually
counts. On the other hand, the appearance of ineffectiveness is what counts too,
and when this sense of ineffectiveness enters into our own sense of self-identity,
the results can be disastrous.

The sense of impotence, and the resultant *resentment* it breeds, might well be
called *corporate poison.* In its milder forms, resentment breeds sloth or indifference and perhaps a modicum of destructive spite, but, in any case, it breeds a
sense of separation between the employee and the company, between "me" (or
"us") and "it" (or "them"). It reduces corporate loyalty to nothing, because
employees no longer feel an effective part of the company. And in more extreme
cases, resentment can even lead to sabotage and rebellion, an active disruption of
the work process. In fact, the milder forms of resentment may be the more insidious. A saboteur or a rebel is easily spotted and can be fired. However, a large
number of quiet, largely submissive, and even superficially satisfied employees
who don't really care and see themselves as just "putting in time" are not so easily identifiable and, in the long run, can do a company much more damage.

Reactions to impotence vary enormously, but they all emerge, sooner or
later, in the form of detachment and resentment. The employer's power comes to
be seen as illegitimate or excessive or "oppressive." Employees come to see their
own work as not mattering much, and the point then becomes to do the minimum,
or just keep up appearances, which in turn, of course, feeds the sense of impotence even more. The typical response to this is increased authority and new
demands from above; however, it is exactly the wrong answer, because it again

reinforces the employee's sense of impotence and resentment. Though it may bring short-term results, it is a sure recipe for longer-term disaster. We need not agree with Nietzsche—that all we really want is power—but to appreciate the importance of feeling potent and effective in our work is a condition for feeling ourselves to be a significant part of any organization. Without power, no role is satisfying; in fact, without power, it may not deserve to be called a role, but perhaps just in the extremely derogatory sense, "a job."

While the negative reaction to impotence is resentment, the positive reaction is an increased assertion of power. But other reactions are harder to detect, and may have very different consequences. One reaction that seems benign and even positive is a tendency to conform, to minimize the vulnerability, and to hide the sense of impotence by being relatively anonymous. This is often true of middle managers, for whom the problem of impotence feels most acute. They feel squeezed from above and not sufficiently effective below. Their accomplishments are hard if not impossible to measure, and so the appearance of power is everything to them, both in the impression it makes on their superiors and in the influence it has on the work of their subordinates. And so, they conform. The stereotypes of the machinelike lackey, the "yes-man," the corporate robot, all represent extreme versions of this reaction to impotence. They are an effort to minimize impotence, in effect, by disappearing into the stereotype.

But impotence can inspire precisely the opposite reaction, an exertion of eccentricity, an effort to stand out and make a role, if not accomplishments, much more visible than anyone else's. The office clown may be reacting to the impotence of the job; not feeling any real sense of accomplishment anyway, the clown tries to be personally important to the group, even to the detriment of work. The office flirt may also be reacting to a sense of job impotence, expressing the power sexually that is not found in work or recognition in the company. Sometimes, eccentricity can be mere rebellion, whether it be the purely private gesture of an extremely obscene (but unseen) pair of undershorts or the more flagrant disruption of the work process with practical jokes or arguments, a favorite expression of resentment and impotence. Or impotence may spur excessive and often uncon-

---

Rules-Mindedness ——

The powerless inside an authority structure often become rules-minded in response to the limited options for power in their situation, turning to "the rules" as a power tool. Rules are made in the first place to try to control the uncontrollable; invoking organization rules and insisting on careful adherence to them is a characteristic response of the powerless in authority positions.

Rosabeth Moss Kantor, *Men and Women of the Corporation*

structive criticism. It may result in dozens of minor rebellions, any one of which is at most annoying but, together, can ruin a department.

The problem of impotence, according to Kantor in *Men and Women of the Corporation*, is particularly critical with women executives. The prejudice against them is still sufficiently strong so that they are perceived as powerless and come to perceive themselves as powerless, no matter what their position or ability. Here again the self-confirming mechanism is at work; a female executive may have much more ability than her male counterparts, but the suspicion of lack of power leads her employees to be cautious, not to trust her and her connections as they would a male executive. This suspicion leads to relative ineffectiveness on her part, which is perceived by her employees and by her superiors too, making her less effective. The solutions to this problem are still forthcoming, but in the absence of sensitive corporate policy that can compensate for the initial suspicions and make an extra effort to establish the authority of executive women, the solutions will inevitably have to be individual ones. This solution must include the need for an extra assertion of power and extra emphasis on its appearances is sometimes misunderstood (or viciously used against women executives) as personal "coldness." In fact, it is one of the new requirements for success, made necessary by the nature of corporate power. Women must not only appear to have power, they must appear to have even more power if they are to have any at all.*

The lesson here is obvious enough: every role requires power and authority as well as responsibilities and a paycheck. People without power are not only ineffective employees, they are undependable and resentful employees. Providing that sense of power, accomplishment, and effectiveness to everyone else may be among the most important, if unspoken, jobs of every manager. Justice is not just a question of fair finances, it is also a question of just distribution of authority. Without the sense that they make a difference and can exercise their autonomy, employees, at any level, are not going to be satisfied.

H.   COERCION: THE LIMITS OF FREEDOM AND POWER

> What distinguishes the capitalist economy from the simple exchange economy is the separation of capital and labor, that is, the existence of a labor force without its own sufficient capital and therefore without a choice as to whether to put its labor into the market or not. Professor (Milton) Friedman would agree that where there is no choice there is coercion.
>
> —C. B. Macpherson, "Elegant Tombstones: A Note on Friedman's Freedom"

---

*See also, Margaret Hennig and Anne Jardim, *The Managerial Woman* (New York: Doubleday, 1978).

One of the keys to economic justice is a "fair return" for our efforts; a primary source of injustice is, therefore, what we call **exploitation,** giving much more than we get back in return. Sometimes, we give more than we get voluntarily, out of love for a friend, compassion for a poor person, patriotism, or admiration. But however admirable such gifts may be, they are not the core of the business world; when we take less than we deserve for a job, it may be presumed that it is because of naivete or trickery, rather than generosity. Or, more likely, it may be because we were *coerced,* that is, *forced* to accept an unfair return.

Coercion is the opposite of freedom as well as the instrument of injustice. Coercion, basically, means *lack of choice,* being unable to refuse an unfair bargain. The most obvious cases in business would be those in which employees are forced to take an unpleasant or dangerous job rather than be fired or demoted. The most troublesome cases involving business are those which involve the worst-off workers, those who have few skills and need jobs just to survive. They are ready targets for coercion and exploitation. Coercion might be thought of as a kind of extortion—either you do something that is against your interests or something intolerable will be done to you.

What makes the question of coercion particularly difficult, first of all, is that the "force" affecting most employees is not so obvious. As classic economics points out quite clearly, the number of workers "in the market" determines wages, and an excess of workers (whether janitors or computer specialists) drives down salaries and decreases the workers' leverage over their jobs. An employee who is thankful just to have a job is not in a position to dictate or even request duties and assignments. But if the market is such that people can earn only a fraction of what would be expected for that particular job, they may still be exploited (assuming, that is, that our sense of a "fair return" is not wholly dictated by the contingencies of the market). We might well want to say that those people are coerced if no other jobs are available. The problem is, however, that it is not at all clear who is doing the coercing, nor is it clear how we are to measure exploitation when not just one particular person, but everyone, is subject to the supply and demand of the market. So long as everyone else acts within his or her own rights, argues philosopher Robert Nozick, the employee who is forced to take an unsatisfying job is not coerced. Necessity is not necessarily coercion.

Second, it is not at all clear when we have *no* choice. If nothing else, we can *choose* to starve rather than work, or even choose to have the family starve too. It is an intolerable choice, to be sure, but it is still a choice. This changes the question from whether or not we have a choice to the much more difficult question: When do we have an *acceptable* choice? The answer here is by no means so easily decided. A middle manager may be extremely dissatisfied with her job but, because of the glut of middle managers or her own lack of visible accomplishments, she cannot move, at least, not at a comparable salary and level of status. She can, of course, choose to take any number of other jobs with much less pay or start a small business of her own. But, given the standard of living to which she has become accustomed, these alternatives are unthinkable. Is she coerced? Another worker with a poor education considers the various jobs that are

Coercion and Integrity ——

Middle managers often complain that pressures within the organization contradict their own feelings of personal integrity. In a treatment of this issue in *Business Week,* two surveys by major corporations confirmed this complaint many times over. A majority of middle managers claimed that they felt pressured to sacrifice personal ethics for company goals. Most insisted that they would not in fact give in to coercion, but many suggested that younger employees tended to go along automatically to show their company loyalty. *Business Week* concluded:

> . . . both surveys, as well as others supporting them, displayed the encouraging fact that most middle managers considered ethics in business extremely important and found it worth their while to resist pressures to compromise. Most defended ethics in business and favored explicit and universal codes of ethics for people in business.

How Two Sets of Managers Share Views on Ethics

	Pitney-Bowes	Uniroyal
Managers feel pressured to compromise personal ethics to achieve corporate goals	59%	70
Most managers would not refuse orders to market off-standard and possibly dangerous items	61%	54%
I personally would refuse to market off-standard and possibly dangerous items	83%	85%
Like the junior members of Nixon's reelection committee, young managers automatically go along with superiors to show loyalty	68%	76%
I would not give gifts to preferred customers even if other salesmen did	80%	55%
Turning in a plausible but incomplete report is unethical	92%	94%
Press reports on unethical business practices reveal a valid need for corrective action	70%	unasked
Business ethics are as good as, or better than, ethics in society at large	90%	88%

Business Week, Jan. 31, 1977

available to him, all without any probability of advancement. Nonetheless, he has a choice of which job he accepts. Is he coerced?

The issue of coercion strikes right at the heart of any discussion of economic rights and justice in a free enterprise system. If people are coerced into working, or into working at boring or unacceptable jobs, then it isn't clear in what sense the market is "free." An entrepreneur is free to invest, or not invest, capital wherever it will most likely make the most profit. Indeed, nothing is more antithetical to the free market system than coerced investment, whether in the mild form created by government regulation or in the extreme form of a "command" economy, in which investors are told quite directly what is to be done. But we cannot be entirely sure that this same freedom to "invest" their time and skills extends to most employees. Most cannot withhold their efforts altogether and live acceptably in this society, and the market is such that they cannot usually switch jobs very easily, as an investor can simply change investments. Something more is needed. Labor unions, essentially, function to short-circuit the supply and demand regarding individual workers in competition with one another and replace it with the increased bargaining power of supply and demand for all of the workers of a certain sort. Ironically, while this has substantially increased the security and somewhat lessened the vulnerability of most blue-collar workers, the brutality of the market for many managers has gotten even worse. Semi-skilled and skilled workers may or may not be easily interchangeable, but unions keep them from being easily replaced. Managers, however, because of the peculiarities of their position and their skills, often are interchangeable, and whatever security there is to be found in modern business life is surely not accountable on the basis of the free market system alone.

The conclusion of this argument, however, is not that we are *all* coerced by "the system"—a popular Marxist summary of the capitalist dilemma. Nor is it that *no one* is coerced, since, short of starvation, everyone could settle for some other job and salary, however minimal. The conclusion is rather that coercion is an *evaluative* concept, in which the language of rights and justice, and ethical conceptions of the good life, already play an intrinsic role. The concept of coercion has to be geared to individual needs and desires. No single standard exists for coercion any more than does a single standard exist for unfairness or "exploitation."

Nevertheless, since we can assume that everyone wants to live and live as well as possible, we can usually assume that threats on a person's life or health are coercive. But what counts as living well, and what counts as a threat on a person's well-being, are also variable. Our middle manager might quite rightly complain that she and her family couldn't possibly exist on less than $60,000 per year, given the country club dues, the house payments, the kids' Ivy League tuition, and so on. This argument will not spark the compassion of a worker making $13 per hour, but we can then go ahead and compare the worker's life with that of a Pakistani peasant, who works just as hard for $13 per year. We can agree that basic subsistence is the outer limit of coercion, but it then becomes much more difficult to decide individual cases. How are we to judge the difference between a case in which a worker is threatened with loss of a job and self-esteem as well as income and one in which a manager is threatened with the loss of a job and even greater loss of self-esteem as a failure?

Coercion plays two crucial and unfortunate roles in business life. First, it is a matter of injustice and therefore, according to the ethics of the free enterprise system itself, morally unacceptable. (Nevertheless, it may be that coercion is built into the system, or any system.) Second, it breeds a sense of impotence and resentment. As an injustice, coercion becomes more blameworthy the less power a person has; coercion of an unskilled, nonunionized woman worker is far more damnable than the pressure placed by the board on an already harried CEO. But just because people who are often and easily coerced learn to accept it as "a fact of life," it is not less of an injustice. Those who are doing the coercing (whether individuals or organizations or the "system" as a whole) have a consequent responsibility to undo the injustice, even if they know that they can continue to get away with it.

The role of coercion in the breeding of resentment and impotence may be a matter of injustice, but we might also recognize coercion and its effects even where there is no injustice. The middle manager who feels coerced by the company may not strike our moral heartstrings, but the resentment may become disruptive to the company, sooner or later. And the CEO who is coerced into making decisions against his will by a demanding board of directors may not represent an injustice of any kind, but we can be sure that, in watching his discomfort, we are also watching a company in trouble, where major decisions may be made only "under protest."

Whether on the grounds of justice or prudence, coercion should be eliminated as much as possible from the business world. In classical economics, with the unbreachable barriers between the people who ran a business and the factory folk who merely worked there, the theory was that the pressure of the market would guarantee good work and cheap wages, at the threat of starvation (which was a very real alternative). In the modern corporation, where the distinction between manager and worker is a matter of degree, this theory will no longer work. People coerced into work may be poor team members, poor employees, or weak links in a complex system. Coercion that is unjust, reported by continuous headlines in newspapers, can inspire consumers to boycott a company as a matter of taste, if not outright moral conviction, and can ruin a company quickly. Coercion that is within the guidelines of justice, however, may still be damaging. People who feel that they are inspired to do their job will work much better than people who feel forced to do it. The psychologist B. F. Skinner showed long ago that even pigeons and rats respond much more favorably to "positive reinforcement" than to punishment and threats. What is true of pigeons and rats is also true of what was once called "the rat race" of the business world; people respond to rewards and offers better than they do to coercion and threats. David Zimmerman has argued that offers can be coercive too* and Marxists sometimes talk about

---

*"Coercive Wage Offers," *Philosophy and Public Affairs.*

people being "co-opted" by an offer that brings them into an organization they formerly rejected. But to speak of "coercion" in these cases loses the force of the concept. As Zimmerman sums it up, "by and large, threats involve coercion and offers do not; mainly because people do not like to be threatened whereas they do like to receive offers." Perhaps there is no single statement in business ethics that will prove more valuable to managers. Even if they are tempted to threaten, they usually will find an offer, even of mere verbal approval, far more effective.

I. Moral Mazes, Moral Courage

> What is right in the corporation is not what is right in a man's home or in his church. What is right in the corporation is what the guy above you wants from you. That's what morality is in the corporation.
>
> —Robert Jackall, Moral Mazes*

Most people in the business world are not entrepreneurs. They work for somebody else, and often they work for a company. But such institutions readily become worlds of their own, and, as we have seen, the pressures within a corporation can often be such that they threaten to compromise or eclipse our normal sense of right and wrong, our common sense, our simple decency. The emphasis on toughness and competition within organizations, while it may to some extent be healthy and motivating, too often tends to become ruthless and cutthroat, an obstacle to teamwork and cooperation. The emphasis on teamwork and "doing your job," while in itself essential, can also be twisted into the demand for blind obedience. We discussed earlier the frequency of those ethical dilemmas in which two or more obligations or sense of loyalty conflict with one another, where there is a conflict of virtues, a clash of loyalties, a disharmony of equally valued values. We can easily imagine a pressured sales manager arguing that too much dependability and forthright honesty can undermine one's skills in negotiation and, in a sense, the business enterprise itself.

It is clear that loyalties often conflict on the job, particularly in a politicized company or institution. One's duty to superiors may well conflict with one's obligations to subordinates, and in any but the best organized company there is always the possibility of conflicting, even contradictory but equally obliging, orders from two different superiors. One's sense of loyalty to an aging and no longer effective manager who provided one's job opportunity in the first place may well clash with a more general sense of obligation to the company. And in all of this, one's own sense of what is right and what is wrong, what is fair and what is not, can easily get lost.

---

*A former vice president of a large firm, Robert Jackall, *Moral Mazes* (New York: Oxford University Press, 1988).

This is what sociologist Robert Jackall has called the problem of *moral mazes*. The problem is the loss of personal integrity due to the pressures of the organization. Corporations may pride themselves on their integrity and efficiency, but the truth in many cases is that, beneath the veneer of good intentions and self-congratulating speeches, the inside of many organizations is chaotic, suffocating, and even dangerous for those who work in them. We become what we do, and under the wrong kinds of pressures, the wrong kinds of demands for loyalty and unquestioning obedience, our personal virtues and ideals may turn out to be obstacles to success. They can wither away or become self-defeating if not nurtured in a climate that recognizes and rewards them. Their survival depends on being exercised in the kind of organization in which they flourish. When "what is right in the corporation is what the guy above you wants from you," personal judgment gets clouded and integrity gets sacrificed to mere exigency.

The problem is not that we are lost or trapped so much as we find ourselves in positions of increasing complexity in which maintaining our larger vision and sense of ethics becomes impossible. Jackall has identified what is surely the most serious threat to personal integrity, and that is the problem of *embeddedness*. People get embedded in their jobs and their positions in the company and they have trouble seeing beyond the pressures that they face. The result is a kind of blindness, a loss of moral vision. Business ethics means looking beyond the walls of one's department or company and beyond (or above) the "bottom line." Unfortunately, this perspective is easy to encourage but difficult to carry out when one is in the midst of a company crisis, and it is the rare executive or manager who can see the bigger picture in the middle of such circumstances. We have all seen corporations sacrifice their best people in the face of a financial downturn, and we all know "survivors" who, while contributing very little (and often slowing things down), manage to remain in the company through the harshest reductions. The secret of their success, it seems, is their embeddedness, their insinuation into a protected pocket under some patron or guardian who may persevere through similar insinuation. Those who get fired, on the other hand, may so suffer despite (or because of) their independence or their accomplishments. They are too visible and not sufficiently embedded. They make the mistake of taking business seriously instead of serving the powers that be. It is with such behavior in mind that Jackall proclaims (summarizing Thorstein Veblen) that there are "no intrinsic connections between the good of a particular corporation, the good of an individual manager, and the common weal."

One might (and must) distinguish between the purposes of a practice and its intrinsic goals and rules. The ethics of a practice, as suggested, consist not only in honoring the rules and pursuing its goals, but in trying to fulfill its ultimate purpose, which in the case of business is general prosperity and a version of distributive justice. But there is an unavoidable shift from ultimate purposes to internal goals, and the danger is that specific tasks and duties will eclipse the overall purposes of business altogether. Most of the time, of course, this is not an ethical problem, for the tasks and duties of a job in a well-organized corporation will already be fine-tuned in order to fulfill the corporate mission and ideals. But in a sleaze-bag corporation, fulfilling one's tasks and duties as instructed is surely not enough. I have a student who recently quit her job as a "telemarketer" for a company that sold (via credit card) nonexistent ("it should arrive within two weeks") surgical equipment to physicians. Hers is an apt and common example. Perceiving the violation of ethics and the wrongness of fulfilling her tasks and duties in such a case did not require any great ethical sensitivity, though it did require a certain amount of sacrifice and courage. "I really needed the job," my student complained. And so do we all. What is essential is to see one's particular job and role in an organization in a larger ethical context, even if (especially if) one "really needs the job." Jackall asks, "How does one act in such a world and maintain a sense of personal integrity?"

If corporate life were (as it often proclaims) a matter of merit, if success really were the natural result of innovation, hard work, and good results, embeddedness would be at worst a distraction and, more often and much better, a welcome camaraderie in which to pursue joint projects and shared goals and interests. But in many, if not most, managerial positions, one's accomplishments are wholly dependent on the actions of others, including those over whom one has no supervisory capacity and no control. And so one gets desperate, seeking out misleading measures and false security, and losing sight (or one's boss loses sight) of the ultimate goals and purposes of the organization. When sight gets blurred, the idea of excellence loses its meaning, only to be replaced by a more rigid and often pathological sense of community known as "teamwork" in that cynical sense that every manager recognizes as "play ball or get out." In other words, shut up and keep your ethics to yourself. This results in the disastrous tendency to measure results by "the bottom line" and ethics by costs and benefits, to succumb to the pressure to compromise not only one's personal values but also the values fostered by the corporation, and the inevitable temptation to engage in office politics.

What is the answer to Jackall's gruesome and all-too-real portrait of many corporations in trouble? Cooperation, in this case, is part of the problem, and integrity, in the face of conflicts of the virtues, is the challenge rather than the answer. The answer is *moral courage.* Moral courage is not just another warrior virtue, transposed from the battlefield into the more civilized realm of the corporation. It is not the same as toughness, although toughness can be a form of moral courage. Moral courage is not self-sacrifice; indeed, this tendency to confuse the virtues with altruism and self-sacrifice is one of the confusions we have been fighting throughout this book. Moral courage is not self-righteous obstinacy and it is not at all opposed to compromise. Indeed, moral courage is more often evident in the willingness to compromise than in the refusal to do so.

Moral courage includes an appreciation of the bigger picture, not just one's immediate work world and its pressures, but the ability to recognize the purposes of the organization and the ways in which the organization or some part of it thwarts its own best intentions. It means sticking with those best intentions and heeding a higher loyalty than one's immediate superior or, on occasion, even the chief executive officer. The price may be high, as we will see in the sad cases of the whistle-blower and the company martyr. But moral courage is often successful as well, and, luckily, most corporations and their top executives take ethics and integrity seriously. They welcome (even if they do not like) advice and criticism from below, and they are well aware that petty politics within the organization can destroy the efficiency of the company as a whole. Indeed, even the most corrupt corporation cannot afford to forget that the customer still has a lot of clout, and whatever upheavals and political battles may be fought within the corporation, the bottom line depends on the marketplace. Someone has to be producing and selling something. The abusiveness and intrusiveness of office politics have their limits, and those limits are set by the need to produce and make a profit. To put the point bluntly, if there were no market, there wouldn't be anything to fight about. The obvious truth is that there is (and must be) considerable correlation between corporate cooperation and contribution in the marketplace. Integrity in business is, accordingly, paying attention to those ultimate powers of the marketplace rather than just the immediate pressures of one's job situation. Thus it is that integrity and success are not so much opposed as mutually supportive. It is a healthy organization that recognizes this and makes sure that it permeates every level and is sought and cultivated in every member of the institution.

J.   "WHISTLE-BLOWING"

> The key question is, at what point should an employee resolve that allegiance to society (e.g. the public safety) must supersede allegiance to the organization's policies (e.g. the corporate profit), and then act on that resolve by informing outsiders or legal authorities? It is a question that involves basic issues of individual freedom, concentration of power, and information flow to the public.
>
> —Ralph Nader, Whistle-Blowing

In the classic movie *On the Waterfront*, the hero Terry (Marlon Brando) is subpoenaed to testify against his mobster-guardian, Joe Friendly (Lee J. Cobb). "But he used to take me to ball games," Terry laments, summarizing in a phrase a lifetime of favors and special considerations. "Don't break my heart," answers the parish priest, who is out to break the mob. Terry's dramatic turmoil is an excellent illustration of the ultimate freedom and power, and the ultimate responsibility, that every employee may have to come to terms with. On the one hand is an employer who has been supportive, helpful, friendly, even almost "like family."

Cheating in School ——

Former Stanford University President Donald Kennedy blamed "infirmities" in the institution's accounting practices for overcharging the federal government more than $160 million over the past decade, including $180,000 for depreciation of the Stanford Sailing Association yacht and $185,000 for administrative costs for a profitable Stanford-owned shopping center. Kennedy said his institution billed the government for many of the expenses "merely because it was lawful to do so."

—Quarterly Review of Doublespeak, January 1992

On the other hand are larger responsibilities that only become painfully evident, sometimes, when the employer runs against the law or seriously against the public interest. Of course, if the employer is an unreasonable tyrant, there will be no turmoil; any employee with half a chance will take the opportunity to put the tyrant out of business. But then, every human enterprise, including every business, has its embarrassments, its errors in judgment, its shadowy underside that everyone would prefer to keep hidden. It is only when the shadows are hiding bloody murder, or some truly serious danger or illegality, that "whistle-blowing" becomes a responsibility that supersedes corporate loyalty. The hard question is, when is that point reached?

"Whistle-blowing is an expression of freedom and an exercise in power. The sometimes pathetic question "What can I do?" *always* has one possible answer, no matter how restricted and impotent we may be inside the organization, a few well-aimed words on the outside can virtually always embarrass even the largest company, and if the information is sufficiently lethal, even bring the corporation to its knees. In a country that so loves scandals and watching the powerful squirm, and where the media are so responsive to the whiff of scandal that even a few words from "an inside source" are virtually guaranteed coverage on the evening news, the power of the disgruntled employee is considerable. But this power means freedom from the total control of even the most "authoritarian" organization. And this freedom, in turn, means the *responsibility* of using such power wisely, as well as using it when necessary.

The importance and also the *pathos* of whistle-blowing depends upon two factors in particular. One is the *prima facie* sense of loyalty required by membership in any organization. This does not mean, as some of the critics of corporations would say, that such loyalty involves blind or terrified devotion or submission or an oath of silence of the sort usually identified with organized crime organizations. What it does mean is that the member has an identity in part

> There is not a crime, there is not a dodge, there is not a trick, there is not a swindle, there is not a vice which does not live by secrecy. Get these things out in the open, describe them, attack them, ridicule them in the press, and sooner or later public opinion will sweep them away. Publicity may not be the only thing that is needed, but it is the one thing without which all other agencies will fail.
>
> Joseph Pulitzer

by *being* part of an organization, by sharing its interests, and by having special concern for its well-being. It may be that the company, like Joe Friendly, even takes employees to ball games and offers any number of other special favors and "perks," but even in the absence of such special treatment, there is a presupposition of loyalty, such that employees will not simply hurt the company without very good reason. The other factor is the overriding responsibilities we all have to society, but, as we argued in earlier chapters, these responsibilities, while *prima facie* dominant, nevertheless must always be weighed in each case against the cost of betrayal and personal risk as well. It is a matter of history that whistle-blowers often take great risks, not only to their careers but to their lives. And this is not just the stuff of great movies. An employee of a scandal-ridden major airplane manufacturer who dared to warn the public (through an influential senator) that the company was playing seriously illegal games that were costing the taxpayers millions of dollars was "literally run out of the plant" and found himself unemployed for years. When the risks are so great that someone's life is in jeopardy, hesitating to "blow the whistle" may usually be excused as a matter of prudence. But when the crime or the danger is *so* great that even risking someone's life may be a perfectly reasonable expectation, the responsibility to the larger society still takes precedence, not only over company loyalty but over personal life and limb as well. Few employees ever face a situation so desperate or dramatic. But such cases are only the extremes of a conflict that many employees meet up with at some time in their career. No organization in the world never makes mistakes, or never, at times, enrages its own employees.

What sorts of situations are serious enough to prompt "blowing the whistle"? Simply summarized, they are situations in which the public safety is endangered or in which the law is being seriously violated (usually to be distinguished from "bending it a little bit"). Sometimes, the dispute itself may be wholly internal, such as those cases in which an employer fails to give due attention to the safety of the workers, employment or promotion practices are unfair, or some other friction between employees and management (or between employees or between managers) seems unresolvable. In these cases an employee (or many employees, as in a strike) may reach outside the company for pressure and support.

Ralph Nader, in his report on the problems that may require employee action, lists the following as examples of causes for overriding employee loyalty and "blowing the whistle"[1]:

1. Selling defective vehicles to unsuspecting customers.

2. Vast waste of government funds by private contractors.

3. Industrial dumping of poisonous wastes.

4. Companies making illegal campaign contributions.

5. Systematic discrimination by age, sex, or race.

6. Misuse of workers' pension funds.

7. Willful deception in advertising a worthless or harmful product.

8. The sale of adulterated foods.

9. Abuse of government power or position for private gain.

10. Lack of enforcement of existing laws, which are supposed to protect the public (as in not allowing use of poisonous chemicals).

11. Corruption (bribes or kick-backs).

12. Suppression of information regarding occupational hazards or disease (such as certain chemicals in the air that cause cancer).

Virtually all of these cases have to be weighed against personal risk and company loyalty, and it should not be supposed that *any* violation of the law or threat to the public will *always* be overriding, for example, if an employee "blew the whistle" on an executive for entertaining a prospective client with an expensive lunch. There is a sense in which false or at least exaggerated advertising is an intrinsic part of the advertising game itself and waste of government funds (though certainly not "vast" waste) is bound to be found in every government contract. But, at the same time, to say that every case is a matter of judgment is not to say that there are no answers, or that it's a "matter of opinion" whether we should blow the whistle or not. Certain cases leap out at us, and it is because of those cases that we are all pretty much agreed that whistle-blowing is an essential responsibility of every citizen; it is an assurance of freedom and a modicum of protected power to be exercised when necessary.

Why is whistle-blowing so important? Why not wait for government investigators to find the company out, and so minimize risk and not jeopardize the company from the inside? The answer, quite simply, is that people on the inside often

---

[1]Ralph Nader, *Whistle-Blowing* (New York: Grossman, 1972), p. 4.

know much more than anyone possibly could on the outside. In cases in which the public well-being or the law is at stake, the difference between the time it would take a government agency to find out anything (if indeed it could do so) and the time it takes an employee to make a phone call could be crucial. But protecting and even encouraging whistle-blowers is also in the interests of the corporations themselves. By making it quite clear that they are open to the rigor of internal scrutiny and criticism, corporations thereby offset the primary reason for government intervention, namely, the suspicion that all is not "above board" and that, furthermore, employee dissent is being forceably silenced. Indeed, as some companies and government figures have learned in the last few years, the cover-up and silencing of those who would do their duty as citizens is often considered far more serious than the original crime itself.

Why be a whistle-blower? What makes it worth the risk? Some moralists would consider this an out-of-order question, insisting that because it is a responsibility, it is not a question of "what makes it worthwhile." But in real life this is a question that must always be answered. The answer may sometimes be "don't take that risk when the risk is great enough but the crime is small enough." Then it is not worth it, and prudential considerations override social responsibilities. But many people feel that when the problem is great enough, they "can't live" with themselves otherwise. They may find themselves "unable to face friends and family," knowing that their lack of courage may have contributed to a major disaster or shameful corruption. They may believe—and often they are right—that though the short-term costs will be dreadful, the longer-term rewards will be more than worthwhile. Or they may just be motivated by the sheer sense of duty and the public good itself, refusing to consider such issues as personal cost or reward or what other people might think. Last but not least, there is always that perennial American emphasis on being a *hero,* and, in many cases of whistle-blowing, that is just what happens. In the midst of risk in the name of the public good, heroes are born.

But how do we know that a particular case is a situation calling for courage and heroism, rather than being a matter just as well dropped and allowed to slip quietly into unrecorded history? How do we know whether to blow the whistle or not? Nader offers the following guidelines, by way of a series of questions to ask ourselves[2]:

1. Is my knowledge of the matter complete and accurate?

2. What are the objectionable practices and what public interests do they harm?

3. How far would I and can I go inside the corporation with my concern or objection?

---

[2]Ibid., p. 6.

4.   Will I be violating any rules by contacting outside parties and, if so, is whistle-blowing nevertheless justified?

5.   Will I be violating any laws or ethical duties by *not* contacting external parties?

6.   Once I have decided to act, what is the best way to blow the whistle—anonymously, overtly, by resignation prior to speaking out, or in some other way?

7.   What will be likely responses from various sources—inside and outside the organization—to the whistle-blowing action?

8.   What is expected to be achieved by whistle-blowing in the particular situation?

■ Summary and Conclusion

Freedom is the key word in our "free enterprise system," not only in our idea that the business world should be free from unnecessary government interference but also in our more basic belief that the free market will contribute to our individual freedom in all aspects of our lives. Freedom is so important to us that it often remains unanalyzed, a mere word or a slogan; freedom is not just an end in itself, but a condition for any number of other good things in life. And even when freedom is something of an end, it must be viewed against a background of many different considerations.

Power on the other hand, is often viewed with suspicion in our egalitarian society. Insofar as power represents superiority over other people, we see it as a danger. But if power means, essentially, the ability to get things done—including the ability to get other people to do their part—then power is not a danger but a necessity, and an essential part of freedom. Responsibility, the topic of previous chapters, presupposes both freedom and power—the freedom to act, the power to get something done. Morality, argued the great German philosopher Immanuel Kant, presupposes freedom and power—"ought implies can."

Lack of freedom and power may also have important ethical considerations. For example, it is because all individuals cannot fight for their share of social benefits or protect themselves against others that the concepts of rights and justice become so important (versus "might makes right"). And lack of freedom and power in business gives rise to many of the most pressing personal problems in corporate life today, particularly through the resentment that the sense of impotence breeds. Gross differences in freedom and power also complicate the ethical picture, particularly in questions of *exploitation* and *coercion*. Indeed, the justifiability of the free enterprise system itself may depend upon the validity of the charge that capitalism exploits and coerces the workers and the consumers, who are not, therefore, free.

In large and complex organizations, any employee, except (sometimes) the chief executive officer, is bound to feel somewhat impotent and bound by rules not of his own making. But it does not follow that there is no freedom or that such employees are completely powerless, nor does it follow that these all-important concepts are meaningless in the modern business world. What it does mean is that we need a more subtle sense of what counts as freedom and power, and an appreciation of how to use the freedom and power that we do have.

■ STUDY QUESTIONS

1. Why is freedom of speech so important to us? Is it an end in itself, or a means? (If so, to what? And how?) What kinds of constraints apply to this celebrated freedom? What other considerations can override this freedom? (Start with yelling "fire" in a crowded, unburning theater.)

2. What freedoms are necessary for business life to go on as we know it? Which of these freedoms must be true in order for the free market system to be justified? Which of these freedoms can be justified *because* it is necessary for the proper working of the free enterprise system?

3. Jean-Paul Sartre, the French existentialist, has claimed that "we are *always* free." Indeed, he goes so far as to say that everyone alive in 1943 is responsible for the Second World War, and that "each of us chooses our own war." What could he mean by that? If he were to say today that "every businessperson is responsible for the current state of the business world, and is free to change it," what would he be saying to you?

4. How important is freedom to you? How much security and status would you exchange in your career in return for increased freedom, and vice versa? Give examples.

5. How would you define "power"? How do you tell which people in your organization have power and which ones do not? What are the "trappings" of power that can easily mislead us into thinking that someone is or is not powerful within the company?

6. Does an employer have a right to inquire about or investigate your sex life, your marital status, your relationship with your spouse or children? Why or why not?

7. In what sense is an employee who has just been fired "free"? What does your answer indicate about the nature of freedom?

8. In your own work, what sorts of abuses would prompt you to "blow the whistle" on your employer? What personal concerns would motivate you to, or keep you from, doing so?

■ For Class Discussion

Whistle-Blowing

Consider the following survey conducted by *Business and Society Review* (#13): A worker in an airplane manufacturing firm's design department is convinced that the latch mechanism on a plane's cargo door is not sufficiently secure and that the door has to be redesigned in order to ensure against the possibility of a crash. He goes to his supervisor with this information and is told that the Federal Aviation Administration has given the legitimate approvals and that he should not "rock the boat." He goes to the president of the firm and gets the same answer.

Would that worker be justified in taking this information to the news media?

Responses:

Yes, 35 (69%). No, 14 (27%). No answer, 2.

Comments:

"The worker, if he is absolutely sure of his technology, should undoubtedly go to the media."

"The worker has an overriding responsibility to the public to ensure the safety of the plan if he is convinced and can provide evidence that a danger exists. Before taking his findings to the media, the worker should take them directly to the Federal Aviation Administration. If this attempt to correct the problem fails and the only avenue of appeal left is the media, the employee is justified in taking that course."

"The worker would be justified in going to the news media with his viewpoint on the safety of the door latch. No question of morality enters into his decision on whether or not to do it."

"Yes—if prepared to accept the consequences." (Three people gave this answer.)

"What do you mean, 'justified'? If he's right, of course the answer is 'yes.' But what if he's wrong and the firm loses a big contract from bad publicity and goes bankrupt?"

"No—he should go next to the FAA." (Four people gave this answer.)

"First to the FAA, then, to get attention, to the courts."

"Yes—after resigning." (Two people gave this answer.)

"No. But he should rapidly double-check the data which originally convinced him of the failure. If still convinced, take to corporate counsel, or even board of directors."

"No—he should write directly to the FAA, after having told the firm's president that he would do so."

"Yes—if he honestly believes there is no other recourse."

"No—I doubt that a worker (a) has sufficient knowledge to conclude that the cargo door is not sufficiently secure or (b) has the engineering expertise to call for redesign. I would recommend that he place his thoughts in writing and give them wide dissemination to all his supervisors. To act otherwise is for him to make the moral judgment that everyone except himself lacks expertise and/or integrity."

How would you answer the question?

How Bad Are Monopolies?

In Adam Smith's classic economic theory, it was competition between numerous small businesses that assured the success of the market system. Concentration of market power, or monopoly, reduced or smothered competition, thus eliminating the mechanism that Smith held to be the one guarantee against economic tyranny and selfish abuse. Ever since, American governmental policy has been aimed at preventing monopolies, first against the "trusts" of the nineteenth century, most recently against the giant corporations in communication and computer technology, including American Telephone and Telegraph (AT&T) and International Business Machines (IBM). The government eventually dropped its multimillion-dollar suit against IBM, but AT&T was eventually forced to break up into many smaller "Baby Bell" companies. IBM has more recently broken up on its own. Both companies insisted that they were not monopolies, but rather combatants in an increasingly aggressive competitive war. Perhaps the most striking new note in this century-old battle was the appearance of foreign competition. The argument is here summarized by economist Lester Thurow:

> The IBM and AT&T cases were the last dinosaurs of the antitrust era. Never again are we apt to witness massive cases that stretch on for decades and grind up hundreds of millions of dollars in corporate and Federal resources.
>
> There has been a massive change in the environment. For the first time in many decades, America faces competitors that are our financial and technological equals. Even some of the largest American corporations are in danger of being driven out of business. Think, for example, of General Motors. For many years it was the largest industrial firm in the world. Today, even if it were the only American auto manufacturer, it would still be in a competitive fight for its life.
>
> What seems large relative to the United States is not large when considered in the context of the world economy. This is particularly

true when it is recognized that foreign firms are often government owned, backed by state banking or belong to larger combines. A government-owned Renault supported by state banking or a company belonging to the Mitsubishi group with its extensive cooperation and lines of credit is simply more powerful than an American firm with the same sales.

The same competitive situation is looming on the horizon in telecommunications. New technologies and foreign competitors are about to engulf the industry. If America is to survive economically, it needs the strongest possible competitors in this industry. A strong AT&T will undoubtedly crush some weak American firms, but these firms were going to be crushed by other strong competitors in any case.

But the problems of antitrust extend beyond that of a changing environment. Enforcement often loses sight of what should be the predominant question. How do we make the United States a more efficient and productive economy? In answering this question, bigness is not always badness, and mergers are not always anticompetitive.

"Are Monopolies Necessarily Bad?" *Newsweek,* Jan. 18, 1982

HISTORICAL INTERLUDE

FREE TO CHOOSE: MILTON FRIEDMAN

A society that puts equality—in the sense of equality of outcome—ahead of freedom will end up with neither equality nor freedom. The use of force to achieve equality will destroy freedom, and the force, introduced for good purposes, will end up in the hands of people who use it to promote their own interests. . . . On the other hand, a society that puts freedom first will, as a happy by-product, end up with both greater freedom and greater equality.

—M. Friedman, Free to Choose

Every applied economic theory, no matter how "value-free" or "scientific," also involves ethics, a set of values and priorities. In Adam Smith's theory, the most obvious of these is the wealth of the nation itself. In Marx's, it is the material and cultural well-being of the worker. In Milton Friedman's, the most pronounced single value is, without question, the value of *freedom.* Freedom is not only the basis of the market itself, it is also the most valuable result of the market system: the freedom of each individual to choose.

Friedman is the most outspoken responsible defender of the benignity of the free market. Like Adam Smith, he attacks government interference in the workings of the market—even in such public concerns as education and urban transportation—as inefficient, ineffective, and, what is much worse, an infringement of our fundamental right to economic freedom. In response to critics who insist that the market cannot do what Friedman claims it can do, he responds that a truly free market has never been allowed to work. As for what it has already done, we need only look at America—as opposed to virtually any socialist country in the world—and a few well-chosen examples of developing countries (Hong Kong or Brazil) that have taken the free enterprise path to progress.

What Friedman means by "freedom" is freedom from coercion. This means, almost always, freedom from government interference. Friedman is not concerned primarily with rights and obligations, but rather with the basic right to economic freedom. Equality is not a central issue for Friedman; indeed, he argues that equality is impossible to achieve, given the obvious differences in skills and talents. Neither is he primarily concerned with the satisfaction of basic needs, although in a truly free market, the general prosperity it will bring to society as a whole will automatically benefit the poor as well. The "right to have basic human needs fulfilled" is not a basic right in itself; instead, ensuring a basic right to absolute freedom of action in a free market system will result in the fulfilling of those needs.

Government's role in the free market scheme is to define and enforce the ground rules under which the free market will operate and no more. For example, Congress should be primarily involved in setting up "the rules of the economic and social game that the citizens of a free society play." These rules include those allowing personal property and binding contracts and punishments for violations. The police enforce the rules (against theft), and the judiciary should be primarily involved in arbitrating disputes over the rules. Government should also provide national defense to protect us from foreign enemies, but the government's role should not be much more than this. At the heart of Friedman's ethical vision is this image of each of us as a "player" in the economic game, pursuing our own individual profit but in so doing enriching us all, even if unintentionally. We should be protected by the government from the "coercion of our fellow citizens," but within the bounds of the economic game, each of us is free to do as we please, and to "vote" with our dollars, thus determining the direction of the market itself.

Friedman, like Marx, is an economic determinist. He argues that the nature of a society's economic arrangements—especially the control of the "forces of production"—determine not only the general style but even the details of each citizen's life. Economic control by the government leads to control in all aspects of life. Economic coercion is coercion in general. A free society, accordingly, must begin with a free economy. Even if a "command" or a "planned" economy could be made more efficient than a free market system (and Friedman argues that this is never so), it would still be objectionable because it would interfere with an individual's freedom. Although the argument is often couched in economic terms, there is still an underlying ethical bias, which is that only a free market guarantees individual freedom.

It is important to distinguish these two general arguments—the efficiency argument and the ethical argument. The first, perhaps, is the most influential, if only because the modern examples of eastern Europe have been so unattractive. When Friedman points to the state of our nationalized railroads, for example, it is hard to deny that government has not lived up to even the most minimal standards of efficiency and attention to the consumer. Similarly, Friedman argues that if all of the money spent by the government in social services were given directly to the poor, instead of administered by the labyrinth of government bureaucracies, every family of four below the poverty line would receive $14,000 (1978 dollars) while the poverty line itself was only $7,000. But this efficiency argument is only half the picture. More important from an ethical point of view is the argument that government planning and social services, even if they were efficient, would still be paternalistic to the poor, and the tax dollars would have to be stolen from the rich, and thus government would be inherently coercive to all. Absolute freedom for individuals would include the *right* to make their own decisions, even if this only means the decision not to compete or not to live well, but only to be left alone.

The idea that citizens "vote" with their dollars is not just a metaphor. This is the very essence of the free market and the ability of citizens to satisfy their desires within it. The government has no way of truly knowing what its citizens want, and, in any case, the demands of the majority must not be allowed to determine the opportunities of a minority. But even worse, the way the American government works, a special interest group, though a minority, tends to tyrannize the majority. Instead, the market allows individuals to choose, through purchasing or not purchasing, exactly what they want, thus voting with their dollars. Thus, "the ballot box produces conformity without unanimity; the marketplace, unanimity without conformity."

Friedman's argument assumes that every individual has the opportunity and the ability to compete in this free market system, and if women, the disabled, racial minorities, or the rural poor are excluded from this free and open competition, the market will eventually right itself. In the meantime, government interference is grossly inefficient and unfair to those who can compete. The beauty of the absolutely free market is that it is impersonal, and this impersonality will eventually result in the marketplacé realizing (no matter how bigoted certain individuals may personally be) that segments of the available work force are underutilized, and the marketplace will extend jobs there, albeit at low wage

The Legacy of Deregulation ——

The orthodoxy of deregulation that characterized the 1980s was supposed to bring with it intense competition. Instead, consumers have seen less competition, higher prices, and deteriorating service in industry after industry. Paul Stephen Dempsey, professor of law at the University of Denver, offers his assessment of the failures of deregulation:

Airlines
- Deteriorating service (unrealistic scheduling, deliberate overbooking, false and misleading advertising, etc.).
- Large number of failures (150 bankruptcies).
- Unprecedented industry concentration (eight firms control 90 percent of the passenger market; only three to five airlines are viable).
- Erosion of the margin of safety.
- Pricing discrimination.
- Prices (in real dollars and adjusted for changing fuel costs) higher than prederegulation trend.
- Deterioration in labor–management relations.

Banks and S&Ls
- More fraudulent transactions.
- More failed institutions.
- Federal deposit insurance funds near bankruptcy.
- Taxpayers will pay $500 billion—more than $2,000 for every man, woman, and child in the United States—to bail out failed thrifts.

Bus Industry
- Unprecedented concentration (industry duopoly becomes an anemic monopoly that faces bankruptcy).
- Deterioration of service (4,500 small communities abandoned).
- Deterioration in labor–management relations.

Cable Television
- Sharply increased prices.
- Deterioration of service.
- Unprecedented concentration.

Railroads

- Unprecedented concentration (seven major railroads control 85 percent of the freight).
- Pricing discrimination (bulk shippers prejudiced).
- Higher coal rates result in significant increase in electricity prices for consumers.
- Deterioration in labor–management relations.

Telecommunications

- Deterioration in service.
- Industry concentration (long-distance service dominated by AT&T).
- Local and rural rate increases outpace declining toll rates.

Trucking

- Large number of failures (60 percent of general freight companies disappear with no significant new entries).
- Unprecedented concentration.
- Deterioration in safety.
- Highly discriminatory pricing (prejudicing small and rural shippers).
- Deterioration in labor–management relations.

Business & Society Review

rates. Even sweatshops that pay below minimum wage are useful, according to Friedman, because they give the otherwise unemployable and untrained worker a chance to climb onto the bottom rung of the economic ladder, learn a skill, and so go on to a better paying job.

Friedman's emphasis on freedom must not be interpreted as a total neglect of rights and responsibilities, but it does suggest that these are more products of the market than its presuppositions. The market itself has no responsibilities, as Friedman himself has argued, and so all responsibilities fall to the individual. But this raises very special problems regarding the nature of social responsibilities, as we have seen elsewhere. Friedman also argues that, as part of the business world, people's responsibilities are limited to their fiduciary responsibilities to others in the business world. Responsibilities to others in society or to the well-being of society as a whole Friedman relegates to the realm of charity and to the indirect (and possibly unintended) effects of the business enterprise. Any effort of society as a whole to affect the social welfare through government interference with business (for example, through taxes or regulation) he baldly labels "socialism."

It is not that Friedman is insensitive to racism or sexism or the plight of the poor, but he considers the cure worse than the disease. Such social problems will disappear, he assures us, if we leave them up to the market system. Racism and sexism will disappear because they do not pay, and poverty will disappear with general prosperity. Support for the arts and protection of the environment will operate in much the same way; they will survive because people are willing to support them, people who have been made prosperous through the free market system. It is a grand promise, but it depends upon the assumption that the ethical and aesthetic concerns of the individual will be well cultivated by the profit-minded free market ethic invoked in its support.

Friedman's model of the free enterprise system assumes that no force in the marketplace has an undue amount of power, especially economic power, over any other group. In fact, he admits that this assumption is not true of our society. Large corporations do exercise an inordinate amount of power, and this seriously distorts the marketplace and threatens precisely those freedoms that the free market is designed to defend. This leads Friedman to proclaim that he is "not pro-business, but pro-free enterprise." And just as he decries government support of individuals, Friedman rejects government aids to business as just another form of welfare and another step towards "socialism."

Some macroethical theorists focus their attention on the abuses and inadequacies of the free enterprise system; Friedman focuses mainly on its virtues and warns against interference with it. For him, paternalism on the part of government is far more of a threat to the well-being of our society: "Expenditures for social security, welfare, medicare, Medicaid and other transfer programs, as well as for the host of new regulatory agencies, . . . generate discontent about waste and efficiency . . . and they involve taking from some to give to others, or imposing some people's values on other people. . . . The rapid growth of the paternal state threatens both national security and domestic harmony."* By contrast, the efficiency and prosperity offered by an unfettered market system will provide just those benefits paternalistically provided by the government, without the cost and without interfering with individual freedom.

---

*"The Paternal State," *Newsweek,* Jan. 22, 1979.

– 13 –

The Meaning of Work

Work is the curse of the drinking class.

—Oscar Wilde

W e often say and think that we work "for a living," and conclude, often regretfully, especially on Monday mornings, that it is one of the necessities of life. We'd rather not do it. We'd rather be rich from birth and not have to worry about all of this, not have to get up early in the morning and waste sunny days working. But as understandable as such daydreams and laments may be, they involve a crucial misunderstanding of the place of work in our ethics, indeed, a place so central that it is often called simply, the "work ethic." The "work ethic" is a conception of life that makes work into something much more than a mere "necessity" for survival and a means of getting the things that we want. It means that work itself is good, that work itself builds "character," and that work is one of the main ingredients in our conception of who we are, what we are worth, and how we feel about our lives.

In the Bible, work is considered quite literally a "curse," an epithet that has endured until the present time. Adam and Eve were expelled from Eden, and part of their punishment was that they henceforth had to toil for a living, instead of simply picking the fruits off trees. In the New Testament, St. Paul sums up the ancient philosophy of work concisely: work or starve. This did not apply to a significant proportion of the community, of course, namely those aristocrats who skimmed the wealth off the top and, while they may have been skilled and carried out important jobs for society as military leaders and statesmen, would not have

421

considered such roles in society as "work." Work was the necessary evil of the lower classes, degrading if also essential to the survival of the society. Whatever the upper classes did to wile away their time, it wasn't "work." It was, Aristotle tells us, an expression of virtue and "excellence," but not work.

One of the most momentous conceptual changes in Western history ushered in much of what we call "modern times" (not coincidentally the title of one of Charlie Chaplin's best movies, in which he satirizes the plight of the modern-day workingman). It was a change that, like all conceptual changes, was a response to new conditions in the world, but also, as in every major change in social conditions, the conceptual change helped make that change possible. The change includes a dramatic growth in urban population and in what we call "the middle class." Consequently, there was great growth in both the demand for material goods and the abilities of society to supply them. Increased trade and increasing use of that abstraction called "money" produced the demand for a new kind of person, or, at least, the respectability of an old kind of person, the merchant and the entrepreneur, ready to make some money with a new scheme, a new mode of production, a new system of supply and distribution. Accordingly, this new kind of person did become respectable (though it took centuries to actually make the change). And "work," which was necessary to supply the new demands, became respectable too. Of course, there was an enormous difference between the "work" of the new entrepreneurs and the work of the people who physically made the products. But now that "work" was respectable, according to John Calvin, it was an exercise of God's gifts rather than His punishment, a proof of moral worth rather than a necessary and degrading evil. There was no longer any need to distinguish "work" in the contemptuous sense from "work" in a more general sense, including those "knowledge workers" (as Peter Drucker calls them) in the offices of management and planning. Indeed, it was with a certain sense of honor that they applied to themselves this term that had formerly been applied mainly to peasants who toiled in the fields and laborers who struggled with heavy loads. They too knew the nobility of such work, even if the amount of sweat and kinetic energy might not have been so measurable.

It is in this perspective that we should understand the *meaning of work,* not as a "necessary evil" or as "a way to make a decent living," but as the key to the modern character. Our jobs are not just something we do; our jobs define what and who we are. Hating our jobs is not just the resentment of an imposed necessity; it is a real confusion about who we are and what we are supposed to do. Indeed, the older language of the Calvinists is revealing here; they spoke of work as a *mission,* the task to which God had appointed us. In America, the new Protestant ethic was spread mainly by the Puritans, the result being the "puritan ethic." It made the virtues of good business into the virtues of good living and goodness itself, which again were dictated by God. The first thing to recognize about work in our society, then, is its momentous importance, not just in our production and acquisition of material goods, but in our psychological and even

The Work Ethic ——

I have been trying to figure out how the new work ethic works, ethically speaking.

I know what the phrase used to mean: that work was at the center of a moral life. I also know that it comes from the Reformation days when Calvin and others tried to exhort people out of their medieval slump by convincing them that the way to heaven was by working hard on earth.

This was more sophisticated than St. Paul's economics. Paul had said simply, if you don't work, you don't eat. The Protestants went beyond the basics, to insist that work was good and leisure evil. It was this belief, along with the notion that hard work produced success, which made the ideal so powerful.

But now when I hear about the work ethic, about how Americans have lost it and don't know where to find it, we seem most worried about two classes of people: the rich and poor. In fact, we seem to be perfecting a two-track philosophy.

According to the politics of the new fiscal year, the rich have lost their willingness to work hard because the government has taken too much money away from them.

The poor, on the other hand, have lost their willingness to work hard because the government has given too much money to them. In response to this grave situation, as of Oct. 1, we have cut the taxes of the rich most lavishly, giving them more money and more incentive to work. We have cut aid to the poor, giving them less money and therefore more incentive to work.

Now no one has explained to me exactly why the rich need money to make them labor while the poor need desperation. No one has explained to me why we choose to entice rich people to work in jobs that are presumably decent and choose to force poor people to work in jobs that are often boring or menial.

Ellen Goodman, *The Boston Globe,* 1981

spiritual well-being. "Work" for us is a *moral* term, an expression indicating personal worth. "Lazy" or "shiftless" is a term of moral condemnation, and unemployment, whatever the cause, is not just a material misfortune but a degradation of character. The modern curse is *not being able to work* instead of, as in the Bible, being forced to work in order to survive.

A.   THE NATURE OF WORK

The gods had condemned Sisyphus to ceaselessly rolling a rock to the top of a mountain, whence the stone would fall back of its own weight. They had thought with some reason that there is no more dreadful punishment than futile and hopeless labor.
                              —Albert Camus, *The Myth of Sisyphus*

From work as a curse to work as doing God's will and proving a person's worth is an enormous change in concepts. But with that change come changes in a great many other conceptions we have of ourselves too. For example, it leads us to think that, as a gift instead of a curse, work should not just be toil and suffering, but *rewarding,* even enjoyable. It leads us to be much more attentive to what our work—and thus ourselves—is *worth,* in terms of both our efforts and what we accomplish. With this, we become extremely sensitive to being "paid what we're worth," to others "earning their own way," and to the danger of being *exploited.*

The change in the nature of work also brought momentous changes. For instance, it used to be that a person could be proud of not having to work; today, that is a matter of shame for most people. Unemployment is a curse, and just quitting a job because we don't like it (without taking another one immediately) strikes many people as the height of irresponsibility. The shift from sheer physical labor to "knowledge work" carries with it a very different conception of the nature of work; it no longer means sore muscles and cuts and scrapes and exhaustion so much as stress and responsibilities, time spent thinking and talking, and filling out assorted slips of paper. For people who work in a company of any considerable size, especially in managerial positions, personal accomplishment is difficult to measure, and this in itself has forced some of the most dramatic changes in the nature of work and our conception of it. Since the actual results are hard to measure, lost in the complex of contributions made by everyone else and often dependent on the actual labor of others, our conception of worth becomes more abstract; it becomes an identification with the company and project as a whole, instead of our own contributions and a function of approval and recognition. This leads to a peculiar phenomenon: the approval and recognition of our peers and superiors now becomes as crucial to job success and, consequently, self-esteem, as actual accomplishment. Our pay for the job becomes not so much the reward for a job well-done as a general measure of our worth. Thus work and the money we get for work become connected in a particularly powerful way.

Even though most people in modern society now do more "knowledge work" than physical labor, the ancient conception of work as physical production (of food, building materials, buildings, and so on) still remains very much with us. The fruits of physical labor are, usually, easy to see; accomplishment can be measured by the bushel, by the number of bricks produced, or by the progress of

Work and Rewards: New Views ──────

Adam Smith argued that specialization made possible the wealth of modern society. He accepted the fact that repetitive routines would ultimately so bore working people that they would eventually become "stupid animals." He maintained, nevertheless, that productivity would increase as long as the wages were adequate.

Recently, however, human resources researchers have come to the opposite conclusion. They have tried ending extreme specialization and given workers more to do, sometimes even the task of building an entire product, when formerly each would have been responsible only for a single operation. Soon after ending the production line assembly, the researchers found that these factories reported increased employee satisfaction and increased productivity.

The assembly line work of earlier years assumed that if workers were paid enough, they would do the most boring job and, collectively, that a great many well-paid people doing such boring jobs would be as efficient and as productive as possible. Now, the language is "job enrichment" rather than simple specialization. With this change, the concept of work is once again going through a major change.

the building under construction. Managers in a modest corporation, however, can at best have the satisfaction of knowing that their company is doing well, that their section is in no way a drain on the company, that they succeed admirably in resolving conflicts on a daily basis, and that they get along well with superiors and get requests granted quickly. However, it is hard to see what "results" exactly mean, or how these might be measured.

For example, when the economy is strong and an industry is thriving because of high demand for its products, the net result may be extremely positive despite even incompetent managers and inept management strategies. The American automobile industry, for example, enjoyed such a situation in the 1960s, and the managers of those corporations quite naturally took some of the credit and congratulated themselves and each other for the great job they were doing and the results they were getting. In fact, they were riding the crest of the wave of consumer prosperity, and their efforts made little difference. With the collapse of the auto industry in the 1970s, with the increasingly poor economy, with foreign competition particularly from Germany and Japan, and with fewer consumers willing to buy large American cars, it became apparent that the much-praised management techniques of the previous decade alone were not enough to have any effect on the industry. Indeed, now the same managers were *blamed* for many of the automobile industry troubles. There were shake-ups. In the midst of the disastrous market situation, no managers could do very well because their sense of accomplishment was tied to a market that made positive feedback and approval almost impossible. Good managers were blamed for the bad performance, just as mediocre managers had congratulated themselves for the industry's good performance. Because it was immeasurable, the actual accomplishment in the job counted for much less than the image projected by the industry as a whole. This became especially problematic as work itself became less tangible and less easily measurable.

The shift from physical production to "knowledge work" has always been accompanied, accordingly, with a certain kind of suspicion. The ancients (Aristotle and Aquinas, for example) warned against people who made profit without

Bertrand Russell: "In Praise of Idleness" ——

Like most of my generation, I was brought up on the saying "Satan finds some mischief still for idle hands to do." Being a highly virtuous child, I believed all that I was told, and acquired a conscience which has kept me working hard down to the present moment. But although my conscience has controlled my actions, my opinions have undergone a revolution. I think that there is far too much work done in the world, that immense harm is caused by the belief that work is virtuous, and that what needs to be preached in modern industrial countries is quite different from what always has been preached. . . .

The wise use of leisure, it must be conceded, is a product of civilization and education. A man who has worked long hours all his life will be bored if he becomes suddenly idle. But without a considerable amount of leisure a man is cut off from many of the best things. There is no longer any reason why the bulk of the population should suffer this deprivation; only a foolish asceticism, usually vicarious, makes us continue to insist on work in excessive quantities now that the need no longer exists.

It will be said that, while a little leisure is pleasant, men would not know how to fill their days if they had only four hours of work out of the twenty-four. In so far as this is true in the modern world, it is a condemnation of our civilization; it would not have been true at any earlier period. There was formerly a capacity for light-heartedness and play which has been to some extent inhibited by the cult of efficiency. The modern man thinks that everything ought to be done for the sake of something else, and never for its own sake.

From In Praise of Idleness

actually producing anything themselves. They would therefore dismiss as "parasites" most of the people in what we now call business, in particular bankers and investors. Calvin and, in this country, Benjamin Franklin were much more appreciative of the talents of good business, but they too insisted that the fruits of our labor be tangible products—food, tools, clothes, and material goods for use and consumption.

Adam Smith also had in mind an economy in which production of consumer goods was the key, and the demand for them, the basic element in the market, was work. This, Smith argued, was the basis of *all* economic value. His "labor theory of value" continued to dominate economic thinking up until the present century. It showed, essentially, that all value—the value of money and the value of self-worth too—was based upon physical labor and its products, as well as (derivatively) the management of labor and the risks of entrepreneurship in employing labor. Karl Marx also accepted the "labor theory of value," but for him it could be used to condemn just those derivative features of the market that Smith had encouraged—management and entrepreneurship. People who didn't actually produce goods, Marx insisted—going back to the ancient and long-standing prejudice—were parasites. Managers and entrepreneurs put nothing into the products produced, so they deserve nothing from them. The person who actually works to make them deserves all the rewards.

This ancient and long-standing prejudice is still with us. It is a perennial problem for most people, who are not "workers" in that narrow sense of working with their hands. Many people still think of "real work" as the physical labor of carrying, digging, scraping, cutting, and so forth. People sometimes drop out of business precisely in order to regain this mythic sense of working with their hands—"real work"—as opposed to the unmeasurable and abstract "knowledge work" of the office and the corporation. Nevertheless, it is "knowledge work" that defines most jobs and careers in business. As Adam Smith argued even before the days of the giant corporation, it is this less tangible form of work that is necessary in a modern society to make possible the distribution and often the production of the more tangible goods formerly produced and distributed by the farmer or the craftsman alone.

Management is a category of work not seriously considered by the ancient critics. (Plato and Aristotle much praised "statesmen," but they never would have thought of them as "working.") Management is primarily the work of *organization,* but it is no less work for that. It is not parasitic on physical labor, as Marx insisted the capitalist was parasitic on the workers' toil; management is necessary for there to be productive physical work, and just as much an accomplishment as planting a fruit tree or making bricks. Otherwise, how does that fruit get to the consumer? How do those bricks ever find their way into a building?

The change in the nature of work and our conception of it is still in the making. We now fully appreciate the importance of management and entrepreneurship and other forms of "knowledge work," though we are still nagged by the ancient sense of work in a very different sense. We now see our careers as not just "ways of making a living" or keeping us from starving, but as a positive source of a sense of accomplishment and self-worth. We measure our success, however, much more in *social* terms of approval and recognition rather than actual physical products, and we think of our jobs primarily in terms of *responsibilities* instead of just physical substance to be transformed into cultural artifact or useful product. Work as *production* has turned into work as role-playing and responsibility, and with this set of dramatic changes in the nature and conception of work, it has, paradoxically, become even more important to us than it was in the days when we simply had to work to eat.

Why Productivity Falls ——

The 1 percent drop in business productivity during the second quarter of 1981 merely underlines the gravity of America's most serious economic problem. Productivity has now been falling since 1977.

The phrase "declining productivity" conjures up popular visions of lazy factory workers and featherbedding unions, but nothing could be further from the truth. America's productivity problem lies not among its unionized blue-collar workers, but among its nonunion white-collar workers. The key to productivity improvements lies not on the factory floor, but in the office.

In the three years from 1977 to 1980, America's production of goods and services rose 7.9 percent after correcting for inflation. Over that same time, blue-collar employment rose 2 percent, while white-collar employment rose 12 percent. Fewer than 600,000 new blue-collar workers were added to the economy, but more than 5.5 million new white-collar workers were added.

The problem is one we do not like to face. American government may be bureaucratic and inefficient, but American industry is just as bureaucratic and inefficient.

What firm has taken the ruthless steps to raise office productivity that it would take without hesitancy to raise factory productivity? What firm does not now have a bigger legal staff? What firm has really used computers to get that much prophesied office revolution under way? What private managers are trying to improve decision-making so that they can fire managers?

The answer: almost none. Those 5.5 million new white-collar workers prove it.

America is becoming a white-collar bureaucratic nation partly because our education system is supplying vast numbers of new workers who are trained to be bureaucrats. And as is now the fashion in supply-side economics, supply creates its own demand.

But there is also a class issue. When a manager raises factory productivity and fires some blue-collar workers, he is firing someone else—someone with a different education and background. When a manager raises office productivity and fires professional and managerial workers, he is firing someone just like himself—someone with the same education and background. If he fires those beneath him, then he can be fired by those above him.

What is worse, we also seem to be inculcating a set of values that implies there is something wrong with blue-collar work: it is better to be an unemployed college English major than an employed skilled blue-collar worker. That attitude, once foreign to America, has now become prevalent.

Lester C. Thurow, *Newsweek,* Aug. 24, 1981

B.   EMPLOYEE RIGHTS AND DUTIES

When a person accepts a position and a role in a business, he or she is, in an important sense, no longer the person he or she was. As an employee of the corporation, one becomes identified with one's title and job description. One is a vice president in charge of procurements or the supervisor of a certain aspect of production. One is an accountant, a teller, an interviewer, or a mediator, and the requirements of the job depend on the specific nature of those roles. Each and every job has its specific duties, and while many of these are specified explicitly in advance, a few of them become evident only as the job progresses. In addition, there are general duties that apply to every person in the company—such as not to cheat or "badmouth" the corporation—as well as duties that apply to every citizen—such as obeying the law and not engaging in illegal practices, harassing others, or discriminating against others in an official capacity on the basis of race or religion. Distinct from duties, employees also have rights and benefits that they can expect in return for their skills and service: the right to a fair wage and safe working conditions, for example. In general, the rights of the employee entail certain duties on the part of the employer. Conversely, the duties of the employee imply certain rights on the part of the employer.

Different jobs have different foundations. Working with some companies, for example, may carry with the job a virtual guarantee of lifetime employment. Many large Japanese firms operate with this as a matter of traditional policy, and until very recently, the American giant IBM had a work-for-life policy as well. Most companies have a policy that allows employees to keep their jobs as long as they keep up their performances, or until the financial situation is so bad that the company cannot possibly retain them. Unfortunately, more and more American companies have found themselves in such circumstances during the past several years, making "down-sizing" and work-force reductions common even in some of the hitherto most secure industries. Nevertheless, employees who are let go are entitled to compensation, and, in general, those companies with the best employment policies tend to have the best compensation packages as well. Justice and the law both demand that a person be let go only "for cause," which means that firing someone merely because you don't like him, for example, is a breach of an employee's rights. Except in those jobs that obviously have a limited duration— for example, building a particular house or completing a particular project—there is a presumption of continuance, the assumption that one will not be let go unless there is good reason for it. Poor performance is one such reason, but, even so, an employer must usually document the poor performance, which often involves repeated evaluations and quality checks. Financial exigency is another good reason, and while the requirements for establishing financial exigency are not always clear, there are certain obvious violations, such as firing one person from a job on the basis of financial exigency and then immediately turning around and hiring someone else for the same job. In addition to such more or less secure work situations, a great many American employees work on an "at will" basis, which means that they work only as long as they want to, and the employer can let them go "at will" as well, even without good reason. Certain reasons for firing someone, however, are not acceptable, notably their race, religion, or gender. Indeed, such reasons are illegal, even if supplemented with other reasons which, by themselves, would not constitute sufficient reasons either.

Business ethicist Patricia Werhane has recently drawn up a "Bill of Rights" for both employees and employers, specifying the *rights* of each and thereby implying the *duties* of each towards the other as well. These rights are all subject to appeal, of course, but many of them are supported and sanctioned by law. However, given the enormous difference in power between large corporate employers and individual workers, as well as the availability of alternative employees, the protection of the law alone is not usually sufficient to protect workers' jobs. Many aspects of work are not adequately covered by law at all. For this reason, collective effort may make all the difference, especially in some industries, between good jobs and ruthless exploitation.

A "Bill of Rights" for Employees ——

1. Every person has an equal right to a job and a right to equal consideration at the job. Employees may not be discriminated against on the basis of religion, sex, ethnic origin, race, color, or economic background.

2. Every person has the right to equal pay for work, where "equal work" is defined by the job description and title.

3. Every employee has rights to his or her job. After a probation period of three to ten years every employee has the right to his or her job. An employee can be dismissed only under the following conditions:

   • He or she is not performing satisfactorily the job for which he or she was hired.

   • He or she is involved in criminal activity either within or outside the corporation.

   • He or she is drunk or takes drugs on the job.

   • He or she actively disrupts corporate business activity without a valid reason.

   • He or she becomes physically or mentally incapacitated or reaches mandatory retirement age.

   • The employer has publicly verifiable economic reasons for dismissing the employee, e.g., transfer of the company, loss of sales, bankruptcy, etc.

   • Under no circumstances can an employee be dismissed or laid off without the institution of fair due process procedures.

4. Every employee has the right to due process in the workplace. He or she has the right to a peer review, to a hearing, and if necessary, to outside arbitration before being demoted or fired.

5. Every employee has the right to free expression in the workplace. This includes the right to object to corporate acts that he or she finds illegal or immoral without retaliation or penalty. The objection may take the form of free speech, whistle-blowing, or conscientious objection. However, any criticism must be documented or proven.

6. The Privacy Act, which protects the privacy and confidentiality of public employees, should be extended to all employees.

7. The polygraph should be outlawed.

8. Employees have the right to engage in outside activities of their choice.

9. Every employee has the right to a safe workplace, including the right to safety information and participation in improving work hazards. Every employee has the right to legal protection that guards against preventable job risks.

10. Every employee has the right to as much information as possible about the corporation, about his or her job, work hazards, possibilities for future employment, and any other information necessary for job enrichment and development.

11. Every employee has the right to participate in the decision-making processes entailed in his or her job, department, or in the corporation as a whole, where appropriate.

12. Every public and private employee has the right to strike when the foregoing demands are not met in the workplace.

From Patricia Werhane, *Persons, Rights and Corporations* (1985)

A "Bill of Rights" for Employers ——

1. Any employee found discriminating against another employee or operating in a discriminatory manner against her employer is subject to employer reprimand, demotion, or firing.

2. Any employee not deserving equal pay because of inefficiency should be shifted to another job.

3. No employee who functions inefficiently, who drinks or takes drugs on the job, commits felonies or acts in ways that prevent carrying out work duties has a right to a job.

4. Any employee found guilty under a due process procedure should be reprimanded (e.g., demoted or dismissed), and, if appropriate, brought before the law.

5. No employer must retain employees who slander the corporation or other corporate constituents.

6. The privacy of employers is as important as the privacy of employees. By written agreement employees may be required not to disclose confidential corporate information or trade secrets unless not doing so is clearly against the public interest.

7. Employers may engage in surveillance of employees at work (but only at work) with their foreknowledge and consent.

8. No employee may engage in activities that literally harm the employer, nor may an employee have a second job whose business competes with the business of the first employer.

9. Employees shall be expected to carry out job assignments for which they are hired unless these conflict with common moral standards or unless the employee was not fully informed about these assignments or their dangers before accepting employment. Employees themselves should become fully informed about work dangers.

10. Employers have rights to personal information about employees or prospective employees adequate to make sound hiring and promotion judgments so long as the employer preserves the confidentiality of such information.

11. Employers as well as employees have rights. Therefore the right to participation is a correlative obligation on the part of *both* parties to respect mutual rights. Employers, then, have the right to demand efficiency and productivity from their employees in return for the employee right to participation in the workplace.

12. Employees who strike for no reason are subject to dismissal.

C. Labor, Unions, and Management

Many countries have fairly strong laws mandating that the firing of any employee requires certain reasons, but in the United States a great many workers are employed strictly on an "at will" basis. This means that even when the firing is unjustifiable or illegal, many employees find that they have no legal recourse. Unskilled workers can be easily replaced from the pool of millions of unemployed and often desperate workers, and even skilled workers regularly feel the threat of discharge. Given the importance of work in our society, both as a means of survival and a source of identity, this sense of powerlessness can be devastating.

Labor unions in this country grew out of the desire of working people to have more say and more power over their working lives. Although such organizations were ruthlessly attacked in their early days, particularly by those employers who did in fact exploit their workers and took full advantage of the ease with which they could be fired, labor unions are not only compatible with economic efficiency and prosperity but essential to democracy as well. Powerlessness in the workplace is antithetical to the autonomy required of citizenship.

Labor unions are often treated as an obstacle or, worse, a betrayal of the capitalist economy, in part because of the original alliance of some labor unions with socialist causes and the Communist Party. Indeed, unionists are still sometimes branded with the now out-of-date epithet "Communist," even though such charges are no longer intelligible. The truth is rather that labor unions originated not in opposition to capitalism but rather as a necessity to maintain the American business system. The right of workers to be protected against reprisals from their employers was established with the passage of the National Labor Relations Act, the "Wagner Act," in 1935, during some of the worst days of the Great Depression. The central concerns of Congress in passing the Wagner Act were the low wages of workers (who thus had little purchasing power) and the frequent disruption of industrial production caused by strikes. The Wagner Act was an attempt to rehabilitate the free market by making labor a stable and dependable factor in production.

Under the Wagner Act, it is illegal for an employer to interfere with or discriminate against workers who are trying to form a union. The act encourages collective bargaining, the process by which a contract covering all workers is negotiated and administered. Acting together in contractual cooperation with industry thus assures stability. Arbitration further stabilizes the process, as "wildcat" strikes get replaced by discussions motivated by mutual interests. The Wagner Act also sets up the framework within which unions represent previously unrepresented workers, although it is a misunderstanding that unions simply come in and "take over." When 30 percent of the workers in a company or an industry "show interest" in establishing or joining a union, an election is held under the auspices of the National Labor Relations Board, the federal agency set up to administer the Wagner Act. If 50 percent or more of the employees vote for a union, the shop becomes "union" and is so represented. Some employees may object, but this situation is no different from any other democratic decision procedure that depends on majority rule.

Arbitration has a privileged position with industrial relations. Especially since 1960, when the Supreme Court ruled in three different decisions concerning the Steelworkers Union, arbitration can be judicially enforced. Again, the aim is industrial stability while at the same time settling disputes and satisfying the demands of both workers and management. Arbitration helps avoid the two most costly and disruptive forms of dealing with such disputes, strikes and "slowdowns" on the one hand, and prolonged litigation on the other. Indeed, since 1960, the tendency of the courts is to assume a "no strike" clause in favor of arbitration, even where there is no such explicit clause in the union contract. But as arbitration has become more and more expensive and time-consuming (although not nearly so much as litigation), mediation has tended to become a first and often final step in coming to agreement. It has also cut down on the adversarial nature of the labor–management relationship. In the face of increasing international competition, cooperation—not mutual antagonism—is obviously in the best interest of all concerned.

The union is the exclusive bargaining representative of all employees, including those who have decided not to join the union. But there are also some obvious problems, and in the history of labor relations there have been a few bloody episodes. With the ascendancy of the unions after the passing of the Wagner Act, many industries had "closed shops," that is, in order to obtain employment in a particular company or industry, one had to already be a member of the appropriate union. There were also "union shops," which did not require prior membership but did require joining the union once on the job. Closed shops, in particular, made possible a new form of discrimination and arbitrariness, not at the hands of employers but at the hands of the union. Some trades and occupations quickly became exclusionary, for if you could not get into the union, you consequently could not get a job. Both closed shops and union shops have gone out of practice, the former now prohibited by law, the latter depleted in substance. What has taken their place is the "agency shop," in which an employee cannot be compelled to join the union but, because he or she benefits from union representation, can be compelled to pay the union a fee equivalent to the proportion of union dues that pays for bargaining and administrative costs. There are advantages for some individual workers who do not join a union. For example, although he or she cannot get involved in internal union matters, he or she is not subject to union discipline either. In case of a strike, the nonunion member is not compelled to join but may nevertheless enjoy the benefits won from the strike. According to the provisions of the more recent Taft–Hartley Act of 1947, however, employees have the right to work in a union-represented workplace even without paying dues, although, again, they are still covered by union benefits. Such "right-to-work" laws even entitle a nonunion member to be personally represented by the union in case of unjust discharge, without paying back the union for its services. Such cases severely undermine the impulse to union membership while taking advantage of the union at the same time.

There is power in collective bargaining and, traditionally, the ultimate weapon of labor unions has been the right to strike. When all else fails, when management will not listen or refuses to agree to what seem to be reasonable demands, there is nothing more effective, in terms of threatening management and gaining public attention, than a strike. Of course, this right has sometimes been abused; indeed, it has been used even when it did not exist, as in the air controllers strike during the very early eighties, which was clearly prohibited by their federal contract. (Then-President Ronald Reagan summarily fired them all.) In other countries, such as England, France, and notably Australia, strikes routinely paralyze public services, showing quite clearly that striking is a weapon that should be used with care and caution. But the right to strike has been limited severely, at least in America, and today's labor practices include the right of the employer to replace a striking worker, making the act of striking a particularly dangerous one. (Technically, the employer is required to offer the replaced employee his job back after the termination of his replacement, but this could be many years or even decades away.) The right to replace a striking worker renders the right to strike all but empty, leaving labor without its ultimate weapon. In these days of cutbacks and high unemployment, it remains to be seen whether the management of most major industries will take seriously their role and responsibilities as "stakeholders" to their employees, or whether they will use this as a license to return to some of the old forms of exploitation.

Labor unions have played an essential role in the evolution of fair and civilized business practices in this country and elsewhere, despite the sometimes violent organizational activities surrounding their formation. Without them, we might still be witness or victim to some of the worst abuses of nineteenth-century capitalism, where children worked sixteen hours a day at dangerous jobs and where most workers received less than subsistence wages. But one of the problems that developed along with the historical confrontation between labor unions and management was the establishment of an attitude of adversarial and antagonistic thinking. It was simply assumed that the interests of the owners and the interests of the workers were naturally opposed. But now, in the face of international competition with countries in which the labor–management relationship is cooperative instead of adversarial—notably Germany and Japan—the very structure of the traditional labor–management confrontation is being called into question. Cooperation, not confrontation, appears to be the way to mutual success as we approach the next century. Moreover, labor unions have been very successful at protecting and promoting the interests of their members, but with each new wave of energetic and skilled immigrants, it appears more and more that many labor unions maintain the role of protecting their members only by keeping others out. What is necessary, accordingly, is to extend to everyone the benefits and fair treatment that is now taken for granted by relatively few, thereby increasing our productivity and competitiveness rather than dwelling on our internal differences.

D. BEYOND ALIENATION: MEANINGFUL WORK

What most people would like, in a phrase, is *meaningful work:* work that they can enjoy, work that makes a difference, work that brings personal fulfillment as well as a good day's pay. But in light of a long history during which work has been viewed primarily as a burden, this is no simple demand. Indeed, the idea of meaningful work threatens to become a rationalization of what would otherwise be a wasted life and a pointless expenditure of time and energy. Or, it can become a source of fraud, in which drudgery is dressed up in disguise. In the following excerpt, business ethicist Joanne Ciulla summarizes this new tendency to exaggerate the meaning of work and diagnoses its problems.

Honest Work ——

Suppose that every tool we had could perform its function, either at our bidding, or itself perceiving the need [and] suppose that shuttles in a loom could fly to and fro and a plucker on a lyre all self-moved, then manufacturers would have no need of workers nor masters of slaves.

—Aristotle, Politics

It's been more than 2,300 years since Aristotle mused about a life without work. Today, the tools and machines that Aristotle dreamed of are becoming the furniture of everyday life in industrialized countries, as the demands of a competitive market catapult us toward a world in which machines replace or simplify most jobs. Aristotle might have rejoiced at this, but Americans don't. Instead of greeting this era with joy, we cling ever more tightly to our work.

Ours is a work-oriented society—one where "all play and no work makes Jack a big jerk." We live in a paradoxical culture that both celebrates work and continually strives to eliminate it. While we treasure economic efficiency, we seek interesting jobs that will offer fulfillment and meaning to our lives.

A Source of Identity

Perhaps the demand for meaningful work grows because we see the supply shrinking.

For many people, work promises more than most jobs can deliver. The corporation is not capable of providing meaningful work for all of its employees.

As things now stand, we have gone beyond the work ethic, which endowed work with moral value, and expect our jobs to be the source of our identity, the basis of our individual worth and the mainspring of happiness. Furthermore, we want our work to substitute for the fulfillment that used to be derived from friends, family and community.

Over the past 60 years, management has capitalized on this "loaded" meaning of work. The social engineer has replaced the time-study man—corporations have become "cultures" that seek to transform employees into a happy family.

The problem of alienation has been licked by "entertaining" that encroaches on employees' leisure time in the guise of business dinners, corporate beer busts and networking parties. Managers, charged with the task of making work meaningful, create new ways of persuading employees to invest more of themselves in their work than their jobs may require. So, banal work is sometimes dressed up to look meaningful.

Emotional Demands

Under the old school of scientific management, the alienated worker did what he or she was told, got paid and went home. The work might have been boring and the wages unfair, but at least everyone knew where they stood.

Today, the transaction is not as honest. While we still trade our labor, we are also required to give away a slice of our private lives.

Workers of the past were often overworked; today, many of us are overmanaged. The exhaustion that pains the faces of office workers at the end of the day may not be physical but emotional, because management may be demanding more of the self than the timely and efficient performance of the task at hand actually requires.

"What Do You Do?"

Work determines our status and shapes our social interactions. One of the first things Americans ask when they meet someone new is, "What do you do?" This used to be considered a rude question in Europe, but in recent years it's being asked more and more. To be retired or unemployed in a work-oriented society is to be relegated to the status of a nonentity.

Young people fanatically pursue careers as if a good job were the sole key to happiness—whether that happiness is derived from the status of the job itself or from the wages that they believe will eventually buy it. They are willing to take drug tests, wear the right clothes and belong to the right clubs, all in the name of obtaining a position that will eventually give them freedom to choose. Many argue that they'll work 70-hour weeks, make their fortunes and retire at 40—few ever do. This attitude has taken a social toll in terms of loneliness, divorce, child abuse and sometimes even white-collar crime.

One-Way Commitments

A consequence of this loaded meaning of work is that people willingly put their happiness in the hands of the market and their employers. Unlike social institutions such as church and community, corporations frequently do not possess a clear moral vision of what is good for people. It is ironic that in an era of hostile takeovers, corporations seem to offer less security but want more commitment and trust from their employees. Yet traits such as trust and loyalty are based on a reciprocal relationship.

In this environment, managers are challenged to find ways of motivating people who want jobs that satisfy a variety of abstract desires and needs, such as self-development and self-fulfillment.

While there doesn't seem to be much consensus on what "self-development" means or what people self-develop for, many feel that this is what they *should* want. So managers, consultants and psychologists guess at employees' needs and develop programs and policies that carry the implicit promise of fulfilling them. This results in a vicious circle—employees desire more, management promises more and the expectation of finding meaning in work rises. Both sides grope in the dark for ways to build a workplace "El Dorado."

The authenticity of a corporation's moral commitment is questionable if the drive for meaningful work is merely another motivating tool or a mask for authority. Young people who enter the workforce are wise to attempts to manipulate them under the guise of caring and skeptical of programs prescribed by the latest management fad that are supposed to create excitement. Managers cannot continually jump-start employees into action. And unlike the organized workers of old, today's young worker doesn't rebel or exert power by picketing with his or her colleagues, but instead stages his or her own silent strike of passive resistance.

Toward a More Just Workplace

Employers have an ethical obligation to recognize that employees have a right to meaningful lives. Businesses might begin by eliminating policies and practices that interfere with that right. Because not all jobs are exciting or engaging, perhaps efforts should be made to make work fit better into people's lives instead of forcing people's lives to fit into work.

The main reasons people give for why they are unhappy at work are that they feel powerless, they do not trust the organization and they feel they are not being treated fairly.

Throughout history, work has involved a relationship of unequal power. Real innovation in management will come when issues like the balance of power are acknowledged and management seeks to create a more just workplace.

In the 8th century B.C., the Greek poet Hesiod pointed out that justice is what makes work worthwhile. He wrote, "Neither famine nor disaster ever haunt men who do true justice; but lightheartedly they tend the fields which are all their care."

Benchmark (1990)

E.   The Importance of Time

One of the changes in our conception of work is the importance of *time*. Of course, the ancient farmer worked far more brutal hours than even the most fanatic careerist today, and even young children worked longer in the factories of the nineteenth century than most workers today. But it used to be that the time put into a job was the time it took to accomplish it. Now, we normally put time into a job regardless of the precise time it takes to do what we have to do. We work hours, not tasks; indeed, an increasing number of jobs are measured just in terms of the time put in, rather than what is actually accomplished. This is not to say that nothing is accomplished. It is rather a natural reflection of the importance of organization as well as the necessity of keeping everyone together in coordinated work schedules and just being sure that "someone is there." It also reflects the difficulty in measuring individual productivity according to a simple quantitative measure. A few people in our society can still be given a task and sent off or sent home to do it (editorial writers, home fix-it craftsmen, a few creative scientists, or consultants), but the majority of people have an office for their work, precisely in order to give them a place and a *position,* which is, as often as not, defined by an actual physical space as much as it is by an abstract category in the business hierarchy.

In physical work, the distinction between working and not working is usually fairly clear; hammering nails in the cornices is building the cabinet, picking fingernails is not. But in the office, the distinction is not clear. Chatting on the phone to a client about fishing, however pleasurable and relaxing, may well count as work. Hard physical labor—moving a file cabinet back and forth across the office—may not be work at all. *How we spend our time,* in other words, is an important ingredient in job accomplishment and work. Indeed, the very concept of "wasting time" makes sense only in a certain kind of society with a businesslike sense of efficiency and productiveness. And in a society in which "time is money," the *amount* of time we put into a job, as well as what we do with our time, becomes greatly significant.

In several recent surveys of managers and executives and their use of time, managerial scientists have discovered that an enormous proportion of the executives' long day is spent just talking. It is not the important talk of strategic meetings—"let's turn this company around"—but simply talk encouraging subordinates, putting up with disgruntled clients or customers on the phone, chatting amiably in the hall, answering questions, forecasting the future of the industry, and, of course, having meetings. A recent *Wall Street Journal* report suggested that many executives spend as much as 40 percent of their working hours in meetings, 30 percent of which is totally wasted.* "Even efficient meetings can be reduced by 30 percent," says Steven Cohen of the American Manage-

---

*Sept. 24, 1980.

ment Association. In such a context, what counts as spending time "getting work done" gets increasingly confusing. Attending meetings and so on is surely "doing our job" in an undeniable sense. At the same time, they are often a "waste of time." What do we *do* in such a meeting? Well, much of it is obviously a kind of

Eternal Recurrence: A Test of Time ——

The German philosopher Friedrich Nietzsche invented an image (or rather, borrowed it from the ancients) that presents the notion of "essential time" in an extremely dramatic way. He called his thesis "the eternal recurrence" and, as a matter of fact, he thought that it was scientifically true. But its truth is not nearly so important as its impact. "How would it be," Nietzsche asks, "if some day or night a devil were to sneak into you and say, 'This life as you now live it and have lived it, you will have to live again and innumerable times more. There will be nothing new in it, but every pain and every joy and every thought and sigh and every thing immeasurable small or great in your life must return to you.' Would you throw yourself down and gnash your teeth and curse the demon who told you thus?" Nietzsche [then] asks, or would you think that this was wonderful, and "crave nothing more fervently than this ultimate eternal confirmation"?

Put into the context of a career, the question becomes, how much of our job is such that the very idea of repeating it (much less an infinite number of times) drives us to despair, and how much of the job is so rewarding that the idea of repeating it (with the sense of reward, each time) strikes us as very desirable? Nietzsche's image is a kind of test; how much, of what we do, do we do just to "get it done with," trying not to think about it any more than necessary and sustained by the knowledge that at least it will soon be done. But what if it is never to be "done," but always repeated? How many people lead their lives from one inessential moment to another, in effect never living for themselves but always for the sake of tasks that they see as inessential to them? And how many of us are doing a job in which, at least some of the time, we feel so fulfilled that we "could do this forever"? Essential time is time infinitely repeatable. It is what work at its best should be, not just a way to "pass the time" or "earn a living" but a satisfying end in itself. This may be a lofty ideal, and no one could expect to feel this way *all* of the time. But if we don't feel this way any of the time, we probably ought to consider another career.

Based on *The Gay Science, The Portable Nietzsche*, trans. W. Kaufmann communications exercise, which may be, even if irrelevant to the point of the meeting (as it often is), essential to the functioning of a department or a committee, just by allowing the sharing of opinions and airing of certain grievances. But it is hard to say what "participating" in such a meeting amounts to, because talking may be wasting time while not talking may indicate serious attention. Indeed, the report concludes, it is also hard to tell who runs such meetings, quoting John Bryan, chairman of Consolidated Food Corp: "I doodle pictures of people at the meeting. And I hope to goodness no one asks me a question."

The subject of wasting time introduces an essential concept, though most people do not have a name for it. We might call it *"essential time,"* time well spent, fulfilling what Calvin called a person's "mission." Time wasted is not essential time. Well-spent time is usually essential time, if the project being worked on is also considered to be essential. Here again is the tie between work and self-identity that we have repeatedly insisted is so important; some tasks define what we think of our character and our "mission," and others do not. We might spend a great deal of creative time working out our income tax for the year, a necessity to be sure, but yet we may not consider that time well spent but rather essential time wasted. On the other hand, a casual but unusually friendly chat with the boss about the best croissants in Paris might seem to be the epitome of essential time, time well spent, insofar as it feeds our conception of ourselves as successful and feeds our self-esteem. Meetings, for most people, are not essential time, even if they are in some sense necessary for the functioning of the business. Routine paperwork, for example, is usually not essential time for most people. Indeed, we can measure the desirability of a job best, perhaps, not in terms of enjoyment or hard-to-measure accomplishment in the usual sense, but in terms of how much *essential time* the job fulfills: in other words, how much of the time spent makes us feel that we are fulfilling our "mission," and how much time is "wasted" on filling out forms, aimless meetings, or annoying phone calls. The "mission" may be a metaphor, of course, but it expresses something absolutely essential in our conception of ourselves and our worth, that we are here *for a purpose* and that we are *spending our time usefully.* Life, after all, is essentially time, and half of our waking adult lives, it is worth remembering, is spent at our jobs.

F. WORK, PLAY, AND LEISURE

Not all essential time is work time, and if Calvin and the puritans sometimes made it seem that way, today we adamantly disagree with them. As contemporary Americans we place an enormous amount of emphasis and stress on *leisure* activities, which we often see as far more important to our personal fulfillment than the work that we do in our careers. Indeed, a great many Americans would answer Nietzsche's question in the preceding section by saying that they have had such an experience of total satisfaction not in the job but rather outside of it, in hobbies, playing various sports, sailing, or simply sunning on some paradi-

Any Number Can Play ——

For twenty years I have felt vaguely that leisure is a much bigger word than is commonly thought; that it is not necessarily identical with recreation, in the sense that playing golf is recreation; that it involves the opposite of rest; and that if mankind ever truly engaged in it he would become a different animal, just as he did after the Fall of Man, when seemingly unto Eternity he forsook leisure, and went to work. . . .

Now free time can be used in two ways. One is "play," which includes all ways of killing time. The other is engagement in leisure activities. . . . such things as thinking or learning, reading or writing, conversation or correspondence, love and acts of friendship, political activity, domestic activity, artistic and esthetic activity. I should add creative travel, which is a kind of conversation with what is past or new or alien. These things are engaged in for their own sakes—that is why they are not labor. Work is done under compulsion. Leisure activities, however, we engage in freely; they are not "externally compensated."

Clifton Fadiman, *Any Number Can Play*

siacal beach. This too is essential time. Unfortunately what is true, and slightly tragic, for a great many Americans, is that all essential time is experienced during leisure hours, and none of it at work.

The work ethic places such importance on work that many other values are too easily brushed aside. In the puritan emphasis on "usefulness," the virtue of "useless" pastimes is ignored, whether these are sports, relaxation, reading, thinking about philosophy, or painting a portrait, except insofar as these contribute to our readiness to be productive. There is a world of difference between simply taking a moment off from work to catch a breath and relaxing just for its own sake, or playing a game, which provides multiple ends of its own. Indeed, "taking time off," relaxation, and play are very different sorts of activities; only the first has any essential reference to work. Relaxation, however important for good work or good (mental and physical) health—which in turn is important for good work—has virtues of its own. This point is often disdained by more fanatic defenders of the work ethic who see usefulness as the only true human good. Indeed, not for health or business reasons, but for reasons all of its own, relaxation is just as much a part of the good life as success or pleasure. Indeed, even to describe relaxation as "pleasure" is to shift it out of a category all its own, by relegating it to something else. For pleasure, we can perform a number of energetic exercises, and there are a great many other things we can do that are not relaxation. If it is relaxation we want, the fact that these other exercises and activities are more pleasurable is beside the point. Just as much as work and pleasure, relaxation is one of the unsung essentials of the good life, even part of its "essential time." In addition to its other virtues, relaxation time gives us the leisure to reflect and appreciate life, to see how good it is or—if something is wrong—to see what it is and how it can be corrected. Thus, the great philosophers from Aristotle to the present have insisted that the good life is, in part, a life of *contemplation,* a life in which we think about and appreciate life, as an essential part of living it.

Work and "Fun" ———

Americans spend $100 billion a year on "fun," according to Dr. John Neulinger of the Leisure Institute in New York City. The problem is, he says, "that so many of us have been conditioned by the work ethic that we think the only meaningful activity is work." Consequently, many people choose leisure activities that are not relief or relaxation at all, but an extension of work, taking up golf "because it is good for business" or getting exercise because it is one more thing that is expected of us. "Some of us enter into recreation as though we were sentenced by a judge," adds Tony Mobley, dean of the School of Health, Physical Education and Recreation at Indiana University.

Ideally, leisure activities should be a contrast and a relief from the stresses and frustrations of work, according to Madelyn W. Carlisle. For example, if your job is sedentary, your leisure activities should probably involve at least some vigorous physical activity. On the other hand, if your work involves a great deal of tension, challenging leisure activity may be just what you don't need; instead, engage in activities that are relaxing and vent aggressive feelings, such as chopping wood or playing touch football. If your job is dull, try mountain climbing or hang gliding; if your work involves constant coping with other people, perhaps try more solitary activities, like hiking or listening to music. (Carlisle suggests raising house plants; "they won't talk back to you.") If you work with a deadline, choose sports and recreation that don't use schedules. If you feel like a failure at work, choose a hobby you can master, collecting something or learning a foreign language. If you feel you're not "contributing to the world" in your work, try volunteering to help the elderly or read to the blind. Leisure is not the "opposite" of work but rather its complement; it should fill out our lives.

Play is a totally different matter. We sometimes treat "relaxation and play" as a unit, as if they were the same thing, or at any rate an established couple. But watching Americans play so hard at games, with so much emphasis on competition and developing skills, makes clear that play is something quite different. Play is stimulating while relaxation is restful. Play is serious, while relaxation is hardly ever serious. Play involves imagination, goals, and skills; getting a chance to relax may also require imagination and skill, but relaxation itself allows none of these. Play, wrote the German writer Friedrich Schiller, is the highest form of human activity, the essential basis of the arts, the single attitude that allows us to rise above the banalities of life. At the same time, we often reduce life to a game or a contest of the imagination.

The distinction between work and play is not always easy to distinguish. Enjoying our work can be one of the greatest rewards of life, a kind of play. We come to apply to our work that sense of imagination and creativity that constitutes the most rewarding games and pastimes of childhood and our leisure time. The ancient connotation of "work" as demeaning and distasteful is still with us, and so "work" is distinguished from "play," the former being what we dislike doing but must, the latter what we enjoy doing and do regardless of the external rewards. But "work" means "getting something done," and there is nothing intrinsic to work that *makes* it unpleasant. Indeed, much of the unpleasantness many people experience is precisely the fact that they perceive what they are doing *as* work; therefore, it is something they must but don't want to do, and therefore is distasteful and unpleasant. Much of what the unplayful puritan ethic calls "the dignity of work" might much better be conceived as the *playfulness* of work, our ability to think positively about what we do, enjoying it and being as creative as possible in doing it, rather than simply getting it done as routinely and as efficiently as possible.

"In every man there is a child," the German philosopher Nietzsche wrote, "and that child wants to play." Nietzsche himself wasn't a very playful fellow (except in his writing), but he saw what Freud, in a much more pessimistic vein, would see a few years later. Much of what we do as adults is repression of the more uninhibited desires of childhood, but we surely make this even worse by thinking of everything "adult" and "mature" and "responsible" as being unpleasant "work," and seeing all of the joys of play as "childish," "immature," and "irresponsible." Revising the Nietzsche aphorism slightly, we might suggest that "in every employee is a child, and that child wants work to be play." Indeed, this is as true of the successful CEO at the top of the pyramid as it is of those doing the tedious and routine jobs at the bottom. In fact, not surprisingly, those at the top are often there just because they know that the better part of work can also be play. So they enjoy it and do it better and more enthusiastically than those who consider their work just "work." Play is not only an essential of the good life, it is an essential of business life as well. It is the difference between drudgery and enjoyment, and often between success and mediocrity as well.

G.   WORK AS CREATIVITY AND EXPRESSION

High is our calling, friend! Creative Art
(Whether the instrument of words she use,
Or pencil pregnant with ethereal hues)
Demands the service of a mind and heart
Though sensitive, yet, in their weakest part,
Heroically fashioned.

—Wordsworth, Sonnets

A sensitive being, a creative soul.

—Wordsworth, "Prelude"

Creativity is one of those concepts that has achieved near-religious status in our society. Part of this is our idea that every individual is "unique," and so has something valuable and different to express. What we call personal *expression* is obviously essential, in one way or another; it is hard to imagine a human being not expressing feelings and thoughts at all. But personal expression is not necessarily creativity. Indeed, the most common modes of expression are rituals and gestures, common phrases and comments that are not at all original, whose power is due to precisely the fact that they are so familiar, so well established, so unoriginal, so uncreative.

In his book *Management,* Peter Drucker comments that creativity is a very rare thing, particularly in the world of management. But, he adds, the manager is not supposed to be creative and, in any case, creativity cannot be *expected* of anyone. Most people are not creative, don't think of themselves as creative, and, except for occasional bouts with one of the muses, have no particular desire to be creative. For them, creativity need not even be a component of the good life. Indeed, we should be far more critical about our insistence that people be "original"; how often is anyone original, as opposed to entertaining, well-read, or insightful? For most people, life in the established modes is enough, with an occasional display of cleverness. Creativity is by its very nature disruptive; it upsets the established order of things. But disruption, sometimes, is also called "progress," which we value very much.

Inventing the new is indeed a drive to be understood in its own right. And even where it does not manifest itself as the dominant drive, it nevertheless can be a powerful means to other forms of self-satisfaction. Inventors sometimes thrive on creativity, advertising executives pride themselves on it, and some managers do indeed boast of their creative management. Plentiful cases bear this out. Some people, in fact, take the need to be creative so seriously that they find work in an organized environment virtually intolerable. But creativity is a value that is overly promoted in our society. It is one thing to appreciate and take advantage of creativity when it appears, and to make room and opportunity for creative persons to prove themselves; it is something else to insist that all people, in order to prove their worth, must be creative too. Creativity is a special case, unpre-dictable, often unintended. In business, as Drucker says, the rule is certainly not "creativity" but organization and order, the tried and the true—which are often the very antithesis of the creative.

H.   WORKING TOO MUCH: WORKAHOLISM, PERFECTIONISM, AND "BURN-OUT"

Believers in the puritan ethic never thought so, but there is always such a thing as working too much, working too hard, and taking work so seriously that it destroys both the rest of the worker's life and, paradoxically, the work itself. "Workaholism" is a fairly new word but the concept itself is as old as work itself. Sometimes, workaholism is like a disease, though psychiatric rather than physi-cal. It can be what Freud called "anal compulsiveness," compulsive because it is as if it is beyond the control of the victim, anal because of, to put it politely, its origins in excessively strict childhood toilet training. Sometimes, workaholism is rather a matter of *avoidance,* not love of work so much as dissatisfaction with other aspects of life, notably, marriage, family, and friends, or lack of them. A Wall Street psychiatrist, Dr. Jay Rohrlich, says that many of his patients are "utterly lost in their personal lives," although they are, in business, "tremen-dously productive and interesting people."* But, Dr. Rohrlich argues, the prob-lem is not always excessive work as compensation for an unhappy personal life, just as often, workaholics are people who genuinely love what they are doing, and the rest of their lives suffer accordingly. For example, people who love the

---

The Workaholic at Work ——

He steps out of his darkened bedroom, leaving his wife asleep. He climbs down the stairs, stepping over the dog. He makes coffee with one hand, dials London with the other to find out the price of gold. A few minutes later he is on the first train to Wall Street—alone. The sun has not yet come up and he is at his desk, ahead of the competi-tion—or so he hopes. He is the ideal image of a man dedicated to his job, climbing the ladder of success. He prides himself on how little he needs to sleep—and the fact that he never leaves the office until everyone else is gone. He loves his work. He is the American success story.

What is wrong with this picture?

The Wall Street Journal, Dec. 18, 1980.

clear-cut criteria for success in business find other aspects of life, in which success and well-being can't be so accurately measured, frustrating. Or else, they try to play business roles at home and with friends, "with totally disastrous results."

Despite the name, workaholism is far more an ethical concept than a medical diagnosis. What counts as working "too much" depends largely on who is doing the working, and who is doing the judging. If a person himself judges that he is working much too hard without satisfaction and at the expense of other more important aspects of life, then a problem is surely present. If a person's family or friends judge that she is working too much, however, the problem may be a conflict of interests, rather than too much work as such. And, it is important not to rule out the possibility that, for some people, work really is the best and most important thing in life. Calling them "workaholics," then, is a way of being offensive and demeaning their efforts rather than a quasi-medical attempt to understand them. What counts as "too much work," in other words, is a general question of priority of values; one individual's "overwork" may be another's dedication.

A related danger is *perfectionism.* Perfectionism is excess concern about the *quality* of the work done, instead of, as in workaholism, the *quantity* of it. We are sometimes told, "there is no such thing as good enough" or "nothing less than the very best." Indeed, part of our puritan ethic is that there is no such thing as "too much concern for quality." But, of course, there can be too much, and too unrealistic attention to quality. A small detail in a report may require a modicum of research but a complete analysis on the same detail, which is completely unnecessary, would take weeks and occupy valuable time. To do a "better" job on the modicum of research than is required, much less a "perfect" job, is to sacrifice a larger more urgent value for a lesser compulsive one. How "well" a job needs to be done depends on the job. Perfection is sometimes the ideal, but it is still an abstraction or a distraction or a plain impossibility.

Perfectionism, in its serious stages, tends to pervade everything. "Wanting to do things right" may be an undeniable virtue, but the perfectionists make themselves, and other people, utterly miserable. As a result of the unreasonable demand to get everything right (considered, that is, out of context and in isolation from all other values), they often fail to do as well as someone who is not nearly so ambitious or cautious. For instance, a study at the University of Pennsylvania Law School showed that a significant number of students were so insistent on being at the top of the class that they had literally disabled themselves with stress; many of them expressed the desire to quit and most were not doing very well.* Many business students, who have also been raised and groomed for the "nothing less than number one" role, display the same self-destructive tendency of demanding too much of themselves. As a result, they make themselves enormously unhappy and, paradoxically, do less well than they might have if they

---

*Psychology Today, Nov. 1980.

cared a little less. Indeed, the liabilities of perfectionism extend far beyond this, from "Type-A" high coronary risk behavior and general tendencies because of high fear of failure, to loneliness and an inability to share thoughts and personal feelings with others. Perfectionists cannot accept what they see as their "faults and failings," and so deprive themselves of the companionship of others who they fear might lend a more reasonable and less critical perspective to their work.

Perfectionism regarding our own work tends to be self-destructive; perfectionism regarding other people's work does too. (The two often go together but not always. It is impossible to have lax standards for ourselves and excessively high standards for others, just as it is possible to have unrealistically high expectations for ourselves but not apply them to other people.) The perfectionist demands of others a job that may well be impossible, or, over a period of time, consistently demands intensity and quality of work that is impossible to sustain. High standards, of course, encourage good work, but we are not just talking about high standards and encouragement. We are talking about *impossible* standards and, eventually, guaranteed failure—the result inevitably being frustration and resentment. Work becomes torture instead of satisfying and the work relationship becomes open conflict instead of cooperation.

The answer to perfectionism, like the answer to workaholism, lies in the question of priorities and perspective. (In extreme cases, of course, there may be psychiatric problems that go beyond this.) Trying too hard and working too much, expecting too much of ourselves as well as pushing ourselves too hard, become inevitable when we focus all of our attention on the job to be done. This leaves no room for a glimmer of an overview of the context that gives the job and its results their meaning, or of the place of the job and its context in our overall ambitions and responsibilities. Therapists sometimes help perfectionists, ironically, by getting them used to insults and criticism, even to the point of heaping insults on them in therapy. Another strategy is simply setting lower goals in which anything above those goals is considered an enjoyable achievement rather than a necessity. Students who convince themselves to be satisfied with "average" may well find that, because of their lower expectations, they actually do better. An employer who stops demanding perfect work of subordinates but praises excellent work as a special effort may well find that subordinates soon respond to the praise with quality work that was not forthcoming when the same quality was a matter of demand.

Some people will object that this is a sacrifice of quality and high standards. That is just the point, however. We can insist on high quality and standards without expecting the impossible, but to think that high quality and standards are the only acceptable results is, all too often, setting ourselves up for inevitable failure.

Working too hard and expecting too much can result in yet another problem, total job exhaustion and despair. The contemporary term for this age-old phenomenon is **burn-out.** It typically affects those who are especially ambitious and hard-working. It can develop slowly or it can apparently come all at once. Novelist Graham Greene describes it in his book, *A Burnt-Out Case:*

Self-expression is a hard and selfish thing. It eats everything, even the self. At the end, you find you haven't even got a self to express. I have no interest in anything anymore, doctor. I don't want to sleep with a woman or design a building.

Burn-out is a kind of stress. Psychiatrist Michael Hurst, for example, runs a clinic for stress-debilitated employees. Burn-out, he claims, affects people who can't cut loose from their work, who, again, have lost their perspective of it. "They haven't learned how to disconnect from it. They feel trapped. They hate themselves for not being able to live the way they like and still be able to do the

How to Avoid Burn-out—and How Your Employer Can Help ——

Psychologist Michael Hurst of Boston said that getting rest, exercise, and de-intensifying the work experience by developing a network of social relationships are important preventive measures. The trick is not to overdo job responsibility—balance it off.

Dr. Harry Levinson, a Cambridge industrial psychologist who runs seminars and workshops for executives, had these suggestions for employers:

Keep track of how long employees are in certain jobs and rotate them out of potentially exhausting positions.

Limit time constraints. "Don't allow your people to work 18 hours a day, even on critical problems. Especially don't let the same people be the rescuers of troubled situations over and over again. Managers tend to rely on their best people, but best people are more vulnerable to becoming burned-out people."

Make sure your organization has a systematic way of letting people know that their contributions are important. "People need information that supports their positive self-images, eases their consciences, and refuels them psychologically."

Provide avenues through which people can express not only their anger but also their disappointment, futility, defeat, and depression.

As technology changes, retrain and upgrade managers. Get them to seminars, workshops and other activities away from the organization.

Remember that employees who are burning out need support from others. Bosses should insist they withdraw, get appropriate help and place themselves first.

Kay Longcope, *The Boston Globe*, Oct. 5, 1981

job." Another psychologist, Harry Levinson, adds, "It happens when there is no relief, no way out. You come to a screeching halt. You just can't take it any more." The typical symptoms are depression, tension, boredom, fatigue, and a strong sense of not being appreciated—all contributing to a sense of hopelessness.

Whenever there is hopelessness, however, the ethical question quickly emerges: what are we hoping for? The answer, in the burn-out case, is almost always "too much." Accordingly, psychiatrists tend to recommend one of two routes, either get out of the job or change those habits and expectations. Burn-out cases feel hopelessness, the doctors say, largely because they take what they do *too* seriously, making every instance a life-or-death situation. Companionship and talking about frustration, again, is an important piece of advice. "Taking a vacation" is usually only a temporary relief (indeed, in some extreme cases of overwork, busy people have had heart attacks on vacation, finding that the *relief* from work stress is more stressful than the original stress itself). What solves the problem is almost always a change in perspective and a reevaluation of those goals and expectations. Burn-out, like workaholism and perfectionism, is largely a matter of wanting and expecting too much. In these cases, unfortunately, too much is sometimes much less than enough.

I.   A QUESTION FOR THE FUTURE: WHY WORK?

The work ethic is not dead, but it is weaker now. . . . While their fathers and grandfathers and great-grandfathers concentrated hard upon plow and drill press and pressure gauge and tort, some younger workers now ask previously unimaginable questions about the point of knocking themselves out. For the first time in the history of the world, masses of people in the advanced industrialized countries no longer have to focus their minds upon work as the central concern of their existence.
—Lance Morrow, Time, May 11, 1981

For most of human history, work has been considered a curse and a brutal necessity. One peculiarity of modern times is that work is now considered something more, "the work of God" or the key to human dignity. We can understand the latter in terms of the former; as work becomes less necessary, it also requires more conceptual praise in its support. A peasant on the farm cannot ask what the virtues of work are; *the only answer is "to eat."* Most business students, however, are in a position to ask perfectly well, and without danger of starvation, whether ambition and work are necessary. Accordingly, what we call the "work ethic" is an ethic that needs to be constantly reevaluated and understood.

What makes people work, once they have assured themselves adequate food, shelter, and the bare necessities of life? We sometimes think in terms of working harder for *things,* a bigger house, a better car, a more extravagant vacation. But this conception of work, though a natural extension of the age-old need to work for the basic necessities of life, leads to serious misunderstanding. Work has had to acquire new meaning and significance, not just because of the "puritan ethic," but because of the changing nature of society in which that ethic became entrenched. Most of us do not work for the basic necessities, we can accomplish that in a few hours a week. Nor do we work for "things," except on special occasions. What we work for is a good life, and perhaps a better life, if not for ourselves then for our children. The material luxuries may fit in, but as symbols rather than as goals in themselves. And, as we have suggested throughout, work itself is not only a means but also a part of that good life. Work, nowadays, is not something we must do to keep alive but something we do to define ourselves as who we are.

What has changed is not only the ease with which we can supply our basic needs. What has changed is the desperation of the motives that many people, but by no means all (or even most) people, feel about work. Lance Morrow suggests

Work is still the complicated and crucial core of most lives, the occupation melded inseparably to the identity; Freud said that the successful psyche is one capable of love and of work. Work is the most thorough and profound organizing principle in American life. If mobility has weakened old blood ties, our co-workers often form our new family, our tribe, our social world; we become almost citizens of our companies, living under the protection of salaries, pensions and health insurance. Sociologist Robert Schrank believes that people like jobs mainly because they need other people; they need to gossip with them, hang out with them, to schmooze. Says Schrank: "The workplace performs the function of community."

Unless it is dishonest or destructive—the labor of a pimp or a hit man, say—all work is intrinsically honorable in ways that are rarely understood as they once were. Only the fortunate toil in ways that express them directly. There is a Renaissance splendor in Leonardo's effusion: "The works that the eye orders the hands to make are infinite." But most of us labor closer to the ground. Even there, all work expresses the laborer in a deeper sense: all life must be worked at, protected, planted, replanted, fashioned, cooked for, coaxed, diapered, formed, sustained. Work is the way that we tend the world, the way that people connect. It is the most vigorous, vivid sign of life—in individuals and in civilizations.

Lance Morrow, *Time,* May 11, 1981

that the ambition of our ancestors to give their children (and therefore us) a better life was a powerful motive that, over and above the needs they had themselves, served to give hard work an undeniable sense of "dignity." But as we benefactors came to assume the advantages of our position, we were no longer concerned that our children live so much better than we ourselves. Motivation has weakened, and most of us work now for ourselves, simply assuming our children will have similar advantages.

Although the dramatic necessities that formerly fueled our ambitions are less dramatic now, the same role of work as definitive of membership in American society remains as essential as ever. What is gone is the desperation. But this being said, let us remember quite clearly that what we have just said of one class of Americans is not at all true of others; the recent immigrants from Asia and South America and other parts of the world are now facing the same situation our grandparents did, with the same ferocious ambitions and the same sense of work

Today's Workers ——

The strike of the Professional Air Traffic Controllers illustrates a new direction for organized labor in this country, a movement emphasizing dignity and quality of work life among an increasingly professional work force.

Like blue collar workers before them, these white collar workers are becoming militant in areas that go beyond wages. The real issue for the controllers has not been money—they were earning about $33,000 a year—it has been frustration at what is viewed as a lack of response by the Federal Aviation Administration to stress on the job.

In the private sector, management has moved to defuse such issues by giving blue collar workers more of a say in their own operations. A major question today is whether such solutions can be transferred to white collar workers, who now make up the biggest part of the nation's work force and, along with their mid-level managers, increasingly share the factory worker's sense of alienation. . . .

Today's workers—many of them veterans of Vietnam, many with high school diplomas, many hostile to authority—take wages and benefits for granted. "They want more," says Richard Balzer of the New York research firm of Yankelovich, Skelly and White. A study by his firm shows that, for 45 percent of today's work force, company loyalty has been replaced by personal fulfillment. For some that comes through work; for others it comes outside the job. And this includes white collar workers.

Ann Wyman, *The Boston Globe,* Sept. 7, 1981

as the grand source of possibilities that we have lost. When Americans these days talk about the loss of the work ethic, what they complain about is bad service, low productivity, shoddy products, or a small number of bored consumers who spent much of their time trying to "find themselves." But for most of humanity, work continues to supply not only the promises for the future but the sense of self in the present. It is work that holds our communities together, and work by which we belong to those communities. To degrade work once again, by supposing that it is simply a means to supply certain things to satisfy our needs, is to misunderstand its purpose and its function in modern society, and its continuing importance as a source of hope for most of our newer citizens.

■ SUMMARY AND CONCLUSION

In a society dominated by the "work ethic," work and its significance becomes central to our conception of ourselves and our worth. Work becomes our membership and defines our role in society. What we work at and how we do it and feel about it defines who we are. But the meaning of work has changed significantly in recent years; for many centuries, it was considered a "curse," a necessary hardship that the less important people in society were forced to do. Only in the past few hundred years has the "work ethic" given some sense of dignity to work as an end in itself, and only very recently has work, in general, begun to be thought of as potentially "rewarding" and even enjoyable. This conceptual change carries with it an important practical management consideration; people now work not just for wages or because "they have to," but because they want to prove themselves, want to be challenged, want to do something "meaningful." The whole world of work, and the success of a business, changes accordingly.

Work carries along with it certain rights and certain duties. A person who is hired for a job has the right to the tools and authority of the job, and a person who is hired for a job has a duty, obviously, to do that job. But there are many other rights and duties as well, including the right to be treated fairly, to be hired (or fired) without prejudice, to be provided with safe and healthy working conditions, and the duty to be supportive or at least not undermine one's employer, to cooperate with one's fellow workers, and to follow the policies of the company as well as obey the law. But there is an obvious imbalance between the company and any single employee, for while the company can always demand that the employee do his or her duty (or threaten dismissal), the employee cannot always make equally reasonable demands of the company. Labor unions have been an important equalizer in this regard, helping employees to make demands and bargain with their companies, no longer as individuals but as a unified block. But the tradition of labor versus management makes cooperation difficult, and a better solution is teamwork in which the efforts and interests of all are taken seriously and mutually respected.

Work is usually contrasted with play, but this distinction too has become less important as our concept of work changes. For people who like their jobs, work itself may include a good amount of play. In pursuit of their leisure time, most Americans work at their play harder than they do their jobs. Furthermore, play differs from relaxation, but relaxation too, in a working life, becomes part of work, as well as a break from it. Indeed, the meaning of work in our lives is such that nothing could be more damaging to our conception of ourselves than to wholly separate work from the rest of our lives, to treat it as a brute necessity, and fail to appreciate its central place in the good life. Whatever else the benefits or the promises, an unfulfilling job is usually a fatal obstacle to living well.

■ STUDY QUESTIONS

1. What kinds of activities do you consider to be work (as opposed to non-work)? What aspects of your career do you consider to be work? What aspects of your career do you consider to be *rewarding* work?

2. What kinds of changes in the jobs to be done in society explain the change from work considered as a "curse" to work considered as a moral virtue? What kinds of changes in our conceptions of ourselves were necessary in order for work—rather than aristocratic leisure—to become an ideal for everyone?

3. What jobs would you be willing to do for minimal (or no) wages? What jobs would you do only for maximum wages? What jobs would you expect to be done only for wages and never "because I enjoy doing it"? What do your answers indicate about the relationship between wages and work?

4. Should people always be paid for their work? Should people be rewarded *only* for working?

5. What is "knowledge work"? How do you measure success in such work?

6. Keep a daily diary for a few days. How do you spend your time? How much time do you consider well spent ("essential time")? How much do you consider not well spent but yet spent doing necessities (the laundry, washing dishes, returning books to the library)? How much time do you consider wasted? What activities fall into each category?

7. Which of your activities do you enjoy the most? If so, why don't you do those more?

8. How do you relax? What do you do with your "spare time"? Do you consider that time well spent? Are you doing the leisure activities that are right for you? What are they?

9. What activities in your life do you consider *creative?* How important are these to you? What creative activities would you like to do more?

10. How do you tell when a person is working *too much?* How can you tell if you are overworking?

11. Why work? ("Because I have to" isn't an acceptable answer.)

12. Should every employee have the right to join a union? Why or why not? Should all employees have the right to strike if conditions become sufficiently unsafe or intolerable? Why or why not? Should an employee ever be forced to join or support a union? Why or why not?

■ FOR CLASS DISCUSSION

Professional versus Social Responsibilities

Sometimes the responsibilities of a practice and social responsibilities conflict head-on in a dramatic way. For example, consider the dilemma of a priest or a psychiatrist who has just heard the confession and future violent intentions of a dangerous criminal. Their professional ethics requires silence; social responsibility dictates a fast call to the authorities. Indeed, in the case of the priest, the obligation of silence is a "sacred" obligation. But it is the wrong question to ask whether society has the right to intrude in his professional obligations. Of course it does; in this case, we would add, it even has an obligation to persuade the priest or the psychiatrist, though not by any means, to disclose the relevant information. The limits of persuasion, however, depend to a large extent on society's general recognition of the legitimacy of priests and psychiatrists and their professions. We do not recognize the legitimacy of oaths of silence amongst gangsters, for example, despite their supposed "sacredness," and this is why we feel free to force and threaten them for information, as we do not with priests and psychiatrists. (Of course, there are still limits to the threats we can use to do so.) A professional obligation is honored because it is sanctioned by society, but this in no way cancels out the social responsibility. What it does is raise a perhaps tragic conflict between the professional and social responsibilities.

Are there instances in business and business practices in which such conflicts can occur? Describe such an instance in detail and describe what you think ought to be done. Do social responsibilities *always* take priority over business responsibilities? Do they *ever* take priority over business obligations? Can you formulate a general rule for yourself about what to do if caught in such a conflict as the one you have described?

HISTORICAL INTERLUDE

ANOTHER KIND OF CAPITALISM: JAPAN, INC.

> In Japan, we tend to think of a business as something that really should go on regardless of short-term performance—not as something to be thrown away or shut down because of temporary difficulties. . . . We learned a great deal about systematic long-range planning from American business, and yet we often feel that in the management of businesses the Japanese have a longer-term orientation than Americans have.
>
> —Yotaro Kobayashi, Fuji Xerox

> In Japan we have a so-called lifetime-employment system. Workers, and executives too, typically spend their entire working life with a single company. People are not judged on performance during a short period of time, under pressure, say, to produce an increase in earnings. Executives can take a longer perspective in guiding the organization, which is considered perpetual.
>
> —Toshio Ozeki, Nikko Securities

Japan is a latecomer to the world of business. When most of Europe was going through the Industrial Revolution, Japan was still a feudal society. As late as only thirty years ago, "made in Japan" was a label for cheap imitations, and Japan was at most a minor economic power. By 1980, however, Japan had beat the Detroit automotive industry in sales of automobiles—the industry that had always symbolized American economic superiority more than any other. How did they do it? They did it with a conception of capitalism quite different from ours, which many of our major corporations have since tried to imitate.

The difference between Japanese business and our own is primarily ethical. Theirs is a way of life that reflects and is reflected in dramatic differences in organization as well as in attitudes towards the individual and the group. Individual initiative and ambition play at most a minor role in Japanese business; in fact, individual ambition is considered a vice, especially if it results in a disruption of the harmony—or *wa*, an essential concept—of the group, in this case, the company. Competition between individuals who should be cooperating for the shared good is similarly considered a disturbance and disruption of productive forces rather than a spur to improve production. But perhaps this well-known cooperation of the Japanese, especially cooperation between labor and management, should be put into historical perspective. It is not as if class conflict and labor–management violence is unknown in Japan. Just over thirty years ago, a decade or so after the end of World War II, there were extremely violent strikes and labor uprisings in Tokyo and other industrializing cities, and it was in reaction to that violent disruption that the current climate of cooperation evolved. The Japanese realized, as now do we (and the British, the Canadians, the Australians, and others), that in the face of harsh economic realities and global competition it is self-destructive to be at each other's throats.

In major corporations, Japanese businesspeople are employed for life, and loyalty to the company and its goals is all-important. Japanese businesses operate on a seniority system that would seem wholly alien to American executives (though it might not seem so to workers and tenured academics). Merit raises and promotion on the basis of good work are relatively rare; time with the company, during which a person has done his job, is the basis of all advancement. But without the spur of competition and the merit system, what motivates improved performance? It is the pursuit of excellence, "the best," not for the individual but for the group. It is pride in work as a contribution to the whole that motivates performance rather than individual rewards or advancement. It is this sense of group identification, instead of merely working for advancement, that some American analysts find most often missing from the American management system—this sense that what we do really matters in terms of advancing the group effort as a whole.

Better Than the Best ——

In the feudal days of Japan, it was the ambition of every samurai or warrior to serve his lord better than did any of his fellow-samurai, and every local lord made efforts to stand higher in the favour of the Shogun and the Emperor than did any other lords in the country. Now that she has entered the world-arena, it is her greatest ambition to be better than the best in the world in any line of culture. In the pre-war days the world charged Japan with exporting commodities cheaper than their manufacturer would cost in other countries. She was not dumping them at all, but, on the contrary, she endeavoured to supply the world with cheaper articles than were supplied by any other countries in the world. In art, science, literature, trade, industry and what-not does every single Japanese aspire to stand higher in his own profession and occupation than anybody else, and in her effort to be better than the best lies indeed the secret of the great progress that Japan has made and will make to rise up from her defeated ruins.

From "Secret of Japan's Progress" in *We Japanese, Being Descriptions of Many of the Customs, Manners, Ceremonies, Festivals, Arts and Crafts of the Japanese*, 1934.

The de-emphasis of the individual does not mean loss of individual power, however. Quite the contrary, the emphasis on the group rather than the individual spreads the power more evenly; and, unlike the American corporation, in which power flows from top to bottom, the Japanese corporation is based on bottom-to-top information flow, based on the assumption that the person who is actually doing a particular job probably has much more understanding of the task at hand than an industrial engineer. This applies particularly to the design of new machinery and to skills. A familiar feature of Japanese industry is the Quality Control Circle, in which workers meet in groups of eight or so to discuss problems they see with the job or the product.

Decision making in general, even at top management levels, is by consensus rather than by an individual passing down judgment. In America, most executives feel that committee work is a waste of time; in Japan, it is essential, because it means that everyone, once again, feels that individual judgment has been considered. Decision making itself is, of course, slower than in the United States, but once the decision has been made, everyone has agreed in advance to support it, and it can then be implemented with impressive speed. If a manager feels that his opinion was considered fully, even if it was not followed, he will not try to undermine the decision or the decision maker. Because of this advance committment, the overall process is more efficient, even if the decision making itself is slower. Both Americans and Japanese know that a decision without support is worthless. In Japan the system assures that there will be no such decisions.

Not only is the competition within the corporation minimized, but also the competition between companies (especially the important exporting companies). Likewise, the antagonism between business and government are minimized too. The cry of American capitalism has always been "laissez faire" to the government—leave us alone. In Japan, cooperation between business and government is accepted by everyone as being in the best interests of society as a whole. This cooperation has been summarized by the phrase, "Japan, Inc." It is important not to overidealize this spirit of cooperation, however, just as it is important not to overstate the extent of antagonism between business and government in America. There is constant friction, of course, as any Japanese businessperson will affirm. But the goal is clearly a shared goal and cooperation is the most rational way to achieve that goal. There is no "invisible hand"; there is careful planning and cooperation. There is fierce competition between companies to establish markets for new products, more fierce, even than the competition here. But the competition is always viewed within the context of shared national interests and in a spirit of ultimate cooperation.

To the American student looking at Japan, the most remarkable difference between Japan and America is the overwhelming sense of security and loyalty for both worker and manager. Not only are jobs guaranteed, but also the survival of the company—even through economic times disastrous enough to bankrupt a comparable American firm. When workers know that they will have a job no matter what, and that the company will share the good times with them (as the

Japanese firms have done), they are willing to help the company weather the rough times. In return, Japanese firms practice paternalistic management of their workers, providing them with subsidized housing and vacations, and many company-funded "freebies." Paternalism, though often despised by Americans as a violation of individual freedoms, is seen by the Japanese as a simple extension of the loyalty that works both ways.

Japanese companies are willing to hire relatively untrained workers (by American standards) and train them themselves. This means that once a company has made a huge investment in a valuable human asset (as opposed to the classical conception of interchangeable laborers), it is willing to move the worker around until it finds him a job that he can do well. This also means that the worker is willing to be moved around in the company and do whatever the company needs, so that the Japanese work force is, by and large, incredibly flexible. There is much less specialization. Workers are highly educated, highly trained, and willing to do whatever job needs to be done. Thus, when asked what he does for a living, a worker is more likely to reply that he is with Toyota than that he is an engineer. Mobility within a firm is often the norm, but mobility between firms, because of the implied stealing of one firm's investments, is virtually nonexistent. Cooperation and job security are the key points of the Japanese management system.

Much of the Japanese attitude towards business can be traced to earlier attitudes and social considerations. For instance, when Japan was a feudal society, with no mobility, loyalty was the key to social organization—including loyalty to family as well as loyalty to the larger community. Loyalty to the corporation is a natural transference of this feudal attitude, which is quite foreign to the "rugged individualism" and puritan attitudes of American society. Similarly, Japan is a relatively homogeneous society with virtually no natural resources except its people, and not a society of immigrants and explorers on a seemingly unlimited continent like our own. Therefore, a singular sense of the whole of society and its well-being is more accessible than it would be in a more varied and mobile society. And yet, the Japanese version of capitalism and its ethics has become obviously attractive to Americans—and only in part by virtue of its financial successes. For a great many Americans, the Japanese sense of *wa* might be a welcome alternative to our own emphasis on competition and the loneliness of "looking out for number one."

Nevertheless, our fascination with the Japanese and their success should be mitigated by the downside of their form of business. That homogeneity is not entirely natural, and many "foreign" yet lifelong residents of Japan are all but shut out of the work force. Women have only recently been able to get jobs in the major corporations; even so, they are still discouraged, their promotions are limited, and they are simply expected to leave the work force when it is "time to have a baby." Furthermore, only a part of the work force has the much-vaunted security of lifetime employment—others are often out of work, taking menial jobs out of desperation. It is definitely a two-tiered system, and even those who enjoy lifetime employment often do so only at the expense of extraordinarily long hours, virtually mortgaging their lives to the corporation. Education tends to be technical and aimed at doing well on tests rather than learning, much less enjoying, the material. Harmony is purchased at the expense of diversity. Furthermore, much of the success of the Japanese corporation has been the product of the building of huge conglomerates, *keiretsu,* which in the United States would be considered serious obstacles to free trade.

It is also worth mentioning that the work ethic in Japan is changing. One *sarariman,* a white collar worker, tells a leading (Japanese) economic journal, "Bluntly speaking, Japanese people are starting to see themselves as underpaid and exploited, long hours, one short vacation, long commutes, and only expensive, tiny homes. I don't think Japanese are hardworking by nature," he says. "The phenomenon came just after World War II, when we were very poor and had to rebuild." But now, the newspapers are filled with stories about teenagers who "just want to have fun" and *sararimen* who care as much for their families as for their companies. Thus it is worth noting that, as America strives to become more like Japan, the Japanese seem to be becoming more like America. Nevertheless, there is much to be learned from the Japanese without emulating them, and foremost among these lessons is the spirit of cooperation. American business doesn't have to be a "jungle," and, indeed, it would be much more successful if it were not.

– 14 –
The Personal Side
of Business:
Friendship, Family,
Sex, and Marriage

I've become rich, friendless and mean, and in America, that's
as far as you can go.

—Mr. Vandergelder, "Hello, Dolly!"

Too much emphasis on the *results* of business life—profits for the company, a salary plus perks for ourself and our family—leads us to ignore the actual content of business life, which consists largely of work relationships, friendships, and more. "For most people," insists a leading sociologist, "their jobs are the place where they make their friends." Furthermore, much of what we call "the personal side of life"—friendships, sex, love, and marriage, for example—spill over into business life and, even more so, vice versa. To pretend that business is one thing, and personal life another, is a form of schizoid separation that very few people can afford. Our role in business has much to do with the friends we make and the friends we keep. Marriages survive or break apart because of business pressures and the way they are mutually handled. Husbands and wives may be as much a part of each other's successes—or failures—as their own efforts. And sex, which according to current gospel is not supposed to be part of business at all, is very much alive, all the time. Business roles do not obliterate personal and biological roles, however, sometimes they do confuse them.

A. FRIENDSHIP

Friendship is one of those values that forms the core of the good life. Aristotle once said that "no one would choose to live without friends." But as obvious as we might find the importance of friendship, it is a truth that too easily escapes our attention in the day-to-day workings of business and in the more abstract worries of ethics. Much of our motive for work comes from the desire to be respected and admired by our friends; indeed, work becomes a means to make friends. And, accordingly, many of our friendships are determined by our work, and our success in work depends upon our friendships.

The idea that success in work depends upon friendships rubs one of the crucial concerns for justice in exactly the wrong way—our strict idea of "advancement on the basis of merit alone." But the ideal of equal opportunity in fact has to be viewed against the background of ongoing human relationships and our natural inclinations as friends and neighbors, as members of families and communities. In many cultures, of course, these latter obligations are taken to the extreme, obliterating all questions of skill, competence, and qualification. In Indonesia, for example, a local manager has an inescapable obligation to hire members of his family, regardless if much better applicants are available. But the idea of pure merit, utterly devoid of interpersonal considerations, puts us off as well. So much of what we do is bound up with personal interaction and cooperation, we need to be comfortable with one another as well as qualified and efficient. In Japan, as noted, business consists of relationships. This does not mean that skills, competence, and merit should be overlooked, but they are not the entire story. Nevertheless, the use of "old boy networks" as a means of excluding women, and the insistence on "feeling comfortable" as an excuse for excluding minority managers and executives, are inexcusable. Friendship and friendliness on the job is essential. Systematic discrimination and favoritism are not.

In today's large corporations, it is generally understood that one special kind of friendship is of particular importance: the **mentor** relationship. Though rarely recognized outside of business circles, one area of common agreement is that few people can possibly make it in the business world without a "friend up above." In the Japanese business world, this mentor relationship is formally built into the system: a senior executive officially takes charge of a number of younger employees, whose progress in the company is his responsibility. In fact, one of the hardships that affected women in the American business world (there are few women at the top in Japan) was the fact that, however hard-working and no doubt talented they may have been, until recently there were few people in high places who would act as mentors for them. The men preferred to choose other men, and all the women were too often shut out altogether. There were too few women already at the top to help the increasing number of younger women entering the business world, and those few women who had made it had to be far more cautious about their relationships with subordinates than their male counterparts.

Friends in High Places: The Advantages of a Mentor ——

While the ideal remains the "self-made" success, employees in most corporations of any size succeed because of the sponsorship of a senior executive, their "mentor" or "sponsor" (sometimes called "rabbi" or even "father/mother"). Mentors serve as coaches for younger employees and take them under their protection. They introduce them to key people in the corporate hierarchy; they encourage them and even fight for them for promotions and job opportunities. Sometimes, mentors help a younger employee to bypass the hierarchy, to cut red tape, get inside information, or go straight to the top for an important consideration. Women especially find that the well-established existence of a "good old boy" network in the corporation can be a handicap to them, although this is now beginning to be corrected by "good old girl" networks of successful women executives who sponsor younger women employees. Indeed, for many junior people in larger corporations, their status and power in the organization is almost wholly a function of their "reflected" power, the status and power of their mentor, without whom they would not have a chance to be a "self-made" success at all.

Based on Rosabeth Moss Kantor, *Men and Women of the Corporation*

The mentor relationship is a kind of business friendship that is, in many cases, a key to success. But in a more subtle way, friendship between peers is also a condition of success, not only in the obvious sense that a person who can't work well with others is of limited value in a cooperative enterprise, but also in the not-so-obvious sense that peer support and encouragement, the mutual inspiration and enthusiasm that comes from close friendships at work, is an important ingredient in success. Having someone to complain to and share concerns with is essential, and it is often the best antidote to such dangers as "workaholism" and "burn-out." These are advantages usually to be gained only in friendships with other people in the same business, in similar positions, usually in the same or a similar company. However sympathetic husbands or wives or golf partners may be, they cannot possibly know the details and the tone of the business situation. Friendship on the job, in other words, is an important and essential part of business life, a key to success, and often a condition for survival. The personal and the professional aspects of life are not easily separated.

The fact that friendships are so important to business success has another side, however. Success has a powerful and often upsetting effect on friendships. For example, almost all successful people have been through the painful experi-

ence of losing a good old friend just because the other person was not so successful. Two people, starting out more or less equally and with the same expectations,
progress at different rates, and the result, no matter how hard they try to separate
the friendship from professional comparisons, is a kind of resentment and conflict. But this is not, as we often think, because the person who has "made it"
starts to "look down on" those left behind; the truth is more often the opposite,
that the person "left behind" finds the progress of a faster colleague a source of
constant irritation, a reminder of his or her own lack of similar success. This
resentment tends to force the friendship apart, much more often than the contempt of someone who has made it for someone who has not. We find this hard to
accept, because our expectation is that our friends will like us better if we are
successful.

The above phenomenon would suggest a fact that psychological studies have
confirmed, that people who are more successful often have fewer long-term
friendships. Success itself does not destroy friendships, nor do successful people
simply "use" their friends to advance and then drop them—a charge made most
often by resentful ex-friends. It is the *rise* to success that destroys friendships,
dislocating peer equivalencies and raising again and again the phenomenon of
resentment, the discomfort of trying to hold together a relationship disrupted by
business rivalry, and the ultimate need to drop it altogether, for it has become
more conflict than companionship. There are people who "use" other people, of
course, but this is a charge often abused and confused with a variety of other
complications in relationships both personal and professional. It is often difficult to tell them apart, and, even then, not always easy to separate them psychologically.

The role of friendship in the good life, like the role of friendship in business
life, is complex and interconnected with a great many other concerns and responsibilities. These complications become most obvious when friendship in a personal sense enters into a professional relationship. For example, this happens
inevitably every time a person tries to get a friend a job, or signs a contract with
someone who also happens to be a friend, or is put in the most uncomfortable
(and sometimes impossible) position of having to hire or promote—or worse,
fire—someone who is also a personal friend. But the complications can be found
even when such obvious conflicts of personal and professional interests do not
arise. Every friendship that is more than casual includes expectations and responsibilities that may conflict with life at many points, most obviously, in terms of
the amount of time friends are willing or able to put into them. When an important meeting is suddenly scheduled, but plans had already been made to meet a
friend for lunch, which takes priority? Suppose the meeting is not all that important? How important does it have to be? Indeed, our general attitude that puts
"work before pleasure," even when the work is not urgent, puts a heavy burden on
friendships. At the extremes, putting work first *all* of the time places an impossible strain on any friendship, which will, eventually, become a friendship
in name only.

The effects of work on friendships can be of a very different kind as well. People who are used to playing the domineering manager-figure at the office may find it difficult to adopt a different role with personal friends, and this, needless to say, puts a severe limitation on the kinds of friends they can have. A domineering person may collect a group of friends who are used to subordinate roles and do not mind playing them—or at least tolerate playing them—in their personal lives as well. Or, a domineering person may have friends who are also domineering because they understand one another better. Or, more rarely, a domineering person may choose friends who are even more domineering, thus getting a chance to play a different role. Friendships, like business positions, consist very largely of mutually defined roles. And whether we choose roles that are similar, complementary, or contradictory is itself an essential part of friendship and its relationship to business life. But worst of all, though all too common, the two roles can become confused to such an extent that *no* personal role ever seems satisfactory and no friendships can develop. In friendship as in business life, almost *any* role (or at least, most roles) are preferable to no role at all. The roles we play determine who we are, and between business and friendship (and the connections between them) that includes an enormous proportion of our self-identity.

We often talk of "friendship" as one type of relationship, but, of course, it is not. Friendships can consist largely of admiration, either mutual or not. Friendships can develop between two people simply for having a good time together but never involving even a serious conversation. There are so-called "friendships"

Friends and Money ——

You get enemies in the business, especially if you're successful. Ones that have grown up and started with you. You want to be liked and you want to help people. I've found out that you can't. It's not appreciated. They never thank you. If you're successful in business, you're around phonies all the time. There's always some guy slappin' you on the back, tryin' to get you to buy something from him or lend him money.

You remember old friends and good times. This relationship is gone. The fun you used to have. They're envious of what you have. They wonder why they didn't do it. When I opened the repair shop in Old Town I was paying my partner $250 a week. I gave him a car and helped with his tuition in college. Someone offered him double what I paid. I said, "If you go, there's no comin' back." So he left. We grew up together, went to grammar school. I lived with him. There's no loyalty when it comes to money.

From Studs Terkel, "Ken Brown," *Working*

that really are no more than casual acquaintances, in that loose sense in which we sometimes call a "friend" someone we have just met once or twice and do not know at all. Intellectual friendships may consist mostly of deep discussion. There are friendships that are concerned mostly with sports—talking about sports, preparation for sport, and the activity itself. Some friendships would not exist apart from a particular business context, while some childhood friendships will survive in some form no matter what the two people go on to do. There are friendships of mutual support and friendships of mutual advantage, and then there are friendships in which mutual enjoyment is so strong that it is considered more important than anything else.

Of the many types of friendships, however, we can distinguish three distinctive varieties. These three varieties were recognized by Aristotle 2,500 years ago, and it should be evident that our ideas about friendship have not changed all that much since then. In his *Nicomachean Ethics* Aristotle listed (1) useful friendship, (2) pleasant friendship, and (3) ideal friendship.

Useful friends help us to get what we want. Mentors are useful friends, to be sure. Indeed, most friendships in business are bound to be "useful" friendships in this sense. This is not to criticize them, and our too easy condemnation of "using people" does not apply here. Sometimes it is quite clear when a friend is "using us" and, when the cost to us is minimal, we do not mind; indeed, it may even give us the pleasant feeling of being "useful." A manager who helps by introducing a friend to other "useful people" need not feel "used," except in the sense that his position is of use to others and such help is considered valuable. Most of the time, of course, useful friends are *mutually* useful, and this is what motivates the friendship. "Using people" becomes a matter of injustice and immorality when the purposes and methods are not clear, such as when one feigns friendship of a more extensive and serious sort while in fact intending only to "use" the person for a few strategic favors. It is the deception and the fraud, *not* the seeking of advantage as such, that makes such a case immoral. Indeed, Kant insisted that this point is one of the cardinal rules of morality by saying "one should never treat a person *merely* as a means, but always as an end as well." But notice that Kant says "merely" as a means not "never" as a means. Treating a person also as an end implies "with respect," and this respect can usually be demonstrated by nothing more than honestly stating what it is that one wants from the other, thus presenting conditions which the other can accept or reject. Most business relationships are like this, and, indeed, it is almost impossible to distinguish whether a great many people are merely business associates or friends in this limited sense.

Friends who share pleasure together are more often personal rather than professional friends, or, at least, the pleasures they share are usually outside of the business setting. Sometimes, of course, the distinction is not so sharp. A good friend who is also an important business associate may be a regular lunch partner. If the purpose of the lunch is business, friendship is not at issue. If the two simply enjoy talking and eating together, it is a "friendship of pleasure" in which neither is trying to "use" the other for anything at all. Of course, sometimes the line between friendly and enjoyable conversation about business and actual negotiations is very vague. But it is important to distinguish the two, and not to confuse "useful" friendships with the very different kind of relationship between two people who enjoy each other's company and doing things together. A cynic may say, "but they are just *using* each other for mutual pleasure"; this only shows that cynics don't understand friendship. There is a difference between using someone and *sharing* with someone. In the first kind of friendship, we can always ask, "What am I getting out of this? What is he or she getting out of this?" In the second kind of friendship, that sort of question seems beside the point: "We are enjoying ourselves, that's all" is a totally adequate answer. Enjoying being together is not the same as "using" one another, just as using one another is not the same as, in the admittedly derogatory sense, "using someone."

The third kind of friendship, which Aristotle calls "ideal," consists not just of mutual advantage and enjoyment (though these might well be there too) but also of mutual inspiration and education. In an "ideal friendship," two people *grow* together; they improve one another and, in so doing, improve themselves. In business life as in personal life we could not be more fortunate than to have an "ideal" friend from whom (and to whom) we obtain not only mutual advantages and the pleasure of doing things together, but a kind of mutual mentorship in which both help and inspire each other. Indeed, Aristotle and his fellow Greeks saw that last kind of friendship as one of the extreme pleasures of life and an absolutely essential component of the good life. They also saw it as the basis for the good society as well, a society bound together not so much by laws and mutual interest as by interpersonal friendship and the desire to improve one another. In contemporary life, this may sound like an implausible ideal, but those who have enjoyed work in a company where personal success and advancement was tied cooperatively to other people who are real friends will attest to it as an ideal well worth working for.

Competition may be the theoretical basis of the marketplace, but friendship is a far more substantial foundation for much of what goes on in business life. Friends within, friends without, and friends who seem to be both in and outside of our business lives make much of what we do possible, and make us want to do it. They also set the tone and the limits, and so, in a crucial sense, they are one of the most important elements, if often unnoticed and unappreciated, in business ethics.

B. SEX (AND LOVE) IN THE OFFICE

The first thing to be said about sex in the office is that discrimination in hiring, firing, and promotion, as well as somewhat less traumatic questions of job assignments, salary raises, and particular responsibilities, is illegal, immoral, and unethical. Whatever else it may be, sex is not a condition of employment, and using sex as a weapon or as a means of demeaning other people, through actual threats or "just joking comments," is also unethical and, increasingly, illegal, as **sexual harassment.** But this being said, without qualification, perhaps the second thing to say is that sex in the office occasionally is a very real factor in business life. The absolute prohibition against sex discrimination can too easily be misinterpreted as the demand that sex be eliminated from the office. Sex, of course, is not just the physical act. It also concerns the way we talk, the way we dress, the way we think of ourselves and, inevitably, the way we think of each other. Sex has been around a lot longer than most business roles. So too it is hardly plausible to totally separate sex and business at the office, given that the bodies with which we show up for work are also the same bodies, with their characteristic shapes and accoutrements, that constitute the basis of our biological life.

Between the requirements of justice and equal opportunity—that sexual differences are not to be considered relevant to hiring, firing, promotion, and job rewards and responsibilities—and the plain fact of sexual differences and sexual identity in the office, the question of business ethics becomes particularly sensitive. It is a set of problems that has been largely ignored by business ethics. To say that sex is irrelevant to job opportunity is not to insist that sex has no place in the office; it is rather the nature of that place, and its complications, that raises the hard questions. Business ethics may begin by condemning the employer who makes sexual "favors" a condition for advancement for an employee, but it does not end there.

In issues such as this the distinction between *moral* considerations and *prudential* considerations must always be kept in mind. It may well be foolish to initiate an office romance, given the amount of suspicion and gossip this will inevitably inspire, given the awkwardness of working together if it succeeds or, much worse, if it does not. However, such concerns are not yet moral concerns, questions of right and wrong. A relationship that is so promising, that makes two people so happy, and, in addition, that allows them to share their social life with someone who also understands the minutest details of their business life is entirely possible. The dangers of such a relationship are far outweighed by the prospects of happiness. On the other hand, there are sexual relations not involving discrimination that are nevertheless immoral if not provably illegal. For example, a male employer makes sexually suggestive comments to a female subordinate, not by way of a "condition for employment" but nevertheless in such a way that, by virtue of her position, she cannot answer back and feels degraded, if not humiliated. Sexual harassment is a breach of morality rather than a mere lapse in taste (which is what the male employer is likely to say when and if he apologizes). This case is an ill-considered action with negative consequences and an intentional degradation of another person, who happens to be in the employer's power and whose protection is, therefore, to a certain extent his responsibility.

The prudential question of sexual ethics in business is enormously complicated, but it usually has a simple answer: "No." The fact of mutual sexual attraction may be inevitable. Being male or female is as much a part of our self-identity at the office as are the details of our particular position and responsibilities. But accepting this and excepting the occasional blossoming of the story-book office romance, the risks and complications of sex in the office, even assuming that questions of discrimination and harassment are not raised, are enormous.

Sex is one of our more noticeable characteristics and is therefore the characteristic most readily seized upon in rationalizations of failure and in malicious office gossip. Two people who are (or are rumored to be) having an affair inspire far more titillation and gossip than two people who play tennis together. That places enormous pressure on them, by virtue of increased attention and also suspicions, in the social dynamics of the office. Small decisions that formerly would have passed unnoticed now become possible "favoritism," small gestures of protection or attention now become stigmatized, and the success of the relationship becomes uncomfortably tied to success in business. If the relationship breaks up, the results can be disastrous, forcing everyone else to take sides as well as setting up an intolerable work situation for the two people themselves. For the woman in the relationship, it is usually even worse. Where there are complications, as there almost always are, it is more often than not the woman who gets blamed, or, removed. Indeed, even when the relationship "works," and the office romance ends in a marriage, it may be the woman who suffers.

In the old office-romance movies, this problem was avoided by ending the movie with the wedding (or earlier), or else, more honestly but without a hint of injustice, it was made to be understood that the woman, not the man, would give up her career. Even still, most companies require one partner to quit or transfer to a different department. In fact, it is seldom the man who does. But for both people, romance in the office can turn out to be a disaster. That doesn't make it wrong, and there are always those cases to the contrary, but no situation is more likely to place personal values and business ambitions in direct conflict. From either a personal or business point of view, the complications are rarely worth it. There may be nothing wrong with an honest office romance, but prudence would usually advise against it.

Sexual harassment is another matter. Sexual harassment is the unwanted *intrusion* of sex into any context including business in which it is inappropriate and degrading. Referring to a person's sex when he or she is trying to discuss an important (or even an unimportant) business issue is sexual harassment. Touching or gesturing towards a person in a sexual way, when he or she is trying not to (or is just not trying to) be an object of sexual attention, is sexual harassment. Putting up a sexually provocative poster or picture within view of a person who is likely to be embarrassed or offended is sexual harassment. And, of course, actual physical assault or obscene language constitutes sexual harassment of the most blatant kind. Sexual harassment is the use of sex to degrade another person or to embarrass or humiliate, even if what is said is intended as "a joke" or as "teasing." However, it is not sex itself that is offensive or intrusive. The characteristic of sexual harassment is its *lack of reciprocity*. Between two mutually consenting people sexual innuendos or suggestions are not wrong or immoral. The *abuse* of sexuality to distract a person from his or her proper job, however, or to shift attention from performance of his or her responsibilities to the unwanted and embarrassing role of "sex object" makes harassment unethical, immoral, and illegal.

The fact of reciprocity, however, does not always make a sexual act acceptable. It may still be in bad taste, of course (though it is important to distinguish bad taste from immorality). More importantly, the mere fact of reciprocity does not guarantee that acceptance on the part of one person might not be a matter of *coercion,* for example, when a superior propositions a subordinate and the latter cannot possibly afford to say "no." Indeed, the possibility of coercion is there even if the intentions of the superior are not at all coercive (for example, if he or she honestly believes that the subordinate is also interested in an affair). In general, the relationship of superior with subordinate is such that the superior should always *presume* that coercion is an intrinsic part of the situation. Some fine romances may thus be prevented, but a great many more tragedies and abuses will thus be prevented too.

Insisting on the absolute prohibition against sex discrimination in business and pointing out the moral abuses attached to sexual harassment, even pointing out the complex dangers of sex and romance in the office, is not an argument against sex and its legitimacy, even in the office. Sex is an important part of our lives, and not surprisingly, it sometimes enters activities that are hardly "romantic," such as daily life in business. But the moral of this most unromantic story is not that sex and love are to be eliminated in such contexts, but to point out the very opposite, that is the *importance* of sex in our lives and the power it has over us is part of ethics. Sex in the office always has consequences. One of the more obvious tenets of ethics in business must be that sex and love are an intrinsic and particularly powerful part of the good life as a whole and, as such, sometimes enter into business life too.

C.   Sexual Harassment: A Crime, Not a Compliment

Until quite recently, sexual harassment was taken seriously by neither the American public nor its court system. "The casting couch" is one of many such metaphors familiar enough to have inured us to what is not a very pretty picture of male-employer female-employee relations. As late as 1975 we found the courts making statements such as "The only sure way an employer could avoid such [sexual harassment] charges would be to have employees who were asexual" (*Corne v. Bausch and Lomb*) and, in 1979, "The attraction of males to females . . . is a natural sex phenomenon and it is probable that this attraction plays at least a subtle part in most personnel decisions . . . it would seem wise for the courts to refrain from delving into these matters" (*Miller v. Bank of America*).

We have some reason to be grateful for the otherwise shocking and disheartening spectacle of Supreme Court Justice Clarence Thomas' confirmation hearings, in which the testimony of Anita Hill made sexual harassment an issue of national importance. People are now less likely to chuckle over cartoons of the boss chasing his secretary around the boardroom table. In fact, we no longer see them in print. When a nominee for one of our nation's highest and most respected offices is publicly accused of sexual harassment, sexual harassment is no longer a joke.

Of course the Supreme Court's acquaintance with sexual harassment did not begin (nor will it end) with Clarence Thomas. As early as 1977 a federal court recognized sexual harassment as a form of sexual discrimination, and thus illegal under Title VII of the 1964 Civil Rights Act, which forbids discrimination in employment on the basis of race, sex, and so on. The most significant change in the perception of sexual harassment by the courts, however, occurred in 1986, with the famous *Meritor Savings Bank, FSB v. Vinson* case. At that time the Supreme Court decided that no court or legislature could create a law which denied that sexual harassment is a crime. The court defined "sexual harassment" as:

> unwelcome sexual advances, requests for sexual favors, and other verbal or physical conduct of a sexual nature. . . . when (1) submission to such conduct is made either explicitly or implicitly a term or condition of an individual's employment, (2) submission to or rejection of such conduct by an individual is used as the basis for employment decisions affecting such individual, or (3) such conduct has the purpose or effect of unreasonably interfering with an individual's work performance or creating an intimidating, hostile or offensive working environment.*

Here the court is following the "Guidelines on Discrimination Because of Sex" established by the Equal Employment Opportunity Commission in 1980. These guidelines remain essentially unchanged today (see box on pages 474–475 with full guidelines). The only significant addition was made in 1991 when President George Bush signed into law the "Civil Rights Act of 1991," which greatly increased the possible remedies for victims of sexual harassment. It is now possible for victims of sexual harassment to seek both compensatory and punitive damages, in addition to lost pay and other less substantial forms of recompense. Prior to this act, the victim could expect, at best, that the harassing behavior would cease, and that a certain amount of lost wages (a maximum of two years) and/or other benefits would be repaid. However, the 1991 act also put a cap on the amount of the damages that may be awarded, with the amount of the award dependent upon the size of the company for which the victim worked so that, in effect, the bigger the company, the more it will likely have to pay.

---

*29C.F.R. § 1604.11 [1986].

There are essentially two sorts of sexual harassment covered by the 1980 guidelines: *quid pro quo* harassment, and "offensive environment" or "hostile work environment" harassment. In *quid pro quo* harassment there is, as the name suggests, an exchange: sexual favors are traded for promotion or other benefits in the company. In fact, there need not be an actual exchange; it is sufficient, for harassment to be present, for the employer or supervisor to suggest that such favors will result in benefits. This develops an interesting wrinkle when favors are granted and another nonparticipant employee misses a promotion or raise that he or she would otherwise have received; in this case the victim is not only the individual whose part in the movie, if you will, depended upon a trip to the casting couch, but also the other actress who was equally or better qualified for the part but didn't get cast. In such cases both victims are eligible for recompense from the harasser. Unfortunately, however, such cases are very difficult to prove without the testimony of the victim who did in fact receive certain benefits from the harassment, and, for reasons which are obvious, that testimony is usually not forthcoming. On the whole, however, *quid pro quo* harassment is comparatively easy to demonstrate, and the cases are more or less clear-cut. A demand for sex is made in exchange for either a benefit—a promotion, raise, or even a first position (sexual harassment occurs very frequently during the actual hiring process)—or the avoidance of some detriment such as, most obviously, the loss of one's job. The earliest cases of sexual harassment brought to court were similar to *Barnes v. Castle,* 1977, in which repeated offers of reward in exchange for sexual favors were made by the employer, and, when these offers were refused, the employee was fired.

Meritor Savings Bank is an example of the other, less obvious, form of sexual harassment in which the harassment creates an unpleasant and ultimately intolerable work environment. Michelle Vinson, the victim, was compelled to have sex repeatedly with a supervisor, and allegedly other incidents of fondling

In a national survey of more than 750 professional women, more than half say they've been sexually harassed at work. But only 32 percent reported these incidents, mainly because they were "difficult to prove" or because women feared they would lose their job. Research by *Working Smart,* a newsletter published by the National Institute of Business Management, shows that harassment includes a wide range of unwanted advances, lewd gestures, and off-color comments. Men and women were also asked to rank the practices they found "unacceptable" at work. Number one was kissing, followed by telling ethnic and sexual jokes and using profanity.

—*Across the Board,* April 1991

and even forcible rape occurred. No exchange took place: she received no benefits from the incidences of sexual favors. Eventually this environment forced her to take extended sick leave, and she was subsequently fired. Other cases are not so extreme: an office in which pictures from *Playboy* are hung on the walls or crude sexual remarks are constantly made will generally qualify as a hostile work environment.

What the victim must prove in order to win a "hostile work environment" case is either that the harassment interferes with the ability of the victim to perform his or her job, or that the harassment has a serious detrimental effect on his or her psychological well-being. Obviously, these cases are more difficult to establish, both for the courts and the victim. What prevents a person from properly performing his or her job will vary from individual to individual, and what is detrimental to one's psychological health will vary even more. One person may find certain behavior absolutely repellent when another would find it relatively inoffensive, depending upon their upbringing, cultural background, and other similar factors. Madonna's just-released, enormously popular book *Sex,* for example, would have been labeled the worst form of pornography twenty years ago in this country, and in Iran, even today, one could serve a very long prison term for merely bringing the book into the country. Our society has become sufficiently diverse and complex as to blur many old boundaries between "acceptable" and "unacceptable" behavior. Especially problematic, perhaps, are those cases in which the accused is unaware of any wrongdoing—what one person might consider friendly flirting, another may well interpret as harassment. The trend is to determine what counts as sexual harassment from the perspective of the victim, and so we can safely predict that these cases will only increase. Nonetheless, the scenario in which seemingly nonthreatening sexual relations between employees are brought to trial is doubtless preferable to the former

The Equal Employment Opportunity Commission guidelines for sexual harassment are: ——

A. Harassment on the basis of sex is a violation of . . . Title VII. . . . Unwelcome sexual advances, requests for sexual favors and other verbal or physical conduct of a sexual nature constitute sexual harassment when (1) submission to such conduct is made either explicitly or implicitly a term or condition of an individual's employment, (2) submission to or rejection of such conduct by an individual is used as the basis for employment decisions affecting such individual, or (3) such conduct has the purpose or effect of unreasonably interfering with an individual's work performance or creating an intimidating, hostile, or offensive working environment. . . .

B. In determining whether alleged conduct constitutes sexual harassment, the Commission will look at the record as a whole and at the totality of circumstances, such as the nature of the sexual advances and the context in which the alleged events occurred. The determination of the legality of a particular action will be made from the facts, on a case-by-case basis.

C. An employer, employment agency, joint apprenticeship committee or labor organization . . . is responsible for its acts and those of its agents and supervisory employees with respect to sexual harassment regardless of whether the specific acts complained of were authorized or even forbidden by the employer and regardless of whether the employer knew or should have known of their occurrence. The Commission will examine the circumstances of the particular employment relationship and the job functions performed by the individual in determining whether an individual acts in either a supervisory or agency capacity.

D. With respect to conduct between fellow employees, an employer is responsible for acts of sexual harassment in the workplace where the employer (or its agents or supervisory employees) knows or should have known of the conduct, unless it can be shown that it took immediate and appropriate corrective action.

E. An employer may also be responsible for the acts of non-employees, with respect to sexual harassment of employees in the workplace, where the employer (or its agents or supervisory employees) knows or should have known of the conduct and fails to take immediate and appropriate corrective action. In reviewing these cases, the Commission will consider the extent of the employer's control and any other legal responsibility which the employer may have with respect to the conduct of such non-employees.

F. Prevention is the best tool for the elimination of sexual harassment. An employer should take all steps necessary to prevent sexual harassment from occurring, such as affirmatively raising the subject, expressing strong disapproval, developing appropriate sanctions, informing employees of their right to raise and how to raise the issue of harassment . . . and developing methods to sensitize all concerned.

G. *Other related practices.* Where employment opportunities or benefits are granted because of an individual's submission to the employer's sexual advancements or requests for sexual favors, the employer may be held liable for unlawful sex discrimination against other persons who were qualified for but denied that employment opportunity or benefit.

fully noted how much easier her life would be if only she had a "wife."

D. But it is an open question whether the lucky male executives are consequently any better at their jobs, much less better as people. The disadvantage to women executives, as Vandervelde points out, is considerable, but without, apparently, making it impossible for women to work as hard or as well as men. Indeed, the successful woman executive may even be performing these functions for her husband. But the real victim of this story, needless to say, is the "wife" who is involuntarily reduced to galley slave and bottle washer, nursemaid and sexual comforter, and whose only real sense of accomplishment lies in the support she gives to her husband. But despite the inevitable reactions, the traditional wife cannot be simply presumed as the standard of marriage.

> Between the early 1960s and 1970s, the divorce rate more than doubled, the birthrate fell to an all-time low, and the number of married women who were working outside the home rose sharply. Now about half of all married women hold paying jobs. And at current rates, half of all recent marriages will end in divorce.
>
> Andrew Cherlin, *Newsweek,* July 27, 1981

It is a simple fact, as well as a demand of equality: more corporate wives now have careers of their own, and more corporate "wives" are now husbands. But at the same time, business life is such that some of the old structures remain, even if without the excessive demand of total passivity and support on the part of the spouse. Corporate life is often extremely demanding and all-encompassing; it does not stop at five o'clock or at the bottom of the elevator. The person we live with must still be an integral part of our business world, even if the role is inevitably that of an outsider. But at the same time, the business world is being forced to take more account of the will and the needs of the significant other: it is no longer to be assumed that a family will pull up stakes and break all ties because the company needs an executive in Des Moines. Gary Cooper, author of *Executive Gypsies,* says that managers no longer believe that moving is a good thing in itself, as opposed to only a few years ago. Dual-career families, with spouses pursuing their own careers, are making this difference. Some of the most basic assumptions about the relationship between employers and employees are changing with it. It is not, as sometimes supposed, merely a changing attitude towards "corporate loyalty"; it is rather the belated recognition of the importance of other loyalties, which in case of a conflict often take precedence.

Robert Seidenberg, in *Corporate Wives–Corporate Casualties,* pushes the challenge one step further, from a simple question about justice and equal opportunities for corporate wives to the accusation that the traditional corporate demand for passivity and total support from the wives has caused tangible psychological damage, especially when moves are involved. The husband sees this as a promotion, in which he retains his ties and his (now increased) status with the firm, plus looks forward to new responsibilities with excitement and a sense of adventure. He carries with him an instantly acceptable set of credentials, automatic acceptance in his new job network, and stays in a company that he already knows and in which he already feels comfortable. His wife, on the other hand, can't similarly transfer *her* identity. She finds that she must develop an entirely new network of friends, find new groups to join, find a new job, and perhaps even a new profession—if she has time to work at all. All in all, she must rebuild her social identity from the start, proving herself all over again in a new place, with entirely new people, with little except the kids, the dog, and the furniture to remind her of what and where she's been. As Seidenberg says:

> All the parties she had given, all the successful affairs she had arranged were in no one's memory. These were things that people had to experience and could not be told about. The 'credit' was now lost.

Insofar as business ethics is not just ethics *in* business but the good life and its responsibilities in general, what White once called "the wife problem" must surely rank high on the list of concerns. The demands of business on our "social life" are enormous, and these inevitably include our wives and husbands. At the same time, surely no concern is more important in life, and more basic to ethics and morals in any sense, than feelings and concern for the happiness and wellbeing of the person we live with. And unlike the more dramatic questions of ethics—whether to bribe the prime minister of Japan or whether to tell the public that a car's gas tank may explode on impact—the question of how to unify our business life and our marriage in a mutually satisfying way is a problem we live with and face every day. It cannot be put aside, and cannot be taken care of by anyone else. Indeed, the connection between business life and the rest of life is never so intimate as this, and never so crucial to the good life as such. In no other question are the priorities of business ethics so urgent, and so essential to happiness and the good life.

E.   Women in Business

The bold application of the mentor technique to a young woman holds special perils—especially for her. A young man's fast rise may cause jealousy and resentment when he is sponsored by a powerful executive. A woman is a more vulnerable target. Whether or not she is romantically linked with her mentor, it's easy for the organization to think she is. Suspicion of a 'casting couch' syndrome can destroy any credibility her link with the mentor could have given her.

—*The Wall Street Journal*, Oct. 13, 1980.

In one sense there is no excluding sex from the office; women and men alike always carry their sexual identities with them, no matter what else they do. A woman dresses to be attractive as a woman, and a man dresses to be attractive as a man. A woman executive may wear a well-tailored business suit instead of a glamorous dress, but the fact that she is a woman is still consciously evident, even if, as a matter of necessity, she tries to downplay femininity and emphasize her more "masculine" business skills—aggressiveness, hard-headedness, straightforward ambition. On the other hand, sex has no place in the office in a quite different sense; sex should play no role in hiring, firing, and promotion, and it should be no consideration in the jobs, rewards, and responsibilities given to an employee. But these two opposing considerations contradict each other; employees and executives are not neuter. Because female executives are rarer than their male counterparts, they inevitably are more visible. With that inevitable visibility the idea of sex-blind neutrality in evaluations of performance, particularly personal and social performance, becomes impossible.

A lone woman on the management level is watched. She is different, if only because she is a woman. She may be the first woman there, and people watch her as a kind of "test case." Some will no doubt believe—or hope—that a woman can't do the job or stand the pressure. Other women may be looking for a heroine to blaze a trail. Some will just find the situation more interesting than usual. Others will simply watch with interest because everyone else is watching. But the net result will be heightened visibility, increased stress and strain, and the sense that she is not doing well just for herself, but "proving something," perhaps even standing up as a representative of half our species.

Heightened visibility has both its advantages and its disadvantages. In any firm of any size, doing well and earning promotion obviously requires visibility, so that people see and appreciate what we are doing. We have to be on management's mind when openings occur, and our participation in a successful project has to be remembered, if some of that success is going to be credited to us. But the heightened visibility can also work against a woman. If an assignment is anything less than an overwhelming success, it is all too easy for detractors or competitors to use the flaws to their advantage. If the members were male, on the other hand, the project would not be so visible, and the less than overwhelming success simply would be counted as a modest achievement. A single failure, in the context of such visibility, could be publicly argued to be proof that a woman—not just this woman, but *any* woman—cannot do the job. The argument is wholly fallacious, but in the charged environment of women new in management and men jealous or envious of their progress, such fallacies have an unfortunate tendency to be taken seriously. It is a fact, as well as a fallacy, that women in high positions tend to be thought of, and tend therefore to think of themselves, as representatives of their sex, and only after that as a capable (or incapable) individual.

Visibility and being seen as a representative of a sex further complicates the already complex and emotional issues in a still male-dominated world. It is natural and acceptable, but always a matter of some envy and suspicion, when someone gets promoted on the basis of a friendship with someone higher up. Indeed, the mentor system is well-established in the American business world and it is a basic fact about organizations: however the more abstract principles of justice might demand total impersonality, people prefer to work with people with whom they already feel comfortable. And yet, there is always the suspicion that a person has been promoted just on the basis of such friendship, without regard to merit, and where merit is hard to measure—as in any complex institution or organization—such suspicions can never be wholly proved to be wrong. But when such suspicions regard a woman who has been promoted, especially promoted by a male mentor, the nastiness that resides in any competitive situation quickly emerges.

Almost inevitably, an attractive woman who gets ahead in the male world will be suspected of having "used her sex to get ahead," and there is hardly an argument or a demonstration that will prove otherwise. Indeed, the liability of having both "brains and beauty" was dramatically demonstrated in a recently publicized case. An extremely talented and also attractive young woman was

---

The Supreme Court, in a major sex discrimination decision, ruled that employers may not bar women of childbearing age from certain jobs because of potential risk to their fetuses.

The high court, by a six-to-three vote, said such "fetal protection" policies, currently used by more than a dozen major corporations with tens of thousands of workers, are a form of sex bias that is prohibited by federal civil rights law.

"Women as capable of doing their jobs as their male counterparts may not be forced to choose between having a child and having a job," the high court said in an opinion written by Justice Harry Blackmun.

Women's rights groups hailed the decision as an important victory, one that averted the threat that the Supreme Court would make it easier for employers to justify practices that discriminate against women.

—*The Wall Street Journal,* March 21, 1991

promoted to the vice-presidency by the male CEO. Rumors spread so quickly and viciously that the CEO felt compelled, unwisely, to issue a statement denying that he and the young woman were anything other than business associates in the traditional mentor relationship.

For the time being, it is almost unavoidable that some people, bitter about their own lack of progress, will voice such suspicions, picking on the most obvious attributes of young and attractive female executives—namely their youth, their attractiveness, and their femaleness. And if she tries to hide her attractiveness and her sex through careful dress and behavior, she will no doubt be similarly accused of being "cold" and "bitchy," and thus incapable of working well with other people. But the moral is not that this is a no-win situation for women; as in so many other aspects of business ethics, there are inevitable conflicts and complications, and being aware of them and ready for them is always better than being caught unprepared. Times are changing and changing fast in business, and what every person does augments, or complicates, that change. But, for now the

Women at Work

- In 1991, there were 4.4 million single working mothers, up from 2.1 million in 1971 (*The New York Times*).

- Some 54.5 percent of mothers with children under age three were employed at the end of 1991.

- For three decades, the percentage of women in the work force has been rising—until 1991, when the proportion of women in the work force fell slightly to 57.3 percent from 57.5 percent (*Business Week,* March 9, 1992).

- Today, about 80 percent of the nation's top companies have a woman on their board of directors. The rate was 3 percent in 1966.

- Today, women earn $0.74 for every dollar earned by a man. Thirty years ago, the wage differential was $0.62 to the dollar.

- In 1992, some 41 percent of the nation's managers, administrators, and executives were women. That's a nine point jump in as many years (*Forbes,* March 16, 1992).

- By 1987, women owned 30 percent of all businesses in the U.S. but, because of their small size, generated only 14 percent of the receipts.

situation is what it is, and women should be ready to defuse the suspicion that they "slept their way to the top." After all, if they can sleep their way to the top, asks *Boston Globe* columnist Ellen Goodman, "then why aren't they there?"

The source of problems faced by women is not always vicious and not always a product of sexual prejudice as such. So many of the accepted ways of doing business are stuck in a world in which for so long it was a matter of fact that only men were involved. There may be nothing objectionable to clubs for men only, any more than there are objections to clubs for sailors, for transvestites, or for college faculty, so long as that is all that the clubs are designed to be. But when it evolves as a matter of fact that it is men's clubs, where women are excluded, that play host to some of the most important business discussions and decisions, then an injustice is involved, for women are being ruled out of not only the clubs, but essential business meetings. Similarly, there is nothing objectionable to having locker rooms that are restricted to men, but when they become the forum for high-powered business talk, women are unjustly excluded. All of this is needlessly confused by the objection against the existence of exclusive clubs as such, but once again that is not the injustice, it is rather the exclusion of women from meetings essential to their success in what is supposed to be a "free" (that is, *open*) enterprise system.

Indeed, this is the ultimate objection, in the name of justice and fair play, to most of the obstacles that face women executives today. It is not the inevitable attention to their sex, nor even the extra fight they have in proving themselves, or the fact that they don't enjoy the advantage of a "wife" at home to pick up the pieces. It is rather the sheer inequity in opportunities and the totally unfair interpretations placed on a woman's activities, even though these are exactly the same as the activities expected of any equally talented and ambitious male employee.

F.   WORK AND THE FAMILY

It is especially this new role of women in the workplace that has forced corporate America, and Western society generally, to reevaluate the relationship between work and the family. As we have just seen, the family can no longer be described as a sort of rest-up, rejuvenation center for the business-weary male provider. In most families, males are in fact no longer the sole providers and, as a Ford Foundation study recently revealed, more and more women are the primary income-earners among married couples with families. Moreover, the family is no longer necessarily composed of Mom, Dad, and kids. Fictional TV character Murphy Brown was quick to respond to the attacks of former Vice President Dan Quayle that the family today may consist of a unit as small as one parent and one child, and that one parent may well be, and very often is, a working woman. A recent definition of family states that even children are incidental to our contemporary way of thinking about families: "A family . . . is two or more people interacting with, responding to, or having the capacity to influence one another for the purpose of accomplishing some goal or sense of shared identity.*

But the key issue today is not *how* we define the family, nor even *what* it may or may not be, but *why* it exists. And the answer to that question, it seems, has remained relatively stable: to provide nurturance for its members, especially its children. The family is the best and just about the only unit we have developed that can give our children the sort of security and love they need to grow into healthy, productive adults. Even in the Israeli *kibbutz,* traditionally a fundamentally antifamilistic societal structure that provides full caretaking of children along with economic independence of spouses, we find that the trend is toward children spending more and more time at home alone with their parents, and parents spending more and more time together. Large families are on the rise. And today many researchers conclude that the *kibbutz* has become "a highly family-oriented society."† In America, Germany, and Denmark, where not too long ago being married was considered very unfashionable among the youth, marriages are on the rise, people are starting families, and starting them at younger ages than they did ten years ago. But the problem remains: how is a loving, nurturant atmosphere to be maintained when the parent or parents are not with the children, when spouses are not with one another, and when work takes priority over the home?

The answer is simple: it can't be. The family, like any other organization or community, like the workplace itself, requires constant attention and time in order to flourish. It was largely corporate indifference to the family that revealed this to us: as spouses entered the work force together, leaving their homes and their children behind them, families began to break down. Divorces increased. Stress increased. And social scientists and corporations realized, doubtless long after the working fathers and mothers, that productivity went down. As William S. Lee, chairman and president of Duke Power Company, remarked in an interview in 1990: "You can't get excited about your work if you are worried about a sick child at home. So the sick child at home is a concern to management." Unhappy families make unhappy workers, and unhappy workers do not work well. Furthermore, well-trained employees, in whom companies have invested thousands or even tens of thousands of dollars, began to quit because of worries about their homes or children.

Obviously, this destructive cycle could not continue, and in the late 1980s corporations developed an awareness of what is now commonly called a "family-friendly workplace." The first ingredient of such a workplace is usually a program for "dependent care": help with finding good child-care programs, pre-tax salary deductions for employees (who are parents or *caregivers*) who set aside such dollars for dependent care (which means that you can spend money on the

---

*Burke and Bradshaw, paraphrased in Zedeck, *Work, Families and Organizations* (Jossey Bass, 1992: San Francisco), p. 20.
†Judith Richter, "Work and Family in Israel," in Zedeck, p. 376.

care of your kids without that money being taxed), child-care centers in the vicinity of or even at the place of work, after-school programs, and so on. The most common, and thus far one of the most effective, responses is that of the pre-tax deduction: in 1990 more than 2,500 companies had such a program. Research and referral programs (or "R&R" programs) are the next most popular, but their impact has not been as great. Least popular, and often involving the highest financial commitment from the employer, are "sick child" programs, in which a nurse is provided to watch and care for the child in lieu of the parent. In these cases the child is generally not so sick that hospital care is appropriate and thus insurance coverage applicable, and so the cost to the corporation can be quite high. Other "sick child" programs, such as "half-time off" for the parent or caregiver, are currently being experimented with by many corporations.

Emerging are programs that focus more on the family as a unit than simply on the care of the child. In 1988, IBM announced a comprehensive flexible leave and work-at-home program that allows employees to take up to three years of leave, with full benefits. They continue to explore the possibilities of workers—especially caregivers—completing many of their work responsibilities in the home. "If the job requires a computer," says J. T. Childs, manager of their 'Work/Life Programs,' "IBM will install one in the home." They also allow flexibility of hours, so that employees may choose to arrive early and leave early, take very long midday breaks (a "midday flex"), or arrive late and leave late.

IBM is not alone. Corporations have now turned their energy toward the problem of the family, and are, predictably, coming up with a tremendous variety of solutions to the problem. Job-sharing teams, in which individuals, as members of a team, may do their work at any time and in any manner, whether at home with the baby or at midnight in the office, are increasingly popular. Certain companies are even encouraging employees to bring their children with them to work during limited hours. In nations that are particularly advanced with respect to this problem, such as Sweden, all these solutions and many more that we have yet to approach are being used with success. The important progress, of course, is not just how a solution is found, but that people have recognized the problem and are striving to improve the situation. The exhausted father coming home to an unhappy, unfulfilled wife and a house full of children he barely recognizes is becoming, or should be, a thing of the past.

■ Summary and Conclusion

Work is not life, and life isn't just work. Life in business is not just business, it is also friendships, peer relationships and apprenticeships, a social world as well as a profession. Furthermore, those other relationships that are so important to us—friendships, love, and marriage—are not wholly separated from our work life either, however we may distinguish them with such labels as "private life" versus "career." If we define ourselves in terms of our work and our roles in society, then these same definitions determine to a large extent the people with whom we associate, the people we will choose as friends, even possibly the person we will marry. The "private" parts of life are intricately tied, for better or worse, to our working lives, and thus are just as central to "business ethics" as the more businesslike questions of morality, justice, rights, and responsibilities.

Once we begin to think about it, friendship is so basic to the good life that it threatens to eclipse all others. Work itself, for most people, is a place to make friends as well as a living, and most of us believe that, where there is a conflict between friendship and work, the former is at least as important as the latter. But there are different kinds of friends and different kinds of friendships. They play different roles in our lives, and face different obstacles too. Success in business can sometimes be detrimental to even the oldest and best friendships, in ways that are not always expected or predictable.

Sex and romantic love would seem to be completely out of place in the business world—or at least insofar as the language of cost-effectiveness and "profit" would imply. But once we look beyond the language at the actual working relationships among people in the business world, sex and sexual awareness, romantic love and the search for it are present in the workplace just as they are in virtually every other human context. But insofar as the business of business is to be businesslike, which means professional and, to a certain extent, impersonal, the extremely intimate phenomena of sex and love are indeed not only a distraction or a disruption but a serious danger to the efficiency and effectiveness of a business.

The relationship between business and marriage, however, is complex. An executive's husband or wife is virtually always a part of her or his professional life, and inevitably affected by it in other ways too. This is a critical question for business ethics, beyond the question about responsibilities within the organization, to the consumer, and the community at large. One person who is greatly affected by business life is the person who lives with a manager, even if he or she is not part of the business world as such. And where there are children in the family, this consideration is multiplied even more. Gone are the days when a businessman could assume that his wife and children would trail along with him, wherever his next promotion would lead. Today, we recognize full well that a primary obligation of every person in business is to the family and the effects of his or her career on them. Increasingly, the general consensus is that if business *always* comes first, a person perhaps should not be married in the first place.

A related change in the business world, of course, is the fact that women now hold executive jobs and find themselves in much the same position regarding their husbands and families that businessmen in general once did. But women face special and difficult challenges in trying to "make it" in a world which is still largely structured by the work-and-family relations of years past. In the context of justice and our sense of equal opportunity, therefore, an essential part of business ethics is the full recognition, on the part of men as well as women, that these difficulties do still exist and that they do, in fact, contradict the sense of fairness and freedom that is basic to our free enterprise system.

■ STUDY QUESTIONS

1. What is friendship? How do you know whether or not someone is your friend? (For example, "a friend in need is a friend indeed"; is that an adequate or fair test of friendship?)

2. Make a list of those people you consider your friends. Who are your "best" friends? Why? Who are your oldest friends? Newest friends? Which friends are mainly "professional" friends, that is, friends regarding work but who you don't see much otherwise? What are the primary differences between your old friends and your new friends?

3. Do you believe that success will make your friends like you more? Less? Explain.

4. In your experience, has a friendship ever conflicted with a work obligation? Explain the conflict. How did you resolve it?

5. Why is sex a danger in an office context? Does this have anything to do with the "morality" of sex? What does it have to do with?

6. What usually happens when an office romance doesn't work out?

7. What happens when an office romance does work out?

8. What is sexual harassment? Why is it not just a matter of "just teasing" or "an innocent joke"?

9. What are the disadvantages of a spouse who is forced to move to a new location along with a husband or wife who is promoted or transferred? Which of these disadvantages do you consider most serious?

10. What are the disadvantages to children who are forced to move along with their parents, one or both of whom is promoted or transferred to a new location? Which of these disadvantages do you consider most serious?

■ FOR CLASS DISCUSSION

"Because She's a Woman?"

She was beautiful, bright, ambitious—and a woman. When Mary Sue Allen was promoted to vice president in charge of strategic planning at Trendix of Chicago, she was simply following the pattern established by her CEO, Nelson Agree. He too had been a youthful protégé and became head of Trendix at thirty-nine. Trendix had a history of promoting young, talented people quickly. Mary Sue Allen was now twenty-nine.

Allen had graduated from Wharton Business School two years earlier, with top honors, while holding down a full-time job. Before that, she spent three years as a junior officer at Chase Manhattan Bank, after beginning as a paralegal. She came to Trendix as assistant to the president, an important role at the time. Trendix was embarking on a shift in emphasis within the corporation, moving towards high technology, and ready to invest some $700 million to do so. Allen's role in forming and conceiving the new strategy was seminal, and the job she did was outstanding. It was on this basis that she was promoted to head of strategic planning and vice president.

The problem was her visibility. Many young men had been promoted to high-ranking positions on the basis of outstanding performance, and virtually all of them had the support of a senior executive who appreciated their talents. This case was not unusual in the slightest way, except that Mary Sue Allen was an attractive woman. Her obvious accomplishments and abilities were not enough to satisfy those who were envious of her rapid successes, and the fact that almost everyone who makes it in the corporate world has a mentor seemed to be forgotten amidst the suspicions and rumors that began immediately after her promotion.

As assistant to the president, Allen was necessarily a step between the president and most other employees, since many plans and much information had to be channeled through her. This created a distance between the CEO and other top management, and resentment too. She became, according to Agree, "his right arm." This in turn bred insecurity among those who did not have such immediate access or visible indispensability. And when Agree was divorced from his wife (a divorce that had in fact been decided upon years earlier), the envy, insecurity, and resentment within the company had a natural target and victim. Allen had also been recently separated from her husband, and the collegial friendship between the president and his fast-rising assistant took on an obvious, if irrelevant, interpretation. A "poison pen" letter to the board made the rumors official: How else, the rumors demanded, could she have risen to the top so quickly?

When the rumors reached Agree, he quickly tried to set the record straight. In a forthright and, some say, defensive speech to the company as a whole at a meeting that was also infiltrated thoroughly by the press, Agree simply reiterated Allen's abilities and accomplishments. She was eminently qualified, and that was that. But rumors and resentment don't disappear easily; a protestation of innocence only serves as further fuel for suspicions of guilt. Allen and Agree were catapulted into the national spotlight.

In a preliminary meeting with the board of directors, Allen had made it quite clear that she would resign if necessary, even though a resignation would look like an admission of guilt (guilty of what?), setting the terrible precedent that rumors can dictate policy and serving notice to young women that they cannot achieve positions of responsibility rapidly. With the publicity, Allen was forced by her prior agreement to ask at least for a temporary leave of absence, which the board denied her, giving her instead a public vote of confidence. But the publicity continued with the rumors, and, two weeks later, she resigned, citing media exposure as impairing her ability to do her job. The board accepted, "reluctantly." After a five-month vacation to consider the hundreds of job offers she received immediately following this, Allen joined Schlenk Co. in New York, as vice president in charge of strategic planning, the same job she had just left at Trendix. The job had been designed, this time, just for her.

The Allen case itself is an unusually public version of a dilemma that is as usual as any other day-to-day problem in the business world. It is a case that happens again every time a male boss orders a female employee to make coffee or type, when that is not her job but, in context, a "lower" form of work. It is a danger every time a woman—especially an attractive woman—accomplishes anything in the competitive business world, since her rivals will always be ready to find excuses to explain how she—not they—has moved another step ahead. It is a very special danger in the more vulnerable world near the top, where competition and resentment are far more powerful and publicity renders every situation more sensitive. And it is an issue that is perplexing to men too, even if it is the woman who is virtually always the victim. Indeed, most of the debate following the Allen case had little to do with her abilities or behavior but almost everything to do with her CEO and mentor, Nelson Agree.

Most at issue, however, is the moral question about a person's private life: was it of any relevance at all, to anyone else, whether or not Allen and Agree were in fact seeing one another "socially"? Agree later insisted that he would never again explain his private life to anyone, and that he had as much right to privacy as a line worker. Allen reflected that when you allow appearances to be paramount, and you do not close the door to have a very private meeting and you do not stay late at work because the appearances might look bad, you end up justifying not hiring women because, in fact, performance will not be as good.

"Was it impossible that a woman could be judged to succeed solely by her wits, rather than her wiles?" asked one business magazine.

Office romances do occur, of course, but it is still general practice as in the Allen case, for the men to stay and the women to leave. And even when there is a personal element in promotion, as well as talent and accomplishment (isn't there almost always?), women are suspected while men are not. "Why haven't all the sons-in-law and 'old college buddies' who have emerged from nowhere to become overnight vice-presidents been harassed into submitting their resignations?" asked a commentator. Indeed, she continued, "if nobody questioned Allen's drive and talent . . . then what was the fuss about?*

---

*Based on an actual case.

HISTORICAL INTERLUDE

A CULTURE WITHOUT CAPITALISM: THE KIRIWINA

Trobriand exchange objects, unlike Western money, cannot be detached from the human experience . . . they are not alienated from the basic concerns of society. . . . If a man has yams, he can find anything else he needs.
—Annette Weiner, *Women of Value, Men of Renown*

The free market system is, according to its supporters, the best means of solving "the economic problem," the problem of producing and distributing goods to the members of a society. Indeed, this seems so obvious to us that the idea of an alternative economic system, not socialism versus capitalism but a truly different exchange system in which the wealth of the nation and the distribution of goods is not at stake, is almost unimaginable. But our conception of economics as production and distribution is but one conception among several, and this short section will put that conception into anthropological perspective by introducing an alternative conception in a society very different from our own.

The noted American anthropologist Annette Weiner has extensively studied the economy of one of the tribal societies of the Trobriand Islands—the Kiriwina. For the Kiriwina people, exchange is primarily communication, the definition of status through ritual exchanges; the distribution of goods (calico, canned foods, tobacco, clay pots, stone ax blades, and yams) is secondary and not a matter of much interest. Exchange may satisfy the function of distribution, but its significance is much deeper than that. It is the communication of a social network, not material accumulation, that is the ultimate goal of the economic practice.

The primary method of exchange for the Kiriwina looks like gift giving to us, but in fact, it is making an investment in a social hierarchy; for them, the mere idea of making a profit would be utterly unthinkable. Giving a gift of yams, banana leaf bundles, or pigs, in particular, establishes a system of obligations. Giving a gift communicates one person's intention of establishing or continuing a relationship; the quality of the gift, in particular, can publicly indicate the status of the recipient in the eyes of the giver. A gift of bruised yams, for instance, might hint disdain and signal the intention of breaking off the relationship, probably causing something of a scandal in the village. The result of the giving is a political network of obligations, and the person who gives the most, accordingly, has the most status and the most power.

When the anthropologist Bronislaw Malinowski studied the Trobriand Islanders many years ago, he came to a very different set of conclusions, but the reason this happened is revealing. He observed mainly the economic activities of the men in the village, assuming that the economic role of women was of limited importance. In fact, however, Weiner showed that the women's exchange activity, not the usual male role of acquirer, defines the economic system. "Behind every wealthy woman is a man—her husband—who has taken his own wealth and labor and converted them into bundles for her." The male acquirer is a secondary figure; the economy that counts, and the political power that goes with it, belongs to the women. A chief does not have many wives because he has status and power as Malinowski supposed, but rather he is chief because he has many wives, who bring to him their status and power. A man of low rank is not allowed to own too many pigs or to let his sows breed too often; the reason is not to protect the porcine market but rather to protect the hierarchy of social relations. If he had more pigs, he would upset the social order, even if he would also enrich the society materially.

Malinowski's mistake illuminates an all-important macroethical warning—that we too readily interpret other cultures and their economic habits in our own terms, instead of searching out the terms of that culture itself. In the Trobriands, economics depends on status, instead of the other way around, as in our society.

For the Trobriand Islands giving gifts can also be a means of acquiring status in another way; giving gifts creates not only social obligations and political power, but it also can be a way of getting access to *magic,* an essential ingredient in Trobriand economics. Magic functions to reduce risk, to guarantee a good fishing catch or a good harvest, and even to ensure that gifts will be reciprocated and not wasted. Magic can ensure that a man's children are beautiful to potential spouses. (A man gives his sister unbruised yams in return for her performing beauty magic for his children.) Magic might seem like a strange ingredient in an economic exchange system, but this should also serve to remind us that the functions of economics are very different, and much less tangible, in the Trobriands than in our society. (Then again, what is "tangible" may also vary from society to society, and a Trobriand woman might well find the status of an American businessman incomprehensible.)

The primary locus of exchange in our society is the market; in Kiriwina society, it is the funeral or mortuary ceremony. If this seems odd to us, it is because social and kinship ties are very essential to Kiriwina economics, and nowhere are they more clearly felt and evaluated than at the inevitable redistribution of wealth that takes place at death. It is in the mortuary ceremony that wealth is redistributed, as women give their gifts of banana leaf bundles and fibrous skirts, establishing their—and their husbands'—status and power in the village. Most inheritance follows the woman's line of descent, and a husband will therefore trade away virtually all of his money and "man's wealth" for "woman's wealth," which his wife will give away. Viewed from the perspective of our market system, in which everyone buys and sells for profit, this seems strange indeed. But once we understand that profit and financial wealth are not the only end of economic exchange, the Kiriwina economy begins to make sense to us. Wealth is giving, not having.

It might be worth noting that even the Trobriand Islands are not safe from the ravages of inflation. As Weiner says, "One day, when women were assembling a large pile of bundles prior to a women's mortuary ceremony, my friend Kadesopi, watching the preparations and shaking her head, said, 'Before, one or two hundred bundles used to be enough [for a particular kind of exchange], but now everybody wants to have three or four hundred bundles in their baskets.'"

A brief account of a very foreign economic system and its ethics will always seem a bit odd, if only because we are ignorant of the many details that hold that system together and allow it to make perfect sense to those who practice it. But this limitation is also an advantage, in that it allows for an overview that the people who practice a system often do not have. Indeed, while any Kiriwina was able to tell Professor Weiner about the details of the system, it would have been difficult for many of them to describe in systematic terms the nature of the framework in which they lived.

So too, it is difficult, as well as odd, when we attempt to describe our own system to a foreign visitor to whom our practices seem as unusual as the practices of the Kiriwina seem to us. This suggests an interesting exercise: put yourself in Professor Weiner's position when asked by an inquisitive Kiriwina how our own system of exchange operates. Write a very brief description of the outlines of our economic value system in such a way that she or he would understand it. Alternatively, imagine yourself a Kiriwina visitor and write a description of an American department store or, perhaps, an afternoon at the stock exchange, as viewed through your eyes.

– 15 –

Doing Good
and Doing Well

Who is the rich man? He who is satisfied with what he has.
—The Talmud

O ne word summarizes all of the ingredients of the good life: "happiness."
Aristotle made this point in his book *Ethics,* but he also insisted that this
word (or more accurately, **eudaimonia,** which literally translates as
"doing well") does not yet tell us what *particular* ingredients constitute the good
life. It only summarizes the fact that we have, in fact, gotten all that we want out
of life—and that, of course, is the good life.

"Happiness" is a concept we often misunderstand, and comparing it with
Aristotle's concept is very revealing. For example, we often think of happiness as
a "state of mind" or "feeling happy." Aristotle would dismiss this as nonsense.
The important thing, he would say, is *being* happy, not "feeling" happy. The idea
of an opium user who "felt happy" all the time would not in any way provide us
with an example of either happiness or the good life. The good life is what we *do,*
not simply what we feel, though presumably if we *are* happy we will feel happy
as well. Aristotle would also insist that happiness is not simply a function of the
individual, but a *social* concept, presupposing a social context and our place
within that context. We tend to emphasize the happiness of a person who is "self-
made" or the happiness of people *despite* the social problems that surround them.
But Aristotle would insist that there is no such person as the "self-made man";
there are only social individuals who have succeeded in ways and with advantages provided by society. And a person who is happy despite being surrounded
by misery and misfortune, Aristotle would say, is simply deluded, not happy.

Happiness is having a good life, and a good life is a life that is shared with others. Happiness, therefore, must also be shared. It presupposes not only our own well-being but the well-being of those who surround us, particularly our friends, families, neighbors, and those we work for, but also, in a more abstract but no less important way, the whole of society. Happiness, and unhappiness, are contagious; it is hard to be happy when "the spirit of the times" is gloom.

Finally, we tend to think of happiness in terms of everything going well and, in particular, in terms of success and satisfaction. But here too, Aristotle had a sense of the good life that we often neglect. The good life is to be found not just in times of good fortune and in perpetual satisfaction; it is also to be found in failure and in perpetual dissatisfaction. With his Greek sense of mortality that we often choose to ignore, Aristotle also emphasized the role of death in the good life too. Indeed, it is a common contemporary argument that life is "absurd" and the good life an illusion, just because of the awful fact that we are destined to die. But this argument can be turned around, of course, as it is in the phrase, "Eat, drink, and be merry, for tomorrow we die." Most of us do not think about death, or, at least, we pay our insurance premiums and simply assume that it will be a long, long way off. But death has an important sobering effect on our conception of the good life. It provides an essential perspective, and it forces us to look at what we are doing with a philosophical eye—what does it all amount to? Are we in fact doing what we want to do? Do we want what we *really* want, or are we so caught up in things we *think* we *ought* to do that we leave no time for what is really important to us? Indeed, without being morbid, we might say that the fact that we are going to die gives life its urgency and much of its meaning. After all, if we could say with assurance, "I'll do that in the next century, or perhaps the one after that," most of our decisions about how to live might be less urgent than they are. The brute fact of the matter, whether or not we believe in an afterlife, is sheer limitation of time.

A. HAPPINESS: MEANS AND ENDS

> A man should get what he wants; otherwise he may learn to like what he gets.
>
> —George Bernard Shaw

In the first chapter, we discussed "the good life" with an eye to its essential ingredients and putting them in order. Of course, this order is not the same for everyone. Part of the good life is simply recognizing this, and not feeling that we can justify our own lives only if everyone else agrees with the same priorities and concerns. But some of the ingredients of our lives have higher priority than others. Some aspects of the good life are more or less desirable "in themselves"; they are "ends." Others are desirable only insofar as they lead to these ends; they are "means." Still others are not clearly means or ends. Pleasure, for example, is an essential ingredient in the good life, but it is clearly not a mere means (at least, not usually) and not clearly an end. We do a job or an activity that we enjoy and that gives us pleasure; we do not do the job or the activity just in order to get pleasure.

Other aspects of the good life seem to be more *preconditions* than ingredients, for example, good health. Good health is something we don't usually think about or enjoy as such when we have it. It is rather something we usually must have in order to enjoy or accomplish anything else. And some aspects of the good life, "happiness" or "success" (in the large sense), seem to be more alternative names for the good life than ingredients as such. A "happy" person essentially is living or has lived a good life. A "successful" person, by which we mean something more than success in a particular profession or enterprise, usually has achieved most of the goals and enjoyed most of the pleasures available, in other words, has lived well.

Leaving aside mere means (which have no desirability in themselves, like having the car tuned up), leaving aside the more obvious preconditions (good health, enough money to live on), and not quibbling over the exact meanings of the broad terms that are synonymous with "the good life," what are the ingredients in living well? We have been discussing many of them, beginning obviously with such good fortunes as success (in the smaller, more particular sense), having more wealth than merely enough "to live on," having friends and a family with whom we feel close and comfortable, being in love and loving, having a *meaningful* and satisfying job, and, more generally, a place and position in a community (or communities) with a satisfying sense of social identity and a generous sense of self-esteem. In addition, there are the *moral* dimensions of the good life, those that provide the connections and limitations in our bonds with other people who are often not friends or family or close associates. These bonds include the emotions of compassion, sympathy, and pity, a sense of other people's needs, a sense of "right and wrong," a clear conception of our own moral and legal responsibilities both in our personal and business life, and a keen sense of justice and other people's *rights*. But it is a mistake to think of these moral ingredients as merely means to the good life for ourselves only; the good life is essentially communal as well as individual. It presupposes a decent community as well as individual good fortune. Furthermore, individual good fortune presupposes that general sense of fitting into the community and being respected and admired (or at least appreciated) that we sometimes refer to as "honor." Morality and the moral dimensions of the good life are, in this sense, ends rather than means, an intrinsic part of the good life rather than simply instruments to enjoy the things we want to enjoy as individuals.

In current discussions of "the good life," we too easily take for granted the social fabric in which the good life is possible. Even worse, we find ourselves succumbing to a mentality that is (temporarily) gripping our country. This mentality is sometimes called "lifeboat ethics" or "every man for himself." (In more chivalrous times, it was "women and children first.") This disastrous and false current view sees life as a matter of individual survival and interpersonal competition for the goods of life. But the question of survival probably has not been a critical question for most of us, especially not on a daily basis. In ancient times Socrates summed it up for all of us when he told his friend Crito, "the point is not just to live, but to live well." And that presupposes (as Socrates also argued) a society in which mutual belonging takes precedence over individual desires.

In this chapter, we want to look a bit closer at some of these ingredients, particularly the personal ingredients, that make up the good life. The meaning of work has already been discussed in some detail, as has the importance of relaxation and play, the importance (both in and out of business) of friendship, family, love and marriage, and the role that sex should and should not play in the good life. Other ingredients now need to be included—literature, art, aesthetics and the finer things in life, a sense of history and the global reach of humanity, philosophy, and religion. But the importance of including these things is not just to assemble a list of the good (and bad) things in life, but to establish a set of clear priorities. It is to avoid the tragedy, brutally summarized by Leo Tolstoy in his short novel *The Death of Ivan Ilych,* of ending our lives with the dreadful suspicion or realization that "we lived it wrong." It is to avoid the realization, too late, that what we really valued all along was friendship and family, despite spending all of our time at the office acquiring wealth or power. It is to avoid the realization that, despite all our efforts, we actually enjoyed life very little or the deflating realization that, in our ruthless quest for success we sacrificed along the way the friendship, respect, and admiration that would have made such success worthwhile.

In the heat of the chase, we sometimes forget what we are chasing and why. This is only natural and desirable, so long as we stop and think occasionally about what we are doing. But in the contemporary folklore of America, the story is often told about the person who wanted too much of the wrong thing and got it. Or, in the even more cynical words of George Bernard Shaw:

> There are two tragedies in life: one is not getting one's heart's desire, the other is getting it.
>
> —"Man and Superman"

B. Success, Ambition, and the Meaning of Money

> Perhaps I am more than usually jealous with respect to my freedom. . . . Those slight labors which afford me a livelihood, and by which it is allowed that I am to some extent serviceable to my contemporaries are as yet commonly a pleasure to me, and I am not often reminded that they are a necessity. So far I am successful. But I foresee that if my wants should be much

increased, the labor required to supply them would become a drudgery. . . . I am sure that for me there would be nothing left worth living for.

—Henry David Thoreau

The first chapter introduced the distinction between success in the particular sense (such as making a million dollars in two years) and success in the general sense (leading a successful life, living well). The particular sense is mainly a choice of means and a matter of skill and fortune, while the choice of ends itself may be totally disastrous, guaranteeing unhappiness and failure in other aspects of life. The general sense, on the other hand, mainly concerns a wise choice of particular ends. Choosing wealth to the exclusion of respect and friendship is almost always a disastrous choice; choosing wealth as a qualified means to a certain kind of life, with clear limitations in terms of both time and morals, is a choice that usually spells success in the large sense, at least in contemporary America. But in between the very particular sense of success as simply fulfilling a goal and success as living well, falls that intermediary and not always clear concept of success that we call "success in business." This is something more than fulfilling a number of particular goals, and it is something more specific than living the good life in general, which is as applicable to a peasant with a rich plot of farmland and a wealth of culture and community as it is to an American urban businessperson. American life is largely defined by business and its activities.

The key to this intermediate concept of success can be summarized in a word—*respect.* Respect by itself doesn't mean living well. But without it, the other trappings of particular successes in business won't mean much at all. A person might retain the respect of colleagues after a tragic business calamity. However, in the fact of failure, losses are multiplied innumerably many times by the loss of respect as well. Of course, in the business world, making money is inevitably going to be one of the *grounds* for respect. And in the business world, which (like most worlds) is structured by hierarchies of success and status, position and power and prestige are also going to be grounds for respect. But these grounds while necessary, are not sufficient. It is possible to make a lot of money and achieve considerable status by stealth and trickery and by being unscrupulous and "stepping on people." That may be success in the very particular sense of achieving goals, but it is certainly not "success in business" in the most important sense we are discussing here. What is missing is the respect of colleagues, as well as admiration from people "below" and "above."

Here morality enters directly into the good life, along with the more general considerations that we are calling "business ethics." Earning respect in business is, among other things, "playing by the rules," not only the moral rules ("don't harm anyone," "don't steal from the customers," and so on) but the understood (though perhaps not sufficiently spoken) rules of fairness and fair play. It means seeing ourselves as a part of a cooperative enterprise (in which competition is a part, rather than being "out for myself") and viewing the competition, not the

The Motives behind Success ——

All goal-oriented behavior is ultimately explained in terms of "motives"—the underlying reasons, desires, and needs that initiate and impel our behavior. Social psychologists have distinguished three primary sets of motives: the need for **achievement,** the need for **power,** and the need for **affiliation.** According to psychologist David McClellan everyone has all three motives, but their strength and proportion varies dramatically from person to person.

Achievement: The need for achievement is directly concerned with setting and satisfying specific goals. Reaching self-set standards is a major source of satisfaction and success. Competition with others is more important than their acceptance or applause. Young people are more likely to seek a sense of achievement from outside authorities and organizations, while older people tend to feel that their own self-set goals are more important. Since the satisfaction of goals gives success, however, the choice of goals is as crucial as working towards them; setting impossible goals is a guarantee of failure. People with high-achievement motivation consequently tend to take more calculated and moderate risks than others. Achievement people also tend to choose activities that make their own abilities evident, instead of merging with a group or organization.

Power: People with a strong motive for power have a need to influence others. Control and influence are more important than achievement, and impotence and humiliation are worse than mere failure. Business managers who emphasize cooperative social power, however, tend to be far more successful than those who seek their power as competitive.

Affiliation: People with a high need for affiliation are concerned with being liked by others more than with success or power. Success and power may be a means for approval, but such people tend to enjoy conversations for their own sake and being part of tight organizations apart from efficiency and effectiveness.

Achievement motivation is more prominent in entrepreneurial ventures, power is the key to effective management in large corporations, but affiliation needs account for much that is more personable and pleasant in the business world. On the negative side, people with high achievement motives are sometimes too individual and restless for long-term effective company positions, people who see power as competition or place the importance of their influence over achievement can often be disruptive, and people with high affiliation needs find coping with problems difficult when these threaten to disturb personal relationships.

cooperation, as ultimate. It means valuing friendships and associations along the way, and honoring them even when they are of no "use." It means earning the respect of people as well as money and position, and this is primarily a *social* virtue. Thus, we began our discussion of success by noting that success is clearly a *social value;* it is not so much a question of "making it" as "fitting in" and being recognized and liked by others. Anything less just isn't good enough.

It is a mistake, however, to think of success, in the above sense, as limited to the business community. Of course, it is perfectly possible and quite common to be successful in the business community and be totally unheard of, except for

---

Fear of Success ——

A vice president at a large institution had eyed the No. 1 job for years, while functioning successfully as the No. 2 man. Finally the boss retired, and he was given the top spot.

Within a week, he tried to kill himself. Deep anxieties in his life surfaced only after he had achieved his goal.

Mental-health professionals call this syndrome "fear-of-success," and they say it is quite common. So, apparently, are other psychiatric conditions that affect occupational performance. The whole subject of emotional difficulties in the workplace is beginning to get more attention—to a large extent because mental-health experts now think many such problems can be identified and treated. . . .

"The classic definition is falling ill on the verge of success," says Jacqueline Fleming, a consulting psychologist with the United Negro College Fund. Dr. Jesse Cavenar [a Duke University psychiatrist] says, "Most of these people have an intense desire to be successful. It may be the one thing they've worked for all their lives."

The vice president who attempted suicide, Dr. Cavenar believes, had a problem stemming from his relationship with an overprotective mother. He became dependent, developed a meek, submissive personality, and ultimately couldn't allow others to depend on him. Moreover, in this analysis, he unconsciously feared retaliation from subordinates if he rose above them. So when he rose he swiftly fell. . . .

He says some executives who become successful also may develop "status anxiety," becoming torn between the desire to be liked by their former peers and the responsibility to the new position. Executives who confuse respect with liking may try to become "nice guys" only to find that subordinates lose respect for them and begin slacking off, he says.

The Wall Street Journal, Dec. 3, 1980

family and a few friends, outside of that community. But even so, the respect of family and friends is at least as important as the respect of many business colleagues. There are many dimensions of respect that involve us every day, from the newspaper vendor who says "hello" every morning to the maitre d' at a favorite restaurant. This becomes quite obvious in the worst of times, when the newspaper vendor, having just read about our company's scandal, hands us the paper with averted eyes, and the maitre d' suggests that we go down to McDonald's for a quick snack (and stay in the car). Indeed, respect often seems like such a small thing, often taken for granted, until we lose it. Then we realize that respect makes success possible and that our conception of success is inconceivable without it.

Success is "the way of the world . . . the law of youth . . . unfolding strength" claimed American poet-philosopher Ralph Waldo Emerson in 1870. It is to "*be* something of worth and value" wrote the Renaissance artist Michelangelo, four centuries earlier. Success *is* the American conception of the good life, and success in business our paradigm example. But success is not just an end; it includes the means, or as Aristotle says, "the life of *activity* in accordance with virtue." We too easily think of success as merely the victory, instead of the hard work, wisdom, good ideas, and responsibilities that go into it. As Emerson pointed out:

> What we ask is victory, without regard to the cause. . . . We Americans are tainted with this insanity, as our bankruptcies and our reckless politics may show.

Indeed, despite what we have said about respect and social recognition, success *also* requires satisfaction in the work itself, not just the recognition. Emerson recognized this also:

> Is there no loving of knowledge, and of art, and of our design, for itself alone? Can we not please ourselves with performing our work, or gaining truth and power, without being praised for it?

Success, in other words, is not just "success" achieving certain ends; success in the sense of "success in business" already has built into it meaningful work that we can enjoy and feel proud of and the attainment of the recognition of other people and their affection rather than their envy or resentment. Being "ruthless" in business is usually stupid rather than immoral, for it often ensures failure in the general sense even as it so desperately strives for success in the particular sense. The puritan ethic, from which all of this stress on success came in the first place, was quite clear that the point of success was to be *useful to others* and a likeable person who was a good member of the community. To think that we have left that ethic behind in the pure effort to "look out for number one" or "prosper in the coming bad times" is to ignore at our peril the parameters within which success in America is still possible and acceptable.

It is within this context too that we might mention the much used and abused word, **ambition.** Ambition is the craving for success. But, again, this word has the same ambiguity; a person may be ambitious in very particular ways and want very particular successes. A person may be ambitious in business, wanting success in a more general way, which necessarily includes the respect of colleagues and other people too. A person may be ambitious in general, but in this context the parallel with success breaks down, for while success in the large sense means living the good life as a distinguished and respected member of the community at large, ambition in the larger sense has an *anti-social* connotation, a hint of voraciousness, a hint of vice rather than virtue. Joseph Epstein sums up this negative sense in his book *Ambition:*

> To say of a young man or woman that he or she is ambitious is no longer, as it once was, a clear compliment. . . . Ambition connotes a certain Rotarian optimism, a thing unseemly, in very poor taste, rather like raging sexual appetite in someone quite elderly. . . . Succeed at all costs but refrain from appearing ambitious.

However, the sense of ambition here is the kind that is too general. It is not the enthusiasm for possibilities and the desire to "get ahead" that has always made certain younger managers appealing to top executives. It is not the ambition that fuels success and achievement (as Epstein goes on to argue), but the kind of obsession with the end that is inconsiderate of the means and of the social fabric in which success is possible. Ambition in the sense of "the desire to achieve" is and always has been the essence of good work and success in business, but ambition that ignores or threatens the cooperation that makes business life possible is oblivious to the larger social good that makes the rewards of business life permissible, and is something quite different. We should keep in mind, in our praise of ambition, that most Europeans view our craving for success as a self-destructive neurosis, just because it puts individual particular successes ahead of concern for the integrity of the social fabric and our place in the community. Of course, the rather rigid European notion of "place" is just what Americans have always been reacting against, but in our quest for individual mobility and improvement, there does exist a social fabric that needs watching out for, even as we watch out for ourselves.

It is in this context too that the *meaning of money* is brought up once again. Money plays a peculiar part in the quest for the good life. On the one hand, in America money is clearly an *almost* essential precondition of the good life, and it surely is essential for life in business. But at the same time, the importance of money is also easily confused; either it is celebrated as the end itself or it is reduced to a mere means. Both are incorrect. Money is not the goal, even in business; other considerations, respect for example, are more important. Even when it is merely the making of money that is in question, the means are as important as the end. The making of money, not just the money itself, is important. But neither

A Horatio Alger Story: Success in America ──

In America, for over a century, the name of "Horatio Alger" has been synonymous with success, with working one's way up from poverty to great wealth through the puritan virtues of honesty, thrift, self-reliance, industriousness, and a familiar cheerfulness. Horatio Alger wrote 135 "rags to riches" books and sold tens of millions of copies. How successful was he?

He was born in Revere, Massachusetts, in 1832. His father, according to Clifton Fadiman, had "maimed Horatio's soul" by the time he was ten, making him "a weak, confused, guilt-ridden fumbler," who "lived in a state of bewilderment relieved only by sharp moments of misery." He graduated from Harvard in 1852, then fled to Paris, "where he sowed two wild oats named Elise and Charlotte, in a manner that suggests that he didn't know what he was doing." He always aimed to write "the great American novel," but he himself knew that what he sold by the millions was essentially "trash." His publishers pocketed most of the profits and he died a myth of success, miserable if not exactly in poverty. "He was a nonentity whose name was known to millions" writes Fadiman, and "he died, having defined the meaning of life for two generations of Americans, without being quite certain why he had lived."

What is the moral of this story?

Based on Clifton Fadiman, "Horatio Alger, Fare Thee Well" in *Any Number Can Play*

is it quite correct to simply say that money is the means to the good life, the means to success (including respect) in business, the means to buy all the good things in life, along with security, protection, and freedom in our personal life. Money is also a *symbol,* and most of the things we buy are symbols too. They are symbols of a certain kind of life, a certain kind of values, a certain kind of success.

Within American business, making money confers a rather obvious distinction and provides a rather obvious (but not exclusive) criterion for success. In personal life too, making money conveys a kind of status. But we should appreciate how this works and what limitations it has. Money alone won't do it; the term *nouveau riche* ("new rich"), though borrowed from the disdainful French aristocracy, still has an air of contempt about it. We need not be an aristocrat or "old money" to appreciate the warrant for that contempt. *Having* money is not yet knowing what to *do* with money, and the newly rich oil baron or real estate speculator who spends lavishly on ostentatious automobiles and ridiculous clothes has always been the butt of American jokes. That is hardly the earmark of success.

On the other side, many of the material status symbols that used to mark a person as a success are now within the reach of a great many Americans— a Mercedes-Benz, expensive clothes, and foreign vacations. Accordingly, the status of these things slips, and other status symbols take their place, many of which have nothing to do with money. The meaning of money, therefore, becomes increasingly ambiguous and puts its status as a symbol itself increasingly in doubt. Not surprisingly, a great many Americans who already live in relative affluence have begun to question the importance of "being rich." They are becoming aware that the good life and status in society are not so obviously tied to wealth as they once were. On the one hand, money is still the measure of our "market value," the importance or rarity of what we do and how much someone is willing to pay for it. On the other hand, the meaning of having or not having money is no longer a clear reflection of our status in society.

From what we have said above, it should now be evident that we should not talk simply about money or the meaning of money so much as about the *many* meanings of money. First, *having* money is a mark of status of sorts, if no longer so dependable as it used to be. But then *spending* money is quite different. Indeed, psychiatrists who deal with successful businesspeople often report that the disjunction between their patients' conception of having money and spending money is virtually schizoid; they may be worth millions but yet live as if they were earning subsistence incomes. And *how* we spend money itself defines a certain kind of meaning of money. A person who has extravagant material desires will find money a very real necessity; a person with more modest desires will find money more of a luxury, perhaps a "security blanket" that may never be used. Second, *earning* money is entirely different again. What we earn represents what our work is thought to be worth, and that may have nothing at all to do with our material needs and desires, with how (or even whether) we intend to spend that money, or what we think of our status in society by having it.

The meaning of money in America is so significant because it plays so many different roles—roles that are often played by other factors in other societies. For example, in a country where social status is determined by family and a fixed place in society, the notion of having money would be of little relevance to status. Or in a country that did not place so much emphasis on the labor market but rather stressed the importance of cooperative efforts, money received for work would not be of such crucial importance in determining the worth of the work. (This is one reason why socialist countries think it is so important not to let differential payments interfere with the cooperative effort. Whether this succeeds is another question.) In a country with fewer consumer goods, the notion of having money to spend obviously becomes less important, and in a country where most of the people's needs are provided outside of "the market," money would play a very small role in their sense of security or well-being.

Of course, this is not to say that Americans are alone in their obsessive pursuit of what used to be called "filthy lucre"; there are few parts of the world where money can't buy power, through which it is always more easy to get status, security, and even friends. But appreciating the many dimensions of the meaning of money is particularly important for Americans, especially because, as in our quest for the good life in general, we are not always clear about the complex ends and means involved. Given the almost religious emphasis on "the almighty dollar" in our society, it is all too easy to get caught up in the gold rush without really having any idea what we want it for, or when enough is enough. ("No such thing as too rich or too thin," wrote one Hollywood philosopher.)

The meaning of money takes us back to the meaning of success. In our society, the two go hand in hand. Not all successes are worthy of the name, as we saw, and not all money is worth the same either. John D. Rockefeller once found that charities and churches refused to accept his money because it was "tainted."

The Value of Money ──

Doolittle: What am I, Governors, both? I ask you, what am I? I'm one of the undeserving poor: that's what I am. Think of what that means to a man. It means that he's up agin middle class morality all the time. If there's anything going, and I put in for a bit of it, it's always the same old story: "You're undeserving, so you can't have it." But my needs are as great as the most deserving widows's that ever got money out of six different charities in one week for the death of the same husband. I don't need less than a deserving man: I need more. I don't eat less hearty than him; and drink more. I want a bit of amusement, cause I'm a thinking man. I want cheerfulness and a song and a band when I'm low. Well, they charge me just the same for everything as they charge the deserving. What is middle class morality? Just an excuse for never giving me anything.

Higgins: I suppose we must give him a fiver.

Pickering: He'll make bad use of it, I'm afraid.

Doolittle: Not me, Governor, so help me I won't. Don't you be afraid that I'll save it and spare it and live idle on it. There won't be a penny of it left on Monday. I'll have to go to work same as if I'd never had it. It won't pauperize me, you bet. Just one good spree for myself and the missus, giving pleasure to ourselves and employment to others, and satisfaction to you to think it's not been throwed away. You couldn't spend it better.

Higgins: This is irresistible. Let's give him ten.

Doolittle: No, Governor. She wouldn't have the heart to spend ten, and perhaps I wouldn't either. Ten pounds is a lot of money; it makes a man feel prudent like; and then goodbye happiness.

George Bernard Shaw, *Pygmalion*

Again, the meaning of money and the meaning of success are tied to the notion of respect and respectability, and there is an all-important difference between being rich and living a rich existence. Indeed, as one of the holy books of the Hebrews instructed long ago, "the rich man is satisfied with what he has." In America, that may have to be much more than the nomad in the Sinai with a goat and two daughters referred to by the Talmud, but the basic lesson is the same. There is no surer way of making ourselves perpetually unhappy than to always want more than we have or need to have, except, that is, for wanting and *getting* what we want when it is the wrong thing to want in the first place. Success is getting what we want, and in this society, in business life in particular, that inevitably means money, at least in part. And the meaning of money is getting what we want, but to think that what we want is merely money is to trap ourselves in a vicious circle whose meaninglessness will, eventually, become all too obvious.

C. THE FINER THINGS IN LIFE

> If a man walks in the woods for love of them half a day, he is in danger of being regarded as a loafer; but if he spends his whole day as a speculator, shearing off those woods and making earth bald before her time, he is esteemed an industrious and enterprising citizen.
>
> —Henry David Thoreau

Much of the good life is intangible, or if tangible it is often "priceless." A great work of art may be bought for a fortune, but the pleasure to be gotten from looking at it (as opposed to the pleasure of owning it) is not to be bought; it is simply to be shared with a culture (perhaps our own, perhaps not). Friendship and love are also invaluable and not to be bought, as Edmund Burke pointed out when he called them "the unbought grace of life." Thoreau's love of the woods is not the possessive love of the landowner; indeed, the landowner may never see the woods or experience that aesthetic satisfaction at all. But the good life clearly consists in part of these "unbought graces," in a sense of ourselves and our place in the world that goes beyond our individual ambitions and successes and our position in the world in some smaller, more provincial and particular sense.

We are members of a culture, whether the cultural heritage of humanity, "Western" culture, American culture, Texas or Southern or New England culture, or the heritage of a particular town or city. We are part of a history, whether the history of the universe, the history of humanity, the history of the "West" or of America or of our family or hometown. And we are participants in a wondrous universe, aestheticized in the eighteenth century as "Nature," full of mysteries and marvels we are in a position to understand and appreciate more than virtually any culture in any time in history. To suppose that the good life is irrelevant to these things is to have a peculiarly truncated conception of the good life, perhaps even excluding ourselves from what is a far better life in which we are not, and need not be, the sole center of attention with the burden of the world on our shoulders. Indeed, the point of "the finer things in life," whether it be listening to good music or looking up at the stars, is that these things give life a larger scope, put our problems as well as our successes in perspective, and allow us to enjoy ourselves more even as we lose ourselves in the panorama of culture, history, or nature.

The problem is—and this is to a large extent a deep criticism of our concepts of education—that these things are often presented to us in the guise of mere means—that is, as chores to be mastered—instead of as ends and values in their own right. The arts, history, and nature are not chores or means, and learning about them is not subjecting ourselves to the often senseless tasks that form too much of the standard school curriculum. Some may quite properly object that a busy business executive doesn't have the time to become an expert in music and art, or to read all the great novels and keep up with *Scientific American.* And, of course, this is so. But what we are talking about here is not merely adding another dimension of work to an already overly busy life, and to "expose" ourselves to the pleasures of culture, history, and science is not to open ourselves up to be tested and flunked by some random examiner. Indeed, one of the major obstacles to the popularity of the arts in America has been precisely this unfortunate tendency to treat them as a field of required and testable knowledge rather than a field to be explored freely by enthusiastic amateurs.

Why this emphasis on the arts and other "useless" aspects of social life? There are many arguments here, too many of them self-serving on the part of academics and professional artists, musicians, and literati. Some say that such enterprises as the arts are "good in themselves." Others say that culture makes us a "better person," though this is doubtful (Caligula and Nero were both well-cultured tyrants). What is essential is that what we call "culture" is not just that effete set of interests entertained by society matrons and others (whom the Marx brothers, for example, used to make fun of in their movies); culture is the very fabric that holds a society together, more fundamental than its laws, its business agreements and economic systems, its politics, or its various fashions of the moment. Particular movements in the arts or in intellectual life, of course, may be merely ephemeral, lasting but a few months or years. But the arts in general and intellectual life in general provide the defining threads and values that we all share, through which we recognize each other and sense our shared belonging to a single culture. We are not saying, of course, that a person who is ignorant of Thomas Eakins does not belong to American culture, but the general style and temper of American art, and the centuries of European art that preceded it, give us our ways of seeing as well as provide the visual imagery through which we define ourselves and think of ourselves. We need not know very much philosophy, and certainly not the particular philosophers, to know that some thinkers (Socrates, Rousseau, and Marx) set the course of Western history, for better or worse, and that, whether or not we know their source, most of our ideas, no matter how crude or "commonsensical," in fact are borrowed from others in our past. Culture, in other words, is an essential dimension of the good life not for its snob appeal or as mere "entertainment" but rather because it adds that dimension of time and genius to our lives, time stretching back to the ancients, genius that, in some vicarious sense, we can call our own and appreciate as part of us. Business life, like most practices, lives for the moment (or at most, a few years at a time); culture expands our world in time, gives it a scope and a meaning that no day-to-day practice can. A person without a culture, no matter how successful or respectable, has only a truncated vision of life.

It is sometimes said that only individuals, not corporations, have responsibility to the arts. But American business is profoundly steeped in the arts. Since 1940, Texaco Oil has made opera accessible to everyone in the country by sponsoring Saturday afternoon radio broadcasts of operas, perhaps the single most important contribution to that art since its creation in the eighteenth century. AT&T casually donates $10 million to the Boston Symphony. The Rockefeller, Ford, and Guggenheim foundations sponsor millions of dollars' worth of fascinating but "useless" research every year, not for making a profit but for enriching the intellectual life of the nation. Great art exhibits are sponsored in museums throughout the country by various corporations. Why then, does the idea continue, even among (especially among) people who are much less cultured than many businesspeople, that businesspeople are "bores," uninterested in "the finer things of life," and interested only in profit?

The answer to this image problem is, again, to be found in the way that business talks about itself. Mobil Oil, one of the sponsors of fine drama on public television, advertises widely its patronizing messages about the joys of free enterprise and the pitfalls of government regulation but seldom discusses its role in the arts. Corporate spokespersons refer to the involvement in the arts, apologetically, as "public relations" or as "good will" or even as "long-term investments," instead of saying what is often true and what everyone would much rather hear, that business considers itself an integral part of American culture and recognizes that it is capable, as most of us are not, of making significant contributions to its support. Also there is the disastrous but continuous ideological insistence that business has only its own "fiduciary" responsibilities to stockholders and therefore no place and no competence in the arts or in the realm of the intellect. This is both false and unflattering, and it has the immediate consequence of once again reinforcing the old image of the businessperson as a bore who knows "the price of everything and the value of nothing."

How much are we expected to know and understand? In our specialist society, the assumption is too often made that there is no point in knowing anything if we aren't willing to try to learn everything, coupled with the occasional defensive reaction of commonsensical ignorance, "I don't know what's good but I know what I like." It takes but minimal "exposure" and involvement in the arts to learn something, to learn to enjoy and appreciate a great deal. With the rich display of the arts on television, the many books available, the now easy access to traveling exhibits of the best art and traveling performances of the best theater and music—not to mention the easy availability of recordings—"culture" is perfectly accessible to everyone. Of course, tastes differ and preferences vary, but being "cultured" never meant an uncritical and indiscriminate love for everything artistic or intellectual. What is unacceptable is feigning the attitude too many people think is expected of them, that *all* such matters are unnecessary and easily neglected, without cost. Indeed, other people, believing the same, might even agree with us when we say, self-defensively, "Oh, I never read; I read all day at the office" or "I don't like classical music" or "I never go to art museums." But in spite of such agreement an alarm still goes off, even if not acknowledged; it is the alarm that says "philistine," for here is a person whose life is limited to the day-to-day, who lacks the scope to see beyond the next deadline. Not surprisingly, many top executives (according to a perennial sequence of articles in *Fortune,* for example) are more and more choosing liberal arts graduates for their top positions, not because they want to discuss Mozart over lunch (though sometimes they do), but rather because it is increasingly evident that "good business," as well as the good life, cannot be confined to "useful" and respectable enterprises alone.

D. DENIAL, DEATH, FAILURE: ON NOT GETTING WHAT YOU WANT

> The non-relational character of death, as understood in anticipation, individualizes [each of us] . . . [our] very being is at issue.
>
> —Martin Heidegger, Being and Time

Our view of the good life, in its quite understandable preoccupation with the good things in life, prefers to ignore the bad, even to deny the bad. We pretend as long as possible that the good life—if it is really good—has no bad or evil in it. But, of course, this is never true; death is the end of every life. Though we might quibble about whether death ought to therefore count as *part* of life, the essential point is clear enough. Death is unavoidable. Even if we see death as simply the end (that is, the terminus, not the goal) of life, the awareness of death, the fear of it, and the anticipation of it are clearly part of life. To ignore death or deny it is not part of or an aid to the good life; it is rather a detraction from the good life. The good life is not based on illusions, and in particular it cannot be based on an illusion as basic as this one would be. We will all die. And though this may not be reason for getting hysterical right now and dropping everything we are doing as ultimately pointless, it is nevertheless a part of the conception of the good life and something to keep in mind, if not neurotically so.

The German philosopher Martin Heidegger (who died in 1976) wrote that knowing we are going to die, but not knowing when, is one of the most critical

> You've had a hard week. You're overworked, exhausted, and you push yourself still further. All of a sudden, you have a heart attack and die.
>
> Write your epitaph.
>
> (Ending as it did, suddenly, this moment, what does your life amount to? What is memorable? What is useful? What do you value, in retrospect? What would you have done differently? Who were you?)

aspects of human existence, for it constantly forces us to think ahead and back, about what we are doing and planning to do, about what we have done and what it all amounts to. Are we doing what makes us the kind of person we want to be? Are we pursing goals that may satisfy us in the short run but would embarrass us for all eternity? Are we acting toward ends that can be achieved, or are impossible? Is the work worth it even if the ends cannot be reached? If we were to die tomorrow, would we be able to feel that we had lived the best life possible up until that point? If we were to live to be a hundred, would we then realize that we squandered most of our talents and resources too early, and so deprived ourselves of so many worthwhile years later on?

Furthermore, there is a sense in which all of us act, not only for satisfaction during our lives, but for a kind of significance *after* our lives. For some people, this means having the best for their children; for others, it means being remembered and admired, or at least, remembered well instead of badly. But this too affects our concept of happiness and the good life in a dramatic way. Aristotle, for example, asked the odd question, "Can we call a man happy even after he is dead?" What he had in mind was the sense in which, even after we are dead and buried, our goals and conceptions may still be alive and undergoing changes. For example, if a person's children come to ruin, bankrupt the family business, and discredit the family name, in a sense, even if the parents are dead, their happiness—that is, their hopes for the future—has been destroyed. Or if a person has worked hard all his life for a good reputation, but that reputation is destroyed after his death, in a sense, again, his life has been a failure, even if he is not there to witness it. The moral of this observation is that living the good life and being happy is not just a matter of being satisfied during our lifetime; it may also be assuring our fortunes after death (and, of course, according to some religions, preparing ourself for eternity as well).

Death is not the only setback in the good life, though admittedly it is the most conclusive. The good life is not the life of undisturbed successes and satisfactions. Even the best life includes failures and misfortunes; what is important is our ability to maintain a sense of self and integrity through failure. ("That which does not overcome me, makes me *stronger*," wrote the German philosopher

Friedrich Nietzsche.) It is not at all difficult to be moral, to be humorous and lightspirited, to be successful and likable, and to be satisfied when all is going well. Quite properly, we do not judge people solely on the basis of how they behave when all is going well. What counts is when life goes badly, and it is character, in turn, that allows us to survive through all but the most crushing failures and to re-emerge with new resolve and determination. Yet, we too easily curse our luck when things go badly, as if such misfortunes were disadvantages and obstacles to the good life, instead of an intrinsic part of it. Life involves risks; indeed, there are few words more central and honored in American business life than "risk." But risks presuppose the possibility of failure and, at least some of the time, actual failures too. Even people who are exceedingly cautious face the possibility of misfortune continuously. The difference between life well lived and life not lived well at all is not the difference between success and failure, but often rather a difference in the ways in which failure is handled; failure may be viewed as the end of a dream and a vacuum to be filled with self-pity and resignation, or as a challenge and a new opportunity.

We want our lives to be satisfying, of course. There is not much point in wanting something if we don't believe we would be happy with it once it's been achieved. But this self-evident sense of satisfaction must always be balanced with a very different concern, our concern for life as an ongoing process rather than a quest with a definite goal. The German poet Goethe saw this point, and in his epic play *Faust* he insisted that "from desire I rush to satisfaction, but from satisfaction, I leap to desire." The most important desires are often those that can never be fulfilled, for these are the desires that not only provide us with our ultimate goal of the good life, but its ongoing fuel as well. Great artists, for example, sometimes describe their work as the quest for the *perfect* poem or painting. Because there is no such perfection (or since perfection is being continuously redefined), they continue to drive themselves throughout their lives in quest of an impossible ideal, which nevertheless produces some wonderful works. At least in some cases, they lead an admirably good life as well, even though it is filled with dissatisfaction. This same sense of endless drive after an unattainable goal can be found in people who never have enough money or power, though there it is not always as clear that the end is itself an ideal, or that the life in which they pursue such an endless quest can survive the dissatisfaction en route. We crave not only what we want but, equally, crave to continue wanting. There is nothing more tragic—though usually not very dramatic—than continuing to live when there is nothing left to live *for.* Indeed, the Gatsby-like urge of many people for a quick fortune and "early retirement" often ends in such quiet tragedy, the tragedy of wanting too little, and finding life empty even though it is full of continuous pleasure and all of their goals have been reached.

The Hawaiian Room ———

They joked a lot about it in the executive dining room, and at least once during every annual officers' banquet someone with a few drinks under his belt would imitate a guitar playing "Aloha" and get a big laugh, but I don't think any of them seriously believed that they would ever end up in the Hawaiian Room. I certainly didn't. . . .

But then last year, the company re-organized some of its division, and my job was abolished. The personnel department assured me that I would be successfully placed elsewhere within the company. To spare me embarrassment, it was suggested I remain at my desk and continue what was left of my normal activities. But I soon learned that others in the company weren't exactly clamoring for the services of a middle-aged man with a large family and a specialized background.

After three months of fruitless search, the personnel officer advised me that all avenues of inquiry had been exhausted. . . . [I moved] on to the Outplacement Center, the infamous Hawaiian Room. . . . Everyone was busy looking for work; some more, some less. Some men had told their families, some were delaying the bad news. And some, perhaps, would die with their secret, or what they hoped was a secret. Some men were continuously close to tears while others pretended a false bravado. Some sat in stunned silence; others were loudly adamant, retelling the story of the fate that had befallen them. For some, it was a blow from which they would never recover, while others just got up, went out and found a job and never looked back.

The most seriously affected seemed to be those who had been with the company all of their lives. Others who had been unbearable snobs, strutting, arrogant peacocks during their careers, were also vulnerable, unable or unwilling to face their misfortune. And some of the saddest cases were those whose wives had left them because they were no longer members of the elite. . . . There were days for rejoicing when a fellow inmate would land a good job, but these times were not that frequent, with many people still there close to a year and still looking. Eventually, they would be dropped from the payroll and never be heard from again. My time came too and, though I didn't have a job yet, my days in the Hawaiian Room were concluded.

Aloha.

John Rocchi, *The Wall Street Journal,* Nov. 29, 1980

Second Chance ——

It happens all the time. A company's profits slump. Or a big project is bungled. Or the chairman clashes with the president in a messy grudge match. No matter; the president (or some other top executive) is blamed and gets fired.

Often, the loser of the match is given a fat severance check and the fig leaf of being called "consultant to the company"—a sinecure, says one president-turned-consultant, "so he won't be arrested for vagrancy."

Despite the headlong fall from grace, a small but growing number of these fired executives are becoming successful management consultants.

Take George Arneson. In 1965, Mr. Arneson, at the age of 40, became president of Vendo Co., a big Kansas City firm listed on the New York Stock Exchange. In 1972, Mr. Arneson was fired—because, he says, the chairman wanted his nephew to be president. Today, Mr. Arneson takes in about $200,000 in annual billings as a management consultant in Leawood, Kan. . . .

Consultants who advise consultants say that such executives, who have been fired or otherwise burned by bad publicity, can nonetheless find eager bidders for some of their talents. A fired executive might be a poor implementer, for example, but an excellent strategic planner. Also, an executive's long stint in the corporate world usually provides him with lots of potential clients in friends and business associates.

Anthony Ramirez, *The Wall Street Journal,* Dec. 4, 1980

E.   RELIGION AND THE LARGER VIEW OF LIFE

What does it profit a man if he gains the whole world but loses his soul?

—Matthew 14:26

We might best understand *religion* and its role in the good life and business life in response to the fear of death, the trauma of failure, and the frustration of a frenzied life that never seems to reach its goal. This is not to say, as Freud once argued, for example, that religion is nothing but compensation for the disappointments of life through the illusion of a beneficent God and a blissful immortal existence. Indeed, to tie our conception of religion in general to a religion (for example, Protestant Christianity) is to miss the point. The purpose of religion as such is not to provide compensation so much as to provide *perspective.* Philosophy and religions have quite properly been classified together, although the language and the techniques are quite different. Both are aimed at providing a kind of understanding that transcends us as isolated individuals and shows us our place in the overall scheme of things. Religion gives some significance, not necessarily compensation, or, for that matter, explanation, for disasters and tragedies and death. It provides an all-embracing vision which gives us a kind of confidence; this can be done by believing in an all-knowing, all-powerful, caring God, or by believing in fate or karma or even the divine indifferences of it all.

Religion enters into a great many conceptions of the good life. Sometimes religion by itself constitutes the good life. Many people would insist that they could not possibly live the good life without religion, but this is itself part of the religious conception of life. With regard to business life, however, a peculiar tension exists between the spiritual and the material that ought to be viewed, in the current context in which religion and business are so mutually supportive, as remarkable. For thousands of years, Christianity looked upon business and businessmen with horror, condemning them outright. In the past few hundred years, however, European and now American theologians have done a most remarkable job in reversing this ancient antagonism, even to the point—first by John Calvin and more recently by any number of unabashedly wealthy American preachers— of making Jesus himself a kind of protocapitalist, and the successful businessperson as such, the "chosen" person in the eyes of God. Indeed, it has now become something of a popular article of faith that the rich person will get to Heaven first (whether or not the camel has learned to thread the needle) so long as he or she has made the money himself or herself, thereby demonstrating for all to see his or her superiority on earth as proof of God's Grace.

It is always an open question to what extent religion provides a view with a perspective on life and to what extent it rather simply rationalizes a certain kind of life and its privileges. While a religious view of life is one of those ultimate conceptual components of the good life that puts all else into focus, religion can also serve as a mere cosmetic embellishment for a life that is in no way religious except for occasional pieties. In other words, the religious conception of the good life and religion as part of the good life is very different from the mere *abuse* of religion, which is probably as much a part of our American heritage as religion and religious freedom. Sinclair Lewis exposed it years ago in his classic *Elmer Gantry,* and the movie *Marjoe* did it again. But the abuses of religion, of course, are no argument against religion as such. The partnership of business and religion may strike us as odd—as it would horrify Aquinas—but there has always been a sense of mutual dependency, at least since the days of John Calvin, between the strictly material concerns of commerce and the spiritual concerns of religion. Indeed, we might well ask why these two have moved so far apart, and why we so easily tend to see the material world as lacking spirituality, and see spirituality as an aspect of life best separated and protected from all the rest.

■ SUMMARY AND CONCLUSION

Happiness: in one word we summarize all of our aims for the good life. But happiness is not merely the feeling of well-being. It requires *being* happy, and that means a life well lived, complete with accomplishments, friendships, and love. Moreover, the happy life is not a life without failures and misfortunes. As a matter of necessity, any effort or achievement carries with it the risk of failure, and just being a mortal human being, living with other mortal human beings, makes tragedy and misfortune an inevitable part of every life, no matter how happy otherwise. To see failure and misfortune as a necessary part of life is not to deny the possibility of happiness; it is rather to revise our conception of happiness and force us to include them within it. A life is happy not because it lacks failure and misfortune, nor in spite of failure and misfortune; it is happy including failure and misfortune. Indeed, sometimes, though we would not initially wish it upon ourselves, we turn out to be happier in our failures than in our successes.

In business life, one ingredient in the good life stands out before all of the others: *success.* It is not to be conceived simply in terms of money, although making money is obviously an important part of it. Respect of colleagues and neighbors is far more important, even if part of the basis for respect is usually (but certainly not always) success at making money. We can be greatly respected without making all that much money, and we can be very rich without being respected at all. Looking at those people who have gained one without the other, we have little doubt who are happier. Making money, like having money, is a means, not an end. Appreciating and aspiring to the good life in business means looking beyond "the bottom line" to the real values that rule our lives.

■ STUDY QUESTIONS

1. Define "happiness" in your own words. What are its most crucial ingredients? How many of these ingredients are directly tied to your business career?

2. What are your ultimate goals in business, as you see them now? How important is it that these goals actually be satisfied? Will you be happy with your life if they are not satisfied?

3. What is the role of a sense of justice in the happy life? Could a person live happily with no concern whatsoever for the well-being of others? Why or why not? What does your answer indicate about the meaning of "happiness"?

4. What does money mean to you? Power? Freedom? Success? The ability to buy things? (What things?) How much money would you consider

"enough," such that the return on future efforts just isn't worth it? Is there any amount of money that would allow you to retire from working? Why or why not? What does this indicate about the meaning of work to you?

5. What is respect? Why is it important?

6. What are "the finer things in life"? Why are they desirable?

7. Why study such a subject as philosophy, which has no "practical" value? Why have such subjects existed so long and been required for an "education" for so many centuries?

8. How is the nineteenth century relevant to you? What do you gain by learning about it?

9. Scientists have now determined that the universe is 12 billion years old. Do you care? (Why learn about science, if it has no technological implications?)

10. What is bad about death?

11. Write your retirement speech, anticipating your regrets and accomplishments.

12. Aristotle writes, "Call no man happy until after he is dead." Why?

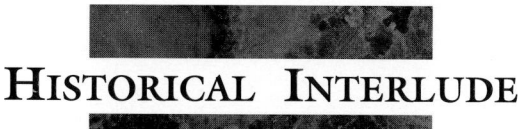

HISTORICAL INTERLUDE

THE FUTURE OF BUSINESS ETHICS

by Tom Peters

Ethics is a hot business topic, and that is a potential boon to us all. Unfortunately, the heightened awareness has spawned an industry of mindless, "do good, be good" writings. But dealing with ethics isn't so easy. The point was driven home after I accepted an invitation to speak about ethics to business students. I spent many a restless night grappling with the easy simplifications that ignore messy reality. This set of somewhat disjointed observations is one byproduct.

• Corporations are created and exist to serve people—insiders and outsiders—period.

• High ethical standards—business or otherwise—are, above all, about treating people decently. To me (as a person, businessperson and business owner) that means respect for a person's privacy, dignity, opinions and natural desire to grow; and people's respect for (and by) co-workers.

• Diversity must be honored. To be sure, it is important to be clear about your own compass heading; but don't ever forget that other people have profoundly different—and equally decent—ethical guidance mechanisms.

• A "pure" ethical stance in the face of most firms' political behavior will lead you out the door in short order, with only the convent, monastery or ashram as alternatives. The line between ethical purity and arrogant egocentricism (i.e., a holier-than-thou stance toward the tumult of everyday life) is a fine one.

• Each of us is ultimately lonely. In the end, it's up to each of us and each of us alone to figure out who we are and who we are not, and to act more or less consistently on those conclusions.

Reprinted from Ethics Digest

Conclusion:
Character
and Integrity

He sacrificed wife and child to his greed for gain; the dollar
was his god, and sordid avarice his demon.
                    —Henry Adams (on the American businessman)

A very natural fantasy recurs in everyone who works for a living—or even who does not work for a living. It is that especially American fantasy of instantaneous, enormous wealth, allowing us to live the good life in every way, without the distracting need to work so hard for it. It is an innocent and natural fantasy in our society, so long as it doesn't obliterate the obvious—that fortunes are made by few of us, and then usually through unusual skill or luck, that most of us will continue to work throughout our lives for much less than a fortune, and the work, not fortune, will define who we are and what we have done. In fiction, F. Scott Fitzgerald's Great Gatsby could disappear for a few years and return with enormous wealth, source unmentioned, to pursue the pleasures of the good life and Daisy, his life-long passion. Similarly, Heathcliff in Emily Brontë's *Wuthering Heights* disappears for years and reappears with a fortune—again we are not told of its origin—and he too pursues his life-long passions, love and revenge. Such stories are misleading; not only can the passions of a novel be portrayed more single-mindedly than the confused and often dull passions of everyday life, but the deleted chapter on "making the fortune" in the novel usually turns out to be most of the book in most of our lives.

The good life and living well, for most of us, is not something that begins *after* we have finished with business and our careers; indeed, that way of thinking, for most of us, guarantees unhappiness. The good life includes our work and career; and they are not mere means, to be pursued ruthlessly, in order to be a more decent and trustworthy person—later. Indeed, even those fortunate people who do succeed in earning considerable wealth and "retiring" fairly early in life soon find that they miss the work, the challenge, and the roles they played in the business world; invariably they get back into it quickly. The fantasy of future fortune can be a playful daydream; sometimes it can be a spur to real ambition. But too often it sets up a portrait of life that is unrealistic if not tragic, a portrait that tries to justify one set of values as pure means, another set of values as the hoped-for end. The problem is it rarely works, and when it does, it is an exceptional case rather than the usual.

It is peculiar that so many people in business talk as if they are forced or pressured into leaving their personal values at home when they go to work, when in fact it is at work as much as at home that most of them prove what and who they are. There are compromising situations, of course, and pressures, obviously. The day-to-day transactions of business are where we show ourselves and establish our sense of integrity. The much-celebrated cases in which otherwise honest and honorable businesspeople are caught giving in to a large bribe or cutting corners to save their job is not the acid test it is often thought to be. To be sure, the integrity of the business world absolutely demands that such people be punished for their "moment of weakness," but such spectacular lapses in character are only a small part of the picture. Most people never have the opportunity to be so grossly tempted, and most tempting opportunities lie at the fringe, not at the center, of 0usiness ethics.

Bribery and products of low quality are controversial precisely because they involve the gray areas of morals; adding a few dollars to an expense account is dishonorable, whether or not it is a clear case of stealing. But most of business life is as morality-bound and as ethical as any walk of life, and often self-consciously more so. Indeed, in the commerce of business life, the concept of *character*—that central ethical notion—is more prominent than in most professions in which skill takes priority over personality. Business, in other words, is as directly involved in and defined by ethics as any other walk of life. Our values are not put aside when we go to the office, but they are instead put to work there. They do not work every day confronted with the temptation that puts them to the ultimate, perhaps impossible, test. But rather they work in our minute-to-minute dealings with each other, in such common and unremarkable features of our behavior as courtesy, basic honesty, and trustworthiness.

A.   THE CONCEPT OF CHARACTER

Character is the term we sometimes use to summarize these features. Of course, character does not collapse at the least temptation, but neither is it to be measured only in extreme situations. Sometimes we use the word "character" to refer to a person who is a bit eccentric or odd, but this is not its usual usage. Character is sometimes a term of *moral* praise, as in "he is a man of character." But here too it is important not to limit our ethical focus merely to the obedience of moral rules. The overall person counts, not only what he or she does *not* do (that is, not breaking moral rules), but what he or she does in a positive way. Character also includes some sense of humor, generosity, living an interesting life, and being a good friend.

From this definition of "character," it might sound as if having a good character (or rather *being* a good character) is more a concern of other people than it is of our own, at least as far as the quest for the good life is concerned. But this again underscores our dubious fixation on the purely personal and individual aspects of the good life, in false contrast to the interpersonal and social nature of our existence. What we are calling "character" is not simply a mask we wear for other people, while privately entertaining ourselves behind it, like a "character actor" in a play. Character is also the way we think of and see ourselves, the way we identify with other people, and, consequently, the source of our own self-esteem as well. Indeed, ultimately, what the good life is all about—over and above pleasure, success, morality, power, freedom, and all the rest of it—is self-esteem, thinking well of ourselves. Whether we like it or not (and why not like it?) our self-esteem is not something we can privately turn on and off at will, regardless of our public actions and the way we relate to other people and they to us. What we think of ourselves is a reflection (though sometimes distorted) of what others think of us. Character, therefore, is the key not only to being an "interesting person" (which is of interest mainly to others), but to the good life as well. Indeed, it was often said by the British moralists (it is a less popular view in success-oriented America) that *character* is the single virtue that could carry a person through all of the troubles and conflicts of life; it is what defines a person as an individual as well as assures him or her an honored place in society. No combination of benefits and other virtues could compensate for lack of character.

In the business world, despite the verbal emphasis on profit and abilities, character is the magical ingredient to the good life and to success as well. It is no secret in executive boardrooms that those who are most successful are not the grinds—no matter how hard working—nor the merely clever, nor even the brilliant strategists who might well be deemed valuable and perhaps indispensable by virtue of their skills. This is not to say, of course, that success is simply a matter of charm and social skills, for character is much "deeper" than that. But it is character that allows a person to survive failures and setbacks, as well as character that makes for maximum influence and promotion. Character makes a company as well as a person attractive. Indeed, this is the intangible element that is so often referred to by managerial studies, hidden behind such phrases as "interpersonal skills" or "communicative abilities," which everyone agrees are a necessary, if not dominant, requirement for success. But the intangibility lies not just in the difficulty of quantifying such factors, but rather in the *synthetic* nature of this all-important ingredient of the good life: character is not just a skill or an ability. It is the integration of a life, the recognition of who we are, the forging of an identity that is distinctly our own, but defined in terms of and integrated with other people and the social world.

B. INTEGRITY: THE KEY TO CHARACTER

Consider the following: You casually offer to split a parking ticket with a business acquaintance with whom you have done, but are not presently doing, business. You offer to pay half of the amount, say, $10. You find that you don't have change: your acquaintance politely says "forget it," and you, equally in form, insist on paying—but later. It is never mentioned again. Your acquaintance would be too embarrassed to bring the matter up over such a small amount; it would make him feel petty and cheap. You know this, but you also know that if you never mention it either, the subject will be closed, and you can get away with never paying the $10 you owe. What would you do?

For most people, the answer here is beyond pondering. Of course you pay. Why? Well, clearly *not* paying is in your own financial self-interest. And let's not suppose that the probability of repeat business is very high. Indeed, you might well know that there is no more business to be done together, but the argument doesn't change much. The point is, ultimately, that just as your acquaintance would feel petty and cheap asking for money, you too would feel petty and cheap not giving it to him. Unlike him, you have an obligation to pay him, whereas he has no comparable obligation to ask you for it. Why pay the money? Why not "get away with it"? Because what is at stake in such cases, and hundreds of others besides, is your own sense of self as a decent human being, a sense of *integrity.* Though that sense might be tenuous in the extremely tempting once-in-a-lifetime context that is the favorite example of moralists, it is the day-after-day sense of integrity that gives a person character and a sense of self-worth. Sacrificing integrity in the single spectacular deal, the once-in-a-lifetime (perhaps illegal) opportunity, may be cause for remorse, punishment, and perhaps the end of a career. But it is the often neglected sense of everyday integrity—paying debts, telling the truth, not acting at every minute as if everything depends on getting "the better deal"—that make us mutually fit to live with.

A businessman at lunch, noting in a quick calculation that his own lunch had been much more expensive than that of his dieting colleague, quickly suggested a 50–50 split of the bill. Of course, it would have been petty and cheap to disagree with him. But in that single small action, the businessman not only saved himself a few dollars; he established himself, perhaps once and for all, as a calculating and deceptive character. What's worse, however, is that while the once-in-a-lifetime temptation comes only once, the opportunities to be petty, cheap, calculating, and deceptive come every day with almost everyone we meet. It is only a matter of time until that stamp of character gets recognized by virtually everyone, whether or not it finally gets internalized as a mortifying self-image as well. Are the combined profits from a few years' lunches, unpaid debts, and broken promises really worth the loss of friends and a likeable image, the general distrust and dislike of colleagues, if not also the loss of self-esteem?

There is a kind of character who combines the above techniques of self-indulgence and manipulation with an extremely self-serving psychological facility for rationalization and insensitivity. These characters take advantage of every small opportunity—and every other person too—but manage to avoid the most painful aspect of being manipulative, petty, and cheap: the recognition of themselves as such and the subsequent loss of self-esteem. They manage to find a way to shift the blame and indignation back to the other person, demanding "What's wrong with him?" or "Why is she being so critical?" They do not see the effects of their actions or the impression they make on other people, but they are content merely with the continuous immediate advantage in every situation and the parade of temporary friends and associates that come by. They may well be happy and contented, and consequently a source of considerable irritation to those manipulated, who quite rightly feel that some form of punishment or come-uppance is in order. Indeed, the victims may on occasion wish they were the same, namely, *so* insensitive and selfish that it is as if they were protected by a cocoon of oblivion from guilt, regret, and remorse.

The lesson of this character type, however, is not the desirability of total selfishness, but the limitations of a merely internal sense of themselves as the determinant of happiness and the good life. We may well wish that such people would get what's coming to them; sometimes they do, sometimes they don't. But the important question is not "Is there ultimate justice?" (indeed, much of religion is concerned with this problem), but rather *"What sort of person do I want to be?"* The good life and living well is not merely a matter of being self-satisfied; a continuous supply of any number of drugs could serve that lowly purpose. It is a matter of being an estimable person, of being happy through as well as with the esteem of friends and colleagues. The good life is an achievement of virtue and integrity, not just "getting everything you want." Indeed, it is necessary even for those in the character type above to convince themselves that they are happy and that other people like and respect them. And there, more likely than not, will be their downfall—if they have one.

Still it is just as important to stress the point—not stressed often enough in moral philosophy—that being a good person does emphatically *not* mean doing good to our own disadvantage, even to the point of making ourselves miserable. Aristotle pointed out long ago that truly virtuous people are not the ones who force themselves to do what must be done, but rather those who actually *enjoy* doing what must be done, just because it is the right thing to do. They see virtuous action as a mark of their own self-worth. According to Aristotle, that alone, together with the esteem of friends (though the two cannot be distinguished), is more than enough to motivate virtuous action in wise people. But even in our age of righteous self-interest and "doing your own thing," most of us recognize that being "a good person," thinking well of ourselves, and having others think well of us are as important as almost any gains that might be made by conniving and deception. Indeed, to what extent are our ambitions for gain motivated by the desire to respect ourselves and be respected by others? We don't need abstract principles or threatened punishments to force us to do what is right. Our very sense of ourselves is such that, seeing the consequences of a bad reputation and feeling the bite of regret, we know it is better to be right than wrong, even when wrong is more profitable or otherwise to our advantage. Of course, totally self-indulgent characters do not recognize this, but the solution isn't to be just like them. Rather, the question is not what would it be like to be them so much as *whether* we would like to be them. And the answer, for most of us, is clearly "no."

The good life is ultimately the cultivated interweavings of self-interest and ambition on the one hand, and public interest and a sense of community on the other. But the fabric of our desires is so subtly a synthesis of these theoretically distinct senses that it is, in practice, virtually impossible to distinguish. Our sense of self-interest and our shared interests with others, our own ambitions, and the kind of place we'd like to live, and the people we'd like to be with are all meshed in the same more or less unified character that defines who we are and how we will live. And if, as cynics are happy to point out, there is almost always some temptation that is likely to tear the fabric for almost anyone, pitting avaricious self-interest against everyone else, this says much less than is usually supposed about "human nature" and its inherent selfishness. What is most important, for most of us, most of the time, is our own sense of integrity—being the person we want to be. And there is little that will compensate us if we don't have that.

C.   Integrity and Business Life

None of what we have suggested above in any way undercuts the legitimacy of the more obvious business motives—to do well, make money, and beat out the competition. It only says that these motives belong in a larger context that gives them meaning; it is *how* we do well, how we make money, and how we beat out the competition that makes success possible and worthwhile. Wealth without honor is worthless. Success that strips away our respectability is not success at all. Indeed, the whole business of business ethics might be summarized in the somewhat pretentious phrase, "profits with integrity." Business ethics, ultimately, comes to just that—to an appreciation of the life of business in a broader perspective than just the obvious goals of fulfilling fiduciary obligations and making a profit. This certainly includes self-respect, first of all, and the respect of colleagues, having friends, people to love and who love you, a community worth living in, and a society worth being proud of. All of the debate about "social responsibility" ultimately comes to this too, not as an extra set of duties imposed on us but as the expression of who we are and where we fit in. Social responsibilities might better be called simply "citizenship"—and being in business does not contradict citizenship in anyway whatever. In fact, it presupposes it, and depends upon it, at every moment.

> A society of organizations is also a society in which a great many people are unimportant and indeed anonymous by themselves, yet are highly visible, and matter as "leaders" in society. And thus it is a society that must stress the Ethics of Prudence and self-development. It must expect its managers, executives, and professionals to demand of themselves that they shun behavior they would not respect in others, and instead practice behavior appropriate to the sort of person they would want to see "in the mirror in the morning."
>
> —Peter Drucker, The Public Interest, Spring 1981

INDEX